S0-BUA-129

Politics in America

The Ability to Govern

THIRD EDITION

Lance T. LeLoup
University of Missouri—St. Louis

West Publishing Company
St. Paul   Los Angeles   New York   San Francisco

Copyediting Marilyn Taylor
Illustration Rolin Graphics
Composition Graphic World
Cover Image Joseph Drivas, The Image Bank
Cover Design Diane Beasley
Index Northwind Editorial Services

50 W. Kellogg Boulevard
P.O. Box 64526
St. Paul, MN 55164-0526

Printed in the United States of America
98 97 96 95 94 93 92 91 8 7 6 5 4 3 2 1

Library of Congress Cataloging-in-Publication Data
Leloup, Lance T.
Politics in America: the ability to govern / Lance T. Leloup. —3rd ed.
p. cm.
Includes bibliographical references and indexes.
ISBN 0-314-79502-2 (hard)
1. United States—Politics and Government. I. Title.
JK31.L45 1991
320.973—dc20 90-12930
CIP

To Molly

About the Author

Lance T. LeLoup is Director of the Public Policy Research Centers and Professor of Political Science at the University of Missouri—St. Louis, where he has taught American politics since 1974. Born in Troy, New York, he earned his B.A. in government with honors from Georgetown University. He received his M.A. and Ph.D. from Ohio State University, where he was a Mershon Fellow. Professor LeLoup has lectured throughout the United States and England. He has taught courses on Congress, the presidency, politics of budgeting, public policy, honors government, and American politics.

Professor LeLoup studies national political institutions and has long been interested in questions of governing and political economy. His books include *Budgetary Politics,* now in its fourth edition, and *The Fiscal Congress: Legislative Control of the Budget,* and he is co-editor of *The Presidency: Studies in Public Policy.* He delivered the 1988 Coleman B. Ransone Lectures at the University of Alabama. His scholarly work is published in the *American Political Science Review,* the *Public Administration Review,* the *Journal of Politics, Comparative Politics, Polity, Policy Analysis, American Politics Quarterly, Legislative Studies Quarterly, Public Budgeting and Finance,* and other journals, anthologies, and edited volumes.

Formerly the legislative assistant to the minority leader of the Ohio Senate, Professor LeLoup has been a frequent observer of Congress and the federal executive branch throughout his research career. An avid student of writing, he has participated in America's oldest writers' conference at Bread Loaf, Vermont. Professor LeLoup is a political commentator on KWMU, the National Public Radio affiliate in St. Louis.

BRIEF CONTENTS

SECTION THREE

NATIONAL INSTITUTIONS AND POLICY MAKING 295

SECTION FOUR

PUBLIC POLICIES 443

CONTENTS

CHAPTER 3

American Political Economy 50

CHAPTER 4

Federalism 79

CHAPTER 5

Civil Liberties 105

CHAPTER 6

Civil Rights 129

Chapter 8

Political Parties 183

Chapter 9

Nominations, Campaigns, and Elections 210

CHAPTER 10

The Mass Media 242

CHAPTER 11

Interest Groups 269

CHAPTER 13

The Presidency 327

CHAPTER 14

The Struggle to Govern: Congress versus the President 357

CHAPTER 15

The Bureaucracy 384

CHAPTER 16

The Judiciary 414

CHAPTER 19

Social Welfare Policy 497

CHAPTER 20

Foreign Policy and National Defense 523

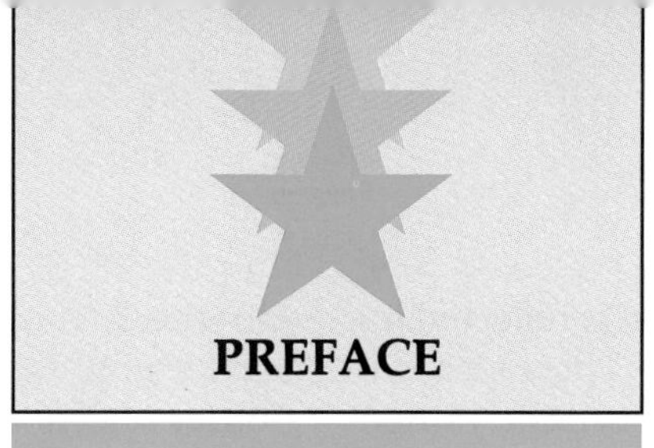

PREFACE

As America's vision of democracy flourishes around the world, concern has grown about the performance of democracy at home. While the Soviet Union and the nations of Eastern Europe face extremely difficult problems in transforming their political institutions and economic systems, challenges confront the American political system as well. The third edition of *Politics in America* is a comprehensive introduction to American government, with particular emphasis on governance and political economy.

Several important thematic changes mark the third edition. First, the chapters reflect the dramatic changes in the international environment with the sudden end of the Cold War and its effects on domestic politics. Second, the discussion of democracy has been expanded, and more material comparing the United States with other democratic systems has been integrated into the text. Third, coverage of political economy has also been made more comparative in scope as American politics is increasingly oriented towards the global economy. Fourth, the theme of governing ability focusing on public policy and governing processes has been strengthened. In addition to the potential for political deadlock under separation of powers, recent trends in electoral politics are examined more critically: negative campaigns dominated by thirty-second television commercials, declining electoral competition, the "decoupling" of congressional and presidential elections, and the spiraling costs of campaigns. These trends seem to be widening the gap between running for office and effectively governing the nation.

Governing

The emphasis on governing offers both relevance to contemporary issues and a framework for explaining outcomes and analyzing the performance of the political system. Exploring the factors that determine governing ability and policy outcomes helps students understand why things happen and what difference it makes. The first chapter outlines the theme of governing ability—the capacity to reach decisions and carry them out while maintaining public trust. This introductory chapter examines a number of cases, describes the policy-making process, and offers some contemporary critiques of the effectiveness of the nation's governing processes. Underlying questions about governing ability guide subsequent chapters concerning the Constitution, parties, elections, interest groups, Congress, the president, and other key institutions. The theme has been sharpened to clarify important relationships. It integrates material that may at first seem vast and disconnected to students, for example, making constitutional choices made two centuries ago less remote to problems and policies today. It encourages students to make comparisons with other democracies and arrive at their own conclusions about the strengths and weaknesses of the American political system.

Political Economy

Political economy remains an essential component of the text because of its growing importance to so many aspects of American politics. Chapter 3 examines the cultural values that underlie American political economy and how the relationship between government and the economy has evolved over time. The chapter compares equity and growth rates among industrialized democracies and outlines the challenges facing the United States in an increasingly interdependent world. Economic factors are an important component of the text's coverage of civil rights, electoral behavior, PACs and interest groups, Congress, the bureaucracy, and many other topics. The growing importance of energy and environmental protection is reflected in expanded coverage in Chapter 18. The focus on political economy remains broad and eclectic, rather than narrow or deterministic. Other important theories, approaches, and issues are not ignored at the expense of economic ones.

THE THIRD EDITION

So much has happened so quickly in recent years that the world indeed seems almost like a different place. The reduction of the communist threat and east-west tensions has consequences for more than just U.S. foreign and defense policy. The end of the Cold War will further internationalize the economy, increasing pressure on the United States to govern more effectively in order to remain competitive. The reduction of the threat of nuclear war may influence the balance of power between Congress and the president. New research findings and new material has been added on topics including: retrospective voting; the growing centralization of power in Congress, black elected officials; court decisions on affirmative action, flag burning, and abortion and the political reaction; the invasion of Panama; Iraq's invasion of Kuwait; negative campaigning and its consequences; President George Bush's popularity and relations with Congress; economic trends and continuing budget battles; the Bush presidency, cabinet, and management style; the drug war; environmental protection and the Clean Air Act revision; and many other political changes in the United States and the world.

Pedagogical Features of the Text

American politics is exciting and important, and a textbook introducing it should be too. To enhance reader interest and comprehension, several pedagogical features are used throughout the text.

Political Close-up Each chapter opens with a "Political Close-up," a selection designed to introduce the topic of the chapter by capturing some of the human drama of politics. Many are new to the third edition. Included are the political meaning of *The Wizard of Oz*, the 1987 stock market crash, a day in the life of a lobbyist, the fall of a Speaker, reflections on democracy by Vaclav Havel, and other selections.

Political Insight Chapters include a number of special insights into American politics that enlighten the text. These "Political Insights" range from excerpts of the 1988 Democratic and Republican party platforms to a look at the identification cards carried by OSHA inspectors under Presidents Carter and Reagan.

People in Politics Some chapters include profiles of people who have made a difference in American politics. From John Maynard Keynes to DNC Chairman Ron Brown, the "People in Politics" features look at individuals who have made a difference.

Appendices So that the text may serve as an important learning and reference work for students, included in the appendices are *Federalist Papers* No. 10 and No. 51, the Declaration of Independence, the Constitution of the United States, and a list of the presidents of the United States.

Ancillaries

An attractive number of ancillary materials make *Politics in America* a complete learning and teaching package.

Politics in America Update Each semester, a special *Politics in America Update* will be sent to adopters. This supplement, which proved popular with earlier editions, will focus on several of the most important changes or political developments in the preceding months. Particular attention will be paid to changes that affect governing, but many other issues and important new research findings will be included.

Instructor's Manual with Test Bank Professor Arnold Fleischmann of the University of Georgia has developed an excellent Instructor's Manual and battery of examination questions. This carefully written manual is one of the most detailed available and will be extremely helpful in preparing lectures. The Instructor's Manual includes chapter outlines, learning objectives, and key terms. The extensive test bank, which includes multiple-choice, true-false, and essay questions in a range of difficulties, is organized by chapter.

Computerized Test Bank The test questions in the Instructor's Manual are also available on WesTest to adopters who want to produce tests using Apple or IBM PC microcomputers.

Transparency Masters Key tables, figures, and artwork from each chapter have been reproduced and placed on transparency masters for instructors using overhead projectors.

Student Study Guide Professor John Todd of North Texas State University has written an outstanding Student Study Guide to accompany *Politics in America*, which students may purchase. Each chapter is outlined, stressing key points, learning objectives, and key terms and concepts. Programmed self-study and sample test questions are also included.

Acknowledgments

I want to thank the following reviewers whose comments and suggestions substantially informed and improved the third edition.

Sudershan Chawla
Marshall DeRosa
Joel Diemond
Manochehr Dorraj
William A. Giles
Marshall R. Goodman
Marjorie R. Hershey
Andrew Merrifield
Margaret V. Moody

Many people have contributed to *Politics in America* through three editions and I wish to acknowledge their invaluable assistance and support. Special thanks and love go to my wife, Laurel Baker LeLoup, for her help, inspiration, and for making it all worthwhile. My colleagues and staff at University of Missouri-St. Louis—particularly those in the Public Policy Research Centers and the Political Science Department—provide a challenging and stimulating environment to work in. Particular thanks go Steve Hause, Barbara Graham, Carol Kohfeld, Bob Baumann, Mike MacKuen, Cosandra Turner, Jane Sweney, and Patrick Taylor, research assistant for this edition. My thanks to the staff at West for their continuing fine work and assistance with the third edition, particularly my editor, Mary Schiller, production editor Mélina Brown, marketing coordinator Stephanie Johnson, and the West sales staff. Finally, perhaps the greatest rewards from writing an American government textbook come from adopters across the country who have taken the time to share their experiences in teaching and the many students whose evolving perceptions of politics in America have been influenced by this book. I am most grateful for their insights and responses, which have strengthened this edition.

PROCLAIM
BY
OF THE
AND

SECTION ONE

The Foundations of Politics

American politics operates under a set of well agreed-upon rules, traditions, and practices—a foundation that has developed over two centuries. The first six chapters examine the components of that foundation. Questions about the ability to govern and an overview of the policy process are introduced in Chapter 1. Chapter 2 considers the Constitution, perhaps the most important foundation of all. The background, issues, and politics of the Constitutional Convention help explain how such key structural characteristics as separation of powers came to be embodied in the blueprint for American government. America's economic foundations are closely tied to its political foundations. Chapter 3 explores American political economy—the traditions and values and changing boundaries between government and economy that helped guide political and economic development in the United States. Chapter 4 examines federalism, the other dominant constitutional feature of the political system. Constitutional foundations not only are of historical interest but also help us understand the ability of the system to govern in the 1990s and current dilemmas in the relationship among cities, states, and the national government. Finally, American politics is also grounded in a foundation of individual rights and liberties. Chapter 5 considers civil liberties. The Bill of Rights to the Constitution has provided the basis for defining the limits of government intrusions into the lives of individual citizens. Chapter 6 looks at the struggle for civil rights, the ability of all Americans to share in the responsibilities and benefits of citizenship. These are the basic elements on which the political system is built and from which public policies are determined.

CHAPTER 1

INTRODUCTION: THE ABILITY TO GOVERN

POLITICAL CLOSE-UP

THE BUDGET BATTLE OF 1990: A GOVERNING CRISIS

It was a spectacle that frustrated political leaders, disgusted average citizens, and amazed foreign observers. For five long months in 1990, the president and Congress deadlocked over the federal budget, unable to reach a compromise despite the fact that the economy teetered on the brink of recession. After a decade of controversy over budget priorities and growing deficits, the United States was threatened by a growing tide of red ink in the 1990s as projected deficits ballooned to $300 billion annually. But in spite of the gravity of the threat, the budget summit failed to produce an acceptable compromise. When President Bush and congressional leaders finally did agree on a five year, $500 billion deficit reduction package, Republican and Democratic members of the House of Representatives rejected it. The government had no budget and was shut down at midnight on October 6. Angry tourists were locked out of national museums, monuments, and parks while the value of the dollar plunged in foreign markets. Was this any way to govern a country?

The political gridlock that gripped Washington had its roots in the

fundamental disagreements between the Democratic Congress and Republican White House over the budget and chronic deficits throughout the 1980s. Confrontations and occasional government shutdowns had occured in the past. Radical remedies such as the Gramm-Rudman-Hollings mandatory deficit reduction law had been tried without success. But the crisis in 1990 was more serious because of the growing threat of recession and the dire consequences of failure. In 1989, President Bush was unable to get Congress to accept his top domestic priority, a reduction in captial gains taxes—the rate of taxation on the sale of securities, land, and other assets. He was able, however, to maintain his most famous 1988 campaign pledge "read my lips—no new taxes."

That pledge would fall by the wayside in 1990 as the president grudgingly recognized that some new revenues were essential to solve the deficit crisis. In May, the administration and congressional leaders convened a budget summit, seemingly the only way to overcome divided government. Through the summer, little progress was made as both sides attacked the other for trying to make partisan political gains rather than solve the problems. The budget numbers grew worse by the week. In September, a mini-summit of eight men retired to the confines of Andrews Air Force Base outside of Washington, D.C. to try to fashion an acceptable compromise. Finally, only hours before the start of the fiscal year on October 1, negotiators announced an agreement that would cut deficits by half a trillion dollars by 1995.

The budget summit agreement reduced the deficits by equal parts of domestic spending cuts, defense cuts, and tax increases. While neither side claimed to like the compromise, they concluded it was the best that they could get. The package was wildly unpopular in Congress and with the public. The elderly complained bitterly about the $60 billion in Medicare cuts. Tax increases fell hard on the middle class in terms of higher excise taxes on beer, wine cigarettes, and higher gasoline taxes, without raising income tax rates on wealthier Americans. President Bush, House Speaker Thomas Foley, and Senate Majority Leader George Mitchell attempted to rally their troops to support the plan anyway. But with elections just weeks away, rank and file members feared a backlash from voters. President Bush went on national television to appeal to voters and Republican legislators to support the package. But leadership attempts were in vain. In the wee hours of the morning on October 5, the House voted down the summit agreement, 254-179. Led by the number two House Republican, Newt Gingrich, House Republicans abandoned the president as the crisis deepened. One day later, President Bush refused to sign a temporary extension, forcing the government to shut down.

House Democrats seized the initiative by developing their own budget plan that raised income tax rates on the wealthy while reducing Medicare cuts. Bush later signed several stop-gap resolutions to allow the government to function. Around the clock negotiations took place in the Capitol through October between the House, the Senate and administration. Finally, on October 28, 1990, just ten days before the midterm elections, Congress passed a compromise budget by narrow margins in both houses. Exhausted, legislators returned home to campaign. Both branches paid a high price for near breakdown of the political system. President Bush saw his popularity plummet from 75 percent in August to 55 percent by late October. Public ratings of Congress were below 20 percent, the lowest ever recorded. The budget crisis of 1990 was a vivid demonstration of growing governing problems in the United States associated with divided party control of government, the decline of party loyalty, and the weakness of presidential and congressional leadership, and the reluctance of legislators—fearful of negative attacks by opponents—to make hard choices. What would it mean for the long-term viability of the political system and the economic prosperity of the nation?

CHAPTER OUTLINE

Introduction and Overview

Governing in a Democracy

Governing: Four Cases

Case 1: Franklin D. Roosevelt's "Hundred Days" (1933)

Case 2: Jimmy Carter's Energy Program (1977-1978)

Case 3: Passing the Impossible Tax Reform Bill (1986)

Case 4: The 1988 Civil Rights Restoration Act

Politics, Public Policy, and Political Economy

Politics

Public Policy

Political Economy

The Policy-Making Process

Foundations

Getting Problems and Issues to Government: The Policy Agenda

Making Policy Decisions

Policies and Their Impacts

Critiques of Governing: Effective Decision-Making or Chronic Deadlock?

Separation of Powers Makes It Difficult to Govern Effectively

Weak Political Parties and "Decoupled" National Elections Increasingly Produce Divided Government

What It Takes to Get Elected Often Makes It Difficult to Govern

Powerful Interest Groups and PACs Exert Undue Influence

Counterpoint: The Policy Process Is Slow but Effective

Why Governing Ability Matters

Summary and Conclusions

INTRODUCTION AND OVERVIEW

Will the American political system successfully meet the difficult challenges it faces in the 1990s and the twenty-first century? Can the United States remain competitive and prosper in the evolving international arena? The answers depend in large part on whether the U.S. government is able to make sound and timely public policy decisions. For centuries, the United States has served as a model of democracy and constitutional government. Today, as democracy movements around the world have raised the hopes of millions of people, Americans are justifiably proud of the example their political system has set. But in an increasingly complex and interdependent international environment, the demands on all governments are increasing. To achieve peace and prosperity in the future, the processes and institutions that embody American democracy must adapt as well.

The challenge to democratic government is to make timely and effective policies while maintaining the trust and support of the people. Concern has grown in recent years in the United States about interbranch conflict, the avoidance of tough choices, and a pervasive stalemate in certain crucial public policy areas. In the 1980s, national government successfully built up the armed forces, bailed out Social Security, reformed the federal tax structure, and made significant progress in arms control and reducing world tensions. But at the same time, Congress and the president deadlocked over critical budget choices leading to record-high deficits that potentially threatened the economy. Differences between the Democratic Congress and the Republican presidency caused stalemates on a host of foreign policy and domestic issues. American politics is often a paradox: sometimes the system works quickly and effectively, yet at other times it sputters and grinds to a halt.

Many experts and public officials express concern about the ability of the American political system to govern effectively. Richard Bolling, former chair of the House Rules Committee, describes it like this:

> Government is not working well, nor has it for some time. Our institutions are out of date. They are not organized in a way that enables them to deal well with our problems. In the Congress, and to a considerable degree in the executive branch, duties are not divided up rationally.[1]

Douglas Dillon, secretary of the Treasury in the Kennedy administration, explains:

> Our governmental problems do not lie with the quality or character of our elected representatives. Rather they lie with a system which promotes divisiveness and makes it difficult, if not impossible, to develop truly national policies. The result of all this is stalemate whenever important and difficult issues are involved. And no one can place the blame. The president blames the Congress, the Congress blames the president, and the public remains confused and disgusted with government in Washington.[2]

John Gardner, founder of the public interest group Common Cause, observes:

> It's very hard today for a president to govern the country. Part of the problem goes back to fragmentation of all the organized special interests that operate with no serious attention to the common good and paralyze the process of governing.[3]

Complaints about changes in political campaigns multiplied in the last decade because of negative attacks, the dominance of thirty-second TV ads, and the avoidance of real issues. One scholar noted that the 1988 campaign suggested that, "there are no incentives at present for campaigners and the media to address the tough problems of governance. The incentives all lead toward the use of symbols and the creation of artificial drama."[4]

Yet despite the problems, some argue that the system was working just as the founders intended—slowly and inefficiently. Former Republican Congressman Barber Conable acknowledges the "well known mess which at any given time clutters up the Washington landscape," but he continues:

> We are better for it. The Founding Fathers didn't want efficient, adventurous governments, fearing they would intrude on our individual liberties. I think they were right, and I offer our freedom, stability, and prosperity as evidence.[5]

Politics in America is an introduction to the foundations, people, institutions, and public policies of government. Of particular concern is the question of governing in a democracy; the factors which promote effective, timely policy-making or leave the system bogged down in stalemate. With the rapid changes in the world economic and political environment, the ability to govern is of particular importance in the 1990s. Public policy choices in the next decade will help determine job prospects, the standard of living, opportunities for higher education, whether drug tests will be mandatory, if Social Security will be available, the ability of women and minorities to compete in the workplace, and whether the United States will become involved in an armed conflict. Chapter 1 explores the following questions:

1. How can democracies and other forms of government be compared and assessed in terms of their ability to govern effectively? How does this provide a framework for better understanding of politics in America?
2. What cases help demonstrate the wide variation in how policies are made and how effectively the political system works?
3. Exactly what is "politics" and "public policy," and what is the relationship between political and economic systems?
4. In general, how are public policies made in the United States? Who are the main participants, what are the stages and elements, and how are the results assessed?
5. What are some leading critiques of governing in the U.S. political system?
6. How can we judge the performance of government? What are some of the consequences of governing problems?

Governing in a Democracy

Democracy made tremendous progress throughout the world in 1989 and the early 1990s. In Eastern Europe, democracy movements toppled repressive Communist regimes with record-shattering speed. After forty-five years, the iron curtain that separated east and west—the United States and the Soviet Union and their respective allies—came crashing down. Made possible by changes within the Soviet Union initiated by President Mikhail Gorbachev, the movement away from one-party rule towards multiparty democracy proceeded from Poland to Hungary, East Germany, Czechoslovakia, Romania, and throughout Eastern Europe. The sudden changes were dramatized by the sight of the Berlin Wall—a vivid symbol of the cold war—being opened and then toppled. In early 1990, the Soviet Union itself abolished the monopoly power of the Communist party. Even the nation that President Ronald Reagan had called the "evil empire" eight years earlier appeared to be moving toward democracy.

A **democracy**, or democratic regime, is a form of government based on the rule of the people, either directly or through elected representatives. A **totalitarian regime**, the dictatorship of a single individual or political party, is a government based on subordination of the individual to the state with strict controls of all aspects of social, political, and economic life. One important characteristic that can be compared across different forms of government concerns *guaranteeing political rights and protecting individual liberties* within the state. This aspect of a political system identifies the degree to which citizens are allowed to participate in or are represented in the affairs of government and enjoy civil liberties, such as freedom of expression, and political rights, such as the right to vote in meaningful elections. By definition, democratic regimes go much farther in protecting political rights and liberties than totalitarian regimes. After two hundred years of a government under a Constitution including a Bill of Rights, Americans often take certain rights and liberties for granted, such as the right to vote, freedom of speech and press, the separation of church and state, and the right to petition the government. In contrast, until the recent democratic revolutions, many citizens of Eastern Europe could not openly criticize their governments, vote in a meaningful election, move freely, or leave their country.

The closest approximation to direct democracy in American politics today is the New England town meeting.

Differences in guaranteeing rights and protecting liberties are more subtle when making comparisons among democratic political systems or within a nation over time. For example, while both nations have a free press, reporters face more restrictions in Great Britain than in the United States. British journalists may not reveal the name of a criminal suspect in the early stages of a case as their American counterparts may. In the United States, protection of civil liberties has sometimes been restricted over the years because of fear of communism or other unpopular ideas. The political rights of blacks and other minority groups were denied for many years and not guaranteed until as late as the 1960s in the South.

A second key characteristic for comparison is the ***ability to govern:*** the capacity of a political system to function effectively, to reach decisions, and to carry them out, while maintaining the public trust.[6] Like an automobile, a government's performance can range from a well-tuned hum to a coughing sputter to a complete breakdown. Politics concerns human beings, not machines, but the mechanics of government are very important. Democracies that function effectively have electoral systems where issues espoused by candidates and political parties relate to policy choices made after the election. Governments must not only be able to reach decisions but also to implement their decisions. Totalitarian regimes can often reach decisions easily without having to worry about public opinion or free elections. This, of course, is no guarantee that sound policy choices are made. Totalitarian regimes do not always move quickly since internal power struggles between factions may delay making decisions. But in extreme cases, totalitarian governments can carry out policies with ruthless disregard of individual rights and liberties. In Cambodia during the late 1970s, the radical Khmer Rouge government led by dictator Pol Pot literally emptied the nation's cities and murdered millions of men, women, and children.

At the other extreme are weak, impotent governments that can barely reach decisions or carry them out. The Weimar Republic, in power in

Germany in the 1920s, was unable to deal with the severe economic crisis. Its virtual inability to govern allowed Adolf Hitler and the Nazi party to come to power. In 1958, the French Fourth Republic floundered, unable to deal with the crisis in Algeria. General Charles de Gaulle stepped in to avert the crisis, and France accepted his new constitution, which gave the president much greater governing powers within the democratic system.

Democratic forms of government differ both in structure and in their ability to reach public policy decisions and carry them out. The United States, with an independently elected Congress and president, is characterized by a separation of legislative and executive powers. Parliamentary systems, like those of Western Europe, are characterized by a fusion of legislative and executive powers rather than by a separation. The executive is drawn from the legislative majority and is assured of support in parliament. Parliamentary systems can change governments quickly in the event of a deadlock because elections can be called on short notice.

The protection of political liberties and the ability of a political system to reach decisions are important in understanding and evaluating governments throughout the world. In many cases, there is a tradeoff between the protection of political rights and liberties and governing ability. The most powerful governments in the world are often the most repressive and least democratic. In the United States, civil liberties have been most abused during wartime or crisis situations when government needed to act with dispatch and decisiveness. As we will see in Chapter 2, limiting government's power in order to protect the rights of individuals goes back to the Constitution itself. Can the United States govern effectively while fully protecting democratic freedoms? If a government cannot make decisions because of fragmentation of power and the inability to break a political deadlock, the danger is drift and inaction at the wrong time. If governments are too weak, unable to deal with economic or social crises, the public may cease to support leaders or even the political system itself. Public confidence will erode if policies are ineffective and do not solve the problems they were intended to. Conversely, the danger of a government that can move too quickly and decisively is the likelihood of hasty, poorly conceived, and ill-advised policies that lack the support of the people.

This text explores American politics—its economic and constitutional foundations, its people, institutions, governing processes and policies. We will explore how institutional structures and political processes affect governing and the public

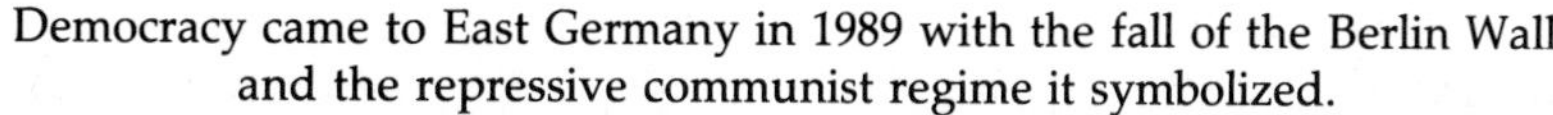
Democracy came to East Germany in 1989 with the fall of the Berlin Wall and the repressive communist regime it symbolized.

policies that result. Some examples of the different patterns of policy-making in the United States will help us get started.

Governing: Four Cases

CASE 1: FRANKLIN D. ROOSEVELT'S "HUNDRED DAYS" (1933)

A cold wind blew on March 4, 1933, as Franklin Delano Roosevelt took the oath of office as president of the United States. Millions listened to their radios with hope in their hearts as the new president addressed the battered nation with strong and reassuring words. Since the collapse of the stock market in 1929, the economy had plunged into the worst depression in history—to this day called the Great Depression. By 1933, the gross national product had fallen to half its 1929 level. One in four Americans was out of work. Across the country, banks were closing in droves. Thousands of businesses had failed. Homeless and hungry, millions lived in "Hoovervilles"—shantytowns named after Roosevelt's Republican predecessor Herbert Hoover.

In his inaugural address, Franklin Roosevelt made clear his intention to move decisively against this severe economic crisis that gripped the nation. "The only thing we have to fear is fear itself," he proclaimed. Confident that Congress would go along with his sweeping proposals, he nonetheless served notice that, if Congress failed to act,

> I shall not evade the clear course of duty that will then confront me. I shall ask the Congress for the one remaining instrument to meet the crisis—broad executive power to wage a war against the emergency, as great as the power that would be given to me if we were in fact invaded by a foreign foe.[7]

The people wanted action, and Roosevelt was prepared to give it to them.

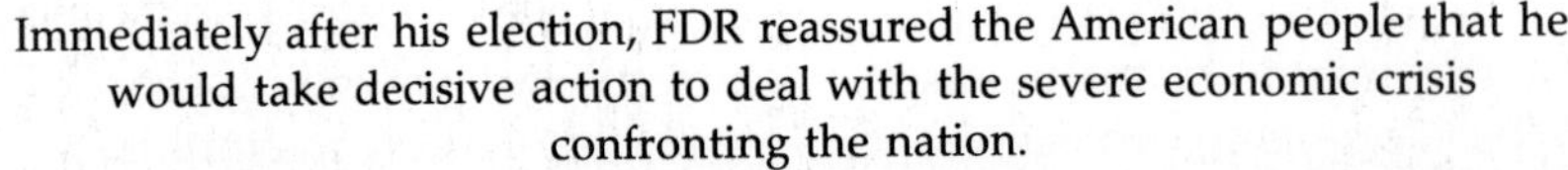

Immediately after his election, FDR reassured the American people that he would take decisive action to deal with the severe economic crisis confronting the nation.

One of his first acts was to declare a bank "holiday," closing the nation's banks while asking Congress for additional powers to deal with banking and currency. The new Congress convened in special session to receive the emergency banking request. The bill, completed at two o'clock that morning, was only partially written. But the members of Congress clamored to do the president's bidding. Forty minutes were allowed for debate. "Vote!" the members shouted. "The house is burning down and the president of the United States says this is the way to put out the fire."[8] The bill passed overwhelmingly by voice vote that very afternoon, and the president signed it into law that evening.

The next day, Roosevelt sent Congress another message, this time on the economy. In the language of crisis, the president requested emergency powers to deal with the federal budget, making cuts where necessary. The bill was passed the following week. During the next one hundred days, one of the most remarkable series of legislative triumphs in American history took place. In this flurry of activity, Congress approved the following:

> The Agricultural Adjustment Act, which overhauled national farm policy, passed overwhelmingly after five hours of debate six days after it was introduced.
>
> The Civilian Conservation Corps, which put 250,000 people to work planting forests and building dams, passed by a voice vote ten days after the president sent the bill down.
>
> Federal unemployment relief to the states, the largest aid program ever approved to that date.
>
> Legislation to regulate securities and the stock market.
>
> The Tennessee Valley Authority, creating a nationally owned electric utility as part of a national plan of electric energy and land management—a landmark bill that was approved by Congress in five weeks.
>
> Legislation to prevent mortgage foreclosure on homes, approved a month after it was submitted.
>
> Emergency railroad legislation, passed within a month.
>
> The National Industrial Recovery Act, passed within a month.

The **New Deal** was under way.

2 Case 2: Jimmy Carter's Energy Program (1977–1978)

In a televised address to the nation on April 18, 1977, President Jimmy Carter unveiled a comprehensive energy program that he planned to submit to Congress. He declared, "Our decision about energy will test . . . the ability of the president and the Congress to govern this nation. This difficult effort will be the 'moral equivalent of war.' "[9]

A month before he presented his energy package, Carter, the self-proclaimed "outsider," decided to cut what he believed were wasteful water projects throughout the country. In March 1977, he had announced the termination of nineteen projects. However, he failed to consult ahead of time with members of Congress for whom water projects were special political plums. "This is [like] motherhood," proclaimed one member. "Carter picked the wrong issue for a showdown with Congress."[10] Senator Edmund Muskie (D-Maine), chair of the Senate Budget Committee, went even further: "No president should have the right, unilaterally, on his own, to frustrate a policy that has been made part of the law of this land, in accordance with constitutional processes."[11] Congress rebuffed the new president. Only a compromise arranged by House Speaker Thomas P. ("Tip") O'Neill prevented a veto and a divisive override attempt. This was not a president enjoying his "honeymoon" with Congress.

By the time President Carter submitted his energy package, less than one hundred days into his administration, he had already strained relations with Congress. In declaring the **"moral equivalent of war,"** Carter tried to spur a recalcitrant Congress into speedy action on his program. Congress went to work, but with little speed. To avoid normal committee rivalries, O'Neill established a Select Committee on Energy in the House to consider the president's requests. It made little difference. The representatives from competing committees simply moved their disagreements to the "supercommittee." On the Senate side, things were worse. Liberal Senators Edward Kennedy (D-Mass.) and Howard Metzenbaum (D-Ohio) actively opposed key elements of the program. Senators from the southwestern oil and gas states were having no part of the president's program. Conservative Senators John Tower (R-Tex.) and Howard Baker (R-Tenn.) also opposed many parts of the package. An uncertain congressional liaison office tried to coax and cajole members of Congress into support. But by the end of 1977, not a single part of Carter's energy package had become law.

Throughout 1978, legislators continued to whittle away at the initial proposals. President Carter himself changed his position on deregulation of natural gas. By the end of the summer, there was little left of the original plan. The *Congressional Quarterly* concluded that the remaining bills "contained only remnants of the tough plan originally presented in 1977."[12] The tax on gasoline, one of the cornerstones of the program, had been dropped early in the process. A tax on imported crude oil also was scuttled. In August 1978, the president made personal telephone calls to twenty-five members of Congress in an attempt to salvage something.

Finally the bill came to a vote in the House in October. It remained a "package" only through the help of Speaker O'Neill, who refused to allow members to separate the items any further. Final passage was by the razor-thin margin of 207 to 206. This is what happened to the president's original package:

Tax credit for home insulation: passed

Reform of utility rates: passed

Gasoline tax: deleted

Tax on "gas-guzzling" cars: a watered-down version passed

Home appliance energy standards: passed

Tax on crude oil: killed by the Senate

Tax on utility and individual use of oil and gas: weakened, then killed in conference committee

Extension of natural-gas pricing: passed in modified form

The Carter administration claimed a legislative victory, even though "victory" took a year and a half and resulted in passage of a fraction of the original plan.

CASE 3: PASSING THE IMPOSSIBLE TAX REFORM BILL (1986)

Not all major domestic policy ideas come from the White House. Comprehensive tax reform was a congressional initiative that President Reagan adopted as the number-one domestic priority for his second term. All the experts said it could never pass, but on October 22, 1986, Reagan signed into law the most sweeping overhaul of federal income taxes in history.[13]

Why had conventional political wisdom concluded that tax reform was an impossible issue for the American political system? First, revenue legislation historically has tended to be highly partisan, highlighting differences in party philosophies about the size and role of government. Second, special tax breaks had become extremely popular in the 1970s and 1980s. As pressure mounted to hold down spending growth, special tax preferences had provided another way to deliver benefits to constituent groups. Third, the congressional tax-writing committees had grown weak and fragmented in the 1980s. They lacked the clout they had enjoyed in the 1960s, when a committee bill was almost assured of passage. The committees' performance in approving President Reagan's 1981 tax cut was characterized as "pigs feeding at the trough"—an unprecedented giveaway that cost the Treasury $700 billion over five years. Finally, tax reform was considered nearly impossible because of the powerful array of special interest groups aligned against it. Interest groups would unite to kill the bill in order to protect their own treasured tax provisions.

With all the obstacles, how was the bill able to pass? **Bipartisanship** was a key factor. From the outset, both parties believed they had a stake in tax reform and ranked it high on their policy agendas. In varying degrees, bipartisan support continued throughout the political process and was instrumental in final passage. Tax reform could have not succeeded in 1985–86 through a party-government approach to policy-making, as it had with the Reagan economic program in 1981. When the Reagan administration sent a proposal to Congress in June 1985, House Ways and Means Chair Dan Rostenkowski quickly pledged Democratic and congressional support for the approach—if not all the particulars—of the president's plan.

Congressional reformers shared a common premise: Tax rates were too high because of the unprecedented growth of tax preferences. If tax breaks could be reduced, rates could be cut. Even so, many potentially fatal obstacles remained. Several rules of thumb minimized conflict. All plans had to be "revenue neutral"—that is, raising the same amount of revenue as current law—not a backdoor tax increase to cut the deficit. Next, reformers agreed that, for any plan to be accepted by the public, at least 75 to 80 percent of all individual taxpayers had to pay the same or less in taxes. Finally, the number of tax brackets would be sharply reduced from fifteen to around three. These agreements assured that the process would get further than in the recent past.

The House passed its version in December 1985, and the Senate approved its bill in May 1986. House approval was more controversial and partisan, with Republicans signing on only after the president promised to insist on certain changes in the Senate package. The Senate bill, engineered by Finance Committee Chair Robert Packwood, was the more sweeping and radical bill. In both houses, a near breakdown within the committee almost scuttled the process. Both Rostenkowski and Packwood took their committee members behind closed doors, away from the lobbyists and reporters who had jammed the hearing rooms.

Perhaps the key breakthrough that led to eventual passage came in closed session of the Senate Finance Committee. Packwood reportedly asked members how low top rates for personal income taxes would have to be for them to give up the preferences they had argued for and already approved in previous open sessions. Most members responded that top rates would have to come down to 30 percent or below. Throwing out their previous decisions, a plan was devised with two brackets and a top rate of 27 percent.

By turning the decision-making process upside down, Packwood succeeded in reporting the bill out of the Finance Committee by the astounding vote of 20 to 0. The magnitude of support for such a dramatic change in tax laws provided political momentum that carried through Senate passage. Final approval of the conference agreement ultimately was reached late in the summer.

Several characteristics of the process that produced tax reform are notable. Private negotiations where bargaining and trading could be done openly and honestly were instrumental. Only ten years after Watergate resulted in the opening up of most congressional deliberations, it appeared that secrecy sometimes helped foster decision making. The strategy of developing a broad bipartisan consensus helped foreclose concerted interest-group opposition. Agreement on the framework for tax revision had to precede fine-tuning the thousands of special provisions. White House support for the process, and a willingness to accept some changes, was also invaluable. This rare combination of factors made the impossible possible.

CASE 4: THE 1988 CIVIL RIGHTS RESTORATION ACT

Patterns of cooperation and conflict between branches extend to the judiciary as well as Congress and the presidency. A controversy between the three branches began in 1984, when the U.S. Supreme Court severely limited the application of four federal civil rights laws in the case of *Grove City College v. Bell.* Over the next four years, a bipartisan coalition of congressional leaders drafted legislation to overturn the Court's decision but were opposed in their efforts by the Reagan administration.

Grove City College was a four-year private institution that did not receive any direct federal assistance, although a number of its students received federal grants. Prior interpretation of civil rights laws, such as Title IX of the 1972 Education Act amendments that bars sex discrimination, held that all programs and activities at an institution must comply if any programs received federal aid. Grove City College officials did not believe that they had to assure compliance with Title IX in athletic programs or in any other activities that did not receive direct federal aid.

In their six-to-three ruling, the Court agreed with Grove City College that only its financial aid programs had to comply with Title IX.[14] The decision had the effect of narrowing the application of three other civil rights laws dealing with discrimination on the basis of race, age, and disability as well as sex. The ruling was greeted with dismay and derision by civil rights groups around the country. Critics in Congress of both parties immediately set out to change the language in all four laws to ensure that failure to comply in any "program or activity" would lead to the elimination of all federal aid.

In the 1984 *Grove City* case, the U.S. Supreme Court ruled that some private colleges did not have to provide equal opportunities for men and women in athletics and other actvities.

The process dragged on for three years with over forty separate hearings held on various versions of the Civil Rights Restoration Act. President Reagan was able to block congressional action in the Republican-controlled Senate until 1987. A number of other issues, including abortion, became entwined and further delayed action. Proponents argued that federal monies should not support any institutions that discriminate and that the bill did little more than restore the standards of application that the Court had taken away. Opponents argued that the proposed bill would represent an unwarranted expansion of federal authority into private institutions. The public debate took on extreme proportions when Jerry Falwell and his conservative Moral Majority group claimed that the act could force religious institutions to hire homosexuals or drug addicts.

The Civil Rights Restoration Act was finally enacted by large majorities in the House and Senate in early 1988. President Reagan vetoed the bill, arguing that it was far too sweeping. Reagan appealed to Republicans in both Houses to uphold his veto. But on March 22, 1988, the House and Senate both overrode the president's veto and overturned the Supreme Court's interpretation. In the House, 52 of 175 Republicans joined the nearly unanimous Democrats to achieve the needed two-thirds majority. In the Senate, while several Republicans who had originally voted for the bill switched to support the president, it was not enough to prevent the veto override. In an election year, members of Congress of both parties wanted to express their support for civil rights and overturned the actions of the president and the Supreme Court.

As the "Political Close-up" and these four cases suggest, governing processes in the United States vary considerably. Franklin D. Roosevelt was able to move quickly and decisively in his first term, making significant changes in public policy. Like Roosevelt, President Jimmy Carter evoked the imagery of war but was unable to act decisively in energy policy. The process of enacting comprehensive tax reform is an example of how carefully crafted governing coalitions must be to successfully confront powerful interest groups. It suggests the importance of bipartisan cooperation between executive and legislative branches when party control is divided. The Civil Rights Restoration Act shows that the policy process can be dominated by the Supreme Court, the Congress, or the presidency. In this case, Congress was united with strong bipartisan majorities in both houses and eventually prevailed over the other two branches.

What shapes the public policy-making process in the United States? What factors determine whether political leaders are able to respond effectively or whether the result is stalemate and inaction in the face of urgent problems? The cases suggest a number of important factors: the nature of the times, economic conditions, leadership abilities, ideology, timing and strategies, majorities in Congress, party control and party loyalty, interest groups, election results, rules and procedures, public opinion, the media, and the constitutional structure of government. These are just some of the elements of politics, public policy, and political economy.

Politics, Public Policy, and Political Economy

POLITICS

Politics pervades our everyday lives—in the workplace, in the university, in the neighborhood, in organizations, all the way to foreign capitals. The term "politics" is used in a variety of ways, frequently with a negative connotation. People are accused of playing "politics" when they favor their own cause over another. It's just "politics" again when someone who knows the right people gets a job over an equally qualified applicant. It's "politics" at a different level when a corporation decides to build a plant in one state instead of another. It's raw "politics" when an angry legislator decries a presidential plan to close a military base in his district.

Definitions of politics are numerous. Fifty years ago, political scientist Harold Lasswell described **politics** as "who gets what, when, and how."[15] "Who" refers to the people and groups involved: average citizens, voters, corporations, minorities, party officials, and various other participants. Groups and individuals often compete with each other, opposing the goals of one another because of different economic interests or values. Politics is the process by which society resolves these conflicts. The "how" of Lasswell's definition describes the political process: the way in which elections are conducted and leaders are chosen, the ways in which Congress passes a bill or the president assembles a budget. The political process depends on the structure of government and rules embodied in constitutions, laws, procedures, and precedents. The "when" in the definition of politics concerns the timing of decisions, from nearly instantaneous events, such as a foreign invasion, to gradual effects, such as the long-term consequences of large government debt. The "what" of Lasswell's definition of politics is the result of politics: an energy policy, a court ruling concerning civil rights, a budget, a Social Security check. The "what" of politics is also called "public policy."

Politics may have many purposes that are not always consistent with each other. For individuals, it might be to achieve personal power, enrichment, or to better humankind. For groups, it may be to obtain specific goals or to minimize restrictions on their activities. A great deal of time, money, and attention is related to electoral politics—the process of running for office. Candidates and political parties work hard to raise money for campaigns. The media devote much of their attention to the "horse race" aspects of electoral politics—who's leading in the polls, what candidates are making a late surge, what charges were leveled against opponents. But the political skills needed to get elected are not necessarily the same as the skills needed to govern. Negative campaigns that avoid real issues can make policy-making more difficult. Spurious campaign promises can tie an official's hands once in office. The late Senator Thruston B. Morton of Kentucky, former chair of the Republican National Committee, often reminded candidates that "the purpose of politics is to establish a government."[16] The distinction between running and governing is an important one in assessing American politics.

PUBLIC POLICY

Public policy is a course of action about a problem. It is what the government does and the effect of those actions on people. Government makes policies on education, labor, health, welfare, agriculture, commerce, defense, the economy, abortion, busing, and dozens of other issues. Policy-making involves choices, and what governments do not do may be as important as what they do. Particularly in the United States, a tradition of limited government restricts the kinds of policies that may be made. Many other Western democracies have government ownership of communication, transportation, and other industries, for example. Most have more-extensive social welfare systems and take a larger share of citizens' income in taxes. Different policy choices have been made in the American political system. Many of those choices are based on the evolution and development of the economic system and its links with the political system.

POLITICAL ECONOMY

Political economy refers to the close relationship between the political system and the economic system. A century ago, no distinction was made between the study of politics and the study of economics. Many of the great thinkers of the time—Adam Smith, Thomas Malthus, David Ricardo, Karl Marx—were called the political economists. Only in this century did political science and economics develop separate disciplines. American political economy is based on shared beliefs about economic relationships between individuals, business organizations, and the state. The dominant economic philosophy in the United States is **capitalism,** a system based on private ownership and the use of markets.

Economic relationships are a fundamental part of American politics. Even those individuals who profess no interest in politics are concerned at a personal level with their own economic survival and prosperity. National economic conditions—inflation, recession, or depression—shape the possibilities for individual success. Surveys have shown that, except for fear of war, economic issues are the greatest concern of the American people. Government plays the major role in setting the rules of economic exchange that often dominate policymaking. Leaders are judged on their economic policy success. Studies have shown that national economic conditions are closely tied to the president's reelection chances, his influence with Congress, and his popularity. Economic issues are prominent in Congress as well. In the 1980s, budget and deficit worries dominated Capitol Hill and resulted in changes in the legislative process.

Political economy is important in explaining many aspects of politics. Chapter 3 examines American political economy in detail—underlying political and economic values, the evolution of the relationship between the government and the economy, and unfolding economic developments of the 1980s and 1990s that will change the policy agenda.

The Policy-Making Process

While the four cases revealed strikingly different patterns in the United States, it is possible to identify the key elements and stages in the policymaking process. Figure 1-1 outlines the compo-

FIGURE 1–1

THE POLICY MAKING PROCESS IN THE UNITED STATES

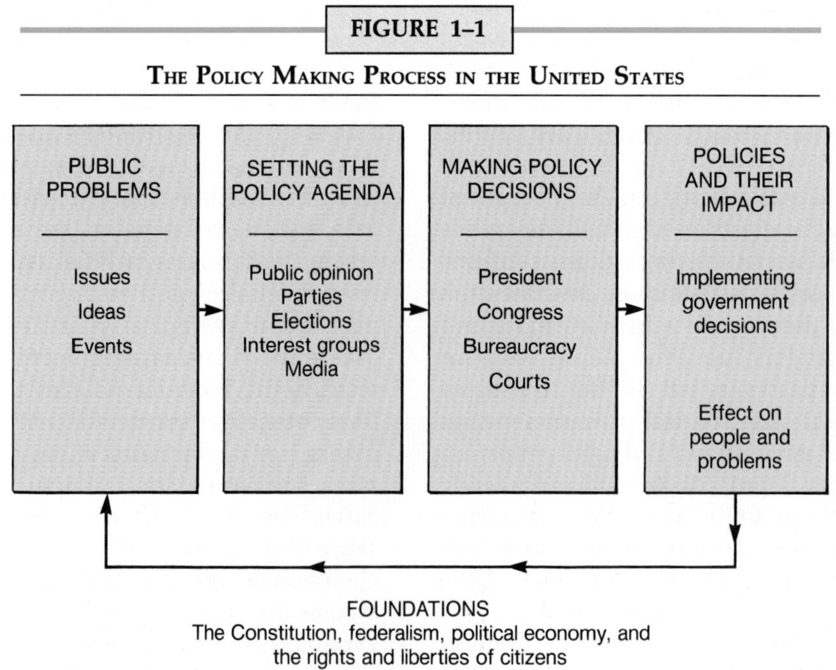

nents and steps in policy-making that are discussed in more detail below.

FOUNDATIONS

The American political system is built on a two-century-old constitutional foundation. The document that the nation's Founders drafted and adopted created a governmental structure and set of principles that still profoundly influences how policies are made today. The Constitution created separate legislative, executive, and judicial branches of government that shared overlapping political powers. Fearing tyranny and the accumulation of excessive power in one branch, the drafters of the Constitution created a system of checks and balances. Separation of powers, checks and balances and other constitutional features help determine how government works.

One distinguishing constitutional foundation of policy-making is ***federalism:*** the division of government powers between state and national government. Not only did the Founders separate powers between legislative, executive, and judicial branches, they also guaranteed that states would retain certain powers. Federalism influences policy-making in a number of ways. State governments may play a coequal or even a leading role in such policy areas as transportation, health and safety, and education. States are often the source of creativity in politics, developing innovations and approaches that are later applied at the national level.

The Constitution not only created a governmental structure but also established certain protections for individual rights and liberties. The Constitution embodies the principle of limited government, restricting the ultimate power of government. Specific protections of liberties and guarantees of rights are found in the Constitution itself and in the Bill of Rights—the first ten amendments to the Constitution. These protections and guarantees remain an important foundation of policy-making today, limiting, for example, what government can do in the war on illegal drugs. Many important policy choices directly concern conflicts over constitutional guarantees and restraints, such as abortion, affirmative action, or mandatory drug testing.

American political economy is also an essential foundation of policy-making. The United States developed as a nation on the basis of certain shared beliefs about the relationship between the political and economic systems. Such principles as private property rights, respect for hard work and material success, and the acceptance of economic inequality, underlie many contemporary policy-making issues. Setting specific rules for economic relations and defining the boundary between the private and public sectors remain two of the most critical policy debates. Section I of the text examines these political and economic foundations.

GETTING PROBLEMS AND ISSUES TO GOVERNMENT: THE POLICY AGENDA

Resting on these foundations, policy-making begins with some sort of problem, issue, event, or idea. For the government to act, the problem or idea must first become part of the policy agenda. In 1933, the Great Depression was an economic crisis so severe that it dominated the policy agenda. In contrast, concern with energy supply and conservation did not have a significant place on the government's policy agenda until the Organization of Petroleum Exporting Countries (OPEC) oil embargo in 1973 dramatized America's dependence and vulnerability. Accidents or natural events, such as the Exxon *Valdez* oil spill in Alaska, Hurricane Hugo, or the San Francisco earthquake, create immediate problems that must be addressed by government. Getting a problem on the policy agenda, however, can sometimes take years. The protection of the civil rights of blacks became part of the policy agenda in the 1950s and 1960s only after decades of struggle.

The **policy agenda** responds both to broad societal changes and public opinion. For example, while the provision of child care was not an important issue in the 1950s, it became one in the 1990s because of the expansion of single-parent households and working couples. Public opinion helps shape the policy agenda and choices that are made. Overwhelming public support for Social Security makes it difficult for elected officials to consider other options. On controversial issues ranging from abortion to defense spending, attitudes of the public help shape the agenda of government.

Issues get on the policy agenda through institutions that link the people to government. **Linkage institutions** include elections, political parties, interest groups, and the mass media. Political parties help shape policy choices in several ways. First, parties recruit candidates for public office and help run election campaigns, determining the quality of public leadership. Second, parties help set the policy agenda by identifying problems and proposing solutions. Parties adopt platforms that define for voters their concerns and positions on issues. Third, parties organize government to make public policy, determining who will lead Congress, run federal agencies, and nominate judges and justices.

Elections determine who will govern, selecting officials to serve in legislative and executive branches across local, state, and national governments. Election campaigns influence the policy agenda. The election of George Bush as president instead of Michael Dukakis in 1988 influenced tax policy and a host of other issues. But party platforms and election results do not always determine policy choices. In 1964, for example, President Lyndon Johnson campaigned against his opponent's support for greater U.S. involvement in Vietnam, but after winning the election, he escalated the war anyway. Elections are critical in any democracy, but the way in which election results are reflected in policy changes differs across political systems.

In modern society, the mass media has become an integral part of policy-making. Americans could sit in front of their televisions and watch the collapse of communism in Eastern Europe as it happened. Television has become the most important component of national election campaigns. The media help shape the policy agenda in a variety of ways, from broadcasting an expose about hazardous waste disposal to annointing a certain presidential candidate as the front-runner. The mass media are also an important element of the policy-making process. Public officials from the president on down need the media to convey information to citizens. News and commentary on controversial issues can influence eventual policy decisions.

Interest groups also help shape the policy agenda and determine what policy choices the government makes. Organized interests influence public policy in several ways. Through political action committees (PACs), interest groups make contributions to finance the campaigns of candidates that they believe will support them. Second, interest groups lobby government officials in legislative, executive, and judicial branches for favorable laws, regulations, or decisions.

The process of defining a policy agenda is complex and dynamic, responding to changes in the political and economic environment. Most often, setting the government's policy agenda is an evolving process of interpreting ambiguous election results, gauging public opinion, and balancing competing interests. Section II of this book examines the linkages between people and politics as part of the policy-making process.

MAKING POLICY DECISIONS

At the heart of the policy-making process of national government are American political institutions: the Congress, the presidency, the bureaucracy, and the judiciary. The process of national policy-making can be examined at three different levels. At the individual level are the people involved in government: the president, members of Congress, civil servants, and judges. Individual interests, motives, and behavior, such as presidential leadership skills or a legislator's concern with reelection, have a profound influence on policy-making. At the second level are institutions and decision-making processes—rules, procedures, precedents that determine the collective behavior of individuals. How effectively can Congress act as a body to enact laws? How does a president shape the presidency, or to what extent is he molded by the office? The third level concerns the political system itself—how national institutions work together to make policy.

Governing ability is determined by how a political system reaches policy decisions, carries them out, and maintains public support. While, to some degree, each institution operates in its own sphere, in most cases policy-making authority is shared. In the case of Jimmy Carter's energy program, because of diverse individual and institutional interests, it took a year and a half to enact a watered-down version of his comprehensive energy policy. In 1989, legislative-executive conflict ultimately killed President Bush's proposal for a capital gains tax cut. In contrast, both branches worked together to overcome interest group oppo-

The president plays a key role in making public policy, such as making decisions about the nations's taxing and spending priorities, but often encounters stiff opposition in Congress.

sition in enacting the 1986 Tax Reform Act. Courts may be the most autonomous of institutions, but as the Grove City College case revealed, their decisions can be altered or overturned. Bureaucracies may seem relatively autonomous in their abilities to make rules and regulations, but they, too, are subject to various controls by both Congress, the presidency, and the courts.

The decision-making stage is one of the most complex and fascinating of the policy process. Section III examines Congress, the presidency, the bureaucracy, and the courts, with a particular focus on executive-legislative relations.

Policies and Their Impacts

The scope of public policies in the 1990s—the government's course of action about problems—is vast. The most important policies are those that profoundly affect peace, prosperity, and the quality of life. The federal budget process and budget choices determine the nation's priorities: how much is spent on everything from space exploration to care for the elderly to the war on illegal drugs. Economic policy determines not only short-term conditions but also the long-term standard of living of Americans. The many facets of economic policy include fiscal policy (the effect of taxing and spending), monetary policy (the supply and cost of borrowing money), international trade, industrial policy, energy policy, and protection of the environment. Social welfare policies determine how society cares for its poor, its children, its elderly, from providing income security to health care. The dramatic changes in the international environment following the end of the cold war are altering U.S. defense and foreign policies. Decisions on the nation's role in the world, what kind of military establishment to maintain, or when armed intervention is justified are among the most important policy choices. Section IV examines these policy areas.

Once public policies are made, they must be carried out, or implemented. Some policy decisions have proven extremely difficult to implement, such as the 1954 Supreme Court decision *Brown v. Board of Education,* which ruled that racially segregated schools were unconstitutional. Thirty-five years later, government is still trying to achieve integration in public education. The federal bureaucracy is often most involved in implementing policies, but all institutions of government play a role. Court decisions may be implemented by lower courts, civil

President Bush speaking to schoolchildren in the Florida Everglades, a unique natural preserve whose future existence depends on the nation's environmental policies.

servants, state legislators, or mayors. Budgets are implemented by the actions of many thousands of individuals.

How effectively policies are implemented has a great deal to do with their impact, the final element of the policy process. Have policies solved the problem or resolved the issue? Has the policy created unintended consequences that create a new issue or problem? Policy impact—the success or failure of government actions—completes the cycle and brings it back to the beginning. With government simultaneously considering hundreds of different policies and problems, the policy-making process is really a series of many overlapping and intertwined cycles.

Politics in America is organized around the stages of the policy process. Each stage, from foundations to agenda-setting to decision-making to policies and their results, provides an opportunity to assess the American political system. Are democratic liberties protected and rights effectively guaranteed? Are the political system and its policy-making processes governing effectively? Critics and defenders provide diverse critiques of American democracy.

Governing in the American Political System: Effective Policy-Making or Chronic Deadlock?

The constitutional structure created for the United States in 1787 was intended to limit government—to prevent tyranny and the concentration of political power. But the problems confronting government have changed dramatically in two hundred years. A governmental framework devised to frustrate potential tyrants may frustrate democratic leaders seeking responsible solutions to public problems. Many observers of politics are concerned that American democracy is not working very well—from its inability to resolve critical issues to declining confidence of citizens in their political institutions. Consider some of the most common complaints about how the political system is working.

Separation of Powers Makes It Difficult to Govern Effectively

One of the oldest concerns about the political system centers on the separation of legislative and executive branches. President **Woodrow Wilson** was one of the first to address issues of governing capacity. In 1885, Wilson wrote:

> As at present constituted, the federal government lacks strength because its powers are divided, lacks promptness because its authorities are multiplied, lacks wieldiness because it processes are roundabout, lacks efficiency because its responsibility is indistinct and its action without competent direction.[17]

The accompanying "People in Politics" explains Wilson's concerns with separation of powers, political parties, and the mixed success he had as president in overcoming legislative-executive conflicts. Under the Constitution, Congress and the president share responsibility for reaching solutions to public problems. But increasingly, the two branches find themselves deadlocked over crucial decisions. Interbranch conflict has been a major cause of chronic budget deficits, which neither side takes responsibility for. Lloyd Cutler, former special counsel to President Carter, explains the problem:

> A particular shortcoming in need of a remedy is the structural inability of our government to propose, legislate, and administer a balanced program for governing. In parliamentary terms, one might say that under the U.S. Constitution, it is not now feasible to "form a Government." The separation of powers between the legislative and executive branches, whatever its merits in 1793, has become a structure that almost guarantees stalemate today. As we wonder why we are having such a difficult time making decisions we all know must be made and projecting our power and leadership, we should reflect on whether this is one big reason.[18]

Critics argue that the Constitution provides too many checks of one branch on the other, resulting in indecision and inaction in the face of urgent problems. Only in times of crisis has the government been able to act consistently with speed and dispatch. Even when policies are enacted, they are often contradictory. For example, at the same time that the federal government spends millions of

PEOPLE IN POLITICS

WOODROW WILSON AND THE PROBLEM OF GOVERNING

The only political scientist (although historians claim him as one of theirs) to occupy the White House was Woodrow Wilson. After a successful career as a professor, Wilson became president of Princeton University. Nursing political ambition, he entered politics and was soon elected governor of New Jersey. In 1912, he won the Democratic nomination for president at a marathon convention after scores of ballots. With the Republicans badly divided, he went on to victory in the general election and was reelected in 1916.

Wilson is notable because he spent much of his career before entering politics writing about government and politics. He is one of the few theorists who actually had an opportunity to put his ideas into practice. Some measure of fame followed the 1885 publication of his book *Congressional Government.* Wilson was concerned about governing. The main problem in American politics, as he saw it, was the need to overcome the fragmentation caused by the constitutional system. The national government he wrote about in the 1880s was dominated by Congress. The presidency was still in a weakened state after the impeachment and near conviction of Andrew Johnson in 1868. Accordingly, Wilson looked inside Congress and was disturbed at what he found: domination by standing committees. Congress, he wrote, was unable to govern because power was too broadly distributed.

The second great obstacle to governing, according to Wilson, was separation of powers. Wilson's answer to both problems was stronger political parties, which could be achieved by self-imposed responsibility and discipline. A great admirer of the British parliamentary system, Wilson wanted to see Congress act more like the House of Commons. He advocated a cabinet system of government for the United States to help overcome the separation of legislative and executive branches.

By the time he was elected president, Wilson had seen power in Washington swing back toward the White House. Still concerned with governing, he backed away from notions of cabinet government and instead saw a strong presidency linked to a strengthened party system as the key to overcoming stalemate. Wilson tried to foster these beliefs while in office, emphasizing partisan appeals and ignoring the Republicans, even when they might have been sympathetic. This strategy ultimately came back to haunt him when the Republican senators blocked the ratification of the Treaty of Versailles at the end of World War I. Wilson audaciously planned a parliamentary-type transition if he failed in his 1916 reelection bid. If he lost, he would appoint his opponent as secretary of state (at that time second in line for the presidency), after which he and the vice-president would resign. Instead of waiting five months for the inauguration, the new president would take over immediately, as in a parliamentary system. His victory in 1916 made this action unnecessary.

Although the differences between American and British politics became more apparent to Wilson later in his life, he continued to admire democratic systems whose institutional arrangements gave them greater ability to govern. His inability to make the American political system work like the British system resulted in political and personal defeat that ultimately broke his spirit. Wilson's ideas remain important bases for contemporary critiques of the American political system.

dollars to conduct research on the harmful effects of smoking, it also spends more millions subsidizing the tobacco industry.

Governing problems associated with **separation of powers** occur in the realm of foreign policy and national security as well as domestic politics. Congress, given the power to declare war under the Constitution, often disagrees with the president, the constitutional commander in chief. Only weeks after President Bush launched an invasion of Panama that was generally supported by Congress, he was barely able to convince one-third of the Senate to sustain his veto of a bill sanctioning China. Opposition to the Vietnam War ushered in an era of greater congressional activism and increasing divisiveness in foreign affairs.

From time to time, the courts get involved as well. Members of Congress filed suit against President Reagan, claiming that he violated the War Powers Act, but the courts declined to rule in the case. In recent years, however, the Supreme Court has handed down a number of decisions reinforcing the strict separation between legislative and executive branches in areas such as oversight of the bureaucracy and the power to order budget cuts. Instead of trying to develop mechanisms for better cooperation, both branches have asserted their constitutional powers. President Bush has taken an aggressive stance against what he considers unwarranted congressional usurpation of presidential authority. He has attempted to expand his veto power and his right not to carry out laws he feels are unconstitutional, as well as to restrict the power of congressional committees and limit the information he has to turn over to Congress.[19]

WEAK POLITICAL PARTIES AND "DECOUPLED" NATIONAL ELECTIONS INCREASINGLY PRODUCE DIVIDED GOVERNMENT

The gap between executive and legislative institutions has widened as a result of changes in the nature of parties and elections. Although not mentioned in the Constitution, political parties proved to be a key element in bridging separation of powers. Party loyalty historically has brought unity of purpose to various elements of government. When a president has strong majorities in both houses of Congress, harmony and cooperation in governing is not certain but more likely.

Many reformers, such as James MacGregor Burns, advocate stronger political parties to avoid divided government and what he calls, "the deadlock of democracy."[20] But instead of getting stronger, parties have gotten steadily weaker in the United States. Today, fewer people consider themselves to be strong party loyalists. More voters split their tickets—voting for candidates of different political parties for president and Congress. Seventy years ago, as much as 95 percent of the electorate cast a straight party ticket. Studies reveal that from half to two-thirds of today's voters split their ticket.[21] As parties have declined, other institutions have gained in importance, such as interest groups and the mass media. Candidates are increasingly independent of parties and get elected based on their own skills and personal appeal.

The result has been a gradual **"decoupling" of elections** for Congress and elections for president, which routinely produce ***divided government***—one party controlling the White House, the other controlling one or both houses of Congress. Today, party control of national government is regularly split between a Democratic Congress and a Republican president. Under the Constitution, the ability to enact policies depends on achieving consensus between the House of Representatives, the Senate, and the presidency. But elections for these offices are held at different times, and each is supported by a different constituency. Nonetheless, when parties were more important in communicating policy issues to voters, congressional and presidential elections were historically more closely coupled together. Presidents often had "coattails" on which they carried party loyalists to victory in congressional elections. But in the last five elections where a party lost the presidency, 92 percent of the congressional candidates of that party were elected anyway.

Divided government was rare during the first 150 years of the republic, occurring less than 25 percent of the time. Since the 1940s, divided government has occurred 60 percent of the time and in the last twenty years, 80 percent of the time. Republicans have had a lock on the presidency since 1968, with the exception of Jimmy Carter's narrow victory in 1976 in the aftermath of the

Watergate scandal. The Democrats have controlled the House of Representatives since 1954: no Republican in the House today has ever been in the majority. Only the U.S. Senate has shown much electoral volatility, changing party control in 1980 and 1986. Congressional incumbents in general are seemingly immune from electoral defeat, creating what some have called the "permanent Congress." House incumbents won reelection at a record rate of 98 percent in both 1986 and 1988.

Although parties have declined in importance, divided government remains highly susceptible to stalemate. When parties disagree sharply on issues, such as on the budget or aid to the Contras in Nicaragua or campaign finance reform, confrontation and deadlock often result. And despite the electoral security of incumbents, other changes in American elections are making it increasingly difficult to govern.

WHAT IT TAKES TO GET ELECTED OFTEN MAKES IT DIFFICULT TO GOVERN

While democratic values flourish around the world, complaints about the performance of democracy at home are multiplying. Critics find electoral politics increasingly nasty, trivial, and irrelevant to the real problems facing the nation. What it takes to get elected often has little to do with governing the nation. Increasingly, it takes lots of money and a good media consultant to get elected rather than issues, ideology, or ideas for solving problems. As one concerned member of Congress recently asked:

> Europe is about to establish a truly integrated trading system with major consequences for our own economy. Japanese industries are challenging America's for world economic leadership. Are not these challenges, along with the challenge of homelessness, rootlessness, and second-rate educational performance sufficiently profound to demand a vigorous, honest, and substantive debate between and within both parties about how they should be met? Is American politics so brain-dead that we are reduced to having political shysters manipulate symbols?[22]

Political campaigns have changed dramatically since the advent of television. As parties have become less important in the electoral process, they have been replaced by media consultants and advertising agencies. Winning elections has become a big business dominated by sophisticated technology—direct mail, computer-assisted polling, and media image-making, all costing millions of dollars. One consultant warns that Washington has become the seat of the "political-industrial complex." Campaigns have become increasingly negative—attacking opponents rather than making positive claims and taking positions on critical issues. So-called "slash and burn" campaign tactics are dominated by the slick **thirty-second spot,** which, according to critics, has drained the content out of campaigns.

Negative campaigns have become a regular part of politics at all levels, where the object is to find a weakness and pound the image into the electorate. In Texas and California, ads for the candidates for governor in 1990 included claims that their opponents were substance abusers or corrupt or would not execute as many criminals as they would. In 1988, the Bush campaign was widely criticized for its negative tactics, from questioning Dukakis's patriotism to blaming him for Willie Horton, a prisoner on weekend furlough who raped a woman. Bush campaign manager Lee Atwater explained, "We had only one goal in the campaign, and that was to elect George Bush. Our campaign was not trying to govern the country."[23]

Negative campaigning is on the rise because it works. "I've had a lot of my friends tell me that they try to run positive campaigns, and their polls just drop," former presidential candidate Walter Mondale observed. "Then they go on the negative, and their numbers go back up. A lot of people are sick about it."[24] The changes in campaign technology and tactics have had a chilling effect on candidates and their ability to govern once in office. Politicians become timid, afraid to take controversial stands or to make tough choices that could be exploited by a potential opponent, a lobbyist, or an aggressive reporter. Officials fear making speeches or writing articles that could be manipulated by clever political consultants. Members of Congress say that on a number of controversial votes, they worry more about how their vote could be used against them than the merits of the issue. Democrats blame Republicans for making it impossible to talk about taxes. Republicans blame Democrats for making it impossible to talk about Social Security. And the process of governing becomes even tougher.

Powerful Interest Groups and PACs Exert Undue Influence

In a political system where political power is dispersed among different branches and different levels of government, organized interests have certain advantages. These advantages have multiplied, according to critics, with the growth of political action committees that have contributed to the rapid increases in the costs of getting elected and staying elected.

In the view of political scientist Theodore Lowi, the power of interest groups to negotiate special treatment in the political process "renders government impotent."[25] As interest groups have grown in number and power, they have been able to dominate certain arenas of public policy in alliance with the bureaucracy and congressional subcommittees. These so-called "subgovernments" have become instrumental in determining policy towards farmers, railroads, automakers, or other groups. But in doing so, the special interests of a few are served rather than the collective national interest.

Powerful interest groups reinforce the changes in election campaigns. They may make governing more difficult because they may exercise a veto power over the government. Groups such as the National Rifle Association have effectively kept gun control off the policy agenda. Senior citizen groups such as the American Association of Retired Persons have helped prevent Social Security cuts and even a discussion of policy options. A government in awe of powerful interests is timid and cautious in making policy. Without dependable alignments or party loyalty, officials must devote most of their efforts building coalitions for each separate issue.

Governing ability within a political system does not equate with "big government." On the contrary, powerful interest groups often result in the unwanted expansion of government. Elected officials must often devise unusual strategies for dealing with the power of interest groups in order to govern. The Reagan administration in its efforts in 1981 to cut domestic spending lumped proposed cuts into a single package to prevent it from being dismantled by interest group pressure. The Tax Reform Act of 1986 was enacted because of an overt strategy on the part of congressional leaders to overcome the opposition of a multitude of special interests.

Interest groups not only affect the policy process by lobbying Congress and the bureaucracy. They also play an increasing role in campaign financing through political action committees. Senator Nancy Kassebaum (R-Kans.) explains how this affects governing:

> This produces two serious problems in the functioning of our democracy. First, the extraordinary importance of money forces elected officials to place a high priority on raising money. Second, the enormous amount of money being spent not only in election campaigns but in single-issue mass mailings and other "grassroots" efforts to influence Congress has tended to shrink, rather than expand, our political debate.[26]

Excessive influence by interest groups, like separation of powers, negative campaigning, and weak political parties, can be a barrier to effective policymaking. Others, however, believe that the political system is working just as the Founders wanted it to.

Counterpoint: The Policy Process Is Slow but Effective

Not everyone is concerned about the performance of the policy process and the ability to govern in the United States. Some, as Barber Conable revealed in the introduction, remind critics that obstacles to policy-making are exactly what the Founders intended. This view held for many generations. The treatises of Senator John C. Calhoun of South Carolina, published in 1852, reveal his belief that the minority should be able to veto the plans of the majority:

> It is, indeed, the negative power which makes the Constitution and the positive which makes the government. The one is the power of acting—and the other the power of preventing or arresting action. The two combined make constitutional government. . . . Where the numerical majority has the sole control of the government, there can be no Constitution.[27]

Those who continue to believe that the policy process should be slow and cumbersome fear a government that governs too easily, moves too quickly. They believe that separation of powers and checks and balances provide crucial safeguards to

Does the constitutional division of power between Congress and the president increasingly cause governing problems?

American democracy. Without them, for example, Congress would never have been able to investigate the Watergate cover-up and force President Nixon from office in 1974. Without them, Congress would not have been able to investigate the Iran-Contra scandal and check the illegal activities being carried out by the National Security Council in the basement of the White House.

A noted historian and former Kennedy administration adviser, Arthur M. Schlesinger Jr., warns against succumbing to the romantic myths of the parliamentary system.[28] Instead of defects in the system producing chronic deadlock, Schlesinger believes that the quality of elected officials is the problem. After all, he says, "separation of powers did not notably disable Jefferson or Jackson or Lincoln or Wilson or the Roosevelts." Schlesinger asks, what is the advantage of acting with decisiveness and dispatch if leaders don't know what they are doing?

Political scientist James Q. Wilson believes that the system governs slowly but effectively. He notes that policies that do get approved by Congress and signed into law by the president reflect broad consensus. They are likely to survive changes in administration, unlike the inconsistency in policy that sometimes characterizes parliamentary systems. According to Wilson:

> The deadlock of democracy is not a deadlock at all. . . . Our system has produced an extraordinary outpouring of legislative innovation because certain ideas were sufficiently coherent to permit change to occur. If we compare American policy with that of most parliamentary democracies, its leading characteristic is moderation. Taken as a whole . . . we tend to temper the enthusiasm of temporary majorities by the need constantly to reformulate that majority.[29]

Given these divergent views, how are students to evaluate the performance of American democracy?

Why Governing Ability Matters

Social scientists generally make two kinds of statements: empirical and normative. **Empirical** statements are objective statements of fact. **Normative** statements are subjective statements of value. Empirical questions ask how something is; normative questions ask how something ought to be. Political scientists attempt to explain the political world by constructing theories, linking together concepts in relational statements. Empirical theories attempt to explain, as objectively as possible, how the political system actually works. Normative theories prescribe a way in which the political system should work.

Judging the performance of American government involves both empirical knowledge and normative values. The emphasis in this textbook is on empirical observations and objective analysis of the dynamics of how the political system actually works today. But the emphasis on governing ability proceeds from a normative concern with growing problems in how the system is working. Since Woodrow Wilson's era, the debate over governing ability has often been characterized as one between liberals who favor stronger government and conservatives who favor weaker government. That no longer seems to be the case. Republicans are just as concerned about obstacles to governing as Democrats. David Stockman, key strategist for conservative President Ronald Reagan, expressed his frustration:

> The true Reagan revolution never had a chance. It defied all the overwhelming forces, interests, and impulses of American democracy. Our Madisonian government of checks and balances, three branches, two legislative houses, and infinitely splintered power . . . hugs powerfully to the history behind it. It shuffles into the future one step at a time.[30]

The analysis of governing in the following chapters challenges readers to evaluate for themselves how well the political system is working. It focuses attention on the relationship between political institutions and processes and policy outcomes that result. It involves contemporary dilemmas, such as deadlock over budget deficits and the consequences of negative campaigning, as well as classic constitutional questions about the effects of separation of powers. But ultimately, governing ability matters because it profoundly affects our future.

Will budget deadlock reduce the nation's standard of living in the coming decades, affecting job prospects or the opportunity to buy a home? Will our air and water be clean and harmful toxic wastes cleaned up? Will American industries be able to compete abroad, or will more and more products be imported? Will access to health care be extended to those who now go without it? Will fewer and fewer Americans bother to vote because they are turned off by politics? Can the scourge of drugs be removed from neighborhoods? Will the streets be safe to walk at night? Will the United States decline as a world power? How these and countless other questions will be answered in the coming decades depends on how well American democracy works and how effectively the nation's leaders are able to govern.

★

SUMMARY AND CONCLUSIONS

1. Governing ability can be defined as "the capacity of the political system to function effectively—to reach decisions, to carry them out, and to maintain public trust." A paradox of the American political system is that at times it works quickly and efficiently, while at other times it becomes deadlocked.

2. The four cases show that the system can at times quickly enact policies with feverish bursts of activity. The more normal situation is a slow process of coalition-building where many groups and individuals have an opportunity to block or modify public policy.

3. Politics can be defined as "who gets what, when, and how." Politics shapes public policy, which is a course of action about a problem. The policy-making process includes getting a problem on the agenda, decision making, and the implementation and impact of that policy. Politics and policy-making are closely related to American political economy.

4. Factors that seem to limit the ability to govern include separation of powers, weak political parties that produce divided government, a growing gap between running for office and governing, and powerful interest groups.

5. Judgments about governing depend on both empirical and normative observations and theories. The performance of government has important consequences for the future.

The constitutional structure created two hundred years ago provides the most important determinant of governing capabilities in the United States. The Constitutional Convention and the blueprint of government it produced is the subject of Chapter 2.

KEY TERMS

bipartisanship
capitalism
"decoupling" of elections
democracy
divided government
empirical versus normative
federalism
interest groups
linkage institutions
"moral equivalent of war"
negative campaigns
New Deal
policy agenda
political economy
politics
public policy
separation of powers
thirty-second spot
totalitarian regime
Woodrow Wilson

SELF-REVIEW

1. How does the ability to govern differ among political systems?
2. What are some of the most notable differences in the four cases?
3. What is politics? public policy? political economy?
4. Describe the stages in the policy process.
5. What are some main complaints about the ability of the American political system to govern effectively?
6. Judgments of the ability to govern depend on what factors?

SUGGESTED READINGS

Burns, James MacGregor. *The Power to Lead: The Crisis in the American Presidency.* 1984.
A discussion of the continuing problems of governing, with a set of proposed reforms that address separation of powers, parties, and the power of interest groups.

Lowi, Theodore. *The End of Liberalism.* 1978.
One of the most provocative, although difficult, books on American politics of the last two decades. Provides some particularly interesting insights into the question of governing.

Mezy, Michael L. *Congress, the President and Public Policy* (1989).
An intelligent analysis of the importance of Congress and the president working effectively together.

Robinson, Donald L. *Reforming American Government.* 1985.
The bicentennial papers of the Committee on the Constitutional System, this volume presents the case for and against constitutional reform and contains the actual drafts of a number of provocative amendments.

NOTES

1. Richard Bolling, "Governing America, A Conversation," *Public Opinion,* February–March 1984, p. 3.
2. Douglas Dillon, quoted in Donald R. Robinson, ed., *Reforming American Government* (Boulder, Colo.: Westview, 1985), 24–26.
3. John W. Gardner, quoted in Charlotte Saikowski, "Does the American Presidency Work?" *Christian Science Monitor,* 5 June 1984, p. 20.
4. Marjorie Randon Hershey, "The Campaign and the Media," in Gerald M. Pomper, *The Election of 1988* (Chatham, N.J.: Chatham House, 1989), 100.
5. Barber Conable, quoted in James Sundquist, *Constitutional Reform and Effective Government* (Washington, D.C.: Brookings, 1986), 4.
6. Lester M. Salamon and Michael S. Lund, *The Reagan Presidency and the Governing of America* (Washington, D.C.: Urban Institute Press, 1985), 3.
7. James MacGregor Burns, *Roosevelt: The Lion and the Fox* (New York: Harcourt Brace, 1956), 165.
8. *Ibid.,* 166.
9. Jimmy Carter, *Keeping Faith: Memoirs of a President* (New York: Bantam, 1982), 91.
10. *Congressional Quarterly Almanac, 1978,* p. 654.
11. *Ibid.*
12. *Ibid.,* p. 439.
13. Jeffrey Birnbaum and Alan Murray, *Showdown at Gucci Gulch* (N.Y.: Random House, 1988).
14. *Grove City College v. Bell* 104 Sct. 1211 (1984).
15. See Harold Lasswell, *Politics: Who Gets What, When, and How?* (New York: McGraw-Hill, 1936).
16. *Washington Post National Weekly Edition,* 22-28 January 1990, p. 23.
17. Lloyd Cutler, "To Form a Government—On the Defects of Separation of Powers," *Foreign Affairs,* Fall 1980, excerpted in Thomas Cronin, ed., *Rethinking the Presidency* (Boston: Little, Brown, 1982), 62.
18. *Congressional Quarterly Weekly Reports,* 3 February 1990, pp. 292–95.

19. Woodrow Wilson, *Congressional Government* (Boston: Houghton Mifflin, 1885), 318.
20. James MacGregor Burns, *The Deadlock of Democracy* (Englewood Cliffs, N.J.: Prentice-Hall, 1963), 323–25.
21. Larry Sabato, *The Party's Just Begun* (Glenview, Ill.: Scott Foresman/Little Brown, 1988), 131.
22. Congressman David Obey quoted in *New York Times,* 18 March 1990, p. 16.
23. Quoted in *New York Times,* 19 March 1990, p. 14.
24. *Ibid.*
25. Theodore Lowi, *The End of Liberalism,* 2nd ed. (New York: Norton, 1979), 295–97.
26. Quoted in Robinson, *Reforming,* 31.
27. Quoted by Peter Drucker, "Calhoun's Pluralism," in Wilmoore Kendall and George Carey, eds., *Liberalism and Conservatism* (Princeton, N.J.: Van Nostrand, 1966), 437. Calhoun, Conable, and those who favor limits on majority rule are often referred to as taking on an "antimajoritarian" position. Those like Woodrow Wilson, Burns, and Cutler take a "majoritarian" position, which favors removing the obstacles to majority rule.
28. Arthur M. Schlesinger Jr., "Leave the Constitution Alone" (1982), in Robinson, *Reforming,* 50–55.
29. James Q. Wilson, "In Defense of Separation of Powers," in Cronin, *Rethinking,* 179–82.
30. David Stockman, *The Triumph of Politics* (New York: Avon, 1987), 9.

CHAPTER 2

The Constitution

POLITICAL CLOSE-UP

Constitutional Amendments That Never Made it

In two hundred years, the United States Constitution has been amended only twenty-six times, and ten of the amendments were added in 1791 as the Bill of Rights. Nonetheless, plenty of amendments have been proposed over the years. During the bicentennial of the Constitution, the National Archives dug out some of the old proposals and put them on display. Some of them reflect novel ideas about how to change America's blueprint of government.

Abolish the presidency and the Senate. Emotions ran high after the controversial election of Rutherford B. Hayes in 1876. One angry citizen, Augustus Wilson, proposed the outright elimination of the presidency to avoid any future controversies over presidential elections. A citizens group from Potter County, Pennsylvania, proposed an amendment to eliminate the Senate. They complained that this aristocratic body "advanced the interest of the money, railroad, and manufacturing speculators to the prejudice of the common welfare."

Appoint a "premier" in Congress. Many reformers in the late 1800s wanted to bridge the separation between the legislative and executive branches. Amendments were proposed to allow cabinet members to participate in congressional debates or to include members of Congress in the president's cabinet. In 1921, William MacDonald proposed an amendment that would require the president to name a "premier" from among members of Congress. The premier would head up a cabinet of legislators; the president would become the ceremonial head of state.

Rename the nation "The United States of Earth." In 1893, Representative Lucas Miller of Wisconsin came up with a novel proposal to rename the country "The United States of Earth." Miller argued that the United States could grow by admitting to statehood all the countries of the world. To administer this vast country, Miller specified in his amendment that the House and Senate would "vote by electricity."

Require a vote of the people in order to declare war. In 1916, a group of isolationists from Nebraska sent a petition proposing an amendment to require a referendum before war could be declared. According to terms of their proposed amendment, records would be kept and all those voting for war would be required to enlist!

Limit individual wealth to one million dollars. During the depths of the Great Depression, Representative Wesley Lloyd of Washington came up with a constitutional amendment that would more equitably distribute income and pay off some of the federal debt. His 1933 amendment would prohibit any individual from accumulating more than a million dollars in wealth. Excess money collected by the government would help pay off the national debt.

Have you heard any good proposals to amend the Constitution lately?

SOURCES: *New York Times,* 3 August, 1987, p. Y12; and James Sundquist, *Constitutional Reform and Effective Government* (Washington, D.C.: Brookings, 1986), chap. 3.

CHAPTER OUTLINE

INTRODUCTION AND OVERVIEW

In the sweltering heat of Philadelphia in the summer of 1787, fifty-five delegates met to draft a constitution for the United States. The goal of the Founders was to create a political system that could govern without making it so powerful that it would infringe on liberty. After all, America had fought a long war against the British Crown because of its arbitrary and unchecked government authority. But the new American nation needed a *national* government. The experience under the weak Articles of Confederation had proven that.

On the two-hundredth birthday of the U.S. Constitution in 1987, Americans celebrated a remarkable document whose durability is unmatched in the modern world. Until 1787, there were very few examples of written constitutions produced by an assembly. Since 1787, virtually all constitutions have followed the American model. Constitutional expert Elmer Cornwell concludes: "The Framers . . . virtually invented both the concept of a written frame of government and the ideal of constitution making by convention."[1] The Constitution has survived, but is survival enough? After two hundred years, is its plan of government outmoded, hopelessly out-of-date? Does it provide leaders with the means to govern in a world of complex problems that the Framers could not have foreseen? In exploring the Constitution and its consequences for governing, the following questions are considered:

1. What was the colonial political experience, and how did it affect the decisions made at the Constitutional Convention? What were other major influences on the Founders?
2. What did the delegates to the Constitutional Convention agree on? What were the major controversies and compromises forged at the convention?
3. What kind of constitutional system was created? How do the basic features of separation of powers, checks and balances, and federalism affect the ability to govern today?
4. How was the Constitution ratified? What were its opponents most concerned about? Why was the Bill of Rights added?
5. How can the Constitution be amended? What are some of the criticisms of the Constitution? Should it be amended to increase governing ability or left the way it is?

The American Political Experience

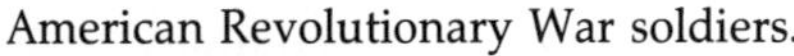

THE ROAD TO AMERICAN INDEPENDENCE

Until the 1770s, colonists thought of themselves not as "Americans" but as British citizens living in the New World. For almost one hundred years, the British had fought the French and their Indian allies. A sense of American national identity began to develop after the **French and Indian Wars** ended in 1765. For the first time, Americans could applaud their own military heroes, such as George Washington. Americans rallied against the Navigation Acts and Stamp Tax imposed by King George and Parliament. Suddenly, they had a common interest that distinguished them from their relatives in England.

The British were displeased with the lack of help and cooperation from the American colonists during the war to drive the French out of North America. In the words of historians Morrison and Commager, "There was a woeful lack of cooperation. Requisitions of men and money were flouted. Commercial regulations were evaded. Trade with the enemy flourished."[2] Let the Americans pay for a war that was waged largely for their own benefit, thought the British. But attempts to exert more control over the colonies ran against the tide of rising American nationalism.

The political situation grew tense in 1773. Under cover of darkness, a group of Americans disguised as Indians vandalized a British East India Company ship. The tea on board was dumped in Boston Harbor. England reacted harshly to the "Boston Tea Party," closing the port of Boston and virtually rescinding the charter of Massachusetts. Political activity within the thirteen colonies increased. In 1774, the First Continental Congress was called to discuss the growing unrest in the colonies and to determine appropriate ways to air grievances. The Second Continental Congress met in 1775, as hostilities between the colonists and the British broke out at Lexington and Concord. Yet even after the actual fighting started, most Americans still hoped for reconciliation with England. Independence was not yet anticipated or desired. However,

American Revolutionary War soldiers.

POLITICAL INSIGHT 2–1

THOMAS PAINE'S *COMMON SENSE*

In January 1776, Thomas Paine made his debut as an international rabble-rouser (he was later to play a role in the French Revolution). Having come to America from England only two years earlier, he brought with him a strong dislike for the class-oriented British society. Common Sense, *excerpted below, combined a powerful message with a vituperative style.*

There is something exceedingly ridiculous in the composition of Monarchy; it first excludes a man from the means of information, yet empowers him to act in cases where the highest judgment is required. The state of a King shuts him from the world, yet the business of a King requires him to know it thoroughly; wherefore the different parts, by unnaturally opposing and destroying each other, prove the whole character to be absurd and useless. . . .

But it is not so much the absurdity as the evil of hereditary succession which concerns mankind. Did it insure a race of good and wise men, it would have the seal of divine authority; but as it opens a door to the *foolish*, the *wicked*, and the *improper*, it hath in it the nature of oppression. Men who look upon themselves born to reign, and others to obey, soon grow insolent; selected from the rest of mankind, their minds are easily poisoned by importance, and the world at large, that they have but little opportunity of knowing its true interests, and when they succeed to the Government, are frequently the most ignorant and unfit of any throughout the dominions. . . .

In short, Monarchy and succession have laid, not this or that kingdom only, the world in blood and ashes. It is a form of Government which the word of God bears testimony against, and blood will attend it. . . .

In England the King hath little more to do than to make war and give away places; which, in plain terms is to impoverish the nation and set it together by the ears. A pretty business, indeed, for a man to be allowed eight hundred thousand sterling a year for, and worshipped into the bargain! Of more worth is one honest man to society, and in the sight of God, than all the crowned ruffians that ever lived.

SOURCE: *The Political and Miscellaneous Works of Thomas Paine* (London, 1819).

harsh reaction by King George and a growing radicalism in the colonies culminated in the Declaration of Independence in 1776.

Public sentiment in favor of independence was swayed by the political pamphlets of the day. One of the most famous pamphleteers was Thomas Paine, whose ***Common Sense*** helped stir up national sentiment for independence from "the royal brute of Great Britain" (see Political Insight 2–1).

On July 4, 1776, the thirteen colonies declared independence with the stirring words of Thomas Jefferson:

> We hold these truths to be self evident, that all men are created equal, that they are endowed by their Creator with certain unalienable Rights, that among these are Life, Liberty, and the pursuit of Happiness. That to secure these rights, Governments are instituted among Men, deriving their just powers from the consent of the governed—that whenever any Form of Government becomes destructive of these ends, it is the Right of the People to alter or to abolish it, and to institute new Government, laying its foundation on such principles, and organizing its powers in such form, as to them shall seem most likely to effect their Safety and Happiness.

The Declaration of Independence was a radical political document containing new ideas about the **natural rights** of citizens relative to government. Jefferson's words in the Declaration reflected the ideas of political philosopher **John Locke,** whose *Second Treatise on Civil Government* was written in 1690.[3] Locke believed that people, because they live in a state of nature, are governed by natural law. These laws of nature, he claimed, are superior to any human-made laws and therefore all governments, which are based on human law, can be challenged. Government must be based on the consent of the governed. If people find themselves in a situation contrary to natural law, they have the "unalienable right" to dissolve the old government and form a new one. Locke's ideas are unmistakable in the Declaration, underpinning the necessity of a break with England and the belief in a constitutional form of government.[4]

CONSEQUENCES OF THE REVOLUTION

One of the first consequences of the war was the drafting of constitutions in the newly independent states. These experiences would prove valuable when it came time to draft a national constitution. Most of the states redrafted their constitutions in 1776 or 1777.[5] Because their drafters feared concentration of power in the head of government (as with the despised King George), most constitutions made the legislature powerful and the governor weak. New York, which got started later than the rest, was an exception. The war was already under way when New Yorkers began to draft their new constitution. The delegates barely managed to stay ahead of the onrushing British troops as they fled up the Hudson River from New York City toward Albany. The need for a stronger governor to take charge in the emergency was apparent. The delegates wrote a constitution giving the governor the power to mobilize the militia and run the state during the war. The governorship of New York would later be an important model for the presidency.

"All men are created equal" was indeed a revolutionary doctrine. Perhaps the most important consequence of the American Revolution was the challenge to the existing order of things. Many old ideas were questioned for the first time, and many new ideas were put into practice. Wealthy, educated men fought side by side with farmers and frontiersmen. Women played an important part in winning the war by farming the land and engaging in trade and manufacturing activities. Royal government and the divine right of kings was rejected. Personal liberty gained new prominence. The American Revolution had a profound impact on revolutionary movements around the world, particularly in France. In America, it opened the door to one of the most important experiments in the history of government, the drafting of the U.S. Constitution.

THE ARTICLES OF CONFEDERATION: A GOVERNING CRISIS

During the war, the United States were loosely governed by the Continental Congress. Articles of union for the thirteen states were drafted in 1777 and submitted by Congress to the state legislatures. They were finally approved in 1781, when the seven states with claims on the land to their west relinquished them to the union. The **Articles of Confederation** became official.

It was a feeble union, barely able to govern. Most of the power remained with the states. Each state was guaranteed "its sovereignty, freedom and independence, and every power, jurisdiction and right" not granted to the national government. The central government was made up of a unicameral (single-chamber) legislature, called the Confederation Congress, which consisted of one representative from each state. Congress was granted the power to make treaties, coin money, regulate trade with the Indians, build a navy, and create a post office. That was about it. Most notable were the powers the national government was denied: powers to levy taxes and to regulate commerce. These were powers the British Crown had abused.

The government lacked a real head and there was no executive branch. John Hanson was elected the first "President of the Confederation Congress of the Confederacy" in 1781. John Hancock was later elected to this post but never bothered to show up! After the experience of British colonial rule and a war filled with cries against tyrants, the states were willing to cede little to the national government.

It was nearly impossible to make public policy under the Articles of Confederation.[6] Foreign nations were not sure with whom they were dealing and had little respect for the new government. Each state printed its own paper money, which was difficult to exchange and confusing to value. National finances were in chaos. It was increasingly difficult for the government to borrow money, and even the states began to default on their payments to the Treasury. An economic crisis was impending.

The consensus won by fighting a common enemy appeared to be crumbling. Conflicts between economic classes—debtor and creditor, farmer and manufacturer—seemed to multiply. A farm debt crisis spread across the country as state legislatures passed laws that resulted in the arrest and imprisonment of indebted farmers. An alarming incident occurred in western Massachusetts when a group of farmers, facing imprisonment because of delinquent taxes, rallied around a local war hero named Daniel Shays. "Shays's Rebellion" occurred when the mob marched into North Hampton and took over the local courthouse. When word spread, the nation was shocked at the inability of the government to deal with the insurrection. Would mob violence rule the new country? Some openly questioned whether a king might be needed after all.

The militia quelled the rebellion when it moved across the border into New York, but its impact had already been felt. Efforts to revise or scrap the Articles of Confederation were accelerated. During the summer of 1786, only five states had bothered to send delegates to a convention in Annapolis, Maryland, to discuss trade regulations between the states.[7] Disappointed, the delegates at Annapolis issued a call for a convention in Philadelphia the following year. Congress sanctioned the convention by approving such a meeting for the "sole and express purpose of revising the Articles of Confederation." Of course, the delegates would do much more than revise. In response to the crisis of governing under the Articles of Confederation, they drafted an entirely new constitution.

The Framers of the Constitution

Fifty-five of the seventy-two delegates named attended the Constitutional Convention in Philadelphia. About thirty attended regularly and played an active role. It was an impressive group, including seven former governors, thirty-nine former members of Congress, and eight who had helped write their state constitutions.[8] George Washington presided, his mere presence an important asset to the convention. Aged Ben Franklin was there, still able to effectively use his wit and humor when tempers flared. James Madison, the primary author of the Constitution, kept a journal of the proceedings. The delegates from Pennsylvania and Virginia dominated the convention.

A few prominent leaders were missing. Thomas Jefferson was in France serving as ambassador. Patrick Henry boycotted the proceedings. Thomas Paine had returned to Europe. The fifty-five delegates consisted of relatively young but powerful, wealthy, and experienced people. Bankers, lawyers, merchants, and estate owners were well represented. Small farmers, laborers, and rural residents were underrepresented. The accompanying "People in Politics" profiles some of the delegates.

THE DELEGATES' DILEMMA

The delegates' problem was to create a political system capable of governing effectively but not so powerful as to abuse liberty. Most of the delegates were suspicious of government and concentration of political power. British abuses were still fresh in their minds: the dissolution of colonial legislatures by the king, the quartering of troops in private homes, the trials of citizens without a jury, the imposition of taxes without consent. Political power and the ability to govern, they agreed, must be limited. But the chaotic years under the Articles of Confederation were also remembered. Delegates knew that during the preceding fifteen years, some of the state legislatures had been as injurious to individual rights as any executive.[9] The experience with the Continental Congress had convinced many delegates that the legislative branch was incapable of running the nation. How could they strike an acceptable balance between governing ability and the protection of liberty? This was their dilemma.

Although the Founders were as much men of practical politics as intellectuals, they were influenced by the dominant ideas of the day. Most of the delegates had read Locke's *Second Treatise.* In addition to his principles of natural law and the

PEOPLE IN POLITICS

THE LEADERS OF THE CONSTITUTIONAL CONVENTION

James Madison

George Washington.
The most famous and popular American, who had led the country to victory in the Revolutionary War, represented Virginia. Washington would have preferred to stay on his lovely Mount Vernon estate with his family and prize horses, but his presence at the convention was essential. He came reluctantly and attended only when he became convinced that the effort to revise the Articles would fail without his participation. Unknowingly, he played another role. The delegates drafted Article II on the presidency with him as the model for that office. Their faith in George Washington gave them confidence to create a strong presidency. He was elected presiding officer and did not participate in the substantive debate.

James Madison.
Only thirty-six years old at the time of the convention, Madison represented Virginia too. Madison is considered to be the main author of the Constitution. A diminutive man with a brilliant mind, he made careful notes of each day's proceedings. Because no official record was kept, Madison's journal is the best record that exists. He was a former member of Congress and a Virginia assemblyman and had helped draft the Virginia Constitution. His careful study of history and the writings of Locke and Montesquieu, combined with his practical political experience, helped him develop the Constitution's unique system of checks and balances.

Alexander Hamilton.
A delegate from New York, the thirty-one-year-old Hamilton was a fiery man of aristocratic leanings who ardently championed a strong national

(Continued on next page.)

consent of the governed, Locke believed in limited government. There were certain things governments may not do, which must be left to the discretion of the individual. Locke emphasized the right of property: "The supreme power cannot take from any man any part of his property without his consent." Gouverneur Morris and other delegates echoed Locke's words at the convention, arguing that the main object of the Constitution should be to protect property. Participation in politics, they argued, should be limited to those who hold property. But their arguments did not prevail. Specific provisions to this effect were not included in the Constitution and instead were left to the states.

The French political theorist **Montesquieu** had suggested a practical means of limiting government to protect liberty. He argued that separation of powers along legislative, executive, and judicial lines would prevent any one part of the government from becoming too powerful. Montesquieu's *Spirit of the Laws* fit nicely with Locke's ideas. James Madison would blend them with his own political experience into the Constitution.

POLITICAL ECONOMY AND THE FOUNDERS

The deteriorating economic situation played a role in convincing delegates that a stronger central government was needed. Economic historians generally agree that the 1780s were characterized by recession, harming some economic interests more than others. Bankers, financiers, and merchants were suffering the most under the Articles of Confederation. They led the call for replacement. The war had damaged the position of American merchants in the world market by removing the guaranteed outlets

PEOPLE IN POLITICS

government. Suspected of being a monarchist, Hamilton proposed the creation of an American nobility to function in the same way as the British aristocracy. Not much inclined toward the common man ("Your people, sir, are a great beast!" he said), he was often out of touch with the sentiment of other delegates and had less influence on the Constitution than he might have had with more moderate views. However, he was very close to George Washington and became the first secretary of the treasury. He would play a critical role as adviser to President Washington, designing the National Bank and shaping U.S. economic policy.

Benjamin Franklin.
The legendary Ben Franklin represented Pennsylvania. Like Washington, Franklin's main contribution to the convention was his presence. At age eighty-one, he was the oldest delegate in attendance—a national figure, slightly eccentric but much beloved. Unlike Hamilton, he had a much more generous view of the common man. Still a ready wit, Franklin helped cool tempers during the hot summer and helped rally support for unanimous approval of all the delegations when the Constitution was finished.

Gouverneur Morris.
Along with Franklin, Morris represented Pennsylvania. Even with only one leg, he was dashing and eloquent, an aristocrat with little patience for the common rabble and some elements of the "commercial class." He savored the sound of his own voice and addressed the convention more than any other delegate. Morris had more influence on the style of the Constitution than on its substance. Head of the Committee on Style, Morris penned many of the sections that have endured so long. In later years, he once started a letter by writing: "The hand that writes this letter wrote the Constitution."

James Wilson.
The third delegate from Pennsylvania, Wilson was a decided contrast to his other two colleagues. He was an unglamorous Scotsman but one of the most able and influential of the delegates. An attorney, he had significant impact on the sections of the Constitution dealing with the presidency and the executive powers. Wilson, a strong advocate of a powerful national government, is largely responsible for the single executive as we know it.

for their products that they had enjoyed as a colony. American industries were underdeveloped and threatened by the importation of cheap foreign goods. Merchants trying to engage in interstate commerce struggled to overcome the growing competition between states. Advocates of a stronger central government became known as **Federalists.** It would have been more accurate to call them nationalists.

On the other side were groups with less to fear from weak government and more to fear from a stronger central government. Small farmers, independent business owners, laborers, and debtors constituted this group. Patrick Henry and George Clinton were among their spokesmen. Opponents of the new national government became known as the **Anti-Federalists.** Although the two groupsdisagreed strongly about how powerful the new government should be, the Constitutional Convention was dominated by the Federalists. Satisfied with the status quo, the Anti-Federalists were poorly represented at the convention. Patrick Henry, for example, was selected but declined, reportedly saying that he "smelt a rat." Although absent from the convention, the Anti-Federalists became a formidable obstacle during the ratification process.

Issues and Compromises: Convention Politics

The Founders are most famous for their disputes, but in fact they began their deliberations with a significant degree of consensus. Within a week of their May 24, 1787, opening, the convention approved a resolution stating that "a national government ought to be established consisting of a supreme legislative, executive, and judiciary." This

George Washington presiding over the Constitutional Convention in Philadelphia in 1787.

was a crucial decision. It signaled basic agreement on a national government of separated powers. It changed the original presumption of reforming a loose collection of states to the goal of creating a real national government. But how far would they go?

Consensus also existed on the need to protect private property. This was not too surprising given the economic circumstances of the delegates. The delegates also agreed on the need for a republican form of government with elected representatives. Alexander Hamilton's plan for a hereditary nobility, as in the British House of Lords, was rejected, but an appointed upper house with longer terms (the Senate) was included as a check on the popularly elected House. Finally, the delegates agreed on the idea of federalism: dividing political power between state and national government. Although the details would have to be hammered out, the general principle of federalism was accepted. What, then, were some of the main areas of conflict?

Three dimensions of conflict dominated the deliberations: small states versus large states, slave states versus nonslave states, and strong executive versus weak executive advocates. The issues were combined in several comprehensive "plans" that were presented to the delegates. Virginia's delegates were well organized and committed to the creation of a stronger national government. A delay in the opening of the first session gave James Madison and his supporters the chance to put together a set of recommendations. Their **Virginia Plan**, by being first, became the agenda of the convention. For the rest of the summer, supporters of a strong national government were able to dominate the agenda despite the efforts of opponents.

THE VIRGINIA PLAN

Madison's proposals came to the floor in the form of fifteen resolutions. They proposed a strong central government with the states clearly secondary in importance. The Virginia Plan called for a bicameral

Congress with both houses apportioned on the basis of population. The House would be elected directly by the people, the Senate would be elected by the House. Madison suggested that the new national government would have the ability to legislate in any matter in which the states are "incompetent." Congress would have the power to "veto" state laws. Under the Virginia Plan, there would be a single national executive and a national judiciary chosen by the Congress.

The convention debated the Virginia Plan for almost two weeks before the small states offered a counterproposal. Believing they had much to lose in the new union, delegates from the smaller states wanted a weaker national government with more powers reserved to the states. William Patterson of New Jersey put together an alternative of nine resolutions and introduced them on June 14.

THE NEW JERSEY PLAN

Patterson's alternative envisioned a central government much weaker than in the Virginia Plan but stronger than under the Articles of Confederation. The states would remain dominant, although surrendering some power to the central government. Fearing domination by the larger states, the small states wanted equal power in the new union. Patterson's **New Jersey Plan** therefore called for a unicameral legislature where all states were represented equally. Powers not expressly delegated to the national government would remain with the states. Patterson also called for a relatively weak plural executive and a strong national judiciary.

After debate, several provisions of the Patterson Plan were included in the draft constitution, but most were rejected. Disappointed, the small-state delegates contemplated walking out of the convention. Disaster threatened. The new union could not survive with only some of the states. The delegates faced a stalemate and the possible collapse of the convention. As the temperature rose, so did tempers. Ben Franklin suggested they start each session with a prayer, but the delegates could not even agree on that. Facing crisis, a committee of eleven—one delegate from each state in attendance—was appointed to work out a compromise over the Fourth of July weekend.

THE CONNECTICUT COMPROMISE

The solution hammered out is known today as the **Connecticut Compromise**, or the Great Compromise. The large-state delegates made a crucial concession on the apportionment of the upper house—the Senate. In return, they demanded that all money bills would originate in the lower house—the House of Representatives. States were to be equally represented in the Senate, whereas House representation would be apportioned on the basis of population. The thorny problem of slavery was skirted in the compromise. Southern states wanted to count slaves to increase their population and their apportioned seats. Northern states did not want slaves counted at all. The delegates finally agreed to count each slave as three-fifths of a free person for census and taxation purposes (the **three-fifths compromise**). Northern delegates also wanted to halt the importation of slaves immediately, but southern delegates made it clear they would have no part of an immediate ban. Northerners settled for a compromise allowing slave importation for twenty more years. No slaves could be imported after 1808. Two of the most difficult issues facing the delegates were settled. The remaining issues were the nature and the powers of the executive.

A STRONG OR A WEAK PRESIDENCY?

Two opposing lines of thought developed during the debate about the executive. The first group of delegates wanted an executive that was weak, subject to the control of the legislature.[10] They were suspicious of executive power or any institution that remotely resembled the hated monarchy. Roger Sherman of Connecticut exemplified this view, as Madison revealed in his diary: "He considered the Executive magistracy as nothing more than an institution for carrying the will of the Legislature into effect, that the person or persons ought to be appointed by and acceptable to the Legislature only."[11] What would the American political system be like today if Congress had been given the power to appoint the president?

Opposing delegates favored a strong executive. Troubled by the inability to govern under the Articles of Confederation, they wanted an independent executive with a veto power. James Wilson of

Pennsylvania was the key spokesperson for the strong executive advocates.[12] Eventually, the following key decisions about the presidency were made.

CREATION OF A SINGLE EXECUTIVE. One of the first decisions was to create a single executive. Edmund Randolph of Virginia criticized the single executive and tried to persuade the delegates that selecting three members to represent different sections of the country would lessen a possible drift to monarchy.[13] Wilson countered that a single magistrate was necessary to ensure "energy, responsibility, and dispatch" in the office. Wilson's motion for a single executive was adopted by the convention on July 17.

The designation of the title "President of the United States" was not made until August. It was accompanied by the phrase "His Excellency," but for some unknown reason the **Committee on Style,** which gave the Constitution its final language, deleted this designation.

REJECTION OF A "CABINET COUNCIL." Many delegates believed that the president should be controlled by some kind of council or cabinet. The Virginia Plan included a "council of revision" to share the veto power with the president. But by the waning days of the convention, with the understanding that George Washington would be the country's first president, the delegates gave up on formally establishing a council or cabinet. President Washington initiated the informal practice of using a cabinet when he conferred with the heads of the executive departments during his first term.

CHOICE OF AN INDIRECT MEANS OF SELECTION. Those who wanted a weak executive favored a system where the president was chosen by Congress. Those who wanted a strong, independent presidency favored direct election by the people. They compromised on something in-between: the **electoral college,** with selection by the House of Representatives if no candidate received a majority of votes. The Founders were worried about the "mob rule" aspect of democracy and wanted to create some barriers between the presidency and the general public. With the electoral college, each state was free to choose its electors any way it wanted (most were chosen by the state legislatures until the 1830s). The electors would then choose the president. Advocates of a strong, independent presidency were generally satisfied. Those who wanted the president to be elected by Congress believed that in most cases, the electoral college would fail to produce a majority and the House of Representatives would pick the president. As it turned out, this has occurred only three times in American history.

ESTABLISHMENT OF A TERM AND PROVISIONS FOR REMOVAL. How long would the president serve? Some delegates favored a six- or seven-year term with no opportunity for reelection, believing this would give the president enough time to carry out his program effectively without having to constantly campaign for reelection. Proponents wanted to place the president "above politics." At first, the convention adopted a seven-year term, but then it reversed itself after agreeing on the electoral college.[14] The delegates finally accepted a four-year term with no limitation on reelection. George Washington established the two-term tradition that held until Franklin D. Roosevelt was elected to a third term in 1940 and a fourth term in 1944. The Twenty-second Amendment, adopted in 1948, now limits the president to two terms.

POWERS OF CONGRESS AND THE PRESIDENT. The Framers delegated specific powers to the president and the Congress. The president was to be head of the executive branch and commander in chief of the armed forces. Constitutional powers include the power to call Congress into session, to commission military officers, to grant pardons, to make treaties, to approve or veto legislation, and to ensure that the laws are "faithfully executed."

Congress, created in Article I and considered the "first branch" of government, was also delegated a number of powers. Some overlapped with the president's. Congress was granted the lion's share of economic powers: the power to impose taxes, excises, and duties, to borrow money, to regulate commerce, to coin money, and to pay debts. Congress also was given the power to declare war, to raise armies, and to call forth the militia. The Founders tried to balance the power of one branch with the other. The potential strength of the presidency would not be known for decades, and the balance between the executive and the legislature continues to evolve after two hundred years. Nonetheless, the advocates of a strong presidency managed to prevail over those who wanted only a weak figurehead for the new government.

FINALIZING THE CONSTITUTION

The long summer had drawn to a close. The delegates had overcome the most divisive issues. The Committee on Style had finished the final draft. It was time to present the finished document to the nation.

First, the convention had to get final approval of the delegates. September 17, 1787, was set for the final vote. Ben Franklin, too infirm to read his own speech, asked his colleague James Wilson to deliver it for him. It was a shrewd effort to unite the delegates. "I confess that there are several parts of this constitution that I do not at present approve," Wilson read for Franklin. "On the whole, Sir, I cannot help expressing a wish that every member of the Convention who may still have objections to it, would with me, on this occasion doubt a little of his own infallibility—and to make manifest our unanimity, put his name to this instrument."[15]

Franklin then moved that the Constitution be accepted unanimously by the state delegations. The final vote was ten in favor, one delegation divided, none opposed. The blueprint for a government had passed, but many questions remained. Would the thirteen states ratify the Constitution? Would it work? Would it create a weak or a strong national government? What kind of a constitutional system had the delegates created?

The Constitutional System

SEPARATION OF POWERS

In his distrust of individual power-holders in government, Madison envisioned a political system in which power was decentralized. The doctrine of **separation of powers** is based on the belief that tyranny is associated with a concentration of power and liberty with a dispersal of power. It is probably more accurate to characterize the constitutional system as separation of *function,* with differentiated but overlapping powers. In the policy-making process, each branch plays a different role but must work together for effective action. Despite the criticism of separation of powers discussed in Chapter 1, some of the delegates felt that the three branches were too intermingled in the Constitution. At the Virginia ratifying convention, one delegate claimed that the executive was, contrary to opinion, "blended with the legislature."[16] Three states wanted to add a "separation clause" to the Bill of Rights to further divide the functions of the three branches. The rejection of this idea indicates that the Founders did not want to separate power absolutely but only to limit the ability of any one branch to dominate. Separating functions was not enough if officials joined together and pooled their authority. Separation of powers had to be supplemented by checks and balances.

CHECKS AND BALANCES

If powers were completely separated, there could be no checks and balances, because each branch would operate independently within its own sphere. **Checks and balances** reflect Madison's desire to protect liberty, not only by dispersing power but also by creating institutional "overlap." Political scientist Louis Fisher explains the relationship between these two doctrines:

> The system of checks and balances is not a contradiction to the separation doctrine. The two are complementary. Without the power to withstand encroachments by another branch, a department might find its powers drained to the point of extinction. The Constitution allocated separate functions to separate branches, but . . . Madison concluded in Federalist 51 that "ambition must be made to counteract ambition."[17]

The three branches were purposely positioned in opposition to one another to "check and balance" the desires, or "ambitions," of each. The president's powers as commander in chief are checked and balanced by Congress' powers to declare war. Two hundred years after the Constitutional Convention,

FIGURE 2-1

CHECKS AND BALANCES

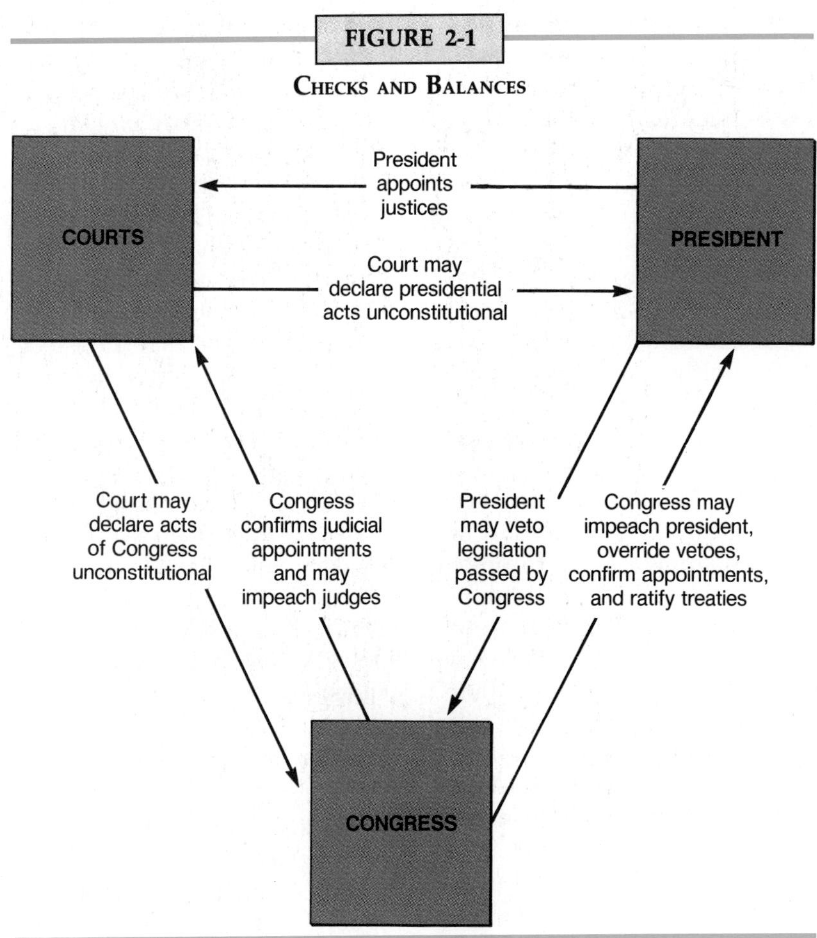

separation of powers and checks and balances are still in controversy. Congress passed the War Powers Act in 1973 to reassert its declining power in foreign affairs. The power of Congress in economic affairs is countered today by the president's power to formulate the national budget and shape fiscal policy (see Chapters 17 and 18). The president can check the Congress by vetoing a bill. Congress can override the veto with a vote of two-thirds of the members of both the House and Senate. The Supreme Court can check the other two branches by declaring an act unconstitutional. The Court can be overcome by passing new legislation to clarify its intent, or more definitively, by amending the Constitution. The former occurred, for example, in the Grove City College case discussed in Chapter 1. The latter occurred after the Supreme Court declared the graduated income tax unconstitutional in the late 1800s. Checks and balances have certainly been used. In the past two hundred years, there have been more than 2,400 presidential vetoes and nearly 100 congressional overrides. In 1984, in a single decision, the Supreme Court invalidated portions of two hundred statutes passed by Congress (see the *Chadha* decision, Chapter 14). Over the years, the Senate has rejected presidential nominees to the cabinet and the Supreme Court and has removed several federal judges from the bench. Figure 2–1 shows, in simplified form, some of the checks and balances included in the Constitution.

Compare a political system with separation of powers and checks and balances to a parliamentary form of government. In parliamentary systems, such as in Great Britain or Germany, the executive "government" comes from the legislature. The British prime minister or German chancellor must be a member of the parliament. The prime minister forms a cabinet composed of other leaders in the majority party. There is no formal separation between executive and legislative functions. The British judiciary lacks the power to declare an act of Parliment unconstitutional, exerting less of a check on the elected government. Parliamentary government is based on the principle of majority rule and is supported by party discipline. German Chancellor Helmut Schmidt was able to govern Germany in the 1970s with a majority of only four votes. He did not lose a single key vote in the Bundestag. When elections are held, the national government is elected at one time. America's Founders placed obstacles in front of potential majorities. Elections for the president, House, and Senate are staggered so that it is more difficult for any majority to take control of the government. To this extent, inefficiency and limits on the ability to govern were built into the structure of American government.

THE FOUNDERS' AMBIVALENCE TOWARD DEMOCRACY

Americans think of their country as the greatest democracy in the world, but the deliberations and decisions of the Founders at the Constitutional Convention reflected a healthy distrust of direct democracy. Contradictory sentiments are reflected in the words and actions of the delegates. Some delegates, like Morris and Hamilton, were outspoken elitists. To them, turning over the delicate task of governing to the poor, uneducated rabble would be the height of folly. Others were more trusting of the ability of citizens to choose wisely through democratic institutions. In the spirit of the American Revolution, a democratic impulse was at work in Philadelphia in 1787, but it was thoroughly tempered by fears of mob rule and direct democracy. The Constitution reflects this ambivalence.

Only the House of Representatives was to be directly elected by the people. Although it was the most powerful and important institution in the new government, the Constitution left senators to be appointed by state legislatures, the president chosen by an electoral college, and Supreme Court justices appointed by the president. The Founders placed barriers between the people and the government. The electoral college, an anachronism today, is a perfect example of indirect democracy.

Thinking about the Constitution today, it is easy to forget the historical context of the 1780s. By the standards of the day, the Constitution was a dramatic departure in the direction of democracy. Over the years, American politics has moved toward increasing participatory democracy. By the 1830s, members of the electoral college were elected by the people, not appointed by the state legislatures. In 1912, members of the Senate were popularly elected for the first time following adoption of the Seventeenth Amendment. The American electorate has expanded in two hundred years from a franchise restricted to landowning white males to one that includes blacks, women, and eighteen-year-olds. The Founders were suspicious of too much democracy, but they created a framework capable of adapting to the increasing acceptance of popular participation.

MOTIVES OF THE FOUNDERS

The delegates to the Philadelphia convention have formed an American pantheon. Jefferson likened the Founders to gods. One writer referred to the convention as the "miracle" of Philadelphia. British Prime Minister William Gladstone, in the 1870s, called the American Constitution "the most wonderful work ever struck off at a given time by the brain and the purpose of man.[18] For nearly a century the Framers of the Constitution were accorded the highest acclaim and praise.

After a century of reverence, a book challenging the motives of the Founders was published. **Charles Beard**, in *An Economic Interpretation of the Constitution* (1913), portrayed those who wrote the Constitution as an economic elite reacting against the rise of the common person to protect the interests of the wealthy, property-owning establishment. Beard suggested that the Constitution was the product of the conflict between two dominant economic interests. The group that controlled the convention, he claimed, had great personal wealth and extensive commercial interests. It was able to dominate the other group, primarily agricultural landowners, to protect their business interests and securities. Can Beard's charges be sustained?

The delegates did represent the elite of American political life. They were all white males; no blacks, women, or Indians were in attendance. Most of the delegates stood to gain from a strong central government and would have lost money if the United States defaulted on its securities. Moreover, the taxing powers of the government under the Constitution were prevented from taking direct aim at private property interests. Taxes were to be levied on the basis of population, not wealth. Without question, economic interests played a role in the creation of the U.S. Constitution. The evidence suggests, however, that these interests were not monolithic; many other interests and objectives were present at the convention.[19] The divisions among the Founders in their debates could not have been predicted solely on the basis of economic interest. Madison's journal reveals that the delegates were concerned as much with human rights issues as with property rights.

The Founders were neither scoundrels nor angels. Although they were elitists who as often as not distrusted the common person, they acted out of complex motives, not just their economic interests. Their most pressing concern was balancing the protection of personal liberty with the obvious need to create a stronger government.

Ratification and Amendment

THE RATIFICATION BATTLE

The delegates returned to their homes having completed a document that completely overhauled American government. The next step was to get it adopted by the thirteen states. Under the Articles of Confederation, amendments had to be unanimously approved by all thirteen state legislatures. Less controversial amendments to strengthen the national government had already failed when they were vetoed by a single state. It was unthinkable that something as far-reaching as the Constitution could be approved unanimously. How, then, could the Framers win approval?

Once the document was completed, the Framers became politicians, pulling out all stops to win adoption of the Constitution. They conceived a special ratification process, bypassing the Articles of Confederation and the state legislatures. The delegates specified that the Constitution would be adopted if it were ratified at special conventions in *nine* of the thirteen states. This sidestepped the state legislatures, jealous of their own power (which would be diminished under the Constitution), and avoided the impossible task of getting unanimous agreement.

Reprinted by permission of UFS, Inc.

Even ratification by nine states was not easy. The Anti-Federalists opposed the Constitution, arguing that the independence of the states and personal liberty were endangered by not providing a bill of rights.[20] The Constitution seemed too radical an instrument for the conservative Anti-Federalists to accept. The changes it mandated were too great. Herbert Storing, one of the leading experts on the Anti-Federalists, concluded:

> The Anti-Federalists did not deny the need for some change, but they were, on the whole, defenders of the status quo. They deplored departures of the Constitution from "the good old way" or "the ancient and established usage of the commonwealth." They shook their heads at "the frenzy of innovation" sweeping the country: "The framing of entirely new systems, is a work that requires vast attention; and it is much easier to guard an old one." . . . In the main, they saw . . . threats to four cherished values: to law, to political stability, to the principles of the Declaration of Independence, and to federalism.[21]

The Anti-Federalists, led by Richard Henry Lee and Patrick Henry, engaged proponents in a public debate in newspapers, pamphlets, and public speeches. The case for ratification was most eloquently stated in a series of letters written by Hamilton, Madison, and John Jay. Called the *Federalist Papers,* the three authors wrote under the pseudonym "Publius." The ***Federalist Papers*** described in great detail the workings of the new system and countered the criticisms of the Anti-Federalists. The *Federalist Papers* are important not only because they helped win ratification of the Constitution but also because they provide important additional information on the meaning and intent of the Framers.

The issue during ratification was not governance but liberty. Opposition focused on the lack of a bill of rights. Although the Constitution included some specific rights, such as trial by jury and the prohibition of religious tests to hold federal jobs (see Chapter 5), freedom of speech, press, and other rights were not expressly protected. "Publius" argued that a separate bill of rights was unnecessary, but in the end, the Federalists decided they would have to concede if the Constitution was to be ratified.

The small states, pleased at the work their delegates had done on their behalf in the convention, ratified quickly. Delaware ratified first by a unanimous vote, but the key battles would take place in the large states. In some states, strong-arm tactics were used to get the legislature to call a ratifying convention. Around the country Federalist proponents moved as quickly as possible in calling state ratifying conventions, hoping to prevent their opponents from getting organized. Pro-Constitution delegates were selected to most of the conventions.[22] As the majority of newspapers favored the Constitution, opponents lacked access to this vital medium in the political battle. The Constitution was passed in Massachusetts by a narrow margin in return for a pledge to add a written bill of rights.

By June 1788, the required nine states had ratified, but the battle was not over. Virginia and New York, two of the three largest states, had not yet approved. The new union could not survive without them. In Virginia, the ratification battle pitted James Madison against Patrick Henry. After impassioned debate, Madison and the Federalists finally prevailed by a narrow margin. In New York, Hamilton struggled to overcome the opposition of most of New York's political establishment. Following Hamilton's threat that New York City would secede from the rest of the state, the Constitution at last was ratified but by only three votes. North Carolina and Rhode Island were the last two states to approve, and the Constitution became the official basis of government of the United States of America.

AMENDING THE CONSTITUTION

To assure ratification, the Federalists had changed the rules in the middle of the game. They made sure that the formal **amendment process** for the new Constitution would not require the unanimous vote of all the states. Nonetheless, it was their intention that changes in the basic plan of government would be very difficult to achieve. Majority rule would *not* be enough to prevail. Two methods for proposing amendments and two methods for ratification were detailed (Table 2–1). Each of the four resulting possibilities requires a *supermajority:* two-thirds to propose, three-fourths to ratify. Amendments can be proposed either by Congress or by a convention called by two-thirds of the states. To date, no

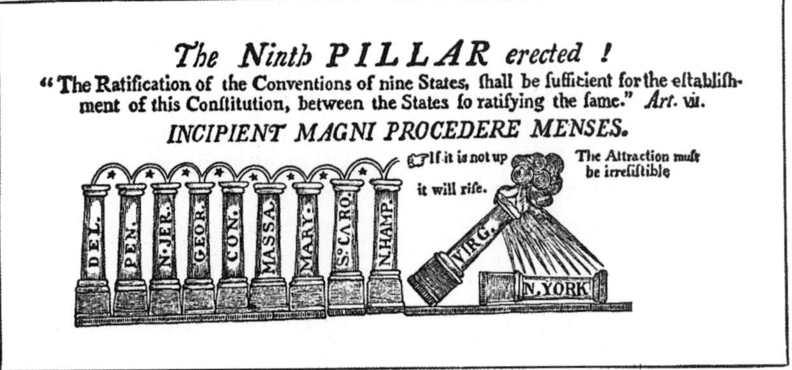

A cartoon published in 1788 that shows the nine states that first ratified the Constitution. These states are shown as pillars that support the arches of government. The pillars Virginia and New York have not yet been erected since these two states had not yet ratified.

amendments have been proposed by a convention, although approximately thirty of the needed thirty-four states have called for a convention to draft a balanced-budget amendment.

Amendments can be ratified either by three-quarters of the state legislatures or by special ratifying conventions. Only the Twenty-first Amendment (repealing Prohibition in 1933) was ratified using state conventions. The other twenty-five amendments have been ratified by state legislatures. In almost two hundred years, only twenty-six amendments to the Constitution have been approved (and the first ten of these were the **Bill of Rights**). Excluding the first ten, the Constitution has been amended on the average of only once every twelve years. The most recent is the Twenty-sixth Amendment in 1971, which extended the right to vote to eighteen-year-olds. A recent failed amendment was the Equal Rights Amendment. Four states short of ratification, it expired in June

TABLE 2–1

AMENDING THE CONSTITUTION

	Method 1	Method 2	Method 3	Method 4
Amendment is proposed by . . .	Two-thirds vote in both House and Senate	Two-thirds vote in both House and Senate	A national convention called for by Congress at the request of two-thirds of the states	A national convention called for by Congress at the request of two-thirds of the states
Amendment is ratified by . . .	Three-quarters of the state legislatures (38 states)	Specially convened conventions in three-quarters of the states	Three-quarters of the state legislatures (38 states)	Specially convened conventions in three-quarters of the states
The method has been used . . .	For all except one	For the Twenty-first Amendment	Never	Never

1982 after a period of seven years and a three-year extension.

Governing under the Constitution

IS THE CONSTITUTION OUT-OF-DATE?

Can a system devised in the 1780s serve the governing needs of a political system in the 1990s? There are as many federal employees today as there were citizens of the country when the Constitution was ratified! The biggest cities in the 1780s had populations in the tens of thousands, not the millions of today. The basic thrust of the Constitution was to give as little power as necessary to the national government to intervene in the lives of citizens. The preservation of public order, national defense, and the regulation of commerce were the most important functions of government. Today, with a population of around 250 million, the demands on the U.S. government are much greater. The public has supported the expansion of public policy into the areas of health care, education, social services, income maintenance, energy and the environment, economic management, agriculture, and many others. Can the political system function adequately with a form of government in which efficiency was purposely sacrificed to a concern for checks and balances?

It should now be clear that most of the Founders had mixed feelings on the question of governing. They wanted a system stronger than the Articles of Confederation provided but not one that would allow majorities to move decisively. Should changes be made today to enhance the ability to govern?

THE COMMITTEE ON THE CONSTITUTIONAL SYSTEM

In the last *Federalist Paper,* Hamilton urged that the Constitution be ratified despite some imperfections, claiming that problems could be solved later through amendments. Thomas Jefferson believed that the process of constitution-making should be repeated every generation. Yet because of the extreme difficulty of the amendment process, in two centuries only a few structural changes have been adopted.

In the 1980s, a group of prominent academics, journalists, business and labor leaders, and elected officials organized the **Committee on the Constitutional System** to review the Constitution and propose possible reforms. They issued the Bicentennial Papers, a series of articles, essays, and drafts of constitutional amendments. The committee members believe that major changes are needed to adapt the Constitution to the realities of today:

> The checks and balances inspired by the experience of the eighteenth century have led repeatedly, in the twentieth century, to governmental stalemate and deadlock, to indecision and inaction in the face of urgent problems. For the most part, rash and arbitrary actions have been deterred. But this benefit has been gained at a growing cost. Except in times of great crisis, the government is now unable to act in a timely manner—or at all.[23]

Constitutional amendments were proposed to accomplish the following:[24]

Create an Electoral System That Encourages Unified Party Control of the Three Centers of Decision-Making—the House, the Senate, and the Presidency. Reformers attempted to devise ways to avoid divided party control of government. One amendment would require candidates for the House, the Senate, and the presidency to run as a ticket. Voters would cast a single vote for all three, eliminating the split-ticket voting that has become so prevalent in recent years and increasing the chances that one party would capture both the White House and Congress.

Lengthen the Terms of Elected Officials and Hold Elections for Congress and the President at the Same Time. The objective of these amendments is to enable leaders to achieve greater statesmanship by having more time to deal responsibly with difficult policy problems. Holding elections for Congress and the presidency at the same time—every four or six years—would also reduce the probability of having a divided government. Many constitutional reformers, from the Founders through the present day, have suggested lengthening the president's term to six years. Many others, including President Lyndon

Johnson, proposed lengthening the term of House members to four years, a term corresponding to the president's.

Reduce Separation of Powers by Creating a Formal Interlocking between Branches. Constitutional amendments in this category are oriented toward achieving greater cooperation, mutual dependence, and collective responsibility between legislative and executive branches. Proposals include repeal of the constitutional provision that prevents members of Congress from serving in the executive branch so that the president's cabinet could be made up of House and Senate leaders. Amendments to this effect were first introduced more than one hundred years ago.

Reduce the Checks and Balances That Now Exist to Allow One Branch to Prevail More Easily and to Make Decisions. Former President Reagan proposed an amendment to give the president a line-item veto throughout his eight years in office. A line-item veto would strengthen the president vis-à-vis the Congress by allowing him to strike down only part of a bill rather than vetoing the whole measure. Most amendments in this category are designed to strengthen the president on the premise that the presidency is the institution most able to act decisively.

Devise Solutions to Breaking a Deadlock When It Occurs Rather Than Waiting until the Next Election. Some of the most radical proposals for constitutional amendments deal with ways to end presidential-congressional stalemate once it occurs. Proposed amendments would move the U.S. Constitution toward a parliamentary form of government. One proposal would allow the president, once each term, to dissolve Congress and call for new special elections. Conversely, Congress could vote a resolution of "no confidence" in the president, requiring that new elections be held in ninety days. These fundamental changes would allow the voters to reconstitute a failed government more quickly than under the current system.

What are the prospects for adoption of constitutional reforms such as those proposed by the Committee on the Constitutional System? Realistically, at the present time, the chances are slim. Why, then, consider such changes? James MacGregor Burns provided justification in testimony before Congress:

> First, because there may well be in the tumultuous century that undoubtedly lies ahead . . . a series of national and worldwide crises in which the capacity of our system will be so sorely tested that many Americans—perhaps rather suddenly—will feel an urgent need for a change. It's very important . . . that we have done our homework, that we have in our intellectual bank the kind of ideas, the kind of analysis, the kind of daring, imaginative posing of alternatives that I think will come out of these hearings. It seems to me that to consider the systemic changes is a matter of hard-headed practicality and not simply a kind of dreamy investigation.[25]

PRESERVING THE OLD ORDER

The proposals of the Committee on the Constitutional System provoked a great deal of healthy debate surrounding the Constitution's bicentennial. As we saw in Chapter 1, some observers believe that the slow, deliberate policy process still has merit. Bipartisan policies—such as the Tax Reform Act of 1986—that make it through Congress are more likely to survive changes in administration. Defenders of separation of powers and limited governing ability find this preferable to parliamentary systems, such as that of Great Britain. There, dramatic policy changes often follow a change in government, perhaps only to be reversed again at the next election.[26]

The debate that began in Philadelphia goes on today, in the third century of the Constitution. The Founders created a system of institutional conflict designed for neither efficiency nor majority rule, but it is a system that has proved durable, flexible, and perhaps even brilliantly successful.

The Constitution has survived longer as a form of government than virtually any other written constitution. It has provided continuity while allowing significant changes to take place. In times of extreme crisis—the Civil War, the Great Depression, the two world wars—the power of the presidency has expanded, enabling leaders to govern during crises, although sometimes in obvious violation of the Constitution (see Chapter 5). The Constitution

Children celebrating in front of Philadelphia's Independence Hall, a symbol of America's enduring political institutions.

is also more than a blueprint for government. It has become the centerpiece of a political culture shared by Americans.

The reality of American politics is that the Constitution is extremely difficult to change. Two hundred years ago, the Founders were able to gain national consensus for the new document only through a combination of persuasion, guile, and strategic maneuvering. Short of a dramatic crisis, it is unlikely that any new framework of government could be agreed to in today's fragmented political world.

Summary and Conclusions

1. The major issue at the Constitutional Convention was how to balance the need for a stronger central government with the desire to limit government to protect individual liberty.
2. The factors that influenced the Framers of the Constitution were the practical political experience that immediately preceded the convention, the political philosophy of such thinkers as Locke and Montesquieu, and various economic concerns and interests.
3. The governing crisis experienced under the Articles of Confederation spurred American leaders to create a stronger government, despite their fears of government.
4. The Federalists were generally people of means who favored strengthening the national government. Anti-Federalists, fearing the loss of personal liberties, opposed a stronger national government and tried to prevent ratification of the Constitution.
5. The key conflicts at the convention were between large and small states, slave and nonslave states, and supporters and opponents of a strong executive.
6. The Constitution in its final form embodied unique principles designed by Madison that divided functions and institutionalized conflict between the branches in the dual doctrines of separation of powers and checks and balances.

7. Ratification was difficult, but by promising to add a written bill of rights, the Federalists were able to prevail. The Founders made it difficult to amend the new constitution, requiring "supermajorities" in a two-stage process.

8. Contemporary questions of governing rest on the constitutional foundations established two hundred years ago. Some suggest that major revisions of the Constitution are needed, but others argue that it has served Americans well and should not be changed.

Whether one wants to revamp the U.S. Constitution or likes it just the way it is, the remarkable features of this document must be acknowledged as it passes its two-hundredth birthday. In the coming chapters, political economy, federalism, and the on-going struggle between government and individual rights and liberties are examined.

KEY TERMS

amendment process
Anti-Federalists
Articles of Confederation
Charles Beard
Bill of Rights
checks and balances
Committee on the Constitutional System
Committee on Style
Common Sense
Connecticut Compromise
electoral college
Federalist Papers
Federalists
French and Indian Wars
John Locke
Montesquieu
natural rights
New Jersey Plan
separation of powers
three-fifths compromise
Virginia Plan

SELF REVIEW

1. Outline some causes of the American Revolution.
2. What were the consequences of the Revolution?
3. Describe the governing crisis under the Articles of Confederation.
4. Discuss the major influences on the Founders.
5. Were there any issues that the delegates agreed on from the start?
6. What were the major controversies of the convention?
7. What were the major decisions that shaped the presidency?
8. Describe the motives of the Founders.
9. How was the Constitution ratified?
10. What are the key principles of the Constitution?
11. How did the Founders provide for changing the Constitution?
12. What is the Bill of Rights?
13. List some proposals for improving governing ability by amending the Constitution.
14. What are some reasons for keeping the Constitution as written?

SUGGESTED READINGS

Barbash, Fred. *The Founding.* 1987.
A dramatic account of the writing of the Constitution, providing a succinct and lively introduction to the drafting of the Constitution.

Jilson, Calvin C. *Constitution Making: Conflict and Consensus in the Federal Convention of 1787.* 1988.
A careful reexamination of the interaction of interests and political principles at the Constitutional Convention.

MacDonald, Forest. *We the People: The Economic Origins of the Constitution.* 1958.
A thorough analysis of Charles Beard's thesis of the economic origins of the Constitution, generally concluding that Beard, at best, oversimplified the case.

Morris, Richard B. *The Forging of the Union, 1781–1789.* 1987.
An examination of the political problems of the new nation leading up to the Constitutional Convention.

Storing, Herbert. *What the Anti-Federalists Were FOR.* 1981.
An interesting review of the often-forgotten, losing side in the ratification debate. Helps clarify what the issues were on both sides.

NOTES

1. Elmer E. Cornwell Jr., "The American Constitutional Tradition: Its Impact and Development," in Kermit L.

Hall et al., *The Constitution as an Amending Device* (Washington, D.C.: American Political Science Assoc., 1981), 4.
2. S. E. Morrison and H. S. Commager, *The Growth of the American Republic* (New York: Oxford University Press, 1937), 9.
3. John Locke, *Second Treatise on Civil Government* (1690). See also Clinton Rossiter, *1787: The Grand Convention* (New York: Macmillan, 1966).
4. Louis Fisher, *The Constitution between Friends* (New York: St. Martin's, 1978), 4.
5. R. R. Palmer and Joel Colton, *A History of the Modern World* (New York: Knopf, 1965), 327.
6. Cornwell, "American Constitutional Tradition," 95; Merrill Jensen, *The Articles of Confederation* (Madison: University of Wisconsin Press, 1940).
7. Gordon S. Wood, *Creation of the American Republic, 1776–1787* (Chapel Hill: University of North Carolina Press, 1969), 280–87.
8. J. W. Pelthason, *Understanding the Constitution,* 6th ed. (Hinsdale, Ill.: Dryden, 1973), 13.
9. Fisher, *Constitution between Friends,* 10.
10. Joseph Kallenbach, *The American Chief Executive* (New York: Harper and Row, 1966), 32.
11. U.S. Congress, "Debates of the Federal Convention of 1787 as Reported by James Madison," in *Documents Illustrative of the Formation of the Union of the American States,* 69th Cong., 1st sess., 1927, p. 664.
12. Kallenbach, *American Chief Executive,* 34.
13. Louis Koenig, *The Chief Executive* (New York: Harcourt Brace Jovanovich, 1975), 22.
14. Kallenbach, *American Chief Executive,* 46–47.
15. Pelthason, *Understanding the Constitution,* 16.
16. Fisher, *Constitution between Friends,* 11.
17. *Ibid.*
18. "Kin Beyond the Sea," *North American Review,* September–October 1878.
19. Countering Beard's views, see Forest MacDonald, *We the People: The Economic Origins of the Constitution* (Chicago: University of Chicago Press, 1958).
20. Robert A. Rutlan, *The Ordeal of the Constitution: The Anti-Federalists and the Ratification Struggles of 1787–88* (Norman: University of Oklahoma Press, 1966).
21. Herbert Storing, *What the Anti-Federalists Were FOR* (Chicago: University of Chicago Press, 1981), 7.
22. Morrison and Commager, *Growth of the American Republic,* 296.
23. Donald L. Robinson, ed., *Reforming American Government* (Boulder, Colo.: Westview, 1985), 69.
24. James L. Sundquist, *Constitutional Reform and Effective Government* (Washington, D.C.: Brookings, 1986), 8.
25. James M. Burns, "Why Think about Constitutional Reform" (1982), in Robinson, *Reforming American Government,* 59–60.
26. See Thomas Mann and Norman Ornstein, rebuttal to Cutler, in Thomas Cronin, ed., *Rethinking the Presidency* (Boston: Little, Brown, 1982), 176–78.

CHAPTER 3

American Political Economy

POLITICAL CLOSE-UP

The Stock Market Crash of 1987

"Black Monday," October 19, 1987, was the day the stock markets recorded their single largest drop in history. It far eclipsed the crash of October 1929, an event closely associated with the Great Depression. On Black Monday in 1987, the Dow Jones Industrial Average—the most common barometer of stock prices—dropped an unprecedented 508 points. A record 604 million shares were traded as prices plummeted out of control in a wave of panic and computer-programmed selling. The index lost 23 percent of its value in one day, far more devastating than the 1929 crash, when the Dow declined 13 percent. Between the market high in August 1987 and October 19, the market lost 36 percent of its value. This represented nearly one trillion dollars in wealth! Some individuals were completely wiped out, but few traders threw themselves out of their Wall Street office windows, as in 1929. The owner of Wal-Mart—one of the wealthiest individuals in the nation—personally lost a billion dollars in one day.

The crash of U.S. markets was matched by precipitous declines in

the stock markets around the world, from Europe to the Far East. What caused this crash?

The most common explanation for the crash was the government's inability to deal with the budget and trade deficits. The political deadlock in Washington made investors nervous and ready to panic. Some felt the overvalued markets were ripe for a crash. Once the panic began, computerized trading made the decline even worse, automatically churning out sell orders. While government officials watched helplessly on October 19 as the market fell, they attempted to move quickly to restore public confidence in their ability to govern. Preventing another catastrophic depression like that of the 1930s was the highest priority.

President Reagan and Congress announced that they would immediately hold a budget "summit" in an attempt to agree on a budget deficit reduction plan. Yet even the fright caused by the stock market crash, was not enough to overcome the institutional conflict between Congress and the president. The summit degenerated into "politics as usual," and a compromise was not worked out for two months.

Despite the dramatic meltdown of stock prices, a depression did not follow the 1987 crash. Contrary to popular myth, the 1929 crash was more of a warning than a direct cause of the Great Depression. The disastrous economic policies pursued after the 1929 crash actually brought on the depression. One critical factor was enactment of the infamous Smoot-Hawley tariff, which led to worldwide protectionism and a closing down of international trade. Another factor was monetary policy. The Federal Reserve Board tightened credit, making it more difficult to borrow and start any kind of sustained recovery. Finally, President Herbert Hoover clung to the inviolable principle of a balanced budget and refused to use any kind of federal aid to help the growing legions of starving and unemployed.

It took an event as frightening as a stock market crash to temporarily overcome the deadlock between Congress and the president. But will governing in this fashion be enough to keep the United States competitive in the global economy of the 1990s?

CHAPTER OUTLINE

INTRODUCTION AND OVERVIEW

Calamitous events like the Great Depression helped change American political economy in the twentieth century. In conjunction with industrial tragedies—coal mine disasters, child labor abuses, packinghouse horrors—the relationship between the private economy and public policy was changed. States began to enact laws mandating minimal safety standards in factories, limiting factory work for children under the age of twelve, and placing other restrictions on mine owners and plant owners. The federal government accepted new responsibility for social welfare and economic management. These changes were but one step in the evolution of American political economy, a critical foundation of policy-making.

There are many approaches to political economy, some doctrinaire and radical, others narrow and deterministic. The approach to political economy in this text is more general, centering on the close interrelationship of the political and economic systems in the United States and other nations of the world. The relationship between economics and politics is a two-way street. On the one hand, economic interests, motives, and power have a potent impact on politics and the policy-making process. Economic factors affect issues and ideology, voting, interest-group formation and membership, congressional reelection rates, and even presidential popularity and success with Congress. On the other hand, public policy decisions critically influence the conditions of economic activity. Government policies affect economic growth, industrial expansion, interest rates, poverty and the distribution of wealth and income, the size of budget and trade deficits, the minimum wage, and Social Security benefits.

Political economy does not mean that politics and economics are one in the same or that economics *determines* politics. Many combinations of economic and political systems exist in the world, even among democratic countries. Noneconomic factors—social, cultural, ideological, historical—influence American politics too. An emphasis on political economy recognizes the conjunction between economics and politics in the realm of public policy. It recognizes that cultural values help shape a nation's political economy, which can influence such outcomes as government ownership or how equitably wealth is distributed. A political economy focus explores the link between economic motives and political behavior as well as the relationship between the governing ability of a political system and the effectiveness of its economic policies. Chapter 3 explores the following questions:

1. How are economics and politics interrelated?
2. What are some of the cultural values and traditions that help shape American political economy, and how have they developed over the past two centuries?
3. How did American political economy develop in the period leading up to the Civil War?
4. How did the industrial revolution transform the U.S. economy, leading to significant social changes, political demands, and expansion of the policy agenda?
5. How did the role of government in the economy change at the time of the Great Depression of the 1930s, leading to the political economy of the last fifty years?
6. How can we compare political and economic systems around the world, and what mix of public and private economic activity produces the best results?
7. Is America in decline as a military and economic power? How does nation's governing capacity influence its economic position in the world?
8. What are the challenges of the new global economic system, and how will they affect American politics in the coming decades?

Economics and Politics

While economic and political systems are closely related to each other, each element remains distinct. Among democratic nations of the world, for example, both the processes and institutions for making economic decisions and economic policies themselves can be quite different. In order to compare other political and economic systems to the United States and to trace the development of American political economy, it is useful to first examine how economics and politics influence each other.

Cultural Values and Traditions Help Shape a Nation's Political Economy

From China to Iran to the United States, the way in which a nation evolved as a culture helps explain certain economic and political choices. Europe, for example, for many centuries was shaped by a rigid class system that defined an individual's economic and political opportunity from birth. The nobility cultivated a sense of noblesse oblige—that the "haves" bore some responsibility for the plight of the "have-nots." The United States, in contrast, had economic elites but a more fluid class structure and developed social welfare policies much later than the European nations. Even with McDonald's in Moscow, Soviet citizens' difficulty in adapting to elements of market capitalism can be traced back not only to seventy years of communism but to centuries of isolation under the czars. In America, shared beliefs concerning the relationships among individuals and between individuals and the state have provided legitimacy and continuity. Common values supporting private property, individual self-reliance, and economic and political liberty helped shape political institutions and the economic system. Over time, however, those cultural values have had to continually adapt to a changing world.

ECONOMIC AND POLITICAL CHANGE ARE CLOSELY RELATED

Political and economic change are interdependent but do not always occur simultaneously. The impetus to scrap the Articles of Confederation in favor of a new constitution was related to severe domestic economic problems in the 1780s. The Civil War was fought not just over the issue of slavery but between two fundamentally different economic systems in the northern and southern states. The Industrial Revolution transformed the United States from an agrarian to an industrial society, leading to unforeseen social problems and new demands on government to regulate business and protect workers. Political change can follow economic decline or collapse, as occurred with the Russian revolution in 1917, leading to radical economic changes. New economic policies followed a critical political change in the United States after the 1932 election, which itself was a response to the Great Depression. The process of democratization that swept through Eastern Europe in 1989 resulted in radical change in those nations' economic systems. While less dramatic, the rapidly changing global economic system is creating growing pressures on the United States to adapt its own political processes or face possible decline as a world economic power.

ECONOMIC MOTIVES HELP EXPLAIN POLITICAL BEHAVIOR

In a democracy, economic concerns have a particularly high priority for citizens and their leaders. Economic issues are usually perceived by the public to be the most important problems facing the nation. Except for issues of war and peace, Americans worry most about the national economy and their own economic circumstances (Table 3–1). The high salience of economic issues has been shown in other ways. The president's prospects for reelection are tied to the performance of the

TABLE 3–1

THE PROMINENCE OF ECONOMIC ISSUES, 1935–1989, AS SHOWN BY ANSWERS TO THE QUESTION "WHAT IS THE MOST IMPORTANT ISSUE FACING THE COUNTRY?"

Year	Issue	Year	Issue	Year	Issue
1989	Economic problems	1970	Vietnam	1952	Korean War
1988	Drugs	1969	Vietnam	1951	Korean War
1987	Unemployment/recession	1968	Vietnam	1950	Labor unrest
1986	Unemployment/recession	1967	Vietnam	1949	Labor unrest
1985	Threat of war and international problems	1966	Vietnam	1948	Keeping peace
1984	Unemployment/recession	1965	Vietnam	1947	High cost of living
1983	Unemployment/recession	1964	Vietnam	1946	High cost of living
1982	Unemployment/recession	1963	Keeping peace	1945	Winning war
1981	Inflation	1962	Keeping peace	1944	Winning war
1980	Inflation	1961	Keeping peace	1943	Winning war
1979	Inflation	1960	Keeping peace	1942	Winning war
1978	Inflation	1959	Keeping peace	1941	Keeping out of war
1977	Inflation	1958	Unemployment	1940	Keeping out of war
1976	Inflation	1957	Race relations	1939	Keeping out of war
1975	Inflation	1956	Keeping peace	1938	Keeping out of war
1974	Inflation	1955	Keeping peace	1937	Unemployment
1973	Inflation	1954	Keeping peace	1936	Unemployment
1972	Vietnam	1953	Keeping peace	1935	Unemployment
1971	Vietnam				

SOURCE: Surveys of the Gallup organization, latest that of June 1989.

national economy. Of all the factors that affect presidential popularity, economic conditions—particularly unemployment—are most closely related. Economic performance and in turn popularity affect how successful the president is in getting his legislative agenda through Congress.

Some of the factors that help economists explain how individuals behave in the market economy help explain how individuals behave in the political process. For example, incumbent members of Congress act rationally to maximize their reelection chances by delivering economic benefits to their districts and raising huge campaign war chests through political action committees. The formation and impact of interest groups is closely tied to economic interests and calculations of economic benefits of membership. The performance of the mass media in modern politics is affected by their status as privately owned, profit-oriented enterprises. The behavior of voters and parties is related not only to economic issues but also to calculations of costs and benefits.

GOVERNING ABILITY HELPS DETERMINE THE EFFECTIVENESS OF ECONOMIC POLICY

Some of the most dramatic examples of the fragmentation of power and obstacles to majority rule are found in the realm of economic policy. Many believe that a frequent consequence of obstacles to governing has been inconsistency in policy and disappointing results. The noted political scientist Samuel Huntington believes that the U.S. institutions of governance are too weak to manage a modern political economy and too porous to restrict demands made on them.[1] Congress, the president, the bureaucracy, the courts, and even state and local governments play varying roles in promoting, regulating, or managing the economy. Key economic choices are linked to cooperation or conflict between the legislature and the executive. In the 1980s, one of the most common complaints about institutional deadlock concerned the problem of potentially disastrous budget and trade deficits that neither Congress nor the president could solve.

Yet governing ability is not the only key ingredient for a prosperous economy. Sound underlying economic institutions and the maintenance of public support are also essential. Communist economies failed despite the powerful governing capacity of the one-party state. In Great Britain, Prime Minister Margaret Thatcher's controversial decision to replace property taxes with a poll tax on all citizens was greeted with riots throughout the country in the spring of 1990. The ability to push an unpopular decision through Parliament could assure neither an effective policy nor legitimacy.

The prominence of economic concerns, economic motives in political behavior, and the relationship between governing ability and policy effectiveness recur as themes throughout this text. This chapter also focuses on the cultural values and traditions that have shaped American political economy over the past two hundred years. This provides the basis for considering how current economic changes will be met and how this response will affect the relative strength of the United States as a military and economic power in the coming decades.

The Roots of American Political Economy

AMERICAN CULTURAL VALUES AND TRADITIONS

The first settlers in America were concerned more with survival than with prosperity, but by the time of the Constitutional Convention, there was a widespread desire to achieve the conditions for economic success. The desire to create a system better able to govern was closely related to the economic problems experienced under the Articles of Confederation. In the early years, both economic and political needs established the values that helped shape the growth of the American economy and define the role of government. Economic and political liberty was an overriding value that found expression as private property rights, individualism, materialism and the work ethic, and acceptance of economic inequality.

PRIVATE PROPERTY RIGHTS. The Constitution reinforced the right of **private property.** Guarantees of individual liberty implied the right to acquire and hold wealth.[2] The British Crown's challenge to property rights was one of the most significant economic causes of the American Revolution.[3] Unlike Europe, where most property was already taken, land in America was cheap, rich in resources, and readily available. With territorial expansion to the west, land continued to be available until the late nineteenth century. Its settlement created a large property-owning middle class resulting in a more egalitarian society.

INDIVIDUALISM. The emphasis in the Constitution on liberty and the nature of colonial life in America both fostered a strong sense of **individualism.** Settlers were widely dispersed, averaging only a few people per square mile. Lack of transportation meant that people rarely had much contact with others. With 95 percent of the population living on small family farms, demands on government were minimal. Self-reliance was essential for survival, and relative isolation enhanced an already strong preference for individualism.

MATERIALISM AND THE WORK ETHIC. Americans were not only individualistic, they were **materialistic** as well. Colonial life and Protestantism forged a strong work ethic and a desire to get ahead. Although the struggle to survive on the frontier hardly seems materialistic by today's standards, increasing one's worldly possessions, even by a cow or a horse, was a constant occupation. Foreign visitors often commented on this aspect of the American character: "The poor struggle to be rich, the rich to be richer," wrote one traveler from abroad.[4]

ACCEPTANCE OF ECONOMIC INEQUALITY. Individualism, materialism, and the **work ethic** in early America contributed to an acceptance of economic inequality. People were believed to be responsible for their own condition, success, or failure. The noted economic historian Louis Hacker observes:

> Easy access to property led to that other aspect of capitalism: acceptance of the uneven distribution of wealth and income and the private decisions made by entrepreneurs. . . . If the man who became wealthy did so because he was an innovator, good for him; . . . the whole society benefited along with him. If the doors of opportunity were open and people could rise, fluidity in the class structure was inevitable. The class hostilities and class exploitation . . . did not appear.[5]

Political and economic liberty—the values of private property, individualism, materialism, and the work ethic—fit nicely with the economic theory that would dominate the nineteenth century: capitalism.

THE AFTERMATH OF MERCANTILISM

From the sixteenth to the eighteenth century, the dominant economic philosophy in the Western world was **mercantilism.** The goal of powerful nations was to increase national strength through a system of colonies, domestic manufacturing, and trade.[6] Commerce was the major activity of the mercantile world. Colonies existed to supply raw materials for manufacturing and to provide a market for the finished products. A strong navy and merchant marine were necessary for a successful nation. Great Britain's main objective in colonizing America was to strengthen itself economically, but the American colonies were never exploited to the extent that the Spanish and French colonies were. For example, the Navigation Acts, which placed sharp restrictions on the commercial activities of Americans, were never strictly enforced. Americans prospered despite them.[7]

After 1763, Great Britain tried to enforce the restrictions and impose other detrimental economic policies on the colonies. Problems quickly mounted. Within thirteen years, the colonies had declared independence. Mercantilism was suddenly dead in America, although the tariffs among states and currency disputes under the Articles of Confederation resembled an internal system of mercantilism. What would replace the old system? What kind of a political environment for economic activity would the Constitution create?

CAPITALISM: ADAM SMITH'S "INVISIBLE HAND"

The same year that Americans declared their independence from Great Britain, a Scottish philosopher named **Adam Smith** published a book that was to have a profound impact on the economic life of the new nation. Smith's 1776 treatise was entitled *The Wealth of Nations.*[8] People initially reacted to its moral implications rather than its economic implications. Efforts by entrepreneurs to maximize individual gain presented a moral dilemma for philosophers because it was believed that such activity made one's neighbors worse off. Smith argued that in a market system the contrary was true. Mercantilism was based on the belief that selfish individualism would result in *less* wealth for a nation and that trade was the route to increasing the wealth of nations. But Smith argued that profit-seeking entrepreneurs operating in the marketplace provided the key to *increasing* national wealth.

Smith attacked the existing set of government regulations, restrictions, and tariffs that made up the system of mercantilism. Left alone, he argued, the "**invisible hand**" of the marketplace produced the best mix of products and prices. Smith emphasized the self-adjusting nature of the market. Even though self-interest motivated individuals, the market would automatically adjust supply and demand to fill the needs of consumers. In this way, both the wealth of the individual entrepreneur and the wealth of the state would increase. Thus, acting to increase one's own wealth actually helped one's neighbors. Smith, considered to be the founder of modern economics, created the ideological basis for capitalism and the theoretical basis for analysis of market systems.

Adam Smith's ideas about political economy corresponded to other major intellectual trends of the time. In writing about a system of "natural liberty," where individuals would be able to pursue their economic interests without interference, he furnished the economic equivalent of the political ideas of Locke concerning natural law and the natural rights of individuals. The ideas of Locke and Smith are sometimes called "liberalism," whose meaning derives from economic freedom and political liberty, not from the current association of liberalism with government-sponsored economic and social intervention. Nineteenth-century liberalism was based on the belief that individuals should be free to pursue their own interests unhindered by government. **Economic liberalism** was popular with business owners, manufacturers, and traders, who liked the idea that they would be free to do as they pleased. Another name for Smith's economic liberalism came from France: **laissez-faire capitalism.** The message given to government by business was "leave us alone." Early political leaders accepted the principles of capitalism but not absolutely. From the start, government intervened in the workings of the private economy.

EARLY ECONOMIC POLICIES

The first secretary of the treasury of the United States, Alexander Hamilton, formulated a series of proposals to define the economic role of the new government. Hamilton, whose elitist and monarchist views were dismissed at the Constitutional Convention, was taken more seriously by the first Congress. On behalf of President George Washington's administration, he called for (1) establishment of a national bank, (2) active encouragement of American manufacturing and commerce, and (3) assumption by the federal government of the accumulated debts of all the states.[9] Although Hamilton generally subscribed to the laissez-faire notions of Adam Smith, he also was an advocate of a strong central government. He believed that tariff protection for fledgling industries and a central bank would not substantially interfere with the free market and would promote the economic development of the new nation.

Most of Hamilton's proposals were approved by Congress, and the National Bank was chartered in 1791. Hamilton also proposed improving the nation's infrastructure—roads, bridges, and canals. Revenue to pay for these improvements was raised through a series of excise taxes grudgingly approved by a Congress reluctant to levy any taxes at all. Despite the controversy over the National Bank and other aspects of Hamilton's proposals, his program helped spur economic growth and development.

Hamilton and the Federalists lost the 1800 election and disappeared from the political scene (see Chapter 8). Thomas Jefferson, who had bitterly opposed the Federalists, as president came to support a strong central government view. But unlike Hamilton, Jefferson believed that the nation would remain primarily agrarian. During the first three decades of the nineteenth century, the economic interests of North and South grew further apart. Much of the debate on national economic policy centered on tariffs, even though tariffs interfere with free markets. And when economic interests were in conflict, it became necessary for government to side with certain economic interests, to the detriment of others. Policy could be described as pro-business as much as pro-free market. Manufacturers, primarily in the North, favored higher tariffs to keep out foreign goods. Large agricultural interests, primarily in the South, came to oppose the tariffs because they increased the prices paid for manufactured goods. Even with these exceptions, in practice the philosophy of laissez-faire capitalism was deeply etched in the nation's value system.

America was ripe for economic growth. The country was rich in natural resources, land, and labor. Between 1790 and 1860, the population grew from 3.9 million to 31 million.[10] Immigration swelled to more than 300,000 a year in 1850, adding to the already rapid natural population increase. Population growth provided a ready labor force for expanding manufacturing and set the stage for the **industrialization** that followed the Civil War.

Slavery was the issue that dominated all others in this period. Although the economics of the plantation system was a crucial element leading to the Civil War, the conflict was brought on by a variety of complex social, economic, and political factors. Slavery was a fatal flaw in American political economy. A fundamental contradiction existed between slavery and the values of individual liberty and freedom. The crisis resulted in the bloodiest war in American history.

Industrialization and Its Political Consequences

The most obvious effect of the Civil War was that the slavery-based economy of the South was destroyed. With the harsh Reconstruction policies of Congress, the economy of the former Confederacy suffered devastating blows from which it would take generations to recover. In the North, it was a different story. Historians Louis Hacker and Charles Beard called the Civil War the "second American Revolution" because the war provided a direct stimulus to the development of industry that reshaped the economy in ways favoring industrialization.[11] New political divisions arose in the United States after 1865. The Republicans, who dominated the political scene in Washington, produced legislation that fostered the interests of industrial capitalists. The National Bank Act of 1864 gave advantages to larger commercial banks. The Homestead Act helped the railroads by giving free land to anyone who would settle in the West—building a market and a dependency on rail services. The Morrill Act created the great land-grant universities in the Midwest and the West, which not only aided American agriculture but also enhanced the development of industrial capitalism by providing technical skills and expertise.

Economic policies after the Civil War allowed industries to grow and flourish.[12] But as rapid industrialization increased the wealth and power of the United States, it also created a variety of new social problems and growing demands on government.

Industrial Expansion

The industrial growth and economic expansion of the United States between the Civil War and World War I were among the most rapid in the history of the world. During this period, the gross national product, the total of goods and services produced, increased a total of 600 percent.[13] Although industrialization was well under way before the Civil War, America was still primarily an agrarian nation. By the time World War I ended, the United States had become one of the leading industrial powers in the world. The movement of people from farm to factory helps tell the story. In 1860, some 19 percent of Americans lived in urban areas. By 1920, more than half lived in the cities.[14] Technology had altered the nature of production. Factories were huge, sprawling operations. Energy sources changed from steam to electricity to internal combustion engines. Revolutions in transportation and communication occurred as well. Products moved across the country over an expanding system of railroad lines. In the twentieth century, the automobile slowly began to replace the horse. First the telegraph, then the telephone, made the country smaller and business and commerce easier.

Although there is some debate about exactly when the "takeoff" period for the rapid expansion of the American economy began, its occurrence is clear.[15] The late 1800s were years when an individual entrepreneur could amass a fortune in steel, oil, or railroads. Government policies helped foster industrialization and allowed the growing concentration of capital. Incorporation became a highly favorable form of business organization, particularly after the Civil War, when the Supreme Court ruled that the due process rights of corporations were protected in the same way as those of individuals (see Chapter 16). But there were storm clouds on the horizon, both in the United States and around the world. Industrialization was a mixed blessing. With industrial wealth came poverty, urban slums, and crime. Across the Atlantic, reacting to the consequences of industrialization in Europe, a man named Karl Marx predicted a radical social upheaval.

THE RADICAL RESPONSE TO INDUSTRIALIZATION: MARXISM

Around the world, concern grew over the social consequences of the industrial revolution: huge inequities in the distribution of wealth, and harsh working conditions for the masses. In Europe, socialism was one reaction to laissez-faire capitalism. Early socialists were utopian, advocating ideal societies where men and women avoided competition, goods were shared, and all lived in harmony and equality.[16] Capitalism is a system based on a competitive market with private ownership of the means of production. Socialism generally favors public ownership of the means of production and distribution through planning, rather than a market system. Of course, there are many variations of both economic systems.

The most famous and influential socialist was **Karl Marx,** who reacted against the naïveté of the

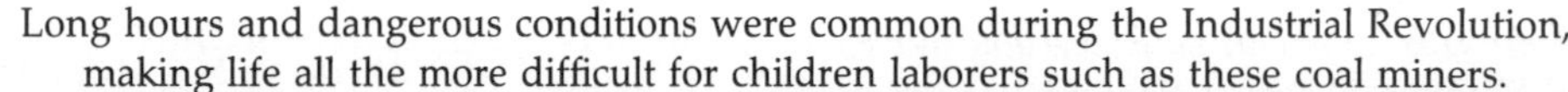

Long hours and dangerous conditions were common during the Industrial Revolution, making life all the more difficult for children laborers such as these coal miners.

POLITICAL INSIGHT 3–1

MARXISM

We have seen . . . that the first step in the revolution by the working class is to raise the proletariat to the position of the ruling class, to win the battle of democracy.

The proletariat will use its political supremacy to wrest, by degrees, all capital from the bourgeoisie; to centralize all instruments of production in the hands of the State, *i.e.*, of the proletariat organized as the ruling class; and to increase the total of productive forces as rapidly as possible.

Of course, in the beginning this cannot be effected except by means of despotic inroads on the rights of property and on the conditions of bourgeois production; by means of measures, therefore, which appear economically insufficient and untenable, but which, in the course of the movement, outstrip themselves, necessitate further means of entirely revolutionizing the mode of production.

These measures will of course be different in different countries.

Nevertheless in the most advanced countries the following will be pretty generally applicable:

1. Abolition of property in land and application of all rents of land to public purposes.
2. A heavy progressive or graduated income tax.
3. Abolition of all rights of inheritance.
4. Confiscation of the property of all emigrants and rebels.
5. Centralization of credit in the hands of the State, by means of a national bank with State capital and an exclusive monopoly.
6. Centralization of the means of communication and transport in the hands of the State.
7. Extension of factories and instruments of production owned by the State; the bringing into cultivation of waste lands, and the improvement of the soil generally in accordance with a common plan.
8. Equal liability of all to labor. Establishment of industrial armies, especially for agriculture.
9. Combination of agriculture with manufacturing industries: gradual abolition of the distinction between town and country, by a more equable distribution of the population over the country.
10. Free education for all children in public schools. Abolition of children's factory labor in its present form. Combination of education with industrial production.

SOURCE: Karl Marx and Friedrich Engels, *Manifesto of the Communist Party* (1848).

utopian socialists. Writing with Friedrich Engels, he advocated "scientific socialism"—a more revolutionary brand of socialism known as communism.[17] Marx and Engels argued that capitalism alienated workers from the product of their labor and that in time the workers (whom Marx called the proletariat) would rise up against the factory owners (the bourgeoisie) and take over the means of production. Marx's theories have attracted the attention of revolutionaries and scholars for more than a century and have been profoundly important in the history of the modern world. Although it is impossible to do them justice in a short summary, Political Insight 3–1 contains some excerpts from the *Manifesto of the Communist Party* that give the flavor of the ideas of Marx.

AMERICAN RESPONSES TO INDUSTRIALIZATION

The ideas of socialism and communism were never accepted in the United States because they run counter to the fundamental values of individualism and laissez-faire capitalism. Although there have been democratic socialist and communist parties in the United States, they never had the broad appeal they had in many European countries. The contrast between American capitalism and the ideas of Marx is stark. Compare the

POLITICAL INSIGHT 3–2

ANDREW CARNEGIE'S "GOSPEL OF WEALTH"

Andrew Carnegie, the man who virtually controlled steel production in the United States by the 1890s, was the embodiment of the American dream to some, a robber baron to others. His ideas about the rich and the poor are contained in the following excerpts from his "Gospel of Wealth," written in 1889.

The contrast between the palace of the millionaire and the cottage of the laborer with us today measures the change which has come with civilization. This change, however, is not to be deplored, but welcomed as highly beneficial. It is well, nay, essential, for the progress of the race that the houses of some should be homes for all that is highest and best in literature and the arts, and for all the refinements of civilization, rather than that none should be so. Much better this great irregularity than universal squalor.

We accept and welcome, therefore, as conditions to which we must accommodate ourselves, great inequality of environment; the concentration of business, industrial and commercial, in the hands of a few; and the law of competition between these, as being not only beneficial, but essential to the future progress of the race. Having accepted these, it follows that there must be great scope for the exercise of special ability in the merchant and in the manufacturer who has to conduct affairs upon a great scale. That this talent for organization and management is rare among men is proved by the fact that it invariably secures enormous rewards for its possessor, no matter where or under what laws or conditions. . . .

Thus is the problem of rich and poor to be solved. The laws of accumulation will be left free, the laws of distribution free. Individualism will continue, but the millionaire will be but a trustee for the poor, intrusted for a season with a great part of the increased wealth of the community, but administering it for the community far better than it could or would have done for itself.

SOURCE: Andrew Carnegie, "The Gospel of Wealth," *North American Review*, December 1889.

philosophy of Andrew Carnegie in Political Insight 3-2 with the views of Marx. In "The Gospel of Wealth," Carnegie claimed that vast inequities in wealth are not only inevitable but also good for society. The very wealthy make further wealth possible, and they also make possible the social and cultural philanthropies that enrich American life. Rich men, in Carnegie's words, have a responsibility to do charitable acts with their wealth. Would either view be satisfactory for America?

Although Americans rejected communism, it was becoming clear that the social consequences of unregulated market capitalism were unacceptable. The market system was not working the way Adam Smith had expected. Rather than increasing competition, industrial capitalism reduced it. **Monopoly**—the creation of trusts through mergers, holding companies, cutthroat pricing, and takeovers—resulted in a single organization that could stifle competition and control prices. Trusts came to dominate railroads, petroleum, steel, sugar, and hundreds of other industries. A compilation of monopolies in 1904 revealed more than three hundred industrial trusts.[18] Trusts represented enormous, unprecendented concentrations of capital and assets, many larger than those of the states in which they operated.[19]

Corporate profits were huge, and the disparity between these profits and workers' wages was correspondingly great. Economist Daniel Fusfeld notes:

> Individualism also had its seamy side. The apologists of wealth had much to apologize for. In 1900, when profits of the Carnegie Steel Company were more than $20 million, the average annual wage for steel

> workers was about $600. The justice of this division of society's income was not self-evident, and it threatened the polarization of social classes that Marx had predicted. Yet the more extreme adherents of the philosophy of laissez-faire went merrily on their way.[20]

There were growing indications of public discontent with the social impact of monopoly capitalism. The trade union movement began in earnest with a series of violent strikes in 1877 following layoffs and wage cuts. Significant amounts of railroad property were destroyed. In the 1880s, an industrial riot took place in Chicago's Haymarket Square. A depression in the 1890s resulted in more violence. A strike by steelworkers was broken in Pittsburgh in 1892 when management strikebreakers clashed with strikers. Twenty were killed.

Farmers were also affected by economic change. Railroads had altered the entire basis of American agriculture. Markets, once locally based, were now regional in scope. A new economic interdependence eliminated the autonomy of the family farmer. Agriculture became a business. Farmers in the Midwest reacted by organizing through such groups as the Grange and by supporting the Populist party, formed in the early 1890s. One of the farmers' biggest problems was "tight money." When credit was tight, farmers had a difficult time getting loans. They believed this was caused by the government's strict adherence to the gold standard. The Populists wanted "easy money," with silver as the basis for currency. Democratic party and Populist party 1896 presidential nominee William Jennings Bryan warned the eastern industrialists not to crucify the farmer on a "cross of gold."

GOVERNMENT REGULATION AND TRUST-BUSTING

The period of rapid industrialization transformed the American economy and the nation. To many observers, industrial growth represented the triumph of capitalism. But unrestricted capitalism also had an ugly side. Marx believed that capitalism would sow the seeds of its own destruction and advocated revolution to hasten the process. Economic reformers in the United States followed a much more modest path to change. Maintaining support for the underlying values, American reaction to industrialization took the form of trade unions, changes in agriculture, and limited government intervention in the economy.

The ideas of individualism, the work ethic, and laissez-faire capitalism were by no means dead. They had in fact blended together into a folklore of Americanism. The rags-to-riches tales in the Horatio Alger books exemplified the American dream. Nonetheless, economic change had expanded the policy agenda of government. By 1890, the public demanded some limitations on the activities of monopoly capitalists. A few states had tried to pass antitrust legislation but were no match for the monopolies. Companies threatened simply to move to another state. In 1890, Congress responded to growing pressure for national action by passing the **Sherman Antitrust Act.** Senator Sherman argued, "Congress alone can deal with the trusts, and if we are unwilling or unable, there will soon be a trust for every production and a master to fix the price for every necessity of life."[21] Business activity "in restraint of trade" was declared illegal.

Continued pressure resulted in the passage of stronger antitrust legislation in 1914. The Clayton Act improved on previous efforts by defining more specific violations and pricing policies. Still, the antitrust acts were more of a legal deterrent to further monopoly than a concerted effort to break up existing trusts. Economist Robert Heilbroner noted that antitrust legislation was up against "a much more fundamental tendency—the tendency of industrial technology to yield decisive advantages to large-scale producers."[22] It also reflected the strength of powerful business interests in the United States and the difficulty for political institutions to move forcefully against them.

The second new thrust of government intervention in the economy was regulation, and in 1887, Congress created the **Interstate Commerce Commission (ICC).** Because of the near chaos in the railroad industry at the time, the ICC was empowered to regulate fares, rates, and routes. For the first time, government policy reflected the view that the free market did not necessarily produce socially desirable consequences. Although at first opposed to regulation, the railroads soon learned how to use the ICC to their own advantage to guarantee their profit margins. Initial efforts at regulation reflected limits in governing ability, but they signaled a significant change in government economic policy. More dramatic changes in economic policies would not occur until after the worst depression in the nation's history.

The Crash, the Great Depression, and Economic Management

THE 1929 STOCK MARKET CRASH

The 1920s were a decade of capitalism gone wild. Everyone seemed to be getting rich or trying to get rich. But underneath the frantic financial manipulations were severe problems that would ultimately lead to economic collapse and depression. Trading in the stock market was dominated by speculation. Stock was bought on margin, people paying as little as 10 percent of face value. In unregulated exchanges, a mania for get-rich-quick schemes was pervasive. The market was manipulated by insiders using information not available to the general public. The economic boom of the 1920s was built on flimsy credit that suddenly disappeared when the market crashed on October 29, 1929.

The crash of the stock market was only part of the reason for the ensuing **Great Depression.** Restrictive monetary policy and protective tariffs adopted soon after the crash made the economy worse, not better. Deficiencies in banking, agriculture, and industry compounded the problem. The business cycle of boom and bust had characterized capitalism since the 1790s, but never had the down cycle cut so deeply into the economy as in the 1930s. The gross national product fell by almost half.[23] The construction of homes decreased by 90 percent. One out of four Americans was out of work, and for the fortunate ones who were employed, wages fell precipitously, to as little as five to seven cents an hour in some cases. The American people cried out for action, but President Hoover was a prisoner of his strong convictions about the limits of governmental responsibility for economic problems. As criticism grew and the economy declined, Hoover held firm. "No governmental action, no economic doctrine, no economic plan or project can replace that God-imposed responsibility of the individual man and woman to their neighbors," Hoover proclaimed. "I am opposed to any direct or indirect government dole. Our people are providing against distress in true American fashion."[24]

True American fashion was about to change. In 1932, Franklin D. Roosevelt was overwhelmingly elected over the discredited Hoover. An anxious nation waited to see how the government would deal with the worst economic crisis in history.

THE NEW DEAL

A profound change in American life was about to take place, reflecting a basic shift in the relationship between the government and the economy. No longer would it be acceptable for officials to sit idle while millions went without adequate food and shelter. No longer would it be acceptable for the business cycle to run its course without attempts by the government to manage and stabilize the economy.

President Franklin Roosevelt acted quickly to restore confidence. With an economic crisis of such magnitude, Roosevelt was able to govern more decisively and quickly than any administration had since the Civil War. The New Deal moved in four key ways to intervene in the working of the market economy.[25] First, the National Labor Relations Act (1935) firmly established the legitimacy of organized labor and collective bargaining as the legitimate method for settling disputes, ending decades of struggle by the union movement for these rights.

Second, the New Deal introduced elements of national planning. Although the Tennessee Valley Authority did not ultimately result in the comprehensive network of national ownership that some of its proponents envisioned, it made important innovations in the role of government in resource planning and management. The New Deal attempted to promote economic stability through cooperative agreements among businesses and between labor and management in specific industries. This effort took form in the National Recovery Act, one of the major failures of the New Deal.

Third, the policies of the New Deal redefined government responsibility to provide a minimum level of economic and social support for its citizens. The Social Security Act, discussed in Chapter 19, created a series of social welfare programs that remain today the bulwark of national policy. The 1935 act created Aid to Families with Dependent Children, Aid to the Blind, Old Age Survivors and Disability Insurance, and unemployment insurance programs. Responsibility for the plight of those victimized by the economic system was partly transferred from the private sector to the public sector. Individualism and self-reliance remained important values, but they were now tempered by a recognition of public responsibility to help those living in poverty. The contradiction between the American work ethic and expanded social responsibility remains a source of conflict in formulating policy.

The fourth and perhaps most profound change was the assumption of responsibility by the government for the management of the domestic economy.

The Keynesian Revolution

The ideas underlying the change in the relationship between government and the economy were provided by **John Maynard Keynes** (pronounced "canes"), a British economist and one of the most famous figures of his day (see the accompanying People in Politics). He challenged the conventional views of economics, arguing that reliance on monetary policy—the money supply and interest rates—was insufficient to guarantee a healthy economy. Keynes published a number of works, but the most influential was his *General Theory of Employment, Interest, and Money,* published in 1936.[26] It synthesized his previous work into a general theory that turned conventional economic thought upside down.

Two major points in Keynes's theory were revolutionary. First, he argued that capitalist economies do not automatically maintain full employment: The invisible hand of the market often does not produce the most desirable balance. Second, he maintained that a balanced budget was not always desirable. The government should intervene either to stimulate or to depress the economy, depending on the level of economic activity in the private sector, by manipulating government spending and taxes—fiscal policy. In the case of a severe depression, through deficit spending (spending more than the revenues collected) the government could stimulate the economy and help compensate for the downward spiral in the business cycle. Keynes's views were extremely controversial; the idea of deficit spending was shocking to fiscal conservatives. But the success of the New Deal and the nearly complete elimination of unemployment through massive doses of government spending during World War II convinced most skeptics.

Keynes actually met with Roosevelt in Washington shortly before the *General Theory* was published.[27] Roosevelt was particularly interested in Keynes's suggestions because they seemed to confirm the direction already taken by New Deal policies. Roosevelt and Keynes died in 1945 and 1946, respectively, leaving behind a legacy of remarkable change in American political economy. In 1946, Congress passed the **Employment Act**, in some ways an embodiment of Keynes's theories and Roosevelt's policies. The Employment Act wrote into federal law the new commitment of the government to stabilize the economy and promote full employment.

The old political economy was not completely dead, but it was permanently changed. The old values were still strong, and at no time was there ever a real threat to eliminate the market-based economy. There was a new realism about the consequences of capitalism and a commitment to prevent devastating depressions in the future. Traditional values were tempered, modernized, given boundaries, and adapted to the new political reality. But a tension between the old and new was created, and it remains in evidence today.

Postwar Economic Policy

Demand-Side Fiscal Policy

The Keynesian approach that dominated post-World War II America centered on demand-side fiscal policy. Demand-side policies are oriented toward consumers to stimulate consumption by raising government spending. Keynesian economics reached its zenith under Presidents Kennedy and Johnson.[28] Economists who were educated in

PEOPLE IN POLITICS

JOHN MAYNARD KEYNES

The most influential economist of the twentieth century, John Maynard Keynes, was no obscure professor. Famous in his own time, he enjoyed the limelight in the company of presidents and prime ministers. Born in Cambridge, England, in 1883, the son of a prominent scholar and logician, he studied under the noted economist Alfred Marshall and in the early 1900s worked for the British Treasury, particularly on problems of the Indian economy. Keynes also lectured at Cambridge University.

Keynes was an integral part of a fashionable coterie of artists, writers, and intellectuals known as the Bloomsbury group. Other notables in the group included Virginia Woolf, E. M. Forster, and George Bernard Shaw. Keynes's friends were critical, often biting, but not revolutionaries—they were from privileged social classes and saw themselves as their generation's natural leaders. Keynes was both a genius and a snob, charming and incisively analytical.

Working for the Treasury during World War I, Keynes had already established a reputation as a financial expert. In negotiating the peace treaty, Keynes saw his pleas to solve the economic problems caused by the war ignored. He resigned and wrote his first book in 1920, a scathing attack on the economic consequences of the Treaty of Versailles, predicting a breakdown of the European economic system and increasing political turmoil. His theories about the workings of capitalist economies began to take shape. At the same time, he made and lost a fortune in the stockmarket, patronized the arts, and married a Russian ballerina.

Keynes questioned the conventional view that reliance on monetary policy—the supply and cost of credit—was sufficient to guarantee a healthy economy. He was particularly critical of the decision of the British government to return to the gold standard in the 1920s. Although Keynes was highly respected, leaders largely ignored his advice because he had not published a clear theoretical statement explaining in detail his rejection of the existing economic orthodoxy. Part of the theory came in 1930 with the publication of his *Treatise on Money.* Already, depression was sweeping the world economies. But it was not until 1936, with the publication of *The General Theory of Employment, Interest, and Money,* that his revolutionary new approach to capitalist economics was fully articulated.

By then, much of what Keynes had predicted had come to pass. During the 1930s, Keynes not only helped the British government formulate economic policies but also successfully advocated his ideas with Roosevelt. When he died in 1946, Keynes had changed basic understandings about how the economy works and fundamental assumptions about the relationship between government and the economy.

SOURCE: Daniel R. Fusfeld, *The Age of the Economist* (Glenview, Ill.: Scott, Foresman 1982), 96–97.

the late 1930s, when the *General Theory* was first published, became presidential advisers. Kennedy attempted to use wage and price "guideposts" to keep inflation down. The Kennedy-Johnson tax cut of 1964 was successful in stimulating economic growth and seemed to confirm the soundness of Keynesian fiscal policy. In 1964, *Time* magazine proclaimed in a cover story, "We are all Keynesians now." At the same time, Johnson's Great Society programs, passed by the large Democratic majorities in Congress, expanded the government's public policy commitments in the areas of education, health care for the elderly (Medicare) and the poor (Medicaid) and programs to enhance job opportunities (the Economic Opportunity Act).

The late 1960s brought economic, social, and political turmoil to the United States. Results of the Great Society's "war on poverty" were disappointing, and funds were increasingly diverted to pay for the war in Vietnam. The low inflation and low unemployment of the early 1960s disappeared, and prices started to increase rapidly. In 1971, President Nixon surprised observers by imposing mandatory wage and price controls to combat inflation. The Arab oil embargo in 1973 touched off a spiral of price increases in energy, which aggravated inflation throughout the decade. Economic policy under Nixon, Ford, and Carter was still primarily Keynesian, but there was growing criticism as Keynesian principles seemed unable to solve the economic problems of the 1970s. Contrary to Keynes's notion that when inflation goes up, unemployment goes down (and vice versa), the 1970s saw both reach unacceptably high levels simultaneously. The phenomenon of double-digit inflation and high unemployment became known as "stagflation."[29] Republicans argued that the United States had outgrown the economic ideas of the 1930s and that it was time for a change.

THE MONETARIST AND SUPPLY-SIDE CHALLENGE

Despite the postwar dominance of Keynesian ideas, the influence of Adam Smith and advocates of free-market solutions were never far from center stage. During the 1970s, conservative critics had sharply attacked increased government spending, calling for greater reliance on the marketplace, less government intervention, and fewer restrictions on entrepreneurs. One of the early and persistent critics of Keynes was economist Milton Friedman. Like the nineteenth-century liberals, he likened political liberty to economic liberty.[30] For years, Friedman argued for the use of monetary policy over fiscal policy to reduce the danger of inflation. Friedman warned that inflation could continue to rise even if unemployment were high. The "stagflation" of the 1970s seemed to bear this out. Emphasis on restraining the growth in the money supply to prevent inflation, as espoused by Friedman, is sometimes

Reprinted by permission: Tribune Media Services

called **monetarism.** Friedman's views were particularly influential in Great Britain after the election of Margaret Thatcher and the Conservative party in 1979.

Some critics of the Keynesian approach proposed **supply-side economics,** a view that rejects government intervention to manipulate aggregate demand and promotes policies that encourage entrepreneurs, investors, and businesses—the producers, or the "supply side" of the economy. Economist Arthur Laffer suggests that when taxes are too high, investment is discouraged and the economy stagnates.[31] His solution was to lower taxes, particularly in upper-income brackets. The supply-side approach generally defines a less active role for government in managing and directing the economy.

Poor economic performance in the 1970s and the growing challenge to Keynesian economics set the stage for the election of Ronald Reagan in 1980. Defections of Democrats and independents who had voted for Carter in 1976 were particularly heavy among those who felt they were worse off than they had been four years before. Political scientist Gerald Pomper notes:

> Economic grievances were at the heart of the Reagan vote. Economic dissatisfaction was the most direct influence of the 1980 vote, and it had a greater impact than any other issue. Despite their philosophy, those liberals who felt worse off financially opposed Carter. Despite their partisanship, those Democrats suffering economically defected to Reagan and Anderson. Traditional supporters of the party . . . remained loyal—but only when their pocketbooks remained full. . . . Jimmy Carter was not defeated in the marketplace of ideas; he was trounced in the marketplace of food and gasoline and mortgages.[32]

After the election, the Reagan administration promised "a clear break with past policy."

> The principal elements of the plan will include slowing budget growth, reducing tax rates, curbing and stabilizing monetary growth, and lightening the regulatory burden. The result will be a speedy recovery of the financial markets, accelerated real growth, and reduced inflation, as saving and investment rise, deficits fall, and the market system works more efficiently.[33]

Reflecting this general approach, Congress passed an across-the-board tax cut of 25 percent in personal income tax rates and tax breaks for business in 1981. Unlike the Kennedy-Johnson tax cut of 1964, the Reagan tax cut was labeled "supply side" because it reduced taxes equally across income brackets. Higher-income persons received the greatest benefit, on the theory that they would then invest and stimulate the economy on the production side. The tax cuts and defense buildup resulted in the highest budget deficits in history during the 1980s.

In attempting to reduce the role of the government in the economy, deregulation was an important part of the Reagan approach to government. Arguing that government regulation had become too intrusive and expensive, the Reagan administration acted to repeal certain regulations (deregulation) and slow down the enforcement of others. Regulation is examined more closely in Chapter 15.

After dominating national politics for nearly forty years, the Democratic party found itself struggling to counter the conservative market approach of Reagan, Bush, and the Republicans. Although Keynesian ideas were not completely dead, a new generation of Democratic leaders sought newer approaches to economic problems. In the 1990s, questions about American political economy are more complex than ever. Neither political party can look only at issues surrounding the management of the domestic economy. Today, crucial questions increasingly involve the relationship of the U.S. economy to the global economy.

Comparing Political and Economic Systems

WHICH MIX OF PRIVATE AND PUBLIC IS BEST?

With the decline of communism in the late 1980s, both market economies and democracy are on the rise around the world. But disputes over the proper mix of public and private economic activity continue, even among democratic nations. What is the best mix of public and private sector activities?[34] The answer depends on what policy consequences are judged to be most important. Two are particularly meaningful.

- *Economic growth:* how much does a nation's total output of goods and services increase?
- *Economic equity:* how evenly or unevenly is a nation's income and wealth distributed among its citizens?

Advocates of greater economic equity are generally concerned with conflict between economic classes in market economies and may advocate a democratic variant of socialism. They note with alarm the uneven distribution of wealth (total value of all assets) and income (monies received in a given year) that often results in a private sector economy. Democratic socialists, unlike Marxists, do not advocate the abolition of all private property and favor democratic processes over the one-party state. They suggest a mix of private and public sector activities that allows sufficient redistribution of income to meet the basic needs of all citizens. Conversely, advocates of greater economic growth usually extol the virtues of market capitalism and the vitality that results from private ownership. They argue that the public sector in general and state enterprises in particular are inherently inefficient and that increasing economic growth is the best way to take care of society's "have-nots."

Among the democratic nations of the world one finds different mixes of private and public ownership, different rates of growth, and varying equity in the distribution of wealth and income. In the past fifty years, Scandinavian nations such as Sweden have been inclined toward democratic socialism, providing redistribution of income through progressive taxes and more government-sponsored social services. Great Britain adopted elements of democratic socialism under Labor governments in the postwar era, with the nationalization of a number of major industries and heavy taxes on the wealthy. As we have seen, market capitalism has always been strong in the United States with limited government ownership and social welfare services. In eras of major economic and social change, however, such as the 1930s and 1960s, government spending on social services and intervention in the economy increased. Marginal tax rates in the early 1960s were as high as 90 percent for the wealthiest Americans, compared to around 33 percent today.

In many nations, the 1980s were a decade of renewed capitalism. The election of Ronald Reagan in 1980 signaled a reemphasis on the private sector and the market economy in the United States. The

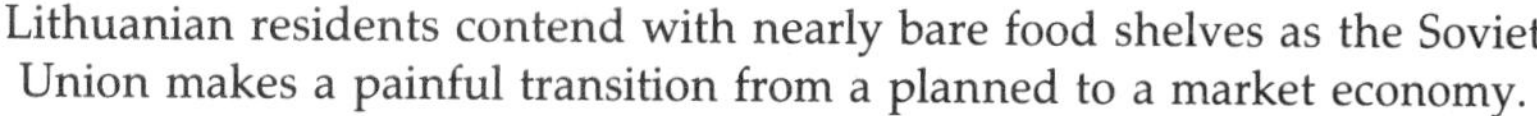

Lithuanian residents contend with nearly bare food shelves as the Soviet Union makes a painful transition from a planned to a market economy.

swing was even more pronounced in Great Britain, where the Thatcher government elected in 1979 privatized the economy by selling off nationalized industries. The ongoing debate on the proper mix between private and public sector activities can be seen in the nations of Eastern Europe as they struggle to transform their planned economies into some mix of market capitalism and public ownership. What policy consequences will result? Both Britain and the United States enjoyed sustained economic growth in the 1980s, but at the same time, the gap between rich and poor widened. Does this mean that robust economic growth translates into greater inequity in the distribution of wealth and income or that government ownership and a larger public sector always equates with weak economic performance?

Not necessarily. Political economist John Freeman believes that many of the claims about the best mix of private and public sector activities are based on shaky evidence.[35] Figure 3–1 compares the amount of government ownership—reflecting the public-private mix—with economic growth. Contrary to many expectations, nations with more state enterprises did not necessarily grow at a slower rate than nations without significant government ownership. For example, the United States, with few state-owned enterprises, did not grow as fast as Norway or Austria in this time period. Conversely, Figure 3–2 suggests that economies with more extensive government ownership do not necessarily have a more equitable distribution of income than predominantly private economies. For example, the distribution of income after taxes in the United States is more equitable than in Italy or France, despite greater levels of public ownership in those nations.

What, then, determines why some economies grow more robustly and why wealth is distributed more equitably in some nations than others? Freeman suggests that the key is how a nation's economic system relates to the workings of its democratic political system.[36] A number of political characteristics are important: social consensus, the role of interest groups, constitutional structure, and the effectiveness of democratic institutions and processes at managing social and economic conflict. In short, economic growth and the distribution of income in a society are not just a function of the relative size of public and private sectors but are closely related to the governing ability of the political system. This essential link between

FIGURE 3–1

ECONOMIC GROWTH RATES AND THE SCOPE OF GOVERNMENT OWNERSHIP

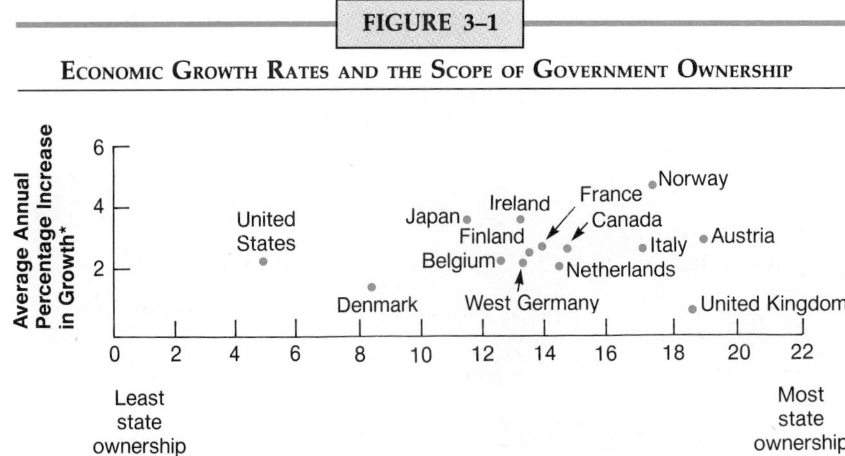

* Measured in GDP, (1974-1980), OECD figures (1982).

** Measured by state enterprises' share of gross fixed capital formulation (1974-1977).

SOURCE: Adapted from John Freeman, *Democracy and Markets* (Ithaca, N.Y.: Cornell University Press, 1989), Figure 1, p. 9.

DISTRIBUTION OF INCOME AND THE SCOPE OF GOVERNMENT OWNERSHIP

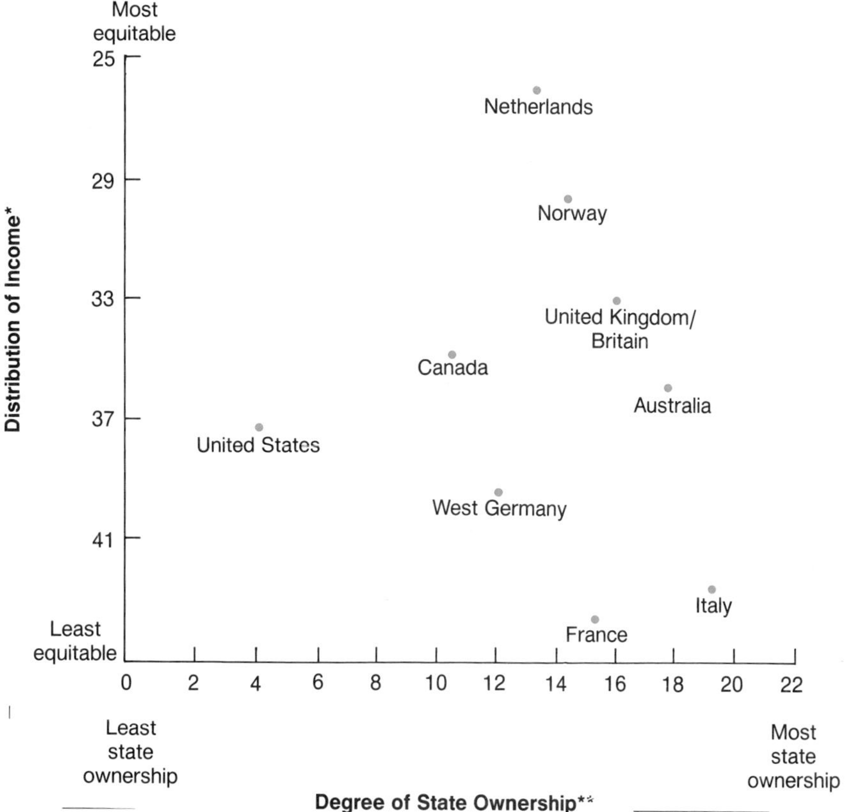

* Measured by difference in post tax shares of national income received by top 20% and bottom 20% of population (OECD, 1976).

** Measured by state enterprises share of gross fixed capital formulation (1974-1977).

SOURCE: Adapted from John Freeman, *Democracy and Markets* (Ithaca, N.Y.: Cornell University Press, 1989), Figure 2, p. 10.

governing and political economy raises several key issues for American politics in the 1990s:

- Do underlying governing problems pose a potential threat to the continued economic prosperity of the United States, even to the point of threatening economic decline?
- Can U.S. political institutions put the nation's finances on sound footing and make policies that keep American industry competitive in world markets?
- Despite the historical acceptance of economic inequality in America, does the growing gap between rich and poor raise the possibility of serious social and political problems?

Governing Challenges in the New Political Economy

FROM DEADLOCK TO DECLINE?

While the U.S. economy was relatively prosperous during the 1980s, many troubling warning signs are on the horizon. Increasingly, many of the economic worries are linked to governing problems that seem to have gotten worse over the past two decades.[37] Divided government and political stalemate helped create chronic budget deficits, a huge trade deficit, and the dubious distinction of being the world's largest debtor nation. Is the United States declining as one of the world's great economic and military powers?

Paul Kennedy's *Rise and Fall of the Great Powers,* published in 1987, provoked widespread discussion of the threat of economic decline in the United States. Kennedy's analysis is based on the hypothesis that over the last five hundred years, nations have risen and fallen as great powers based on their global economic balances, which ultimately determine global military balances.[38] Kennedy traces what he calls "imperial overstretch" of once-great powers, such as Spain and Great Britain. Economic strength originally allowed the great powers to become militarily dominant. But expansive empires ultimately committed them to massive doses of military spending, eventually stagnating the domestic economy. Decline occurred when the gap between economic strength and military commitments simply grew too large.

Does the pattern fit the United States and Soviet Union today? Like the great powers before them, their economic strength allowed them to become superpowers in the twentieth century. In the postwar era, each spent large amounts on defense and the arms race and dominated the world. But the balance of economic power has shifted since 1945. Output from the Third World has steadily increased, Europe has become the world's largest trading unit, and Japan has grown so rapidly that it has surpassed the Soviet Union in total output. While the economic problems of the Soviet Union are obviously much more serious than those of the United States, a revolution of sorts is being attempted through President Gorbachev's "perestroika." In contrast, complacency in the United States despite economic and governing problems could lead the nation down a dangerous path.

Indicators of the United States's changed role in the world economy since 1945 are clear:[39]

- In 1950, some 40 percent of the world's goods and services were produced in the United States. By 1990, this had declined to well below 20 percent. Europe's production increased from 20 to 30

Can U.S. industries compete in world markets? Many heavy industries, such as this steel mill, have had to close their gates.

FIGURE 3–3

The Transformation of the United States from Creditor to Debtor

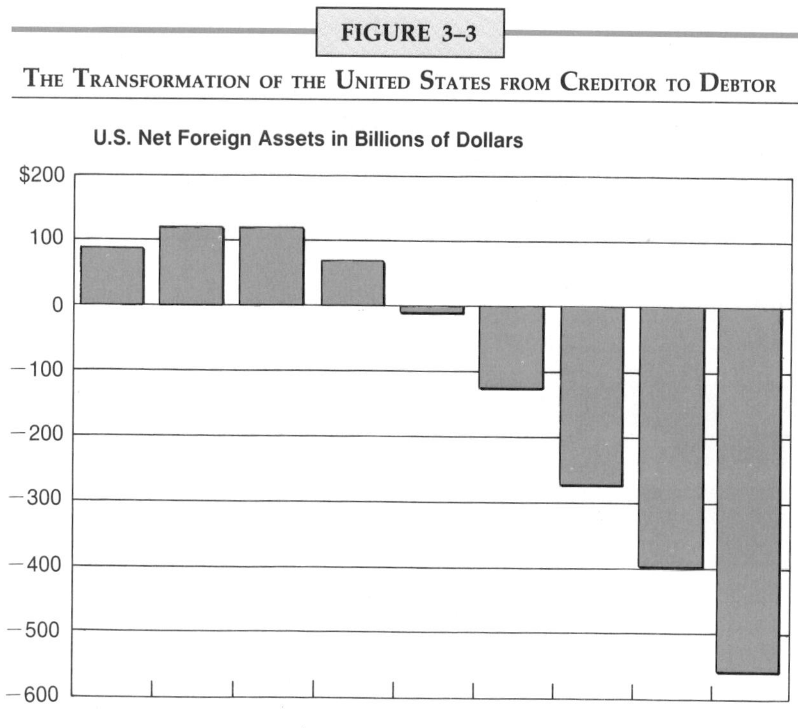

SOURCE: Federal Reserve Board, 1989, U.S. Net Foreign Assets in Billions of Dollars

percent of the world's total, while Japan's climbed from 2 percent to 10 percent of the total.

- In the mid-1970s, two-thirds of the world's advanced technology was designed in the United States. By the mid-1980s, this had dropped to half and by the mid-1990s will decline to below one third.
- By the mid-1980s, the United States imported more high-technology products than it exported, products representing the cutting edge of industrial development. Increasingly, American exports consist of raw materials and agricultural products.
- Productivity, the amount of output by workers, has increased in the United States but at a slower rate than that of its competitors, such as Japan and Germany.
- In the late 1980s, Germany passed the United States to become the world's largest exporter of goods, and Japan is about to become second largest.
- In record time during the 1980s, the United States went from being the world's largest creditor nation (other nations owe money to Americans) to being the world's largest **debtor nation** (Americans owe money abroad). Figure 3–3 shows the rapid turnaround that occurred in the 1980s. These long-term debts threaten to lower living standards in coming years.
- The United States experienced record budget deficits in the 1980s, tripling the total national debt from around one trillion dollars to three trillion dollars.

Do these dramatic changes mean that the United States is declining as a world economic power along the lines of Paul Kennedy's historical patterns? Not yet. While the United States is not as dominant in the world economy as it was after World War II, its economy remains healthy and is still the largest in the world in absolute terms. While many nations have grown more rapidly in the last forty years, the United States is not necessarily declining as a great economic power. Long-term economic prosperity will depend on savings and investment in the private sector, which will be affected by policies adopted by Congress and the president in the coming years. But to avoid decline, the United States must overcome some of the governing problems of the past two decades. One of

Changes in international economic balances affect many aspects of political and social life. Japanese collectors, like the man shown here bidding for a Van Gogh portrait, have recently gone on an international art buying spree.

the most important challenges is to manage the nation's finances more effectively.

MANAGING THE NATION'S FINANCES

Both political parties and both legislative and executive branches claim to be against budget deficits, but they continue to exist anyway. The **budget deficit** is the difference between what the government collects in taxes and what it spends. The difference is made up by borrowing money. The sum of all deficits over time (minus any surpluses) equals the **national debt.** Despite the fact that most politicians are against big deficits and the growing debt, economists dispute their effects on the economy. Deficits can be a useful economic tool during a recession for fostering economic growth. Most agree, however, that sustained deficits during periods of prosperity, such as the 1980s, have the potential to weaken the economy in the long run. Uncontrolled, deficits could lead to higher interest rates, reduced savings and investment, inflation, and reduced living standards down the road.[40]

Hence, one of the most important challenges of the 1990s for political leaders of the United States is to gain control of the nation's finances. Divided government has made this extremely difficult. Election campaigns by both parties have restricted budget options by politicizing, taxing and spending issues. Congress has tried mandatory deficit reduction plans, such as the Gramm-Rudman-Hollings law, without much success.[41] To foster rational management of the nation's finances, Congress and the president must adopt methods for governing that avoid the deadlock and incapacity that has plagued the budget process in the past decade. Solving that problem can help meet another challenge: keeping the nation's industries competitive in the world economy.

ENHANCING AMERICAN COMPETITIVENESS

Despite the fact that there is little government ownership of industry in the United States compared to most other democratic countries, government policies are an important determinant of **competitiveness.** The globalization of the economy has presented new problems and political challenges. Many heavy industries in the United States, such as steel, shipbuilding, and automobile manufacturing, have declined, bringing economic hardship to areas dependent upon them. Many American manufacturers have shifted operations to low-wage countries or buy parts and assembled products from overseas. Two million high-paying manufacturing jobs were lost in the 1980s. While millions of new jobs were created, they were often minimum-wage jobs in the service sector.[42] Americans buy billions of dollars more of imported goods than the United States sells as exports, creating a large **trade deficit** and prompting demands for protection for domestic industries from foreign competition.

But while significant changes have taken place within the U.S. economy, the United States is not deindustrializing. Manufacturing remains essential to the economy, with one-quarter of the work force employed in manufacturing jobs. A strong interdependence exists between service and manufacturing industries.[43] The challenge for decision-makers is to increase the competitiveness of American goods in the world market, not to close off the economy from the rest of the world. Continued leadership in computers, robotics, and semiconductors could form the core of a highly competitive U.S. economy in the future. Government policies necessary to promote competitiveness include budget and fiscal policies, trade legislation, and could even include specific proposals to foster high tech industries. As with the nation's finances, the ability to govern effectively is a prerequisite for promoting economic competitiveness.

THE GAP BETWEEN RICH AND POOR

As we have seen throughout this chapter, one fundamental aspect of a nation's political economy is the gap between rich and poor and policies designed to help those on the bottom of the economic ladder. Figure 3–4 compares American attitudes on economic equity with those of citizens of other nations. A smaller percentage favors a guaranteed basic income or government efforts to redistribute income in the United States than in any of the other countries included. But despite continued acceptance of economic inequality, many are concerned with the growing gap between rich and poor in the United States. The prosperity of the 1980s was not enjoyed equally throughout the economic scale and a growing polarization between rich and poor is possible if the trend continues. With private inheritance, wealth is more unequally distributed than income. The top 10 percent of the population owns one-third of all the nation's

FIGURE 3–4

CROSS-NATIONAL COMPARISON OF ATTITUDES ON GOVERNMENT AND ECONOMIC EQUITY

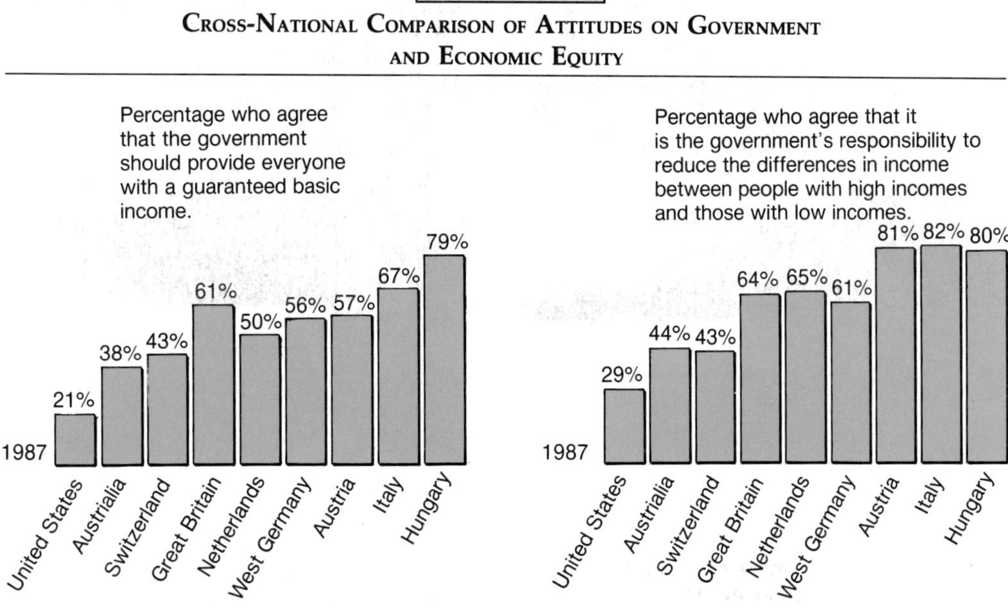

SOURCE: *The American Enterprise*, May/April 1990, p. 113. Reprinted with permission.

private wealth and holds 62 percent of all corporate stock. In 1970, the very richest 1 percent of families in the United States held 27 percent of the wealth. By 1988, the proportion was greater than 36 percent of all wealth, near the peak share attained in 1929. At the bottom of the economic ladder, the poorest 10 percent of the population owes more than they own!

Income is slightly less skewed. Table 3–2 shows the proportion of income received by Americans divided into fifths (quintiles) from 1950 to 1988. It reveals that inequity in the distribution of income in the United States has been increasing steadily since the 1970s. By 1988, the bottom fifth received only 4.6 percent of all income, compared to 5.4 percent in 1970. At the other end, the top fifth received 44 percent of all income, compared to 40.9 percent in 1970.

Annual income for the poorest fifth of Americans has declined in real purchasing power by one-third since 1970. Income earned by the middle class has declined as well. Fifty times more corporate executives earned more than a million dollars per year in 1988, compared to 1980. While stockbrokers and traders on Wall Street frequently earn in the upper six figures, one out of five children, two out of five Hispanic children, and three out of five African-American children live in poverty today.[44] Nearly half the jobs created in the 1980s were at minimum wage. Even with the minimum-wage increases in the early 1990s, many employees supporting a family on a full-time minimum-wage job fall below the poverty line. The number of homeless people, including many families and children, increased at a dramatic rate in the last decade. As with other challenges, the performance of American democracy will have a profound effect on whether political leaders can develop policies concerning access to health care, hunger, homelessness, and poverty in the 1990s.

Poverty amidst plenty has remained a part of the American political economy.

TABLE 3–2

DISTRIBUTION OF INCOME: PERCENTAGE SHARE OF INCOME RECEIVED BY EACH FIFTH OF FAMILIES, 1950–1988

	1950	1960	1970	1980	1984	1988
Poorest fifth	4.5	4.8	5.4	5.1	4.7	4.6
Second fifth	12.0	12.2	12.2	11.6	11.0	10.7
Third fifth	17.4	17.8	17.6	17.5	17.0	16.7
Fourth fifth	23.4	24.0	23.8	24.3	24.4	24.0
Richest fifth	42.7	41.3	40.9	41.6	42.9	44.0

SOURCE: U.S. Census Bureau, 1990.

When the stock market crashed in October of 1987, much of the nervousness among investors was created by deadlock between Congress and the president over the budget and other economic issues. While the crash pushed the president and congressional leaders to the bargaining table, underlying governing problems were not solved. President Bush began his administration with an early summit agreement on the budget, but by the end of the year, Congress and the president had reverted to the familiar pattern of conflict and stalemate. In 1990, alarming increases in the size of the budget deficit forced Bush to back away from his campaign pledge of no new taxes. Throughout the past two hundred years, the American political system has demonstrated the capability to govern decisively and effectively in times of crisis. But does it take a crisis to make the system work? Many even more difficult governing challenges will arise in the future. For example, how can the government of any one nation, no matter how powerful, regulate corporations that are genuinely multinational in their operations and ownership? In meeting the challenges of the new political economy, the institutions and processes of governing must work effectively if the United States is to remain prosperous and avoid decline.

SUMMARY AND CONCLUSIONS

1. A nation's political economy involves its values and cultural traditions, how it responds to change, the economic motives behind political behavior, and how effectively a political system can govern in the economic realm.
2. American political economy has strong traditions of market capitalism, which include private property, individual liberty, materialism, the work ethic, and acceptance of economic inequality.
3. Territorial expansion and the divisions over slavery dominated economic and political development before the Civil War. The rapid industrialization between 1865 and 1920 transformed the economy, creating new social and political problems.
4. Americans recognized the limitations of unrestricted capitalism and supported government intervention into the private economy to regulate trusts and counteract swings in the business cycle. A more activist economic role for government emerged in the 1930s out of Keynesian economic theory and the policies of Franklin D. Roosevelt.
5. Confronting new and more complex economic problems in the 1970s, the Keynesian approach was increasingly challenged. Policies after the election of Ronald Reagan in 1980 represented elements of monetarism and supply-side economics: less government regulation, lower taxes, reduced social spending, and greater emphasis on market solutions.

6. Nations can be compared by looking at equity in the distribution of income and rates of economic growth, but neither are determined exclusively by what mix of private and public sector activities is chosen. Governing ability is often a crucial determinant of which political systems are most economically successful.
7. Although the nature of the U.S. economy and its role within the global economy have changed dramatically, the nation is not necessarily declining. Preventing decline will depend, however, on the performance of both government and business.
8. Governing challenges in the new political economy include managing the nation's finances better, increasing the competitiveness of U.S. goods and services, and addressing the growing gap between rich and poor in society.

American political economy displays elements of both stability and change. Political and economic liberty and market capitalism remain important foundations, but their application continues to change. The ideas of Locke and Smith became Americanized as they took hold in the vast territorial expanse of the United States. The Industrial Revolution reshaped the economy and the policy agenda. While many fulfilled the American dream of getting rich, others struggled long hours in unsafe conditions at subsistence wages. Today, as the economy becomes globalized, new problems and challenges have arisen. Underlying values of individualism and self-reliance still conflict with values of equity and social justice. To successfully meet these new challenges, the American political system must constructively manage these conflicts while reaching timely, effective decisions.

KEY TERMS

Adam Smith
budget deficit
competitiveness
debtor nation
economic liberalism
Employment Act (1946)
Great Depression
individualism
industrialization
Interstate Commerce Commission (ICC)
BUSINESS CYCLE
CAPITALISM
DEMOCRATIC SOCIALISM
GROSS DOMESTIC PRODUCT (GDP)
INCORPORATION
MOBILITY OF LABOR
TRUST CARTELS
SOCIALISM
"invisible hand"
John-Maynard Keynes
laissez-faire capitalism
Karl Marx
mercantilism
monetarism
monopoly
national debt
private property
Sherman Antitrust Act (1890)
supply-side economics
trade deficit
work ethic

SELF-REVIEW

1. In what ways are politics and economics related?
2. What are some of the cultural values and traditions that underlie the American political economy?
3. What dilemma did Adam Smith solve?
4. Describe the nation's first economic policies.
5. What role did economic factors play in the outbreak of the Civil War?
6. What was the Marxist reaction to industrialization?
7. What was the American reaction to industrialization?
8. How did the U.S. government intervene in the economy in the face of growing monopolies?
9. What happened to the U.S. economy after 1929?
10. How did Keynes's theories "revolutionize" capitalist economics?
11. What were the main economic changes of the New Deal?
12. Describe the key features of monetarism and supply-side economics.
13. How has America's position in the world economy changed since 1945?
14. How does the mix of private and public economic activity affect economic growth or the distribution of income?
15. How is political deadlock associated with budget deficits, trade deficits, and foreign debt?
16. How has the distribution of income in the United States changed since the 1970s?
17. How does governing capability effect the way in which the United States will meet the challenges of the global economy?

Suggested Readings

Fusfeld, Daniel. *The Age of the Economist.* 1982.
A readable review of economic history focusing on the life, times, and ideas of the world's most famous economists.
Friedman, Benjamin. *Day of Reckoning.* 1988.
Troubling look at the possible consequences of the deficits of the 1980s.

Kennedy, Paul. *The Rise and Fall of Great Powers.* 1987.
A long but fascinating thesis on economic power, military might, and eventual decline.

Ransom, Roger L. *Coping with Capitalism.* 1981.
An intelligent, nontechnical discussion of economic change and its consequences.

Stein, Herbert. *The Fiscal Revolution in America.* 1969.
An excellent, detailed review of the impact of Keynes on presidents from Franklin Roosevelt to Nixon, written by a Republican Keynesian.

Notes

1. Samuel Huntington, "The United States," in M. Crozier, S. P. Huntington, and J. Watanuki, eds., *The Crisis of Democracy* (New York: New York University Press, 1975).
2. Roger L. Ransom, *Coping with Capitalism* (Englewood Cliffs, N.J.: Prentice-Hall, 1981), 33.
3. Gilbert Fite and Jim Reese, *An Economic History of the United States* (New York: Houghton Mifflin, 1965), 148.
4. *Ibid.,* 33.
5. See Louis M. Hacker, *The Course of American Economic Growth and Development* (New York: Wiley, 1970), 10–11.
6. August C. Bolino, *The Development of the American Economy* (Columbus, Ohio: Merrill, 1966), 21.
7. Ransom, *Coping,* 29.
8. Adam Smith, *An Inquiry into the Wealth of Nations* (New York: Modern Library, 1937).
9. Hacker, *Course,* 55; Bolino, *Development,* 67–68.
10. Fite and Reese, *Economic History,* 136.
11. Charles Beard and Mary Beard, *The Rise of American Civilization* (New York: Macmillan, 1927); and Louis Hacker, *The Triumph of American Capitalism* (New York: Columbia University Press, 1940).
12. Ransom, *Coping,* 46–49.
13. *Historical Statistics of the United States from Colonial Times to 1970* (Washington, D.C.: Government Printing Office, 1976).
14. Bolino, *Development,* 82.
15. W. W. Rostow, *The World Economy* (Austin: University of Texas Press, 1978), reviews some arguments on the takeoff period of industrial growth.
16. See, *e.g.,* Robert Owen, *A New View of Society* (1816).
17. Karl Marx, *The Communist Manifesto* (1848), *A Contribution to the Critique of Political Economy* (1859), and *Capital* (1867).
18. John Moody, *The Truth about the Trusts* (New York: Moody, 1904).
19. Robert Heilbroner, *The Making of Economic Society* (Englewood Cliffs, N.J.: Prentice-Hall, 1962), 122–23.
20. Daniel R. Fusfeld, *The Age of the Economist,* 4th ed. (Glenview, Ill.: Scott, Foresman, 1982), 67.
21. Thomas Cochran and William Miller, *The Age of Enterprise* (New York: Harper and Row, 1961), 122–23.
22. Heilbroner, *Making,* 124.
23. *Ibid.;* all figures in paragraph taken from Heilbroner, *Making.*
24. Quoted in James David Barber, *Presidential Character* (Englewood Cliffs, N.J.: Prentice-Hall, 1977), 30.
25. Fusfeld, *Age,* 91.
26. See Robert Lekachman, *The Age of Keynes* (New York: Random House, 1966); and Roy Harrod, *The Life of John Maynard Keynes* (London: Macmillan, 1951).
27. John Kenneth Galbraith, "Came the Revolution," *New York Times Magazine,* 16 May 1965.
28. Herbert Stein, *The Fiscal Revolution in America* (Chicago: University of Chicago Press, 1969).
29. Congressional Budget Office, *The Fiscal Response to Inflation,* January 1979, p. 67.
30. Milton Friedman, *Capitalism and Freedom* (Chicago: University of Chicago Press, 1962).
31. D. I. Museman and A. B. Laffer, eds., *The Phenomenon of Worldwide Inflation* (Washington, D.C.: American Enterprise Institute, 1975).
32. Gerald M. Pomper, "The 1980 Presidential Election and Its Meaning," in Thomas Cronin, ed., *Rethinking the Presidency* (Boston: Little, Brown, 1982), 22.
33. See David Stockman's comments in *Atlantic Monthly,* December 1981.
34. John R. Freeman, *Democracy and Markets: The Politics of Mixed Economics* (Ithaca, N.Y.: Cornell University Press, 1989).
35. *Ibid.,* 8.
36. *Ibid.,* 13.
37. See Benjamin Friedman, *Day of Reckoning* (New York: Random House, 1988).
38. Paul Kennedy, *The Rise and Fall of Great Powers* (New York: Random House, 1987).
39. *Washington Post National Weekly Edition,* 4 May 1987, pp. 6–7.

40. Lance T. LeLoup, *Budgetary Politics* (Brunswick, Ohio: King's Court, 1988), 63–65.
41. Lance T. LeLoup, Barbara Graham, and Stacey Barwick, "Deficit Politics and Constitutional Government: The Impact of Gramm-Rudman-Hollings," *Public Budgeting and Finance* (Spring 1987): 83–103.
42. *Business Week,* 3 March 1986, p. 57.
43. Congressional Office of Technology Assessment, *Paying the Bill: Manufacturing and America's Trade Deficit,* OTA-ITE-390 (June 1988).
44. *New York Times,* 21 June 1987, p. E25.

CHAPTER 4

Federalism

POLITICAL CLOSE-UP

If the States Had Not United...

We sat in an incredibly long line of cars at the border crossing to enter the Republic of Delaware. As citizens of the United States of New England (the USNE), we had to show our passports and fill out a declaration of goods. It was spring break at the University of New England, and we were heading south to the sunny beaches. We would be going through the Confederate States of America (the CSA), where a civil rights movement was in full swing, on the way to Florida.

Whenever we drove through Delaware, we were amused at how small a country it was, in a class with Liechtenstein and Monaco. We remembered our history lessons. After the collapse of the Constitutional Convention in 1787, Delaware and the other states tried to carry on under the Articles of Confederation. After the British War of 1812, the loose confederation disintegrated. New York, the New England states and the Maritime Provinces formed the USNE, our home (we live in Massachusetts). The Confederate States were formed in the 1830s, encompassing Virginia, Maryland, the Carolinas, Alabama, Georgia, Kentucky, Delta, and Tennessee.

Delaware, Pennsylvania, and New Jersey remained independent for years, before Pennsylvania expanded to the Mississippi River on the west, the Ohio River on the south, and the Great Lakes on the north. New Jersey joined the Pennsylvanian Republic in 1884, but little Delaware remained an independent state to this day.

We finally got through the border crossing with no problems except the delay. Since Delaware has a free public transportation system that covers the state, the roads leave something to be desired. We stopped to buy some imported *biere* from St. Louis in New France.

Although we in New England like to think we are the leading nation in North America, the Pennsylvanian Republic and California actually have a higher gross domestic product than the USNE. The CSA, after lagging behind the other North American nations, is in the midst of an industrial boom, although its agriculture has steadily fallen behind the Great Plains states of New France, which extend to the Rockies. Despite the many negotiations in the last two decades in an attempt to form a common market—the North American Economic Community—the problems of language and sharp regional differences have so far proved insurmountable.

It seems impossible, from the vantage point of today, that the states could ever have been united. The People's Free Indian Republic (PFIR) in the southwestern part of the continent was particularly hostile to the Confederate States. It had fought three wars in the past century, and the situation was still unstable. Although the United States of New England and our ally, Pennsylvania, have military superiority, there remains a threat that we will be drawn into another conflict on the side of the Indian Republic. This has not yet occurred because our government under Prime Minister Kennedy and his Labour party are suspicious of

Communist Premier Longknife of the PFIR.

Driving my Pennsylvania-made Pontiac (almost all the cars in the USNE are imported), I was half dreaming. What would it have been like if they had been able to unite the states of America back in 1787, I wondered. Would the North and South have been able to live together in one country? What leaders would have been able to govern such diverse states? Could we have become a single huge, rich nation?

CHAPTER OUTLINE

INTRODUCTION AND OVERVIEW

Who would really govern in a system that gave some powers to the national government and others to the state governments? Federalism divides authority between the central (national) government and state and local (subnational) governments. Almost every political system has some kind of **subnational governments,** but the differences are in the power granted to these units.[1]

Much of the bargaining that took place in Philadelphia at the Constitutional Convention concerned the division of power between the states and the national government. Some sort of power-sharing was inevitable. The question was, how much power would the states surrender? One of the main contentions of the Anti-Federalists, who opposed ratification of the new Constitution, was that the states were giving up too much power to the central government. Were they to be proven right? Is the federal government too powerful? Should there be greater reliance on state and local government, where officials are closer to the people and their problems? Or does the federal system, as it currently exists, fragment political power to such an extent that it seriously limits the ability to govern?

Federalism is relevant today for nearly 80,000 reasons: 50 state governments, 3,000 counties, 19,000 municipalities, 17,000 townships, 15,000 school districts, and 25,000 special districts in the United States.[2] State and local government spending constitutes about one-third of the total public sector, or almost 13 percent of the gross national product (GNP). There are many times more state and local government employees than federal employees. Local and state governments employ millions of teachers, police officers, fire fighters, clerks, registrars, legislators, and bureaucrats.

An analysis of federalism begins with the Constitution but goes beyond it. Many questions were left unanswered by that document, leaving the courts to fill in the missing pieces over the years. Today federalism involves questions about, the states: How much variation in public policy is found among the states? Does federalism lead to chaos, or is it a source of vitality in American politics? Federalism also involves questions about the problems of the local governments: How can America's older cities cope with a growing dependent population while their economic base is shrinking? How do newer cities cope with rapid growth? Many of these questions have to do with political economy as finances have become a critical link in the relationship between the states and the national government.

Chapter 4 looks at the following questions:

1. What is the constitutional basis of federalism? How has the balance of power between state and national governments developed over the years? How does it affect the ability of the American political system to govern effectively?
2. What is fiscal federalism? Have financial questions come to dominate intergovernmental relations in the United States?
3. What are some of the current policy issues concerning federalism? What are the Bush administration's views on federalism?
4. What is the state of the states? What are some important similarities and differences among states? What are their most serious problems in the 1990s?
5. How did American cities develop, and where do they stand in the federal system? How are they governed? Is there a fiscal crisis in the major urban areas?

★

Federalism and the Ability to Govern

THE CONSTITUTIONAL BASIS OF FEDERALISM

Most political systems have lower units of government to help implement policies. The distinction between *confederal, federal,* and *unitary* forms of government lies in the constitutional basis and distribution of powers. **Federal** systems divide power between subnational and national governments. They constitutionally guarantee specific powers to state governments. In a federal system, the central government is constitutionally prohibited from taking away powers reserved to the subnational units. **Unitary** systems constitutionally guarantee specific powers only to the national government. Subnational units in a unitary system are "creations" of the national government, and their powers are determined by the national government. In **confederal** systems, most power remains with the subnational governments, as was the case with the states under the Articles of Confederation. States remain sovereign, and only limited powers are granted to the national government.

The United States, Germany, Mexico, and Switzerland are examples of nations with federal governments. France, Great Britain, Israel, and Italy are examples of unitary governments. A classic example of centralization in a unitary system was the French education minister who claimed that at any hour of the day he could tell what every child in a particular grade was studying. Exaggeration or not, such centralization is unthinkable in the United States, where local school districts and administrators have autonomy in determining what will be taught.

"Federal" in the name of a country or in its constitution does not always mean it is really a federal system. The Soviet Union, for example, has a federal constitution, but, until recently, power was exercised almost exclusively by the central government. Recent moves toward democracy in the U.S.S.R. have allowed the Soviet republics to strengthen their power vis-a-vis the national government in Moscow.

Imagine creating state and local governments from scratch today. That is what Poland did in 1990 as the nation transformed both its political and economic systems. Under communist rule, Poland was governed from the top down through an extensive party bureaucracy. Suddenly, Poles had the opportunity to create local democracy. The task was to establish some 2,000 new governing units and an administrative officer for each and elect over 140,000 representatives to fill the seats on newly created local councils. Looking around the world, Poles found many different ways to structure local government and divide power between levels of government.

Why a federal system for America? Mainly because at the time the Constitution was written the states were the existing source of government power. Moving from confederation to a federal government was controversial enough. Moving to a unitary system was unthinkable. The debate over federalism in the ratification process centered around the idea of "small republics." Basing their arguments on the writings of Montesquieu, the Anti-Federalists insisted that liberty could be reasonably protected only in small governing units—that is, the states.[3] Madison countered by arguing that liberty could be well protected in a larger republic because of the diversity of interests in the society.[4] The practical problem for the Founders was to balance the need for a stronger central government with the desire of the thirteen states to retain their autonomy. The Framers tried to be specific. Certain powers were reserved to the states, others were delegated only to the national government, and some were left for both levels to share. Table 4–1 compares some of the main powers assigned in the Constitution and in amendments to date.

Despite the specific delegations of authority, the Constitution left many questions open and its language subject to interpretation. Over the years, the forms of federalism—local governments, counties, cities, states, national government—have remained essentially the same, but the *content* of federalism has changed significantly.[5] How were the actual practices and powers as they are known today established?

NATIONAL SUPREMACY

Federalism fragments power, and by doing so, it generally reduces the ability of the central government to govern. This is exactly what the Founders wanted and what American politics in 1787 and 1788 demanded. The **Tenth Amendment,** the last item in the Bill of Rights, was added to assuage public fears that the new national government would run roughshod over the states. The amendment reads: "The powers not delegated to the United States by the Constitution, nor prohibited by it to the States, are reserved to the States respectively or to the people." Would this prove to be a fatal impediment to the growth and development of the Constitution in succeeding decades by placing severe restrictions on the ability of national institutions to govern? No, because of several important developments.

Even though the Tenth Amendment appears to favor the states, the Constitution was sufficiently vague to leave open the question of supremacy. Thirty years after the Constitution was ratified, the Supreme Court handed down one of its most important rulings. The decision in ***McCulloch v. Maryland*** (1819) established national supremacy and an expansive interpretation of the ability of the national government to act.

One of the first controversies in American politics was over the National Bank approved in the 1790s. The bank was given extensive powers to print money and engage in credit activities. Popular with the Federalists, the bank was despised by many Anti-Federalists and state governments as an infringement on states' rights. In 1818, the state of Maryland levied a tax of $15,000 on the Baltimore branch of the National Bank. The officers of the bank refused to pay, and James McCulloch, the cashier in the bank, was sued for payment. State courts in Maryland upheld the tax, but the case went before the U.S. Supreme Court.

Chief Justice John Marshall had presided over the Supreme Court since he was named by President John Adams in 1800. The Federalists had long since disappeared as a political force, but Marshall continued to represent the Federalist viewpoint on the Court. Daniel Webster argued the case for the National Bank. He made an eloquent defense of a broad interpretation of the powers of the national government in justifying Congress's decision to establish a national bank. Sympathetic to Webster's argument, Marshall and the Court ruled against Maryland, in favor of the bank.

Marshall's opinion settled some important questions and established principles that would permanently affect the distribution of governing authority between the states and the national government. The Court held that the federal government had the authority to create a national bank because of the elastic clause (the "necessary and proper" clause) in

TABLE 4–1

CONSTITUTIONAL POWERS UNDER FEDERALISM

	Powers Granted	Powers Denied
National government	To coin money To conduct foreign relations To regulate commerce with foreign nations and among states To provide an army and a navy To declare war To establish courts inferior to the Supreme Court To establish post offices To make laws necessary and proper to carry out the foregoing powers	To tax articles exported from one state to another To violate the Bill of Rights To change state boundaries
State government	To establish local governments To regulate commerce within a state To conduct elections To ratify amendments to the federal Constitution To take measures for public health, safety, and morals To exert powers the Constitution does not delegate to the national government or prohibit the states from using	To tax imports or exports To coin money To enter into treaties To impair obligations of contracts To abridge the privileges or immunities of citizens (Fourteenth Amendment)
State and national government	To tax To borrow money To establish courts To make and enforce laws To charter banks and corporations To spend money for the general welfare To take private property for public purposes, with just compensation	To grant titles of nobility To permit slavery (Thirteenth Amendment) To deny citizens the right to vote because of race, color, or previous servitude (Fourteenth Amendment) To deny citizens the right to vote because of sex (Nineteenth Amendment)

Article I, section 8 of the Constitution. The implication of the ruling was that the national government had certain "implied powers" (not stated but allowed under the Constitution) and was not just limited to "enumerated powers" (spelled out specifically in the Constitution). Second, the Court ruled that neither Maryland nor any other state had the authority to tax a creation of the federal government. The bank was a creation of the sovereign will of *all* the people, and no state—the reflection of only one segment of the people—could be allowed to tax it. Noting that "the power to tax is the power to destroy," the *McCulloch* decision established the supremacy of the national government over the states. Marshall's expansive views of the power of the national government as written in the Court's opinion became famous:

> Let the end be legitimate, let it be within the scope of the Constitution, and all means which are appropriate, which are plainly adapted to that end, which are not prohibited, but consistent with the letter and spirit of the Constitution, are constitutional.[6]

The broad interpretation of implied powers had an important impact on American politics. Restriction of the federal government to enumerated powers would have severely limited the ability to govern, particularly in the twentieth century. A decision in favor of state supremacy or a narrow interpretation of constitutional powers might have required major structural changes in the Constitution in later years.

THE EVOLUTION OF FEDERALISM

The *McCulloch* decision may have been the most important turning point in the history of federalism, but it was not the only one. The struggle between **states' rights** advocates and the supporters of Marshall's national supremacy view continued until the Civil War. President Abraham Lincoln and the Republican party denied the states' right to secede and ultimately fought to enforce their stand. The states' rights view was premised on the notion that the Constitution was only a "compact" between the states and that the states were free to "nullify" federal laws by ignoring them. The Civil War put this interpretation to rest and in doing so further strengthened the power of the national government over the states.

After the Civil War, most of the disagreement over federal-state relations concerned the interstate commerce clause. The interpretation of federalism at this time was sometimes called **dual federalism,** meaning that the states and the national governments operated primarily in their own separate spheres. The doctrine of dual federalism was based on the assumption that there was a clear distinction between commerce within a state (intrastate commerce) and commerce between states (interstate commerce). In the late nineteenth century, the Court struggled to draw the line between the two and to determine what the states could regulate and what the federal government could regulate. The results were frustrating as the economy grew more complex. In time, the Court began to expand the definition of interstate commerce and hence what Congress could constitutionally regulate. By the 1940s, virtually all businesses were subject to national regulation. In the 1960s, the Congress used the interstate commerce clause to end segregation in public accommodations in the South (see Chapter 6).[7]

The idea of dual federalism gave way to one of **cooperative federalism,** where both levels of government share responsibilities across a number of policy areas. Using the analogy of a cake, political scientist Morton Grodzins described dual federalism as a layer cake, with separate, distinct levels. Cooperative federalism today is much more

As residents moved out of central city areas, sprawling suburbs created new political problems and demands.

like a marble cake, with powers and responsibilities swirled together.[8] Education is an example of this blending. Once considered strictly a function of state and local governments, the federal government began taking a more active role in education in the 1950s. In response to the Soviet launching of *Sputnik,* the first artificial satellite to orbit Earth, national policy-makers moved quickly to enhance scientific and technical education in the United States by passing the National Defense Education Act in 1957. Federal aid increased markedly in the mid-1960s with passage of the Elementary and Secondary Education Act in 1965.[9]

Federal-state relations have not simply been a history of the national government encroaching on state governments, but this has certainly been the most prominent pattern. One of the last gasps of the old states' rights position came in reaction to the 1954 *Brown v. Board of Education* decision, which outlawed segregation in public schools. Southern members of Congress issued a manifesto declaring their intent to disobey the Supreme Court, and southern state legislatures passed "**nullification acts,**" declaring the ruling invalid within their borders. The eventual acceptance of integration in the South effectively ended a chapter in the history of federalism.

The courts are still called on to settle questions of political power between the states and the federal government. After nearly half a century of legal defeats, advocates of state and local government finally won a major court decision in the case of *National League of Cities (NLC) v. Ussery* (1976). One observer noted: "The Supreme Court unearthed the remains of the Tenth Amendment. Although interred for nearly four decades, the resulting legal autopsy revealed the constitutional provision to be alive and kicking."[10] The Court sided with the states, remarking, "Congress may not exercise power in a fashion that impairs the states' integrity or their ability to function effectively in a federal system." The decision was hailed as a victory for state and local control, but it was a fleeting one. Between 1976 and 1985, the Court consistently ruled for the federal government over states whenever their interests collided. The rather broadly stated doctrine in the *NLC* case appeared to be a limited one.

The Supreme Court made it official in 1985 when it overruled *NLC v. Ussery* in a 5-to-4 decision, giving Congress almost unlimited ability to force state and local governments to comply with federal regulations. In the case of ***Garcia v. San Antonio Metropolitan Transit Authority*** (1985), the Court ruled that the federal Fair Labor Standards Act, which sets minimum-wage and overtime requirements, applied to local governments. Writing for the majority, Justice Harry Blackman stated that the Court "now reject[s], as unsound in principle and unworkable in practice, a rule of state immunity from federal regulation that turns on a judicial appraisal of whether a particular governmental function is 'integral' or 'traditional.'" Critics were quick to attack the decision. In a forceful dissent, Justice Lewis F. Powell, Jr., wrote that the decision "effectively reduces the Tenth Amendment to meaningless rhetoric." He complained that the decision "rejects almost two hundred years of the understanding of the constitutional status of federalism." Unhappy state and local officials feared that the Tenth Amendment had been laid to rest for good.

Is "cooperative federalism" an adequate description of the relationship between Washington and the state capitals? State and national governments often seem to be in an adversarial relationship, not a cooperative one. The president and members of Congress, even those who claim to support strengthening the states, have not hesitated to attach strings to federal money. States like to blame Washington for their problems, and they resent having the federal government tell them what to do. A recent example was legislation concerning the legal drinking age, which traditionally had been a police power reserved for the states. Congress passed a law intended to pressure states to raise the legal drinking age to twenty-one. Although compliance by states was "voluntary," they risked losing billions in federal highway monies if they refused. The Reagan administration, although avowing the concept of more power to state governments, strongly supported the measure. Regulations for mandatory passive restraints (air bags) in automobiles revealed an innovative twist in intergovernmental relations. Responding to pressure from the automobile industry, Congress said that if at least fifteen of the largest states passed mandatory seat-belt laws (active restraints), then the regulations requiring air bags would not take effect. States have more real choice in the latter case, but it is still the federal government that is calling most of the shots.

The constitutional division of power between the national government and the states has had an important impact on the ability to govern. The preexistence of the states at the time of the Constitutional Convention and the strong sentiment for keeping their autonomy could have resulted in an extremely weak national government. Flexible constitutional language, critical Supreme Court decisions, and the Civil War established national supremacy and enhanced governing capacity. But the federal system may still pose barriers to governing. Leaders in the 1960s complained about state intransigence in protecting civil rights, state variations in social welfare programs, and erratic implementation of other federal programs. Officials of the federal government often believe it is more efficient to set uniform policies in Washington than to work through the states.

The perspective is very different from the states and cities. State and local politicians see limits on the national government as highly desirable. States believe that in many areas, they can govern more effectively and efficiently than Washington. In their view, reforms to enhance governing should strengthen the states vis-à-vis the federal government, not vice versa. A debate continues over which level of government is the most competent. As Figure 4–1 shows, the public believes that state and local governments are better able to solve problems than the federal government. As federalism has evolved from dual federalism to cooperative federalism with a competitive edge, relations among levels of government are increasingly based on money—what is often called **fiscal federalism.**

Fiscal Federalism: The Political Economy of Intergovernmental Relations

For many years, the federal government provided some financial assistance to state and local governments, but as late as 1950, federal aid amounted to less than 10 percent of all state and local revenues. As policy initiatives expanded at all levels of government, intergovernmental relations in the United States increasingly centered on questions of finances. By 1978, one dollar out of every four spent by state and local government came from Washington. The increasing financial dependency on of American states and cities on federal funds was accompanied by greater penetration of the national government into the domain of state and local politics. Renewed controversy erupted over the division of political power among national, state, and local governments.

FIGURE 4–1

LEVEL OF GOVERNMENT BEST AT SOLVING PROBLEMS

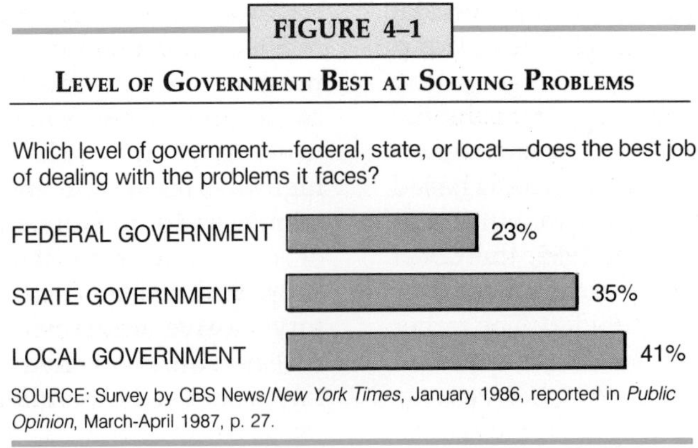

SOURCE: Survey by CBS News/*New York Times*, January 1986, reported in *Public Opinion*, March-April 1987, p. 27.

Relations between states and cities and the federal government are increasingly dominated by money. Checks, like this one presented by President Reagan, have shrunk in the past decade.

FEDERAL GRANTS TO STATE AND LOCAL GOVERNMENTS

CATEGORICAL GRANTS. Direct grants-in-aid, **categorical grants** can be used only for one specific purpose. States usually must provide some matching funds. (With highway trust funds, for example, the states contribute 10 percent, and the federal government contributes 90 percent.) Categorical grants require the states and cities to establish an agency to administer the funds, have plans and procedures for allocating the money approved in Washington, and be subject to regular review by the federal government.

In 1965–66 alone, the Johnson administration and the Eighty-ninth Congress created sixty-seven new categorical grant programs in health, education, urban redevelopment, and economic assistance. By 1972, there were a total of more than five hundred different categorical grants. Using categorical grants, federal officials maintained maximum control over how money was to be spent in an attempt to achieve national objectives. Categorical grants ensured that more consistent national standards would be applied across the country. Antidiscrimination clauses in the categorical grants proved to be particularly effective methods for achieving national civil rights goals. But the extensive strings on the money and the multitude of programs resulted in confusion, waste, and duplication in many cases. States and cities became increasingly competitive with one another in the battle for federal monies. State and local officials complained about the excessive difficulty in getting the money and what they perceived as constant interference by "the feds" in running their programs. But with growing social and fiscal needs, cities and states could not afford to pass up a single opportunity for money, even if they were dubious about the requirements. By the 1970s, there was growing criticism of categorical grants and pressure for change.

BLOCK GRANTS. As an alternative to more-restrictive categorical grants, **block grants** provide state and local governments with monies for broadly defined purposes. Block grants give more discretion to state and local officials. For example, local leaders may define "community development" as stabilizing housing patterns in one city and developing recreational or physical facilities in another. In the 1970s, categorical grants were consolidated into block grants in such policy areas as crime control and law enforcement, health care, education, and employment and training.

Block grants have obvious attractions for state and local officials. But as more categorical grants were folded into block grants, critics charged that the national government was giving up too much control. In the area of crime control, for example, opponents charged that not enough money was going to the central cities where money was really needed. Instead, state officials were allowing too much money to go to rich suburban police departments. Despite some problems with block grants and lingering support for categorical grants, the political climate of the 1970s and 1980s clearly favored greater state and local control.

REVENUE SHARING. Simply put, **revenue sharing** is a revenue turnback from the national government to state and local governments. The idea for revenue sharing originated with Thomas Jefferson in the 1800s and had proponents in both political parties in the 1950s and 1960s. In the early 1970s, President Nixon announced his plan for a "New Federalism" to balance the relationship between the states and the national government.[11] The centerpiece of his plan was the revenue-sharing bill. Some $6 billion a year would be turned back; two-thirds of the monies would go to local governments, the remaining third to the states.

Strong support from state and local politicians helped spur passage of the bill in 1972. Congress worked long and hard writing the specific formula for distribution. Perhaps the greatest complaint about the program was that revenue sharing did not target the money to areas of the greatest need. With each member of Congress guarding local district interests, nearly every government got something whether they were relatively rich or poor.[12] Cities in the worst financial shape had to use the funds for their regular budget to prevent layoffs and cuts in essential services.

Congress was satisfied enough with the results to extend the program in 1976. In response to critics who wanted to see money better targeted, Congress also passed "countercyclical" revenue sharing in 1976 to send additional monies to areas with the highest levels of unemployment. Revenue sharing was extended again in 1980, but countercyclical aid was allowed to lapse, and states were dropped from the formula to concentrate on local governments. After years of steady growth in federal aid to state and local government, dramatic changes would occur in the 1980s.

FEND-FOR-YOURSELF FEDERALISM

THE REAGAN LEGACY. One priority of the Reagan administration in the 1980s was to swing political power and economic responsibility back to the states. In 1982, President Reagan proposed his own version of the **"New Federalism,"** a plan to turn certain federal programs back to the states. Under the Reagan proposal, the federal government would take over financing Medicaid in return for states assuming full responsibility for welfare and food stamps. In addition to this swap, sixty-one other categorical grants would be turned over to the states.

Congress ultimately did not approve Reagan's New Federalism plan, but significant changes in fiscal federalism did occur. Many categorical grants were folded into a smaller number of block grants, cutting total outlays at the same time. More important, the message the states got was: "Start looking to your own fiscal resources from now on."[13] Federal aid to state and local governments had reached a high-water mark in 1978 (see Figure 4–2). By 1978, nearly 27 percent of all state and local spending came from money provided by the federal government through various grant programs. By 1988, however, the federal share had slipped to less than 17 percent of all state and local outlays. What happened?

In the decade between 1978 and 1988, state and local treasuries were subjected to three shocks. The first was the so-called "tax revolt" that began in 1978, when California voters approved a statewide proposal, **Proposition 13,** that set limits on property taxes. Other states followed suit, adopting a variety of tax and spending limitations. The second shock came in 1981–82, when state and local governments

FIGURE 4-2

THE RISE AND DECLINE OF FEDERAL AID, 1958–1988 (AS A PERCENTAGE OF STATE-LOCAL OUTLAYS)

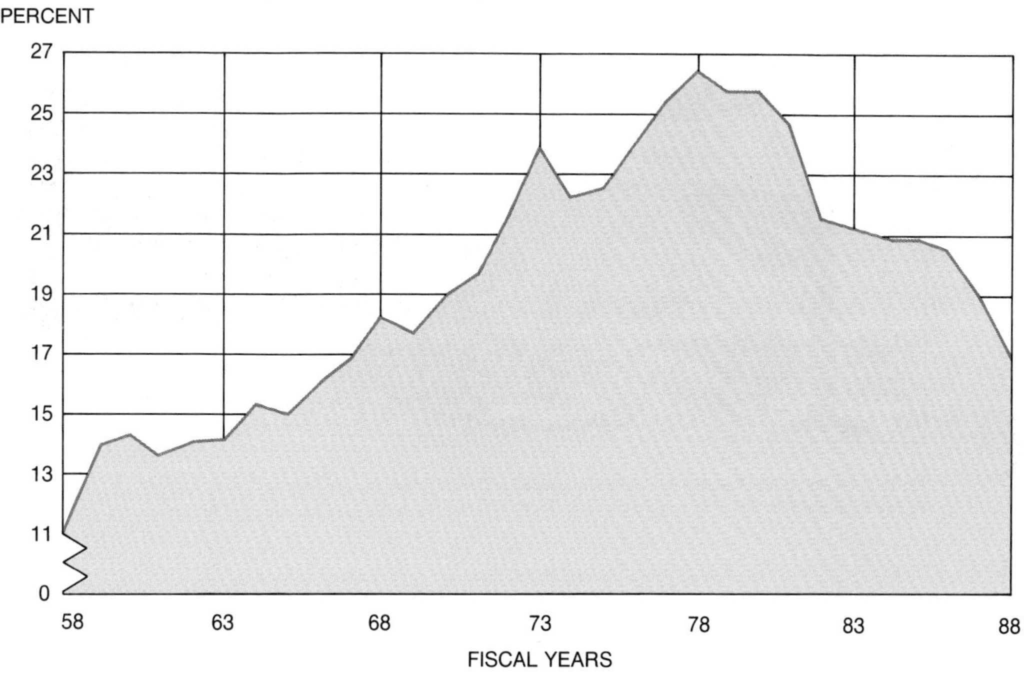

NOTE: Figure for 1988 is an estimate.

SOURCE: Advisory Commission on Intergovernmental Relations, 1987.

were badly hurt by the recession—the most severe since the Great Depression. The third and most critical shock came when the Reagan administration and Congress turned the federal money tap off in the 1980s. As part of the Reagan administration's plan to reduce government spending at all levels, federal aid to state and local governments sustained major cuts.

In 1981–82, the federal government provided no countercyclical aid, as earlier administrations had. Farm belt states received no special aid during the farm crisis of the mid-1980s. The clear signal from Washington in the 1980s was that state and local governments were to fend for themselves financially. By 1988, more than half the states had created "rainy day" funds to help cushion the shock of future economic and political downturns.

FEDERALISM UNDER THE BUSH ADMINISTRATION

The trends in fiscal federalism that began under Reagan are continuing under the Bush administration. President Bush has argued in favor of greater powers and responsibility for subnational governments. The difference, according to the executive director of the National Association of Counties, is that Bush wants government to do more than President Reagan did in such areas as education, the environment, transportation, and child care, but he wants state and local governments to pay for it.[14] As a result, although tax burdens are steady or decreasing at the federal level, they are increasing at the state and local level in the 1990s. This has led some to call state and local governments the "designated taxers" in the federal system. In the past decade,

state taxes rose 144 percent, while city and county taxes grew more than 135 percent. Since 1978, state and local spending as a percentage of GNP has increased from 11.3 percent to 12.7 percent. Will this lead to another tax revolt like the one in the late 1970s? A number of governors in financially strapped states in the Northeast, including 1988 presidential candidate Michael Dukakis of Massachusetts, declined to run for reelection in 1990.

The financial predicament of American state and local governments in a risky fiscal environment contrasts with how subnational governments are funded in other federal systems. In Germany, the states receive revenues from a tax-sharing arrangement with the central government in Bonn. The Australian states receive unconditional grants from the national government. In Canada, the provinces are also financed partially through a federal-state tax-sharing plan. In all three of these nations, the financial arrangements between state and national governments are based on uniform distribution formulas that reduce interstate variation. In the United States, each of the fifty states is on its own. The result is a great deal of variation in terms of level of services, level of tax burdens, and the kinds of taxes that are used.

The decline in federal aid has intensified the competition among states for new business and industry. This serves to place some limits on fiscal variation between states. High-service and high-tax states may limit expansion of services for fear that their tax burdens may drive prospective businesses to another state. Low-tax and low-service states may forgo further cutbacks lest poor services and a substandard educational system have a similar deterrent effect on economic development.

American states and local governments are a fascinating array of political units, colorful in their political history, rich in diversity. What are their policies, politics, and problems? The rest of this chapter explores these and other questions.

States

The union of American states grew quickly. Westward expansion and rapid population growth resulted in the addition of new states, but slavery was the main issue over which each new admission was fought. Compromises balancing the number of slave states and free states in the Union in 1820 and 1850 kept the lid on the seething controversy for a time. When it could no longer be contained, the resulting Civil War became a milestone in federalism by firmly establishing the dominance of the national government. After 1865, more western states were admitted to the Union. The era of expansion came to an end in 1912 with the admission of Arizona and New Mexico. Since then the national map has been expanded only by granting statehood to Alaska in 1958 and to Hawaii in 1959. Many of the political and economic differences that exist today are related to the history, geography, and economic development of the states.

STATE GOVERNMENTS

Most state constitutions created strong legislatures to govern their states. But political corruption and resulting reform movements in the late nineteenth century reduced the power and prestige of state legislatures. Industrialization spawned powerful business interests anxious to extend their influence into the political realm, and many state legislators were only too anxious to help.

Reformers responded both to economic change and to political corruption. Many state constitutions were revised, giving governors greater powers and often limiting the length of legislative sessions. Changes seemed to reflect the ironic view that "no person's liberty is secure while the legislature sits in session." By the twentieth century, it was apparent that governors could be as corrupt as state legislatures. Former Maryland governor Spiro T. Agnew was still receiving payoffs while he was in the White House as Richard Nixon's vice-president. His successor as governor, Democrat Marvin Mandel, was convicted of fraud and sent to jail. Former Illinois governor Otto Kerner was sent to prison for his part in a racetrack scandal. Tennessee governor Ray Blanton ended his term in office by selling pardons to a number of convicted criminals.

Today, the balance of power between governor and legislature varies across the fifty states. In states where the governor is more powerful, he or she has a longer term of office, greater control of state offices, greater budget authority, and a stronger veto power. Many governors have an **item veto,** where portions of a bill can be eliminated without vetoing the entire measure. President Reagan unsuccessfully requested that Congress consider giving him a similar veto to combat spending excesses on the federal level. Table 4–2 compares the veto powers of state governors. Political Insight 4–1 examines some of the more fanciful proposals from

TABLE 4–2

STATES RANKED AS TO GOVERNORS' VETO POWERS

Very Strong		Strong	Medium	Weak
Alaska	Minnesota	Alabama	Florida	Indiana
Arizona	Mississippi	Arkansas	Idaho	Maine
California	Missouri	Kentucky	Massachusetts	Nevada
Colorado	Nebraska	Tennessee	Montana	New Hampshire
Connecticut	New Jersey	West Virginia	New Mexico	North Carolina
Delaware	New York		Oregon	Rhode Island
Georgia	North Dakota		South Carolina	Vermont
Hawaii	Ohio		Texas	
Illinois	Oklahoma		Virginia	
Iowa	Pennsylvania		Washington	
Kansas	South Dakota		Wisconsin	
Louisiana	Utah			
Maryland	Wyoming			
Michigan				

SOURCE: Compiled from *The Book of the States, 1980–1981* (Lexington, KY: Council of State Governments, 1981), 110–111.

POLITICAL INSIGHT 4-1

THE FRIVOLOUS SIDE OF STATE LEGISLATION

Not all policy-making in the state legislatures across the United States is concerned with hard budget choices or difficult moral issues. Over the years, a number of zany bills have been introduced and occasionally enacted. Legislators love to enact official state "stuff" from a state song to a state insect. Kentucky, South Dakota, and Michigan each recently designated an official "state soil." Colorado made the yucca moth the state insect, and Alaska designated the "senior hoary marmot" as the official state marmot.

A number of other interesting bills were proposed. In Pennsylvania, a bill was introduced to increase the number of toilets for women in stadiums and other public places to eliminate long waiting lines and establish "potty parity." In South Carolina, legislation was introduced to ban "toad licking" after it was discovered that South American cane toads secrete a hallucinogenic toxin. Another legislator there introduced a bill to ban the discharge of a firearm within 300 yards of a chicken coop to prevent scared chickens from jumping in a pile and suffocating themselves. A state senator in New Mexico introduced a bill creating a new county named after himself. A representative in Tennessee introduced a measure to encourage citizens to assault flag burners by reducing the fine to one dollar. The West Virginia legislature considered legislation to give people lottery tickets if they wore their seat belts. Other less than notable proposals including paying people to vote, exempting ostrich steaks from sales tax, and bringing back the whipping post. Who says state politics isn't exciting?

SOURCE: Source: *St. Louis Post Dispatch,* 15 February 1990, p. A2.

state legislators that may explain why governors want a strong veto power.

An important political event in the states in the 1960s was legislative redistricting. Until 1962, congressional and state legislative districts could be drawn without regard to population. Districts were based on such traditional boundaries as counties and tended to overrepresent rural districts. One district in New Hampshire's lower house had only thirty constituents! Although the Supreme Court had earlier avoided deciding the issue of redistricting because it was a "political question," it finally declared malapportioned districts to be unconstitutional. In the 1964 decision of ***Reynolds v. Sims,*** the Court applied the doctrine of "one person, one vote" to state legislative districts.[15] The court ruled that districts had to be approximately equal in population, noting that representation was based on people, not trees or cows. Every state had to redraw legislative district lines, some as many as three times. Rural areas lost representation, urban areas remained about the same, and the newer suburban areas made the largest gains. Despite these boundary changes, studies of redistricting have revealed little change in party balance or the ideological stance of state legislatures.[16]

STATE POLITICAL CULTURE

A drive along a busy interstate highway reveals license plates of many hues and slogans. But the differences among states go beyond mottoes, birds, and flags. States vary in political traditions and "personality"—what political scientists call **political culture.**[17] Political culture can be simply defined as the way citizens orient themselves to politics. Political scientist Daniel Elazar developed three general categories for the American states. States with a tradition of "leaving politics to the professionals," where participation is more limited, have what he called an *individualistic culture.* Included are such states in the Northeast as Ohio, Indiana, New Jersey, Maryland, and Pennsylvania. Some of these states—for example, Maryland and New Jersey—

have been plagued with political corruption more than others, giving rise to the claim that the political culture in those states is somehow more conducive to official illegalities.

Corruption is much less prevalent in the states of the upper Midwest and the Northwest, where a *moralistic* culture prevails. Elazar found that these states have citizens who tend to participate more actively and public officials who are more oriented to government intervention to solve public problems. Oregon, Michigan, Wisconsin, and Minnesota are examples of the moralistic political culture. The Populist and Progressive movements (1890–1920) were particularly strong in the upper Midwest. One result was a series of reforms including the direct primary, the recall petition (where public officials may be removed from office), and the referendum (where voters may place issues directly on the ballot rather than leaving them for legislative action).

Traditionalistic political culture dominates the southern states. Citizens in the South support a conservative, limited role for state government with a greater orientation by governing elites to preserving the existing order. Georgia, Alabama, Mississippi, Virginia, and South Carolina are examples of the traditionalistic culture. This culture was enhanced by the one-party system that existed for a century following the Civil War. Antipathy toward the Republicans meant that the Democratic party operated unchallenged in the "solid South." Winning the Democratic primary was tantamount to winning the election, making it easier to restrict participation to a smaller group of people, mainly whites.

Three categories cannot capture the wealth of variation among state political systems, but they do suggest interesting lines of difference. Some states show remarkable divergence within their own borders. New York, Illinois, and California all exhibit distinct political personalities in upstate and downstate areas. Political culture can change over time. The voter registration efforts surrounding Jesse Jackson's candidacy for president and the development of a more competitive two-party system resulted in important changes in the participation of voters in the South.

Among the states, there are leaders and followers. Some states have pioneered solutions to public problems in such areas as tenant-landlord relations, education and child welfare, protection against child abuse and for battered wives, prisoner release and rehabilitation, and local ownership of failing corporations. A study by political scientist Jack Walker, who examined state policy innovation since World War II, found that New York, California, and Massachusetts were the most innovative states, whereas Nevada, Wyoming, and Mississippi were the least innovative.[18] New York, in 1984, was the first state to pass a mandatory seat-belt law. Although the leaders among the states include many of the largest, wealthiest states, smaller states, such as Massachusetts, Colorado, Oregon, and Rhode Island, are often out front in policy innovation.

Policy Variations among States

The three main policy responsibilities of state governments are public education, social welfare, and highways. These functions account for more than two-thirds of all state expenditures across the country. Health and hospitals are other important responsibilities. Figure 4–3 shows state spending by function, averaged across the fifty states.

Some states choose not to follow the leads of other states. Others simply cannot afford to do so. Comparisons show that significant policy variation exists among the states. The average welfare recipient in New York receives more than four times more money than the average recipient in Mississippi. Tax laws differ. Residents of Massachusetts cross the border into New Hampshire to purchase liquor because of lower taxes and lower prices. State services—education, social services, mental health, and highways—differ. For example, for many years students in California state universities paid no tuition, whereas students in other states paid substantial amounts to attend public universities.

An indicator of state policy efforts is per capita spending (see Table 4–3). Way out in front is oil-rich and people-poor Alaska. State government there spent more than $9,000 per person in 1986. Variations are less dramatic for the rest of the states, but the top states spend from 50 percent to 100 percent more per person than the bottom states.

The cause of policy variations among states is a question that has intrigued political scientists and generated a great deal of empirical research. Initial

FIGURE 4–3

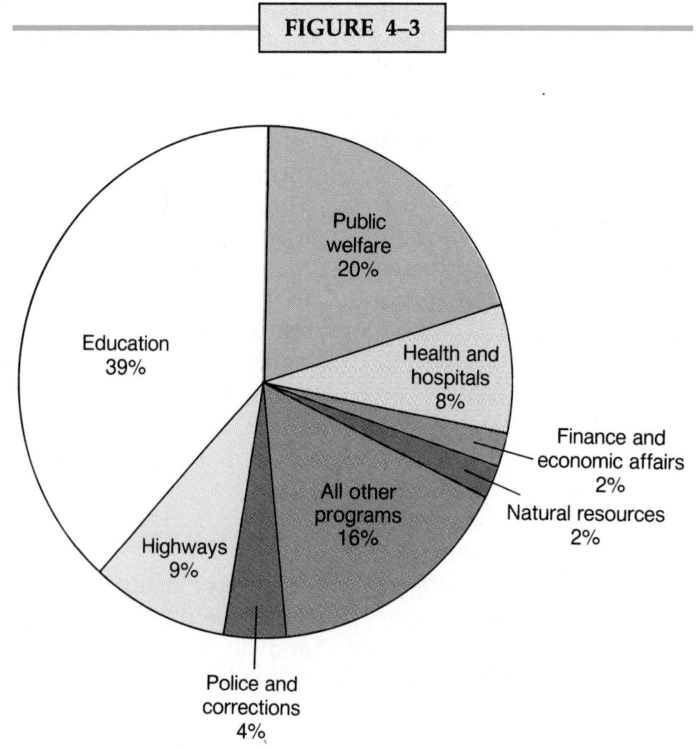

SOURCE: *The Book of the States, 1986–1987* (Lexington, KY: Council of State Governments, 1987), 242–243.

findings revealed that the main explanation was economic: wealthier states tended to do more because they could afford to do more.[19] However, many political scientists believed that political factors, such as competition between the political parties, resulted in more-progressive policies. Subsequent studies have found that although economic factors continue to explain much of the variation among states, political differences, such as party competition and legislative capability, are also important.[20]

States and the Abortion Controversy

The complexities of governing in a federal system are dramatically demonstrated by the intense political conflict over legalized abortion. Long considered a state issue, abortion was prohibited in the United States until the late 1960s and early 1970s, when New York, Hawaii, Alaska, and Washington legalized it. It became a national issue when the U.S. Supreme Court legalized abortion in the decision of *Roe v. Wade* (1973). For sixteen years, opponents dominated the headlines while advocates considered the issue settled. Outspoken support of legalized abortion was perceived to be a dangerous political issue, and many candidates at both the state and national level tried to avoid taking a position altogether. But the decision of *Webster v. Reproductive Health Services* in 1989 caused a sudden change in political calculus. Without reversing *Roe,* the Court upheld a Missouri law restricting abortions performed in a public facility or by any public employee using public funds unless it was necessary to save the life of the mother. The issue swung back to the states as the *Webster* decision opened the door to intense campaigns by both opponents and proponents of abortion.

Fearful of the Supreme Court overturning *Roe* altogether, pro-abortion forces mobilized in record numbers. In Florida, Republican Governor Bob Martinez called a special session of the legislature to enact new restrictions. He failed to get a single bill approved. Two gubernatorial races in November 1989 demonstrated the changes. In Virginia, Douglas Wilder became the nation's first elected black governor by making his support for legal abortion the main issue in the campaign. In New Jersey, pro-abortion Democrat James Florio, who had lost two previous attempts at the governorship, handily defeated his antiabortion Republican opponent. Their success suddenly made support for abortion look not merely acceptable but politically advantageous.

In 1990, a number of candidates either became more outspoken in their support or switched from the "pro-life" to the "pro-choice" camp. In Ohio, Attorney General Anthony Celebrezze, the leading contender for the Democratic nomination for governor, reversed his position. After a career of outspoken opposition to abortion, Celebrezze pledged to veto any legislation restricting abortion and promised to support public funding. His stance angered antiabortion forces, who called his switch a flip-flop for personal political gain. In Illinois, Attorney General Neil Hartigan, the leading Democratic contender for governor, settled an abortion case pending before the U.S. Supreme Court that could have been the vehicle for overturning *Roe.* In Idaho, the legislature passed a restrictive abortion law. Pro-abortion opponents threatened to boycott Idaho potatoes across the country if Governor Cecil Andrus, who opposed abortion, signed it into law.

TABLE 4–3

PER CAPITA EXPENDITURES OF THE FIFTY STATES AND DISTRICT OF COLUMBIA, 1985–1986

1.	Alaska	$9,452	27.	Louisiana	$2,423
2.	Dist. of Columbia	4,694	28.	Nebraska	2,395
3.	Wyoming	4,473	29.	Kansas	2,382
4.	New York	3,629	30.	Illinois	2,351
5.	Minnesota	3,049	31.	Maine	2,309
6.	California	2,872	32.	Ohio	2,289
7.	Delaware	2,818	33.	South Dakota	2,254
8.	New Jersey	2,801	34.	Oklahoma	2,228
9.	Montana	2,785	35.	Virginia	2,212
10.	Michigan	2,780	36.	Texas	2,204
11.	Wisconsin	2,736	37.	Georgia	2,199
12.	Massachusetts	2,731	38.	Pennsylvania	2,189
13.	North Dakota	2,707	39.	West Virginia	2,158
14.	Hawaii	2,702	40.	Alabama	2,125
15.	New Mexico	2,696	41.	Florida	2,123
16.	Rhode Island	2,681	42.	New Hampshire	2,024
17.	Oregon	2,672	43.	Indiana	1,998
18.	Nevada	2,666	44.	Idaho	1,979
19.	Connecticut	2,582	45.	South Carolina	1,972
20.	Maryland	2,580	46.	Mississippi	1,957
21.	Vermont	2,577	47.	Kentucky	1,921
22.	Washington	2,569	48.	Tennessee	1,918
23.	Colorado	2,568	49.	Missouri	1,916
24.	Arizona	2,542	50.	North Carolina	1,911
25.	Utah	2,483	51.	Arkansas	1,843
26.	Iowa	2,443			

SOURCE: Bureau of the Census, *Government Finances in 1985–1986,* Series GF–86/No. 5 (Washington, D.C.: Government Printing Office, 1987).

To the dismay of antiabortion forces, Andrus vetoed the bill.

While the new political calculus affected both parties, it created a bigger problem for Republicans, who featured opposition to abortion in their national platforms since 1980. With most Democrats in favor of legalized abortion, Republicans appeared split down the middle. Perceiving abortion as an issue that could help them at both the state and national level, Democrats characterized abortion as a "defining" issue, much as support for civil rights or opposition to the war in Vietnam had been in the 1960s. Republican National Chairman Lee Atwater claimed that there was room for both positions within the party, but many Republican strategists were concerned. If the Court eventually reverses the *Roe* decision, each state will once again have to set its own policy on this divisive issue.

POPULATIONS AND ECONOMIC TRENDS

Americans have been on the move in recent decades, leaving the cold of the **Snowbelt** for the sunshine and economic opportunity of the **Sunbelt.** Since the 1950s, the populations of the Northeast and North Central parts of the United States have stagnated, while the South and Southwest have boomed. In 1976, for the first time, more Americans lived in the South and West than in the North. The U.S. population is aging, and more and more retired people are choosing to spend their golden years at the poolside rather than shoveling snow. In addition, it is often more economical for companies to build new facilities in wide-open spaces than it is to modernize an old plant. People have followed jobs. Table 4–4 shows the shifts in population by census region between 1980 and 1989.

Today, states are in competition for jobs, businesses, and government grants. States try to outbid each other. When General Motors (GM) announced it would build a huge new facility to manufacture its new Saturn automobile, state leaders tried to outdo one another to land the plant. Governors traveled to GM headquarters to make slick presentations, offering free land, tax abatements, new transportation systems, and other incentives. Tennessee finally "won."

In Congress, competition for such pork-barrel projects as dams, bridges, monuments, federal buildings, and parks is fierce. It is not uncommon to see members of Congress carrying pocket calculators on the floor of the House and Senate to figure

TABLE 4–4

REGIONAL SHIFTS IN POPULATION, 1980–1989

	1989 (thousands)	1980 (thousands)	Percent change
Totals			
United States	248,239	226,546	9.6%
Northeast	50,772	49,135	3.3%
New England	13,047	12,348	5.7%
Middle Atlantic	37,726	36,787	2.6%
Midwest	60,148	58,865	2.2%
E. North Central	42,298	41,682	1.5%
W. North Central	17,851	17,183	3.9%
South	85,523	75,372	13.5%
South Atlantic	43,115	36,959	16.7%
E. South Central	15,406	14,666	5.0%
W. South Central	27,002	23,747	13.7%
West	51,796	43,172	20.0%
Mountain	13,513	11,373	18.8%
Pacific	38,283	31,800	20.4%

SOURCE: U.S. Census Bureau, reported in *New York Times*, 4 January 1990.

FIGURE 4-4

MAP OF CENSUS REGIONS

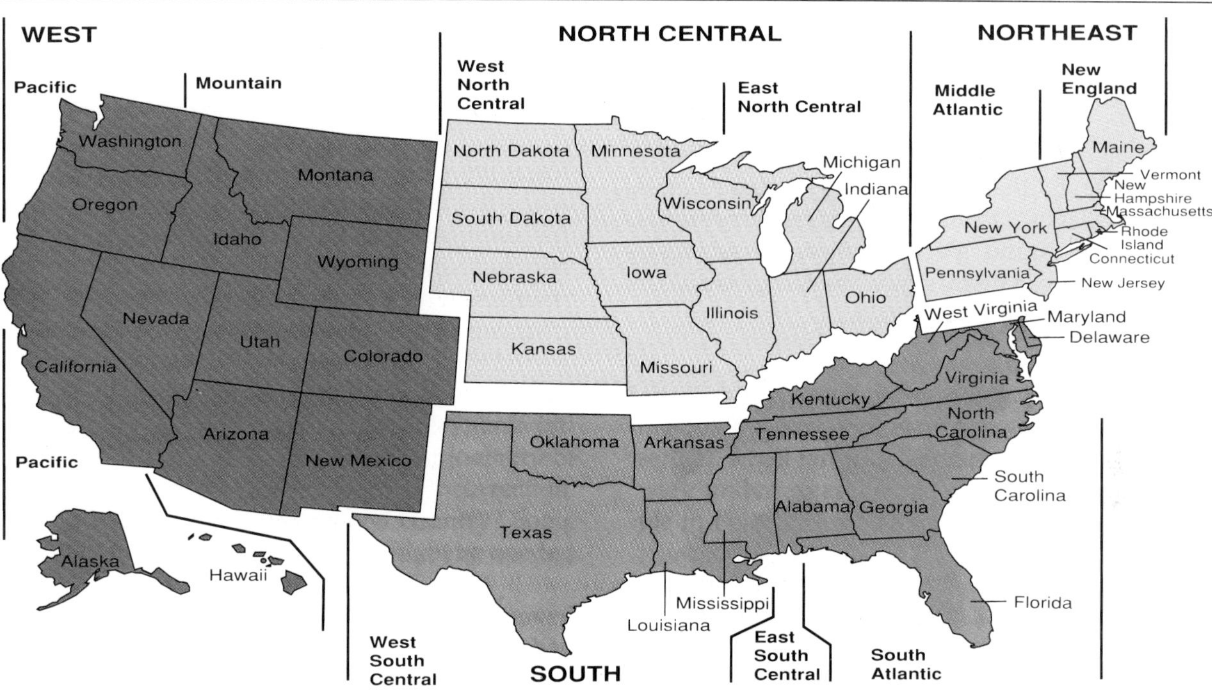

SOURCE: U.S. Census Bureau

benefits to their state and region. Today's states and cities have full-time lobbyists in Washington to work for higher funding. Incumbent legislators face embarrassing questions from election challengers if their state has not done well in getting federal dollars.

The controversies surrounding the 1990 census reflect the growing importance of population and income data to states and cities as the shrinking fiscal pie is subdivided. They also reveal the growing reluctance of Americans to cooperate. In 1990, only 63 percent of households returned their census forms, 12 percent less than had responded in 1980. As a result, the Census Bureau had to send census takers to some 37 million households around the country. State and local leaders roundly criticized Census Bureau officials and the billions of dollars they were spending. On the first mailing, census forms were not delivered to entire apartment complexes, streets, towns, and even zip codes. Many officials, particularly in large urban areas, argued that it was impossible to get an accurate head count and that statistical estimation should have been used instead. The census stakes are high, and the disputes will have to be resolved in court. Cities will sue because those who are not counted tend to be urban poor, the homeless, undocumented aliens—groups most in need of assistance. States on the verge of losing representation in Congress are also prepared to challenge the 1990 census in court. These conflicts over the census are one more example of the difficulties of governing in a multilayered federal system.

Regional shifts will continue to alter the balance of political and economic power, but such changes have occurred throughout American history. Regional conflict is less today than it was in the country's first century. The North-South split has continued to narrow. Yet there are some disturbing trends. Is federalism and regional competition threatening the ability to govern in the broad national interest?

Cities and Local Governments

Below the states in the hierarchy of government come local governments, even though cities like New York and Los Angeles have a higher population than most states. The legal relationship between state government and local government is comparable to that of a unitary system. Cities, towns, villages, hamlets, counties, townships, school districts, and special districts are subject to the laws of the state in which they are located. In 1868, the Supreme Court declared:

> Municipal corporations owe their origin to, and derive their powers and rights wholly from the [state] legislature. It breathes into them the breath of life, without which they cannot exist. As it creates, so may it destroy. If it may destroy, it may abridge and control.[21]

In a legal sense, states control local government. In a political sense, they do not. The state of Illinois, for example, could not abolish the city of Chicago or Cook County. Cities have the same strong political heritage and traditions as state and national governments, some of them even more colorful. Municipal governments provide the services that touch people directly: trash collection, street repair, police and fire protection. How did cities develop? How are they governed now, and how were they governed in the past? What is the condition of America's cities today?

THE URBANIZATION OF AMERICA

Rural life was the norm in early America. In 1790, when the first census was taken, only 5 percent of the population lived in cities of more than 2,500 people. New York was the largest city, with a population of 33,000.[22] Many of the Founders distrusted cities and city life. Irving Kristol suggested that individualism in the American tradition resulted in an antiurban bias. Jefferson, Washington, Lincoln, and, in the twentieth century, Coolidge and Hoover expressed a dislike for cities.[23] In *Democracy in America,* the astute nineteenth-century French observer of American politics, Alexis de Tocqueville, revealed his own strong antiurban bias:

> I regard the size of some American cities and especially the nature of their inhabitants as a real danger threatening the future of democratic republics of the New World, and I should not hesitate to predict that it is through them that they will perish, unless

Early Chicago.

their government succeeds in creating an armed force which, while remaining subject to the wishes of the national majority, is independent of the peoples of the towns and capable of suppressing their excesses.[24]

Despite this bias, urbanization in the 1800s was swift. Table 4–5 charts the rapid growth of America's largest cities between 1820 and 1870. New York and St. Louis, for example, increased their population by around 1,000 percent in these fifty years! The industrial revolution with its railroads and steam power and factories brought millions of people into the cities. Urbanization was further fueled by the massive influx of immigrants who provided cheap labor for the new mills and factories. Urban housing patterns never really corresponded to the mythical "melting pot." At first, wealthy and established residents dominated the city center, and poor immigrants congregated around the fringes in ethnic ghettos with poorer housing. Improvements in public transportation made it possible for the affluent to build new homes on the periphery of the city.[25] Movement into the neighborhoods they vacated began a housing cycle that changed the ethnic and racial composition of neighborhoods in a few decades. Irish, Italians, Germans, Poles, Jews, and African Americans were all involved.

The process of **suburbanization** began after World War I when the automobile made it possible for people to live still farther from the central city. After World War II, millions more in the middle class moved to suburbia, helped in their migration by the "GI bill," which made it easy to get home loans.[26] Blacks migrated in large numbers from the Deep South to the cities of the Northeast and the Midwest. By the late 1950s, the interstate highway system enabled commuters to live beyond the suburbs, in so-called exurbia. The central cities began to lose their dominance as economic and commercial centers. Suburban shopping centers and office complexes not only competed for consumers and businesses but often won.

City Politics

The immigrants who landed on Ellis Island in New York to be processed as new residents of the United States became the raw material of the urban political machines of the late 1800s and early 1900s. Democratic party workers might have been the first people they encountered as they disembarked. Political machines in the big cities were something akin to benevolent dictatorships. They provided social services in an era when official government policy furnished little or none. All that was asked in return was loyalty.

"I got two rules," one of Chicago's long-term ward committeemen is reported to have said. "The first one is, 'Don't make no waves.' The second one is, 'Don't back no losers.'"[27] Such a creed might have passed the lips of any one of a dozen machine politicians, from Boss Tweed of Tammany Hall in New York to Kansas City's Tom Prendergast to Boston's James Curley. **Machine politics** solved the problem of fragmentation of politics, creating a tightly disciplined governing unit. The machine was based on a strong political party capable of controlling the election process by giving something to everyone. Machines were able to govern, but with the concentration of political power came what the Founders had feared: tyranny and corruption. As often as not, citizens were robbed through systematic graft. Reform movements swept away most of the political machines in the twentieth century.

Today's big city mayors are not nearly as powerful as those who ran the machines. Modern mayors face governing problems, both in the diverse demands of constituents and the fragmentation of urban political power. Mayors must work with a council or board of aldermen and oversee a bureaucracy that administers most of the city's services.

TABLE 4–5

Rapid Urbanization in the Nineteenth Century: America's Five Largest Cities in 1820 and 1870

1820		1870	
New York	152,000	New York	1,478,000
Philadelphia	65,000	Philadelphia	674,000
Baltimore	63,000	St. Louis	311,000
Boston	43,000	Chicago	299,000
New Orleans	27,000	Baltimore	267,000

SOURCE: U.S. Census Bureau.

URBAN POLITICAL ECONOMY

Many of America's older cities suffer from difficult financial problems. As jobs and people leave, the taxable economic base of a city declines. The residents who stay in the central city tend to be elderly or very young, mostly poor, and in need of public assistance. At the same time, the costs of public services continue to rise. Detroit, for example, lost 19 percent of its jobs during the 1960s, while the dependent population and cost of services jumped rapidly. Many cities had to eliminate or cut back on services they once provided—hospitals, mental health facilities, museums, parks, libraries, public transportation systems—concentrating instead on sanitation, police and fire protection, streets, and public works, to keep the gap between revenues and spending commitments from growing larger. In the face of severe financial crisis, as in the case of New York City in 1975, congressional authorization of loan guarantees helped the city out of its immediate crisis. The city of Cleveland went bankrupt for a time, defaulting on its obligations.

As federal aid to state and local government declined in the 1980s, many cities have had to make hard financial choices by cutting services, firing employees, and tightening management and budget procedures. Figure 4–5 shows the cuts in funding in four federal programs to assist cities between 1980 and 1988.

GOVERNING AMERICA'S CITIES IN THE 1990S

Big-city politics in the United States has long had strong racial and ethnic underpinnings. Cities were rarely the "melting pots" popularly portrayed, as groups tended to live in ethnic enclaves both by reason of common culture and discrimination. The achievement of political power was often symbolized by winning the mayoralty, as generations ago, Irish and Italians eventually displaced Yankee mayors. In the last two decades, African-Americans have been elected mayors in

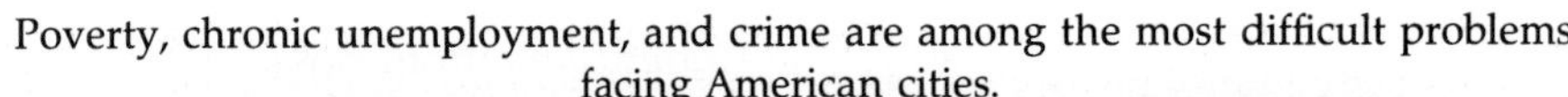

Poverty, chronic unemployment, and crime are among the most difficult problems facing American cities.

many of America's largest cities, reflecting the changing composition of big cities and the results of a long struggle for civil rights. Voters in Cleveland, Detroit, Atlanta, Chicago, Philadelphia, Seattle, Baltimore, and Washington all elected black mayors since the late 1960s.

New York, the nation's largest city, elected its first black mayor in 1989. David Dinkins, who is profiled in the accompanying People in Politics, won in a city increasingly divided along racial lines with a campaign that emphasized tolerance. Racial voting has appeared in most mayoral elections where white and black candidates opposed each other. In the 1983 contest for mayor of Chicago, Harold Washington became that city's first black mayor despite the fact that many white Democrats defected to the Republican candidate. Turnout in that racially charged contest was nearly 80 percent, far above average. The coalition that united behind Washington fell apart after his death, however, and the son of legendary Chicago boss Richard Daley was elected. In New York, Dinkin's margin of victory was substantially below election-eve polls, a phenomenon observed in other elections involving black candidates.

Ethnic cleavages continue to evolve in city politics, further propelled by growing income disparities. In cities of the South and Southwest, Hispanic candidates are emerging to challenge both black and white candidates. By 2010, Hispanics will become the nation's largest minority group. But despite the continued importance of racial and ethnic factors in big city politics, there is some evidence that it may be beginning to decline in importance in the 1990s. David Dinkins was elected mayor of New York, where blacks make up only one quarter of the electorate, by winning nearly one-third of white votes. In Seattle, with a black population of only 10 percent, African American Norman Rice defeated a white candidate who campaigned against busing. In New Haven, a city with long traditions of ethnic politics, a black candidate received 70 percent of the vote, a substantial portion of it from whites. Much depends on the city and the candidates' approach to the electorate.

The real challenge for today's mayors is governing: building coalitions in the fragmented world of local politics to find constructive solutions to a growing array of problems. Mayors want to foster economic development and construction without displacing the poor, destroying neighborhoods, or tearing down historic sites. They must provide better transportation, health care, sanitation, recreation, and housing at a time when federal assistance continues to decline. Urban dwellers demand action on drug pushers, crack houses, and drug-related crime by mayors who lack the independent power to increase law enforcement, build new jails, or relieve overcrowded court dockets. Many school systems in major cities are failing despite huge sums already spent. Urban political economies, like their national counterpart, are increasingly part of a complex global network. Federalism today requires policy-making that must encompass cooperation between local, state, and national leaders if these difficult governing challenges are to be met.

FIGURE 4–5

Federal Aid to Cities

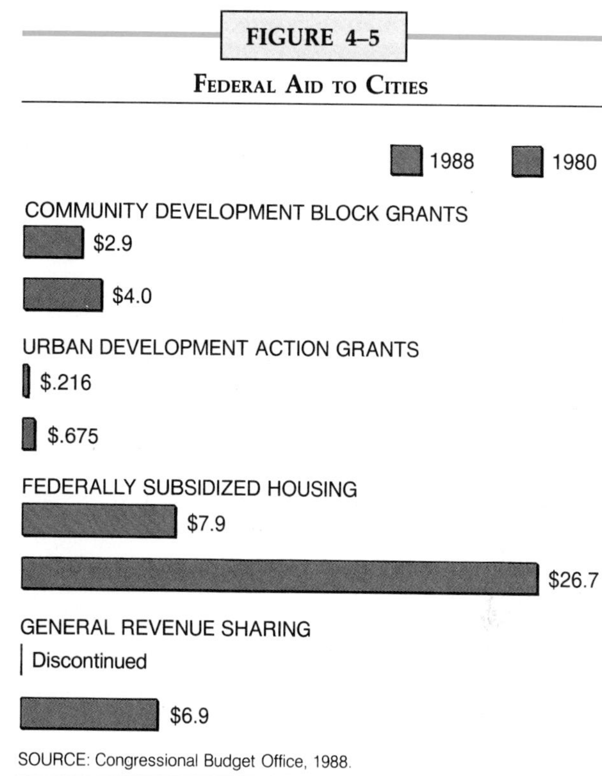

SOURCE: Congressional Budget Office, 1988.

PEOPLE IN POLITICS

DAVID DINKINS
MAYOR OF NEW YORK

Mayor of New York City—many think it's a harder job than president of the United States. In 1990, David Dinkins was inaugurated as the first black mayor of the nation's largest—and perhaps most ungovernable—city. Dinkins defeated three-term incumbent mayor Ed Koch in the Democratic primary in 1989 and won a narrow victory over Republican Rudolf Giuliani in November. How did he succeed in getting elected in New York's rough-and-tumble political world, and what challenges did he face?

Dinkins, 62 years old at the time of his election, grew up in a world where bigotry was open and widespread; black children never thought of themselves growing up to become mayor. His father was a barber in Trenton, New Jersey. His parents divorced when he was young, and his mother moved to Harlem and worked as a domestic. David and his sister spent time with both parents, who remember him as the glue that helped keep the family together. His low-key, conciliatory style developed from these early personal challenges. He went to college at Howard University in Washington, D.C., and moved back to New York to begin a political career in the early 1950s.

Dinkins started at the bottom, moving up steadily through a succession of positions in government. He married Joyce Burroughs, daughter of a Harlem Democratic ward leader. His first electoral victory was for a seat in the state legislature, but the seat was cut in redistricting, and he only served one term. He remained a part of the political organization that had sacrificed his seat and eventually won a job as ward leader. Despite failing to pay federal income taxes for four years in the 1970s, he became city clerk and continued his upward climb.

By 1989, New Yorkers had grown tired of Ed Koch, the affable, hard-nosed former congressman who had helped rescue the city from the brink of financial collapse. New economic woes plagued the city, which was increasingly divided between rich and poor and suffering under a growing climate of racial hostility. When a gang of white teenagers in Bensonhurst shot a young black man to death, Koch was accused of intensifying polarization. Dinkins, instead, urged racial harmony. When Democrats went to the polls a month later, they gave Dinkins a substantial win over Koch.

Despite the five-to-one advantage the Democrats had in registered voters, Dinkins was not a sure bet to win. Giuliani, his well-financed Republican opponent, was both attractive and well known for his vigorous prosecution of organized crime figures. Dinkins ran a moderate, nonconfrontational campaign as the candidate most likely to promote harmony among New York's various ethnic and racial groups. With blacks making up only one-quarter of the vote in New York, he won the election with 30 percent of the white vote to go along with his 90-percent support from blacks.

His political skill and coalition-building style would be sorely tested in the 1990s. With a budget of over $25 billion and 300,000 city employees, New York City is larger than most countries. With a severe AIDS epidemic, 700,000 drug addicts, a growing murder rate, and both white-collar and blue-collar jobs declining, the problems are staggering. Being mayor of New York has always been tough, but insider David Dinkins faces an exceptionally difficult challenge in an era when cities are receiving less and less help from Washington.

Summary and Conclusions

1. Because states were the basic political units of colonial America, the Founders created a federal system for the United States. The supremacy of the national government evolved through court decisions, the Civil War, and changes in public policy. Although federalism sometimes makes governing more complex and difficult, it does so in a way that has advantages as well as disadvantages.

2. Since World War II, the relationship among states, cities, and the federal government has been increasingly dictated by fiscal issues. Federal aid to state and local governments declined sharply in the 1980s. Presidents Reagan and Bush sought to enhance the role of the states by consolidating categorical grants into block grants and by turning responsibility for a number of programs back to the states.

3. States play an important role in policy-making, particularly in education, welfare, and social services. Variations in state policies reflect economic and political differences, as well as the political culture of states. Although the states are competing with each other, the level of conflict between regions is not unusually high by historical standards.

4. Local government is the level of government closest to the everyday problems of the people. Many of the nation's largest cities have faced serious financial and political problems in recent years. The diversity of interests in a modern city, combined with the fragmentation of power and the decline in federal aid, makes effective policy-making very difficult.

As a result of *McCulloch v. Maryland* and the Civil War, which established national supremacy, federalism has not caused major governing crises in the twentieth century. Although the old states' rights arguments cropped up as recently as the 1960s, the dominance of the national government is well established. Yet state and local governments continue to play an important role in the political system. Someone once claimed that if America did not have states, something like them would have to be invented. The creation of local democracies in Poland suggests this is probably correct. State and local governments add vitality to the governing process. They have a different vantage point from which to view public problems. Many important policy innovations have been pioneered at the level of state and local government. The public believes that state and local government does a better job of dealing with problems than the federal government, and the margins of difference have increased in the past decade.

Key Terms

block grants
categorical grants
cooperative federalism
dual federalism
fiscal federalism
Garcia v. San Antonio Transit Authority
item veto
machine politics
McCulloch v. Maryland
nullification acts
political culture
Proposition 13
Reagan's New Federalism
revenue sharing
Reynolds v. Sims
Snowbelt
states' rights
subnational government
suburbanization
Sunbelt
Tenth Amendment
unitary, federal, and confederal systems

Self-Review

1. Describe a federal, confederal, and unitary system of government.
2. How was national supremacy established?
3. What is fiscal federalism?
4. What kinds of grants-in-aid does the federal government provide for states and cities?
5. What were President Reagan's New Federalism proposals?
6. What are the trends in federal aid to state and local governments since the late 1970s?
7. What are the key institutions of state government?
8. How do the states differ?
9. List the policy priorities of the states.
10. How does the abortion issue demonstrate policy-making at different levels of government?

11. How were cities governed in the late nineteenth century?
12. What are some of the difficult challenges facing big-city mayors in the 1990s?

SUGGESTED READINGS

Garreau, Joel. *The Nine Nations of North America.* 1981.
An entertaining suggestion for a political and economic reorganization of North America.

Judd, Dennis, *The Politics of American Cities* 3rd ed. 1988.
An examination of private power and public policy in the nation's cities.

Rakove, Milton. *Don't Make No Waves, Don't Back No Losers.* 1975.
Written by a political scientist with an inside view of the Daley machine, this is an insightful if somewhat apologetic account of Chicago politics.

Rosenthal, Alan. *Legislative Life.* 1982.
An excellent analysis of legislative politics across the fifty states.

NOTES

1. See William Riker, *Federalism: Origin, Operation, Significance* (Boston: Little, Brown, 1964).
2. U.S. Census Bureau, *Census Reports,* 1982.
3. See Herbert J. Storing, *What the Anti-Federalists Were FOR* (Chicago: University of Chicago Press, 1981), 15–23.
4. Martin Diamond, "The End of Federalism," in Daniel Elazar, ed., *The Federal Polity* (New Brunswick, N.J.: Transaction, 1974), 129–52.
5. Michael Reagan, *The New Federalism* (Oxford: Oxford University Press, 1972), 4.
6. *McCulloch v. Maryland* (1819).
7. See *Heart of Atlanta Motel v. United States* (1964).
8. Morton Grodzins, *The American System* (Chicago: Rand McNally, 1966).
9. See Steven Bailey and Fredrick Mosher, *ESEA: The Office of Education Administers a Law* (Syracuse N.Y.: Syracuse University Press, 1968).
10. Advisory Commission on Intergovernmental Relations, *Intergovernmental Perspective* (Winter 1983): 16.
11. See Richard Nathan, *The Administrative Presidency* (New York: John Wiley, 1982).
12. See Richard Nathan, Allen D. Manuel, and Susan E. Caulkins, *Monitoring Revenue Sharing* (Washington, D.C.: Brookings, 1975).
13. John Shannon, "The Return to Fend-for-Yourself Federalism: The Reagan Mark," *Intergovernmental Perspective* (Summer–Fall 1987): 34–37.
14. "Designated Taxers," *National Journal,* 31 March 1990, pp. 774–77. Figures on growth of state and local tax burdens in this paragraph are taken from this article.
15. The decision in *Baker v. Carr* (1962) gave federal courts the jurisdiction to apply the "one person, one vote" standard to congressional districts (in *Wesberry v. Sanders* [1964])) and to state legislative districts (in *Reynolds v. Sims* [1964]).
16. See Thomas Dye, "Malapportionment and Public Policy in the States," in Richard Hofferbert and Ira Sharkansky, *State and Urban Politics* (Boston: Little, Brown, 1971), 260–73.
17. See Daniel Elazar, *American Federalism: A View from the States,* 2nd ed. (New York: Harper and Row, 1972), 93–126.
18. Jack L. Walker, "The Diffusion of Innovations among the American States," *American Political Science Review* 63 (September 1969): 880–899.
19. Richard E. Dawson and James A. Robinson, "Inter-Party Competition, Economic Variables, and Welfare Policies in the American States," *Journal of Politics* 25 (May 1963): 266.
20. See Lance T. LeLoup, "Reassessing the Mediating Impact of Legislative Capability," *American Political Science Review* 72 (June 1978): 616–21.
21. *City of Clinton v. Cedar Rapids and Missouri Railroad Co.* (1868).
22. Congressional Quarterly, Editorial Research Reports, *The Future of the Cities* (Washington, D.C., 1974), 10.
23. Irving Kristol, *Horizon Magazine* (Autumn 1972): 36–41.
24. Alexis de Tocqueville, *Democracy in America,* quoted in Edward K. Hamilton, "On Nonconstitutional Management of a Constitutional Problem," in Charles Levine, ed., *Managing Fiscal Stress* (Chatham, N.J.: Chatham House, 1980), 53.
25. Edward C. Banfield, *The Unheavenly City* (Boston: Little, Brown, 1970), 26–29.
26. *Ibid.,* 31.
27. Milton Rakove, *Don't Make No Waves, Don't Back No Losers* (Bloomington: Indiana University Press, 1975), 11.

CHAPTER 5

Civil Liberties

Political Close-Up

"Red, White, and Blue, We Spit on You"

On the steps of Dallas City Hall during the Republican National Convention in 1984, Gregory Lee Johnson doused an American flag with kerosene, lofted it over his head, and set it ablaze. Johnson's supporters, members of the Revolutionary Communist party, cheered as the Stars and Stripes burned. Onlookers were disgusted as the protesters chanted anti-American slogans: "Red, white and blue, we spit on you; you stand for plunder, you will go under." The event abruptly ended as Dallas police arrived and arrested Johnson for violating the Texas penal code, which made it a crime to desecrate a venerated object. Gregory Johnson's flag-burning set the stage for a bitter and controversial court battle over the rights of free expression under the U.S. Constitution.

Johnson was convicted but successfully appealed to the Texas Court of Criminal Appeals on the grounds that flag-burning was constitutionally protected free expression. The state of Texas appealed to the U.S. Supreme Court, arguing that its statute was constitutional. The Court decided the case in 1989, the first case to be decided solely on the basis of flag desecration. Noting the generally conservative drift of the Supreme Court since President Reagan had named four of the nine justices, Texas officials were fairly confident of victory. But they were in for a surprise as the Court announced its highly unpopular decision: despite its distasteful nature, Johnson's flag-burning was protected by the First Amendment of the Constitution.

Justice Brennan wrote the opinion for the 5-to-4 majority, in which the Reagan appointees split two to two. The decision rested on two key issues. First, the majority argued that since Johnson was protesting at the Republican convention, his purpose was to express his political beliefs. Second, the state of Texas did not have sufficient grounds to deny free expression since there was no serious breach of peace. While the majority opinion agreed that a state has the right to encourage proper treatment of the flag, it cannot be at the expense of violating the First Amendment. The four dissenters on the Court disagreed vehemently with the majority, arguing that the flag deserved special protection.

The decision in *Texas v. Johnson (1989)* was extremely unpopular with the American people. Politicians, from the White House to Congress to statehouses, lambasted the Supreme Court. President Bush and many members of Congress proposed a constitutional amendment to ban flag-burning. But after the initial burst of outrage, concern over tampering with free speech convinced legislators to settle for passing a federal statute to protect the flag. While the sponsors believed that the new law would meet the test of constitutionality, it was immediately challenged by a group that burned the flag on the steps of the Capitol. The Supreme Court would have to rule again.

In 1990, the Court reaffirmed its decision of the previous term. In a 5 to 4 decision, the new federal law was struck down as an unconstitutional violation of the First Amendment's guarantee of free speech. Once again, the Court's ruling was assailed. This time it was clear that only a constitutional amendment could effectively prevent desecration of the American flag. The House took up the amendment first. Opponents argued that the First Amendment was too essential to liberty and that no exceptions had been added to the Constitution in two hundred years. While a substantial majority voted for the amendment, proponents failed to gain the needed two-thirds majority. The Senate vote also fell short of the sixty-seven votes that were needed. Justice William Brennan argued in the initial decision that, "the flag's deservedly cherished place in our community will be strengthened, not weakened by the Court's action." Do you agree?

CHAPTER OUTLINE

INTRODUCTION AND OVERVIEW

After his invasion of Kuwait caused international economic sanctions, Iraq's Saddam Hussein threatened to execute any housewives in the country caught hoarding food. In Argentina in the late 1970s and early 1980s, thousands of political dissidents, or just suspected "troublemakers," were killed by right-wing extremists with the active complicity of the government. Opponents of the shah of Iran in the 1970s were imprisoned, tortured, and killed by SAVAK, the shah's feared secret police. Citizens of many countries have only limited rights to speak, to protest, to oppose the government. Americans often take civil liberties for granted, forgetting they are not enjoyed by many peoples of the world.

Even in the United States, civil liberties have not always been secure. The Alien and Sedition Act in 1798 made it a crime to publish or speak anything "false, scandalous, and malicious" against the president, the Congress, or the government. In two hundred years, the government has periodically abridged freedom of speech, press, and other civil liberties. The illegal wiretapping, "enemies list," break-ins, and covert activities during the Nixon administration reminded Americans that threats to civil liberties are not just a thing of the past.

Political systems with the greatest governing ability are often the worst violators of civil liberties. As the discretion of the government to act is increased, so is the threat to the rights and freedoms of citizens. The worst infringements of civil liberties in the United States occurred in periods when the government has been most powerful, particularly when national security is invoked. During the Civil War, Confederate sympathizers living in the North were arrested and held without charge and without trial. During World War II, Japanese Americans, many of them U.S. citizens, were rounded up and interned in prison camps. The Founders' fear of the power of the central government was based partly on their concern for preserving liberty. Does the history of civil liberties in the United States confirm their fears? The following questions are considered in this chapter:

1. What are civil liberties and civil rights, and how do they differ?
2. What rights and liberties are guaranteed in the Constitution and the Bill of Rights? Why do rights frequently come into conflict with each other?
3. What is free expression, and how have the courts determined acceptable limits on freedom of speech and the press?
4. How has the "wall of separation" between church and state created controversies over such issues as prayer in public schools? What are the limits to the free exercise of religion?
5. What rights do people accused of crimes retain? Have the courts gone too far in protecting criminals?

The Politics of Rights and Liberties

WHAT ARE CIVIL LIBERTIES AND CIVIL RIGHTS?

Perhaps no words in our political vocabulary are more loosely used than *rights* and *liberty*. In fact, the distinction between rights and liberties is murky, and scholars often disagree about the precise definitions. The approach adopted here defines *liberty* as protection from government power and a *right* as a privilege guaranteed by government.

The Founders came of age in an era of state religions, when a person could go to jail for criticizing the king. Troops were quartered in people's homes without permission. Citizens could be locked up without explanation. The notion of

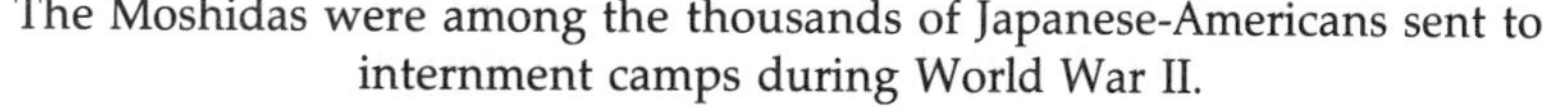

The Moshidas were among the thousands of Japanese-Americans sent to internment camps during World War II.

liberty that developed in America was a negative one: something that the government could *not* do. **Civil liberties,** then, are *freedom from* state actions, legal guartantees that the government will not interfere with certain activities. This conception of a civil liberty is based on the view that government poses the greatest threat to individual liberty and must be restricted—hence the importance of limited government in American political traditions and culture.

Yet the history of the United States, particularly slavery and racial segregation, indicates that negative liberties—freedom from government—are insufficient to guarantee that all citizens will have equal right to participate in democratic government and society. As a result, increasing emphasis has been placed on civil *rights:* the opportunity to participate equally in the state. **Civil rights** are the *freedom to* share fully in the political system. While civil liberties are generally protected by limiting what government can do, civil rights are protected by positive action by government. For example, under the 1965 Voting Rights Act, the government sent federal examiners to southern states to be sure that blacks had the opportunity to exercise their right to vote.

Civil liberties, even if they are written down in a constitution or bill of rights, are only as meaningful as government actions taken in their defense. Some civil liberties and civil rights are little more than rhetoric. For example, the constitution of the Soviet Union gave citizens the rights of free speech, free movement, and other traditonal liberties guaranteed in the U. S. Constitution. However, government policy has not backed them up in practice until recently. Political Insight 5–1 examines some of the provisions of the Soviet Constitution. Notice the emphasis on positive rights—such as the right of all adults to a job, to leisure, and to a secure retirement—compared with the U. S. Constitution.

Just what does it mean when the Bill of Rights states, "Congress shall pass no law abridging freedom of speech?" In fact, we have a long history of laws and court decisions *restricting* the exercise of free speech. Although the Constitution guarantees "free exercise of religion," it does not always apply to polygamists, snake handlers, or faith healers. Civil liberties and civil rights may seem straightforward, but they are not. Rights are in conflict with other rights; the process of balancing competing rights, favored by competing interests, is extremely political. Issues of civil liberties often pit the interests of the state against the interests of individuals.

THE CONSTITUTION AND THE BILL OF RIGHTS

Many of the fundamental rights and liberties of Americans are in writing. Unlike Great Britain, where civil liberties are protected through common law and tradition, early American political leaders wanted the guarantees in writing. "All Men are created equal," proclaims the Declaration of Independence, and are "endowed by their Creator with certain unalienable Rights," among which are "Life, Liberty, and the pursuit of Happiness." But such generalities were not enough to satisfy many people, so the Founders guaranteed civil liberties in the Constitution itself in a number of areas.

Habeas corpus. People arrested have the right to be formally charged with a crime within a reasonable time or released. If they believe they are being held unconstitutionally without charge, they may apply for a writ of **habeas corpus** and be released.

Bills of attainder. The Constitution guarantees that no legislative body can declare in a **bill of attainder** that some group or individual had committed a crime; only a court and jury can determine guilt.

Ex post facto laws. The Constitution bans **ex post facto laws,** which declare an act to be a crime retroactively.

Trial by jury. Article III gives every citizen accused of a federal crime the right to a trial by peers, not just by a judge. Trial in the Senate to impeach an official is the only exception.

Location of a trial. All citizens accused of a crime have the right to be tried in the state in which the crime was committed.

Treason. Treason, defined as making war against the United States or giving aid and comfort to itsenemies, is the only crime defined in the Constitution. The Founders attempted to

POLITICAL INSIGHT 5–1

EXCERPTS FROM THE SOVIET CONSTITUTION

Article 34. Citizens of the Union of Soviet Socialist Republics (USSR) are equal before the law, without distinction as to origin, social or property status, race or nationality, sex, education, language, attitude to religion, type and nature of occupation, domicile, or other status.
Article 35. Women and men have equal rights in the USSR.
Article 36. Citizens of the USSR of different races and nationalities have equal rights.
Article 40. Citizens of the USSR have the right to work (that is, to guaranteed employment and pay in accord with the quantity and quality of their work, and not below the state-established minimum), including the right to choose their trade or profession, type of job, and work in accordance with their inclinations, abilities, training, and education, with due account of the needs of society
Article 41. Citizens of the USSR have the right to rest and leisure.
Article 42. Citizens of the USSR have the right to health protection.
Article 43. Citizens of the USSR have the right to maintenance in old age, in sickness, and in the event of complete or partial disability or loss of the breadwinner.
Article 44. Citizens of the USSR have the right to housing.
Article 45. Citizens of the USSR have the right to education.
Article 50. In accordance with the interests of the people and in order to strengthen and develop the socialist system, citizens of the USSR are guaranteed freedom of speech, of the press, and of assembly, meetings, street processions, and demonstrations.
Article 52. Citizens of the USSR are guaranteed freedom of conscience, that is, the right to profess or not to profess any religion, and to conduct religious worship or atheistic propaganda. Incitement of hostility or hatred on religious grounds is prohibited.
Article 54. Citizens of the USSR are guaranteed inviolability of the person. No one may be arrested except by a court decision or on the warrant of a procurator.

protect people who express unpopular views from prosecution by requiring the testimony of two witnesses or confession in open court (Article III, section 3).

Religious tests. The Constitution prohibits requiring a religious oath or a specific belief as qualification for a federal job.

Although the Founders were concerned about protecting the liberties of Americans, in drafting the Constitution they were even more concerned with hammering out the details of the government. As a result, the biggest obstacle to the ratification of the Constitution was the failure to include more explicit guarantees of basic civil liberties. As part of the political bargain reached to get the Constitution ratified, the proponents agreed to amend the original document by adding a bill of rights. The first ten amendments to the Constitution were ratified in 1791 and became known as the **Bill of Rights.** (See Appendix C for a list of amendments to the Constitution.)

The First Amendment to the Constitution, guaranteeing freedom of speech, press, religion, petition, and assembly, is probably the most important protection of civil liberties. The Second and Third Amendments are less relevant today, but the Fourth, Fifth, Sixth, and Eighth Amendments have all been invoked in defining the rights of people accused of crimes. First Amendment rights and the rights of the criminally accused are examined in more detail in the remainder of this chapter.

Rights and liberties are not absolutes. Although the very language of rights has the connotation of an absolute, in practice the judicial process defines limits to rights or chooses between competing rights. Abortion foes proclaim the "rights of the unborn," while those supporting legal abortion espouse the "rights of women to control their own bodies." Which "right" is right? Who decides when rights are in conflict?

Legislatures and courts are the main forums for the politics of rights and liberties. The process of defining civil liberties is a never-ending search for tolerable, constitutional limits and boundaries. Federalism affects civil liberties and civil rights because the original Bill of Rights limited what the national government could do but not what the states could do. Some believed that the Bill of Rights would apply to the states as well, but the Supreme Court took a narrow view of its application.[1] In the case of *Barron v. Baltimore* (1833), Chief Justice Marshall wrote for a unanimous court that the Constitution was ordained by the people "for themselves, for their own government, and not for the government of the individual states."[2]

The narrow interpretation was a serious problem. What good was it to have a civil liberty as a citizen of the United States if it would be violated by the individual states? The Court began to move away from the view of *Barron* in 1925 when it ruled in the case of *Gitlow v. New York:*

> For present purposes we may and do assume that freedom of speech and of the press which are protected by the First Amendment from abridgement by Congress are among the fundamental personal rights and liberties protected by the due process clause of the Fourteenth Amendment from impairment by the States.[3]

This began a process called **selective incorporation.** The Fourteenth Amendment's language stating that no state shall deprive citizens of due process or equal protection of the laws became a vehicle for incorporating Bill of Rights protections to the states. Incorporation was selective. The courts ruled that it must be done on a case-by-case basis, rather than by applying the entire Bill of Rights to the states on the basis of the Fourteenth Amendment. On several occasions, the Supreme Court ruled that certain provisions, like the protection against double jeopardy, did not apply to the states.[4]

Some justices argued for **total incorporation** based on the legislative history of the Fourteenth Amendment.[5] Though the total incorporation view has never been officially sanctioned by the Court in an opinion, the effect in the past two decades has been nearly the same. Only a few provisions of the Bill of Rights have not been incorporated through the Fourteenth Amendment to apply to the states.

The Constitution, particularly the Bill of Rights and the Fourteenth Amendment, is the basis for decisions on civil liberties. But the Constitution leaves difficult questions unanswered when rights come into conflict. Courts operate in a political setting at a given point in history within a context of evolving social values. American civil liberties, although constantly being refined, remain well protected, thanks to the highly supportive political and economic environment created by the Founders and early leaders. Many other countries lack such a history and commitment. The needs of the society as a whole, as opposed to individual needs (as defined by the government), are more important in Second and Third World countries. Table 5–1 ranks nations by degree of protection of civil liberties. Although these rankings represent subjective judgments, clearly most of the world's people do not enjoy the political liberty Americans have come to expect.

First Amendment Liberties: Freedom of Speech

Freedom of speech gives a person the right to express opposition to the government. Having experienced political life without the ability to comment and criticize freely, the Founders wanted protection against the possible tyranny of those in power. They incorporated this protection in what to them was the most important amendment—the First Amendment.

TABLE 5–1

CIVIL LIBERTIES AROUND THE WORLD

Most Liberty 1	2	3	4	5	6	Least Liberty 7
Argentina	Belize	Antigua and Barbuda	Chile	Bahrain	Afghanistan	Albania
Australia	Cyprus	Bahamas	Egypt	Bangladesh	Algeria	Angola
Austria	Dominica	Bolivia	Fiji	Bhutan	Brunei	Benin
Barbados	Ecuador	Botswana	Hungary	Guyana	Burkina Faso	Bulgaria
Belgium	Finland	Brazil	Mexico	Haiti	Burma	Cambodia
Canada	France	Taiwan	Nepal	Indonesia	Burundi	Chad
Costa Rica	Germany	Colombia	Nicaragua	Jordan	Cameroon	Equatorial Guinea
Denmark	Greece	Cyprus	Sri Lanka	Kuwait	Cape Verde Islands	Ethiopia
Grenada	Israel	Dominican Republic	Tunisia	Lebanon	Central African Republic	Guinea-Bissau
Iceland	Jamaica	El Salvador	Turkey	Liberia	China	Iraq
Ireland	Kiribati	Gambia	Vanuatu	Madagascar	Comoros	North Korea
Italy	Malta	Guatemala		Malaysia	Congo	Malawi
Japan	Mauritius	Honduras		Morocco	Ivory Coast	Mongolia
Luxembourg	Nauru	India		Nigeria	Cuba	Mozambique
Netherlands	Portugal	South Korea		Panama	Czechoslovakia	Romania
New Zealand	St. Kitts-Nevis	Pakistan		Poland	Djibouti	Saudi Arabia
Norway	St. Lucia	Papua New Guinea		Qatar	Gabon	Somalia
Sweden	St. Vincent	Peru		Sierra Leone	Ghana	Syria
Switzerland	Solomon Islands	Phillippines		Singapore	Guinea	Vietnam
Trinidad and Tobago	Spain	Thailand		Sudan	Iran	South Yemen
Tuvalu	Suriname	Tonga		Uganda	Kenya	
United Kingdom	Uruguay	Western Samoa		Soviet Union	Laos	
United States	Venezuela			United Arab Emirates	Lesotho	
				North Yemen	Libya	
				Yugoslavia	Maldives	
				Zambia	Mali	
				Zimbabwe	Mauritania	
					Niger	
					Oman	
					Paraguay	
					Rwanda	
					Seychelles	
					South Africa	
					Swaziland	
					Tanzania	
					Togo	
					Transkei	

SOURCE: Raymond D. Gastil, *Freedom in the World, 1989* (New York: Freedom House, 1989). Reprinted with permission from Freedom House, Inc.

"Speech" is not just saying what one wants to about a member of Congress or a senator. "Speech" can include symbolic acts, such as wearing a black armband or burning an American flag. It can include hostile statements about others as well. Is it a fair exercise of free speech to make an anti-Semitic speech in a Jewish neighborhood? Does free speech allow a person to slander or libel another—that is, to knowingly utter or publish false and damaging statements about someone?

PUBLIC SUPPORT FOR FREE SPEECH

Freedom of speech has never been interpreted as an absolute right. The history of free speech in the United States is a history of the courts trying to balance constitutional protections against other legitimate interests. The guarantee of free speech is intended to protect the rights of the minority to express unpopular or critical views, to prevent the tyranny of the majority.

Abstract support for the principle of free speech is very strong. More than 95 percent of the American people say they back this First Amendment guarantee. Support in practice is much weaker. A large proportion of respondents oppose allowing a communist to speak in a public school, for example. Although free speech may be accepted in theory, both citizens and governments are often anxious to put limits on its actual exercise, particularly in times of war or in national security crises. Despite the generally high marks the United States receives for its protection of civil liberties, the right of free speech has often come under sharp attack. Free speech is in greatest danger when real or imagined threats to national security are involved.

NATIONAL SECURITY LIMITS FREE SPEECH

THE SEDITION ACT (1798). Less than ten years after the ratification of the First Amendment, a perceived threat to national security led to the first government curbs on free speech. The American party system that began to emerge saw a growing rift between the Federalists and the Anti-Federalists (see Chapter 8). The Federalists, led by Adams and Hamilton, were angered by the vocal opposition to their efforts to promote war with France. The Anti-Federalists, led by Jefferson, still saw France as America's strongest ally and fiercely opposed the government's moves. Anti-Federalist newspaper editorials vilified President Adams and the other Federalists, and the Federalists responded with a series of bills to limit free speech and press. The most famous of these, the **Sedition Act,** made it a

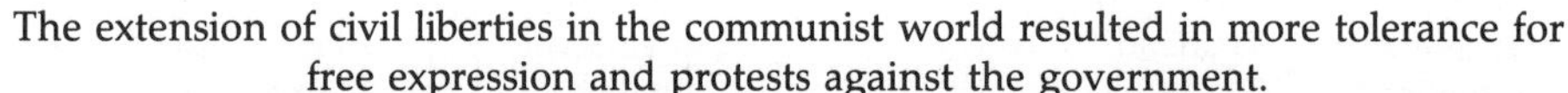
The extension of civil liberties in the communist world resulted in more tolerance for free expression and protests against the government.

Speaker's corner in Hyde Park, London, where crowds gather to listen to all manner of "free speech."

crime to speak or print anything "scandalous" or "malicious" or to attempt to defame the government. Several dozen newspaper editors were prosecuted, and a number were sent to jail. This particular restriction on free speech was never reviewed by the courts. After the Federalists lost the election of 1800, Jefferson reaffirmed his commitment to freedom of speech and of the press and pardoned all those convicted under the statute. The law itself expired in 1801, but a pattern had been set.

THE ESPIONAGE ACT (1917). The courts did not become actively involved in defining the acceptable limits on free speech until the twentieth century. The courts have not only tried to decide specific outcomes of cases but also attempted to establish broader principles to guide future decisions. Establishing "tests" and principles has proven frustrating. Many have been tried and discarded.

As the United States entered World War I, concern about sabotage by Germans within the country surfaced. Fears of internal subversion were flamed by the Bolshevik Revolution and ensuing instability in Russia. In 1917, Congress passed the Espionage Act, which made it a crime to utter "false statements" that might interfere with or cause disloyalty or mutiny among U.S. armed forces. Prosecution and the resulting court decisions produced the first judicial guideline for free speech.

Charles T. Schenck, who opposed U.S. entry into World War I, urged young recruits to resist the draft. Schenck was indicted and convicted under the Espionage Act, and the case was eventually heard by the Supreme Court. Justice Oliver Wendell Holmes wrote the opinion for a unanimous Court in the decision of ***Schenck v. U.S.*** (1919). In his opinion, Holmes observed that the First Amendment did not protect someone who "falsely shouted fire in a theater causing panic."[6] He went on to say, "The question in every case is whether the words used in such circumstances are of such a nature as to create a clear and present danger that they will bring about the substantive evils that Congress has a right to prevent."[7] Under the "**clear and present danger**" test, Schenck's conviction and the Espionage Act were upheld.

The clear and present danger test was soon found wanting; it did not effectively define what was protected speech and what was not. Soon after the *Schenck* decision, the Court ruled on a New York State statute limiting certain kinds of utterances. In that 1925 decision, the Court said that speech could be limited if it created a "bad tendency" and if the law that prohibitied it conformed to a standard of "legislative reasonableness."[8] Although the "clear and present danger" test and the "bad tendency" test were applied in several other cases, they were clearly unsatisfactory. Nonetheless, a number of people were convicted, and the laws limiting speech were generally upheld.

THE SMITH ACT (1940). Again fearing internal subversion during wartime, Congress passed the **Smith Act** in 1940. Designed to protect the United States from both Nazi and communist subversion, the law made it illegal to advocate the overthrow of the government by force. Only a few prosecutions were brought under the Smith Act during the war, but in the postwar period, as tension between the Soviet Union and the United States grew, more cases came before the courts. In ***Dennis v. U.S.*** (1951) the Justice Department prosecuted the leader of the American Communist party under the Smith Act in 1948. The Supreme Court upheld the lower court conviction of Dennis, the majority applying the "evil scale" concept developed by Judge Learned Hand in the lower court. Judge Hand believed that free speech could be curtailed when "the gravity of the evil, discounted by its improbability, justifies such invasion."[9] The majority reasoned that overthrow of the government was so serious, despite little probability of success, that prosecution of the communist leaders was justified. The government used the *Dennis* decision to prosecute a number of other lesser officers in the Communist party.

As times changed, judicial guidelines changed. Several years after the *Dennis* decision, the Supreme Court began to retreat. In 1957, the Court overruled *Dennis,* stating that, to be convicted, communists had to actively advocate overthrow of the government, not just express a belief in general doctrines of revolutionary violence.[10]

VIETNAM ERA CASES (1965–1974). Because of the divisiveness it caused, the Vietnam War was unlike previous wars, except that in this war too there were those who wanted to silence its opponents. Congress passed a law in 1965 making it a crime to burn a draft card. Those prosecuted under the law argued that they were engaging in "symbolic speech"—the communication of ideas by conduct—and were therefore protected by the First Amendment. The Supreme Court disagreed in 1968, upholding the statute and noting that "an apparently limitless variety of conduct can be labeled 'speech' whenever the person engaging in the conduct intends to express an idea."[11] In 1969, a case was brought against Sidney Street, who burned the American flag in disgust after the assassination of black civil rights activist James Meredith. In a close decision, the Court set aside Street's conviction, ruling that the state law prohibiting flag-burning was too broad and that the right to differ includes "the right to publicly express one's opinions about our flag."[12] The case of *Texas v. Johnson* (1989) in the chapter's political closeup, differed from the *Street* decision because physical violence against the flag was the only reason for conviction.

THE SEARCH FOR BALANCE. By the end of the Vietnam War, the attitudes of society and the courts had grown more tolerant of dissent. Gone were the "clear and present danger" test, the "bad tendency" test, the "evil scale." The Supreme Court adopted a stricter interpretation of the meaning of the First Amendment. But free speech was still not absolute. Although the late Justice Hugo Black believed in an absolute interpretation of the First Amendment, Political Insight 5–2, which looks at Black's views, indicates that even the strictest interpretation must be open to some restrictions. Cases like the flag-burning cases demonstrate the continued tension between national security and patriotism and the right of citizens to express their views. The courts still labor to find a balance between them. Freedom of speech is related to other rights guaranteed under the First Amendment: expression, solicitation, demonstrations, and distribution of pamphlets and other printed materials. As a foundation of American democracy, freedom of speech has been given a preferred position by the courts when it comes into conflict with other rights and interests—a position that freedom of the press also enjoys.

POLITICAL INSIGHT 5–2

AN ABSOLUTE READING OF THE FIRST AMENDMENT: INTERVIEW WITH JUSTICE HUGO BLACK

INTERVIEWER: You said, "It is my belief that there are 'absolutes' in our Bill of Rights, and that they were put there on purpose by men who knew what words meant and meant their prohibitions to be 'absolutes.'"

JUSTICE BLACK: My first reason is that I believe the words do mean what they say. I have no reason to challenge the intelligence, integrity, or honesty of the men who wrote the First Amendment. The beginning of the First Amendment is that "Congress shall make no law." I understand that it is rather old-fashioned and shows a slight naïveté to say that "no law" means no law. It is one of the most amazing things about the ingeniousness of the times that strong arguments are made, which almost convince me, that it is very foolish of me to think "no law" means no law.

INTERVIEWER: Some of your colleagues would say that it is better to interpret the Bill of Rights so as to permit Congress to take what it considers reasonable steps to preserve the security of the nation even at some sacrifice of freedom of speech and association. Otherwise, what will happen to the nation and the Bill of Rights as well? What is your view of this?

JUSTICE BLACK: My answer to the statement that this government should preserve itself is: yes. The method I would adopt is different, however, from that of some other people. I think it can be preserved only by leaving people with the utmost freedom to think and to hope and to talk and to dream if they want to dream. I do not think this government must look to force, stifling the minds and aspirations of the people. Yes, I believe in self-preservation, but I would preserve it as the founders said, by leaving people free. I think here, as in another time, it cannot live half slave and half free.

INTERVIEWER: Do you make an exception in freedom of speech and press for the law of defamation? That is, are you willing to allow people to sue for damages when they are subjected to libel or slander?

JUSTICE BLACK: My view of the First Amendment, as originally ratified, is that it said Congress should pass none of these kinds of laws. As written at that time, the amendment applied only to Congress. I have no doubt myself that the provision, as written and adopted, intended that there should be no libel or defamation law in the United States under the United States government, just absolutely none so far as I am concerned.

INTERVIEWER: Would it be constitutional to prosecute someone who falsely shouted "fire" in a theater?

JUSTICE BLACK: I went to a theater last night with you. I have an idea if you and I had gotten up and marched around that theater, whether we said anything or not, we would have been arrested. Nobody has ever said that the First Amendment gives people a right to go anywhere in the world they want to go or say anything in the world they want to say.

INTERVIEWER: Is there any kind of obscene material, whether defined as hard-core pornography or otherwise, the distribution and sale of which can be constitutionally restricted in any manner whatever, in your opinion?

JUSTICE BLACK: So far as I am concerned, I do not believe there is any halfway ground for protecting freedom of speech and press. If you say it is half free, you can rest assured that it will not remain as much as half free. I realize that there are dangers in freedom of speech, but I do not believe there are any halfway marks.

SOURCE: From Black and Cahn, "Justice Black and First Amendment 'Absolutes': A Public Interview," *New York University Law Review* 37 (June 1962): 549.

First Amendment Liberties: Freedom of the Press

Libel, pornography and obscenity, and standards for radio, television, and cable television all involve questions of a free press. Is it legitimate exercise of free press for a magazine to reveal how to manufacture a hydrogen bomb? Is it constitutional for a former Pentagon employee to publish classified documents showing that the government lied? Does freedom of the press mean that reporters and television cameras have a right to cover a rape trial? Should a reporter be required to reveal his or her sources, even when a crime has been committed? Do high school students have the right to publish what they want in their school newspaper? These are just a few of the questions that the courts have had to grapple with in trying to clarify the meaning of freedom of the press.

PRIOR RESTRAINT AND LIBEL

Courts have consistently ruled against censorship of the press—sometimes called **prior restraint,** or the requirement of government approval before material is printed or broadcast. Perhaps the clearest case was the Supreme Court's prohibition of prior restraint in the case of ***Near v. Minnesota*** (1931). A vituperative newspaper editor in Minnesota had published a series of articles calling public officials "gangsters" and "grafters" and some other colorful names. The state of Minnesota responded by closing down the paper. In his decision for the majority, Chief Justice Charles Evans Hughes strongly emphasized the need for "a vigilant and courageous press" and ordered the paper reopened.

Although the *Near* opinion was clear enough to discourage most instances of prior restraint, newer circumstances have tested the boundaries of the doctrine. One such set of circumstances concerned the *Progressive* magazine and its attempt to publish an article on how to build a hydrogen bomb. The author of a 1979 article put together information on how to build the bomb using only nonclassified sources available to anyone. Nonetheless, the government moved quickly to squelch the article. It obtained a temporary restraining order and prevented immediate publication, pending a hearing. The Supreme Court, however, never made a final ruling on the legality of the government's action because other periodicals released the information, making the case moot.

While newspaper publishers remain largely free from government censorship, the same is not true for high school students writing for their school newspapers. In the case of ***Hazelwood v. Kuhlmeier*** (1988), the Supreme Court ruled that a principal could censor two controversial articles from the student newspaper.[13] Students at Hazelwood East High School in St. Louis published the *Spectrum* as part of a journalism class. The two articles in question concerned students' reactions to the problems of parental divorce and coping with teenage pregnancy while in school. The principal felt that the articles were inappropriate and that the identities of people quoted in the article were not sufficiently concealed. He censored the articles from the paper, to the dismay of the student editors, who filed suit claiming infringement of their First Amendment liberties.

Writing for the majority, Justice Byron White concluded that the deletion of the two articles was constitutional because the newspaper was part of the school's regular curriculum. Although public school students "do not shed constitutional rights to freedom of expression at the schoolhouse gate," he wrote, officials of the school have the right to "refuse to lend its name and resources to the dissemination of student expression" that they consider inappropriate. The decision left unclear exactly what the limits of free expression might be in public colleges and universities.

Although the government has rarely been given the right to censor an article before publication, rights past publication are not so protected. The right of free press has always been balanced by the right of citizens to be protected from **libel**—lies knowingly printed for malicious purposes. Libel laws have sometimes been used in an attempt to prevent reporters and editors from criticizing public officials. In the case of *New York Times v. Sullivan* (1964), the Supreme Court limited protection from libel when printed statements involve political issues. During the civil rights movement in the South in the early 1960s, a number of politicians tried to stifle criticism of their anti-civil rights conduct by filing libel suits.[14] A county commissioner in Montgomery, Alabama, L. B. Sullivan, claimed that an editorial advertisement appearing in the *New York Times* had damaged his reputation as a public official. The trial court awarded him half a million dollars, but the Supreme Court reversed the lower court decision, stating that "debate on public issues should be uninhibited, robust, and wide open, and that it may include vehement, caustic, and sometimes unpleasant sharp attacks."[15] In their concurring opinion, Justices Black and Douglas stated that the writers had "an unconditional right to publish- . . . criticisms of the Montgomery agencies and officials."

The *Sullivan* case was particularly important in reaffirming a strict interpretation of the First Amendment. It made a crucial distinction between political and nonpolitical expression, establishing much greater tolerance in the area of public affairs than in private cases. Yet even political reporting can come into conflict with and be limited by the government when it confronts national security.

Two prominent libel cases captured the headlines in the 1980s. Israel's defense minister, Ariel Sharon, sued *Time* magazine for $50 million over a story about his role in the massacre of Palestinians by Lebanese Christians in a refugee camp. While the jury agreed that the story was incorrect, they held that Sharon had not been libeled by *Time* because there was an absence of malice on its part. In the second case, General William Westmoreland, former commander of American forces in Vietnam in the 1960s, sued CBS for $100 million, alleging that the television program "60 Minutes" and newsman Mike Wallace had libeled him by claiming that Westmoreland had altered enemy troop strength estimates in his reports to President Johnson and other top officials. After a long and highly publicized trial, Wallace and CBS were largely exonerated when Westmoreland dropped the charges. The verdict and settlement ultimately supported the broad freedom for political expression; it also reminded print and electronic media of the boundaries of that freedom.

National Security Limits Freedom of the Press

Perhaps the most important case since the 1931 *Near* decision affirming freedom of the press was the **Pentagon Papers case.** Disillusioned over U.S. policy in Vietnam, former Pentagon employee Daniel Ellsberg made copies of confidential documents he had seen while working for the Defense Department and showed these documents to reporters at the *New York Times.* Stunned at the government cover-ups and duplicity revealed in the documents, the editors decided to publish excerpts verbatim in the *Times.* The Nixon administration tried, legally and illegally, to stop Ellsberg and the *Times* (including a bungled attempt to burglarize Ellsberg's psychiatrist's office). The government moved to halt publication on the grounds that it would damage national security. Because of the immediacy of the case, the Supreme Court ruled in a matter of days.

The majority ruled that the government had failed to prove that prior restraint against the *Times* was justified, but there was tremendous disagreement within the Court (nine separate opinions were filed). In a 6-to-3 split, the majority concluded that even in cases of national security, the government must assume a full burden of proof to justify prior restraint. It had not met that burden of proof in the Pentagon Papers case.

The Right to a Fair Trial versus Freedom of the Press

Civil liberties guaranteed in the Bill of Rights occasionally come into conflict with each other. The right to a fair trial, guaranteed under the Sixth and Seventh Amendments, can be put in jeopardy by free exercise of the press. In general, courts have decided that limitations on the activities of the press are legitimate when those activities threaten the ability of an individual to receive a fair trial.

Trials of cases that include sex, violence, or lurid testimony often make good copy and sell papers. Such coverage may also make it difficult or impossible to find an unbiased jury. In the early 1960s, in one of the most infamous murder trials in the country, a prominent Ohio physician, Sam Sheppard, was accused of murdering his wife.

Angry local papers were full of gory details and unfavorable publicity. The state court convicted Sheppard, but he appealed the guilty verdict to the U.S. Supreme Court, where the conviction was reversed. Noting the "Roman holiday"atmosphere that permeated the trial, Justice Tom Clark, writing for the majority, was highly critical of the "circulation-conscious editors catering to the insatiable interest of the American public in the bizarre."[16] In throwing out the verdict, the Court served notice that self-restraint on the part of the press would be required if convictions were to be upheld.

When the Founders drafted the First Amendment, television and other technological wonders were not even imagined. Should stations have a right to film and televise trials? In a 1963 decision, the Supreme Court ruled that courts had the right to exclude television cameras from the courtroom.[17] It was likely, the majority in a 5-to-4 decision said, that television would inject an "irrelevant" factor into the proceedings that was likely to negatively affect the defendant's ability to get a fair trial. Although bans against television cameras in courtrooms remain in most parts of the country (which is why you see an artist's sketches, not footage, on the television news), some states have recently experimented with allowing televised trials.

After twenty years of limiting media coverage of trials, the courts seem to be easing restrictions. In a 1976 case, the Supreme Court ruled against a "gag order" by the state of Nebraska that prohibited *any* press coverage of a brutal mass murder trial, stating that a blanket ban on coverage was too vague and constituted unacceptable prior restraint.[18] In a 1980 Virginia case, the Supreme Court ruled against a judge who had closed a murder trial to the press. Such a trial, the Court said, must be open to the public.[19] These rulings raise a question: Will it be more difficult to get a fair trial with increased access of both the public and the press to criminal proceedings?

PORNOGRAPHY AND OBSCENITY

Does freedom of the press mean that anything can be published, or are some materials too filthy, lewd, licentious, and obscene for society to tolerate? Supreme Court Justice Potter Stewart once said of pornography, "I can't define it, but I know it when I see it." As it turns out, that is exactly what the Supreme Court justices have had to do over the years: view films, look at pictures in magazines, and read books in an attempt to define a standard.

Pornography raises basic constitutional issues. The public's presumed right to protection from violent, sadistic, exploitive material conflicts with the First Amendment rights of free speech and press: "Congress shall pass *no* law. . . ." The problem with censorship is how to determine where to draw the line and who draws it. Throughout most of American history, the First Amendment was ignored when it came to obscenity and pornography. State and local governments were given complete latitude in defining and banning what they considered offensive. Over the years, some works now considered tame were censored: D. H. Lawrence's *Lady Chatterley's Lover,* James Joyce's *Ulysses,* Vladimir Nabokov's *Lolita,* and others. By the 1950s, with social norms changing, the Court was called on to set some kind of standard.

The Supreme Court grappled with the problem in *Roth v. U.S.* (1957) and a companion case and finally determined that anything with "redeeming social value" must be protected under the First Amendment.[20] However, any material that, to the average person, by contemporary community standards, appealed to "prurient interests" may legitimately be banned. Although the *Roth* standard seemed reasonable, it provided no meaningful guidance. Just what is "redeeming social value"? Who should define "community standards"? What exactly is "prurient interest"?

The justices of the Supreme Court paid the price for this vagueness. Case after case had to be reviewed in an attempt to clarify the standard. Between 1957 and 1968, the Court issued more than fifty separate opinions in thirteen obscenity cases as the nine justices struggled to define what was protected by the First Amendment and what could be banned. In 1962, the Court narrowed the scope of "prurient interest" by adding that material must be "patently offensive."[21] In 1964, the Court tried to clarify "redeeming social value" and "contemporary community standards," noting that the society at large must be considered the relevant community. In 1966, the Court reversed a Massachusetts lower court decision that banned the novel *Fanny Hill,* ruling that this popular high-school "classic" of the 1960s had a "modicum of social value."[22]

Many blame the Supreme Court's extension of the right to free expression for the increase in porn strips in the nation's cities.

A more permissive attitude toward explicit sexual material characterized the late 1960s and early 1970s. Films, magazines, and sex shops sprang up throughout the nation. Many blamed the Supreme Court for this rash of "filth." The justices' concern with protecting free expression under the First Amendment had resulted in a number of indefinite tests and confusion over what was obscene. The Court took a new direction in the case of ***Miller v. California*** (1973), modifying the notions of redeeming social value and community standards. The majority argued that, instead of redeeming social value, a work only had to be shown to "lack serious value when taken as a whole." Community standards were redefined as local standards, not national standards. Chief Justice Warren Burger noted in his opinion in *Miller* that it is not necessary "that the people of Maine or Mississippi accept public depiction of conduct found tolerable in Las Vegas or New York City."[23]

Did this finally clarify what is obscene? No. In its very next case, the Court overturned a Georgia court decision banning the film *Carnal Knowledge.* The justices still seemed to be reviewing on a case-by-case basis. Since *Miller,* the Court has continued to limit what state and local governments may censor. In 1981, it ruled that a small town in New Jersey could not ban nude dancing by passing an ordinance prohibiting all live entertainment.[24] The ordinance, they stated, was unconstitutionally broad and banned a wide range of expression long recognized as permissible.

In 1987, the Court backed away from the community standards doctrine of *Miller.* A majority of justices, in the case of *Pope v. Illinois,* declared that community standards were not sufficient to determine the artistic, scientific, or literary value of a work. Justice White, writing for a 6-to-3 majority, noted that the value of a work "does not vary from community to community based on the degree of local acceptance it has won." The proper standard is "whether a reasonable person would find such value in the material, taken as a whole."[25] To determine whether a work is obscene, and therefore may be banned, a more objective national standard must be used.

In an 1989 case, the Supreme Court unanimously overturned a law passed by Congress banning "dial-a-porn" telephone services. The Court ruled that the law was too broad, covering messages that were indecent but not obscene.

The controversy over pornography and the First Amendment is yet another demonstration of competing "rights." Freedom of expression is limited by concerns over national security, the right to receive a fair trial, the right to be protected from libel, and the right of citizens to be protected from obscenity. The process of balancing these rights is one of the most difficult in politics. Responsibility has fallen to the courts, and they continue to struggle to define the boundaries of civil liberties under the First Amendment.

First Amendment Liberties: Freedom of Religion

Many Americans came to the New World to escape religious persecution. Guarantees of their right to worship freely were of paramount concern. The First Amendment proclaims: "Congress shall make no law respecting an establishment of religion, or prohibit the free exercise thereof." The first part is known as the **establishment clause,** the second part as the **free exercise clause.** The language certainly seems clear. The government cannot establish a state religion and cannot interfere with how people practice religion. What competing rights could come into conflict? Yet one of the most emotional political issues of recent times has surrounded prayer in public schools. Other conflicts have also surfaced. Is it constitutional to provide state aid to parochial schools? Does it constitute establishment of Christianity to have nativity scenes in front of city hall? Can a state require the teaching of creationism? Over the years, there have been controversies surrounding the free exercise clause as well. Do Mormons have the right to practice polygamy? Do religious views justify withholding medical treatment from children, even if they will die without it?

Does Prayer in Public Schools Constitute Establishment of a State Religion?

The U.S. Constitution has erected a "wall of separation" between church and state. But how high should the wall be? The courts have been called on to make that determination. Difficulties arise when the establishment clause conflicts with the free exercise clause. For many years public schools began each day with Bible reading or some sort of school prayer. The state of New York used a short prayer composed by the state Board of Regents that went as follows: "Almighty God, we acknowledge our dependence upon thee and beg thy blessings upon us, our parents, and teachers, and our country. Amen." The prayer was voluntary and nonsectarian. Nonetheless, in the case of *Engel v. Vitale* (1962), the 6-to-1 majority on the Supreme Court ruled that the prayer violated the establishment clause because it was an "officially prescribed prayer."[26] The following year, the Court extended the ruling in a Maryland case and a Pennsylvania case involving Bible reading and the Lord's Prayer.

The school prayer decisions were among the most unpopular in the history of the Supreme Court. The justices went to great lengths to explain that they were not antireligion but were simply making a difficult decision to ensure that the rights of minorities are protected constitutionally. What could the Court's opponents do? Change the Constitution. A movement to legalize school prayer began in 1962 and continues today. In 1984, the U.S. Senate spent nearly two weeks debating a constitutional amendment to allow voluntary prayer in public schools (the **school prayer amendment**) that was supported by President Reagan. The language of the amendment debated in 1984 was virtually identical to that of amendments considered in the early 1960s. In 1966, a constitutional amendment to allow school prayer fell only nine votes short of the sixty-seven needed to meet the two-thirds requirement for passage. In 1971, a similar proposal fell twenty-nine votes short in the House of Representatives.[27]

Proponents of the school prayer amendment argue that by interpreting the establishment clause too rigidly, the Court had in fact taken an antireligion position, denying citizens the right to pray: "Our purpose here is to render the state a neutral party in the exercise of religion rather than have the state compel or forbid that exercise in any public facility."[28] But opponents disagreed: "The issue really is not prayer in schools for our children. They have that right today. No court case, no law, no Supreme Court ruling prevents any individual child or adult in this nation from praying wherever or whenever they wish."[29] The text of the amendment that finally came to a vote read as follows:

> Nothing in this Constitution shall be construed to prohibit individual or group prayer in public schools or other public institutions. No person shall be required by the United States or any state to participate in prayer. Neither the United States nor any state shall compose the words of any prayer to be said in public schools.

The final vote of 56 to 44 in favor was 11 votes shy of the two-thirds needed. Outside the Capitol, hundreds of demonstrators held prayer vigils and lobbied for the amendment. Other religious groups—Protestant, Catholic, and Jewish—lobbied against it. The continuing debate over prayer in public schools is one example of how political the process of clarifying rights can become. In June 1985, the Supreme Court, by a 6-to-3 vote, reaffirmed its 1962 decision, overturning an Alabama law providing for a period of silent prayer. No vote on the school prayer amendment has been taken on the floor of Congress since 1984.

OTHER ESTABLISHMENT CLAUSE CONTROVERSIES

School prayer is not the only issue surrounding the establishment clause. Another is state aid to parochial schools—sometimes called "parochiaid." One of the first court tests of parochiaid arose in New Jersey in the case of *Everson v. Board of Education* (1947). The state of New Jersey had allowed school districts to subsidize bus transportation of students to parochial schools. When challenged by a citizen who felt this violated the establishment clause, the Supreme Court disagreed. In a close 5-to-4 decision, the majority opinion emphasized the "secular legislative purpose" of the statute.[30] The favorable decision encouraged large and varied numbers of proposals in the states for programs to aid nonpublic schools. In subsequent decisions, the courts have upheld assistance in providing textbooks but have overturned other kinds of aid to nonpublic schools, such as teachers' salaries, instructional aids and materials, tuition, and general upkeep of grounds. Anything beyond "buses and books" has been ruled as breaching the separation of church and state.[31]

Over the years, the Court has tried to settle a number of other establishment controversies. In 1970, it ruled that it was constitutional for the state to exempt church property from taxation.[32] The Court has also upheld the right of states to require Sunday closing or "blue laws." Opponents of blue laws argued that such laws established Sunday, a Christian holy day, as the official holy day of the state. But the Court ruled in 1961 that it was legitimate for the state to legislate a "day off," even if there were strong religious reasons for the choice of day.[33] In the 1980s, the Court showed signs of continuing flexibility in its interpretation of the establishment clause. A 1984 ruling allowed a Rhode Island city to retain its Christmas nativity scene in front of the city hall, noting the widely accepted secular elements of the Christian holiday. A ruling in the 1989–90 Supreme Court term held that public high schools can be required to allow student religious clubs to meet on the same basis as other extracurricular activities.

The Court's flexibility in interpreting the establishment clause of the First Amendment does not extend to the teaching of the Bible's version of creation in public schools. In the case of *Edwards v. Aguillard* (1987), a 7-to-2 majority struck down a Louisiana statute that forbade the teaching of evolution in public schools unless "creation science" was also taught. Writing for the majority, Justice Brennan said that the law violated the establishment clause because its "primary purpose . . . is to endorse a particular religious doctrine."[34] Rejecting arguments that the statute was designed to promote academic freedom, the Court concluded that it was a case of the state advancing the religious viewpoint that a supernatural being created humankind.

THE FREE EXERCISE GUARANTEE

The guarantee of free exercise of religion has also caused constitutional trouble. How far does the Constitution go in protecting a group calling itself a religion? One of the first cases of this type arose when Utah was still a territory in the late nineteenth century. Concerned about the Mormon practice of having multiple spouses, Congress banned polygamy from the territories. In 1878, a man convicted of violating the law challenged the statute in court, arguing that his religion dictated that he have a large number of wives. The Court spoke clearly: while the Constitution protected all religious *beliefs*, it did not protect all religious *practices*.[35] Public laws passed by Congress or the states had superiority over religious beliefs when the two came in direct conflict, despite the free exercise clause.

The issue seemed to be settled until the Jehovah's Witnesses issued a number of challenges beginning in 1940. Jehovah's Witnesses had refused to allow their children to participate in the flag salute and Pledge of Allegiance in public schools, believing it was a violation of their religious views not to worship graven images. Some of their children were subsequently expelled from school. Arguing that the salute and Pledge of Allegiance requirement interfered with the free exercise of their religion, the Witnesses took their case to court.

Although the lower courts ruled in favor of the children and their parents, the Supreme Court overturned the verdict in the decision of *Minersville School District v. Gobitis* (1940). In siding with the school district, the Court argued that the flag was an important symbol of national unity that transcended religion. The tenor of the times undoubtedly played a role in the decision, coming as it did at the outset of World War II. Patriotism won over religious tolerance. Just three years later, the Supreme Court reversed itself completely on the issue in a decision written by Justice Robert Jackson. "To sustain the compulsory flag salute," he said, "we are required to say that a Bill of Rights which guards the individual's right to speak his own mind left it open to public authorities to compel him to utter what is not in his mind."[36]

Jehovah's Witnesses were unpopular in many communities because of their door-to-door proselytizing. Another case arose when the city of Jeanette, Pennsylvania, required Jehovah's Witnesses to obtain "peddlers' licenses" before they could use this technique to convert others to their faith. The Supreme Court ruled in 1943 that this requirement interfered with the free exercise of religion and was unconstitutional.[37]

Like freedom of speech and press, the free exercise of religion has never been absolute. The courts, however, have allowed certain kinds of behavior in a religious context that would be illegal in any other circumstances. For example, they ruled in 1964 that it was legal for American Indians to use the drug peyote in certain religious ceremonies.[38] But the courts refused to go along when LSD guru Timothy Leary argued that smoking marijuana was necessary to his practice of Brahmakrishna (the religious beliefs of a Hindu sect).[39] With growing concern over drugs, the court ruled in the 1989–90 session that government may proscecute American

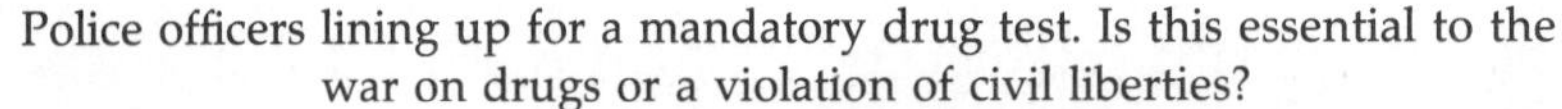
Police officers lining up for a mandatory drug test. Is this essential to the war on drugs or a violation of civil liberties?

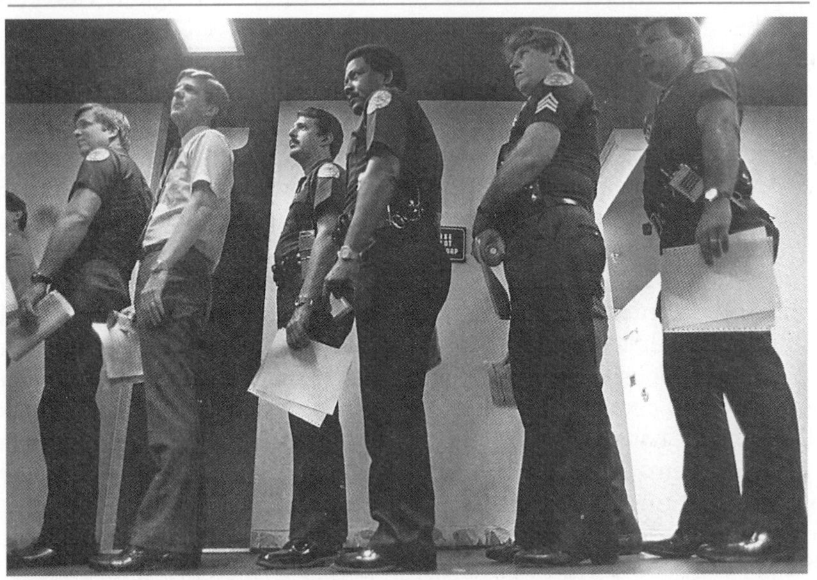

Indians who use illegal drugs even if only for sacramental purposes. Since the turn of the century, the free exercise provision has been limited by the government's power to protect public health. Courts have consistently rejected claims on religious grounds when someone's life is threatened, ordering blood transfusions for minors and, in a recent case, chemotherapy for a twelve-year-old cancer victim.

Over the years the courts have shown a high level of support for First Amendment rights, recognizing that these rights form the very basis of liberty and individual freedom in the United States. But civil liberties—particularly First Amendment liberties—are not simple. They involve comparisons of fundamental values and complex principles that continue to be a vexing dimension of American politics.

The Rights of the Accused

The civil liberties of Americans also involve the justice system—police, courts, criminals, and those accused of crimes. In many countries around the world, there are few if any limits on what police can do. American colonists were periodically subjected to unannounced searches by the British and had their personal property seized. In many nondemocratic nations, government power is not checked by concern and safeguards for individual liberties. Many of these nations are rated low in the comparisons of civil liberties presented in Table 5–1. Protection of civil liberties requires some limitations on the actions of internal security forces. The controversy in the United States today, however, has to do with presumed overlimitations. As the courts have acted to protect the rights of people accused of a crime, some claim the system has tilted to the side of the criminals. Critics complain that in defining limits to police activities the rights of law-abiding citizens and victims are sacrificed.

The rights of the accused are protected by the Fourth, Fifth, Sixth, and Eighth Amendments. The Fourth Amendment protects citizens from "unreasonable searches and seizures." The Fifth Amendment protects citizens against self-incrimination and double jeopardy (being tried twice for the same crime). The Sixth Amendment guarantees "a speedy and public trial, by an impartial jury." The Eighth Amendment prohibits "cruel and unusual punishments." How much time between an accusation and a trial is deemed "speedy"? Is the death penalty "cruel and unusual" (see Chapter 16)? Is it an unreasonable search and seizure to pump the stomach of a suspect who has swallowed evidence?

The Exclusionary Rule

Despite the guarantees of the Fourth Amendment, many states allowed illegal searches and seizures, and courts admitted evidence seized in raids conducted without search warrants. The Supreme Court first ruled in 1914 that illegally obtained evidence would not be allowed in federal courts.[40] But this did little to alter state practices, where virtually all criminal prosecution occurs. After wavering for several years, the Supreme Court in 1961 finally applied the search and seizure provisions of the Bill of Rights to the states. In the case of *Mapp v. Ohio,* the Court reversed a pornography conviction where evidence was obtained by forcible police entry without a search warrant. The Court applied the **exclusionary rule,** which stated that any evidence obtained in an illegal manner must be excluded from the trial even if it would have proven the defendant guilty. The rule was designed to give meaning to the protection guaranteed by the Fourth Amendment.

Prosecutors and police were less than enthusiastic about the *Mapp* decision and the exclusionary rule, but there was more to come. The Supreme Court, under Chief Justice Earl Warren, handed down a number of important decisions that extended the rights of the criminally accused—angering the law enforcement community. Did the *Mapp* decision go too far and handcuff the police? Many thought so. A new era emerged under Chief Justice Warren Burger and the Nixon appointees in the 1970s. One of the first areas of "modification" was the exclusionary rule as the Court retreated from the *Mapp* decision. In 1976, the Burger Court refused to invoke the exclusionary rule in a federal tax case, arguing that the likelihood of deterring the conduct of the police did not outweigh the social costs of excluding the evidence.[41] Although hold-over justices from the Warren Court sharply dissented, the new direction of the Burger Court was clear. Justice Thurgood Marshall argued that the majority was engaged in the "slow strangulation of the exclusionary rule."[42]

In 1984, the Supreme Court took further steps to narrow the protections that had been extended to the accused over the previous two decades. In a major revision of the *Mapp* decision, the Court ruled 6 to 3 in *U.S. v. Leon* (1984) that illegally seized evidence could be used if a search was "objectively reasonable," even if the search warrant proved to be defective.[43] The ruling means that even if magistrates and judges make mistakes in issuing search warrants, defendants will not be able to use this "technicality" to have the case dismissed. In a related ruling, the Court ruled that evidence could be admitted if it were "inevitable"—that is, it would have been obtained anyway by lawful means.[44] In 1988, under Chief Justice William Rehnquist, the Court took another step to narrow the scope of the exclusionary rule. In companion cases, the Court ruled that when drugs were seized with a legal search warrant but after an earlier illegal search, the evidence was independent of the improper search and could be included.[45] The exclusionary rule was narrowly upheld in a 1990 decision. A 5 to 4 majority refused to allow a proscecutor to introduce illegally-obtained evidence to undermine the credibility of a defense witness where the defendant himself did not testify.[46]

THE RIGHT TO COUNSEL

The specter of secret police and totalitarian "justice" may seem farfetched to most Americans, but U.S. history is replete with examples of miscarriages of justice and abuse of individual rights. The Scottsboro cases of the early 1930s demonstrated some of these abuses. A number of young black men were accused of raping a white woman. Denied meaningful representation by counsel, they were convicted in an arrest, arraignment, and trial process rife with abuses. The Supreme Court ruled that defendants had the right to a lawyer because it was a capital case and that denial of counsel violated the Fourteenth Amendment's guarantee of due process.[47] Although the decision guaranteed the right to counsel in capital cases, it did not extend the right to other criminal cases.

In 1963, in ***Gideon v. Wainwright,*** the Supreme Court ruled that all defendants have a right to be represented by counsel in state criminal proceedings. The accompanying People in Politics profile of Clarence Earl Gideon shows how one person without resources was able finally to get his day in court. The *Gideon* decision guaranteed that defendants would be represented by competent legal counsel at the trial. The year following *Gideon,* the Court overturned a murder conviction because the defendant was denied access to his lawyer during interrogation.[48] Law enforcement officials continued to complain about the Warren Court's extension of civil liberties. Supporters of the Court noted that although it is always lamentable when a guilty party goes free, protection against police break-ins, brutality, and coercion of confessions ensured the basic liberties for everyone.

Police interrogations were not always conducted in a "constitutional" manner. Beginning in the 1940s, the Court ruled that confessions obtained by physical coercion, and later psychological coercion, were inadmissible.[49] In 1966, the Court made one of its most important and controversial rulings on the rights of the criminally accused in *Miranda v. Arizona.* As you may know from television, in *Miranda* the Court set out strict guidelines for police interrogation practices. When the suspect is arrested the arresting officers must inform the accused of his or her rights: "You have the right to remain silent; anything you say can be used against you in a court of law; you have the right to counsel; if you cannot afford a lawyer, the court will appoint one for you."

A wave of internal domestic violence in the 1960s and a rapid increase in violent crime led to renewed calls for "law and order." During the 1970s, the Burger Court moved to limit the applicability of the ***Miranda* rule.** In June 1984, the Court modified the *Miranda* rule in two seemingly contradictory ways. The first case concerned an arrest in New York City where a gun was seized as evidence before giving the suspect his *Miranda* warnings. The Court ruled this was an acceptable exception to the *Miranda* rule. For the 6-to-3 majority, Justice William Rehnquist wrote: "We do not believe that the doctrinal underpinnings of "*Miranda*" require that it be applied in all its rigor to

PEOPLE IN POLITICS

CLARENCE EARL GIDEON

Clarence Earl Gideon was a pauper. At the age of fifty-one, he was serving five years in a Florida prison for the crime of breaking and entering. A gambler and a drifter, he had been in prison before for minor offenses. He was the last person in the world that anyone would expect to change the basic rights granted all people accused of a felony.

Gideon had been arrested for breaking into a pool hall in Panama City, Florida. He was brought to trial. Gideon could not afford a lawyer, so he asked the judge to appoint one for him. Because it was not a murder case, the court was under no obligation to do so and refused. The jury quickly found Gideon guilty and sentenced him to prison.

In prison, Gideon remained angry at the miscarriage of justice of which he had been the victim. He knew he was innocent, and he believed that a competent attorney would have gotten him acquitted. Using a procedure called *in forma pauperis* (in the manner of a pauper) Gideon wrote to the U.S. Supreme Court, requesting that it hear his case.

Gideon carefully printed his letter in pencil. He wrote: "When at the time of the petitioner's trial he asked the lower court for the aid of counsel, the court refused this aid. Petitioner told the court that the Court made a decision to the effect that all citizens tried for a felony crime should have aid of counsel. The lower court ignored this plea."

A clerk in the Supreme Court read this letter, and the impossible began to happen.

The Court had ruled twenty years earlier that defendants do not automatically have the right to counsel, but in 1961, the Court took a new look. It agreed to hear Gideon's petition. Over the next two years, a process unfolded that gave Gideon his day in court. In 1963, the Supreme Court announced the landmark decision of *Gideon v. Wainwright,* granting the right to counsel to all those accused of a felony under the due process clause of the Fourteenth Amendment. For Clarence Earl Gideon, it meant he would receive a new trial, this time with counsel. At his new trial, the jury pronounced Gideon "not guilty." One destitute person's determination succeeded in overturning an unfair verdict. In the process, he extended civil liberties to all those accused of a crime.

SOURCE: Anthony Lewis, ***Gideon's Trumpet*** (New York: Random House, 1964).

a situation in which police officers ask questions reasonably prompted by a concern for public safety."[50] Was this simply introducing greater flexibility, or was it a "sweeping exception" that could undermine the entire ruling? Dissenters claimed it would cause chaos among the nation's police. In the second case, two weeks later, the Court extended the *Miranda* decision to include misdemeanors as well as felonies.

The *Miranda* decision continued to be controversial into the 1980s and 1990s. In the last two years of the Reagan administration, the Justice Department and Attorney General Edwin Meese launched an all-out assault to get the *Miranda* rule overturned. In two 1987 decisions, the Supreme Court refused to extend the reach of the 1966 decision but gave no indication it was willing to alter the basic requirements. The Court ruled, first, that law enforcement officers need not inform suspects of all the crimes they might be questioned about in order for suspects to waive their right to remain silent.[51] In the second case, the Supreme Court ruled by a 7-to-2 majority that a confession by a suspect who agreed to answer questions orally but who would put nothing in writing without a lawyer was constitutional. Writing for the majority, Chief Justice Rehnquist explained: "*Miranda* gives the defendant a right to choose between speech and silence."[52] Once the accused had waived that right to silence, his confession was valid. In 1990, by a 8 to 1 majority, the court ruled that a videotape of a drunken-driving suspect could be admitted as evidence, even though the suspect did not first receive Miranda warnings.[53]

The process of balancing governing in the interest of the people as a whole with the liberties of individuals continues to be one of the most difficult challenges of politics. Because of the Constitution, which limits government, and the written Bill of Rights, civil liberties have generally been protected in the United States. But during emergencies and times of crisis, when governing ability in the American political system expanded, violations of civil liberties have been most severe. The debate will continue, because one person's "legal technicality" limiting the power of government officials is another person's fundamental liberty.

SUMMARY AND CONCLUSIONS

1. Civil liberties are "freedom from" state control; civil rights are "freedom to" share in the privileges and benefits of the state. The United States has traditionally emphasized individual liberty more than positive rights.

2. Protection of civil liberties is stronger in the United States than in most other countries in the world. But even in the United States there are constant challenges to civil liberties, particularly in times of war or national crises, when the government takes on special or emergency powers.

3. Most of the civil liberties of Americans are written down in the Constitution and the Bill of Rights. However simple and straightforward these guarantees may seem, rights are often in conflict, and it is up to the government, particularly the courts, to balance the competing rights and political interests.

4. The First Amendment guarantees of freedom of expression have a preferred position, but neither free speech nor free press has been interpreted as an absolute right. They have been constitutionally limited by considerations of public health and safety, libel, the right to a fair trial, national security, and other factors.

5. The wall of separation between church and state has produced a number of controversies. In maintaining the wall, many critics believe the courts have become antireligious, as in prohibiting school prayer. The courts generally protect religious beliefs but not all religious practices (such as polygamy).

6. In the 1960s, the Warren Court made a number of decisions extending the rights of the accused by acting to restrict police procedures and to provide all defendants with attorneys and a knowledge of their constitutional rights. Critics charged that such restrictions hampered law enforcement. Modifications to *Miranda* and other decisions under the Burger Court and the Rehnquist Court indicate the continuing attempts to reach an acceptable balance between the defendant's rights and the needs of law enforcement.

Protection of individual civil liberties is a key foundation of American politics. Civil liberties are guarantees that the government will not engage in certain practices. Only when one looks at other countries around the world does the relative status of American civil liberties become clear. Many nations place little value on individual liberty. Their governments fear political opposition and repress dissent, placing few limits on what internal security forces may do to keep order. The balance between the power of the government and the rights of the people often tilts to the side of the government. Protection of individual civil liberties limits the ability to govern but in a way that is fundamental to American democracy. Civil liberty in the United States is a strong tradition, and respect seems to be increasing. Yet threats to civil liberty exist, particularly in the electronic age. Civil liberties are part of an ongoing process of interpreting constitutional guarantees within the current social and political environment.

Key Terms

bill of attainder
Bill of Rights
civil liberties
civil rights
"clear and present danger" test
Dennis v. U.S.
establishment clause
exclusionary rule
ex post facto laws
free exercise clause
Gideon v. Wainwright
habeas corpus
Hazelwood v. Kuhlmeier
libel
Miller v. California
Miranda rule
Near v. Minnesota
Pentagon Papers case
prior restraint
Schenck v. U.S.
school prayer amendment
Sedition Act
selective incorporation
Smith Act

Self-Review

1. What is the difference between civil liberties and civil rights?
2. Compare the features of the U.S. Constitution with those of the Soviet Constitution.
3. How have questions of national security limited freedom of expression?
4. What, according to the courts, are legitimate restrictions on freedom of the press?
5. How has the Court attempted to define pornography and obscenity?
6. On what constitutional grounds did the Court ban prayer in public schools?
7. How has the Court interpreted the free exercise of religion guarantee of the First Amendment?
8. What is the exclusionary rule?
9. What rights do the *Miranda* and *Gideon* rulings guarantee?

Suggested Readings

Barker, Lucius J., and Twiley W. Barker, Jr. *Civil Liberties and the Constitution.* 6th ed. 1990.
An excellent discussion and review of the most important civil liberties cases and the social and political context in which they were decided.

Friendly, Fred. *Minnesota Rag.* 1981.
A well-written account of the case of *Near v. Minnesota* and the issue of prior restraint.

Irons, Peter., *The Courage of their Convictions: Sixteen Who Fought their Way to the Supreme Court.* 1990.
A look at the actual persons who fought for their liberties in the areas of religion, privacy, race and other areas.

O'Brien, David. *The Public's Right to Know: The Supreme Court and the First Amendment.* 1981.
An exploration of some of the classic problems of civil liberties when rights come into conflict.

Schwartz, Bernard. *The Great Rights of Mankind: A History of the American Bill of Rights.* 1977.
A look at the origins and developments of the written sources of civil liberties.

Notes

1. See Lucius J. Barker and Twiley W. Barker, Jr., *Civil Liberties and the Constitution,* 5th ed. (Englewood Cliffs, N.J.: Prentice-Hall, 1986).
2. *Ibid.,* 13.
3. *Gitlow v. New York* 45 S.Ct., 625. 1925.
4. *E.g., Adamson v. California* (332 U.S. 46, 1947).
5. See Justice Black's dissent to the *Adamson* decision in *ibid.*
6. *Schenck v. U.S.* (249 U.S. 47, 1919). See also Barker and Barker, *Civil Liberties,* chap. 3.
7. *Ibid.*
8. *Gitlow v. New York.*
9. *Dennis v. U.S.* (1951) 86 S.Ct. 1840.
10. See *Yates v. United States* (354 U.S. 298, 1957).
11. *U.S. v. O'Brien* (391 U.S. 367, 1968).
12. *Street v. New York* (394 U.S. 576, 1969).
13. *Hazelwood v. Kuhlmeier* (1988) 107 Sct 926.
14. Barker and Barker, *Civil Liberties,* 145.
15. *New York Times v. Sullivan* (376 U.S. 255, 1964).
16. *Sheppard v. Maxwell* (384 U.S. 333, 1966).
17. *Rideau v. Louisiana* (373 U.S. 723, 1963).
18. *Nebraska Press Assoc. v. Stuart* (427 U.S. 539, 1976).
19. *Richmond Newspapers Inc. v. Virginia* (444 U.S. 896, 1980).
20. *Roth v. U.S.* (354 U.S. 476, 1957).
21. *Manual Enterprises v. Day* (370 U.S. 478, 1962).
22. *A Book Named "John Cleland's Memoirs of a Woman of Pleasure" v. Attorney General of Massachusetts* (383 U.S. 413, 1966).
23. *Miller v. California* (413 U.S. 15, 1974).
24. *Schad et al. v. Borough of Mount Ephraim* (101 S.Ct. 2176, 1981).

25. *Pope v. Illinois* (1987) 107 S.Ct. 1918.
26. *Engle v. Vitale* (370 U.S. 471, 1962).
27. See *Congressional Quarterly Weekly Reports,* 18 February 1984, p. 315.
28. *Ibid.,* 10 March 1984, p. 538.
29. *Ibid.,* p. 540.
30. *Everson v. Board of Education* (330 U.S. 1, 1947).
31. Barker and Barker, *Civil Liberties,* 38–41.
32. *Walz v. Tax Commission* (397 U.S. 664, 1970).
33. *McGowen v. Maryland* (366 U.S. 420, 1961).
34. *Edwards v. Aguillard* (1987) 107 S.Ct. 2573.
35. See *Reynolds v. U.S.* (98 U.S. 145, 1878).
36. *West Virginia State Board of Education v. Barnette* (319 U.S. 624, 1943).
37. *Murdock v. Pennsylvania* (319 U.S. 105, 1943).
38. See *People v. Woody* (394 P. d. 813, 1964).
39. *Leary v. U.S.* (383 F. d. 851, 1967).
40. *Weeks v. U.S.* (232 U.S. 383, 1914).
41. *U.S. v. Jones* (428 U.S. 433, 1976).
42. Quoted in Barker and Barker, *Civil Liberties,* 291.
43. *U.S. v. Leon* (No. 82-1771, 1984).
44. *Nix v. Williams* (No. 82-1651, 1984).
45. *Murray v. U.S.; Carter v. U.S.* 108 S.Ct. 2529, 1988.
46. James v. Illinois 110 S.Ct. 648, 1990.
47. *Powell v. Alabama* (287 U.S. 45, 1932).
48. *Escobedo v. Illinois* (378 U.S. 478, 1964).
49. *Brown v. Mississippi* (297 U.S. 278, 1936) and *Chambers v. Florida* (309 U.S. 277, 1940).
50. *New York v. Quarles* (No. 82-1213, 1984).
    Colorado v. Spring (1987). 107 S.Ct. 851.
    Connecticut v. Barrett (1987). 170 S.Ct. 828.
53. Pennsylvania v. Muniz 110 S.Ct. 2638, 1990.

CHAPTER 6

Civil Rights

POLITICAL CLOSE-UP

The 1960 Civil Rights Filibuster

In the year 1960, eighteen southern senators were staunchly committed to preventing the passage of any civil rights bill in the United States. Even though the rest of the senators were in favor of some kind of civil rights legislation, the southern bloc members believed their chances to veto the wishes of the majority were good. In view of their past successes, they had cause for optimism. Following the 1954 decision of *Brown v. Board of Education,* which declared segregated schools unconstitutional, congressional attempts to pass civil rights laws had been blocked by southern members. A modest bill creating the Civil Rights Commission was approved in 1957, despite the attempts of Senator Strom Thurmond (D-S.C.) to halt it single-handedly (Thurmond later switched to the Republican party). Using Senate rules that allow unlimited debate, he undertook a one-man filibuster to talk the bill to death. Thurmond held the floor of the Senate for twenty-four hours and eighteen minutes on August 28–29, 1957, a record for a single individual, but he failed to receive additional help from his southern colleagues. As a result, a watered-down

version of the bill was finally enacted, and the stage was set for the great civil rights debate of 1960.

In 1959, the Eisenhower administration submitted a limited bill to help blacks register and vote in the South. Congress in 1960 was divided into three groups over civil rights. The southern bloc was opposed to all legislation. Moderates generally supported the limited approach of the Eisenhower administration. Progressive northern Republicans and Democrats wanted more direct comprehensive action to guarantee civil rights. No action was taken in 1959, but the congressional leadership, particularly Senate Majority Leader Lyndon Johnson (D-Tex.) and Minority Leader Everett Dirksen (R-Ill.), promised a civil rights debate in 1960. And what a debate it was.

Johnson wanted the full Senate to take up the civil rights question, but no bill could make it out of committee. On the House side, the civil rights bill was locked up in the Rules Committee, chaired by segregationist Howard Smith (D-Va.), who was hostile to any legislation. Lacking a legitimate bill to present to the Senate, Johnson drew on his considerable creative resources, as he would through the weeks that followed. He called up a minor bill on another matter and "invited" senators to offer civil rights amendments to it. So began a debate that lasted from February 15 to April 8, 1960.

The band of eighteen was determined to block this effort. They began a massive filibuster, using every conceivable delaying tactic. But Johnson and the majority were also determined. The majority leader kept the Senate in session around the clock to wear down the southerners. Working hand in hand with Dirksen and the Republicans, the leadership sparred with the southerners in a classic battle of legislative strategy and parliamentary technique. The southern bloc, led by Richard Russell (D-Ga.) and Thurmond, warned that some of the older senators could not stand up to the rigors of all-night sessions. As the filibuster and other delaying tactics dragged on, all other work of the Senate ceased. Cots were set up around the chamber. The southerners demanded quorum calls (where at least half the Senate must be on the floor) in the wee hours of the morning in an attempt to force the Senate to adjourn. This would have opened up additional opportunities for delay. Johnson was able to keep the Senate in continuous session so that the legislative "day" of February 15 did not actually end until March 8! As the Senate mired down in seemingly endless debate, the House finally broke the legislative logjam in the Rules Committee. With the membership threatening to use a rarely invoked "discharge petition" to force the bill out of committee, the Rules Committee finally sent a civil rights bill to the floor. The House passed the Civil Rights Act on March 24 by a vote of 313 to 106. This provided new impetus in the Senate. The eighteen southerners were weakening as the debate entered its eighth week. Despite motions to table and other last-ditch efforts, the civil rights bill finally came to a vote on April 8 and passed the Senate by a vote of 71 to 18. A small but determined group had almost succeeded in thwarting the will of the Senate, the House, and the White House (and it did succeed in diluting the original legislation). President Eisenhower, who had not played an active role during the long Senate debate, signed the historic 1960 Civil Rights Act in May.

SOURCE: *Congressional Quarterly Almanac, 1960,* 185–200.

CHAPTER OUTLINE

INTRODUCTION AND OVERVIEW

The apparently broad truth that "all men are created equal" contained in the Declaration of Independence actually meant something narrower to the Founders. It meant that only some white men—not black slaves or American Indians or women—are created equal. While the Founders acted to create a limited government that would protect individual liberties, they did not worry much about extending the full responsibilities, opportunities, or benefits of citizenship to all people. Over the past two hundred years, American politics has been characterized by significant struggles for civil rights. The most dramatic has been the struggle for African-American civil rights, but women have also had to fight for full equality. Recently, Hispanics, Indians, gays, disabled, and incarcerated and institutionalized people have all entered the political arena to fight for their civil rights.

As noted in Chapter 5, civil liberties are the "freedom from" certain government actions, while civil rights are the "freedom to" enjoy the full benefits of citizenship. Civil rights include:

- The right to vote and participate in politics
- Equal protection of the law and the assurance that there are not two standards of justice
- Equal opportunity to participate in the economic system
- Equal access to such social institutions as schools and universities, churches, and the military

Although Americans may take their civil rights for granted, even today all citizens do not have equal political rights. In the recent past, large numbers of people were systematically denied civil rights afforded others. This chapter explores the quest for civil rights, particularly civil rights for blacks, from slavery through the Civil War and the establishment of segregation to the civil rights movement of the 1950s and 1960s. It also examines the women's movement for equal rights as well as recent controversies surrounding civil rights policy.

Civil rights sheds a different light on the problem of governing. What happens when Congress and the president are unwilling or unable to take action? What happens if courts make policy but are unable to carry it out? Is it possible for a grassroots movement to create enough political pressure to force the government to make laws and apply them equally throughout the nation?

The following questions are examined in this chapter:

1. How did a system of discrimination and segregation of blacks arise even though Congress enacted laws to guarantee equal rights immediately after the Civil War?
2. What events marked the emergence of the civil rights movement in the twentieth century? What were some of its major milestones?
3. Why did the Supreme Court rather than the president or Congress finally act to end segregation? What were some disadvantages of having this branch of government take the lead?
4. What kind of leadership was provided in the presidency and Congress in the area of civil rights?

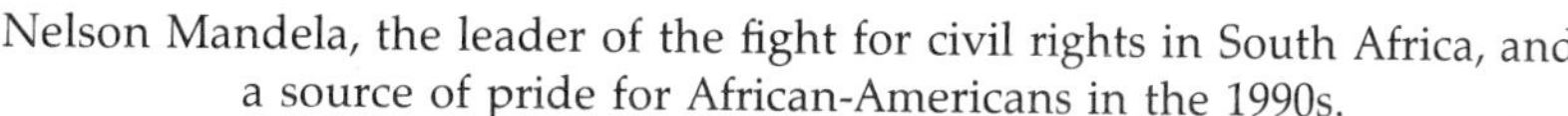
Nelson Mandela, the leader of the fight for civil rights in South Africa, and a source of pride for African-Americans in the 1990s.

What were the major legislative landmarks in civil rights policy?
5. How are civil rights laws enforced by the bureaucracy? How effective is compliance with the law? What are the current issues concerning civil rights?
6. How have women attempted to gain equal rights? What are some of the current issues, strategies, and tactics of the women's movement?
7. What is the new civil rights agenda in the United States? What groups are pressing their claims for equal rights? Why has the right to privacy become a civil rights issue for some groups?

Black Civil Rights: Won and Lost

THE CIVIL WAR: THE ULTIMATE GOVERNING CRISIS

During the first half of the nineteenth century, slavery was the most pervasive and divisive issue in American politics. It represented fundamental regional economic differences that challenged the ability of the nation to remain under one government. A series of compromises kept the union together through the 1850s, but change was inevitable. The ***Dred Scott*** decision in 1857 was a misguided effort by the Supreme Court to uphold the institution of slavery (see Political Insight 6–1). It only intensified efforts in the North to abolish slavery, and it may have hastened the Civil War. Seventy years after the ratification of the Constitution, the United States faced its ultimate governing crisis, resolved only by a bloody war. But in the years of Reconstruction that followed the Civil War, another governing problem arose. Despite ratification, constitutional amendments guaranteeing equal rights for blacks were subverted by southern states and the Supreme Court.

How could this happen? Constitutional amendments are the most difficult but most definitive way to make policy. Southern states first circumvented the **Thirteenth Amendment,** which banned slavery, by passing "black codes." Not to be thwarted, the Radical Republicans, who dominated Congress, responded to these acts by pushing through the **Fourteenth Amendment,** which was ratified in 1868. Its language seemed clear: "No state . . . shall deprive any person of life, liberty, or property without due process of law; nor deny . . . the equal protection of the laws."

The **Fifteenth Amendment** was intended to ensure voting rights for blacks. It said that the right to vote could not be abridged because of a person's race, color, or previous slave status. These three amendments (see Appendix C for the full text of the amendments) would seem to have closed the question of equal rights for blacks. Yet within twenty years, virtually all semblance of equal rights in the South was wiped out.

LEGAL SEGREGATION IN THE SOUTH: JIM CROW LAWS

It took the Supreme Court only three years to make its first rulings on these amendments. In the *Slaughterhouse* cases in 1873, the Court chose the narrowest possible interpretation of what it meant for states to abuse the "privileges and immunities" of blacks. Congress reacted by passing a law that forbade discrimination against blacks in such public accommodations as hotels and restaurants. In a series of decisions in 1883, called the "Civil Rights Cases," the Court ruled that Congress could not prevent discrimination by private individuals, opening the door to a series of "Jim Crow" laws in the South (so named from a minstrel-song slang expression for blacks). The effect of the Civil Rights Cases was that it was legal for private businesses to either segregate or refuse to serve blacks altogether. But what about public facilities, such as parks? Could state governments discriminate when the Fourteenth Amendment specifically stated that they could not deny equal protection?

Despite the guarantees of the Thirteenth, Fourteenth, and Fifteenth Amendments, a new system of racial discrimination developed. The courts sanctioned the creation of separate societies. In Louisiana, a law passed in 1890 required blacks and

POLITICAL INSIGHT 6-1

THE *DRED SCOTT* DECISION

Courts, like other political institutions, have made mistakes over the years. Some have been disastrous. The case of *Dred Scott v. Sanford* (1857) was a misguided attempt by the Supreme Court to settle judicially an issue that was tearing at the very fiber of the nation. Four years after the decision, the tear was complete, and the Civil War under way.

Dred Scott was a slave who moved with his owner to a state where slavery was illegal. Scott sued in court, claiming that because he was no longer in a slave state, he was a free man. The conservative Court was dominated by southerners, and the opinion in the case was delivered by Chief Justice Roger B. Taney, a strong advocate of states' rights.

The Court ruled first that Dred Scott, because he was black, could not be a citizen in any state and therefore could not sue. This ran counter to the practice in most northern states, where blacks were considered citizens. The Court also used judicial review (for only the second time in its history) to strike down the 1820 Missouri Compromise, which had prohibited slavery in Maine and what was then the Louisiana Territory. Slaves are property, the Court noted, and it is unconstitutional to deprive people of their property without due process of law.

The decision is considered to be perhaps the worst in the country's history, for several reasons. First, the Court's ruling went counter to growing national opinion favoring abolition of slavery. Second, not content just to rule against Dred Scott, the Court invalidated a forty-year-old political bargain and said that Congress could not ban slavery anywhere. A majority of citizens in the North responded angrily to this decision, which denied the basic humanity of blacks. It took the Civil War and the Emancipation Proclamation in 1863 to settle the question of slavery.

whites to ride trains in separate Pullman cars. A man named Plessy refused to sit in the car reserved for the "colored races" and was ejected and imprisoned. Plessy, noting that he was only one-eighth black, claimed he was entitled to every right, privilege, and immunity guaranteed to members of the white race. In *Plessy v. Ferguson* (1896), the U.S. Supreme Court ultimately upheld the law and argued that the Constitution would allow "**separate but equal**" facilities. The *Plessy* decision in some ways represented the final triumph of the forces that wanted to make segregation in the South legal. In ruling that the equal protection requirement could be satisfied by separate, segregated facilities, the Court ignored the obvious effect of its decision with its claim that separation of the races did not imply that one was superior to the other. The Court had given its blessing to discrimination in both public and private sectors.

DISENFRANCHISEMENT OF BLACKS

The rollback of civil rights for blacks was not limited to discrimination in Pullman cars and schools or at drinking fountains. It included taking away the right to vote as well. Immediately after the Civil War, politics in the South changed radically. Blacks were elected to the U.S. House of Representatives, to state legislatures, and to various other political offices. Black participation in politics grew steadily in the 1870s and 1880s. In Mississippi until 1890, more blacks than whites were registered to vote.[1] But just ten years later, most of the black voters had been taken off the rolls. In Louisiana, there were more than 130,000 registered black voters in 1896; eight years later, there were less than 1,400.[2]

This disenfranchisement was accomplished by a series of devious means. One was the **grandfather clause,** which allowed a voter automatic registration if his grandfather had voted before 1865. Of course, this included only white voters. Those whose grandfathers had not voted often had to pass a **literacy test.** Three black Ph.D.'s failed the exam in Alabama. In a city in Mississippi where no white had ever failed the test, three black teachers with master's degrees were determined to be too illiterate to vote.[3] Another exclusionary device was the *poll tax,* which often kept poor whites as well as blacks out of the voting booth. Finally, the **white primary** was another form of Jim Crow law. Because political parties were ruled to be private entities, it was legal for them to open their membership to whites only. In the "solid South," this meant the Democratic party only. Winning the Democratic primary was tantamount to election. If all these exclusionary devices failed, and they rarely did, there was always private intimidation and threats. Some southern towns published the names of blacks who tried to register to vote, and economic ostracism by the white community followed. The Ku Klux Klan and its burning crosses were another very real threat to blacks and sympathetic whites.

Two generations after the Civil War, separate societies existed side by side in many states. Although racism, discrimination, and segregated housing patterns existed in the North, no northern state approached the dual society of the old Confederacy. "Separate but equal" was a fantasy. Only in the largest cities were separate facilities provided for blacks, and they were almost always inferior. In the smaller towns, facilities were for whites only. Political scientists Harrell Rodgers and Charles Bullock describe discrimination in the public sector in the South:

> In the South virtually every service provided by the government was offered on a segregated basis. Separate hospitals and health centers looked after the health needs of blacks and whites. In public buildings such as courthouses, whites and blacks drank from separate water fountains and urinated into segregated toilets. Justice was dispensed in courtrooms in which segregated seating was enforced and white and black witnesses took the oath using different Bibles. Those who were imprisoned were confined in racially homogeneous cells or were sent to work on the roads in uniracial chain gangs. Some police departments had black officers, but these men were often forbidden to stop or arrest whites. In some cities they received no salary but were compensated with a portion of the fines levied on blacks whom they arrested. A standing joke in the South was that the only public facility not segregated was the highway system.[4]

The Civil Rights Movement

The struggle for black civil rights began before the Civil War with the activities of abolitionist groups and some groups of free blacks. However, a concerted effort to provide equal rights did not begin in earnest until the early twentieth century. In 1909, the National Association for the Advancement of Colored People (NAACP) was organized in New York. A group of both black and white activists, it was dedicated to change through the legal system. In 1911, the Urban League was formed by whites to improve the living conditions of blacks in the big cities. Although both these organizations were mostly conservative in their approach to change, they played an active role when the civil rights movement took on national significance in the 1950s and 1960s. The NAACP was instrumental in bringing to court the crucial case of ***Brown v. Board of Education*** (1954), which overturned the "separate but equal" doctrine of *Plessy* and began the era of integration.

THE *BROWN* DECISION AND THE JUDICIAL ERA OF CIVIL RIGHTS

The Supreme Court had created the legal basis for segregation. Later, however, the Court was the institution that moved most forcefully against racial discrimination. Twenty years after *Plessy,* the Court began to chip away at some of the most obnoxious elements of Jim Crow laws. In 1915, it found the grandfather clause to be unconstitutional.[5] The "separate but equal" doctrine was challenged by blacks in the 1930s, 1940s, and 1950s, with many of the lawsuits sponsored by the NAACP. In 1938, a qualified black person was denied admission to the University of Missouri law school solely on the basis of race. The Court held that Missouri's providing the black plaintiff with a scholarship to attend a law school out of state did not satisfy the test of equality.[6] The Court did not overturn the "separate but equal" doctrine, but it raised the standard for equality. If Missouri had provided a separate law school for blacks, presumably there would have been no case. So Missouri and five other southern states did exactly that. Blacks then sued on the grounds that the black law school was inferior and did not satisfy the equal protection clause. In 1950, the Supreme Court ruled against such a school in the state of Texas, finding that it provided inferior education for the students, compared with the all-white University of Texas law school.[7] Although the Court stopped short of declaring the "separate but equal" doctrine invalid, the doctrine was clearly on its last legs.

Four years later, on May 17, 1954, the Supreme Court finally overthrew the "separate but equal" doctrine in the landmark case of *Brown v. Board of Education.* The decision was based on a combination of cases from seven cities brought on behalf of students by the NAACP. Thurgood Marshall, attorney for the NAACP, argued the case before the Supreme Court. (Marshall would become the first black person to serve on the Supreme Court). In the unanimous decision, written by Chief Justice Earl Warren, the Court attacked the basic nature of segregation in public education: "Separate is inherently unequal," the justices declared. Segregated school systems in the southern and border states were declared illegal. The modern era of civil rights had begun.

As we saw in Chapter 1, governing is more than simply announcing policies. To be meaningful, policies have to be effectively implemented. Although the Supreme Court was able to end the legal sanctions for racial discrimination, it was not able to make the required changes. In its decision, the Court instructed school districts to desegregate "with all deliberate speed." The lack of a specific timetable encouraged resistance from southern politicians, school boards, and citizens. More than thirty years after the *Brown* decision, some school desegregation cases are still in court. Insulated from reelection pressures, the Court was best able to change national policy. But lacking its own enforcement mechanisms, it was least able to carry out the new doctrine. As a result, progress was slow and other institutions had to take up the task of guaranteeing civil rights.

Reaction to the *Brown* decision was predictable. Civil rights advocates, both white and black, were elated. In the South, where segregation was a way of life, reaction was swift and often violent. Southern state legislatures passed "nullification acts," announcing that they would refuse to obey the Supreme Court. One hundred members of Congress signed the "Southern Manifesto," pledging to fight the decision at every step. Implementation was difficult and often ugly. In 1957, President Eisenhower ordered the National Guard into Little Rock, Arkansas, when Governor Orville Faubus refused to allow black students to attend the white high school. Despite the setbacks, school desegregation proceeded, and the civil rights movement began to move against other aspects of racial discrimination.

The 1950s were the judicial era of civil rights. Although the courts continue to play an important role in civil rights today, in the 1950s, they acted virtually alone. It took more direct action to finally stir the executive and legislative branches.

ECONOMIC SANCTIONS AND THE CIVIL RIGHTS MOVEMENT

On December 1, 1955, Rosa Parks had finished her work as a seamstress in Montgomery, Alabama, and stepped onto the bus for the ride home. She sat down in the front of the bus rather than walking back to the "colored" section. Ordered out of the seat so a white man could sit there, Rosa refused and was arrested. This small act of defiance became a major event in the civil rights movement. A young black minister, the Reverend Martin Luther King, Jr., decided to strike back at white businesses where it hurt—in the pocketbook. King organized a black boycott of the Montgomery bus system.[8] Montgomery blacks, a sizable share of the bus riders, walked rather than ride in the back of the bus. A year later, the Supreme Court ruled that segregation of public transit systems was unconstitutional.

Economic sanctions became an important component of direct action to achieve civil rights for blacks. Increasing numbers of whites participated, often traveling from northern cities to help. One of the most effective strategies was the **sit-in.**

Although blacks could shop in local southern department stores, they could not get served at the lunch counters. In Greensboro, North Carolina, in February 1960, a group of black and white college students staged a series of lunch counter sit-ins, occupying the seats and refusing to leave until they were served. Owners were quick to call in the local sheriff, who was happy to drag the troublemakers off to jail. But the numbers swelled. By August 1961, more than 70,000 people had participated in sit-ins, and more than 3,500 had been arrested.[9] The results were impressive. Across the South, hundreds of facilities previously closed to blacks were opened.

Civil rights workers faced danger and even death in the South. Whites from the North were as despised as black demonstrators. Refusing to use segregated waiting rooms, drinking fountains, and other separate facilities, "freedom riders" rode interstate buses throughout the South, challenging segregation. Through its political and economic tactics, the civil rights movement had become a truly national phenomenon by the early 1960s. There was much to do. Pressure was growing in Washington for the president and Congress to take meaningful actions to secure civil rights for blacks.

Martin Luther King Jr.

THE PRESIDENT, THE CONGRESS, AND CIVIL RIGHTS

In the summer of 1963, Martin Luther King, Jr. led a march on Washington of blacks and whites impatient for change. His stirring speech to the crowd of a quarter of a million people had tremendous impact (see Political Insight 6–2). The struggle for civil rights had grown from a small movement to one that had captured the attention of the nation. People looked to President John F. Kennedy and Congress to act. Before 1963, presidents had provided relatively little leadership in civil rights, although President Harry Truman had taken an important step when he desegregated the armed forces of the United States by executive order. In 1948, the Democrats adopted a pro-civil rights platform (leading to a walkout by some southern delegates), but little legislative action resulted. President Eisenhower demonstrated to the nation that he would enforce the law of the land, but in general he did not push civil rights, believing "you can't change men's hearts with laws."[10] One observer characterized Eisenhower's stance toward civil rights as "benign neutrality."[11] Two civil rights bills were passed during his administration. The 1957 Civil Rights Act created the Civil Rights Commission and made it a federal crime to prevent a person from voting. The 1960 Civil Rights Act, as difficult as it was to enact, did relatively little to actually achieve equal rights.

During the 1960 campaign, John Kennedy voiced strong support for the civil rights movement. Civil rights activists were therefore all the more disappointed with Kennedy's record in the first two years of his administration. Although he remained committed, Kennedy recognized the continued unpopularity of civil rights legislation in Congress. He feared alienating southern senators and representatives, who still dominated crucial committees and could obstruct his entire legislative program.

POLITICAL INSIGHT 6–2

I HAVE A DREAM (MARTIN LUTHER KING, JR., AUGUST 1963)

. . . So I say to you, my friends, that even though we must face the difficulties of today and tomorrow, I still have a dream. It is a dream deeply rooted in the American dream that one day this nation will rise up and live out the true meaning of its creed—we hold these truths to be self-evident, that all men are created equal.

I have a dream that one day on the red hills of Georgia, sons of former slaves and sons of former slave-owners will be able to sit down together at the table of brotherhood.

I have a dream that one day, even the state of Mississippi, a state sweltering with the heat of injustice, sweltering with the heat of oppression, will be transformed into an oasis of freedom and justice.

I have a dream my four little children will one day live in a nation where they will not be judged by the color of their skin but by content of their character. I have a dream today!

I have a dream that one day, down in Alabama, with its vicious racists, with its governor having his lips dripping with the words of interposition and nullification, that one day, right there in Alabama, little black boys and black girls will be able to join hands with little white boys and white girls as sisters and brothers. I have a dream today! . . .

With this faith we will be able to work together, to pray together, to struggle together, to go to jail together, to stand up for freedom together, knowing that we will be free one day. This will be the day when all of God's children will be able to sing with new meaning—"my country 'tis of thee, sweet land of liberty, of thee I sing; land where my fathers died, land of the pilgrim's pride; from every mountainside, let freedom ring"—and if America is to be a great nation, this must become true.

And so let freedom ring from the prodigious hilltops of New Hampshire.

Let freedom ring from the mighty mountains of New York.

Let freedom ring from the heightening Alleghenies of Pennsylvania.

Let freedom ring from the snow-capped Rockies of Colorado.

Let freedom ring from the curvaceous slopes of California.

But not only that.

Let freedom ring from Stone Mountain of Georgia.

Let freedom ring from Lookout Mountain of Tennessee.

Let freedom ring from every hill and molehill of Mississippi, from every mountainside, let freedom ring.

And when this happens, and when we allow freedom to ring, when we let it ring from every village and hamlet, from every state and city, we will be able to speed up that day when all of God's children—black men and white men, Jews and Gentiles, Catholics and Protestants—will be able to join hands and to sing in the words of the old Negro spiritual, "Free at last, free at last; thank God Almighty, we are free at last."

SOURCE: From Roy L. Hill, ed., *Rhetoric of Racial Revolt* (Denver: Golden Bell Press, 1964), 371–75.

But by 1963, Kennedy became convinced that strong action had to be taken despite the potential political consequences. Racial incidents helped spur his resolve. Medgar Evers and three civil rights workers were murdered in Mississippi. Police responded violently to peaceful demonstrations in Selma and Birmingham, Alabama. In June 1963, Kennedy sent a major civil rights bill to Capitol Hill. By November 1963, the bill was out of committee and awaiting action by the full House, but Kennedy never lived to see it passed.

As a southerner, Lyndon Johnson had been conservative on civil rights early in his political career. But when he entered the spotlight of national politics, Johnson became a civil rights champion.[12] As president, he used his considerable legislative skills and the residual support for the slain president's bill to push through the 1964 Civil Rights Act. Even with this momentum, a major battle erupted in the Senate over the bill. The debate lasted more than two months, and final victory was achieved only after once again breaking a southern filibuster. Johnson's landslide victory in the 1964 elections filled the Congress with new Democrats and cleared the way for easy passage of the 1965 Voting Rights Act. These two pieces of legislation represented for the first time meaningful guarantees of equal rights.

THE 1964 CIVIL RIGHTS ACT. During Reconstruction, Congress tried to assure open access to public accommodations based on the equal protection clause of the Fourteenth Amendment. As we have seen, the Supreme Court in the 1880s struck down these laws. How could Congress and the president write a bill that the Court would uphold? Strategists came up with an alternative to the equal protection clause, making it unnecessary for the Court to reverse its previous decisions. They invoked the *interstate commerce clause* of the Constitution to ensure open access to public accommodations in the **1964 Civil Rights Act,** making it a federal crime to refuse service to any person if (1) a business served people traveling from state to state or (2) if a "substantial portion" of the products used in the business had moved in interstate commerce.[13] Motels and restaurants would go out of business if they flouted the law, as much of what they use or serve is manufactured out of state. Virtually no business could escape the law, but some still refused to comply. In Atlanta, Georgia, Lester Maddox, later elected governor of the state, used an ax handle to repel black customers from his chicken restaurant. But on the whole, compliance was high and significant changes occurred.

THE 1965 VOTING RIGHTS ACT. Despite the elimination of many of the discriminatory practices, such as the grandfather clause and the white primary, and despite the passage of the Civil Rights Acts of 1957 and 1960, blacks still had difficulty registering and voting in the South. The **Voting Rights Act of 1965** took positive measures to assure black registration and voting. It provided that in any state where less than 50 percent of eligible voters were registered to vote, prima facie discrimination existed (that is, no further proof of discrimination was needed). The law did three things: (1) it authorized the appointment of federal officials to oversee registration and elections; (2) it eliminated remaining tests and devices used to prevent blacks from voting; and (3) it made it possible to move against an entire county or state in the courts, rather than taking each individual occurrence of discrimination on a case-by-case basis.[14]

Federal examiners, poll watchers, and registrars were stationed in six states (Alabama, Georgia, Mississippi, Louisiana, South Carolina, and Virginia) and in a number of counties in North Carolina. A comparison of black and white registration before and after the 1965 Voting Rights Act in the six states and other southern states (see Table 6–1) shows that in just a few years the proportion of black voters increased dramatically. White registration increased as well, bringing the South as a region closer to national figures for voter registration.

UNMET EXPECTATIONS AND REDIRECTION TO ECONOMIC ISSUES

Martin Luther King, Jr. had established the civil rights movement in the tradition of nonviolent protest. Despite the progress resulting from federal legislation in the 1960s, the civil rights movement split into different camps. More-radical groups, impatient with the slow pace of change and seeing little improvement in the position of blacks, urged a more militant approach. Stokely Carmichael, an original founder of the Student Nonviolent Coordinating Committee, provided an increasingly radical perspective with his call for "Black Power" in the mid-1960s. Black Muslims, like Malcolm X, pushed for black nationalism and separatism. The Black Panthers urged their members to carry weapons. Beginning with the riots in the Watts section of Los Angeles in 1965, the late 1960s saw a number of "long hot summers" of racial violence in America's cities. Detroit, Newark, and Gary exploded in destructive violence.

The expectations of the civil rights movement were high. King's nonviolent strategy of direct action and economic sanctions had worked. The grassroots movement had brought significant legislative victories. But to many blacks, particularly the young, the victories were hollow. Many were still poor and unemployed. The focus of the civil rights movement began to shift to questions of political economy. Blacks wanted more than the ballot and the right to sit at the lunch counter; they wanted to share in the economic prosperity of the nation.

King reflected this change in emphasis in his own activities. As the most important black leader in the United States, he helped focus attention on poverty by leading a "poor people's" march on Washington in early 1968. A month later, King was dead, the victim of an assassin's bullet in Memphis. More cities erupted in violence, including the nation's capital. Two months later, the white leader most respected in the black community was gunned down in Los Angeles. The assassinations of King and Senator Robert F. Kennedy marked a turning point in the civil rights movement. The nation was tired of violence. Public opinion surveys revealed that a majority believed enough change had occurred in civil rights. The Vietnam War sapped the nation's energies and resources. The civil rights movement entered a new phase, one concerned with consolidating and enforcing gains already made in the legal area while extending them into the economic realm.

Civil Rights Enforcement: Problems of Implementation

INTEGRATION OF PUBLIC SCHOOLS

One of the most important changes made by the 1964 Civil Rights Act turned enforcement of school desegregation over to the Department of Health, Education, and Welfare (HEW—today the HHS, Department of Health and Human Services), giving that agency the power to terminate federal assistance to school districts that discriminated. Financial incentives and penalties were a potent weapon to achieve integration. HEW developed a set of

TABLE 6–1

PROPORTIONS OF BLACKS AND WHITES REGISTERED BEFORE AND AFTER THE VOTING RIGHTS ACT OF 1965

	Registration Before the Act (% of Voting-Age Population)		Registration After the Act (% of Voting-Age Population)	
	Black	White	Black	White
Alabama	19.3	69.2	51.6	89.6
Arkansas	40.4	65.5	62.8	72.4
Florida	51.2	74.8	63.6	81.4
Georgia	27.4	62.6	52.6	80.3
Louisiana	31.6	80.5	58.9	93.1
Mississippi	6.7	69.9	59.8	91.5
North Carolina	46.8	96.8	51.3	83.0
South Carolina	37.3	75.7	51.2	81.7
Tennessee	69.5	72.9	71.7	80.6
Texas	*	*	61.6	53.3
Virginia	38.3	61.1	55.6	63.4
Total	35.5	73.4	57.2	76.5

*Figures unavailable.

SOURCES: Commission on Civil Rights, *Political Participation* (Washington, D.C.: Government Printing Office, 1968), 12–13. In Harrell R. Rodgers Jr. and Charles S. Bullock, *Law and Social Change* (New York: McGraw-Hill, 1972), 271.

guidelines for compliance in 1965. By the beginning of 1967, it had cut off funds to 34 school districts and was in the process of terminating aid to 157 more.[15] In addition to HEW, the Civil Rights Division of the Justice Department filed suit against noncomplying school districts. The politics of civil rights had moved from the courts acting alone through Congress and the presidency to the federal bureaucracy. By the end of the 1960s, more changes were in the wind.

Ten years after the *Brown* decision, the Supreme Court warned school districts that there had been "entirely too much deliberation and not enough speed."[16] The case of *Alexander v. Holmes* (1969) made it clear that delays in desegregating schools would no longer be tolerated. Suddenly the political calculus changed. By 1970, fewer blacks attended integrated schools in the North than in the South! **De jure** segregation (segregation by law) was a southern problem. But **de facto** segregation (segregation in practice, caused by housing patterns) was a northern problem. Justice William O. Douglas argued that the distinction between de jure and de facto segregation was being used to justify segregation in the North: the distinction should be abandoned, and segregation should be attacked wherever it existed.[17] This cooled the enthusiasm of many white northerners for further change, particularly when it involved the busing of schoolchildren to achieve racial balance.

Other factors affected the change in the handling of civil rights in the 1970s. President Nixon's reelection bid in 1972 was to be based on a "southern strategy," capitalizing on the growing disenchantment of conservative southerners with the Democratic party. Although Nixon gave support to the gains and the goals of civil rights, he was reluctant to alienate southerners. The Nixon administration ordered less-aggressive enforcement of existing laws and judicial rulings, announcing that some delays might be necessary. Busing to achieve school integration had become one of the hottest issues in the country. In a speech to the nation, Nixon expressed his opposition to busing in cases of de facto segregation. Despite the reluctance of the White House, the courts kept up the pressure on school districts to desegregate. In the case of *Swann v. Charlotte-Mecklenburg Board of Education* (1971), the Supreme Court ruled that a transportation plan was a constitutionally acceptable solution to eliminate a dual education system.[18]

As school desegregation and court-ordered plans moved North, many whites fled the cities for the suburbs, often resulting in more heavily segregated schools. More than thirty-five years after the *Brown* decision, busing remains extremely unpopular and controversial. Many politicians make federal judges scapegoats for enforcing the guidelines established by the Supreme Court, fanning local prejudices. Lower courts continue to be the most important institution implementing school desegregation as they struggle to end racial separatism in public education. In the 1980s, courts employed a variety of approaches to achieve desegregation. In general, courts have not supported cross-district busing to achieve racial balance. In some cases, such as one involving Norfolk, Virginia, the courts have actually terminated busing plans.

EQUAL OPPORTUNITY VERSUS AFFIRMATIVE ACTION

As the civil rights movement shifted to economic issues, new controversies developed over how far and how fast to overcome past discrimination in the workplace against blacks, women, and other minorities. During the 1960s, a number of actions were taken to improve employment opportunities for blacks. Presidents Kennedy, Johnson, and Nixon all issued executive orders prohibiting discrimination in federal agencies. The 1964 Civil Rights Act banned discrimination in private sector employment. Kennedy and Johnson issued orders prohibiting the government from doing business with contractors that discriminate. The **Equal Employment Opportunity Commission (EEOC)** was created by the 1964 Civil Rights Act to enforce these provisions. Although civil rights advocates accused the Nixon administration of a slowdown in school desegregation enforcement, the administration won praise in the area of employment. For example, the "Philadelphia plan" approved by the administration guaranteed a certain number of minority jobs in the construction industry. The plan was a two-edged sword, however, leading to controversies over the question of racial "quotas."

Once society has made a commitment to giving the same political and economic rights to all its citizens, is it enough to provide **equal opportunity,** or is it necessary to take **affirmative action** to overcome disadvantages as a result of past discrimination? Affirmative action is a standard that says when all other factors are equal, preference will be given to the target group (this standard applies to women as well as blacks). In practice, affirmative action has sometimes been defined in a more limited fashion (such as assuring a broad pool of applicants) and at other times in a more interventionist fashion (such as establishing quotas). When affirmative action is equated with preferential treatment, quotas, and reverse discrimination, it is strongly opposed by the public.

The Supreme Court has upheld affirmative action but has limited preferential treatment or quotas. In 1979, the Court tried to clarify the standard in the ***Bakke*** case. Bakke was a white male who claimed reverse discrimination when he was denied admission to medical school at the University of California at Davis. The admissions committee had reserved a certain number of places in the incoming class for minority group members, even if they had poorer academic qualifications than majority applicants. The Court ruled in favor of Bakke and against explicit quotas, although the Court also said it was permissible to take race into account in admissions as long as race is considered with other factors.

In 1980, the Court upheld a preferential training plan for blacks at the Kaiser Aluminum Company. In the *Weber* case, the Court said it was permissible to reserve half the training slots for minority members, even if they had less seniority than white employees. In 1984, however, the Court ruled against an affirmative action plan that in effect required that someone with more seniority be fired to preserve a minority-filled job.[19] In its 6-to-3 decision, the Court ruled that the Memphis, Tennessee Fire Department wrongly insulated black fire fighters from the possibility of layoffs or demotions. Preferences to make up for past discrimination could be given only if current minority members could prove actual victimization. The Court said that the Civil Rights Act of 1964 expressly protects white workers with seniority. This case went beyond *Bakke* because it appeared to undermine the remedial use of race as a factor and affirmative action as a standard.

In 1986 and 1987, however, the Supreme Court clarified its endorsement of affirmative action as limited preferential treatment for women and minority groups to remedy the effects of past discrimination. In the case of *Sheet Metal Workers v. EEOC* (1986), the Court upheld a lower court order requiring the union, which had refused to admit blacks, to increase minority membership to 30 percent.[20] In 1987, the Supreme Court approved a decision by the Santa Clara (California) Transportation Department to promote a woman over a man who had scored marginally higher on a qualifying interview. The city had no women dispatchers. Until 1988, the Court prohibited rigid racial or gender quotas and preferential treatment of blacks but endorsed other more modest plans. Decisions more consistently went against affirmative action, however, after Bush replaced Reagan in the White House.

Civil Rights during the Bush Administration

INFLUENCE OF THE REAGAN APPOINTEES

Support for affirmative action began to decline after Anthony Kennedy, President Reagan's fourth appointment to the Supreme Court, was sworn in. A series of decisions handed down in 1989 raised fears among civil rights activists that progress of recent decades might yet be reversed. This put the Court and Congress in growing opposition, leaving President Bush in the middle. In the case of *Richmond v. Croson,* by a 6-to-3 vote, the Court struck down an affirmative action plan for Richmond, Virginia, that set aside 30 percent of city construction contracts for minority-owned firms. Croson, a white-owned firm, lost a city contract and sued, arguing that the minority set-aside plan violated the equal protection clause of the Fourteenth Amendment. The Court agreed, ruling that the city was unable to show compelling evidence that specific discriminatory practices had occurred in the past to justify the plan.[21] This ruling put minority preference plans across the country in jeopardy.

A number of other decisions handed down in 1989 tended to weaken existing civil rights protections. The Court, in *Patterson v. McLean Credit Union,* ruled 5-to-4 that an 1866 law forbidding discrimination applied only to hiring, not to discrimination on the job.[22] In another case, the Court decided that affirmative action plans can be challenged as reverse discrimination even years after they are adopted.[23] Conversely, the Court ruled that seniority plans cannot be challenged as discriminatory unless it is done right away.[24] In another narrow 5-to-4 decision, the Supreme Court changed who must bear the burden of proof in employment discrimination cases. For eighteen years, employers had to show why discriminatory practices were a business necessity. But in the case of *Wards Cove Packing v. Atonio,* the Court ruled that employees must prove that an employer has no legal justification for exclusionary practices, no matter how strong the discriminatory effect.[25]

CONGRESS VERSUS THE COURT

Congress successfully overturned the *Grove City College* decision in 1988 by enacting the Civil Rights Restoration Act over President Reagan's veto (see Chapter 1). A coalition of legislators led by Edward Kennedy (D-Mass.) and Howard Metzenbaum (D-Ohio) aimed to negate several of the Court's 1989 rulings in the same fashion. The Civil Rights Act of 1990 was drafted to reverse the decisions based on interpretation of congressional statute. Of particular concern was reversing the *Patterson* decision to strengthen protection against racial discrimination on the job and overturning the *Wards Cove* decision to return the burden of proof in discrimination cases to employers. The 1990 Civil Rights Act also attempted to reverse the Court's decisions dealing with legal challenges to seniority plans and affirmative action plans.

The Bush administration took a middle ground, offering legislation to overturn the *Patterson* and *Wards Cove* decisions but not the others. But Bush ultimately vetoed the 1990 Civil Rights Act and the Senate failed to override by a single vote. The Supreme Court heard additional cases challenging affirmative action. In 1990, the Court heard a case challenging the Federal Communications Commission's (FCC) minority-ownership programs. In an unusual division within the Bush administration, the FCC and the Justice Department filed separate briefs, on different sides of the issue.[26]

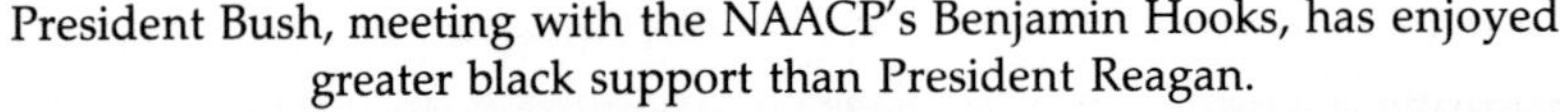

President Bush, meeting with the NAACP's Benjamin Hooks, has enjoyed greater black support than President Reagan.

George Bush, who enjoyed significantly higher approval ratings among blacks than Ronald Reagan had, tried to avoid the criticism leveled at his predecessor over opposition to civil rights measures. Yet he found himself in an uncomfortable political position because of civil rights reversals emanating from the increasingly influential Reagan-appointed justices.

PUBLIC ATTITUDES

The political environment for civil rights in the United States today is quite different from what it was in the mid-1950s. The days of "massive resistance" to integration, lunch counter sit-ins, freedom riders, and Governor George Wallace standing on the schoolhouse steps are gone. Public opinion has changed as well. Figure 6–1 and Table 6–2 reveal a growing acceptance of racial equality in the last twenty-five years or at least a growing reluctance to admit bigotry.[27] Table 6–2 shows a steady upswing in the number of people who report they would vote for a black president. Between 1958 and 1987, the number doubled from 38 percent to 79 percent. The survey results suggest that, in principle at least, a large number of Americans are ready to accept a black presidential or vice-presidential candidate. The election of Douglas Wilder as governor of Virginia and David Dinkins as mayor of New York demonstrate the ability of moderate black candidates to generate significant white support. Yet their narrow margins of victory compared to their election-eve polls and the larger margins of victory enjoyed by Wilder's white running mates reveal the continuation of some racial bias in voting.

Figure 6–1 indicates a decline in the proportion of whites who claim they would be upset if blacks moved into their neighborhoods. Note also the relationship between education levels and racial tolerance. Attitudes toward integrated schools have also changed. At the time of the *Brown* decision, only half the whites in the nation believed that black children and white children should go to the same school. By the 1980s, almost 90 percent of whites favored integration.

Racism and prejudice have not been eradicated in American society. A residual segment of the population clings to racial stereotypes. Although the proportion holding this belief has declined over the past decades, obstacles to racial harmony still remain. Overall, greater acceptance of racial equality by the public has convinced some that the battles have been won and that it is no longer necessary to enforce civil rights aggressively.

TABLE 6–2

CHANGING ATTITUDES ON RACE OF PRESIDENTIAL NOMINEE

Answers to the question "If your party nominated a generally well-qualified man for president and he happened to be black, would you vote for him?"

	Yes, Would (%)	No, Would Not (%)	No Opinion (%)
1987	79	13	8
1983	77	16	7
1971	70	23	7
1969	67	23	10
1967	54	40	6
1965	59	34	7
1963	47	45	8
1958	38	53	9

SOURCE: *Gallup Report*, no. 262 (July 1987): 19.

Equal Rights for Women

THE MAJORITY "MINORITY"

Blacks were not alone in having the full rights of citizenship denied them. Another "minority" that has had to struggle for equal rights actually composes a majority of the U.S. population—women. Discrimination against women has taken different form than discrimination against blacks. Segregation and Jim Crow laws were intended to place blacks in a subservient position because the majority perceived them as inferior. Laws limiting the rights of women were intended to "protect" them. Discrimination upheld the traditional role of women as the "second sex," whose proper place was in the home raising a family rather than in positions of power or responsibility in society. The results of this view of women were state and federal laws that treated women significantly differently from the way men were treated. In 1908, the Supreme Court justified such distinctive treatment

FIGURE 6–1

CHANGING ATTITUDES ON RACE

Percentage of nonblacks who agree with the statement, White people have a right to keep (Negroes/blacks) out of their neighborhoods.

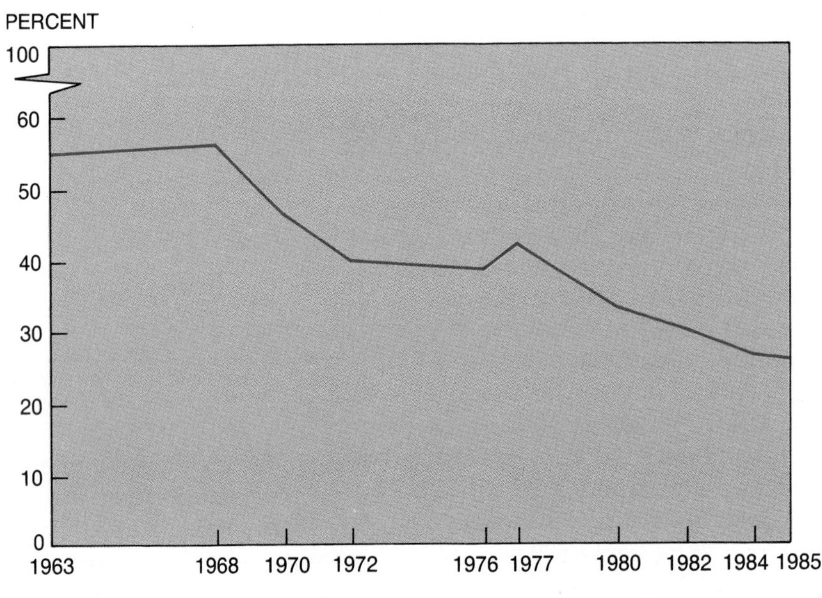

BY EDUCATION (Nonblacks' response):	1963	1985
	AGREE STRONGLY/SLIGHTLY	
Less than high school graduate	64%	45%
High school graduate	49	25
Some college	46	18
College graduate	37	12

SOURCE: *Public Opinion*, July–August 1987, p. 24. Reprinted with permission of American Enterprise Institute for Public Policy Research.

because of differences in "structure of body, in the functions to be performed . . . [and] in the capacity for long-continued labor."[28] It was not until the 1960s that a majority of Americans began to change their attitudes on the role and rights of women, both in the workplace and outside it.

ROOTS OF THE WOMEN'S MOVEMENT

No women were present at the Constitutional Convention, but some played key roles during the Revolutionary War. Still, it is fair to say that during the eighteenth and nineteenth centuries, women who wanted to take an active role in public affairs were considered unwomanly, if not worse. A number of women were instrumental in the movement to abolish slavery before the Civil War. Yet some of the men who were "progressive" in their views on slavery were less progressive when it came to women. At a Connecticut antislavery rally in 1840, the male chair resigned because a woman was allowed to address the meeting.[29] At an antislavery conference in London, the female delegates from the United States were allowed only to watch from the balcony behind a curtain. Offended by this treatment, the women in the antislavery

Suffragists demonstrating at turn of the century for women's right to vote.

movement called a Women's Rights Convention in Seneca Falls, New York, in 1848. Led by pioneer feminist Elizabeth Cady Stanton, the conference drafted a Women's Declaration of Independence. But as national tensions worsened, they temporarily put aside women's issues for the fight against slavery and for the duration of the Civil War.[30]

After the war, the movement resumed, taking two directions. The Thirteenth, Fourteenth, and Fifteenth Amendments did little for women, particularly in terms of political rights. Dissatisfied, some women heeded Stanton's 1848 call for the vote and began to push actively for women's suffrage. The concerns of the second group were with the stability of the family rather than with women's political rights. Troubled by the effects of alcohol on the family, they sought to make intoxicating drinks illegal and to gain other legal protections from the government for the family, such as legislation limiting child and women's labor and prostitution. Their main organization was the **Women's Christian Temperance Union (WCTU),** which grew rapidly from its founding in 1874. The WCTU succeeded in its primary objective when the Eighteenth Amendment, ushering in Prohibition, was ratified in 1919. The **women's suffrage movement** won its victory the next year when the **Nineteenth Amendment,** giving women the right to vote, was ratified in 1920.

By 1900, the women's suffrage movement had grown to significant proportions. The state of Wyoming, which had allowed women to vote when it was a territory, refused to join the Union without women's suffrage. Despite some congressional opposition to this "petticoat provision," Wyoming became the first state to intentionally allow women to vote. (Before the Civil War, New Jersey had accidentally left gender out of its constitutional qualifications to vote, so several women succeeded in doing so. This oversight was quickly amended.) Political Insight 6–3 shows some of the major milestones in the women's movement.

THE WOMEN'S MOVEMENT AND THE EQUAL RIGHTS AMENDMENT

World War II saw a great increase in the labor force participation of women as they left the home for the factory. But soon after the soldiers returned, most women returned to their more traditional roles. The modern women's movement began to gather steam

POLITICAL INSIGHT 6-3

MILESTONES IN THE WOMEN'S MOVEMENT

1790 Judith Sargent Murray publishes first American essay on women's rights.

1821 Emma Willard opens first secondary school for women in Troy, New York.

1824 First strike by female workers in United States, by Pawtucket, Rhode Island, weavers.

1833 Oberlin College (Ohio) founded as first coeducational college.

1837 Mount Holyoke College (Mass.) founded as first women's college.

1839 Mississippi adopts first United States Married Women's Property Act.

1845 Margaret Fuller publishes *Woman in the Nineteenth Century.*

1848 First U.S. women's rights convention meets at Seneca Falls, New York.

1849 Elizabeth Blackwell becomes the first female physician in the United States.

1853 Antoinette Brown ordained as first female minister in the United States.

1868 Susan B. Anthony begins publication of a weekly newspaper, *The Revolution.*

1869 Anthony and Elizabeth Cady Stanton found National Woman Suffrage Association.

1869 Wyoming Territory becomes the first place in United States to permit women to vote.

1870 Ada H. Kepley becomes first female law graduate in United States.

1872 Anthony arrested and convicted for registering to vote.

1872 Victoria Woodhull campaigns as first female candidate for president.

1875 Supreme Court rules that the Fourteenth and Fifteenth Amendments do not give women equal protection.

1876 Frances Willard becomes head of Woman's Christian Temperance Union.

1878 Woman Suffrage Amendment first introduced in Congress.

1889 General Federation of Women's Clubs founded.

1890 Suffragists unite as National American Woman Suffrage Association.

1898 National Association of Colored Women founded.

1898 Utah becomes first state to permit women to serve on juries.

1903 National Women's Trade Union League founded.

1913 Alice Paul leads suffrage demonstration at President Wilson's inauguration.

1916 Emma Goldman arrested for advocating birth control.

1916 Jeanette Rankin of Montana becomes first woman elected to Congress.

(Continued on next page.)

in the 1960s, following publication of Betty Friedan's *The Feminine Mystique* and other writings critical of sexist institutions and roles. Unlike their WCTU great-grandmothers, those in the women's movement turned away from protectionism and challenged the gender-based distinctions embodied in law and social norms. They formed several organizations that have had significant political impact. The **National Organization for Women (NOW)** and the National Women's Political Caucus (NWPC) became active in promoting one of the key goals of the women's movement: the **Equal Rights Amendment (ERA).**

The failure of the ERA in 1982 represented a setback to the women's movement, but the defeat does not obscure the social change that occurred in the preceding two decades. The ERA was passed by both houses of Congress in 1972 by substantial margins. At first, it appeared fairly noncontroversial, reading simply: "Equality of rights under the law shall not be denied or abridged by the United States or by any state on account of sex." Its primary objective was to replace the presumption that women should be treated differently from men with a presumption that they should be treated equally under the law. The amendment would have

POLITICAL INSIGHT 6–3

1917	Arrest of militant suffrage demonstrators in Washington, D.C.
1919	Congress passes the Woman's Suffrage Amendment.
1920	Nineteenth Amendment gives women the vote.
1920	Suffrage leagues reorganized as League of Women Voters.
1922	Rebecca Felton of Georgia becomes first woman in Senate (appointed).
1923	Alice Paul writes the Equal Rights Amendment (ERA).
1925	Nellie Taylor Ross of Wyoming becomes the first female governor.
1932	Hattie Caraway of Arkansas becomes the first female elected to the Senate.
1933	President Roosevelt names Frances Perkins secretary of labor, the first woman in the cabinet.
1957	Civil Rights Act permits women to serve on federal juries.
1961	President Kennedy establishes first Commission on the Status of Women.
1961	Betty Friedan's *The Feminine Mystique* is published.
1963	Equal Pay Act mandates equal pay for equal work.
1964	Civil Rights Act (Title VII) forbids sex discrimination in employment.
1966	National Organization for Women (NOW) founded.
1968	Shirley Chisholm of New York becomes first black congresswoman.
1970	New York State legalizes abortion.
1970	President Nixon names first female generals in the United States.
1972	Congress passes the ERA, banning discrimination on account of sex.
1972	Congress passes Equal Employment Opportunity Act to extend Civil Rights Act.
1973	Supreme Court legalizes abortion in all states.
1975	International Women's Year.
1981	Sandra Day O'Connor becomes first woman on Supreme Court.
1982	Deadline expires for ratification of the ERA.
1984	Geraldine Ferraro becomes first female candidate for vice-president.
1987	Supreme Court rules that states may require private all-male clubs to admit women members.
1988	Episcopal Church elects Reverend Barbara Harris the first woman bishop in the world-wide Anglican communion.
1990	Captain Linda Bray becomes first woman to lead an American military unit in combat, during the invasion of Panama.

SOURCE: Professor Steven C. Hause, Department of History, University of Missouri—St. Louis.

affected thousands of provisions of federal law that make gender-based distinctions and even more provisions of state law, such as those dealing with property and inheritance rights, head of household and homestead, family structure, child custody and support, criminal acts against wives, statutory rape, and equal pay laws.

Something happened to the ERA on the way to ratification. Following an initial period, when a large number of states ratified quickly, the amendment question burst into controversy. Conservatives, including many women, opposed the amendment on substantive and symbolic grounds. A few states tried to rescind their initial ratification. Opponents argued that women should not lose the protections of the laws. There were charges that the amendment would lead to unisex bathrooms, marriages between homosexuals, and women in front-line combat. By 1979, advocates were only a few states short of the necessary three-fourths needed to ratify. Congress agreed to extend the time period for ratification for three more years, but it was to no avail. The amendment died in 1982, three states short of ratification. President Reagan opposed ratification of the ERA during his 1980 campaign. The WCTU, still around and

Women have more occupational choices today than a decade ago, including traditionally male occupations such as auto mechanic.

claiming several hundred thousand members, also opposed it.

Legal Equality and Inequality

Courts, like other institutions, react to both social and political changes in applying the Constitution to legal conflicts. The Supreme Court's decision in 1908 on the legal status of women would seem as out-of-date in today's world as the *Plessy* decision. While fighting for the ERA in Congress and the state legislatures, women have taken their cases to court to challenge "gender-based discrimination."[31] Resulting decisions have affected men as well as women.

The courts were slow to change. As late as 1948, the Supreme Court upheld a Michigan law that prohibited a woman from tending bar unless she was the wife or daughter of the male owner.[32] In 1971, however, a similar law in California was overturned as a violation of both the Fourteenth Amendment and the 1964 Civil Rights Act.[33] In the 1970s, the Court took up an increasing number of gender-based discrimination cases. In one case, it ruled that a company could not refuse to hire women with preschool-age children if they also hired men with young children.[34] In 1975, the courts acted to clarify the rights of pregnant women, ruling that it was "arbitrary and unreasonable" to require an expectant mother to take maternity leave three months before she was due.[35] The Supreme Court ruled in the 1970s that states could not automatically exclude women from juries or make "being female" grounds for an automatic exemption from jury duty.[36] Further, the Court overturned gender-based discrimination in cases of the legal age of majority, height and weight requirements for employment, and the legal drinking age.

In a number of other areas, however, the courts have allowed **gender-based distinctions** in the law. In 1974, the Supreme Court upheld a California ruling that excluded pregnancy-related complications from the awarding of disability benefits.[37] In the same year, the Court allowed the state of Florida to grant a property tax exemption to widows that was not granted to widowers.[38] Under a decision announced by the Court in 1975, the Navy can legally retain women passed up for promotion, even though men must be discharged if not promoted in the same time.[39] Perhaps the most important case upholding gender-based discrimination in recent years was the 1981 case concerning the all-male draft. In *Rostker v. Goldberg* (1981), the Supreme Court ruled by a 6-to-3 vote that although it recognized its responsibility to determine legitimate gender-based distinctions, here it would defer to Congress. In his opinion, Justice William Rehnquist noted:

> The reason women are exempt from registration is not because military needs can be met by drafting men. This is not a case of Congress arbitrarily choosing to burden one of two similarly situated groups, such as would be the case with an all-black or all-white, or an all-Catholic or all-Lutheran, or an all-Republican or an all-Democratic registration. Men and women, because of the combat restrictions of women, are simply not similarly situated for the purposes of a draft or registration for a draft.[40]

The Court has chosen a path of determining on a case-by-case basis whether the distinction based on gender is legitimate or an illegitimate violation of equal protection for women. The failure of the ERA means that the battle for women's rights will continue to be fought primarily in the courts.

WOMEN IN POLITICS

Like other minorities, women have sought greater influence in American politics in a number of ways, including running for office. Since 1972, the "equal division rule" of the Democratic party guarantees that 50 percent of the national convention delegates will be women. On Capitol Hill, twenty-seven women served in the House of Representatives and Senate in 1990. Congresswoman Geraldine Ferraro of New York became the first woman nominated by a major party for the vice-presidency, in 1984.

The political objectives of women are varied. Conservative women hold views very similar to those of conservative men and oppose many of the goals of the women's movement as threatening to the family structure. Abortion is a particularly divisive issue. Feminists generally support the right to choose abortion. There is greater consensus among women on the need for equal pay for equal work. Laws guaranteeing equal pay have been adopted in many states, but significant gaps in earning still exist.

By 1978, for the first time in American history, more women were out working than remained in the home. The percentage of women in the work force has continued to rise and with it the importance of economic issues relating to working couples and single-female-headed households. Day care, retirement benefits, and medical and maternity benefits are of more concern to women than they were a generation ago. In many areas, men and women have very similar attitudes, but in the 1980s, a "gender gap" existed, a problem for presidential candidate George Bush. Some preelection polls found a gender gap as large as 25 percent in terms of his support among males and females.

How are female candidates perceived by the electorate, compared with male candidates? Gallup polls taken over a period of fifty years show growing acceptance of the idea of electing a woman president. The proportion of voters who would not vote for a qualified woman has declined from 65 percent in 1937 to 12 percent in 1987 (see Table 6–3). A poll conducted for the National Women's Political Caucus found widespread if not complete acceptance of women in politics.[41] A majority of the respondents believed that a woman could do the job of president as well as a man could. Many perceptions of female candidates were shared by men and women alike. On such issues as day care, education, and helping the have-nots in society, women were thought to be more capable than

TABLE 6–3

CHANGING ATTITUDES ABOUT FEMALE PRESIDENTIAL NOMINEES

Answers to the question "If your party nominated a woman for president, would you vote for her if she were qualified for the job?"

	Yes (%)	No (%)	No opinion (%)
1987	82	12	6
1984	78	17	5
1983	80	16	4
1978	76	19	5
1971	66	29	5
1969	54	39	7
1967	57	39	4
1958	52	44	4
1949	48	48	4
1937	31	65	4

SOURCE: *Gallup Report*, no. 262 (July 1987): 17.

men. Men were perceived to be better on technical issues, such as arms control and trade. Yet compared with their male counterparts, women still face many obstacles when running for political office. The survey revealed that resistance to having women in public office increased with the importance of the office. For example, 31 percent of respondents believed that a female president could not do as good a job as a man, compared with only 5 percent who felt the same about election to school board. While some resistance to female candidates still exists, women are now closer to being accepted as full partners in the electoral arena.

New Civil Rights Concerns

Economic Equality versus Political Equality

Despite some progress in recent years, significant differences in the education, income, and employment status of white males compared with blacks, women, and other minorities still exist. In pursuing economic equality, the civil rights movement has come up against norms of American political economy generally opposing redistribution of wealth. Some old civil rights supporters who favored granting legal equality oppose the economic agenda of the new civil rights leaders. Morris Abram, an early civil rights supporter well regarded by black leaders in the 1960s but opposed by them in the 1980s, describes what he sees as the distinction between civil rights and economic equality:

> The new movement treated economic claims as civil rights, by embracing an idea of "rights" that included economic entitlement—a "right" to shelter, a "right" to health care, a "right" to day care for children. The [civil rights] movement demanded these "rights" although none of them are to be found in the Constitution.
>
> The allocation of economic resources is obviously important to the social progress of American blacks. But . . . people do not have a constitutional right to health care or housing subsidies, any more than a farmer has a constitutional right to a tobacco subsidy, or Chrysler to a bailout. There may be sound reasons—moral, practical or otherwise—for providing these things, but they are not civil rights.[42]

What are the civil rights goals in the 1990s? Jesse Jackson's campaigns have focused on economic justice. Black leaders want to link civil rights with economic issues—employment, fiscal and monetary policy, and other policies—in an effort to promote greater economic equality in the United States. Many women's groups advocate the concept of "comparable worth"—equal pay for jobs that require equivalent skills, training, and education. For example, comparable worth regulations would require that secretaries be paid as much as meter readers or grounds keepers. The U.S. Civil Rights Commission has rejected comparable worth as a policy. Chapter 19 takes a closer look at economic inequality and social welfare policy.

New Civil Rights Groups

As the battle to achieve full civil rights for blacks and women has entered a new phase, other racial and ethnic minorities in society have begun pressing their claims. Hispanics, the third largest group in the United States, are now represented in a number of elective offices. Economic issues are major concerns for Hispanics—like other minorities, they tend to be among the have-nots in society—and immigration from Mexico is a particularly important issue. The exception is Cuban refugees in Florida who tend to be affluent and conservative. The Hispanic caucus in the House opposed the 1984 Simpson-Mazzoli immigration bill, which provided penalties for employers hiring illegal aliens and in the caucus's view threatened the civil rights of all Hispanic Americans. The caucus has also been very concerned about government policy in Central America.

Native Americans, once run off their land, slaughtered, or put on reservations, were quiet for decades. Recently, through groups like the **American Indian Movement,** they have taken an active role in politics to achieve full civil rights and economic betterment. Indians, like other minorities, have beseeched the courts to right old wrongs. Their victories in a number of cases have resulted in financial compensation for lands illegally taken from them by state governments.

The disabled emerged from obscurity to become a political force in recent years. Among other goals, the estimated 43 million Americans with some sort

Mourners at the AIDS quilt in Washington, D.C., signifying dissatisfaction with government policy towards gays.

of disability want the right to physical access to allow them to exercise their full political rights and to compete more effectively in the economic world. Federal statutes and regulations made some strides in increasing access to public buildings. In 1975, the Education for All Handicapped Children Act passed the Congress, mandating special education programs across the country.[43] Although the disabled enjoy sympathy and support from the majority population, some resistance to increased program spending accompanied the antiregulation, antigovernment mood of the 1980s. In 1990, however, the landmark Americans with Disabilities Act extended to the disabled rights already guaranteed to women, racial, religious, and ethnic minorities under the 1964 Civil Rights Act. The bill protects disabled people from discrimination in employment and public accommodations. It also requires that public transportation systems, telecommunications, and other public services be accessible to all.

One of the last groups to press claims for full political and social rights is the gay community. Homosexuals long stayed out of the public view, but recently have taken a more direct approach to politics. In cities such as New York and San Francisco, the gay community is a powerful voting bloc, and several homosexuals have won elective office. Gays have brought a number of lawsuits to the courts in an attempt to prevent discrimination in employment and other areas, but they have met resistance from the judicial system. Homosexuality is still a crime in many states, and the U.S. Supreme Court has upheld the constitutionality of such statutes. Estimates are that as much as 10 percent of the population is gay, suggesting that the group will be heard from more in the future.

THE RIGHT OF PRIVACY

When President Reagan nominated Robert Bork for the vacancy on the Supreme Court in the summer of 1987, cries of protest arose from groups representing women and minorities. Representatives of blacks, women, Hispanics, and homosexuals condemned Bork for his judicial writings and decisions hostile to civil rights and the right of privacy. After a monumental battle, the Senate voted not to confirm Bork's nomination.

The **right of privacy** has become a key issue for civil rights groups, particularly women and homosexuals. While the right of privacy has deep roots in American history, it has only recently been recognized by the Supreme Court. In 1965, in the case of *Griswold v. Connecticut*, the Court ruled by a vote of 7-to-2 that a state law prohibiting dissemination of birth control information was a violation of the marital right of privacy. Justice William O. Douglas wrote for the majority that "zones of privacy" older than the Bill of Rights existed, even if not spelled out in the Constitution.[44] Bork and others countered that the Court had erred and that there was no such thing as a right of privacy.

The *Griswold* decision became an important precedent in the controversial *Roe v. Wade* (1973) decision, which legalized abortion.[45] Privacy, particularly sexual privacy, continues to be an issue of utmost concern in the 1990s. In one of the most controversial decisions of the 1980s, the Supreme Court ruled in 1986 that despite the right of privacy, it was constitutional for states to ban homosexual conduct, even in private. In ***Bowers v. Hardwick*** (1986), a narrow 5-to-4 majority upheld Georgia's antisodomy law. Some twenty-four states and the District of Columbia outlaw homosexual conduct, even in private between consenting adults. Dissenting opinions were sharply worded. "Depriving individuals of the right to choose for themselves how to conduct their intimate relationships poses a far greater threat to the values most deeply rooted in our nation's history than tolerance of nonconformity could ever do."[46]

Civil rights battles in the 1990s reflect many new issues and concerns, encompassing both economic and political claims by African Americans, Hispanics, women, gays and lesbians, Native Americans, and the disabled. The Supreme Court will continue to play a critical role in determining public policy in civil rights, but Congress, the president, the bureaucracy, and state governments are also heavily involved. As the Supreme Court reverses the course of recent decades, dissenting justices have issued increasingly bitter complaints. In his dissent to the *Wards Cove* decision, Justice Harry Blackmun wrote, "One wonders whether the majority still believes that race discrimination—or, more accurately, race discrimination against nonwhites—is a problem in our society, or even remembers that it was."[47]

SUMMARY AND CONCLUSIONS

1. Throughout American history, certain groups in society have not been afforded the same political rights and economic opportunities as others. The politics of civil rights concerns the attempt of these groups to achieve equal rights.
2. American blacks were subject to pervasive discrimination deriving from the practice of slavery. The Civil War, the ultimate governing crisis in American history, was fought over fundamental differences in the social and economic systems of North and South.
3. During Reconstruction, Congress attempted to provide civil rights for blacks, but Supreme Court rulings upholding states' actions undermined those attempts, and complete segregation of the races was established in the South.
4. The decision in *Brown v. Board of Education* (1954) began the new era of the civil rights movement when the Court ruled that "separate was inherently unequal."
5. Progress was slow during the judicial era of civil rights because of massive resistance to desegregation in the South. Successful implementation of civil rights required legislative and executive participation in addition to judicial enforcement.
6. The Civil Rights Act of 1964 and the Voting Rights Act of 1965 furnished the strongest legal basis for black civil rights in American history.
7. The civil rights movement has changed in recent years, with a growing emphasis on economic issues. Civil rights remain controversial, particularly on questions of affirmative action, quotas, and reverse discrimination.
8. The women's movement for equal rights has a long history but only recently has affected significant change. Although the ERA was not ratified, progress has been made in eliminating many gender-based distinctions that discriminate against women.
9. The civil rights movement in the 1990s includes many new groups making demands on the political system for greater civil rights, including the right of privacy.

Voting is a right that most Americans take for granted. But for many years, blacks, women, and others were denied the opportunity to take part in this essential act of a representative democracy. In the preceding pages, the movement to guarantee equal rights to blacks, women, and other minorities has been examined. It is still an ongoing struggle. As with civil liberties, the politics of civil rights involves conflict: affirmative action versus seniority; the rights of the majority versus the rights of the minority.

The ability to govern in the United States has been sorely tested over questions of civil rights. The Civil War was the most serious crisis, but others have followed. In the 1950s and 1960s, civil rights bills in Congress were bottled up by a determined opposition willing to use every conceivable delaying tactic to prevent the majority from passing legislation. The limits of the Supreme Court's ability to carry out its decisions became apparent after the *Brown* decision. Lower courts dragged their heels, and state legislatures, governors, and school boards all obstructed enforcement. The fragmented structure of Congress and the entire federal system with its multiple layers of government limit governing capacity when a determined group wants to stall or delay. How will the political system respond to growing economic inequities between the majority and minorities in America?

KEY TERMS

affirmative action
American Indian Movement
Bakke case
Bowers v. Hardwick
Brown v. Board of Education
Civil Rights Act of 1964
de facto and de jure segregation
Dred Scott case
Equal Employment Opportunity Commission (EEOC)
equal opportunity
Equal Rights Amendment (ERA)
gender-based distinctions
grandfather clause
literacy test
National Organization for Women (NOW)
Nineteenth Amendment
right of privacy
"separate but equal" doctrine
sit-in
Thirteenth, Fourteenth, and Fifteenth Amendments
Voting Rights Act of 1965
Women's Christian Temperance Union (WCTU)
white primary
women's suffrage movement

SELF-REVIEW

1. Why was the Civil War a governing crisis?
2. How did "Jim Crow" laws institute segregation?
3. How were black voters disenfranchised?
4. What was the effect of the 1954 *Brown* decision?
5. How did political economy affect civil rights strategies and enforcement?
6. What did the Civil Rights Act of 1964 and the Voting Rights Act of 1965 provide?
7. How did the civil rights movement change in the 1960s?
8. How has school integration been implemented?
9. Explain equal opportunity, affirmative action, and preferential treatment.
10. How have public attitudes on race changed in the past decades?
11. Describe changes in affirmative action during the Bush administration.
12. What is the background of the women's movement?
13. What is the ERA?
14. What are some court rulings against gender-based distinctions?

SUGGESTED READINGS

Bell, Derrick. *And We Are Not Saved: The Elusive Quest for Racial Justice.* 1987.
An allegorical discourse on racial equality.

Friedan, Betty. *The Feminine Mystique.* 1961.
The book some say started the "women's liberation movement" still provides perspective on sexual stereotyping and roles.

Kluger, Richard. *Simple Justice.* 1977.
A long but brilliant account of the 1954 *Brown* decision and the events that led up to it.

Thernstrom, Abigail. *Whose Votes Count?* 1987.
A controversial analysis of affirmative action and how the Voting Rights Act has been enforced.

NOTES

1. Harrell R. Rodgers, Jr. and Charles S. Bullock, *Law and Social Change* (New York: McGraw-Hill, 1972), 17.
2. Charles E. Silberman, *Crises in Black and White* (New York: Vintage, 1964), 23.
3. U.S. Commission on Civil Rights, *Voting, 1961* (Washington, D.C.: Government Printing Office, 1961), 91–97.
4. Rodgers and Bullock, *Law and Social Change*, 57.
5. *Guinn v. U.S.* (238 U.S. 347, 1915).
6. *Missouri ex rel. Gaines v. Canada* (305 U.S. 337, 1938).
7. *Sweatt v. Painter* (339 U.S. 629, 1950).
8. See Martin Luther King, Jr., *Stride toward Freedom* (New York: Harper, 1958).
9. See Joel B. Grossman, "A Model for Judicial Policy Analysis: The Supreme Court and Sit-in Cases," in Joel Grossman and Joseph Tanenhaus, eds., *Frontiers of Judicial Research* (New York: Wiley, 1969), 247.
10. Rodgers and Bullock, *Law and Social Change*, 203.
11. Bruce Miroff, *Pragmatic Illusions: Presidential Politics of John F. Kennedy* (New York: David McKay, 1976), 269.
12. Eric Goldman, *The Tragedy of Lyndon Johnson* (New York: Knopf, 1969), 488.
13. See Rodgers and Bullock, *Law and Social Change*, 62.
14. *Ibid.*, 29.
15. Congressional Quarterly Inc., *Revolution in Civil Rights* (Washington, D.C., 1968), 93.
16. See *Griffin v. County School Board* (377 U.S. 218, 1964).
17. Lucius J. Barker and Twiley W. Barker, Jr., *Civil Liberties and the Constitution*, 4th ed. (Englewood Cliffs, N.J.: Prentice-Hall, 1982).
18. Also see *North Carolina State Board of Education v. Swann* (402 U.S. 43, 1971).
19. *Firefighters v. Stotts* (No. 82-206, 1984); *New York Times*, 17 June 1984.
20. *Local 28 of the Sheet Metal Workers International v. EEOC* 106 S.Ct. 3019 1986.
21. *City of Richmond v. J.A. Croson Co.* (109 S.Ct. 706, 1989).
22. *Patterson v. McLean Credit Union* (109 S.Ct. 2363, 1989).
23. *Martin v. Wilks* (109 S.Ct. 2180, 1989).
24. *Lorance v. AT&T Technologies* (109 S.Ct. 2261, 1989).
25. *Wards Cove Packing Co. v. Atonio* (109 S.Ct. 2115, 1989).
26. *Wall Street Journal*, 26 March 1990, p. 1.
27. American Enterprise Institute, *Public Opinion*, July–August 1987.
28. *Muller v. Oregon* (208 U.S. 412, 1908).
29. Lillian O'Connor, *Pioneer Women Orators* (New York: Columbia University Press, 1954), 36.
30. See Judith Hole and Ellen Levine, *Rebirth of Feminism* (New York: Quadrangle, 1971).
31. Barker and Barker, *Civil Liberties*, 568.
32. *Goesaert v. Cleary* (335 U.S. 464, 1948).
33. *Sail'er Inn Inc. v. Kirby* (485 P.2d 529 fn 15, 1971).
34. *Reed v. Reed* (404 U.S. 71, 1972).
35. *Lafleur v. Cleveland Board of Education* (414 U.S. 632, 1975).
36. *Taylor v. Louisiana* (419 U.S. 522, 1975) and *Duren v. Missouri* (439 U.S. 357, 1979).
37. *Geduldig v. Aiello* (417 U.S. 484, 1974).
38. *Kahn v. Shevin* (416 U.S. 361, 1974).
39. See *Schlesinger v. Ballard* (419 U.S. 498, 1975).
40. *Rostker v. Goldberg* (101 S.Ct. 2646, 1981).
41. Morris Abram, "What Constitutes a Civil Right?" *New York Times Magazine, 10 June 1984, pp. 52–58.*
42. See Erwin L. Levine and Elizabeth M. Wexler, *P.L. 94–142: An Act of Congress* (New York: Macmillan, 1981).
43. *Griswold v. Connecticut* (381 U.S. 479, 1965).
44. See *Roe v. Wade* (410 U.S. 113, 1973).
45. *Bowers v. Hardwick* (1987) S.Ct. 2841.
46. *Congressional Quarterly Weekly Reports*, 8 July 1989, p. 1697.
47. *Ibid.*

SECTION TWO

PEOPLE AND POLITICS

The second section of *Politics in America* looks at the occasions in democratic politics where the people and the government come together most closely. Parties, elections, the media, and interest groups serve as linkage institutions between the public and its leaders. Chapter 7 examines public opinion—what the people think about their political system and the issues confronting it. The sources of opinions, the interrelationship of opinions, and public participation in politics are also considered. Political parties—the coalitions of interests seeking political office to affect public policy—are explored in Chapter 8. The role of parties in bridging institutional gaps and fostering effective governing is of particular interest. Voting and elections, key elements of a representative democracy, are the subject of Chapter 9. Important developments in the contest for the presidency are investigated and analyzed. Some of the most dramatic changes in elections have been brought about by the increasing impact of the mass media. Chapter 10 focuses on the mass media in the United States—its organization and impact on people and politics. Finally, Chapter 11 looks at how people organize to promote common interests through groups and political action committees to influence both the outcome of elections and the policy-making process. The key linkage institutions examined in this section not only define the public's role in politics but also go a long way toward determining the ability of the political system to govern.

CHAPTER 7

Public Opinion and Political Behavior

POLITICAL CLOSE-UP

The Poll with the Money-Back Guarantee

The name most associated with public opinion polls is that of an Iowa farm boy who became interested in discovering how people responded to what they read in the newspaper. In the late 1920s, George Gallup wrote a doctoral thesis on a new objective technique for measuring reader interest in newspapers. His technique contained the basic concepts of random sampling that would make public opinion polling accurate.

In 1935, Gallup founded the American Institute of Public Opinion and conducted the first Gallup poll. But the first real test was the 1936 election. Gallup went up against the well-established *Literary Digest* poll that had successfully predicted the outcome of presidential elections in the 1920s. The *Digest* poll was huge, made up of responses from subscribers plus people culled from lists of automobile registrations and the telephone directory. With more than 3 million responses, the *Digest* confidently predicted an Alf Landon landslide in 1936. Using only about 1,500 respondents, Gallup grew increasingly nervous as November approached and his results continued to predict a strong Franklin Roosevelt victory. Gallup had given a money-back guarantee if he were wrong to the newspapers that subscribed to his poll . Not only his reputation but also his fledgling polling institute hung in the balance.

George Gallup.

The results are history. The *Literary Digest,* lucky in previous predictions of Republican victories, had a systematic bias in its poll that Gallup avoided. The outcome made his reputation. He was soon joined in the business by Louis Harris, Burns Roper, and others. In one of his first columns in 1935, Gallup explained the benefits of objectively measuring the opinions of the "unorganized majority":

> There is now being conducted and published each week a nation-wide poll, the purpose of which is to ascertain public opinion. . . . The weekly poll . . . seeks to make public opinion articulate. In polls published to date the public has expressed its opinion of the federal relief and recovery expenditures, has indicated President Roosevelt's present political popularity, and expressed its opinion on the effects of repeal [of Prohibition.] Future issues will . . . include such questions as the immediate payment of the bonus, the power of the Supreme Court, government regulation of business, and others of equal national interest and importance.
>
> Many political writers have said that the organized minorities in America, with their pressure organizations and their lobbyists in Washington, exert a preponderant influence on legislation. Whatever the ultimate value to the process of democratic government, this weekly poll will make it possible, for the first time, to learn what the unorganized majority thinks about the issues and laws which affect the daily lives of American citizens.*

But half a century later, have politicians become obsessed with polls and maintaining their own popularity?

SOURCE: *Gallup's 15 November 1935, column reprinted in *Washington Post National Weekly Edition,* 13 August 1984, p. 37.

CHAPTER OUTLINE

INTRODUCTION AND OVERVIEW

In a nation exemplifying freedom of expression, why are U.S. politicians so reluctant to tell the public the truth about hard choices and tough issues? Fear of public opinion seems to stifle meaningful debate about key issues. A liberal legislator is warned by his pollster not to make a speech calling for deep cuts in the military because it is too far out in front of public opinion. A conservative law clerk is afraid to publish law review articles because of what happened to Judge Robert Bork in the Senate confirmation hearings over his nomination to the Supreme Court. A U.S. senator retiring after twenty-four years in Congress cited his frustration with the new breed of "wet finger politicians" who spend more time testing the political winds than reading policy papers.[1]

Public opinion has a profound effect on governing. It reflects concern with public problems and establishes boundaries for policy responses. But while democracy embodies following the will of the people, it also involves leadership—efforts to inform and enlighten public opinion. The Founders had doubts about mass opinion and participatory democracy, fearing the rise of demagogues fostering mob hysteria. Therefore, in creating a representative democracy, they placed buffers between the people and their leaders. Disagreement over leading or following public opinion continued at the beginning of the twentieth century. James Bryce claimed that public opinion "towered over" presidents, congresses, and state legislatures.[2] Walter Lippman, echoing Alexander Hamilton's doubts, wrote, "The unhappy truth is that the prevailing public opinion has been destructively wrong at the critical junctures."[3]

The growing prevalence of scientific public opinion polls of the kind pioneered by George Gallup have changed the nature of American politics. Have elected officials in the United States become too preoccupied with polls and their approval ratings? Does declining voter turnout indicate that many Americans are turned off by the feel-good platitudes they hear from politicians? These are difficult but essential questions about the performance of American democracy in the 1990s. In this chapter, we will explore what Americans believe, how public opinion is measured, how opinions are formed, and how people act on their opinions and attempt to clarify the link between public opinion and governing. The following questions are addressed:

1. How does public opinion shape boundaries for governing?
2. What do Americans believe? What are their attitudes concerning political economy? Do Americans trust their government?
3. How is public opinion measured? Are polls and surveys dependable?
4. What are the sources of public opinion? How does political socialization take place?
5. Are Americans ideological? How are liberalism and conservatism to be understood in the context of American politics?
6. How do citizens participate in politics? What determines whether a person is very active or a nonparticipant?

Public Opinion and the Ability to Govern

WHAT IS PUBLIC OPINION?

Public opinion is the collective beliefs and attitudes of the people. Our concern here is with political opinions—attitudes about issues, candidates, political parties, rights, and government in general. Despite the legions of pollsters at work, public opinion is complex and often difficult to explain. Public opinion is often fluid and changing, but polls and surveys are only a snapshot at a given moment in time.[4] In the 1988 presidential primaries, polls taken on Friday before Tuesday voting often missed actual totals by 15 or 20 percent after last-minute weekend media blitzes. Even when politicians are able to accurately gauge popular sentiment, they often find it difficult to govern effectively and successfully appeal to the public. Public opinion has a critical impact on governing throughout the policy process, from agenda-setting through policy approval to implementation.

Opinions have certain characteristics.[5] First, opinions have a *direction:* for or against, positive or negative. Second, opinions are held with different levels of *intensity:* some people are dead set against welfare, others are just mildly against it. Opinions on moral issues—such as abortion, the draft, and capital punishment—tend to be held the most intensely. Third, opinions have varying degrees of *stability*. Some, like support of broad democratic principles, are highly stable over time. Others, like support for increased defense spending, change rapidly in a relatively short period of time.

Political opinions on public policy issues form their own unique pattern. The president or Congress may find that a favorable pattern can quickly disintegrate when policies are proposed or enacted. Political institutions and leaders are constantly trying to ascertain opinion, respond to opinion, and manipulate opinion to their advantage.

PUBLIC INFORMATION ABOUT POLITICS

Representative democracy, in theory, translates the views of the citizens into public policy through a representative process. But a number of factors prevent this ideal from becoming reality. First, many people do not have relevant opinions on issues. Second, it is often very difficult to determine just what public opinion is even when it exists. Third, the relationship between public opinion and policy-makers is a two-way street: opinion shapes policy, leaders shape opinion.

Politics is not the most important thing in life for most people. Many Americans are not well informed about politics, lacking basic information about officeholders, institutions, and policies. Table 7–1 examines the public's level of political information measured in surveys taken since 1945. Although many would like to see a better informed and more active citizenry, public opinion

TABLE 7–1

LEVEL OF POLITICAL INFORMATION AMONG THE ADULT PUBLIC, 1945–1987

		Year	Source[a]
94%	Know the capital city of the United States	1945	AIPO
94%	Know the president's term is four years	1951	AIPO
93%	Recognize a photograph of the current president	1948	AIPO
89%	Can name the governor of their home state	1973	Harris
83%	Are aware of the right to jury trial	1987	Hearst
80%	Know the meaning of the term "veto"	1947	AIPO
79%	Can name the current vice-president	1978	NORC
78%	Know what the initials FBI stand for	1949	AIPO
74%	Know the meaning of the term "wiretapping"	1969	AIPO
70%	Can name their mayor	1967	AIPO
69%	Know which party has the most members in the U.S. House of Representatives	1978	NORC
68%	Know that the president is limited to two terms	1970	CPS
63%	Know that China is communist	1972	CPS
63%	Have some understanding of the term "conservative"	1960	SRC
58%	Know the meaning of the term "open housing"	1967	AIPO
52%	Know that there are two U.S. senators from their state	1978	NORC
46%	Can name their congressman	1973	Harris
41%	Are aware that the Bill of Rights is the first ten amendments to the U.S. Constitution	1987	Hearst
39%	Can name both U.S. senators from their state	1973	Harris
38%	Know Russia is not a NATO member	1964	AIPO
34%	Can name the current U.S. secretary of state	1978	NORC
31%	Know the meaning of "no-fault" insurance	1977	AIPO
30%	Know that the term of a U.S. House member is two years	1978	NORC
28%	Can name their state senator	1967	AIPO
23%	Know which two nations are involved in SALT	1979	CBS/*NYT*

[a] See source note below for abbreviations.

SOURCE: American Institute of Public Opinion (Gallup) (AIPO); Center for Political Studies (CPS); Lou Harris and Associates; National Opinion Research Center (NORC), CBS/*New York Times* (CBS/NYT), Hearst Corporation. Reported in Robert Erikson, Norman Luttbeg, and Kent Tedin, *American Public Opinion* (New York: Macmillan, 1988),42.

nonetheless is important in shaping public policy. Even if people do not have a sophisticated understanding of specific issues, a majority have general impressions about how things are going and how well leaders are performing.

Citizens have help in their efforts to keep public policy attuned to public opinion. Linkage institutions such as political parties, interest groups, and the media help bridge the gap between the people and the government. Those who are particularly interested in and informed about politics are often opinion-leaders.[6] Friends, neighbors, and work associates may look to them for cues on complex issues. Even if a majority of people are not following the ins and outs of politics, "attentive publics" do. Relatively low levels of public information, and interest in politics do not mean there is little accountability or responsiveness in the system. Quite the contrary. The concern today is that politicians have become timid, afraid to say or do anything risky or unpopular.

PUBLIC OPINION AND THE BOUNDARIES FOR GOVERNING

Different patterns of public opinion shape the options of policy-makers. Figure 7–1 shows some of these patterns. Two basic elements are the percentage of the population that holds the opinion (vertical axis) and the direction and intensity of the

FIGURE 7–1

GENERAL PATTERNS OF PUBLIC OPINION

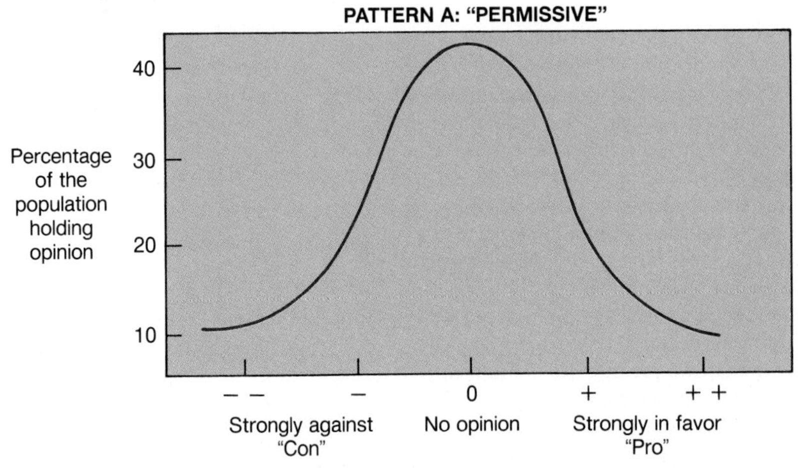

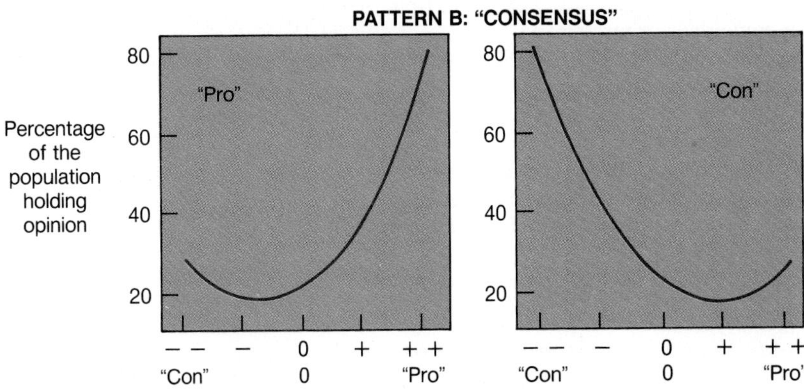

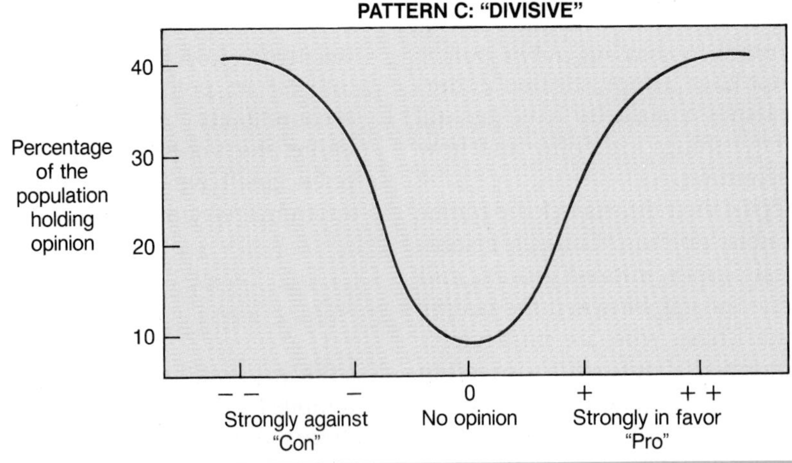

opinion (– – to + +, horizontal axis). Note the portion of the population with no opinion or weak opinion (clustering around the center). Pattern A is a "**permissive" pattern.** Supporters and opponents are approximately equally divided, but most people have no opinion. Facing such an opinion configuration, leaders may act freely without fear of much public reaction. An example might be public attitudes on whether or not to make the Environmental Protection Agency a cabinet department: most citizens have no opinion, and those that do hold them without much intensity. The patterns in B represent a "**consensus" pattern** of opinion. Agreement exists, but this time most people have an opinion. Politicians' options are more limited with this pattern; they increasingly fear opposing the majority. An example of a supportive consensus would be approval of Social Security; an example of a nonsupportive consensus would be opposition to tax increases.

NBC conducting exit poll.

The "**divisive" pattern** of public opinion in C reflects deep conflict in public sentiment—significant numbers on both sides holding opinions very intensely. This pattern poses grave problems for politicians. Most politicians try to avoid divisive issues altogether. Public opinion about slavery before the Civil War may have been the most divisive in American history. Ultimately, if the divisions are sharp enough and if attitudes are held intensely enough, they may render a political system completely ungovernable.

Actual configurations of opinion are rarely as neat as the models in Figure 7–1, and how questions are asked often has a significant effect on the result. Figure 7–2 shows the distribution of opinion on abortion, one of the most divisive contemporary issues. This survey indicates a split between those who believe abortion should be available to all and those who feel it should be available but more difficult to obtain. Only 18 percent oppose abortion under all circumstances. What makes this issue so divisive is the intensity of opinion by substantial numbers on both sides. Measuring public opinion on abortion is very tricky and depends on how questions are asked. For example, 88 percent of the people support abortion if the woman's health is in danger, but 90 percent oppose abortion as a means of birth control.[7]

What Americans Believe

Democratic Values, Trust, and Government Power

The ability to govern is affected in the short run by particular patterns of public opinion. In the long run, the stability and strength of a political system are built on a foundation of public support for the general principles on which that system is based. The rapid collapse of communism in Eastern Europe reflected the lack of public support for the principles and institutions of those political systems. The U.S. government is based on a solid foundation of shared political and economic values. Although Americans may have different opinions

FIGURE 7–2

DIVISIVE PATTERN OF OPINION ON ABORTION

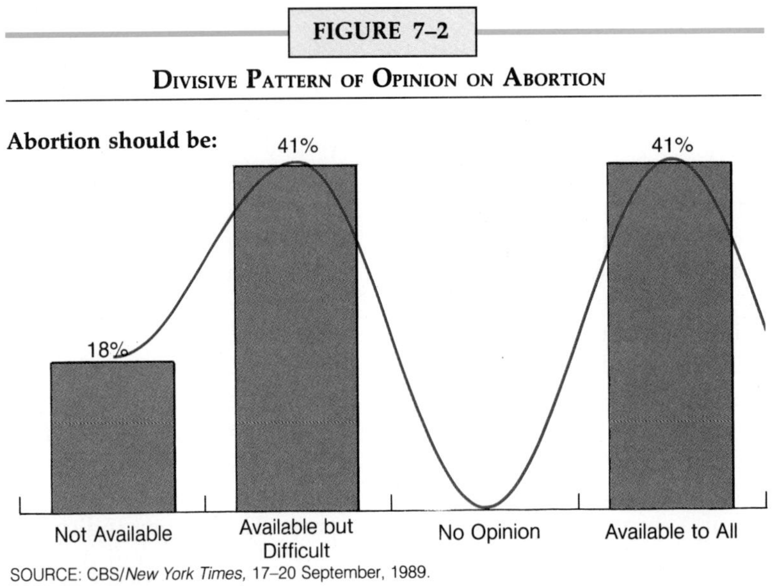

SOURCE: CBS/*New York Times*, 17–20 September, 1989.

about such issues as school prayer and abortion, both Republicans and Democrats, and liberals and conservatives, support the Constitution.

Americans express strong support for the principles of democracy—government by the people, freedom of speech, freedom to petition the government, and so on. But there is a significant gap between what Americans support in principle and what they support in practice. While 95 percent of the American public support the principle of freedom of speech, almost half believe that a communist should not be allowed to make a speech in public.[8] And despite support for freedom of the press, only 60 percent of Americans believe that a book written by a communist should be in a public library. Tolerance toward homosexuals has increased slightly over the past ten years, but less than 50 percent of Americans believe a homosexual should be allowed to teach.

Opinion surveys continue to reveal that considerable intolerance of unpopular views exists in the United States. Political tolerance is related to a person's education, income, and social status. More highly educated people are more politically tolerant and more likely to support democratic principles both in theory and in practice. Important differences also exist between political leaders and the public. Political leaders display greater support for democratic practices, and greater tolerance of unpopular viewpoints, than the general public.

Despite the consensus on the Constitution and on basic political and economic values, public trust in government has eroded over the past two decades. The assassination of President John F. Kennedy, racial violence in the cities, the war in Vietnam, student protests, and the Watergate scandal shook public confidence in the political system. In 1960, only 24 percent of Americans agreed with the statement "Public officials don't care what people like me think." By 1980, this figure had increased to more than 50 percent.[9] Trust in government declined precipitously between 1964 and 1980. In 1964, some 22 percent of Americans responded that the government could rarely or never be trusted, compared with 74 percent in 1980. By the end of the 1980s, only half believed the government could be trusted most of the time. Many are concerned about the implications such fluctuations between trust and cynicism have for the stability of the political system.

Public opinion affects governing by creating expectations relative to particular problems and solutions. Americans, however, are ambivalent about the role of government, sometimes wanting more programs while at the same time wanting a smaller government. By the late 1970s, a plurality of Americans believed that the federal government had too much power. This sentiment was echoed by Ronald Reagan's 1980 campaign for the presidency on a platform promising to shrink government and to "get the government off our backs."

Public attitudes about the power of the federal government were fairly stable until 1982, with the exception that even fewer respondents believed the government should use its power more vigorously (Figure 7–3). Beginning in 1982, however, attitudes toward government power changed. By the late 1980s, the proportion who felt that government was too powerful had declined to 28 percent, while those who believed the government should use its power more vigorously increased to 41 percent. More people responded that government was using about the right amount of power. These attitudes suggest important correlations with governance during the 1980s.

Americans express strong support for the principles of democracy, but in recent years, public trust in government has eroded.

Political Economy and Public Opinion

Despite widespread support for individualism and limited government, Americans have high expectations of government. Over the past two decades, public opinion displayed two somewhat opposing tendencies. In the relatively affluent society of today, Americans want government to provide a variety of services, from transportation and education to medical care for the aged. At the same time, the public tends to oppose actions that seem to restrict individual autonomy and often blames public problems on "big government." These conflicting sentiments are often seized on by opportunistic politicians. Those who want to reduce government cite findings about citizens' opposition to the size and scope of government. Advocates of expanded government note the public's zeal for more and bigger programs. In fact, both sentiments exist side by side.

The public's expectations of government responsibilities are related to the economy (see Figure 7–4). Over 80 percent of Americans believe old-age security and health care are the government's responsibility. Perhaps more surprising is the base of support for government intervention in the economy in terms of helping industry. A majority also supports policies to control inflation and to help the unemployed. On the other hand, Americans are split evenly on providing a decent standard of living to the unemployed and oppose both income redistribution and providing jobs for everyone who wants one.

Economic policy is complex and confusing to the average person. Yet a large majority of Americans have some understanding of inflation, depression, recession, and other elements of American political economy. And virtually all citizens have clear perceptions of their own economic situation and their future prospects. Public approval of economic performance played a major role in the 1984 landslide reelection of Ronald Reagan. During Reagan's first term, public opinion about the economy turned around remarkably. In early 1981, only 9 percent of the public believed the economy was getting better, but by 1984, this figure had grown to 49 percent.

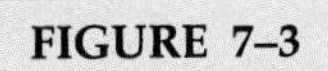

PUBLIC ATTITUDES ABOUT THE POWER OF THE FEDERAL GOVERNMENT, 1978–1986

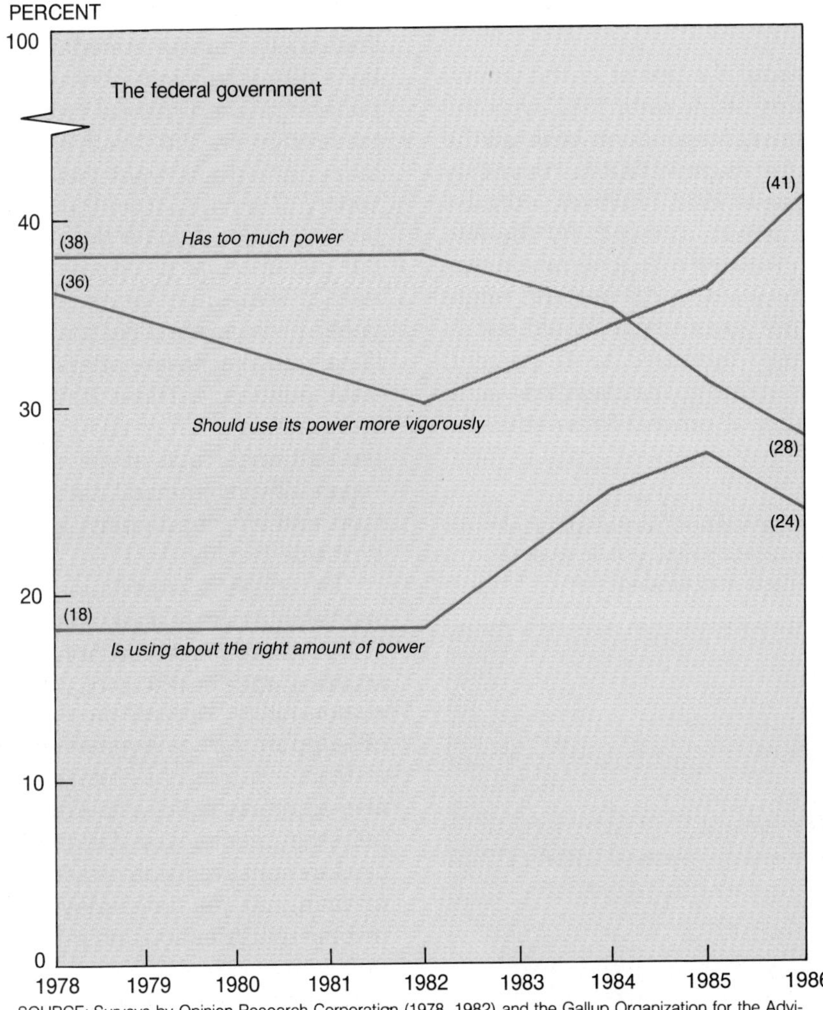

SOURCE: Surveys by Opinion Research Corporation (1978, 1982) and the Gallup Organization for the Advisory Commission on Intergovernmental Relations, latest that of 17–18 May, 1986. As reported in *Public Opinion*, May-April 1987, p. 29. Reprinted with permission of American Enterprise Institute for Public Policy Research.

Inconsistencies in public opinion are apparent in attitudes toward government spending. While over 80 percent support cuts in federal spending, when the question is asked generally, majorities support more spending in specific areas. The public supports budget cuts only in the areas of foreign aid and welfare, not for health, education, or the environment (see Table 7–2). And although the public consistently supports the nation's taking an active role in world affairs, most people dislike spending for foreign aid.[10] Both attitudes have remained stable for the past two decades, but public opinion on defense spending has fluctuated considerably. In the aftermath of Vietnam in 1973, only

FIGURE 7–4

THE PUBLIC'S ATTITUDES ABOUT GOVERNMENT AND THE ECONOMY

On the whole, do you think it should or should not be the government's responsibility to....

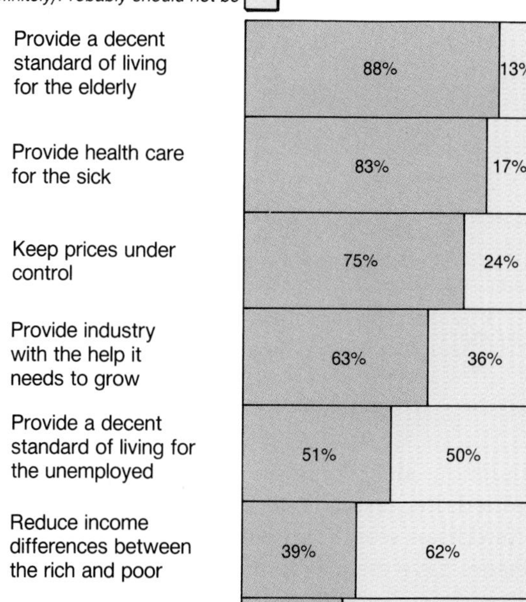

NOTE: "Can't choose" and "No answer" calculated out.

Survey by National Opinion Research Center, General Social Survey, February-April, 1985. Reported in *Public Opinion*, March-April 1987, p. 23. Reprinted with permission of American Enterprise Institute for Public Policy Research.

11 percent of the public believed the United States was spending too little on defense. But after the efforts of the Carter and Ford administrations to increase defense, and after President Reagan's warning about deteriorating U.S. defense capabilities, in 1980, some 56 percent of the public believed too little was being spent on defense. With the massive infusion of money into the Pentagon's budget in the early 1980s, by 1988, less than 20 percent of Americans felt that too little was being spent on defense.

Americans have many opinions that are important to politicians and to the policy process. Support for democracy and trust in government are fundamental values that underpin the entire political system. Attitudes on the economy and on public spending are important for policy decisions made every year. Poll results on abortion and other difficult moral issues affect candidates' platforms and election results. How can opinions be most accurately measured? Can politicians be confident that they really know what Americans believe?

Measuring Public Opinion

SURVEY RESEARCH

Public opinion can be measured in a variety of ways. An interviewer can go to a street corner and talk to whomever happens to walk by. The nature of the responses will vary, of course, depending on whether the corner is in the financial district or in a drug-riddled slum. Or people can be asked to fill out a questionnaire printed in the newspaper and send it in. The opinions obtained this way reflect the views of people who read that particular paper and have the time, the inclination, and a postage stamp to respond. Letters to Congress or letters to the editor can also be counted. By this measure, Barry Goldwater was the overwhelming favorite for the presidency in 1964. In addition, presidents like to count telegrams. But of all the methods available, there is only one reliable way to measure public opinion—by a scientific survey.

Public opinion polling and survey research have come a long way in the last fifty years. Recall from this chapter's political closeup that the editors of the *Literary Digest* were convinced their prediction about the 1936 election was accurate because they received several *million* ballots. Confidently, they predicted the outcome: Landon in a landslide. Why did the *Literary Digest* poll fall flat on its face? Because the sample of their readers was not remotely representative of the voting public. Millions of Americans were unemployed, standing in

TABLE 7–2

PUBLIC SPENDING PRIORITIES

	Government Should Spend More On	Government Should Spend Less On
The homeless	68%	6%
Education	66	5
Social Security	63	5
Health	63	6
Aid to the poor	63	11
Job creation and training	61	8
Environmental protection	47	11
Agriculture subsidies	40	21
Science and basic research	36	13
Mass transit and bridges	36	14
Aid to states and cities	27	23
Space exploration	17	42
Defense	14	48
Foreign aid	5	71

SOURCE: Roper Poll, reported in *Washington Post National Weekly Edition*, 9 June 1987, p. 38. Responses of "Government is spending the right amount" and "no opinion" are not shown.

breadlines, homeless. Few of them subscribed to a magazine that was largely found in the drawing rooms of affluent Republicans. George Gallup's more scientific methods correctly picked Franklin Delano Roosevelt as the winner. A new era in measuring opinion was born.

Since the 1930s, survey researchers have developed an array of techniques for taking reliable polls. Two of the most important steps include drawing the sample and designing the questionnaire.[11]

SAMPLING. All polls attempt to determine the opinions of the entire population by looking at only a relatively small sample. The minimum number for a good sample is around 500 respondents, and based on this sample, the poll results will have an error margin of around plus or minus 5 percent. The optimum number for a national survey is around 1,500 respondents, which produces an error margin of about plus or minus 2 to 3 percent 95 percent of the time. For example, if a sample of 1,500 indicates that 55 percent of respondents favor tougher drunk driving laws, we can be confident that in 19 out of 20 cases, the actual range in the population is 52 to 58 percent. The most important characteristic of a sample is that it be **random**—each individual in the population must have an equal chance of being included. Because a completely random sample of all Americans would be extremely difficult to obtain, pollsters have devices to make sampling easier but still random. To facilitate the process of surveying while protecting randomness, a sample may be *stratified*—that is, subpopulations are selected within different regions in communities of varying sizes. Samples can also be *clustered:* small geographical units are selected so that the respondents are close together and easier for the interviewer to reach.

The best way to conduct a survey is to send interviewers directly into homes, but the high cost of personal interviews has led commercial polling organizations to turn to the telephone survey. Here a sample may be drawn by random digit dialing. Refusal of people to participate in telephone interviews can be a problem if there is some nonrandom reason for turndowns (such as the fearfulness of the elderly in high crime areas). Recently, exit polls, in which people are interviewed right after they vote, have become popular and highly accurate. Exit polls are controversial because some people consider it an invasion of privacy to be asked how they voted and because the projections of exit polls on the East Coast have been released before voting was completed on the West Coast, possibly affecting the vote in the latter region. The state of Oregon passed a law banning exit polls, but it was struck down by the courts as a violation of the First Amendment. Regardless of the kind of poll, the principle of random sampling is essential to the accuracy of the result.

Design of the Questionnaire. Survey questions are carefully written before they are asked, and then each respondent is asked the question the same way. Closed-ended questions give the respondent a limited number of choices to respond to (yes, no, no opinion; strongly agree, agree, no opinion; and so on). Open-ended questions give the respondent the freedom to give any answer (for example, "What is the most important problem facing the nation today?"). The advantages of open-ended questions are that the question is less likely to structure the response and the information gained is broader. A disadvantage is that responses are more difficult to classify. Most commercial polls with rapidly reported results rely on closed-ended questions.

Survey questions should be as neutral as possible. Respondents can be influenced by even the slightest variation in wording. For example, in a question about China, it makes a difference if the interviewer asks about "Red China" or the "People's Republic of China" or if a question uses the term "pro-life" as opposed to "antiabortion" or "welfare" instead of "income assistance." Unscrupulous pollsters can structure questions to obtain almost any responses they want, but most pollsters are extremely careful to eliminate sources of bias.

Problems with Public Opinion Polls

"No one's ever asked me for *my* opinion" is often heard from those who doubt pollsters and their craft. Despite the elaborate methodology just described, the public remains skeptical of polling. Some of the problems are apparent in the survey techniques: error in the sample design, poorly trained interviewers, poorly designed questions. But difficulties can arise even when all those technical problems have been dealt with.

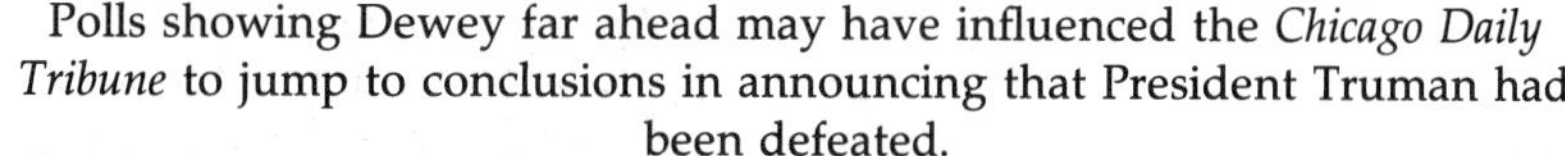

Polls showing Dewey far ahead may have influenced the *Chicago Daily Tribune* to jump to conclusions in announcing that President Truman had been defeated.

Chicago Daily Tribune — Home

DEWEY DEFEATS TRUMAN

G.O.P. Sweep Indicated in State; Boyle Leads in City

TABLE 7–3

GALLUP POLL ACCURACY RECORD

Year	Gallup Final Survey		Election Results		Deviation
1988	56.0%	Bush	53.9%	Bush	−2.1
1984	59.0	Reagan	59.1	Reagan	−0.1
1982	55.0	Democratic	56.1	Democratic	−1.1
1980	47.0	Reagan	50.8	Reagan	−3.8
1978	55.0	Democratic	54.6	Democratic	+0.4
1976	48.0	Carter	50.0	Carter	−2.0
1974	60.0	Democratic	58.9	Democratic	+1.1
1972	62.0	Nixon	61.8	Nixon	+0.2
1970	53.0	Democratic	54.3	Democratic	−1.3
1968	43.0	Nixon	43.5	Nixon	−0.5
1966	52.5	Democratic	51.9	Democratic	+0.6
1964	64.0	Johnson	61.3	Johnson	+2.7
1962	55.5	Democratic	52.7	Democratic	+2.8
1960	51.0	Kennedy	50.1	Kennedy	+0.9
1958	57.0	Democratic	56.5	Democratic	+0.5
1956	59.5	Eisenhower	57.8	Eisenhower	+1.7
1954	51.5	Democratic	52.7	Democratic	−1.2
1952	51.0	Eisenhower	55.4	Eisenhower	−4.4
1950	51.0	Democratic	50.3	Democratic	+0.7
1948	44.5	Truman	49.9	Truman	−5.4
1946	58.0	Republican	54.3	Republican	+3.7
1944	51.5	Roosevelt	53.3	Roosevelt	−1.8
1942	52.0	Democratic	48.0	Democratic	+4.0
1940	52.0	Roosevelt	55.0	Roosevelt	−3.0
1938	54.0	Democratic	50.8	Democratic	+3.2
1936	55.7	Roosevelt	62.5	Roosevelt	−6.8

Average deviation for 26 national elections:
2.2 percentage points
Average deviation for 19 national elections since 1950, inclusive:
1.5 percentage points

Trend in Deviation

Elections	Average Error
1936–1950	3.6
1952–1960	1.7
1962–1970	1.6
1972–1988	1.4

SOURCE: Gallup Poll, *Gallup Report*, no. 278 (November 1988).

Even with the best methods, there is still an error factor. In a close election, this can be crucial. If the error is at the maximum, an election pegged "too close to call" (such as the 1980 presidential contest) may turn out to be a near landslide. The credibility of the polls suffers. Another cause of error is that some voters may shift at the last minute. Carter's personal polls showed a rapid change in voter sentiment over the weekend, just days before the 1980 election, after the commercial polls had completed their last interview. Another difficulty for pollsters is predicting turnout, which can strongly affect results. The polls' worst performance was the 1948 presidential election, where virtually all (including Gallup) predicted Republican Thomas Dewey would defeat Harry Truman for the presidency. Methodologies have improved since then, but the polls still make mistakes.

During the 1988 elections, more polls than ever were taken. The public was inundated with a steady stream of findings about races and potential races at all levels of government. But polls are being used to influence results, not only to predict them. In polls that were made public, candidates invariably did better in their own surveys than in surveys conducted by the opposition. The hope is that poll results will become self-fulfilling by portraying the candidate as ahead and invincible.[12] Early polls may convince a potential candidate to enter the race or to drop out. Nonetheless, polls are increasingly important in American politics and have gotten better over the years. Table 7–3 examines the record of the Gallup poll since 1936. Note that while the average error was 3.6 percent in the earliest period, average error declined to 1.4 percent in the last sixteen years.

Sources of Opinion: Political Socialization

ACQUIRING POLITICAL VALUES

A political system must continually regenerate itself to survive. Each succeeding generation must learn the norms, values, and processes of the system. In a primitive society, children learn from an early age who is chief, who is witch doctor or medicine man, and what rites they must go through to become part of the adult community. American children learn something about how people behave in a democracy, that there is someone powerful called the president, and that people are Republicans or Democrats or independents. The process of learning is called **political socialization**—the transmission of political values and political norms from one generation to the next. Political socialization transmits a broad array of values and opinions, from general feelings about trust in government to specific opinions about the economy or national defense.

Political socialization is a lifelong process, although it makes its greatest mark in childhood and adolescence.[13] Political learning begins at a remarkably early age. By the second grade, most children already have a sense of nation and are able to identify with symbols like the flag. The political system is ill-defined but personified by the president. Children's orientations toward government are usually positive: the president is seen as a good person who is likely to protect them. Through the elementary years, children develop a more sophisticated view of government. Aware of the right to vote as an element of democracy, they learn that good citizens pay attention to politics and current events. Early learning provides a crucial foundation for their eventual performance as adult citizens and develops a strong sense of the legitimacy of the government.

During the elementary years, children develop attachments to social and political groupings, acquiring a "we-they" sense of America versus the world. They recognize that they are black, white, or Hispanic; rich or poor; Republican or Democrat; Catholic, Jewish, or Protestant. Perceptions and identifications learned in childhood are very deep and are carried into adult life. By adolescence, young people see the political world more critically. Junior high school students recognize that the president is not all-powerful, that Congress and the courts and bureaucracies share power. Politics becomes less personified. The average adolescent can disagree with the president without losing faith in the larger political system. By high school, a number of important political attitudes have already formed. Many students have clear opinions on international affairs and domestic issues. Political socialization slows down at this point but does not stop. Socialization continues as a person reacts both to personal experiences (such as unemployment) and to political events (such as the Vietnam War or Watergate) in their later life.

THE AGENTS OF POLITICAL SOCIALIZATION

What **agents** in society are the source of political learning? A television news program showed the children of parents who were active in the American Nazi party. The children, some as young as four or five years old, were already indoctrinated into racial and ethnic hatred. Although most families do not set out to instruct their children in a particular ideology, the family is a key source of political learning.

THE FAMILY. Through its behavior, the family affects how a child feels about authority and helps

Schools play an important role in political socialization by developing children's identification with and attachment to the nation.

shape a child's likes and dislikes in politics. One of the family's most important influences is in the transmission of *party identification*—the psychological attachment to one of the two major parties. Most children adopt the party identification of their parents. Transmission of party identification is strongest when both parents agree, weakest when they disagree or have low attachments. Those who differ from their parents tend to label themselves independent, rather than making the larger change from Democrat to Republican or vice versa.

Parents have a monopoly on children's time and devotion in the early years, but the transmission of party identification is usually not a conscious process. By the time children are in the fifth grade, more than half of them identify with one of the two major parties, even though they are unsure about the differences between the parties. About 60 percent of students reported the same party identification as their parents.[14]

The transmission of specific political attitudes on issues has been found to be much weaker than the transmission of party identification. By the time young people are old enough to form political opinions, they are subject to many more influences than just those in the home. But despite adolescent rebellion, parents and children agree on many issues. A recent survey found considerable agreement between students and parents about drugs, religion, and sex.[15]

SCHOOLS. Formal education plays an important role in political socialization. Although American students may be less overtly indoctrinated than Soviet youth used to be in the Young Communist Leagues, schools actively promote and inculcate American values. Elementary school students learn about American history, explorers, pioneers, and democracy—American heroes and the institutions of government. Unlike the family, the school does not try to instill particular feelings about social groupings or party affiliation. Its primary role in political socialization is to provide factual information about the political system and to develop a general attachment to the nation.

High school civics courses affect a student's sense of citizen duty more than they foster any particular set of political opinions. College education, opening students to new experiences and influences, has an impact on political attitudes.

Students often learn to attack problems more analytically. If they are from conservative backgrounds or socially homogeneous schools, they may be exposed to faculty with more liberal and diverse viewpoints. Their peers may be from different racial, ethnic, and social backgrounds. The relationship between level of education and adult political behavior is strong. The more highly educated people are, the more likely they are to vote, to participate and feel effective in politics, to have substantive knowledge of issues, and to tolerate diverse points of view.

THE CHURCH, PEERS, THE MEDIA, AND LIFE EXPERIENCES. In addition to family and schools, religion can influence political attitudes. Jews tend to be more liberal, white Protestants somewhat more conservative. Catholics tend to be more liberal on economic issues than Protestants but conservative on social issues. Churches rarely have a pervasive role in socialization unless the child's environment is dominated by religion or the issue is particularly important for the church. The Catholic church and fundamentalist Protestant churches have been particularly active in the antiabortion movement, and this has affected the attitudes of many young adherents. Friends and peer groups are also important in shaping attitudes, including political attitudes. Television can provide information that challenges the influence of both parents and schools, forming children's images of politics and politicians.

Political socialization continues throughout life. Monumental events may affect the attitudes and perceptions of entire generations. The Great Depression of the 1930s and World War II had an important impact on the people who lived through them. More recently, the Arab oil embargo and the emergence of the Organization of Petroleum Exporting Countries and high energy prices caused a widespread change in political perceptions, especially of energy needs, and attitudes toward conservation, production, and pricing of energy. Political socialization is an ongoing learning process. Some older people have become politically active for the first time in their lives after feeling the financial pinch of retirement. Growing membership in organizations such as the Gray Panthers and the American Association of Retired Persons reflects this new awareness.

Ideology: The Interrelationship of Opinions

POLITICAL IDEOLOGY

Political discourse in the United States is dominated by the terms **liberal** and **conservative,** by analysis of *left* versus *right.* What do these familiar but confusing terms really mean? Political labels identifying people or parties on a spectrum are a form of shorthand, a way to translate often complex political attitudes into a single dimension. As with any simplification, they can be deceptive and misleading. The great array of issues in American politics cuts many different ways. Some people who are liberal on economic issues may be conservative on social issues. In addition, the meaning of "liberal" and "conservative" has changed over the centuries. Liberalism in the nineteenth century, as described in Chapter 3, supported laissez-faire capitalism and minimal government intervention. This describes the position of conservatives today. Since the 1930s, liberalism has come to mean support for greater government involvement in the economy and in solving social problems. Because of their ambiguity, it might be easier to avoid using the terms "liberal" and "conservative" altogether, but journalists, politicians, and many others continue to rely on them.

Political ideology is a set of interrelated beliefs about government and public policy. Although doctrinaire appeals have been made from time to time in American politics, they have never been very successful. Accordingly, some argue that the American people and their political parties are not highly ideological. Communist parties with strict sets of beliefs are cited as prime examples of ideological parties. In contrast, the Republicans and Democrats are seen as broad coalitions encompassing a variety of opinions.

Is this an accurate view of ideology in American politics? Others suggest that, in a broader sense, Americans are as ideological as anyone. The values of America—market capitalism, individualism, materialism, liberty—form the basis of a distinctive political ideology. America's commitment to capitalism now appears stronger than the

Soviet Union's commitment to communism. Consensus over political and economic values reflects the success of political socialization in the United States.

Within the boundaries of American politics, the degree of ideology can be measured in three ways. First, how do Americans identify themselves ideologically? Do they consider themselves liberals or conservatives—and how do these divisions correspond to the two major political parties? Second, do voters respond to politics in ideological terms? Do they make voting decisions based on some coherent ideological framework? Third, are Americans' attitudes on issues closely related to one another? Are they ideologically consistent?

IDEOLOGICAL SELF-IDENTIFICATION

Most people are able to locate themselves on a political spectrum as either liberal, conservative, or middle-of-the-road. In the late 1980s, 20 percent labeled themselves liberal, 45 percent moderate, 28 percent conservative, and 7 percent no ideology.[16] Identification on a liberal-conservative dimension is not equivalent to partisan identification. While most Republicans consider themselves conservative, Democrats tend to be spread more evenly across the political spectrum, including a large segment who label themselves conservative. The proportion of the population that considers itself liberal has declined since the 1960s; only one in five felt "liberal" described their political viewpoint in 1988, compared with one in three in 1964.

Is self-identification accurate? What two people mean by the term "conservative" may be quite different. More rigid tests of the meaning of "liberal" and "conservative" in American politics include the content of attitudes and the interrelationship of opinions.[17]

DO AMERICANS CONCEPTUALIZE POLITICS IN IDEOLOGICAL TERMS?

In the classic study of voting behavior of the 1950s, *The American Voter,* political scientists from the University of Michigan found that only a small minority of voters conceptualized politics in ideological terms. Using a fairly strict definition of "ideological response," they counted only 12 percent of the electorate as **ideologues** in the 1956 election.[18] How did other voters conceptualize politics? Around 40 percent described candidates and parties in terms of benefits to groups they identified with (for example, some liked the Democrats because they were "for the working man"; some liked Republicans because they were "good for business"). Another 25 percent of the voters evaluated politics by the nature of the times (for example, "Things haven't been too prosperous under the Republicans"). The final group, 22 percent of the voters, reflected no issue or ideological content at all. They just liked one party or candidate (for example, "My family have always been Democrats" or "He's a good man—I just like him").

The findings of *The American Voter* about the nonideological nature of voters created a number of controversies about the study's methodology, assumptions, and interpretation. Later research in the 1960s and 1970s tempered the earlier views in several ways. Analysis of subsequent elections revealed that more ideological candidates, like Barry Goldwater or George Wallace, evoked a more ideological response from the voters.[19] The proportion of voters who could be classified as ideologues rose to 27 percent and 26 percent in the 1964 and 1968 elections, respectively.[20] Other scholars suggested that too stringent a test had been applied earlier and that most voters did consider issues in evaluating candidates and parties. It may have been that many voters were not able to articulate the underlying approach clearly and that *The American Voter* researchers imposed their own notions of ideology.

OPINION CONSISTENCY AND INTERRELATIONSHIPS

Another test of voters' ideological or nonideological stance is whether opinions on one issue are related to opinions on other issues. If a person is conservative on, say, the issue of government regulation, is he or she also conservative on the issue of domestic spending cuts? Many complicated studies on this question have been carried out in the past two decades.[21] Viewing attitudes on a range of policy issues, one can see that most citizens are not "pure" liberals or conservatives. People hold a variety of opinions on the many issues on the policy agenda. Respondents may be more liberal on domestic policy and more conservative on foreign policy, for instance (organized labor has a tradition of this pattern).

A consistent pattern of liberalism or conservatism is expressed by only a small, active, and informed segment of the population. Most people do not employ a tightly structured ideology to serve as their guide to American politics. This has led some to conclude that the old categories of liberal and conservative are no longer sufficient to describe the ideology of the American electorate.

PUBLIC OPINION, IDEOLOGY, AND DIVIDED GOVERNMENT

Divided party control of Congress and the presidency, which often makes governing more difficult, may be influenced by political attitudes and ideology as well as institutional arrangements. Shortly before the 1988 election, a survey revealed that three out of four of the crucial "swing voters"—independents and undecideds—preferred Congress and the presidency controlled by different parties.[22] Some scholars argue that this reflects a rational desire by middle-of-the-road voters to balance a Republican president with a Democratic Congress.[23] Another explanation is based on voters' contrary views on government spending observed above. Their preference for fiscal conservatism and low taxes is reflected by voting for Republican presidents, but their desire for more services and local benefits results in voting for Democratic representatives. According to this view, divided government allows voters to have it both ways.[24]

The assertion that voters deliberately decide to split their tickets for ideological reasons seems implausible given what we know about levels of information and ideological consistency. Even the suggestion that inconsistencies in public expectations from government foster divided government lacks evidence. A survey taken by the Republican party revealed that barely a majority of respondents even knew that Congress was controlled by the Democrats and 21 percent believed that the Republicans had a majority in Congress![25] Nonetheless, even though voters may not prefer divided government, neither is there evidence that they are concerned with its recurrence.

Acting on Opinions: Political Participation

PARTICIPATION IN POLITICS

Political participation can take many forms, from pulling the lever or punching the card in the voting booth, through canvassing door-to-door, to donating money. Table 7–4 shows the different ways in which Americans participate in politics, comparing presidential election years. Using a list of political activities, political scientists Sidney Verba and Norman Nie developed a classification of participation.[26]

COMPLETE ACTIVISTS. Those in the most involved group are the **complete activists**—writing letters, giving time and money to candidates, always voting, perhaps even running for office. This group makes up about 11 percent of the population. The complete activists are skilled, highly educated, and relatively well off. They are a small but politically crucial element of the population.

CAMPAIGN ACTIVISTS. Campaigners are faithful voters who frequently get involved in campaign activities. Unlike the complete activists, they do not participate actively in the community or concern themselves with broad social issues. Campaigners prefer the heat of a campaign to sitting through hours of testimony at a legislative hearing. They make up about 15 percent of the population and tend to be very partisan.

COMMUNITY ACTIVISTS. The last group of high participators is in some ways the mirror image of the campaigners. Community activists take an active role in local affairs and social issues but are generally less partisan and stay out of election campaigns. Activists in such groups as the League of Women Voters stress competence and community service rather than partisan politics. This group makes up about 20 percent of the population.

SELECTIVE PARTICIPANTS. A small group of what are called "selective participants" make up only 4 percent of the population and are somewhat unusual.

TABLE 7–4

HOW AMERICANS PARTICIPATE IN POLITICS, 1952–1984 (IN PERCENTS)

Activity	1952	1956	1960	1964	1968	1972	1976	1980	1984
Belong to political club	2	3	3	4	3	5[a]	5[b]	3	4
Work for political party	3	3	6	5	5	5	4	4	4
Attend political rally or meeting	7	10	8	9	9	9	6	8	8
Contribute money to campaign	4	10	12	11	9	10	9	16	12
Use political sticker or button	–	16	21	16	15	14	8	7	9
Give political opinions	27	28	33	31	30	32	37	36	32
Vote in election	62	59	63	62	61	55	55	53	53

[a]Data are from 1974.

[b]Data are from 1977.

All data, except for voting and political clubs 1972–84, are from the National American Elections Studies conducted by the Center for Political Studies at the University of Michigan. Voter turnout is Bureau of the Census data as reported by M. Margaret Conway, *Political Participation in the United States* (Washington, D.C.: Congressional Quarterly Press, 1985), 6. Political club data 1972–84 are from National Opinion Research Center, General Social Survey. Reported in Robert Erikson, Norman Luttbeg, and Kent Tedin, *American Public Opinion* (New York: Macmillan, 1988), 5.

Selective participants are not even regular voters, but they periodically become active in politics over a specific issue, responding to needs and problems when they arise and when problems affect them personally. Typically, selective participants contact government officials and attempt to organize to get something done, such as stopping a freeway from being built through their neighborhood.

REGULAR VOTERS. A group of citizens referred to as "regular voters" limit their role to expressing their views in the polling booth and stay out of the rest of politics. Regular voters tend to be strong party identifiers, although not active in party affairs. They make up 21 percent of the population.

INACTIVES. Those at the bottom of the political participation scale are inactives. They are uninvolved, rarely or never voting, not taking part in community activities, or even talking about politics much. Inactives make up 22 percent of the population—more than twice as many as the complete activists. The people who fall into this category tend to be of disproportionately lower socioeconomic status and not highly educated.

What accounts for such a range of participation? Because politics can be difficult, confusing, and time-consuming, levels of participation are related to a variety of socioeconomic factors. More highly educated people tend to vote more and participate in more ways than less well educated people. They have a better grasp of the issues and feel more at ease in the often complicated world of politics. Race is related to participation, with whites generally participating more than blacks. However, blacks participate at a somewhat higher rate than whites at their comparable income level.[27] Wealthier people participate disproportionately more than the poor. They have more time, more resources, and an easier life, all of which allow them to participate in politics. Gender is also a factor. Women tend to participate more than men, although the differences are not great. Finally, age is a factor. The most active age-group is people in their middle years—the thirties through the fifties. The young and the old tend to participate less frequently.

PROTEST AS A FORM OF PARTICIPATION

Participation in politics is not limited to the traditional activities just described. Political life in many countries is characterized by strikes, demonstrations, terrorism, assassination, and political violence. **Political protest** can be peaceful and nonviolent, but unfortunately, in much of the world direct action is often bloody and extreme.

The United States has not been immune to violence. Four presidents have been felled by assassins' bullets, and more than that number have survived attempts on their lives. Barely three months into his first term, President Reagan was wounded by a would-be assassin. The United States was born of violent revolution against Great Britain. A violent protest movement, Shays's Rebellion, helped spur the drafting of a new constitution to strengthen the national government. Violence and vigilante movements characterized much of the nineteenth century. The Civil War was a violent and costly solution to an apparently unsolvable political problem. Violence has been used both by labor unions and by strikebreakers and government troops. Many peaceful protests have turned violent at the same time that many peaceful protests have been met by government violence.

Protest and direct action have been an important part of politics in recent years. The civil rights movement gained its greatest momentum when Martin Luther King and his supporters urged peaceful disobedience of segregation laws. Hundreds of thousands of people descended on the nation's capital in 1963 to protest racial discrimination, giving impetus to passage of the Civil Rights Act and the Voting Rights Act in 1964 and 1965. The war in Vietnam stirred protests on college campuses and elsewhere in the mid-1960s. Although a majority of Americans supported the war through the end of the decade, the antiwar movement grew to large proportions. President Nixon showed contempt for the growing demonstrations, at one point announcing that he was watching a football game while the protests were going on outside the White House. When it was revealed that the administration had violated previous promises and invaded Cambodia in the spring of 1970, protests erupted across the country. Tragedy struck when national guardsmen fired on and killed students at Kent State and Jackson State. This time hundreds of campuses were closed down by student strikes.

Are protest and direct political action effective means of participation? Protest is not the same as violence. Most political protests in the United States have been peaceful. Only about one-third of them have involved violence, which as often as not was instigated by the police or troops.[28] Overall, the record of protest is mixed. Violence and terrorism can backfire, creating the opposite of the effect desired. But protest can often be effective. In the 1960s, the civil rights movement and the antiwar movement both had important if delayed effects. When people take to the street with banners and

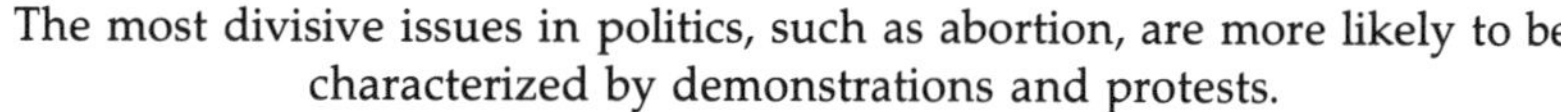
The most divisive issues in politics, such as abortion, are more likely to be characterized by demonstrations and protests.

TABLE 7–5

A DIFFERENT LOOK AT THE AMERICAN ELECTORATE

		% WHO VOTED FOR REAGAN, 1984	% OF ADULT POPULATION, 1990	% WHO PREFER DEMOCRATIC CONGRESS, 1990
Republicans				
Enterprisers	Affluent, educated, 99% white, this group forms one of the two bedrocks of the Republican party. Enterprisers are pro-business and antigovernment and express tolerance and moderation on questions of personal freedom. They overwhelmingly disapprove of tax increases, and oppose increased spending for health care, aid to the homeless, and programs for the elderly.	96%	12%	6%
Moralists	Middle-aged, middle-income, with a heavy concentration of southerners, this group forms the second bedrock of the Republican party. Moralists are regular churchgoers with a large number of "born-again" Christians. They are strongly antiabortion, pro-school prayer, in favor of the death penalty, anticommunist, prodefense, and in favor of social spending except when it is targeted to minorities.	97	11	4
Independents				
Upbeats	Young, optimistic, and strong believers in America, this group leans solidly to the GOP. They are middle-income with little or no college, 94% white, under 40, strongly pro-Reagan. They identify the deficit and economic concerns as top problems and give moderate support to "Star Wars."	86	8	14
Disaffecteds	Alienated, pessimistic, skeptical of both big government and big business, this group leans Republican. They are middle-aged, middle-income, and feel significant financial pressure. They are strongly antigovernment and antibusiness, but pro-military, strongly support capital punishment and oppose gun control.	81	12	32
Bystanders	Young, poorly educated, and marked by an almost total lack of interest in current affairs, Bystanders are nonparticipants in American democracy. They tend to be under 30. Their top concerns are unemployment, poverty, and the threat of nuclear war.	NA	12	47
Followers	With a very limited interest in politics, this group has little faith in America. They tend to be young, poorly educated, blue-collar, eastern and southern, mostly under 30, and have little religious commitment. They oppose "Star Wars" and favor increased spending to reduce unemployment.	54	5	68

TABLE 7–5

Independents (continued)		% WHO VOTED FOR REAGAN, 1984	% OF ADULT POPULATION, 1990	% WHO PREFER DEMOCRATIC CONGRESS, 1990
Seculars				
	The only group in America that professes no religious belief, this well-educated, white, middle-aged group combines a strong commitment to personal freedom, moderate beliefs on social questions, and a very low level of anticommunism. They favor cuts in military spending and oppose "Star Wars," school prayer, antiabortion legislation, and relaxing environmental controls.	34%	7%	66%
Democrats				
1960s Democrats				
	This upper-middle-class, heavily female (60%) group of mainstream Democrats has a strong commitment to social justice and a very low militancy level. They strongly identify with the peace, civil rights, and environmental movements. They favor increased spending on programs for minorities and most other forms of social spending and strongly oppose "Star Wars."	25	9	84
New Deal Democrats				
	They are blue-collar, union members with moderate incomes and little financial pressure, religious, intolerant on questions of personal freedom but favoring many social spending measures, older (66% over 50). They favor most social spending, more restrictions on abortions, school prayer, and protectionism and are less concerned about the environment.	30	7	87
God and Country Democrats				
	Older and poor, this solidly Democratic group has a strong faith in America and is uncritical of its institutions and leadership. Committed to social justice, the Passive Poor are also moderately anticommunist. They favor all forms of increased social spending, oppose cuts in defense spending, are moderately antiabortion, and favor relaxing environmental standards.	31	8	88
The Partisan Poor				
	The Partisan Poor have very low incomes and feel great financial pressure. They are very concerned with social justice issues. Some 37% black, they are also southern, urban, and poorly educated. They are strong advocates of all social spending but oppose tax increases. They favor death penalty and school prayer amendment but are divided on abortion.	19	10	82

SOURCE: Adapted from *The People, Press, and Politics: A Times Mirror Study of the American Electorate Conducted by the Gallup Organization, September 1987* (Times Mirror Company, 1987). Updated, Sept. 19, 1990.

placards, they are making a visible statement much more likely to make an impression than simply petitioning public officials. The media are an important key to the effectiveness of protest movements. Television cameras were trained on the Chicago police as they clashed with protesters at the 1968 Democratic National Convention, causing public antipathy toward protesters and police alike. In the 1980s, several members of Congress were arrested in demonstrations at the South African embassy, protesting that nation's policy of apartheid (racial separation). Their arrest helped focus media attention on apartheid, and they received support from their more conservative colleagues in Congress, who agreed with their goals if not their tactics.

Most often, protest serves to spur action through the traditional political process. But protests can stiffen opposition. Public opinion surveys reveal that most Americans believe civil disobedience or direct action are not legitimate forms of participation.

Redefining the American Electorate: Opinions, Partisanship, Ideology, and Participation

The weakening of party ties, shifts in social and economic divisions, the limitations of liberalism-conservatism in describing ideology, and variations in levels of political participation have led to a search for new ways to define the American electorate. One effort is the result of an extensive study conducted by the Gallup organization for Times Mirror in 1987 and updated in 1990.[29] Its survey, consisting of in-depth interviews with more than 4,000 Americans, resulted in a typology that divides the electorate into eleven different groups. The categories are a product of combining basic social and political values with political and ideological self-identification. The results, although not definitive, are an interesting set of classifications. Table 7–5 profiles what the authors call "the real electorate" and compares each group as a percentage of the adult population, presidential vote in 1984, and the percent favoring a Democratic congress in 1990.

The study led to some intriguing findings. The researchers concluded that the Republican party is composed of two distinct groups—the enterprisers and the moralists—that differed on conservative social issues and commitment to free enterprise. This split was reflected in the 1988 nomination contest between Robert Dole, former Vice-President George Bush, and Pat Robertson, the evangelical Christian. The Democrats fell into four separate groups divided by generation, class, tolerance, and attitudes toward communism—a complex coalition of Democrats to unite behind a single candidate. Independents consist of five groups, one that does not participate, two that lean Democratic, and two that lean Republican. The outcome of elections, according to their findings, will often be decided by how effectively the two major candidates can attract these different "independent" groups. How well do people you know fit into these groups, profiled in Table 7–5?

SUMMARY AND CONCLUSIONS

1. Public opinion is the collective attitudes and beliefs of the public on a range of political questions. It creates boundaries for governing ranging from a permissive flexibility to sharp constraints on what can be done.
2. Americans have attitudes on many political issues. Support for democratic principles is higher in the abstract than in practice. Trust in government has declined significantly in the past two decades. Although Americans do not understand all the nuances of modern economics, they are attentive to economic questions.
3. Public opinion is most accurately measured by scientific, random sample surveys.
4. Political socialization is the process of transmitting political values and norms from generation to

generation. It occurs primarily during childhood and early adulthood but continues through life. Family, schools, church, peers, and the media are the main agents of socialization.

5. In general, Americans are not highly ideological. Political debate in the United States takes place within the boundaries of shared values and customs. Most people can identify themselves as liberal or conservative, but there are often no sharp differences between them.

6. Participation in politics varies from the complete activist to the totally inactive. Participation is related to education, income, and socioeconomic status. Protest and direct action have been an important part of the political process in the United States throughout its history.

Even if public opinion rarely binds the hands of elected officials, in many instances fear of it seems to produce a reluctance to confront voters with hard choices. This can block a full and open discussion of alternatives, stifle creative problem solving, and breed an insensitivity to serious, long-term issues. This situation might seem puzzling, given what we know about public opinion. On many important issues, the public is not well informed and does not hold strong opinions. Citizens have contradictory expectations of government. There is little evidence of sharp ideological divisions among citizens. Yet the reluctance on the part of many politicians to veer out of the mainstream keeps many policy options off the agenda. Candidates often exploit issues that may make it easier to get elected but more difficult to govern once in office. Effective governing in a democracy depends on the relationship between leaders and the public. That relationship has grown more troubled in the 1990s, as we will see in the remaining chapters of this section, with the rise of "slash and burn" campaign tactics, the growing importance of television and media consultants, and the proliferation of money in the electoral process. Chapter 8 examines the changing role of political parties.

KEY TERMS

agents of socialization
complete activists
"consensus" pattern of opinion
"divisive" pattern of opinion
ideologues
liberal versus conservative
"permissive" pattern of opinion
political ideology
political participation
political protest
political socialization
public opinion
random sample

SELF-REVIEW

1. How does public opinion influence governing?
2. What is the public's understanding of economics?
3. What is public opinion?
4. How is public opinion measured?
5. What are some of the problems with the polls?
6. How do citizens acquire their attitudes and political values?
7. What are the agents of political socialization?
8. Explain political ideology.
9. How do Americans identify themselves in ideological terms?
10. Describe the different forms of political participation.
11. Give a brief profile of the type of person most likely to participate in politics.
12. What are the effects of protest and violence as a form of participation?
13. Who are "independents," according to the Times Mirror study?

SUGGESTED READINGS

Erikson, Robert, et al. *American Public Opinion.* 1988.
An excellent overview of public opinion, its measurement, and its impact.

Flanigan, William H., and Nancy H. Zingale. *Political Behavior of the American Electorate.* 6th ed. 1987.
A good summary of the current findings on political behavior.

Hess, Robert D., and Judith Tourney. *The Development of Political Attitudes in Children.* 1967.
The classic study of political socialization of children.

Verba, Sidney, and Norman Nie. *Participation in America.* 1972.
Still the most thorough study of political participation in the United States.

NOTES

1. *New York Times,* 18 March 1990, p. 16.
2. James Bryce, *The American Commonwealth,* vol. 2 (New York: Macmillan, 1916), 251.
3. Walter Lippmann, *The Public Philosophy* (New York: New American Library, 1955), 23–24.
4. W. Lance Bennett, *Public Opinion in American Politics* (New York: Harcourt Brace Jovanovich, 1980), 12.
5. V. O. Key, *Public Opinion and American Democracy* (New York: Knopf, 1961).
6. Elihu Katz and Paul Lazersfeld, *Personal Influence* (New York: Free Press, 1955), is an early classic on the impact of opinion leaders.
7. CBS/*New York Times* poll, 17-20 September 1989.
8. James Prothro and Charles Gregg, "Fundamental Principles of Democracy," *Journal of Politics* 22 (1960): 285.
9. Center for Political Research, Institute of Social Research, University of Michigan Election Studies, 1960 and 1980 results.
10. See *Public Opinion,* October–November 1982, p. 29.
11. The following material on sampling and questionnaire design relies on William H. Flanigan and Nancy H. Zingale, *Political Behavior of the American Electorate,* 5th ed. (Boston: Allyn and Bacon, 1983), 179–87. See also University of Michigan, Survey Research Center, *Manual for Coders.*
12. *Washington Post National Weekly Edition,* 13 April 1987, p. 37.
13. Robert D. Hess and Judith Tourney, *The Development of Political Attitudes in Children* (Chicago: Aldine, 1967).
14. M. Kent Jennings and Richard G. Niemi, "The Transmission of Political Values from Parent to Child," *American Political Science Review* 62 (March 1968): 173.
15. *Washington Post National Weekly Edition,* 16 April 1984, p. 38.
16. Gallup poll, 11–14 April 1986, released 19 June 1986.
17. Flanigan and Zingale, *Political Behavior,* p. 107.
18. Angus Campbell, Phillip Converse, Warren Miller, and Donald Stokes, *The American Voter* (New York: Wiley, 1960), 124–44.
19. John Sullivan, James Pierson, and George Marcus, "Ideological Constraint in the Mass Public," *American Journal of Political Science,* May 1978, pp. 233–49.
20. Flanigan and Zingale, *Political Behavior,* p. 108.
21. Phillip Converse, "The Nature of Belief Systems in Mass Publics," in David Apter, ed., *Ideology and Discontent* (New York: Free Press, 1964), 206–61.
22. *Wall Street Journal,* 28 October 1988, p. A10.
23. Morris P. Fiorina, "The Reagan Years" in Cooper, Kornberg, and Mishler, eds., *The Resurgence of Conservatism in Anglo-American Democracies* (Durham, N.C.: Duke University Press, 1988).
24. Gary Jacobsen, "Congress: A Singular Continuity" in Michael Nelson, ed., *The Elections of 1988* (Washington, D.C.: Congressional Quarterly Press, 1989) 144–46.
25. *Congressional Quarterly Weekly Reports,* 6 May 1989, p. 1063.
26. Sidney Verba and Norman Nie, *Participation in America* (New York: Harper and Row, 1972), 118–19.
27. *Ibid.,* 151–59.
28. Jerome H. Skolnick, *The Politics of Protest,* Staff Report to the Commission on the Causes and Prevention of Violence (New York: Ballantine, 1969).
29. Times Mirror Co., *The People, Press, and Politics* (1987). Update issued 19 September, 1990.

CHAPTER 8

POLITICAL PARTIES

POLITICAL CLOSE-UP

PARTY POLITICS AND THE WIZARD OF OZ

The Munchkins, witches, magic slippers, and wonderful Wizard of Oz of Frank Baum's book published in 1900 remain famous today because of the 1939 film starring Judy Garland. But is *The Wonderful Wizard of Oz* just a children's story?

The formation of the Populist party was a reaction of midwestern farmers to industrialization, changes in agriculture, and the gold standard for currency that kept interest rates high and money "tight." Frank Baum moved to South Dakota just about the time the Populist party was forming. The leader of the Populist party, William Jennings Bryan, made one of history's most famous speeches when he accused the eastern bankers of crucifying the midwestern farmers on a "cross of gold." In 1896, Frank Baum campaigned for Bryan, who became the nominee of the Democratic party as well. So where does *The Wonderful Wizard of Oz* fit into all this?

The story takes place in Kansas, a place of exceptional virtue and innocence, where we meet Dorothy, her dog Toto, Auntie Em, and Uncle Henry. When the cyclone carries Dorothy and Toto to Oz, she lands on and kills "the wicked witch of the East" (the Populists blamed eastern industrialists and bankers for the severe problems of the farmers), leaving only the West under the hands of the other wicked witch. When Dorothy encounters the Tin Woodsman on her way to Emerald City, he is "rusted solid," the condition of many factories following the depression of 1893. But the Woodsman's biggest problem is his lack of a heart. The Populists saw industrialization as dehumanizing, turning people into machines, devoid of human sensitivities and values.

Scene from the 1939 film, *The Wizard of Oz.*

Dorothy sets out for Emerald City to meet the wonderful Wizard to help her get back to Kansas. Although the film version had ruby slippers, in the original story Dorothy wears magic silver slippers as she follows the "dangerous" yellow brick road (representing, of course, the gold standard). The Populists' most important proposal was to place currency on a standard of both silver and gold, not just gold, to ease credit and make it easier for farmers to borrow money. Dorothy next encounters the Scarecrow, who is in need of a brain to replace the straw in his head. Who could it be but midwestern farmers themselves, in desperate need of greater "smarts" concerning their political interests? With the Tin Man and the Scarecrow, Dorothy meets the Cowardly Lion, in need of courage. Could the Lion be William Jennings Bryan himself? When the Lion first sees the Tin Man, he strikes him but can make no inroads with his claws on the tin, just as Bryan could make no inroads with the labor vote in the 1896 election.

Bryan was no coward, and eventually in the story neither is the Lion. Together the band marches to Emerald City—symbol of Washington, D.C.—reminiscent of "Coxey's Army" of indigents and unemployed who marched on Washington in 1894 to demand jobs. In Emerald City, they find a bungling old man hiding behind a facade of noise and deception, able to be all things to all people—the Populists' cynical view of the Republican president. After the wicked witch of the West is done in with the help of Dorothy's magic silver slippers, the Wizard departs in a balloon. He leaves Oz under the care of the Scarecrow while the Tin Man rules the West, a hopeful Populist vision of the farmers gaining national political power as industrialization moves West. The Lion is sent to the forest to protect the "weaker creatures," perhaps symbolic of Bryan's retirement from politics.

Dorothy finally goes back to Kansas using the magic silver slippers. But what about the silver standard so urgently desired by the Populists? In the story, the magic slippers fall off in flight and are forever "lost in the desert"—the replacement of the gold standard never came about.

Populist sympathizer Frank Baum claimed *The Wonderful Wizard of Oz* was nothing more than a children's story. Do you still think so?

SOURCE: Henry M. Littlefield, "The Wizard of Oz: Parable on Populism," American Quarterly 16 (Spring 1964):47–58.

CHAPTER OUTLINE

INTRODUCTION AND OVERVIEW

Political parties play an important role in insuring democratic political processes and in determining how effectively a nation is governed. As the nations of Eastern Europe altered their political systems and discarded one-party communist rule, the formation of competitive multiparty systems was an essential step. In East Germany in 1990, dozens of political parties competed in the first free elections held since 1932. Once democratic elections are held, political parties are strong forces in how parliamentary democracies are governed. Elected leaders may rely on strict party discipline when necessary. Some governments have been able to work with majorities as slim as one or two votes.

Parties can also be important in political systems where governmental power is fragmented and dispersed, as in the United States. Although the Founders initially feared them, within a few years, political parties had become an essential element of American politics. Party loyalty can help bridge the separation of powers by providing a common bond between executive and legislative branches. For most of American history, parties played a crucial role in both the electoral process and the governing process. Congress and the presidency were controlled by one party 75 percent of the time.[1] Nine out of ten voters voted a straight party ticket. Parties dominated election campaigns and helped voters clarify issues. But the role of political parties declined in the twentieth century.

Parties are now less important in elections. The attachment of voters to parties has weakened as campaigns are increasingly dominated by television. Instead of emphasizing platform positions and issues, the media focus on the candidates' personalities and the horse race aspect of campaigns. The importance of parties in governing also has declined. Elections for Congress and the presidency, once closely linked, have become "decoupled," producing a government divided between a Democratic Congress and a Republican president. Under divided government, partisanship and party loyalty produces conflict and stalemate rather than effective governing.

Many factors contributed to the movement away from political parties by voters. With more sources of political information, voters became less dependent on parties. Political parties no longer printed ballots, ran elections, or performed welfare services. Suburbanization created a population more isolated and more difficult to organize. The number of independents increased while strong identifiers in both parties declined, a phenomenon called "dealignment." Candidates moved away from parties as well. Primary elections made potential nominees independent of the party organization. With the arrival of the television era, candidates could raise their own funds, run their own campaigns, create their own message. And while both parties undertook renewal efforts in the 1970s and 1980s to reverse their declining role, their impact on both elections and governing has been permanently altered.

This chapter explores the creation, evolution, and changing role of political parties in American politics and considers the following questions:

1. What are political parties, and how do they affect elections and governing?
2. How does the American two-party system compare with party systems in other countries?
3. How did the American party system develop?
4. Why does the United States have a two-party system?
5. How do the people relate to the two major parties, and how do the parties affect voters?
6. How are political parties organized at the national, state, and local level?
7. How does a party affect the organization of government and policy-making?
8. What are the problems and prospects for the Republicans and Democrats in the 1990s?

Political Parties, Elections, and Governing

THE FUNCTIONS OF POLITICAL PARTIES

A political party is a collection of individuals having common interests organized to seek and gain political office. Parties perform three important functions in politics. First, *political parties recruit candidates for public office.* The degree to which parties control access to politics varies among countries, but virtually all candidates run with some party label. In this way, the parties facilitate electoral choice. They provide a way for voters to recognize candidates and distinguish them from other candidates.

Second, *political parties help set the policy agenda* by identifying major public problems and proposing solutions. A party is a coalition of interests, which distinguishes it from a single-issue group. Because parties contain competing interests, they must weigh various priorities in developing their platform. Parties bring together multiple interests and balance them within a larger framework. Parties vary considerably, however, in their breadth of interests and the specificity of their proposals.

Third, *political parties organize government to make public policy.* They serve as a pool for executive appointments and as a basis for dividing power in the legislature, and they furnish a method for forging links between the executive and legislative branches. Political parties can foster governing by providing the means to formulate, approve, and implement public policy.

THE ELEMENTS OF POLITICAL PARTIES

In addition to their political roles, parties are complex social structures comprised of three main elements: party in the electorate, party organization, and party in government.[2]

PARTY IN THE ELECTORATE. The men and women who belong to a party, who psychologically identify with a party, or who frequently vote for a party form the **party in the electorate.** The clients of parties are a broad group of citizens, not just people who officially register with a party. A majority of U.S. citizens identify with one of the two major parties without actually joining. The party in the electorate is an open and inclusive group.

PARTY ORGANIZATION. The party organization is the formal apparatus of a political party. In the United States, it ranges from the national chairperson down toward committeemen and committeewomen. The **party organization** consists of the people who run political campaigns, who donate time and money to the party, and who continue the party activities between elections. Acting in the name of the political party, officials make decisions about party rules, primaries, convention delegates, and other aspects of the party machinery.

PARTY IN GOVERNMENT. Elected officials who win under a party label (this includes almost all public officials) make up the **party in government.** In the United States, this includes governors, state legislators, the president, members of Congress, and

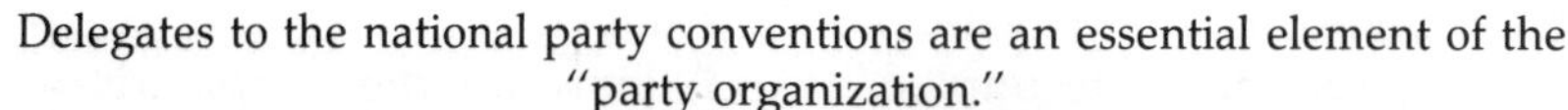
Delegates to the national party conventions are an essential element of the "party organization."

various state and local officials. As party members in official positions, they become spokespersons for the party and are responsible for organizing policy making. Figure 8–1 shows the three major components of political parties.

FIGURE 8–1

THE THREE ELEMENTS OF POLITICAL PARTIES

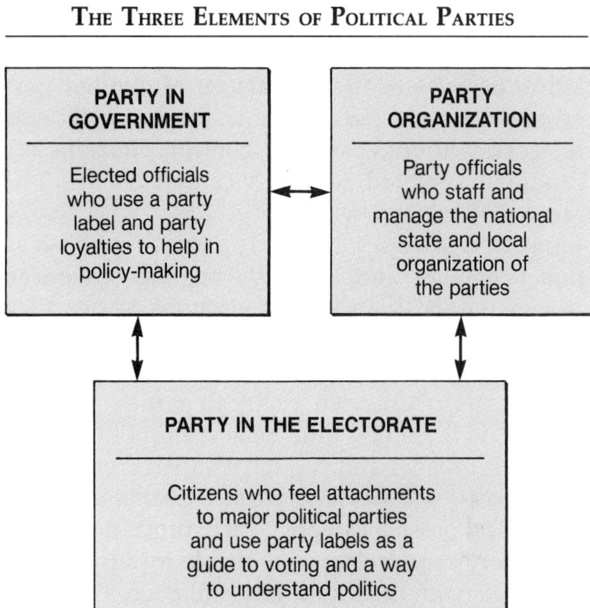

COMPARING PARTY SYSTEMS

Political parties in the United States are among the oldest in the world. They are also unique. Comparisons with party systems around the world can help clarify the nature of the U.S. party system and identify ways to evaluate the impact of parties on politics.

NUMBER OF PARTIES. Party systems may be one-party, two-party, or multiparty. One-party systems are on the decline throughout the world, with additional political parties beginning to emerge even in the Soviet Union. One of the most important constitutional changes in the nations of Eastern Europe was eliminating the monopoly of the Communist party. In recent years, Mexico was an example of a democratic system with a single dominant party—the Party of Revolutionary Institutions (PRI), which dominated government for over sixty years without opposition. In 1988, however, opposition parties gained enough strength to challenge the PRI, and Mexico appeared to be in transition from a one-party system to a multiparty system. The southern states in the United States in the one hundred years after the Civil War were examples of one-party (Democratic) subsystems.

Many nations, like the United States, are two-party or predominantly two-party systems. Great Britain has been a predominantly two-party system, although a third party, the Social Democratic/Liberal Alliance, captured 23 percent of the vote in the 1987 general election. Canada has two dominant parties: the Liberal party and the Conservative party, but a third party, the New Democrats, is growing.

The third variant is a **multiparty system,** where a number of parties win seats in the parliament on a regular basis. Italy is an example of a multiparty system. In general, such nations often have coalition governments made up of several parties. Multiparty systems are often less stable than two-party systems, and the parties tend to be narrower and more ideological in their appeal. In contrast to ideological parties in a multiparty system, Republicans and Democrats in the United States are **coalition parties** that represent rather diverse interests. Compared with a multiparty system, bargaining and the balancing of interests takes place within the party before the election, rather than between different parties after elections. Although instability is a result of many factors, Italy has had more than forty-five governments since World War II.

Party strength is determined by how effectively the party selects candidates and works for their election, how clearly and specifically it formulates policy in party programs, and how disciplined it is in organizing government and making policy. How do American parties measure up?

CONTROL OF CANDIDATE SELECTION. American parties do not have a monopoly on candidate selection. The *direct primary,* where candidates are selected by virtually anyone who wants to vote and where nearly anyone can run, supersedes the ability of the party organization to select candidates. Although the great majority of candidates in the United States run as Democrats or Republicans, the party must bow to the popular candidate, not vice versa. In most party systems, prior approval by the regular party organization is necessary to gain political office. Because of the prevalence of divided government, the American political system must be able to work without one-party control. Elections are candidate centered, not party centered.

IDEOLOGICAL APPEAL. Political parties establish a policy agenda and a party program. American parties emphasize winning elections rather than articulating a specific ideology. British parties, in contrast, are more programmatic and issue-specific.

Although American political parties are concerned with issues and policy proposals, their appeal is broader and vaguer, compared with most other party systems. The parties' goal is to secure the widest possible support. Party professionals are often very nonideological and able to support any candidate with the right party affiliation. Although a party platform is drawn up at the convention every four years, the presidential candidate is not bound to follow it. Because the president and Congress are held less accountable to their party's platform, less importance is placed on the document than in other party systems. Believing that its platforms had been too specific in the past, the 1988 Democratic party platform was the shortest since 1932, emphasizing basic principles and goals rather than specific proposals.

ORGANIZATIONAL STRENGTH. Differences in the role of ideology between American and other parties can be partly explained by the organization and structure of the parties, as well as by the nature of parliamentary government. British parties have strong organizational structures. The leader of the party becomes prime minister if his or her party wins the election. The loser becomes leader of the opposition. If the U.S. president is the titular head of the party, who is the leader of the opposition? The defeated candidate? Possibly, but defeated candidates often have no further influence in party affairs. Would it be the Speaker of the House? The chairperson of the national committee? The front-runner for the next presidential nomination? In the United States, there is often no clear leader of the party that loses the presidency.

PARTY DISCIPLINE AND GOVERNING. Throughout the world, parties differ in how they organize government and make policy. Powerful parties control more resources to encourage **party discipline.** As a result, most parliamentary parties are disciplined in their voting, generally approving what the prime minister and the government propose. Members are subject to severe sanctions if they desert the party, including an early end to their political careers. Members realize that defeat on a key vote in parliament could topple the government, requiring new elections (the exact nature of this requirement varies across countries). No such sanctions or dangers confront members of the U.S. Congress. Members are perfectly free to oppose the president (whether of their party or not) and the party leadership with little fear of reprisal or serious consequence. The nature of the party system in the United States has important consequences for governing. The president and congressional leaders have limited ability to maintain party unity. Candidates can even switch parties, as Representative Phil Gramm did in 1983, and get reelected in the same district! How did this party system develop in the United States?

The Development of American Political Parties

THE FIRST AMERICAN PARTIES

Early political leaders agreed: they should *not* divide into opposing political parties. The Constitution was silent on the subject of parties, but clearly the intention of the Founders was for government to respond directly to public opinion without using political organizations as linkages. Yet political parties emerged very quickly, and the leaders who were so opposed to them—Jefferson, Madison, Hamilton—helped foster their creation. Why?[3]

The creators of the first American parties disagreed fundamentally over the power of the national government. The **Federalists,** led by Alexander Hamilton, were increasingly suspicious of the group led by Thomas Jefferson. Jefferson's followers eventually took the name **Democratic Republicans** (to imply that Hamilton and the Federalists were still monarchists). Hamilton feared that Jefferson would destroy the concept of a national government. Jefferson in turn felt Hamilton would erode federalism and limited government. The opposing camps did not see this as a minor squabble but as two incompatible views of the Constitution. Historian Paul Goodman concludes, "Federalist and Republican alike regarded themselves not as parties but as embodiments of the nation's will."[4]

There were other issues. Under President Washington, Hamilton's economic program fostered commerce and attempted to protect domestic manufacturing. The National Bank, authorized in 1791, was an important component of this policy. Hamilton's policies seemed to favor industry over agriculture, furthering the split between the Federalists and the followers of Jefferson. Attitudes toward the French Revolution reflected growing political cleavages in the new nation. Jefferson and his followers viewed it approvingly as an extension of the American Revolution—a contest between the common people against the upper classes. Hamilton and the Federalists saw it as a dangerous threat to society and strong government. Basic differences could no longer be masked by the popularity of George Washington. Political leaders divided into two camps, the basis of the first political party system in the United States.[5]

The conflict came to a head with the election of 1800, where Jefferson and Aaron Burr opposed the incumbents, John Adams and Charles Pinckney. Jefferson and his supporters won the election and carried both houses of Congress. The Federalists quietly faded away (although Federalist judges, especially Chief Justice John Marshall, continued to have important influence for decades). The party system had begun. Table 8–1 shows the development of American political parties since the first party system.

ANDREW JACKSON AND THE SECOND PARTY SYSTEM

The election of 1824 signaled important changes in American politics.[6] Andrew Jackson was defeated by John Quincy Adams, even though Jackson won more popular votes. The House of Representatives chose Adams when the electoral college failed to produce a majority. Until this time, presidential candidates had been nominated by Congress, but when the popular Jackson was denied the presidency, that method was discredited.

The demise of the congressional caucus nomination system led to the innovation of party nominating conventions to select presidential candidates. The first major party convention was held by the Democrats in 1832, when they nominated Jackson and Van Buren. The nominating convention was a great popular reform at the time, reflecting an enlarged electorate and increased popular participation in politics. The old caucus system allowed selection by an elite group, whereas the convention reflected grassroots mobilization of support. Ironically, conventions later would be the target of similar charges of elitism, leading to the increased popularity of direct primaries.

Other electoral changes marked the Jacksonian era. Not only did the number of voters triple between 1824 and 1828, but also by the 1830s, most members of the electoral college were selected by popular vote, rather than by the state legislatures. Jackson expanded the power of the presidency with this new popular base. Political parties became continuing organizations—similar to their contemporary counterparts—during this second party system.

The modern Democratic party began with Jefferson's Democratic Republicans, who became just "Democrats" in Jackson's time. Their opponents had a more uneven course. In the 1820s, the National Republicans represented some of the old Federalist positions but were replaced by the Whigs in the 1830s. Not until the formation of the Republican party in 1856 were the two modern parties in place.

REPUBLICANS VERSUS DEMOCRATS: THE EVOLUTION OF THE MODERN PARTY SYSTEM

The polarizing issues of slavery and sectionalism redivided party loyalties and resulted in the emergence of the two-party system as it is known today.[7] Once the two major parties in the United States were established, three additional eras (or "party systems") can be identified (see Table 8–1).

TABLE 8–1

Party Systems in American History

Party System	Dates	Competing Parties	Characteristics/Comments
First party system	1788–1824	Federalists vs. Democratic-Republicans	Parties emerge in 1790s. One-party factionalism within the Democratic-Republican party after 1820.
Second party system	1828–1854	Democrats vs. Whigs	Balanced two-party competition, with Democrats the dominant party.
Third party system	1856–1896	Republicans vs. Democrats	Republican dominance from 1862 to 1874; balanced two-party competition from 1874 to 1896. Sectionalism in political conflict.
Fourth party system	1896–1928	Republicans vs. Democrats	Republican dominance except for period of intraparty schism in 1912. Continued sectionalism.
Fifth party system	1932–	Republicans vs. Democrats	Democratic dominance and formation of the New Deal coalition. After 1950s, the New Deal coalition is weakened, and sectionalism declines, giving rise to competitive two-party politics for president and statewide elections.

SOURCE: John F. Bibby, *Politics, Parties, and Elections in America* (Chicago: Nelson-Hall, 1987), 22.

Following the Civil War, the Republican party dominated national government. The party of Abraham Lincoln, the Republicans were also the party of the Union and the North. The Democrats became the party of the South; a strict one-party system existed in the states of the old Confederacy. The Republican party would not emerge in the South for more than one hundred years.

The era of Republican dominance shifted in the mid-1870s as a period of balanced two-party competition emerged. Party control of Congress was often divided, but only one Democrat, Grover Cleveland, was elected president in this period. One of the legacies of the third party system was the emergence of political party "machines." Areas of one-party dominance increased the internal strength of party organizations. Because there was little competition for office, a great deal of political power became entrenched within the dominant party. Using patronage to build political "machines," parties came to be a central force in politics.

Political parties rose to their apogee in the sprawling urban centers of the nation. Big-city machines with their political bosses were a product of local party organizations. Their use of *patronage*—the dispensing of political favors and jobs based on party loyalty—helped build political empires. Organizational skill combined with a little graft and corruption maintained their smooth-running machines. Before the introduction of federal social welfare programs, political parties were mother, father, social services agency, and rich uncle all wrapped up in one. One of the bosses of New York City's Tammany Hall, George Washington Plunkitt, explained how it was done:

> What holds your grip on your district is to go right down among the poor families and help them in the different ways they need help. I've got a regular system for this. If there's a fire in Ninth, Tenth, or Eleventh Avenue, for example, any hour of the day or night, I'm usually there with some of my election district captains as soon as the fire engines. If a family is burned out, I don't ask whether they are Republicans or Democrats, and I don't refer them to the Charity Organization Society, which would investigate their case in a month or two and decide they were worthy of help about the time they are dead from starvation. I just get quarters for them, buy clothes for them if their clothes were burned up, and fix them up 'til they get things runnin' again. It's philanthropy, but it's politics, too—mighty good politics. Who can tell how many votes one of these fires bring me? The poor are the most grateful people in the world, and, let me tell you, they have more friends in their neighborhoods than the rich have in theirs.[8]

In the late nineteenth century, the urban machines flourished. Party workers met immigrants coming off the boat and signed them up as members of the Democratic party before they had even cleared immigration (which then became easier). Political machines slowly died out during the twentieth century. Big-city political machines are the only real example of highly centralized, powerful political parties in the American experience. Corruption made the machines the target of reformers, who considered them a threat to democracy. Between 1890 and 1920, Populists and Progressives initiated a number of reforms to erode the machines' power. In some jurisdictions, nonpartisan elections were mandated, and the establishment of merit systems at the state and local level limited patronage. Tighter voter registration requirements were adopted. Perhaps the most important change was the invention of the *direct primary*, allowing the rank and file—not party leaders or bosses—to choose candidates for office. The Progressive movement was particularly strong in the midwestern states of Minnesota, Wisconsin, and Nebraska and in California and some of the western states. Many current state party procedures date back to the Progressive reforms early in the twentieth century.

Elections that reshape the partisan loyalties of the electorate are called "realigning elections." The election of 1896 between Republican William McKinley and Populist-Democrat William Jennings Bryan was such an election. It ushered in another era of Republican dominance, broken only by a split within Republican ranks in 1912. The final party system to date followed the realigning 1932 election, when a majority of the electorate shifted from identifying with Republicans to identifying with the Democratic party. Since 1932, the Democrats have remained the majority party, although by the 1980s, the New Deal coalition had largely disintegrated.

Events of the most recent decades reflect a period of declining party strength and divided control of government. Democrats have dominated control of Congress, while Republicans have a lock on the presidency. Political parties have weakened because of the expansion of presidential primaries, the growing importance of the mass media, and the increasing importance of political action committees and candidate organizations over traditional party organizations. But despite its ups and downs,

President Andrew Jackson

the two-party system of Republican versus Democrat has existed for 130 years. Minor parties or "third parties" have not survived. Why has the two-party system proven so durable?

WHY DOES THE UNITED STATES HAVE A TWO-PARTY SYSTEM?

Despite the diverse background of the two political parties, the United States has maintained a two-party system through eras of political and economic change. Political scientists have come up with a number of explanations for this.

CONSENSUS. One explanation of the two-party system is based on the contention that Americans seem to have fewer political differences than citizens of other countries. Politics in the United States is based on common agreement on broad principles of politics and economics, and therefore voters are not responsive to ideological appeals. Because the Republican and Democratic parties have such broad constituencies, there is little room for third and fourth parties.

PARTY IDENTIFICATION. Most Americans still identify with one of the two major parties, and this contributes to the stability of the party system. Third parties have no historical pattern of psychological identification. They must either appeal to independents or lure identifiers away from their party. With clear evidence that **dealignment** (people leaving both parties) has taken place, the two-party system may be in increasing jeopardy if it depends on voter identification with the parties.

THE ELECTORAL SYSTEM AND LAW. A persuasive explanation of two-party dominance focuses on the nature of the electoral system. French political scientist Maurice Duverger suggests that electoral systems with **single-member districts** (only one person elected per district) and plurality elections (the candidate with the most votes, not necessarily a majority, wins) tend to support a two-party system.[9] The example of the Social Democrat/Liberal Alliance in the 1987 British general election is a classic case of how third parties in a two-party system are hurt by these election rules. Although the Alliance garnered 23 percent of the vote nationally, it won less than 4 percent of the 600-plus seats. In a system with *multimember districts* (more than one person elected per district) and **proportional representation** (where seats are allocated on the proportion of votes), the Alliance might have had as many as 150 seats.

Even though some multimember districts exist at the state level, the electoral system in the United States promotes a two-party system. All House members are elected every two years in single-member districts, and senators, with staggered elections, are elected in the practical equivalent. Winner-take-all rules in the electoral college similarly penalize minor parties.

State election laws are written in a way that tends to perpetuate two parties. In many states, it is very difficult for a third-party candidate to get on the ballot. Legal limitations make it cumbersome for third parties to organize and compete. Parties that concentrate their strength in a certain area (like George Wallace's American Independent party in the South in 1968) have the best chance to overcome the advantages the current system confers on the two parties.

The two-party system in the United States has proven extremely durable. Custom, history, partisan identification, and the electoral system combine to make it difficult for minor parties to take root. But change can occur—in the United States as elsewhere. The Republican party captured the presidency just four years after it was founded. The Social Democratic party in Great Britain made a strong showing less than two years after it was founded. The right circumstances could produce a new party to replace one of the current parties or usher in a multiparty era in American politics.

THIRD PARTIES IN THE UNITED STATES

Occasionally third parties have arisen to challenge the two dominant parties.[10] Every four years, a number of minor parties contest the presidential election. The total vote for all "third" parties was less than 1 percent in 1988. Only the eleven third parties shown in Table 8–2 have garnered more than 5 percent in a presidential election. Most of them eventually disappeared or were absorbed by one of the major parties.

The **Populist party** was one of the more notable third parties. In spite of some initial political

TABLE 8–2

AMERICA'S MOST SUCCESSFUL THIRD PARTIES

Third Party	Year	% of Popular Vote	Electoral Votes	Fate in Next Election
Anti-Masonic	1832	7.8	7	Endorsed Whig candidate
Free Soil	1848	10.1	0	Received 4.9% of vote
Whig-American	1856	21.5	8	Party dissolved
Southern Democrat	1860	18.1	72	Party dissolved
Constitutional Union	1860	12.6	39	Party dissolved
Populist	1892	8.5	22	Endorsed Democratic candidate
Progressive	1912	27.4	88	Returned to Republican party
Socialist	1912	6.0	0	Received 3.2% of vote
Progressive	1924	16.6	13	Returned to Republican party
American Independent	1968	13.5	46	Received 1.4% of the vote
John B. Anderson	1980	7.1	0	Did not run in 1984

SOURCES: Congressional Quarterly, *Guide to U.S. Elections* (Washington, D.C.: Congressional Quarterly, 1975); *Statistical Abstract of the United States, 1986.*

success, the Populists did not survive as a separate party, thanks to the Democrats also choosing William Jennings Bryan—the Populist presidential nominee—as the Democratic nominee in 1896. Bryan lost to William McKinley and was left to further the cause of populism within the Democratic party. When third parties raise important new issues, their concerns are often taken over by one of the major parties, preserving the two-party system.

Third parties are often launched by personalities instead of issues. The most successful third-party challenge in recent years was by a "personality" party. George Wallace made significant inroads in presidential primaries and captured 14 percent of the vote in the 1968 election. Without Wallace, however, his American Independent party fizzled. In 1980, John Anderson—a liberal Republican—ran as an independent candidate, campaigning on a number of issues he believed were being ignored by the major party candidates. But Anderson had no organized political party behind him. His support in preelection surveys was as high as 23 percent in June 1980, but it declined steadily until election day, when he received 7 percent of the national vote. Although Anderson's presence in the race could have had an impact if the election had been closer or if he had drawn votes from one candidate rather than from both, his candidacy had relatively little effect on the outcome. Because many people are reluctant to "waste" their vote, independent or third-party candidates usually suffer a sharp drop-off in support in the actual vote count. Were he not loyal to the Democratic party, based on his strong showing in the past, it is clear that Jesse Jackson could gain a significant number of votes as a third-party candidate.

Third parties have played a relatively minor role in elections, but they have a potential impact. A third-party candidate could tip the balance of votes between the two major parties. In a close presidential election, a candidate carrying only a few states could throw the election into the House. Third parties may affect the policy agenda of the two major parties. Despite the dominance of the two-party system, a new candidate or new issue could someday upset the traditional two-party balance and reshape American political parties.

Grassroots Support: Party in the Electorate

PARTY IDENTIFICATION

Party identification, the psychological attachment to one of the major parties, bonds ordinary citizens to the Republicans or Democrats. Party identification is measured by asking the following question: "Do you consider yourself a Republican, a Democrat, or an independent?"

Table 8–3 shows the historical distribution of party identification in the United States. Since the days of Roosevelt and the New Deal, the Democrats have been the majority party. In the postwar period, less than one-third of the electorate have considered themselves Republicans. Between 1960 and 1980, this figure declined to about one-fourth, despite the substantial presidential victories of Nixon in 1972 and Reagan in 1980. Between 1940 and 1980, Democrats were the favored party of from 40 percent to 50 percent of the population. But the 1980s saw interesting and important changes.

Between 1940 and 1980, the most notable trend in party identification was the decreasing number of strong partisans and the increasing number of independents. Those who identified themselves as independents increased from 20 percent in 1940 to as high as 35 percent in the late 1970s—a fairly widespread movement toward dealignment. Throughout most of the 1960s and 1970s, Republican identifiers lagged behind both Democrats and independents. But by the mid-1980s, Republican identifiers were on the rise. Political analysts began to speculate about a possible party **realignment,** making the Republicans the majority party instead of the Democrats.

The advantage enjoyed by the Democrats showed some signs of slipping during the 1980s, although they temporarily increased their edge after the Iran-Contra scandal in 1987. By 1989, the Democratic identifiers maintained only a slight margin over Republican identifiers, 38 percent to 34 percent. The trend toward dealignment stopped in the 1980s, with the proportion of citizens identifying themselves as independents stabilizing at around 28 to 30 percent. Data on the party identification of younger voters is more suggestive of a long-term realignment taking place. In 1989, 43 percent of those under thirty considered themselves Republicans compared to only 25 percent Democrats.[11] The older generation that was influenced in its partisan preferences by Franklin D.

The most successful third party candidate in recent years was independent John B. Anderson, who, in 1980 received over 7 percent of the national vote.

TABLE 8–3

Party Identification, 1937–1990

	´37	´44	´50	´54	´60	´64	´68	´72	´76	´80	´81	´82	´83	´84	´85	´86	´87	´88	´89	´90
Democrat	50%	41	45	46	47	53	46	43	47	46	42	45	44	40	38	39	41	42	38	39
Independent	16%	21	22	20	23	22	27	29	30	30	30	29	31	29	29	29	29	28	28	26
Republican	34%	38	33	34	30	25	27	28	23	24	28	26	25	31	33	32	30	30	34	35

SOURCE: Gallup Poll, *Gallup Report* no. 286 (July 1989); 1990 data from Gallup Poll, *Gallup Report*, no. 296 (May 1990).

Roosevelt is being replaced by a younger generation influenced by Ronald Reagan.

Party identification influences political behavior in a number of ways. Effects can be seen more clearly when party identification is broken down further by asking a follow-up question. Those who identify with the Republicans or Democrats are asked if they consider themselves a strong or a weak Republican (or Democrat). Independents are asked if they lean to one party or the other, resulting in the seven categories shown in Table 8–4. The most direct effect of party identification is on voting. But it is not a perfect relationship, or the Democrats would have won all the contests for president for the last fifty years. Table 8–4 shows the association between party identification and voting in 1988. In recent years, defections have been much greater for Democrats than for Republicans. This was particularly true in 1984, when one Democrat in six voted for Ronald Reagan. Party identification serves as a cue to voting, but it is an increasingly unreliable cue at the presidential level.

Identification with a political party affects political behavior in other ways as well. Party identification provides a perceptual screen that helps voters evaluate the complicated political messages that bombard them. It furnishes a political frame of reference, affects their attitudes on issues, and colors their feelings about different candidates. Yet it is never a complete guide to political behavior or a substitute for individual judgment or reaction to changes in the political environment. Table 8–4 shows that strong identifiers of both parties are more likely to vote than independents and more likely to participate in other ways. But independents play a crucial role in democratic politics. It is often their movement to the Democratic or Republican candidate that swings the election.[12]

The important role of party identification in models of political behavior has been firmly established in research published over the past thirty years. Its stability over time compared to other attitudes led political scientists to conclude that party identification affected issue positions, candidate assessment, and voting rather than being influenced itself by other short-term factors. However, recent findings by Michael MacKuen, Robert Erikson, and James Stimson have cast some doubt on those well-accepted conclusions.[13] They analyzed national party identification trends since 1945 and found them less stable than previously thought. More importantly, they demonstrated that the movement of party identification (such as the figures shown in Table 8–3) was systematic, not simply sampling error. The authors found that aggregate trends in national party identification can be explained in part by both economic conditions and presidential approval ratings in the preceding time period. Their findings that variations over time in party identification are related to political and economic factors will lead to additional research and insights into both the causes and effects of party identification.

Social Characteristics of Partisans

Before political scientists focused their attention on party identification as an important variable in political behavior, early voting studies concluded that socioeconomic factors determined the vote. Analysts concluded that a voter who was white, Protestant, and college-educated, had a white-collar job, and lived in a small town outside the South would be very likely to vote Republican. The typical Democratic voter was Catholic, a blue-collar worker with less education and lower income, and

TABLE 8–4

THE IMPACT OF PARTY IDENTIFICATION ON VOTING, 1988

	% Who Voted Democrat	% Who Voted Republican	Rate of Voter Turnout
Strong Democrat	93	7	68
Weak Democrat	68	32	54
Independent Democrat	86	14	56
Independent	35	65	41
Independent Republican	13	87	56
Weak Republican	16	84	63
Strong Republican	2	98	76

SOURCE: Center for Political Studies, National Election Study, 1988, reported in Abramson et al, *Change and Continuity in the 1988 Elections*, (Washington, DC.: Congressional Quarterly Press, 1990), 110, 211.

lived in a city. Voting studies of the past three decades have provided a clearer understanding of the relationship between social characteristics and how people vote. Party identification acts as a variable that intervenes between socioeconomic status and voting. Race, occupation, income, and religion also are related to party identification.

The Democratic party has fared poorly in presidential elections since the mid-1960s. In 1984, Walter Mondale and the Democratic party were portrayed as pawns of special interests, renewing questions about group support for political parties. A recent study by Stanley and associates examined the marginal difference that groups made in the Democratic party's support coalition between 1952 and 1984.[14] The core groups supporting the Democratic party over the years are blacks, Catholics, Jews, women, southern whites, union members, and working-class people. Table 8–5 shows how likely members of these groups are to identify with the Democrats and that group support for the Democratic party has varied over the years. Blacks have significantly increased their support for the Democratic party, while support from southern whites has declined significantly. This tends to confirm the hypothesis that there was a realignment of blacks in the middle 1960s. Note the dramatic shift in the probability of black Democratic identification between 1960 (45 percent) and 1968 (85 percent). White southerners significantly declined in their probability of identifying with the Democrats from 75 percent in 1952 to 42 percent in 1984. For Jews, Catholics, females, union members, and working-class people, identification with the Democratic party declined overall between 1952 and 1984.

Racial differences in partisanship and voting increased over the last decade. The increase in identification with the Republican party has been substantially greater among the white electorate and was partially masked in the aggregate figures by shifts among the black electorate towards the Democratic party. In 1988, among whites, Republican identifiers and leaners outnumbered Democrats 46 percent to 40 percent. In contrast, among blacks, Democrats held an 81 percent-to-11 percent advantage.[15] Despite efforts by the Republican party to appeal to black voters, in 1988, only 1 percent of blacks considered themselves strong Republicans.

Tenuous at the Top: The Party Organizations

NATIONAL PARTY ORGANIZATION

American political parties are bottom-heavy, dominated by state organizations rather than ruled from above. Figure 8–2 shows the structure of the two parties. Each party is governed by a national chairperson and a national committee. The main activities of the national parties have to do with the presidential nominating conventions. The rest of the time, national parties exercise little political power and are little more than confederations of state party representatives.

National party chairs are important but rarely wield great power. If the chairperson's party controls the presidency, he or she must be compatible with the president. The party chairperson is often ideologically close to the president, as Lee Atwater was with President Bush after 1988. If the party is not in control of the presidency, however, the party chairperson needs to be acceptable to the different factions in the party. In this situation, the party chairperson's job is more organizational than policy oriented. He or she must concentrate on fund-raising, planning the convention, overseeing various party commissions and committees, and managing the affairs of the national parties.

National leaders of the Republican and Democratic parties play a role in defining the image and approach of the party. After his 1988 presidential victory, George Bush's choice of top campaign strategist, Lee Atwater, to head the party was endorsed by the Republican National Committee (RNC). Atwater was particularly disliked by Democrats because of his role in shaping the aggressive media campaign against Michael Dukakis during the 1988 campaign. Atwater was named to the Howard University board of trustees but had to resign after vehement protests by African-American students angry at what they believed were racist messages in some of the Bush campaign ads. Following the defeat in 1988, the Democratic National Committee chose Ron Brown of California to chair the national Democratic party. Brown, the first black to chair a major U.S. political party, is profiled in the accompanying People in Politics.

The national committees are made up of representatives of the fifty states. Members are chosen either by state convention, by the state central committee, by the delegates to the national convention, or in a few states through primaries.[16] As a group, the national party committees are weaker than party organizations in other countries, meeting infrequently and having little group identity. Analogous to the states under the Articles of Confederation, most of the power of American political parties resides at the state and local level.

STATE AND LOCAL PARTY ORGANIZATION

Across the nation, there are still sharp differences in how competitive the two parties are with each other. Pockets of one-party dominance still exist. In the southern states, some Republican party organizations remain weak after a century of Democratic control, but they are growing rapidly. Although Republicans have done well at the presidential level, Democrats still monopolize state and local elective offices in the South. The Republican party is increasingly strong in the West and Southwest, and it maintains its traditional strength in some parts of New England.

State parties play under fifty different sets of rules. Some states allow parties to control the

TABLE 8–5

OVERALL PROBABILITY OF DEMOCRATIC IDENTIFICATION FOR GROUP MEMBERS, 1952–1984

Group	1952	1956	1960	1964	1968	1972	1976	1980	1984
Blacks	.53	.50	.45	.79	.85	.68	.70	.70	.65
Catholics	.56	.51	.65	.61	.54	.50	.50	.42	.42
Jews	.70	.60	.50	.52	.54	.52	.57	.69	.59
Females	.47	.43	.49	.59	.51	.43	.42	.42	.40
Native southern whites	.75	.70	.72	.71	.52	.50	.52	.46	.42
Union households	.54	.50	.57	.67	.53	.45	.47	.44	.46
Working-class people	.54	.48	.51	.64	.55	.45	.46	.44	.42

NOTE: Cells are the mean of the predicted probabilities of identification for group members each year.

SOURCE: H. W. Stanley, W. T. Bianco, and R. G. Niemi, "Partisanship and Group Support over Time: A Multivariate Analysis," *American Political Science Review* (September 1986): 969–976.

FIGURE 8–2

THE STRUCTURE OF AMERICAN POLITICAL PARTIES

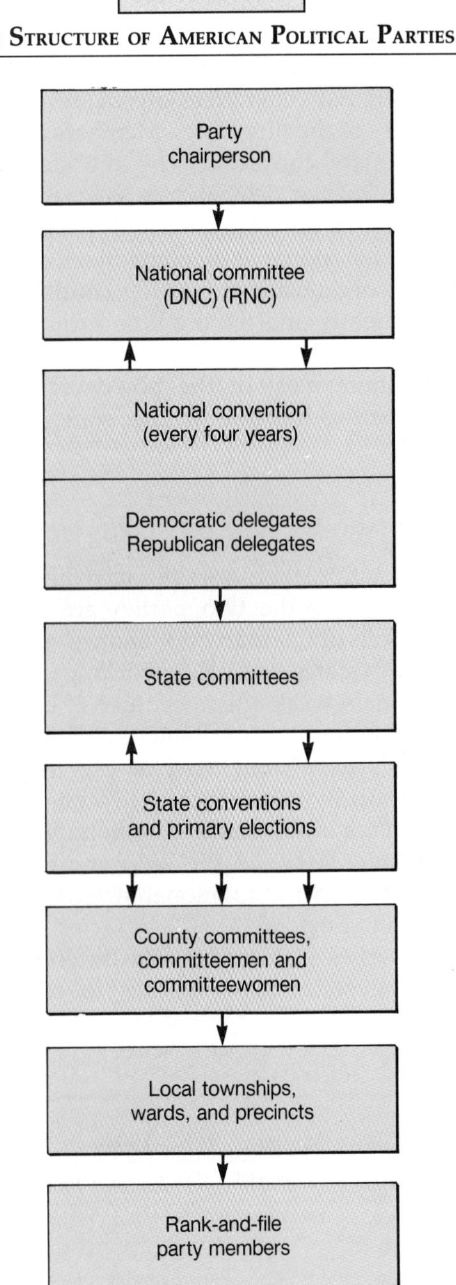

political process more than others. At the low end of the scale with weaker parties are Alabama, California, Kansas, Maryland, Nevada, Oklahoma, and Tennessee.[17] States that allow greater party authority are Connecticut, Delaware, Indiana, Michigan, New Jersey, New York, and South Dakota. One important way that parties exercise their authority is by controlling the recruitment of candidates. In Connecticut, where parties are strong, 83 percent of the state legislative candidates are recruited by the state parties. In Wisconsin, where parties were weakened by Progressive-era reforms, the figure is only 13 percent.[18]

Each state party system is a variation on a theme. Powerful individuals or families dominate some states: the Kennedys in Massachusetts, the Byrds in Virginia, the Longs in Louisiana. Big-city party organizations may control the state party. The Daley machine in Chicago, for example, exerted powerful influence over the Illinois Democratic party.[19] Certain state parties are splintered into competing geographic factions. In New York State, Democrats dominate in New York City, while Republicans dominate in upstate areas. In California, liberal Democrats control the northern part of the state, and conservative Republicans dominate the area around Los Angeles. California, with relatively weak parties, has produced a diverse group of political personalities. "Governor Moonbeam" Jerry Brown, former actors Ronald Reagan and George Murphy, the enigmatic Richard Nixon, S. I. Hayakawa (the college president who squashed student protests in the 1960s), and Tom Hayden (a state assemblyman who once led student protests) all came from the Golden State. As traditional party loyalties break down, state party politics become more fluid and unpredictable. But American political parties are not dead yet. Despite the organizational decay over the years, signs of national party revival and renewal abound.

NATIONAL PARTY REFORM

The 1970s and 1980s witnessed important changes in the political parties in the direction of strengthening their organizations and their political influence.

THE REPUBLICANS: MODERNIZING THE PARTY APPARATUS. The Republican party has been the more stable of the two parties, avoiding the divisive internal reforms that have characterized the Democrats since 1968. For years, the national Republican party was little more than an office in Washington, a few national committee meetings, and the convention every four years. The Republicans hit bottom after

People in Politics

Ronald Brown, Democratic Party Chairman

Following the defeat of Michael Dukakis in 1988, the Democratic party sought a new leader. The problem of selecting a national chair acceptable to the diverse elements of the party is not unlike the problem of selecting a presidential candidate. Although Jesse Jackson lost the nomination in 1988 to Dukakis, the Democratic National Committee (DNC) turned to his convention manager, Ron Brown, to head the party. By the time the DNC voted for a new national chair on February 10, 1989, all of Brown's rivals for the job had withdrawn. His appointment brought with it a challenging agenda.

Ron Brown was born in the Harlem section of New York City in 1941. His parents managed the once-famous Theresa Hotel where politicians, entertainers, and sports heroes congregated. It was at the Theresa in 1952 that the young Brown had his photograph taken with vice presidential candidate Richard Nixon. Brown later joked, "I immediately decided I wanted to become a Democrat." His mother and father, both graduates of Howard University, stressed the importance of education. Attending school on New York's upper east side, he experienced the extremes of poverty and affluence that existed only a matter of blocks from each other. When he enrolled at Middlebury College in Vermont, he was the only black in his class.

At Middlebury, Brown pledged a fraternity that had racial restrictions in its charter. With the support of his fraternity brothers, he was instrumental in breaking down the restrictions for Sigma Phi Epsilon and

all other fraternities at the college. After a tour of duty in the military, he returned to New York in the mid-1960s. Brown took a job with the Urban League and attended law school at night at St. John's University, where he became close friends with one of the university's most feared professors, Mario Cuomo. Their paths would cross many times again. Brown moved to Washington, D.C., in the early 1970s and made many acquaintances among the Democratic elite in the nation's capitol. In 1980, he headed Ted Kennedy's campaign in the California primary and remained active in Democratic circles while practicing law.

Brown initially turned down Jesse Jackson when he was asked to manage Jackson's 1988 campaign for president. But after the primaries, and with a growing sense of the importance of the Jackson candidacy, he agreed to take over during the convention. Although Jackson would not win the nomination, Brown had a profound effect on the convention. His performance as a tough but pragmatic negotiator and his concern with party unity impressed the Dukakis forces and thrust him into contention for the party chairmanship after the election. He faced three former members of Congress, the Michigan Democratic party chairman, and other prominent Democrats. His political skills paid off with early endoresements from Governor Cuomo and Senator Bill Bradley (D-N.J.), as the other challengers bowed out.

Many saw Brown's close association with Jackson as a liability in efforts to unify the national party. But the new party chairman distanced himself from Jackson, endorsing Chicago's Democratic mayoral nominee, Richard M. Daley, while Jackson supported an independent black candidate. Brown's selection reflects the importance of black voters to the Democratic party, but Democrats know that to win a national election, the party must recapture moderate white voters. Some critics objected not to Brown's race but his close ties to the "Eastern liberal establishment." Ron Brown will face many difficult controversies over divisive issues and party rules as the 1992 election nears. But after a dismal decade in terms of presidential elections, he has an opportunity to change the strategies and fortunes of the Democratic party in the 1990s.

Watergate and Gerald Ford's defeat in 1976; then they changed strategies. Under William Brock, national chairperson, the Republican party strengthened its national organization and fund-raising apparatus. Party operations were computerized, and a highly effective direct-mail fund-raising campaign was developed. The national party undertook organizational reform, stressing improved services to state parties and candidates.[20] It established fifteen regional political directors to work with the states, provided technical assistance for fund-raising, and established a national data-processing network. From their low point in 1976, the Republicans staged an impressive comeback. They captured the presidency and the Senate in 1980, raising significantly more money than the Democrats and effectively exploiting a superior organization.

THE DEMOCRATS: TOWARD BROADER REPRESENTATION AND PARTY DEMOCRACY. The Democratic party since 1968 has followed a controversial path of procedural reform implementing fundamental changes in the national party structure and rules to broaden representation and foster intraparty democracy. The controversy within the Democratic party has focused on five key issues: (1) the role of party officials in the national convention, (2) quotas for women and minorities in the convention, (3) proportional representation in state primaries, (4) the right of presidential candidates to pick delegates, and (5) restricting participation in primaries to Democratic voters.[21]

Changes in party rules have broadened representation within the party but have been disruptive and divisive. Five reform commissions within the Democratic party were formed between 1968 and 1988. The McGovern-Fraser Commission (1968–71) implemented the **equal division rule,** requiring that delegates be divided equally between men and women, as well as affirmative action guidelines that resulted in significant increases in the number of minorities as delegates. The blacks, women, and young people who went to the convention for the first time in 1972 replaced many traditional party leaders. Loyal Democratic regulars felt they had been pushed out by a group of outsiders. The massive McGovern defeat led to the formation of the Mikulski Commission in 1973, which relaxed requirements in order to include more party officials. The Winograd Commission (1975–78) extended the effort to regain party leaders and elected Democratic officials as convention delegates.

After the 1980 election defeat, the Hunt Commission (1981–82) proposed a number of major changes in the presidential selection process that were adopted by the Democratic National Committee.[22] Equal division and affirmative action were maintained, and there was some movement away from proportional representation. The primary season was shortened by five weeks, and 550 "super-delegates" were added, which meant automatic convention seats for national committee members, state Democratic legislative leaders, and three-fifths of the Democrats in Congress.

After the 1984 loss, the Democratic party convened the Fairness Commission, which added more party leaders to the convention. Some 80 percent of the Democratic members of the Congress were delegates in 1988, compared with 60 percent in 1984. In addition, all Democratic governors and all 372 members of the Democratic National Committee automatically received delegate seats. The new delegates expanded the total number of delegates at the Democratic Convention from 3,933 in 1984 to 4,133 in 1988. In response to the complaints of Jesse Jackson, the panel recommended lowering the threshold for receiving delegates from 20 percent to 15 percent of all votes cast in a state primary. As it turned out, Jackson ran well across the country in 1988 and did not need the lower threshold. The Democratic party restored the "open primary" in Wisconsin and Montana. In prior years, Wisconsin election law allowed a "crossover" primary, where all voters, regardless of party registration, could participate in either primary. Hunt Commission reforms, however, required all states to hold primaries for "Democrats only"—either registered Democrats or people declaring themselves to be Democrats on election day. The experiment with the closed primary was judged a failure by Wisconsin Democrats, who noted that turnout was the lowest in thirty years. Others argued that, in the face of the Mondale debacle, Democrats had to make a greater effort to reach out to independents.

Spurred by complaints from the Jesse Jackson campaign, the Democratic party agreed on yet another rules change for the 1992 nomination process. Despite the fact that Michael Dukakis and many party professionals felt the process worked well in 1988, they made concessions to Jackson for the sake of party unity. Two key changes were adopted. The first would tie the number of delegates more closely to a candidate's actual primary vote. This was accomplished by banning bonus delegate allocation systems used in large states such as New York and Florida. Second, it was agreed that the total number of super-delegates would be reduced to around 400. Under the 1988 rules, Dukakis was able to translate his 42 percent of the primary vote into a clear majority at the convention by capturing bonus delegates and the lion's share of the super-delegates. Had these new rules been in effect in 1988, the prospect for a "brokered" convention where no candidate commanded a majority of delegates would have been much greater. Critics within the party complained that these changes sacrificed the long-term strength of the national party for the short-term interests of individual candidates. After two decades of tinkering with the party machinery, Democrats would use yet another set of nominating rules in 1992.

Uncertain Allegiance: Party in Government

RESPONSIBLE PARTIES: THE DESIRE TO ENHANCE GOVERNING

Over the years, a number of observers have linked governing problems in the United States to the weakness of political parties.[23] The Republicans and Democrats are portrayed as "me-too" parties, too middle-of-the-road to have any meaningful differences. The parties confuse voters who have to rely on image, personality, or some other criterion to make a voting choice. Weak parties are unable to transform platform proposals into concrete policies. Advocates of responsible parties particularly decry the lack of party loyalty and discipline in government.

Woodrow Wilson is considered the founder of the doctrine of **responsible parties.** An admirer of the British party system, with its strong parties and clear policy differences, Wilson believed the winning party in an election should have a clear mandate to govern by virtue of its distinctive party program. Disciplined parties would bridge the gap between the executive and legislative branches brought about by separation of powers and the Madisonian system of checks and balances. Disciplined parties would bind congressional majorities to the president, making the national government better able to govern efficiently and effectively. Disciplined parties would be more responsible as well. With clear-cut party programs, the electorate would be able to choose more clearly between the candidates and would be able to hold the officials more accountable in their actions.[24]

The responsible-parties doctrine holds the following:

1. Political parties should *not* be broad-based coalitions of different ideologies, but instead each party should present clear and specific programs.
2. Parties presenting distinct alternatives are more responsible because voters can choose between them more definitively and the party that wins has a clear mandate to govern.
3. Once in power, party discipline would be high and Congress would pass the party program as presented by the president, enhancing both the ability to govern and accountability.

On occasion, something approaching party government has prevailed in American politics. Franklin Roosevelt was able to command the loyalty and support of congressional Democrats and pass dramatic new legislation in his first "hundred days." More recently, with a little help from conservative Democrats, Ronald Reagan created a Republican-conservative majority to achieve passage of his far-reaching 1981 economic program. But such cases are the exception, not the rule. More frequently, presidents cannot count on support from their party in Congress. Would the United States be better off with more responsible, disciplined parties? Is it possible to achieve responsible parties within American politics? How much difference really exists between the Republicans and Democrats?

DIFFERENCES BETWEEN THE TWO PARTIES

The Republican and Democratic parties have been compared to Tweedledum and Tweedledee, the indistinguishable twins from Lewis Carroll's *Through the Looking Glass.* Obviously, there are differences between the two parties, but are these differences meaningful enough to give voters a real choice?

While the Republican party has been successful at the presidential level, it has not yet emerged as the majority party in the nation.

Does the election of one party's candidate over the other's change the course of public policy? Voters in the 1964 election presumably had a clear choice between the highly conservative Republican Barry Goldwater and the very liberal Democrat Lyndon Johnson. Yet soon after the election, Johnson escalated the war in Vietnam—just as he had charged Goldwater would do if elected. Republican Richard Nixon not only formed diplomatic ties with the People's Republic of China but also submitted a comprehensive welfare reform package to Congress. These were policies that an observer might have thought more "Democratic" than "Republican."

Party platforms hold important clues to the differences between the two parties. Written every four years, the platform summarizes the party's stands on a broad range of issues. Sensitive to the charge that it catered to special interests, the Democratic party streamlined its platform in 1988. The 1988 platform was much shorter and less specific across a wide range of issues. Yet caution must be exercised when attempting to determine real party differences. Platforms are political documents designed to make the two parties look as different as possible. More than lists of goals and proposed actions, the platforms are frontal attacks on the record and positions of the opposition. Political Insight 8–1 compares key provisions of the 1988 Republican and Democratic platforms.

Even though politicians and journalists emphasize conflict and divergence, party differences are limited. The platforms of both the Democratic party and the Republican party are built on broad social consensus and agreement on basic values. Both parties share reverence for the elderly, for family farms, for small business and free enterprise, and for a strong national defense.

The responsible-parties doctrine requires that parties translate their program into public policy. Yet even if meaningful differences exist between the parties, Congress rarely divides along party lines. Over the past decade, only around half of all roll-call votes in Congress found a majority of Democrats opposing a majority of Republicans.[25] Most bills reflect a compromise between the majority and minority parties in each house. Rarely is the president's program passed exactly as requested. Input from a variety of sources, including elements of both party platforms, alter proposals before they become law. Political parties remain important to the way government is organized to make public policy, but unlike parliamentary democracies, party alone does not form the basis for policy-making. Some policies are determined by interest groups, not by parties. Some policies are determined by regional divisions that cut across party lines. Some policies, notably foreign affairs policy, are often characterized by a bipartisan approach. Party is only one of many important factors in making policy.

Because of the limited ability of parties to determine public policy, some people are extremely skeptical about the party platform. The presidential candidate may not have supported all parts of the platform and may not push very hard for its proposals. But political scientist Gerald Pomper studied the translation of platforms into policy and concluded that things are not as bad as the cynics claim. Looking at the platforms over twenty years, Pomper found that a majority of items actually became policy. He concluded: "Democrats and Republicans are not 'Tweedledum' and 'Tweedledee', but neither are they practitioners of 'party government.'"[26]

Rational Parties: The Desire to Get Elected

If one looks at American political parties from a strategic perspective, they act more like **rational parties** than responsible parties. The programmatic similarity of the parties is fostered not only by underlying consensus but also by rational electoral strategies. Parties place more emphasis on winning elections than on ideological purity, dictating that they stay close to the political center of the electorate.

In his *Economic Theory of Democracy,* Anthony Downs argues that where prevailing public opinion tends to be middle-of-the-road, rational parties will tend to be centrist.[27] If a party goes too far to the right or left, the other party will quickly fill the void and capture the majority of the vote. Some argue this is what happened in 1964 with Barry Goldwater (too conservative) and in 1972 with George McGovern (too liberal). Differences are minimized, according to Downs, because both parties hug the middle. Third parties, as a result, have a tough time. The political middle, where most of the voters presumably are, is already co-opted by the two major parties. Third parties are left to appeal to a small number of voters to the right or left. Downs's theory seems to fit the British parties in the 1980s. When the Labor party moved left and the Conservative party moved right, a gap was left in the political middle. It was quickly filled by a new political party, the Social Democrats.

If American parties cling to the middle of the road, why do they portray each election as a choice between stark alternatives? Such a portrayal is an effort to push the opposition party out of the mainstream in the minds of the voters. The Republicans pictured the Democrats in 1980 as the party of declining national defense and weakening traditional family values, the party of economic doom, despair, and failure. The success of the Republicans in the election was not lost on the Democrats. Seeking to reestablish their hold on the majority of voters, Democrats in 1988 emulated the Republicans by emphasizing their commitment to economic growth in the private sector, family values, and a strong national defense. In the 1982 elections, Democrats tried to push Republicans out of the political center on the sensitive Social Security issue. After midterm election losses in 1982, President Reagan went to great lengths to affirm his support for Social Security in the 1984 election, promising to make no cuts. Trying to win majority support, parties usually act rationally by moving toward each other, instead of moving further apart, as advocated by the responsible-parties doctrine. Is this good for the voters?

Research on the American voter since the 1950s suggests that the responsible-party model does not fit the U.S. political system very well because of the nature of the electorate, the organizational weakness of the national parties, the broad coalitions included in each party, and the fragmentation of the political system. Opponents of the responsible party doctrine note the advantages of the rational-party system. Broad coalition parties promote consensus and reduce conflict. They produce less dramatic shifts in public policy when there is a change in the party in power. Nonetheless, the appeal of a stronger party system remains, particularly when deadlock appears to cripple the process of governing. Three decades ago, even though the United States did not have disciplined parties, party ties were stronger than today. Congressional party leaders had greater control of members. If there is no other way to structure political loyalty or form lasting coalitions, will the ability to govern be sufficient to make tough policy choices in the 1990s? What looms ahead for America's political parties?

The Future of Party Politics

There is little consensus among analysts and experts about the future of American political parties. One book title proclaims *The Party's Over,* while another author responds in a book entitled *The Party's Just Begun.*[28] Claims and counterclaims are made about dealignment, realignment, decline, and

POLITICAL INSIGHT 8–1

COMPARISONS OF THE 1988 REPUBLICAN AND DEMOCRATIC PARTY PLATFORMS

In 1988, the Democratic party produced a short platform stating general principles and goals. The Republicans produced a much longer, more detailed list of positions and objectives. Despite the very different styles of the two platforms, one can find among the various planks some similarities among sharp differences.

THE ECONOMY

Republican platform. Our nation of communities is prosperous and free. In the sixth year of unprecedented economic expansion, more people are working than ever before; real family income has risen; inflation is tamed. By almost any measure, Americans are better off than they were eight years ago.

Democratic platform. We believe that the time has come again for America to take charge once again of its economic future, to reverse seven years of "voodoo economics," "trickle down" policies, fiscal irresponsibility, and economic violence against poor and working people that have converted this proud country into the world's largest debtor nation. . . .

DEFENSE

Republican platform. Peace through strength is now a proven policy. We have modernized our forces, revitalized our military infrastructure, recruited and trained the most capable fighting force in American history. And we have used these tools with care, responsibility and restraint. . . .

This underscores the need for the deployment of the Strategic Defense System commonly known as SDI. SDI represents America's single most important defense program and is the most significant investment we can make in our nation's future security.

Democratic platform. We believe that our national strength has been sapped by a defense establishment wasting money on duplicative and dubious new weapons instead of investing more in readiness and mobility; that our national strength will be enhanced by more stable defense budgets and by a commitment from our allies to assume a greater share of the costs and responsibilities required to maintain peace and liberty. . . .

CENTRAL AMERICA

Republican platform. Central America has always been a region of strategic importance for the United States. . . . Today, thousands of Nicaraguans are united in a struggle to free their homeland from a totalitarian regime. The Republican Party stands shoulder to shoulder with them and with both humanitarian and military aid. If democracy does not prevail, if Nicaragua remains a communist dictatorship dedicated to exporting revolution, the fragile democracies in Central America will be jeopardized.

Democratic platform. We believe in an America neither gun-shy nor trigger-happy, that will promote peace and prevent war—not by trading weapons for hostages, not by sending brave Americans to undefined missions. . . . We believe that this country should provide new leadership (in Central America) to deliver the promise of peace and security through negotiations.

WOMEN'S RIGHTS AND ABORTION

Republican platform. We renew our historic commitment to equal rights for women. . . . We must remove remaining obstacles to women's achieving their full potential and full reward. That does not include the notion of federally mandated comparable worth, which would substitute the decisions of bureaucrats for the judgment of individuals.

(Continued on next page.)

POLITICAL INSIGHT 8–1

We believe . . . that the unborn child has a fundamental right to life which cannot be infringed. We there reaffirm our support for a human life amendment to the Constitution. . . .

Democratic platform. We further believe that we must work for the adoption of the Equal Rights Amendment to the Constitution; that the fundamental right of reproductive choice should be guaranteed regardless of ability to pay. . . .

TRADE

Republican platform. To make the 1990s America's decade in international trade, Republicans will advance trade through strength. We will not accept the loss of American jobs to nationalized, subsidized, protected foreign industries and will continue to negotiate assertively the destruction of trade barriers.

Democratic platform. We believe that America needs more trade, fair trade, an administration willing to use all the tools available to better manage our trade in order to export more American goods and fewer American jobs, an administration willing to recognize in the formulation and enforcement of our trade laws that workers' rights are important human rights abroad as well as at home, and that advance notice of plant closings and major layoffs is not only fundamentally right but also economically sound.

DRUGS

Republican platform. The Republican Party is committed to a drug-free America. Our policy is strict accountability, for users of illegal drugs as well as for those who profit by that usage. . . .

The Republican Party unequivocally opposes legalizing or decriminalizing any illicit drug. . . .

We know the most powerful deterrent to drug abuse: strong stable family life, along with the absolute approach summed up in "Just Say No."

Democratic platform. We believe that illegal drugs pose a direct threat to the security of our nation from coast to coast, invading our neighborhoods, classrooms, homes and communities large and small; that every arm and agency of government at every federal, state and local level . . . should at long last be mobilized . . . and that the legalization of illicit drugs would represent a tragic surrender in a war we intend to win.

EDUCATION

Republican platform. Republican leadership has launched a new era in American education. Our vision of excellence has brought education back to parents, back to basics, and back on a track of excellence leading to a brighter and stronger future for America.

. . . We must make America a nation of learners, ready to compete in the rapidly changing world of the future. Our goal is to combine traditional values and enduring truths with the most modern techniques and technology for teaching and learning.

Democratic platform. We believe that the education of our citizens, from Head Start to institutions of higher learning, deserves our highest priority; and that history will judge the next administration less by its success in building new weapons of war than by its success in improving young minds. We believe that this nation needs to invest in its children on the front side of life by expanding the availability of preschool education for children at risk; to invest in its teachers through training and enrichment programs, . . . to commit itself for the first time to the principle that no one should be denied the opportunity to attend college for financial reasons. . . .

party renewal and reform. Just what does the future hold for party politics in the United States? Will the parties become more or less important in election campaigns and voting? Will they have a greater or lesser role in governing? What are the problems and prospects for the Republicans and Democrats?

STILL WAITING FOR THE REPUBLICAN MAJORITY

The Republican party seemed doomed in 1964 after one of the biggest landslides in history when Lyndon Johnson overwhelmed conservative Barry Goldwater. But since that defeat, the Republicans rebounded to capture the White House in five out of six elections. Even the 1976 election, the party's only loss, was close despite the Watergate fiasco and a divisive nomination battle. The national Republican party made important strides as an organization. Despite the growing independence of candidates, the national Republican party has become a more important force in financing and assisting Republican candidates. The Republicans captured the U.S. Senate in 1980 for the first time in twenty-six years and made gains in state and local offices in the early 1980s. The Republican party has dominated its Democratic rival in the battle over ideas among the American electorate. The party became more conservative in 1980 with the nomination and election of Ronald Reagan, presenting a clearer ideological image to the American people. Throughout the 1980s, the Republican party has retained its advantages in the minds of a majority of voters as the party better able to maintain prosperity, prevent war, and tackle the nation's top problems. Entering the 1990s, Republican George Bush enjoyed record public approval ratings.

Nonetheless, many Republicans are disappointed at gains made outside the presidency. Despite pulling nearly even with the Democrats in terms of voter identification and their advantages among the young, a clear Republican realignment has not yet occurred. Republicans lost the Senate in 1986 and have virtually no prospects for controlling the House of Representatives. Many of the gains of the early Reagan years in the numbers of Republican state and local officials were reversed by the late 1980s. The Republican party is increasingly a white party, making few inroads in growing segments of minority voters. Republican advantages among voters remain incomplete and fragile. As we saw in the last chapter, public opinion is inconsistent; Americans want lower taxes but more spending on social programs. The perception of the Republican party as stronger on national defense may become less important with the end of the cold war and growing public pressure for defense cuts. Perceptions of the two parties also depend on economic trends and continued prosperity. The growing battle over abortion threatens to divide the "enterprisers" and the "moralists," the two main components of the Republican coalition (see Chapter 7).

IN SEARCH OF A DEMOCRATIC PARTY IDENTITY

The Democratic party would appear to have more serious problems than the Republicans. As the New Deal coalition of the 1930s has faded, Democrats have failed to create a clear identity for voters at the national level. Democrats have been called the "everybody party." The party's broad array of groups and interests include social and environmental activists who are heavily female and highly educated; older blue-collar workers who are economically liberal and socially conservative; gays, minorities, and poor people. This coalition has proven problematic at the national level but more workable at the state and local level, where the party has been successful. Unlike their presidential candidates, Democratic candidates for statewide office and Congress can more carefully tailor their campaign issues and appeal to constituents in their region and locality. At this level, they have succeeded, entering the 1990s with stable majorities in Congress and significantly more governors, state legislators, and mayors than the Republicans.

Despite problems with its identity as a national party, many Democratic issues and programs have proven durable.[29] Social Security, Medicare, protection of the environment, equal rights for women, and opposition to unfair practices by big corporations remain popular with the American people even after the 1980s. The Democratic party has adapted its positions to better compete with Republicans. Support for strong defense, law and order, free enterprise, and family values has become more pronounced as Democrats have responded to public opinion and behaved rationally in altering their message. This response may have prevented or at least delayed a partisan realignment.

Tinkering with the rules of the game for the presidential nomination process has also hampered Democratic efforts nationally. In attempting to create rules that are fair to its diverse constituencies, it has created problems for party nominees. Lagging behind Republicans in terms of organizational reforms and financial strength, Democratic candidates have had to rely on contributions from political action committees and have encouraged direct contributions to state party organizations (referred to as "soft money" contributions) to skirt spending limits. This has put the party in a difficult position regarding campaign finance reform. Although uncomfortable with their dependence on PACs, Democrats are reluctant to relinquish their sources of funding unless the national party can compete more equally with the Republicans.

PARTIES AND GOVERNING

The issue of realignment is less relevant in today's politics than it was fifty years ago because parties themselves are less critical to the processes of organizing elections and governing. While both parties have renewed themselves in important ways, parties are not as important for voters as they are in other nations and as they once were in the United States. Political scientist Larry Sabato concludes:

> As long as the parties remain irrelevant to the public's view of the political world, ticket-splitting will flourish, volatility in the electorate will be the norm, and shifts between party identification and Independency or "leaning" status will be casual in response to the current fads in issues and personalities. Further, the concept of realignment itself will not be germain, both because voters will not take parties seriously enough to adopt a new label with any permanency and because realignments under these conditions can be nothing more than . . . transient adjustments to the candidates and circumstances of the moment.[30]

Given inconsistent voter preferences and the structural features of American political institutions that produce divided party control of government, parties—at least for the time being—cannot become the critical element for effective governing. Government must develop procedures for resolving conflicts, overcoming deadlock, and making hard policy choices that do not depend on responsible parties or party government. This may mean bipartisan summits between legislative and executive branches. It may necessitate greater reliance on bipartisan commissions to provide political "cover" for acting on controversial issues. More autonomous (and less democratic) institutions like the Federal Reserve Board or the federal courts may become more important. Political parties have been an enduring feature of American politics and will continue to be so in the future but in less critical ways than in the past.

SUMMARY AND CONCLUSIONS

1. American political parties, although weaker than parties in most other democracies, perform the same basic functions: recruit candidates for office, help shape the policy agenda, and organize the government to make policy. More than anything else, U.S. parties organize to win elections. In general, the two parties are broad-based coalition parties seeking the support of a majority of Americans.

2. Disagreement over the powers of the national government and economic issues resulted in the emergence of the first American political parties. The current Republican-Democratic division emerged at the time of the Civil War.

3. Explanations for the durability of the two-party system include national consensus, party identification, and the nature of the electoral system and state laws. Third parties have occasionally been important but have not cracked the two-party system.

4. Party in the electorate is the foundation of political parties consisting of people who identify with one party or another. Parties help people understand politics and provide important cues for voting and other political behavior, but this seems to be less important than in the past in presidential voting. Party identification in the electorate has declined, a phenomenon called "dealignment."

5. The second element of party is party organization. American political parties do not have strong national organizations, and in fact are extremely weak at the top. State and local parties are stronger.

6. The third element of party is party in government. Compared with the importance of party in other democratic political systems, party affiliation in American politics does not supply a steady or dependable allegiance. American parties act more like rational parties than like responsible parties.

7. The two political parties face different problems in the 1990s. Evidence suggests that a Republican realignment has not yet taken place. The Democrats have had trouble finding an identity and have a diversified coalition to unite under one party.

As political parties have declined, other institutions in politics have taken over some of their traditional functions. For example, interest groups and political action committees are an increasing source of policy guidance and election financing. But this takeover has certain political costs. Parties aggregate interests. Interest groups have much more specialized, limited aims. When parties are replaced by interest groups, politics becomes more fragmented as narrower interests attempt to achieve dominance. Growing interest-group power puts more of a burden on institutions like Congress. In the absence of effective parties, Congress is left to aggregate interests and choose relative priorities by itself, making governing more difficult. Weak parties encourage more and stronger interest groups, putting more pressure on Congress and the presidency in the process of governing.

The mass media have also begun to perform the traditional roles of political parties in the grooming, evaluation, and "coronation" of presidential candidates. Television has given citizens an opportunity to make their own judgments about potential candidates. With television and primaries, parties have little control over nominations. Neither interest groups nor the national media can perform all the functions of political parties. Unlike parties, they are as likely to further limit governing ability as they are to foster it.

KEY TERMS

coalition parties
dealignment
Democratic Republicans
equal division rule
Federalists
multiparty system
party discipline
party in government
party in the electorate
party organizations
party platforms
Populist party
proportional representation
rational parties
realignment
responsible parties
single-member districts

SELF-REVIEW

1. How do parties affect governing?
2. How do American political parties compare with parties abroad?
3. Under what conditions did political parties emerge?
4. How did parties change during the Jackson era? after the Civil War?
5. Why does the United States have a two-party system?
6. What has been the significance of third parties in the United States?
7. What are the patterns of party identification in the electorate?
8. Describe the social characteristics of partisans.
9. How are the national parties organized? state and local parties?
10. What caused the demise of big-city machines?
11. What is the responsible-party model?
12. What are the differences between the parties?
13. How do rational parties act?
14. Describe the coalitions of voters that support the Republican and Democratic parties.

SUGGESTED READINGS

Bibby, John F. *Politics, Parties, and Elections in America.* 1987.

A good overview of political parties and their contemporary role in American politics.

Chambers, William N. *Political Parties in a New Nation.* 1963.

A scholarly examination of the roots of the American party system.

Downs, Anthony. *An Economic Theory of Democracy.* 1957.
The classic theory of why political parties stick to the middle of the road.

Sabato, Larry J. *The Party's Just Begun.* 1988.
An agenda for political party renewal in the 1990s.

NOTES

1. Lloyd Cutler, "The Cost of Divided Government," *New York Times,* November 22, 1987, p. E27.
2. Frank Sorauf, *Party Politics in America* (Boston: Little, Brown, 1980), 9–11.
3. William N. Chambers, *Political Parties in a New Nation* (New York: Oxford University Press, 1963).
4. Paul Goodman, "The First American Party System," in William N. Chambers and Walter Dean Burnham, eds., *The American Party Systems* (New York: Oxford University Press, 1975), 56–89.
5. William N. Chambers, "Party Development and the American Mainstream," in Chambers and Burnham, *American Party Systems,* 3–32.
6. Richard P. McCormick, *The Second American Party System: Party Formation in the Jackson Era* (Chapel Hill: University of North Carolina Press, 1966).
7. Eric L. McKitrick, "Party Politics and the Union and Confederate War Efforts," in Chambers and Burnham, *American Party Systems,* 117–51.
8. William L. Riordon, *Plunkitt of Tammany Hall* (New York: Knopf, 1948; originally published in 1905).
9. Maurice Duverger, *Political Parties* (New York: Wiley, 1951).
10. Daniel Masmanian, *Third Parties in Presidential Elections* (Washington, D.C.: Brookings, 1974).
11. *Gallup Report,* no. 286 (July 1989) p. 2.
12. V. O. Key, *The Responsible Electorate* (Cambridge, Mass.: Harvard University Press, 1966).
13. Michael MacKuen, Robert Erikson, and James A. Stimson, "Macro Party Identification: A Preliminary Analysis" (Paper delivered at the annual meeting of the Midwest Political Science Association, Chicago, Illinois, 14–18 April 1988).
14. H. W. Stanley, W. T. Bianco, and R. G Niemi, "Partisanship and Group Support over Time: A Multivariate Analysis," *American Political Science Review* 80 (September 1986): 975–76.
15. Paul Abramson et al. *Change and Continuity in the 1988 Elections,* (Washington, D.C.: Congressional Quarterly Press, 1990) 206–8.
16. Cornelius Cotter and Bernard C. Hennessey, *Politics without Power* (New York: Atherton, 1964).
17. Ronald E. Weber, "Competitive and Organizational Dimensions of American State Party Systems" (Paper prepared for annual meeting of the Northeast Political Science Association, 1969).
18. Malcolm Jewell and David Olsen, *American State Political Parties and Elections* (Homewood, Ill.: Dorsey, 1978), 87.
19. Milton Rakove, *Don't Make No Waves, Don't Back No Losers* (Bloomington: Indiana University Press, 1975).
20. John Bibby, "Party Renewal in the National Republican Party," in Gerald M. Pomper, ed., *Party Renewal in America* (New York: Praeger, 1980), 107.
21. Carol F. Casey, "The National Democratic Party," in Pomper, *Party Renewal,* 88–89.
22. *Congressional Quarterly Weekly Report,* 3 April 1982, pp. 749–51.
23. James McGregor Burns, *The Deadlock of Democracy* (Englewood Cliffs, N.J.: Prentice-Hall, 1963).
24. American Political Science Association, *Towards a More Responsible Two-Party System* (New York: Rinehart, 1950).
25. *Congressional Quarterly Weekly Reports,* 15 January 1983, p. 107.
26. Gerald Pomper, *Elections in America* (New York: Dodd Mead, 1968), 198–200.
27. Anthony Downs, *An Economic Theory of Democracy* (New York: Harper and Row, 1957).
28. David Broder, *The Party's Over* (New York: Harper and Row, 1972) and Larry J. Sabato, *The Party's Just Begun* (Boston: Little, Brown, 1988).
29. Sabato (1988), 170–71.
30. *Ibid.,* 170–71.

CHAPTER 9

NOMINATIONS, CAMPAIGNS, AND ELECTIONS

POLITICAL CLOSE-UP

CHOOSING A RUNNING MATE

The first "presidential"-level decision that a major party nominee must make is the selection of a running mate. Although the choice of a vice-presidential candidate is rarely decisive in determining the outcome of the election, it can be critical in a close election. It is a choice that provides both opportunity and risk for the presidential candidate. It offers an opportunity to broaden the regional and philosophical base of the ticket, adding political strength and appeasing certain factions within the party. But it can be risky if the vice-presidential candidate runs into problems and distracts attention from the presidential candidate and the campaign. George Bush's selection of Dan Quayle in 1988 demonstrated some of the pitfalls of choosing a running mate.

The Constitution originally provided that the candidate placing second in the electoral college balloting would be made vice-president as a sort of consolation prize. That system was eliminated by the Twelfth Amendment after the 1800 election ended in a tie in the electoral college. Since then, presidential candidates have chosen their own running mates and

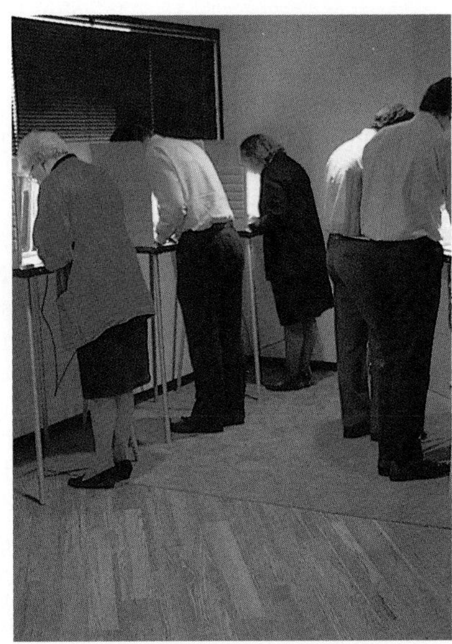

campaigned as a ticket. A number of vice-presidential candidates have caused problems. Eisenhower's selection of Richard Nixon in 1952 was met by questions concerning financial impropriety, and Nixon was kept on the ticket only after an emotional television speech. George McGovern's choice of Thomas Eagleton in 1972 turned into a fiasco when he dropped Eagleton from the ticket after saying he backed him "one-thousand percent." Geraldine Ferraro, Walter Mondale's 1984 running mate, could not shake questions about her husband's financial dealings, which diverted attention from the campaign.

And in 1988, Bush's controversial choice of Indiana Senator Dan Quayle became the main story during the Republican Convention and for weeks afterward.

In July 1988, Democratic nominee Michael Dukakis skirted disaster after naming Texas Senator Lloyd Bentsen without first informing rival Jesse Jackson of his choice. Dukakis and Jackson patched up their differences and avoided a damaging split in the Democratic ranks. A month later, George Bush announced he would not make his vice-presidential selection public until the last day of the Republican Convention, in hopes of boosting the prime-time ratings. Predicting his choice was the favorite pastime of politicos and the press. Preconvention speculation focused on nomination rivals Robert Dole and Jack Kemp, but at least a dozen other names were still on the list. Extensive background checks were made and an attorney hired by the Bush campaign conducted interviews with the leading candidates to forestall any potentially damaging relevations if they were chosen.

At an impromptu press conference on Tuesday of convention week, Bush surprised reporters by announcing his choice for vice-president: a little-known, forty-one-year-old senator from Indiana, Dan Quayle. Critics within the Republican party were dismayed with the choice since Bush had passed up more experienced and better known candidates like Dole who would have more vote-pulling power. With over 13,000 media people at the convention desperately in search of a story, it took only hours for controversy to erupt. Quayle's service in the National Guard during the Vietnam War, and whether his wealthy family exerted influence to get him in, was at the center of the controversy. His trip to Florida with several members of Congress and then-lobbyist and Playboy model Paula Parkinson was raised. Quayle was bombarded with tough questions. Several Republican leaders suggested that Bush should immediately dump Quayle, but Bush stood behind his choice. In the week after the convention, questions about his service in the Guard continued to plague Quayle. Parkinson claimed Quayle had propositioned her. His voting record in the Senate came under scrutiny. Through it all, George Bush continued to defend his choice for the number two spot on the ticket.

While attention to Quayle abated after several weeks, political experts concluded that some damage had been done. The furor had diverted attention from Bush's acceptance speech at the convention and had dominated other campaign issues for several weeks. Quayle lambasted the press for harassing him and attempted to turn the situation into an advantage. A poll revealed that a majority of Americans thought the media had been overzealous in pursuing Quayle. Yet in some quarters, the sentiment remained that Bush had blundered in his first big decision. The entire episode was a vivid reminder of the possible pitfalls in choosing a running mate. It renewed questions about whether, in a presidential nomination process that lasts for months, some better method for choosing vice-presidential nominees could be developed.

Chapter Outline

Introduction and Overview

The right to vote in free elections is the cornerstone of democracy. After signing the Voting Rights Act in 1965, President Lyndon Johnson spoke passionately about its importance:

"The right to vote is the most basic right without which all others are meaningless. It gives people—people as individuals—control over their own destinies.... The vote is the most powerful instrument ever devised by man for breaking down

Long lines did not deter Nicaraguans from waiting for the chance to vote in that nation's first free election in many decades.

injustice and destroying the terrible walls which imprison men because they are different from other men."[1] But has electoral politics in the United States lost its way even as its vision is realized abroad?

Campaigns cost millions of dollars, and incumbents, who spend more and more of their time raising money, seem unbeatable. Campaigns, dominated by slick thirty-second commercials, have taken on a nasty tone. Sixty-eight percent of the American people felt the 1988 campaign for president was more negative than campaigns of the past.[2] The process of running for office is increasingly irrelevant to the difficult challenges of governing. And not coincidentally, voter turnout in the United States is the lowest in the world.

Elections are crucial for governing, but today, they too often produce avoidance and paralysis rather than bold initiatives. The institutions and processes of governing have not kept pace with the rapid development of electoral technology: efficient fund-raisers, clever strategists, experienced pollsters, and producers who create highly effective negative television commercials. Elected officials live in fear of the "four horsemen" of modern politics: negative television attacks by opponents, close scrutiny of their lives by the media, growing public cynicism, and the need to raise huge amounts of money to stay in office.[3] Many promising leaders simply choose not to run at all.

This chapter looks at national elections in the United States, from nomination to campaign to the final vote. It examines how elections have evolved, building on earlier chapters about public opinion and political parties. We look at congressional elections, presidential elections, and recent trends in the electoral process. In focusing on how elections relate to governing, the following questions are considered:

1. How has the electorate expanded, and what are the historical trends of voting and turnout?
2. What characterizes congressional elections?
3. How has the system for choosing presidential candidates evolved, and what are its implications?
4. What strategies are used by the successful candidates for the nomination for president?
5. How are delegates to the national convention chosen, and what role does the convention play today?
6. How are general election campaigns conducted? What difference do they make?
7. What key factors determined the 1988 election results?
8. How do elections shape the ability to govern?
9. What are some of the recurrent problems with elections and some of the possible reforms?

Changes in American Elections

The Constitution left each state in control of its own procedures for elections and requirements for voting. Voting was generally limited to property-owning white males, although some states were less restrictive than others. In the most permissive states, up to 80 percent of the white males could vote. In the most restrictive states, only 10 percent could vote.[4] But over the next two hundred years, suffrage was gradually extended as restrictions on voting fell, and in many respects, elections became nationalized.

THE EXTENSION OF SUFFRAGE

Voting was originally a privilege too important to entrust to the masses. The first extension of suffrage came with the elimination of property requirements for voting, a reform undertaken for pragmatic reasons in the new western states and territories.[5] In the sparsely settled areas, allowing all white males to vote simplified administration. The most significant increases in the electorate came in the Jacksonian era, when the number of eligible voters tripled between 1824 and 1828 and doubled again by 1840. Except for in a few states such as Louisiana, which kept property restrictions on voting until 1852, by 1830 virtually all white males could vote.

Few blacks could vote before the Civil War, even those who lived in free states. The Fifteenth Amendment to the Constitution enfranchised black males for the first time, decreeing that the right to vote "shall not be denied or abridged by the United States or by any state on account of race, color, or previous condition of servitude." These seemingly clear guarantees were swept aside in the states of the old Confederacy (see Chapter 6). Although northern blacks continued to vote, virtually all black males in the South were **disenfranchised** by the year 1900.

The single largest increase in the number of eligible voters in the nation occurred in 1920 with the ratification of the Nineteenth Amendment. After nearly fifty years of pressure from the women's suffrage movement, women achieved the right to vote. Although opponents feared a massive change in electoral politics if women got the vote, there was no immediate electoral change after 1920.

As late as the 1950s, as few as 10 percent of the black population in the Deep South was registered to vote. Although some of the exclusionary devices, such as the grandfather clause and the white primary, were ruled unconstitutional (in 1914 and 1944, respectively), intimidation and threats kept blacks from registering and voting. The major increase in southern black voting came after the passage of the Voting Rights Act of 1965. The results were dramatic. Hundreds of thousands of blacks registered and voted for the first time.[6]

The most recent extension of the franchise was the granting of suffrage to eighteen-year-olds. It seemed hypocritical not to allow young men who faced the draft and the Vietnam War at age eighteen to vote until age twenty-one. The Twenty-sixth Amendment, ratified in 1972, extended the vote to all citizens eighteen years old and over. Because of the student protests of the 1960s, some believed that the increase in younger voters would have a pronounced effect on elections, but no such change occurred. In the 1972 election, Richard Nixon narrowly carried the eighteen-to-twenty-five-year-old age-group, most of whom did not vote. In the 1988 election, George Bush carried this group by a large margin.

THE NATIONALIZATION OF ELECTIONS

Election laws and practices still show tremendous variation across the fifty states. The patchwork quilt of primaries and caucuses in selecting the 1988 presidential candidates is vivid proof. Offices that are elective in one state may be appointed in others. Certain states allow "crossover voting" in primaries (that is, Republicans are allowed to vote in the Democratic primary and vice versa). A number of states make it easier for citizens to place propositions on the ballot or to propose recall petitions to remove officials from office. Compared with the early days of the republic, however, there is more standardization today. Elections have been partly "nationalized" through statutes, constitutional amendments, and national party rules. As the vote was extended to nonproperty owners, blacks, women, southern blacks, and youth, the standards for voting eligibility became unified. The main

POLITICAL INSIGHT 9-1

THE ELECTORAL COLLEGE: COUNTING THE "REAL" BALLOTS FOR PRESIDENT

By the morning of November 9, 1988, the nation knew who would be the next president of the United States. But under the Constitution, the "real" balloting was more than a month away, and the actual counting of the ballots two months away!

The electoral college devised by the Founders was a compromise between those who wanted direct election of the president by the people and those who wanted the president chosen by Congress. Electors were apportioned to the states on the basis of their total number of senators and representatives. Originally appointed by the state legislatures, the electors compose a "college" that never meets as a group. The electors ballot for president in December, meeting in their respective states. Electors were anticipated to exercise free and open judgments in selecting the president. Since political parties had not yet emerged in 1787, most government leaders doubted that any candidate after George Washington would receive the necessary majority of votes from the electors, throwing the election into the House of Representatives. Only three times in American history has this occurred: 1800, 1824, and 1876.

Actual operation of the electoral college turned out differently from what the Founders envisioned. By the 1830s, most electors were elected by the people rather than appointed by the legislature. As political parties gained strength, states initiated the "general ticket"—a winner-take-all system where all electoral votes would go to the winning candidate rather than be split. The presumptions about the electoral college changed. Electors would not be free agents but would be expected to vote in accordance with the voters' preference. Today, electors are usually party loyalists pledged to a certain candidate. Even though their names do not appear on the ballot in most states, voters actually vote for a slate of electors, not the presidential and vice-presidential candidates. Despite the changes in practice, the original constitutional language remains.

Today, the electoral college is an anachronism, a legacy of a bygone era. Yet the president is not officially elected until the 538 electors vote and the ballots are counted by Congress. In 1960, fifteen electors pledged to John F. Kennedy voted for Harry Byrd of Virginia, but it did not affect the outcome of the election. Could it happen again? Only faith and tradition, not law, prevent it. Many proposals to eliminate the electoral college have been offered over the years. Most recently, a constitutional amendment to provide for direct election of the president fell fifteen votes short of the necessary two-thirds majority needed in the Senate in 1979.

In December 1988, presidential electors met in the fifty states to cast their secret ballots for president. The ballots were transported to Washington to be opened the first week of January (enough time to make it on horseback) after the new Congress convened. Two senators and two representatives opened the envelopes containing the electoral votes. The results were as expected. But what if some year the electoral vote tally is within a few votes? What if a single elector's vote could change the outcome of the election?

---

differences today concern registration procedures and residency requirements, and even those are limited by federal court rulings.

The Constitution originally required only that members of the House of Representatives be elected directly by the people. Under the Constitution, the president is selected by the electoral college—a group of electors chosen by each state. The presidential election was actually a series of state contests for members of the electoral college. (The electoral college is examined more closely in Political Insight 9-1.) Congress established only the date on which the electors from the various states actually cast their votes for president. Methods for choosing electors and date of that selection were left to the states. Presidential electors were at first chosen by state legislatures, but by 1830, the great majority were chosen by voters. States balloted on different days: Missouri balloted in August, while Maine traditionally voted in September for president. Congressional elections also varied, with some states electing House members at large, others using multimember districts, and some using the single-member districts that are used today. A few states held their elections in odd-numbered years. Some required a majority rather than a plurality to win, requiring run-off elections after the initial balloting.

By 1850, Congress had put an end to much of this variation. House members were required to be elected by district. The date for federal elections was set for "the Tuesday following the first Monday in November of even-numbered years." In the twentieth century, the Republican and Democratic parties established rules governing the conduct of presidential primary elections and delegate selection. In the 1980s, the Democrats set time limits for the dates of primaries and other requirements, pointing to the possible role of the parties in further nationalizing presidential elections. Compared with other nations, however, the presidential selection process remains decentralized.

Voter Turnout

In 1988, only 50.2 percent of voting-age Americans cast their vote for president, the lowest total since 1924. Table 9-1 examines turnout in presidential and off-year congressional elections since 1948. Turnout has steadily declined since 1960, when 62.8 percent voted in the Nixon-Kennedy contest. Even the total number of voters declined by over a million between 1984 and 1988. Voter turnout for off-year elections has also declined, down to 36.4 percent in 1986. This leaves the United States at the bottom of the list of democratic nations, as shown in Table 9-2. Turnout for state and local elections is even lower than for presidential elections in most cases.

Why is turnout so low in the United States? This question has concerned and baffled observers for decades. One explanation centers on the registration procedures adopted around the turn of the twentieth century to eliminate voting fraud. Most eligible voters must register with local election boards up to a month before the actual balloting. Since 1976, several states have adopted procedures that allow voters to register at the polling place on election day. In the last four presidential elections, turnout in these states has averaged 14 percent higher than in states without election day registration.[7] Differences in voting levels vary with socioeconomic factors. Wealthier, more highly educated, middle-aged Americans are the most likely to vote. Even so, turnout among comparable groups remains far below levels in other democracies.

TABLE 9–1

National Voter Turnout: 1948–1988

	Presidential Election Years			Nonpresidential election years	
	Number*	Percent**		Number*	Percent**
1988	91,591,486	50.15	1986	64,991,128	36.41
1984	92,652,680	53.10	1982	67,615,576	39.78
1980	86,515,221	52.56	1978	58,917,938	37.20
1976	81,555,789	53.55	1974	55,943,834	38.23
1972	77,718,554	55.21	1970	58,014,338	46.60
1968	73,211,875	60.84	1966	56,188,046	48.17
1964	70,644,592	61.92	1962	53,141,227	47.05
1960	68,838,204	62.77	1958	47,202,950	45.13
1956	62,026,648	60.37	1954	43,850,995	43.75
1952	61,551,543	62.98	1950	41,684,212	43.12
1948	48,261,189	51.30			
Average Percent		56.80			42.54

*Total national number of persons voting for the highest office.

**Percentage of the total national voting age population who voted for the highest office.

Congressional Research Service

TABLE 9–2

AVERAGE VOTER TURNOUT SINCE 1945

Country	Percentage of Votes
Australia	95.4
Netherlands 1971–81	94.4
Austria	94.2
Italy	92.6
Belgium	92.5
New Zealand	90.4
West Germany	86.9
Denmark	85.8
Sweden	84.9
Israel	81.4
Norway	80.8
France	79.3
Finland	79.0
United Kingdom	76.9
Canada	76.5
Ireland	74.7
Japan	73.1
Switzerland	64.5
United States	56.8*
OVERALL AVERAGE	81.0

SOURCE: Gary Orren and Sidney Verba, "American Voter Participation: The Shape of the Problem," paper presented to the symposium on American Voter Participation, sponsored by Harvard University and the American Broadcasting Companies, Inc., Washington, D.C., October 1983, p. 13.
*From Table 9–1.

A number of other factors are associated with the continuing decline in voter turnout in the United States.[8] Enfranchisement of eighteen-year-olds at the time when significant numbers of baby boomers were reaching voting age contributed to declining turnout because younger voters are the least likely to go to the polls. Since strong partisans are more likely to vote than independents or weak partisans, the dealignment that occurred in recent decades also affected turnout. That does not explain decline in the 1980s, however, since the proportion of independents remained relatively stable. Declining voter turnout is also linked to increased cynicism on the part of voters and a decreasing sense that politicians are responsive or can be trusted. Turnout is also linked to actions taken by the parties and candidates. In 1984, both parties engaged in efforts to get potential voters registered, but turnout increased by only about half of one percent. In 1988, both parties as well as private foundations cut back their voter registration efforts. In addition, many analysts believe that the negative tone of the campaign contributed to the 3-percent drop from 1984.

What are the consequences of low voter turnout? George Bush won the presidency in 1988 by 7 million votes but was the choice of only 27 percent of the eligible voters. Obviously, the millions of nonvoters could have elected Dukakis in 1988 if they were so inclined. But surveys of nonvoters indicated that Bush held a comparable edge among them. Some argue that low turnout does not matter unless the policy preferences of nonvoters are different than voters. The evidence suggests that is rarely the case.[9] Others argue that low turnout reflects general satisfaction and the lack of serious cleavages with American society. To many, however, the low levels of turnout are of growing concern. If campaigns increasingly turn off voters and if elections are regarded as irrelevant, where will guidance for policy-makers come from? If the results of congressional elections consistently differ from the results of presidential elections, where will the impetus to govern the country come from?

Congressional Elections

RECENT TRENDS

Congressional elections shape the boundaries of the relationship between the president and the Congress. In recent years, the results of congressional elections seem increasingly separated from those of presidential contests. The Republican landslides in 1972 and 1984 produced Republican gains in the House of only a dozen or so seats. If the ability to govern depends on election results to provide direction in government, recent trends suggest that clear direction is increasingly unlikely.

The most important factor in congressional elections today is the power of incumbency. House members seeking reelection are on average successful from 90 to 95 percent of the time. Senators are less successful, but incumbents are usually returned to office from 80 percent to 90 percent of the time. In 1986 and 1988, a remarkable 98 percent of House incumbents running for reelection were successful.

POLITICAL INSIGHT 9-2

THE 1990 ELECTIONS

Despite voter anger over tax increases and spending cuts and worries about the Middle East, congressional incumbents once again were highly successful in the midterm elections. Governors fared less well, as voters ousted the governing party in 14 states. Democrats increased their margins in Congress by picking up 8 seats in the House and one seat in the Senate. The 102nd Congress began with Democrats holding a 56-44 margin in the Senate and a 267-167 advantage (with one independent) in the House of Representatives. While these gains were not large by historical standards for midterm elections, it meant that President Bush would face even stronger Democratic majorities in 1991 and 1992. Divided government, partisan conflict, and veto fights would continue in the 1990s.

Senate incumbents proved extraordinarily safe in 1990. Only Senator Rudy Boschwitz (R-Minn.) was defeated by a challenger. The result was an overall reelection rate of 97 percent, the highest since 1854! This was in contrast to recent elections where Senate incumbents had more trouble, such as 1980, when only 55 percent were reelected. Although some incumbents had close calls, their 3 to 1 advantage in campaign spending proved decisive. House incumbents continued to be successful as 96 percent were reelected, down slightly from the record 98 percent reelection rates in 1986 and 1988. Several House veterans were defeated including 16-term House Democrat Robert Kastenmeier of Wisconsin, and several members of Congress saw their margins of victory reduced over previous elections. House Majority Leader Richard Gephardt (D-Mo.) was reelected by less than 57 percent of the vote, controversial House Minority Whip, Newt Gingrich (R-Ga.) squeaked by with less than 51 percent of the vote, and Senator Bill Bradley (D-N.J.) barely won against an unknown and underfinanced challenger. Vermont independent Bernie Sanders became the first Socialist elected to the House since the 1920s.

Races for governor in 36 states showed the electorate to be more volatile. Incumbent governors in both parties were upset and party control of the governorship changed in 14 states. With crucial redistricting plans to be approved before the 1992 elections, the gubernatorial contests took on special importance. The final breakdown in governorships after the election was 28 Democrats, 19 Republicans, and 2 independents, with a runoff scheduled in Arizona.

In an ironic reversal of the Founders' intentions, more incumbents were defeated in the Senate, with only 34 seats up for election, than in the House, where all 435 seats were contested. Incumbents are successful at getting reelected for a variety of reasons, not the least of which is the vast array of resources they have at their disposal. Incumbents are in an advantageous position to attract campaign contributions, particularly from political action committees.

Recent trends in congressional elections have profound implications for governing.[10] The power of incumbency is based on the popularity and recognition of candidates more than on specific issues. While members of Congress reflect the general policy preferences of constituents, they increasingly try to campaign on noncontroversial issues emphasizing service to the district.[11] The growth of negative campaigns has pushed issues even farther from center stage, as challengers focus on such things as morals and ethics, substance abuse, or attendance records. When issues come into play, the focus is often on a single vote. Representative David Obey (D-Wis.) describes the effect on governing:

> When the main question in a member's mind every time he votes is, "What kind of a thirty-second spot are they going to make out of this vote?" then truly the ability of the political system to make complicated and tough decisions in the long-range interest of the United States is atomized.[12]

The other main trend in congressional elections that most affects governing is the "decoupling" of

TABLE 9–3

PROJECTED GAINERS AND LOSERS AFTER 1990 CENSUS

States Expected To Gain Seats	Current Number of Seats	Expected Gain	Seats in 1990s
California	45	+7	52
Florida	19	+4	23
Texas	27	+3	30
North Carolina	11	+1	12
Virginia	10	+1	11
Georgia	10	+1	11
Arizona	5	+1	6
States Expected To Lose Seats	**Number of Seats**	**Expected Loss**	**Seats in 1990s**
New York	34	−3	31
Pennsylvania	23	−2	21
Illinois	22	−2	20
Ohio	21	−2	19
Michigan	18	−2	16
Massachusetts	11	−1	10
Iowa	6	−1	5
Kansas	5	−1	4
Kentucky	7	−1	6
New Jersey	14	−1	13
West Virginia	4	−1	3
Montana	2	−1	1

SOURCE: *Congressional Quarterly Weekly Report* 5 May 1990, p. 1339. Revised to reflect Census Bureau preliminary 1990 results, August, 1990.

congressional and presidential elections. This is a state of affairs that often leaves the legislative and executive branches attuned to different constituencies with conflicting priorities and agendas. In 1988, George Bush assumed the presidency with the lowest proportion of members of his own party in Congress of any president in history. Whether some voters actually prefer divided government or whether divided government simply reflects recent institutional and political trends, the decoupling of elections often results in drift, avoidance, and paralysis.

APPORTIONMENT AND REDISTRICTING

The linkage among elections, representation, and governing is forged in 435 congressional districts and 50 states. House districts, as established in the Constitution, are apportioned to the states on the basis of population. Following the census taken every ten years, the seats in the House of Representatives are **reapportioned** among the fifty states. Until 1920, the size of the House expanded as the population increased. The first House of Representatives had only 65 members, but by 1832, it had grown to 242.[13] In 1913, the House achieved its present size of 435, but that figure was not fixed by law until 1929, following a nine-year battle waged by states that stood to lose seats.

Today, the apportionment stakes are high. More than twenty lawsuits were filed against the Census Bureau after the 1980 census, which reflected major population shifts from the Snowbelt to the Sunbelt states. New York was the big loser, dropping five seats.

The stakes are just as high following the 1990 census. By 1986, the average congressional district population was 553,000, up 6.4 percent from 1980.

Some 34 of the 435 districts grew by more than 20 percent in the 1980s—and all of these were in the South and West. Conversely, districts that actually lost population or grew at a slower pace than the national average were generally found in the Northeast and the Midwest. States in these regions will lose additional seats to states in the Sunbelt through reapportionment following the 1990 census. Table 9-3 shows projected winners and losers after the 1990 census. If current trends hold, California will be the big winner, gaining seven seats for a total of 52. New York is projected to lose three seats, with four large industrial states expected to lose two seats each.

Once congressional seats are apportioned to the states, an even more difficult process begins. **Redistricting,** the drawing of new district boundaries within states, must occur. Redistricting becomes particularly painful when there are fewer seats than before. Even if district lines are established in the most unbiased, objective manner possible, someone suffers. When one or more seats are lost through reapportionment, redistricting often places two incumbents in the same district. States that lost seats after the 1980 census went through a series of pitched political battles involving commissions, state legislatures, governors, and ultimately the courts. Federal judges are increasingly called on to settle district boundaries when other parties fail to reach agreement.

Redistricting has always been highly politicized. The people who draw up the boundaries of congressional districts are not completely objective, unbiased, or unaffected by the outcome. Effectively drawn boundaries can help a party retain control of a state delegation for a decade. **Gerrymandering** (named after Governor Elbridge Gerry of Massachusetts) refers to manipulating the boundaries of a district to benefit a certain candidate or party. Even today, the shape of some congressional districts almost defies imagination. In the 1960s, the Supreme Court ruled that congressional districts must be drawn according to the principle of "one person, one vote" (see Chapter 4). Since that time, many feel that while district populations are nearly equal, political gerrymandering has become even worse. The creation of safe seats through gerrymandering may be a factor contributing to the success of

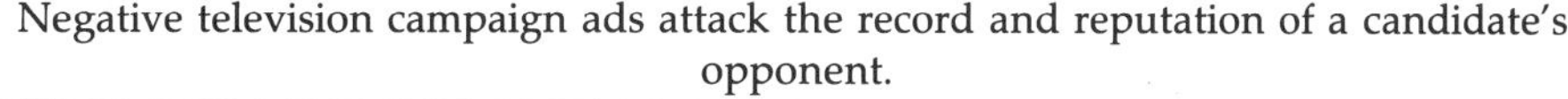
Negative television campaign ads attack the record and reputation of a candidate's opponent.

incumbents, the decoupling of congressional and presidential elections, and the recurrence of divided government.

Congressional election results will affect the legislative record of a president and his ability to govern effectively. One might expect that a presidential candidate would spend time trying to carry sympathetic members of Congress in on his coattails, yet few have succeeded when they tried. Candidates for president must spend most of their time on their own race as they travel the long and arduous path to the White House. President Reagan's efforts to campaign for Republican senators in order to keep Republican control in 1986 were a failure.

Presidential Elections: The Road to Nomination

THE POOL OF PRESIDENTIAL TALENT

At one time, a little-known politician could go to a party nominating convention and end up as a presidential candidate. Warren G. Harding, nominated by the Republicans in 1920, was hardly mentioned as a possibility before the convention. The days of getting nominated by party bosses in a smoke-filled room are gone. Today, many candidates decide to run immediately after the last election is over. After Reagan's decisive victory in 1984, Republicans Dole, Kemp, and Bush and Democrats Hart, Gephardt, and Dukakis began to maneuver with an eye toward 1988. Some maneuverings are less subtle than others. Robert and Elizabeth Dole stayed in suite "1988" at their hotel at the 1984 Republican Convention. Meanderings through the political wilderness between elections are sometimes called the **"invisible primary."**[14] Candidates find out if they have the "right stuff." Can they arouse the interest of rank and file members? Can they take the pace, the long hours, the time away from their family? Can they begin to develop a constituency, an identity?

Probably the most important qualification for running for president is prior political experience. Dwight Eisenhower was the last in a long line of war heroes elected president; today, some political experience is a must. In recent years, U.S. senators and state governors have been the main source of presidential candidates, but the most dependable route to the nomination is still the vice-presidency. Nixon, Johnson, Humphrey, Ford, Mondale, and Bush all served as vice-president before becoming a candidate for president. A decade ago it looked as if the Senate had become the main presidential breeding ground. The candidacies of former governors Carter, Reagan, and Dukakis have revived the governors' mansions as presidential incubators.

Most presidential candidates, such as George Bush (Texas), come from large states. A candidate could carry the ten largest states and come within a handful of electoral votes of winning the election. Recent exceptions to candidates from large states are Goldwater (Arizona) and McGovern (South Dakota), who both lost miserably. Carter (Georgia), Mondale (Minnesota), and Dukakis (Massachusetts) came from medium-sized states.

Religion and age are not as important as they used to be. In 1928, Al Smith was the first Catholic nominated and the only one until Kennedy was elected president in 1960. Most presidents have been Protestants. Kennedy was the youngest president at forty-three, and Reagan's reelection in 1984 successfully countered suggestions that he was too old at seventy-three. The voters, reflecting broader social changes in the United States, are also more tolerant of divorce. Reagan was the first elected divorced president. Other barriers to office are also breaking down. While George Bush's family had been in the United States for centuries, Michael Dukakis was the first generation son of Greek immigrants.

Americans have high expectations of their leaders. Presidents should be attractive and intelligent, decisive but reflective, honest yet crafty, articulate but sincere, should possess a good sense of humor without being a clown, and be politically experienced while appearing fresh and new. Candidates must appear to be decisive and strong and avoid showing signs of weakness. Early in the 1972 campaign, Democratic front-runner Edmund Muskie was caught by the television news cameras with tears in his eyes as he angrily responded to the *Manchester* (N.H.) *Union Leader's* attacks on his wife. He quickly fell out of the race and later commented, "It changed people's minds about me. . . . they were looking for a strong, steady man and here I was weak."[15] Gary Hart was forced out of the race in 1988 over allegations of an extramarital affair. Senator Joe Biden dropped out because of negative publicity surrounding a speech he took verbatim from the leader of the British Labor Party.

The road to the White House is fraught with hazards. A candidate must convince large numbers of voters that he or she is the best of all possible choices. Behind the candidate's calculations lie considerations such as: Do I want it badly? Do I have the qualifications? Do I have the regional base? Do I have the right image? But the most important question for a candidate today is, Can I raise enough money? If the answer is yes to all of these (in the candidate's own mind, at least), then the decision is "go." The next step is to build a campaign organization. A successful candidate's staff must be experienced, specialized, and highly professional. With an official declaration of candidacy, a campaign organization established, and the contributions rolling in, the candidate is ready to compete for the nomination. For all the complexities of presidential politics, the basic goal of a candidate is simple—to get one more than 50 percent of the votes of the delegates to the party's nominating convention.

THE HUNT FOR DELEGATES

Convention delegates are apportioned to the states on the basis of the size of their congressional delegations and the results of the previous presidential elections. States where the party did well in the previous election will get more delegates. In 1988, the Democratic party had a larger convention with 4,162 delegates compared to 2,277 delegates at the Republican Convention.

Each state determines how convention delegates will be selected. Delegates are chosen either through presidential primaries or by a **caucus-convention system.** The number of states using presidential primaries has varied in the twentieth century but has been on the increase since 1968. In 1988, a record number of delegates were chosen through presidential primaries; thirty-seven presidential primaries were held, selecting over three-fourths of the convention delegates. Nonetheless, the caucus-convention states remain important, particularly the early caucuses. In the caucus-convention system, the delegate selection process often takes several months to complete. It begins with a series of meetings at the grass-roots level (townships, precincts, wards) to measure relative candidate strength and select representatives to a district or state convention. Each caucus state has its own particular rules, but basically, the more people who initially show up to support a candidate, the more actual convention delegates that candidate will eventually earn through district and state conventions.

A primary, derived from the Latin word for "first," is the first election, one taking place within the party. The general election, which determines who will hold office, takes place between parties. Primaries, like caucuses, also vary from state to state.[16] Some states hold **nonbinding preference primaries**—beauty contests—that are only advisory to state party leaders. Some states allocate delegates to the convention on a "one person-one vote" basis; if a candidate received 50 percent of the vote, then he or she would receive half of the delegates. While Democratic party rules prevent "winner-take-all" primaries, some states have what are called "winner-take-more" primaries. Bonus delegates are awarded to the top vote-getter.

Some states, such as Illinois, New Jersey, and Pennsylvania, award delegates on a winner-take-all basis within congressional districts. In 1988, Jesse Jackson complained that such rules were unfair to his campaign. For example, while Jackson received 28 percent of the primary vote in Pennsylvania and 33 percent in New Jersey, he received only 8 percent of the delegates in each state.[17] Finally, in addition to delegates selected by caucuses and primaries are "super-delegates." These are delegates selected from among elected officials and members of the national committees. Despite the different method of selecting delegates across the fifty states, the system comes close to translating primary votes into convention delegates. For example, in 1988, Jesse Jackson received 29 percent of the primary vote nationally and won 27 percent of the delegates to the Democratic National Convention. This was a marked improvement over 1984, when he received 18 percent of the primary vote but won only 12 percent of the delegates.[18]

The debate over primaries versus caucuses continues in many states. Advocates of caucuses argue that primaries weaken political parties, giving

1990 nominee for governor of Texas, Democrat Ann Richards, survived a bitter primary fight within her party.

disproportionate power to the media that emphasize the "horse-race" aspect of the process. Caucus supporters want state and local party leaders to have a greater say in determining the nominee. Critics contend that primaries discourage the most qualified candidates while encouraging more glamorous, superficial candidates. The skills needed to win primaries are not necessarily the skills needed to govern effectively. Would Abraham Lincoln be able to win a presidential primary? But primaries have their strong defenders. Advocates of presidential primaries contend that the caucus system is elitist and limits democratic participation. In many states, only several thousand participate in caucuses, often less than 1 percent of eligible voters. In 1988, over 35 million voters participated in the presidential primaries, a record level of participation.

Whatever their merits or faults, primaries are popular and have become the central feature of the presidential nominating system. Before 1968, only a small proportion of delegates were selected by primaries. Hubert Humphrey won the 1968 Democratic nomination without entering a single one of the seventeen primaries held that year. Michael Dukakis and George Bush entered thirty-six and thirty-seven primaries respectively. Today's delegate selection process is more candidate-centered and less party-centered than twenty years ago. Campaigns are longer and more oriented to the mass media than before. The process is increasingly "front-loaded": not only have more states opted for primaries over caucuses, but they have scheduled their primaries earlier. In 1968, only one of the seventeen primaries was held before the end of March. In 1988, twenty-three of thirty-seven primaries were held before the end of March. This will be the case even more so in 1992, when California moves its primary to the beginning of the process.

CRITICAL CAUCUSES AND PRIMARIES

The nomination process winnows out candidates until only one or two are left within each party. At the start of 1988, seven Democrats and six Republicans were poised to mount serious campaigns during the primary and caucus season. Many speculated that no Democratic candidate could win a majority of delegates, forcing multiple ballots and a "brokered" convention. Yet only a few months later, both nominations were sewed up. By the time the votes had been counted on Super Tuesday, March 8, George Bush had locked up the Republican nomination. Michael Dukakis's convincing win in the New York primary on April 19 over Jesse Jackson virtually assured Dukakis of the nomination.

More than ever, early momentum is critical in winning the party nomination for president, which heightens the importance of the first few contests. Under current party rules, states must schedule their primary or caucus within a three month **"window" period** from late February to June. Iowa and New Hampshire are permitted to hold their contests earlier. By virtue of going first, Iowa and New Hampshire play a special role in presidential nomination politics. Many critics feel that role is out of proportion to their size and representativeness.

In the cold and snow of mid-February, the citizens of Iowa hold caucuses around the state to determine the first delegates. Iowa came to national prominence in 1976 when dark-horse Jimmy Carter emerged as the winner of the Democratic caucuses. In 1988, Iowa was a major focus for the multitude of Democratic and Republican candidates. Led by Democratic contender Richard Gephardt, who spent over 130 days campaigning in Iowa, the candidates crisscrossed the state through 1987 and early 1988, going from PTA meetings to pig roasts. But Iowa's prominence in the presidential selection process suffered a blow in 1988. The winners—Democrat Gephardt and Republican Robert Dole—did not translate their Iowa triumph into victory in the New Hampshire primary or the eventual nomination.

New Hampshire, on the other hand, continued its history as the proving ground of successful presidential candidates. Traditionally the site of the first primary, this rocky little New England state has a legendary role in nomination politics. In 1988, as other presidential hopefuls have for decades, George Bush began his successful quest for the White House with a victory in the New Hampshire primary. In 1968, Eugene McCarthy's strong showing in New Hampshire led to Robert Kennedy's entry into the campaign and Lyndon Johnson's surprising withdrawal from the race several weeks later. The same year, Richard Nixon soundly defeated George Romney to establish himself as the Republican front-runner. New Hampshire was critical in establishing the viability of dark-horse candidates George McGovern in 1972 and Jimmy Carter in 1976, particularly since they were not from the Northeast.

Not all candidates are enamored of Iowa or New Hampshire and the important role they play in nomination politics. Morris Udall expressed his distress with the system:

> We all said we weren't going to let New Hampshire do it to us again, and New Hampshire did do it. We all said that the Iowa caucus was not that important, and the press made it that important. . . . Once the avalanche starts down the ski slope, get out of the way. . . . The people want winners and losers and if you make twenty-seven points in a football game and I make twenty-six, you're called a winner and I'm called a loser.[19]

In 1988, the key development in the increasingly front-loaded primary calendar was Super Tuesday. Concerned that not enough attention was paid to southern states in presidential politics, Democratic leaders agreed to hold their presidential primaries on the same day, creating the first regional primary in American history. Tables 9-4 and 9-5 show the Republican and Democratic primary results in 1988. A total of sixteen primary contests and five caucuses were held on Super Tuesday, March 8, choosing around 30 percent of the delegates on a single day. Republican George Bush was the primary beneficiary of Super Tuesday. As Table 9-5 shows, he swept to victory over Robert Dole in every primary on March 8, sewing up the nomination. On the Democratic side, Dukakis, Jackson, and Tennessee Senator Albert Gore divided the votes and the delegates in nearly equal proportions. Southern leaders who had designed Super Tuesday gave it mixed reviews. Many of the smaller states and border states were disenchanted with Super Tuesday because they were ignored.

The early contests and Super Tuesday in particular showed the importance of money and the media in the presidential nomination process. The two best financed candidates—Bush and Dukakis—were the winners and eventual nominees. On the Democratic side, only Jesse Jackson was able to maintain significant support without massive amounts of campaign spending. Gephardt had spent most of his money in Iowa and was unable to counter negative advertising in the week before Super Tuesday. Gore's media blitz skyrocketed his standing in the polls that week, but lacking funds, his campaign fizzled afterward. Dukakis was the best financed Democrat, and he spread out his expenditures carefully through the primary season.

TABLE 9–4

1988 DEMOCRATIC PRIMARY RESULTS

	Turnout	Dukakis	Jackson	Gore	Gephardt	Simon	Others/ Uncommitted
New Hampshire (Feb. 16)	123,360	35.8%	7.8%	6.8%	19.8%	17.1%	12.8%
South Dakota (Feb. 23)	71,606	31.2	5.4	8.4	43.5	5.6	5.9
Vermont (March 1)	50,791	55.8	25.7	x	7.7	5.2	5.6
Alabama (March 8)	405,642	7.7	43.6	37.4	7.4	0.8	3.1
Arkansas (March 8)	497,544	18.9	17.1	37.3	12.0	1.8	12.8
Florida (March 8)	1,273,298	40.9	20.0	12.7	14.4	2.2	9.9
Georgia (March 8)	622.752	15.6	39.8	32.4	6.7	1.3	4.2
Kentucky (March 8)	318,721	18.6	15.6	45.8	9.1	2.9	7.9
Louisiana (March 8)	624,450	15.3	35.5	28.0	10.6	0.8	9.7
Maryland (March 8)	531,335	45.6	28.7	8.7	7.9	3.1	5.9
Massachusetts (March 8)	713,447	58.6	18.7	4.4	10.2	3.7	4.4
Mississippi (March 8)	361,811	8.3	44.4	33.3	5.4	0.6	8.1
Missouri (March 8)	527,805	11.6	20.2	2.8	57.8	4.1	3.6
North Carolina (March 8)	679,958	20.3	33.0	34.7	5.5	1.2	5.4
Oklahoma (March 8)	392,727	16.9	13.3	41.4	21.0	1.8	5.6
Rhode Island (March 8)	49.029	69.8	15.2	4.0	4.1	2.8	4.2
Tennessee (March 8)	576,314	3.4	20.7	72.3	1.5	0.5	1.6
Texas (March 8)	1,766,904	32.8	24.5	20.2	13.6	2.0	7.0
Virginia (March 8)	364,899	22.0	45.1	22.3	4.4	1.9	4.3
Illinois (March 15)	1,500,928	16.3	32.3	5.1	2.3	42.3	1.6
Puerto Rico (March 20)	356,178	22.9	29.0	14.4	3.0	18.2	12.5
Connecticut (March 29)	241,395	58.1	28.3	7.7	0.4[1]	1.3	4.2
Wisconsin (April 5)	1,014,782	47.6	28.2	17.4	0.8	4.8[2]	1.3
New York, (April 19)	1,575,186	50.9	37.1	10.0[3]	0.2	1.1	0.8
Pennsylvania (April 26)	1,507,690	66.5	27.3	3.0	0.5	0.6	2.2
District of Columbia (May 3)	86,052	17.9	80.0	0.8	0.3	0.9	0.1
Indiana (May 3)	645,708	69.6	22.5	3.4	2.6	1.9	x
Ohio (May 3)	1,376,135	62.7	27.5	2.2	x	1.1	6.6
Nebraska (May 10)	169,008	62.9	25.7	1.5	2.9	1.2	5.7
West Virginia (May 10)	322,148	78.9	14.0	3.6	x	0.7	2.8
Oregon (May 17)	388,932	56.8	38.1	1.4	1.7	1.2	0.7
Idaho (May 24)	51,370	73.4	15.7	3.7	x	2.7	4.5
California (June 7)	3,89,164	60.8	35.2	1.8	x	1.4	0.8
Montana (June 7)	120,962	68.7	22.1	1.8	2.8	1.3	3.2
New Jersey (June 7)	640,479	63.2	32.9	2.8	x	x	1.1
New Mexico (June 7)	188,610	61.0	28.1	2.5	x	1.5	6.9
North Dakota (June 14)	3,405	84.9*	15.1*	x	x	x	x

[1] *Gephardt withdrew from the race March 28.*

[2] *Simon suspended his campaign April 7.*

[3] *Gore suspended his campaign April 21.*

NOTE: Results based on official returns from state election bureaus except for Ohio, West Virginia, California, and Montana, where only unoffical returns were available. An "x" indicates that the candidate or the uncommitted line was not listed on the ballot. No Democratic candidates filed to be on the ballot for the June 14 North Dakota primary; an asterisk (*) indicates write-in votes.

SOURCE: *Congressional Quarterly Weekly Report*, 9 July 1988, p. 1894. Reprinted with permission from Congressional Quarterly, Inc.

TABLE 9–5

1988 REPUBLICAN PRIMARY RESULTS

	Turnout	Bush	Dole	Robertson	Kemp	Others/ Uncommitted
New Hampshire (Feb. 16)	157,625	37.6%	28.4%	9.4%	12.8%	11.8%
South Dakota (Feb. 23)	93,405	18.6	55.2	19.6	4.6	1.9
Vermont (March 1)	47,832	49.3	39.0	5.1	3.9	2.7
South Carolina (March 5)	195,292	48.5	20.6	19.1	11.5	0.3
Alabama (March 8)	213,515	64.5	16.3	13.9	4.9	0.3
Arkansas (March 8)	68,305	47.0	25.9	18.9	5.1	3.1
Florida (March 8)	901,222	62.1	21.2	10.6	4.6	1.4
Georgia (March 8)	400,928	53.8	23.6	16.3	5.8	0.5
Kentucky (March 8)	121,402	59.3	23.0	11.1	3.3	3.2
Louisiana (March 8)	144,781	57.8	17.7	18.2	5.3	1.0
Maryland (March 8)	200,754	53.3	32.4	6.4	5.9	2.0
Massachusetts (March 8)	241,181	58.5	26.3	4.5	7.0	3.7
Mississippi (March 8)	158,872	66.0	16.9	13.5	3.4	0.2
Missouri (March 8)	400,300	42.2	41.1	11.2	3.5	2.1
North Carolina (March 8)	273,801	45.4	39.1	9.8	4.1	1.5
Oklahoma (March 8)	208,938	37.4	34.9	21.1	5.5	1.0
Rhode Island (March 8)	16,035	64.9	22.6	5.7	4.9	1.9
Tennessee (March 8)	254,252	60.0	21.6	12.6	4.3	1.5
Texas (March 8)	1,014,956	63.9	13.9	15.3	5.0	1.9
Virginia (March 8)	234,142	53.3	26.0	13.7	4.6[1]	2.4
Illinois (March 15)	858,256	54.7	36.0	6.8	1.5	1.0
Puerto Rico (March 20)	3,973	97.1	2.7	0.1	x	0.1
Connecticut (March 29)	104,171	70.6	20.2[2]	3.1	3.1	3.1
Wisconsin (April 5)	359,294	82.2	7.9	6.9	1.4	1.7
Pennsylvania (April 26)	359,294	82.2	7.9	6.9	1.4	1.7
District of Columbia (May 3)	6,720	87.6	7.0	4.0	x	1.4
Indiana (May 3)	437,655	80.4	9.8	6.6	3.3	x
Ohio (May 3)	794,904	81.0	11.9	7.1	x	x
Nebraska (May 10)	204,049	68.0	22.3	5.1	4.1	0.5
West Virginia (May 10)	122,346	89.3	x	8.6[3]	x	2.1
Oregon (May 17)	274,451	72.9	17.9	7.7	x	1.5
Idaho (May 24)	68,275	81.2	x	8.6	x	10.2
California (June 7)	2,193,579	82.8	12.9	4.2	x	x
Montana (June 7)	85,907	73.2	19.5	x	x	7.4
New Jersey (June 7)	242,272	100.0	x	x	x	x
New Mexico (June 7)	88,744	78.2	10.5	6.0	x	5.3
North Dakota (June 14)	39,434	94.0*	x	x	x	6.0

[1] *Kemp withdrew from the race March 10.*

[2] *Dole withdrew from the race March 29.*

[3] *Robertson suspended his campaign May 16.*

NOTE: Results are based on official returns from state election boards, except for West Virginia, California and Montana, where only unofficial returns were available. An "x" indicates that the candidate or uncommitted line was not listed on the ballot. Republicans did not hold a preference vote in new York; the April 19 primary was for election of delegates only.

SOURCE: *Congressional Quarterly Weekly Report*, 9 July 1988, p. 1896. Reprinted with permission from Congressional Quarterly, Inc.

Television advertising and media coverage are critically important during the primary season. Candidates able to spend on television advertising in the days before a primary proved successful. Candidates unable to counter negative television commercials suffered. The impact of the media is greatest during the primary season. The electorate proved to be extremely volatile; polls taken four or five days before a primary often proved to be off by as much as 15 to 20 percent.

News coverage of the candidates is often as important as paid political advertising, and because of this, the media came under sharp attack in 1988. Candidates must beware of the blunder or misstatement that can dominate the news. Many felt that Gary Hart, Joe Biden, and later Dan Quayle were all abused by an overly aggressive media. Media critics also note the emphasis on the "horse-race" aspect of the nomination process rather than the candidates' records or issue stands. But news coverage can help a candidate. Jesse Jackson was particularly effective at using news coverage as a means of advertising his campaign. The presidential selection process continues to evolve as the rules of the game change. Despite the large number of candidates in 1988 and initial speculation about a brokered convention, the system has a strong tendency to narrow the field to one or two serious contenders. A lull in the election-year turmoil usually occurs in the preconvention period, especially if the nomination is sewn up. All eyes are directed to those quadrennial political circuses, the national conventions.

The Conventions

The primaries are over. Thousands of delegates have trooped into the convention city brimming with enthusiasm, wearing buttons, crazy hats, and carrying the placards of their heroes. By the time the convention convenes, there is probably little doubt who the nominee will be. The convention has assembled more to coronate than to nominate. So why bother with a convention at all?

CHOOSING THE PARTY NOMINEE

The nominating convention, now 150 years old, is still the major event of the national parties. In the preprimary era, the outcome of the convention was very much in doubt. For many years, the Democratic party required two-thirds of the delegates to nominate a candidate. Multiple ballots, sometimes more than one hundred separate votes, were needed to choose the nominee. The Democratic party dropped the **two-thirds rule** during Franklin Roosevelt's administration. Since then, the only convention to go beyond the first ballot was in 1952, when Adlai Stevenson was nominated on the third ballot.

Some of the key decisions of conventions are made by the **credentials committee,** which settles controversies over the seating and legality of delegations. Eisenhower's victory over Robert Taft in 1952 was helped by key credentials committee decisions that seated delegates favorable to him.[20] In 1964, the Democrats' credentials committee refused to seat an all-white delegation from Mississippi. Party reforms guaranteeing black and female representation at the convention were an outgrowth of this action. A credentials fight brewing at the 1988 Republican Convention over the Michigan delegation was settled just before the convention.

Another important convention committee is the **rules committee,** responsible for establishing the rules and procedures for voting at the convention. Rules can be critical to the outcome in a closely contested convention. In 1980, Ted Kennedy's forces at the Democratic Convention unsuccessfully attempted to push through a rule that would allow delegates selected in primaries (mostly Carter delegates) to switch candidates on the first ballot. Kennedy saw this as his only chance since Carter already had more than 50 percent of the delegates. The other major convention committee is the platform committee.

WRITING THE PLATFORM

The **platform committee** is responsible for assembling the party manifesto—a statement of positions on a host of major (and minor) national issues (see Political Insight 8-1). Platforms are often the center of controversy, despite efforts by party leaders to present a united front. Reagan supporters had a significant effect on the 1976 Republican platform even though Ford won the nomination.[21] Ford allowed the Reagan forces to include a statement critical of détente and a number of other conservative provisions. The Ford camp refused to budge, however, on the Reagan forces' desire to oppose the Equal Rights Amendment (opposition to the ERA was included in the 1980 and 1984 Republican platform).

The Kennedy-Carter confrontation at the 1980 Democratic convention also saw the platform significantly altered by the supporters of Kennedy, the losing candidate. In 1984, even though the Reagan forces were in total control of the Republican Convention, there was behind-the-scenes maneuvering between the ultraconservatives and the moderates. Most of the platform controversies between Dukakis and Jackson in 1988 were negotiated before the convention. At the convention, Dukakis forces agreed to allow floor votes on two controversial platform proposals: renouncing first use of nuclear weapons and higher taxes for corporations and the rich. Both were defeated. All other controversial proposals were kept off the floor completely. But to do so, the Dukakis camp allowed Jackson to insert nine planks of his own without floor debate. Dukakis effectively balanced party unity with the need to have a platform that was ideologically compatible.

CHOOSING THE VICE-PRESIDENTIAL NOMINEE

As we saw in the Political Close-up that opened this chapter, choosing a running mate can be a tricky business. Every four years, about convention time, the method of choosing a running mate comes under fire. The current system is simple—the presidential candidate chooses a running mate, and the convention ratifies the nominee's choice. Traditional political wisdom dictates balancing the ticket geographically and ideologically. Candidates obviously want someone who will make the ticket more attractive, but poor choices are not always fatal. Nixon defeated Humphrey in 1968 despite the fact that the Democratic vice-presidential nominee, Edmund Muskie, was seen much more favorably than Spiro Agnew, the Republican running mate. Successful candidates may turn to their closest competitor to foster party unity, as John Kennedy did with Lyndon Johnson and Reagan did with George Bush. George Bush was selected despite the fact that during the primary campaign, he labeled Reagan's proposals for taxing and spending "voodoo economics."

Ronald Reagan made two of the more interesting moves in the history of the vice-presidential selection process. The first was in 1976, when he became the first candidate to name his running mate before the convention. Surprising everyone, and infuriating conservative Republicans, Reagan chose liberal Republican Richard Schweiker of Pennsylvania. Reagan proposed a rule change that would require all candidates to name their running mate before the first ballot, but Ford allies successfully defeated this proposal. The second innovation came in 1980, when Reagan tried to promote a "dream ticket": himself as president, Gerald Ford as vice president. Reagan courted the former president by promising to create a corporate board structure in the White House. Reagan was to be the chairman of the board to oversee the overall management and Ford the corporation president running the day-to-day operations. The deal fell through and Reagan chose Bush, avoiding what could have been an interesting but potentially disastrous division of labor in the White House.

Walter Mondale made history when he selected Congresswoman Geraldine Ferraro of New York as his running mate. Women's groups had lobbied hard for the selection of a woman. In the weeks before the convention, Mondale interviewed a number of potential running mates, including several women, blacks, and an Hispanic. Under growing pressure from such organizations as NOW, Mondale chose Ferraro before the convention, ending speculation. Soon after her nomination, the media exhibited a sudden flurry of interest in Ferraro's family finances. It took nearly a month of valuable campaign time to answer all questions about her personal finances. In 1988, Michael Dukakis put political considerations above ideological compatibility in choosing Texas Senator Lloyd Bentsen. Bentsen was chosen and announced before the convention, even though he and Dukakis disagreed on a number of issues, such as aid to the Contras. It was an effective effort to shore up support for the ticket in the South, particularly in George Bush's home state of Texas. In 1970, Bentsen defeated Bush for the U.S. Senate. It was a message to conservative Democrats that a Dukakis-Bentsen ticket would be responsive to their desires. Bush, on the other hand, created a political storm with the selection of Indiana Senator Dan Quayle. It once again highlighted sharply contrasting selection processes: while presidential candidates are subject to microscopic scrutiny for many months, vice-presidential candidates are often chosen after a brief screening process.

THE IMPACT OF THE CONVENTION

The convention is the start of the presidential campaign. After all the screaming and the "spontaneous" demonstrations are over, after the roll is called state by state, after all the exhausted delegates fly home, the public is left with an impression. Does this party have its act together? One of the most important functions of a convention is to launch the candidacy of its standard bearer. After a convention, the candidate's ratings in the polls are supposed to jump. Michael Dukakis got a huge "bounce" from the successful 1988 Democratic Convention, surging to a 17 percent lead in the polls. But the impact turned out to be short-lived. Despite the controversy over Quayle, the surge for Bush after the Republican Convention gave him a slim lead in the polls.

One of the most disastrous conventions in its impact on the public was the 1968 Democratic meeting in Chicago, which was marred by violent confrontations between police and demonstrators. The assassinations of Martin Luther King and Robert Kennedy hung over the convention like a shroud. Conflict about the war in Vietnam and Lyndon Johnson's withdrawal from the race left nominee Hubert Humphrey with as many liabilities as assets. The disarray manifested at the 1972 convention also crippled the Democratic party. Support for the candidate *declined* after the convention, instead of making the usual jump.

Party officials continually stress the need for unity. The conventions signal an end to intramural fighting as the parties prepare for political combat. Finally, the conventions are over. On Labor Day weekend, the campaign officially begins.

The Presidential Campaign

Campaigns matter. Although the early voting studies revealed that most voters made their mind up by the time the campaign actually started, voters have become more volatile. With the reduced importance of party ties, more voters are deciding later or changing their minds. This was particularly true in 1988. Dukakis went from a 17-percent lead to a 10- to 15-percent deficit in a matter of weeks. Nearly one-fourth of the voters said they did not decide until the last month of the 1988 campaign, more than enough to throw the election either direction.[22] Despite the fact that voters may have disapproved of **negative campaigning,** there is evidence that it worked and may become more prevalent in the future. Skillfully designed attacks by the Bush campaign succeeded in making Dukakis's liberalism, patriotism, and prisoner furlough program important while in turn minimizing Bush's potential liabilities.[23]

As campaigns have come to be dominated by consultants and media advisors, a number of strategic decisions must be made.

FORMULATING CAMPAIGN STRATEGIES

SHARPENING THE CANDIDATE'S IMAGE? Presidential politics increasingly centers on image making. Reagan may have been the first real "media" president, but he was not the first president to capitalize on image. Franklin Roosevelt was able to convince millions of poor Americans that a New York patrician was the source of their salvation. John Kennedy was an attractive media candidate, helped by his exposure on television in face-to-face confrontation with Richard Nixon. But even if a candidate's personality or image is not just right, changes can be made. Richard Nixon won the presidency twice despite his image liabilities. The marketing analyst that helped "package" Nixon in 1968 described the task:

> Let's face it, a lot of people think Nixon is dull. Think he's a bore, a pain in the ass. They look at him as the kind of kid who always carried a bookbag. Who was forty-two years old the day he was born. They figure

A nostalgic whistle stop campaign, reminiscent of how campaigns used to be conducted. Today, national campaigns are conducted primarily on television.

> other kids got footballs for Christmas, Nixon got a briefcase and he loved it. He'd always have his homework done and he'd never let you copy.
>
> Now you put him on television, you've got a problem right away. He's a funny looking guy. He looks like somebody hung him in a closet overnight and he jumps out in the morning with his suit all bunched up and starts running around saying, "I want to be president." I mean this is how he strikes some people. That's why these shows are important. To make them forget all that.[24]

Media consultants for George Bush tried to combat his "wimp" image through a confrontation with anchorman Dan Rather on CBS News and at other stages throughout the campaign.

GOING NEGATIVE OR POSITIVE? Candidates must decide how much to attack an opponent (negative) versus how much to emphasize their own attributes (positive). Virtually all campaigns are a combination of both strategies, but the mix varies considerably. Negative approaches can backfire, creating sympathy for the opponent, reflecting poorly on the attacker for his or her bad manners and mudslinging. Johnson in 1964 picked up on some of the popular reservations about Goldwater and presented himself as a candidate of moderation. Meanwhile, his television ads hinted that his opponent was a dangerous warmonger. Most candidates let others sling the mud, but in 1980, many thought Carter went too far in attacking Reagan. Despite the fact that no one seems to like negative campaigning, it appears to work. Not only did negative campaigns in the U.S. Senate races increase in the 1980s, but, as we will see below, most observers believe that George Bush overcame the big deficit in the polls in 1988 through aggressive attacks that increased negative perceptions of Michael Dukakis.

ISSUES: HOW SPECIFIC? In 1976, Ford attacked Carter for being indecisive on issues, for changing his tune to suit the audience. "He waivers, he wanders, he wiggles, he waffles," charged Ford. "In California, he tried to sound like Cesar Chavez; in Chicago, like Mayor Daley; in New York, like Ralph Nader; in Washington, like George Meany; then he comes to the farm belt and he becomes a little old peanut farmer."[25] Carter, avoiding specific issues, struck the theme of the outsider, a "Mr. Clean" who was not tarnished by the Washington establishment. But what proved to be effective in getting elected was a disadvantage when he became president and had to work with the establishment he had derided.

American presidential elections are contested more on competing themes than on specific issue proposals. Recent candidates presenting specific, detailed proposals have lost badly. Walter Mondale promised to raise taxes because of huge federal deficits and presented a set of tax and spending proposals. His specificity was a liability, playing directly into Reagan's portrayal of the Democrats as big taxers and spenders and the Republicans as tax cutters. In 1988, while both Bush and Dukakis promised to reduce the deficit, neither produced a specific plan to do so.

Successful candidates talk about peace, prosperity, low taxes, reductions in nuclear weapons, strong national defense. They are more interested in discussing their general policy agenda than specific proposals. Dukakis campaigned on the theme of "competence," while Bush emphasized "experience." Such a strategy is rational from the perspective of the candidates and parties. Rival candidates find it is much harder to oppose general notions, such as "honesty and morality" in government, or "getting the government off our backs."

HOW PARTISAN? In the past three decades, the majority-party Democrats were more likely to inject partisan appeals in the election than were Republicans. Kennedy, Johnson, Carter, and Dukakis all made attempts to tie themselves to Roosevelt and his legacy. Ronald Reagan, appealing for Democratic votes, mentioned Roosevelt, Truman, and Kennedy throughout the 1984 campaign. A frustrated Walter Mondale finally demanded he stop! As the two parties have pulled closer in terms of party identification, the Republican party has run a series of television spots—so-called generic advertisements endorsing no particular candidate—to help boost Republican candidates nationally. While party label is less important in determining the outcome of presidential elections, public perceptions of the two parties remain significant. Equally important is the electoral college map and the pattern of two-party support in presidential elections over the past twenty years.

WHERE TO CAMPAIGN? Presidential elections are not determined by the national popular vote but by separate contests in the fifty states. Despite the fact that the Democrats remain slightly ahead in terms of partisan identification, the Republicans have a stronger electoral base in presidential elections.[26] Only the District of Columbia voted Democratic in each of the six preceding elections and only Minnesota voted Democratic in five of the six prior presidential elections. Five states, Hawaii, Maryland, Massachusetts, Rhode Island, and West Virginia, voted Democratic in four of the six prior elections. This core group of solid Democratic states makes up only fifty electoral votes. In contrast, while only Arizona has voted Republican in all six prior elections, twenty-two states voted Republican in five of six, and fourteen states voted Republican in four of the six previous elections. This group of solid Republican states makes up 360 electoral votes, more than enough to win the presidency.

WHETHER TO CAMPAIGN? Historically, incumbency has been a powerful advantage for a presidential candidate, although in recent years problems of incumbents have pointed to the liabilities as well. Still, many important benefits accrue to the candidate who is already president. Ronald Reagan's landslide reelection in 1984 and masterful use of incumbency suggest its assets.

A popular response from an incumbent president is the so-called **rose garden strategy.** The president acts as a nonpartisan leader, conducting presidential business such as meeting foreign officials and signing bills in the rose garden of the White House. He campaigns by not campaigning, refusing to treat the opponent as an equal. He plays the role of statesman, while the nominee of the out party must play the politician. A classic rose garden strategy was followed by Lyndon Johnson in 1964. Realizing a big early lead in the polls, LBJ ignored Goldwater, concentrating on the affairs of state and declining to debate his opponent. Nixon in 1972 followed a similar script, taking highly publicized trips abroad and refusing to debate McGovern. Reagan did not play a straight rose garden script in 1984. He actively campaigned against Mondale and debated him twice. Nonetheless, Reagan used the advantages of acting presidential equally well.

Sitting in the rose garden can backfire in a close election. Ford tried it in 1976 and watched Carter gain in the polls. As a result, Ford shifted gears and came out swinging. Carter used the rose garden strategy in the early stages of the primaries in 1980 against Edward Kennedy. Capitalizing on public support after the seizure of the hostages in Iran in November 1979, Carter refused to campaign against Kennedy as his standing shot up in the polls. By election time, however, the public had grown impatient with the hostage situation. Reagan forced Carter to come out and campaign. They debated, and the result is history. Despite the mixed record of incumbents and challengers in recent elections, incumbents' advantages appear to outweigh their disadvantages.

FINANCING PRESIDENTIAL CAMPAIGNS

The financing of presidential campaigns has changed dramatically since the early 1970s. The 1972 campaign remains as one of the sleaziest in history: flagrant abuses, illegal corporate contributions, "laundered" money, and million-dollar gifts from wealthy individuals. Nixon, in an exercise in political overkill, raised $60 million, more than double the amount raised by McGovern. CREEP, the Committee to Reelect the President, had trouble spending all the money. Watergate revelations disclosed many irregularities and illegalities in campaign financing and led to passage of significant campaign finance reform in 1974.

The most radical change was the shift to a system of public financing, funded by the one-dollar checkoff on individual tax returns. The **Federal Election Campaign Act (FECA)** of 1971 was amended in 1974 to provide public financing, limits on individual contributions, limits on the gifts of political action committees, and ceilings on overall spending. The provisions of the act and limits on campaign contributions are summarized in Political Insight 9-3. The act was weakened by the 1976 Supreme Court decision of **Buckley v. Valeo,** where the Court ruled it was unconstitutional to limit what an individual could contribute to his own campaign and altered the law in other ways.[27]

While the FECA has had significant impact in cleaning up the financing of presidential elections, several problems remain. One of the unintended consequences of the act was the growth of political action committees and the rapidly expanding amounts of money they contribute to federal elections. In addition, several loopholes exist that allow expenditures beyond the official spending limits. Independent expenditures by PACs—monies spent to help a candidate but not given directly to the campaign—do not count against the totals. Independent expenditures grew from $317,000 in 1977-78 to over $8 million a decade later. Second, because the limits apply only to direct expenditures on federal elections, parties and candidates have increasingly made what are called "soft money" expenditures. These are expenditures aimed at influencing state and local elections or strengthening state party organizations. While these do not directly affect the presidential election, they clearly have an indirect impact and are targeted to key states. With independent expenditures by PACs and soft money expenditures by parties and candidates, actual spending in presidential elections is far greater than the totals permitted under the Federal Election Campaign Act.

Explaining Voting Behavior: The 1988 Election

Many complex factors determine how voters choose a candidate, and social scientists disagree about which theoretical perspective is best. Abramson, Aldrich, and Rohde, in their analysis of presidential elections since the 1950s, identify three main approaches to explaining voting behavior:[28]

- The first approach emphasizes individual socioeconomic characteristics (age, race, income, occupation, etc.) and membership in certain groups (union membership, religion, etc.). This approach is favored by sociologists who argue that social characteristics determine political preferences. We saw in Chapter 8 the growing importance of race in relation to party preferences and will examine other social characteristics and voting results in 1984 and 1988.
- The second approach emphasizes social-psychological factors, particularly attitudes towards parties, candidates, and issues immediately before the election. This approach, favored by political scientists, is closely tied to the University of Michigan and the pioneering work *The American Voter,* published in 1960.[29] As we saw in the previous chapter, party identification emerged as the most important variable. It serves as a perceptual screen that influences how voters perceive candidates and

POLITICAL INSIGHT 9-3

REQUIREMENTS UNDER THE FEDERAL ELECTION CAMPAIGN ACT

Federal Election Commission. The commission consists of six people chosen to monitor and enforce campaign finance requirements for federal candidates. They receive the required campaign spending reports from the candidates, distribute federal funds, and adjudicate certain questions and complaints raised under the law.

Federal Matching Funds. Candidates may choose to use public funds for their campaign and abide by a set of rules and requirements or raise all their money privately. Candidates must qualify for matching funds by raising $5,000 in twenty states through contributions of $250 or less (this demonstrates support in terms of both number of donors and geographic distribution). Up to the spending limits, candidates receive federal funds equal to their private contributions.

Spending Limits. The original limits set for the 1976 election were $10 million before the conventions and $20 million in the general election. Adjustments for inflation pushed the limit on total spending for each candidate to $27.6 million for the nomination and $46.1 million for the general election in 1988. In addition, 20 percent of the total may be used for fund-raising, which does not count against the limits. Each party received $9.2 million to pay for the national nominating convention.

Contributors. Candidates may spend as much of their own money on the campaign as they wish (the Supreme Court struck down a limit of $50,000 of a candidate's own money) within the general limits for total spending. Other limits are as follows:

From Individuals:

To a candidate or his or her committee: $1,000 per election

To national party committees: $20,000 per calendar year

To any other committee: $5,000 per calendar year

Total Contribution Limit: $25,000 per calendar year

From Political Action Committees:

To a candidate or his or her committee: $5,000 per election

To national party committees: $15,000 per calendar year

To any other committee: $5,000 per calendar year

Total Contribution Limit: None

From Party Committees:

To a candidate or his or her committee: $5,000 per election

To national party committees: no limit

To any other committee: $5,000 per calendar year

Total Contribution Limit: None

From Any Other Group or Committee:

To a candidate or his or her committee: $1,000 per election

To national party committees: $20,000 per calendar year

To any other committee: $5,000 per calendar year

Total Contribution Limit: None

issues, which in turn influences turnout and voting (see Table 8-4).

■ The third approach comes from economics. Voters are considered rational actors who make retrospective evaluations of incumbents and their parties, looking to the recent past to judge performance and policy preferences.[30] Perceptions of the recent performance of the economy are particularly important. This approach suggests that voters retrospectively evaluate the performance of the party in power more than they prospectively judge the promises for the future of the two candidates. This **retrospective voting** hurt Carter in 1980, for example, but helped Reagan in 1984 and Bush in 1988.

Analyzing a combination of sociological factors, partisan factors, and retrospective evaluations in the context of the 1988 campaign, we can better understand the Bush victory. Bush's advantages were peace, prosperity, and the popularity of Ronald Reagan. The Bush campaign took an aggressive—many said negative—approach in attempting to create an image of Michael Dukakis for the voters. Bush and his surrogates attacked Dukakis for his veto of a mandatory Pledge of Allegiance bill, the Massachusetts prisoner furlough program, and his liberalism. The Bush camp seemed to dominate the agenda of the campaign, while Dukakis was slow in responding to many of the charges. While a large majority of Americans were happy with the nominee of their respective party in the summer, by fall a majority wished their party had nominated someone else. The negative perceptions of Dukakis in particular increased markedly during the campaign. Some polls revealed that Democratic vice-presidential nominee Senator Lloyd Bentsen was preferred to both presidential candidates. In the election postmortem, many were critical of the Dukakis campaign. His lackluster performance in the second debate and on ABC's "Nightline" were cited as lost opportunities. His eleventh-hour acceptance of the "liberal" label was thought to have come too late, after the damage had been done. Bush, on the other hand, was acknowledged to have run a slick, professional campaign.

The electoral college maps in Figure 9-1 show the geography and magnitude of the Bush victory in comparison with recent presidential elections. Republican George Bush carried forty states with a total of 426 electoral votes, compared to ten states and the District of Columbia, a total of 112 electoral votes, for Democrat Michael Dukakis. Bush forged his electoral coalition from the same base of support as recent Republican presidential victors. He swept the South and most of the West and made substantial inroads in the industrial states of the Midwest and Northeast.

Appeals to different social groups, attitudes toward the parties, candidates, and issues, as well as retrospective evaluations of the performance of the Reagan administration were all important determinants of the outcome of the 1988 presidential election. Table 9-6 indicates some of the key concerns

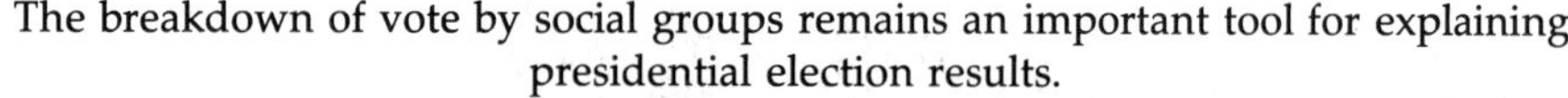

The breakdown of vote by social groups remains an important tool for explaining presidential election results.

FIGURE 9–1

Results of Presidential Elections, 1968–1988

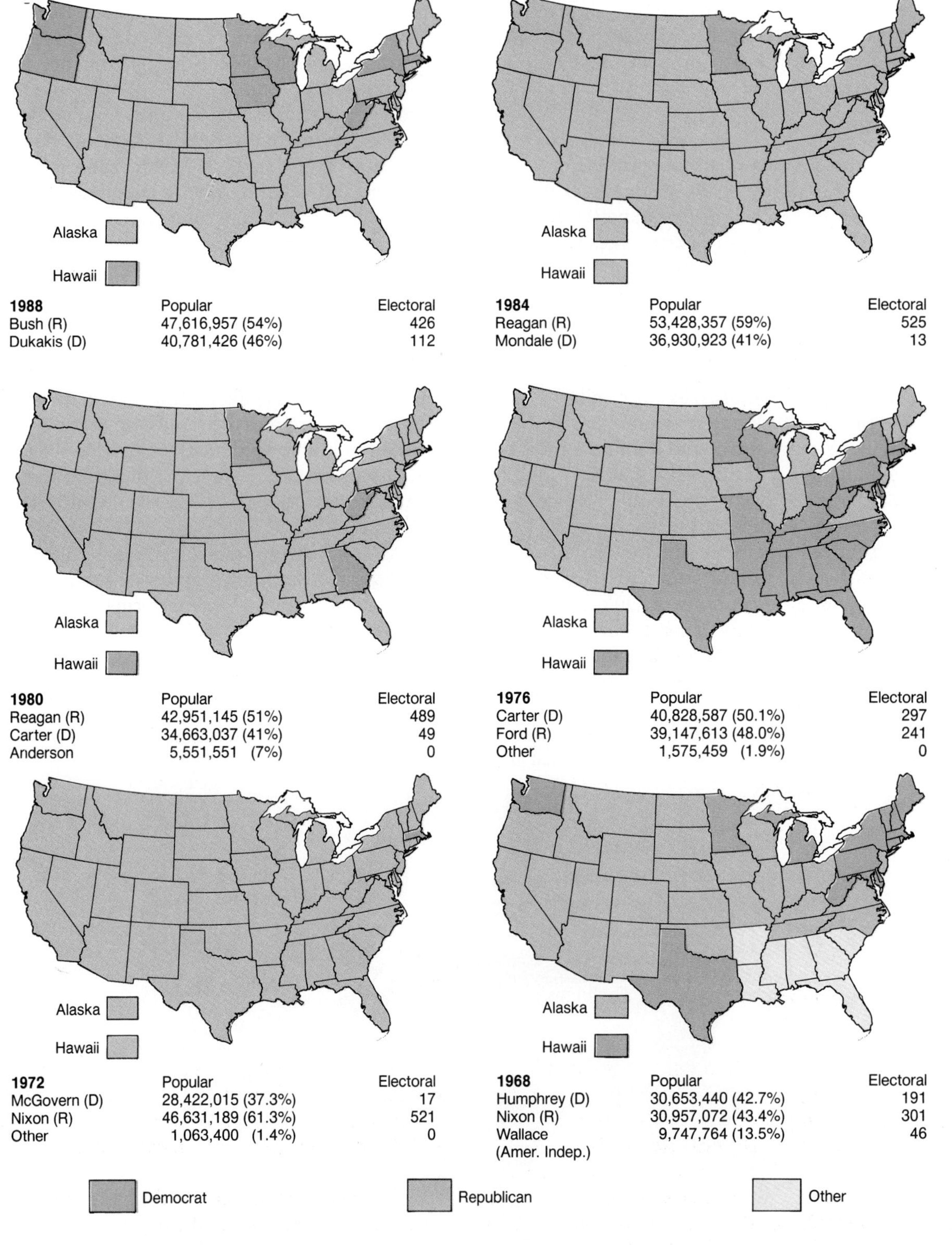

TABLE 9–6

EXPLAINING THEIR VOTE

	Percent Voting for	
	Bush	Dukakis
Why did you vote for your candidate?		
He has more experience (34%)	97%	3%
He's more competent (27)	73	26
He seems to care about people like me (24)	25	75
It's time for a change (18)	5	92
He has a clearer vision of the future (17)	52	46
He has a better vice president (13)	14	86
My party didn't nominate the best man (10)	50	44
He impressed me during the debates (7)	54	46
He will avoid a recession (4)	80	19
He's more likable (3)	52	46
What did you like least about his opponent?		
His views are too liberal (28%)	94%	6%
He ran a dirty campaign (28)	30	69
He has shown bad judgment (24)	46	53
He just leaves me cold (19)	55	43
He's too risky (15)	76	24
He's too close to the special interests (13)	26	72
He's too tied to the past (10)	10	88
He won't stand up for America (8)	65	33
He's too much of a wimp (7)	38	60
He isn't going to be elected (4)	63	34
Which issues were most important to your vote?		
The federal budget deficit (25%)	39%	60%
National defense (23)	84	15
Abortion (20)	63	36
Crime (18)	67	31
Ethics in government (17)	31	67
Taxes (15)	70	29
Drugs (14)	41	58
Unemployment (10)	35	64
Protecting the environment (11)	28	70
Foreign trade (5)	57	42
No issue, really (12)	52	45

SOURCE: Cable News Network-*Los Angeles Times* exit polls, November 8, 1988. Reported in *National Journal*, 12 November 1988.

of voters in 1988 and which candidate benefited. One-third of the voters reported that experience was one of the most important factors in their decision. Of this group, a nearly unanimous 97 percent voted for Bush! Bush also succeeded among the 27 percent of voters who mentioned competence as the main reason for their vote. Three out of four of them chose George Bush. Dukakis had a marked advantage among voters who wanted a candidate who cared about people like them, those who felt it was time for a change, and those who reported that the vice-presidential candidate influenced their vote.

Table 9-6 also shows some of the negative perceptions and positive issues that were important to voters. Bush clearly succeeded in convincing a significant proportion of voters that Michael Dukakis was too liberal. On the other hand, the 28 percent who were concerned about a dirty campaign favored Dukakis over Bush by a margin of 69 to 30 percent. The issue most frequently mentioned by voters was the federal budget deficit. These voters favored Dukakis. On the other hand, among the next three most frequently cited issues—defense, abortion, and crime—voters overwhelmingly favored Bush. The success of the Bush campaign in portraying Dukakis as soft on defense is apparent. Of the one in four voters who mentioned defense as important, 85 percent favored George Bush.

The breakdown of the 1988 vote by social groups tells us much about the evolving American electorate and the nature of party coalitions in the 1990s. Table 9-7 examines who voted for Bush and Dukakis in 1988 compared to the Reagan-Mondale contest in 1984. In virtually every category, the Republican advantages were reduced from those of the Reagan landslide four years earlier. But the breakdown reflects the continuing Republican majority coalition in presidential elections. The gender gap was evident. Men voted for Bush by a margin of 58 to 40 percent, while women favored Dukakis by a narrow margin. Sharp differences based on race remain. Blacks continued to favor the Democratic candidate but by a slightly reduced margin from 1984. Whites favored Bush by 57 to 41 percent. Among southern whites, the margin was 68 to 31 percent.

The 1988 election displayed much greater regional variation than the 1984 contest, when Ronald Reagan's margins were uniform across the country. The largest reversal was in the East, where Dukakis outpolled Bush 53 to 45 percent. Only in the South was Bush's margin of victory comparable to Reagan's. Little variation was evident by the age of voters. Bush carried every age group, with his margin reduced only among those over 60 years of age. Dukakis carried only those with very low incomes, low education, and union households and those who considered their financial situation the same or worse. Republicans continued to support their party's candidate more loyally than Democrats (by 95 percent compared to 89 percent), but some of the so-called Reagan Democrats came back to their party in 1988.

Evaluations of the issues and promises of the candidates were relatively even in 1988. Democrats were perceived as the party more likely to help the poor and the middle class and the party more likely to improve education. Republican advantages came in the areas of the economy and defense. But George Bush gained a significant advantage over Michael Dukakis because of positive retrospective evaluations of the Reagan administration. Table 9-7 includes voting preferences by those who reported their financial situations to be better, worse, or the same. Those who were better off voted for Bush by a ratio of 7 to 3. While those who were worse off favored Dukakis by the same proportion, nearly three times as many voters were better off (44 percent) than were worse off (17 percent). Abramson, Aldrich, and Rohde conclude:

> Our evidence strongly suggests that retrospective voting was widespread in all recent elections. . . . Presumably, voters find it easier, less time-consuming, and less risky to evaluate the incumbent party on what its president did in the most recent term of office than on the nominees' promises for the future. Dukakis . . . failed to convince the public that the Democratic party would better handle their concerns.[31]

Elections and Governing

WHAT GUIDANCE FOR POLICY-MAKERS?

What impact did the 1988 elections have on how the nation is governed? The message of the elections is obscure if it exists at all, since voters not only kept the Democratic party in control of Congress but increased its majorities in both houses while expressing their satisfaction with the performance of Republicans in the White House. George Bush had no coattails whatsoever; it was the worst showing by a winning presidential candidate in terms of House seats in twenty-eight years. Governing problems are worsened by the increasing use of "slash and burn" campaign tactics. Many Democrats were incensed by the attacks by Bush on Dukakis's patriotism and by the infamous Willie Horton ads. The bruising and bitter battle over Bush's nomination

TABLE 9–7

WHO VOTED FOR BUSH AND DUKAKIS

	1984		1988		1984–88 Republican Change
	Rep.	Dem.	Rep.	Dem.	
All (100%)	59%	41%	54%	45%	−5%
Men (50)	63	37	58	40	−5
Women (50)	56	44	49	50	−7
Whites (85)	67	33	57	41	−10
Blacks (8)	9	91	11	86	+2
Hispanics (4)	47	53	38	61	−9
East (25)	59	41	45	53	−14
South (28)	58	42	58	40	0
Midwest (30)	59	41	52	47	−7
West (17)	59	41	54	43	−5
Southern whites (24)	73	27	68	31	−5
Nonsouthern whites (61)	64	36	53	45	−11
Protestants (56)	61	39	58	40	−3
Catholics (30)	59	41	49	50	−10
Jews (4)	32	68	24	74	−8
"Born again" white Protestants (18)	80	20	71	27	−9
Age 18–24 (11)	59	41	55	44	−4
25–29 (12)	61	39	54	45	−7
30–39 (23)	57	43	52	46	−5
40–49 (19)	59	41	55	43	−4
50–59 (12)	62	38	57	42	−5
60+ (23)	60	40	51	47	−9
	45	55	33	64	−12
Family income: −$10,000 (10)					
$10–20,000 (17)	56	44	45	53	−11
$20–30,000 (21)	61	39	51	47	−10

	1984		1988		1984–88 Republican Change
	Rep.	Dem.	Rep.	Dem.	
$30–40,000 (20%)	66%	34%	60%	39%	−6%
Over $40,000 (32)	68	32	62	37	−6
Didn't finish high school (8)	48	51	39	60	−9
High school grad (34)	56	44	53	46	−3
Some college (21)	62	38	57	42	−5
College grad (21)	63	37	59	39	−4
Postgrad (16)	52	48	49	49	−3
Union households (31)	48	52	43	55	−5
Nonunion (69)	64	36	59	40	−5
Financial situation:					
Better (44)	81	19	69	30	−12
Same (39)	51	49	48	50	−3
Worse (17)	27	73	29	69	+2
Democrats (30)	16	84	10	89	−6
Independents (37)	67	33	55	42	−12
Republicans (31)	97	3	95	5	−2
Liberals (24)	32	68	18	81	−14
Moderates (37)	59	41	55	42	−4
Conservatives (39)	82	18	82	17	0
1984 votes					
Reagan-R (55)	100	0	82	17	−18
Mondale-D (27)	0	100	8	91	+8
Did not vote (12)	—	—	45	53	—

SOURCE: Cable News Network—*Los Angeles Times* exit polls, November 8, 1988. Reported in *National Journal*, 12 November 1988.

BY WRIGHT FOR THE MIAMI NEWS

of former Senator John Tower for secretary of defense reflected some of the lingering partisan resentment from the campaign. While Bush took a more conciliatory approach to Congress than Reagan, partisan divisions between branches remained wide.

Presidential campaigns are too long, hampering the functioning of the presidency and executive branch for nearly a year.[32] They are endurance tests that do not necessarily produce the best candidates. Many of the most competent candidates simply refuse to put themselves or their families through it. Presidential campaigns tend to isolate candidates from members of Congress; the system does nothing to see the presidential nominees can work with members of their own party within Congress. As Michael Robinson observed:

> The primary system is a disaster. It costs too much; it makes pseudo-enemies out of true political allies, and it makes pseudo-winners out of true losers. And, more importantly, the primary system has made the process of becoming president so dispiriting, so distasteful, that those who would become, shouldn't.[33]

CAN ELECTIONS BE IMPROVED?

A number of reforms have been proposed to improve and shorten the process. In 1988, Congress considered bills to establish regional primaries.[34] One proposal by Senator Alan Dixon (D-Ill.) would create six regional primaries to be held every other week beginning in late March. The order would be determined by lottery. More radical approaches suggest a single national primary. This idea was first proposed in 1911 and since then, over one hundred proposals have been submitted in Congress. Proponents believe it would increase participation, shorten the process, equalize individuals' votes across states, and improve governing by forcing candidates to concentrate on national issues. Opponents fear it would permanently cripple already weak political parties and make the electorate even more subject to media manipulation, big spending, and negative campaigning.

Linking the electoral process more closely to the governing process is an extremely difficult challenge. It would mean more competitiveness in congressional elections. It would mean more substance and less negative campaigning in both congressional and presidential campaigns. Campaign financing reform, including limits on total spending, could help level the playing field for challengers and free legislators from endless fund-raising. Around the world, national campaigns are more heavily regulated than in the United States, and their democracies function perfectly well. In many nations, for example, commercial air time is donated free, not purchased by candidates. In France, polls may not be released the week before the voting.

Stricter requirements could be applied in the United States within constitutional guidelines. Presidential candidates accepting public funds could be required to participate in debates. While the debates are not perfect, they are a vast improvement on thirty-second commercials. Limits could be placed on advertising purchased with public funds. As one critic concluded,: "It is perverse that the public has been subsidizing presidential candidates (in the amount of $46 million in 1988, of which more than half was used for advertising) to pay for thirty-second commercials that influence the vote mainly through slogans and visual imagery."[35] Ads of a minimum length (five to thirty minutes, for example) could be required. Proposals have been advanced to limit negative advertising by requiring candidates to appear personally when the record of an opponent is attacked. Others have suggested establishing a nonpartisan national review board to make determinations of fairness and fact in campaigns.

The ultimate sanction against negative campaigns is in the hands of the voters. Negative campaigning is on the rise because it works. Until voters reject such appeals and respond to substance over symbols, the prospects for change are dim and the consequences for governing severe.

SUMMARY AND CONCLUSIONS

1. Through U.S. history, suffrage has been extended to all white males, blacks, women, again southern blacks, and finally eighteen-year-olds. Elections have been partially nationalized over the years, although states still control many aspects of their own election laws.

2. Voting turnout in the United States is lower than in most democratic countries, and its continued decline is a source of concern to many. Only 50 percent participate in presidential elections, and the total is even less for congressional, state, and local elections.

3. Incumbents' domination of congressional elections has raised fears about a growing isolation of Congress from national trends. Seats are reapportioned every ten years after the national census, requiring each state to go through the politically volatile redistricting process.

4. The system of choosing presidential candidates has evolved from selection by congressional caucuses through nominating conventions to a system dominated by presidential primaries. The results of the changes have been to open up the nomination to "outsiders" and "dark horses" and to weaken the role of traditional party leaders.

5. The successful presidential candidate faces a long and arduous struggle to obtain delegates through primaries and caucuses to gain the nomination. Potential candidates must possess certain qualities, have great stamina, start early, and generate the necessary momentum to create a bandwagon effect. The national media have the greatest influence on the election before and during the primaries.

6. The nominating convention is still the major event of the two parties, but in recent years the conventions have been reduced to endorsing the predetermined candidate. Convention delegates also approve the party platform, endorse the vice-presidential nominee, and try to launch the campaign on a successful note.

7. Although many voters have made up their minds about whom to vote for by the start of the campaign, more and more voters now decide during the campaign. The campaign is in part an exercise in professional image-making, with media advisers as important as policy advisers.

8. Candidate image and relative economic prosperity are critical in determining the outcome of the election. As a result, even landslide elections do not offer policy-specific mandates to govern but do provide important political resources for the president. Critics are dissatisfied with many aspects of the current system, and some have proposed regional primaries or a national primary.

Elections remain the keystone of democratic government, even though they do not convey a clear or unambiguous message. In a complex society, it would be exceedingly unusual if the electorate spoke with a single voice. Cynics note that a single vote does not give the average citizen a say over how the government is run and what it does. Are elections therefore meaningless and voting unnecessary? No, because the nation is more than individuals. It is a collectivity, an aggregation of communities, groups, interests, and concerns,. Acting in concert with others, voting can have meaning and impact, but only if the link between elections and governing remains strong.

KEY TERMS

Buckley v. Valeo	nonbinding preference primary
caucus-convention system	platform committee
credentials committee	reapportionment
disenfranchisement	redistricting
Federal Election Campaign Act	retrospective voting
gerrymandering	rose garden strategy
invisible primary	rules committee
negative campaigning	two-thirds rule
	"window" period

SELF-REVIEW

1. How has suffrage been extended through U.S. history?

2. In what way have elections been nationalized?

3. Describe the changes in voter turnout over the years.

4. How are seats in Congress apportioned to the states?

5. What are the advantages of incumbency to members of Congress?

6. How are convention delegates apportioned to the states?

7. How do the caucus and convention systems operate?

8. What are the different types of primaries?

9. What is a "brokered" convention?

10. How is the vice-presidential nominee chosen?

11. What are the major factors in campaigns?

12. What are the advantages of incumbency to a president?

13. How are presidential campaigns financed?

14. How can the 1988 election result be explained?

15. What is retrospective voting?

16. What are the consequences for governing of the current electoral system?

SUGGESTED READINGS

Abramson, Paul, Aldrich, John and Rohde, David. *Change and Continuity in the 1988 Elections.* 1990.
More detailed analysis of various approaches to explaining election behavior.

Asher, Herbert. *Presidential Elections and American Politics.* 1984.
A good overview of models of voting behavior and changes in the conduct of campaigns.

Malbin, Michael J., ed. *Money and Politics in the United States.* 1984.
Analyses of campaign finance and elections in the 1980s.

White, Theodore. *The Making of the President.,* 1960.
An insightful narrative of one of the closest presidential elections.

NOTES

1. *New York Times,* 7 August 1965, p. 8.
2. *New York Times,* 18 March 1990, p. 16.
3. *Ibid.*
4. William H. Flanigan and Nancy H. Zingale, *Political Behavior of the American Electorate,* (Boston: Allyn and Bacon, 1983), 5.
5. Charles Williamson, *American Suffrage from Property to Democracy, 1760-1860* (Princeton: Princeton University Press, 1960).
6. Harrell Rodgers and Charles Bullock, *Law and Social Change* (New York: McGraw-Hill, 1972).
7. *Congressional Digest* (April 1990), p. 101.
8. Paul Abramson, John Aldrich, and David Rohde, *Change and Continuity in the 1988 Elections*

(Washington D.C., Congressional Quarterly Press, 1990), 87-113, is the source of this section.

9. Raymond Wolfinger and Steven Rosenstone, *Who Votes* (New Haven: Yale University Press, 1980), 109–14.
10. Gary Jacobsen, *Congressional Elections* (Boston: Little, Brown, 1982).
11. Morris Fiorina, *Congress: Keystone of the Washington Establishment* (New Haven: Yale University Press, 1977).
12. Quoted in *New York Times,* 18 March 1990, p. 16.
13. Randall B. Ripley, *Congress: Process and Policy* (New York: Norton, 1983), 8.
14. Arthur Hadley, *The Invisible Primary* (Englewood Cliffs, N.J.: Prentice-Hall, 1976).
15. Theodore White, *The Making of the President, 1972* (New York: Atheneum, 1973), 106.
16. Frank Sorauf, *Party Politics in America* (Boston: Little, Brown, 1980), 271.
17. *Congressional Quarterly Weekly Reports,* 11 June 1988, p. 1576.
18. *Ibid.*
19. Louis Cannon, "Udall Complains 'Orgy of Publicity' Benefits Carter Drive," *Washington Post,* 17 April 1976, p. A4.
20. V. O. Key, *Politics, Parties, and Pressure Groups* (New York: Crowell, 1969), 418.
21. Richard A. Watson, *The Presidential Contest* (New York: Wiley, 1980), 33.
22. Abramson et al., *Change and Continuity, 1988,* 52.
23. *Washington Post,* 16 November 1988, p. A12.
24. Joe McGinniss, *The Selling of the President 1968* (New York: Trident Press, 1969), 103.
25. Quoted in Watson, *The Presidential Contest,* 49.
26. Paul Abramson, John Aldrich, and David Rohde, *Change and Continuity in the 1984 Elections* (Washington, D.C.: Congressional Quarterly Press, 1984), 85.
27. *National Journal,* 13 September 1980, p. 1512.
28. Abramson et al., *Change and Continuity, 1988,* 81–84.
29. Angus Campbell, Phillip Converse, Warren Miller, and Donald Stokes, *The American Voter* (New York: Wiley, 1960).
30. Morris Fiorina, *Retrospective Voting in American National Elections* (New Haven: Yale University Press, 1981).
31. Abramson et al., *Change and Continuity, 1988,* 193–94.
32. Cyrus Vance, "Reforming the Electoral Reforms," in Thomas Cronin (ed.), *Rethinking the Presidency* (Boston: Little Brown, 1982), 47.
33. Michael Robinson, "An Idea Whose Time Has Come—Again," *Congressional Record,* 19 June 1975, p. E3336.
34. *Congressional Quarterly Weekly Reports,* 9 July 1988, pp. 1892, 1895, 1897.
35. Paul Quirk, "The Election," in Michael Nelson, ed., *The Elections of 1988* (Washington, D.C.: Congressional Quarterly Press, 1989), 89.

CHAPTER 10

The Mass Media

POLITICAL CLOSE-UP

"Thirty-Second Politics": Exploiting Fear of Crime

—Texas, a campaign commercial before the 1990 primaries: former Democratic governor and candidate Mark White walks into a room hung with huge black-and-white photographs of criminals executed while he was governor. White speaks:

"These hardened criminals will never again murder, rape, or deal drugs. As governor, I made sure they received the ultimate punishment—death—and Texas is a safer place for it.

"But tough talk isn't enough. Criminals know how to tangle up the courts and delay executions. To bring them to justice takes strength and dedication. Because if the governor flinches, they win.

"Only a governor can make executions happen. I did, and I will."

—Florida, a campaign commercial before the 1990 primaries: Republican Governor Bob Martinez, seeking re-election, sits in his office and speaks:

"I have now signed some ninety death warrants in the state of Florida. Each one of those committed a heinous crime that I don't even choose to describe to you."

Then, for a few seconds, the evil smirk of mass murderer Ted Bundy, executed in 1989, appears on the screen. Martinez returns.

"I believe in the death penalty. I believe it is the proper penalty for one who has taken someone else's life."

These are the stark images of modern media campaigns, and Martinez and White were not alone. In the Texas primary election, White's opponent, Jim Mattox, bragged in his commercials that as attorney general, he carried out thirty-two executions. In California, gubernatorial candidate Diane Feinstein ran ads touting her strong support for the death penalty.

Her opponent, Attorney General John Van de Kamp, on the defensive on the crime issue, soft-pedaled his opposition to the death penalty by noting that he believed in carrying out state law.

Creators of these death penalty commercials claim they are "positive" because they show what the candidate stands for. They can be "negative" when used to suggest an opponent is soft on crime. Perhaps the most famous examples are the infamous Willie Horton ads used by George Bush against Michael Dukakis in 1988. The idea for the strategy came from Dukakis's arch political enemy, New Hampshire Governor John Sununu. In 1987, Sununu saw a story about a convicted murderer who raped a woman in Maryland while on furlough from prison in Massachusetts. It was passed on to the Bush campaign in 1988, where campaign manager Lee Atwater promised that by the time the election was over, Willie Horton would be a household name. One commercial that aired during the fall campaign featured stone-faced criminals—mostly black—filing through revolving doors. The voice-over said that Dukakis allowed weekend passes to be given to murderers and that many had escaped while on furlough. Later commercials featured the white victims of Willie Horton's crime spree.

Fear of crime and criminals among the American people is a powerful force for candidates to tap into in the 1990s. Support for the death penalty has risen to nearly 80 percent in recent years, up from only 50 percent only a few years ago. Fear of crime, and its exploitation by media consultants, has been heightened because of the drug crisis. The consultant who tested Mark White's ads found them "devastatingly effective." Less vivid images and descriptions, claim the consultants, "just don't get through."

SOURCE: Dan Balz, "Electric Chair One-Upmanship," *Washington Post National Weekly Edition,* 12-18 March 1990, p. 11.

CHAPTER OUTLINE

INTRODUCTION AND OVERVIEW

How important is the mass media for governing? A dramatic aspect of the democratic revolutions in Eastern Europe was the wresting away of control of the mass media from communist rulers. In Romania, during the bloody overthrow of President Nicolae Ceausescu, the television station itself became the focal point of revolution. A reporter in Bucharest described the scene:

> The National Salvation Front clung to the television like a mantle of power, running the country from a barricaded studio while Ceausescu's fanatical guard tried to blast it into silence. Sniper fire smashed windows, and heavy shells blew holes in the walls.
>
> Until the revolution, the station broadcast only two hours daily, a deadening litany of the heroic and generous qualities of Ceausescu.... Suddenly it was on the air around the clock, and Romanians who once scorned television sat glued to their screens.
>
> In the assault, section chairs and janitors alike beamed with pride at the unflickering image they broadcast across the nation. In the face of rumors and threats, the reassuring voices on television maintained the momentum of the revolt.[1]

Even in democratic nations, the mass media are recognized as a great source of political power. In France, control of television networks has sparked sharp confrontations between political parties. After the Socialists lost the 1987 parliamentary elections, the new conservative majority rescinded private broadcast licenses to Socialist sympathizers and replaced directors of three government-owned television stations with conservatives. We have entered the media age of politics where both running for office and governing increasingly center on television.

Television opened a window on the world, allowing people to see things they had never seen, but it soon became clear that television is more than a window. Television is a **medium of communication** that inevitably screens and alters what it reveals. Today, 98 percent of the homes in the United States have television sets; most have more than one. The average high school graduate has spent as much time in front of the television set as in school.[2]

"Media" is the plural of "medium," meaning a vehicle through which something is transmitted. Like the gypsy in front of the crystal ball who puts her trusting client in touch with the departed, newspapers, magazines, radio, television, and other media transmit messages from a *source* to the *receiver.* The word **mass** refers to **media** that reach large numbers of people simultaneously. Whether it is the *New York Times,* a televised presidential debate, or radio coverage of the Super Bowl, information is transmitted to large numbers of people in identical form.

In transmitting messages from sources to receivers, the mass media function as a crucial linkage institution in American politics. The media provide impressions, sounds, pictures of politics and politicians. The media show public problems, crises, wars, and political conventions. The media bring images of demonstrations and riots into the White House and the homes of members of Congress and bureaucrats. How do the media affect what people think and do? Are Americans vulnerable to media messages or resistant to manipulation? How do the mass media affect political socialization and general support for the political system? How do the mass media affect the ability to govern? Have media campaigns widened the gap between running for office and governing?

To develop a fuller understanding of the relationships between the media, politics, and governing, the following questions are explored:

1. How have the mass media evolved?
2. How are the media regulated in the United States, compared with the media in other democratic and nondemocratic systems?
3. What are the "mass media"? How are they organized, and what are the economic and political pressures on them?
4. How do the media affect public attitudes, political socialization, and election campaigns?
5. What is the relationship between the media and public officials? Why do they need each other? How do they use each other?
6. What is news? How do the media gather or create news? Is election news biased?
7. How does the government control and regulate broadcast media compared with the print media?
8. Can journalists help clean up campaigns?

The Development of Independent Media

The Evolution of Journalism and the Mass Media

Within hours of President John F. Kennedy's assassination in 1963, more than 95 percent of Americans were aware of what had happened. Americans now accept instantaneous communication as a simple fact of life. How startlingly different it is from communication in the early days of the nation. In 1790, it took an average of five days for news to travel from Philadelphia to New York, ten days to Richmond and Boston, fifteen days to Portland, and more than twenty days to Charleston.[3]

In addition to the slowness of communication, early forms of mass communication were rudimentary and limited. Political pamphlets, such as Thomas Paine's *Common Sense,* were a popular method of expressing political opinions. Early newspapers were not independent observers of politics. They were published by political factions and the fledgling parties to express partisan viewpoints to a limited audience. Much political communication took place by word of mouth—discussions and debates among the educated segments of the population. The popular press, with widespread public circulation, did not become prevalent until the mid-nineteenth century, when technological changes allowing faster and cheaper printing made it possible for newspapers to reach larger numbers of people.[4] The invention of the telegraph rapidly increased the speed of communication and led to creation of the first news wire service (the Associated Press) in 1848.

Newspapers quickly became big business. They were profitable and popular with the public, many basing their appeal on splashy, sensational stories. Huge newspaper empires, owned by such magnates as William Randolph Hearst and Joseph Pulitzer, came to play an important role in American politics. Although independent in the sense that they were privately owned and not affiliated with a political party, newspapers were highly partisan and opinionated. The popular press began to shrink the world for Americans, creating a common experience, a shared political culture. By the late nineteenth century, magazines such as *Harper's, Atlantic,* and *Scribner's* became important vehicles of opinion on contemporary public policy questions. "Muckrakers"—who might be called investigative journalists today—used the power of the press at the turn of the century to push for antitrust legislation, child labor laws, and other reforms.

Broadcast journalism created a second communications revolution. The development of radio in the 1920s brought listeners into direct personal touch with politicians, allowing citizens to hear politicians' own words in their own voices. Al Smith, the Democratic nominee for president in 1928, may have been the first politician to run afoul of this new medium. His strong New York accent did not appeal to many voters across the country. If radio hurt Smith, it proved to be a great ally of Franklin D. Roosevelt, whose "fireside chats" are still legendary in the history of political communication. David Halberstam describes the effect of Roosevelt's broadcasts:

> He had an intuitive sense of radio cadence. Unlike most people, who speeded up their normal speech pattern on radio, Roosevelt deliberately slowed his down. . . His very first words reflected his ease: "My friends," he began. *My friends.* That was it, they were his friends. Nor were they a passive audience. At that desperate moment in American history the American people were not cool, not aloof, they needed him and they wanted him to succeed; what could be more stirring than to be told by that man with the rich assured voice that the only thing they had to fear was fear itself.[5]

Relations with the press changed as well. Roosevelt was the first president to have a press secretary and to recognize the political importance of the media. He used the media for his own political purposes, as the media had used the presidency as a source of stories and news for decades. Thus began the pattern of mutual dependency, tempered with mutual suspicion, that characterizes the relationship between the media and the president today.

Television was the next stage of technological advance, one that had a profound effect on the conduct of American politics. Not only voices but also pictures, expressions, and gestures were now shared simultaneously by millions of people. The first national conventions were televised in 1952, bringing the hullabaloo of politics into American living rooms. Politicians were quick to exploit the dramatic possibilities of television. Nixon's emotional "Checkers speech"—where he denied any financial impropriety beyond accepting a puppy named Checkers—was instrumental in Eisenhower's decision to keep him as his running mate in 1952. The Army-McCarthy hearings in the 1950s, the Nixon-Kennedy debates in 1960, Johnson's dramatic withdrawal from the presidential race in 1968, Nixon's resignation in 1974, and Oliver North and the Iran-Contra hearings in 1987—all became part of American political history, directly involving millions of Americans. What next? Cable networks already exist where viewers can "talk back" to a program. Satellites, home computers, and home video all continue the process of rapid change in communication.

The Mass Media around the World

One indication of the importance of mass media in politics is the degree to which governments feel they must control them. Domination of the media

Iraq's Saddam Hussein unsuccessfully tried to manipulate world public opinion after his invasion of Kuwait.

is overt and direct in authoritarian regimes. Operating under the assumption that because their governments always act in the interests of the people, such regimes hold that interference from the media is antisocial and cannot be tolerated.[6] The mass media become organs of government propaganda. Little separates "news" and "opinion." Both must support the government and conform to the dominant ideology. The media play a propaganda role, whether explicitly teaching party doctrine or simply avoiding stories about crime and other social problems (which are not supposed to exist). After his invasion of Kuwait sparked international outrage, Iraqi President, Saddam Hussein, tried to use television to sway world opinion. His crude attempts backfired, however, with western viewers shocked at his display of frightened British and American hostages.

The role of the mass media is much different in most nonauthoritarian countries. Governments are viewed as imperfect manifestations of the public interest that must be kept under careful scrutiny, and mass media fulfill this function.[7] But practice is not always in concert with the ideal. Mass media, even in most democratic nations, are generally supportive of the political system. They may knowingly withhold information that would be damaging to the government, as they have done in the United States in not reporting certain activities of the Federal Bureau of Investigation (FBI) and the Central Intelligence Agency (CIA). Although the media may play a more subtle propaganda role in democratic nations, that is not their main function. They exist to inform and entertain, although the distinction between the two is not always clear. Media in most democracies play the ambivalent role of social critic and government supporter.

All nations place some limits on the operation of the media. Nondemocratic nations control the media by strictly limiting who may publish or broadcast. Those who are disloyal are put out of business or worse. Political dissidents are denied access to the media, and those who are critical of the government are often punished. Direct government ownership of the main organs of communication is the common practice. Even in this circumstance, the ruling elite is careful to censor what the government-owned media present, thereby determining what the public hears and sees.

Democratic societies are much less restrictive, but they attempt to control the media in other ways. Great Britain, Canada, France, and many other nations own the major national television networks. Although the network may be relatively independent, its broadcast decisions may be affected by political pressures. In the summer of 1985, journalists and staff of the British Broadcasting Corporation (BBC) staged a one-day strike to protest the cancellation of a television documentary on Northern Ireland because of sharp pressure from the Thatcher government. Doris Graber suggests there are four main controls over the media in democratic societies: (1) treason and sedition laws, (2) government secrecy in sensitive areas, (3) slander and libel laws protecting individual reputations, and (4) limits on material that might offend portions of the audience.[8]

The media in the United States have greater freedom than their counterparts in almost any other country. The print and broadcast media are more diverse than in Great Britain, for example. Slander and libel laws are much less restrictive in the United States, allowing the media more leeway in presenting material, especially political material. Newspapers in Great Britain must be much more careful of what they print. During the abdication crisis in the mid-1930s, British newspapers carried virtually nothing about the relationship between Mrs. Wallis Simpson and King Edward VIII, but it was widely covered in the U.S. newspapers. Sunshine laws and open-meeting laws make the U.S. government much more accessible to the media than it is in a number of other democratic nations. Although the United States places more restrictions on pornography than many other democratic countries, in general, the mass media in the United States are among the most diverse and independent in the world.

Organization and Ownership of the Media

The Major Communications Media in the United States

Four politically important major media exist in the United States (in addition to books, movies, recordings, and other entertainment media).

Television. Perhaps the most pervasive medium, television is dominated by the three major national networks: the National Broadcasting Company (NBC), the American Broadcasting Company (ABC), and the Columbia Broadcasting System (CBS). These three giants supply 90 percent of the programming for some seven hundred local television stations licensed to broadcast by the Federal Communications Commission (FCC). The Fox Network (home of Bart Simpson) and other independents began to challege the dominance of the three major networks in recent years. In addition to the privately owned television stations is the Corporation for Public Broadcasting, which was created by the Public Broadcasting Act of 1967 to present educational or cultural programming that could not be supported by private networks. The Public Broadcasting System (PBS) consists of around 280 television stations. Run by political appointees, PBS was intended to be independent of government control, but recent administrations have attempted to guide programming in various ways.

Almost every American home has a television set, and more than half have two or more. Some of the most highly rated shows on television may be seen by more than 50 million people. The average "sitcom" may be watched by 15 million to 40 million people. The nightly news of the major networks is watched by about 11 million each, or a total of more than 30 million people daily. Since 1962, television has been the major source of news for Americans, and by the 1980s, it was the major source for almost 80 percent of Americans.

Newspapers. Currently, around 1,750 daily papers are published in the United States. Despite the well-publicized demise of many large dailies, such as the *Washington Star* and the *Philadelphia Evening Bulletin,* which was published for nearly 150 years before it folded, about the same total number of dailies are published today as were published at the end of World War II. However, the number of competing daily papers within major cities has declined significantly. Some of the newspapers with the largest circulation (such as the *National Enquirer*) are not well respected—circulation is *not* a good indicator of a publication's influence. The *New York Times, Washington Post, Chicago Tribune, Los Angeles Times, Wall Street Journal,* and *Christian Science*

Monitor are among the papers with substantial reputations and considerable national influence.

Most newspapers in the United States are still local enterprises. Great Britain's *London Times* and *Guardian* (formerly the *Manchester Guardian*), France's *Le Monde,* and the Soviet Union's *Pravda* are all primarily national papers. A trend toward nationalization is beginning in the United States and may significantly change the character of the newspaper business by the next century. With the advent of new transmission and printing technologies, the *Wall Street Journal* and the *New York Times* are printed at various locations across the country and are available for daily delivery without waiting for transportation from New York. *USA Today* began publishing in the early 1980s and has become a popular national newspaper.

RADIO. The third-ranking source of news and information for Americans, radio survived all the predictions of its demise after television arrived on the scene. Around 4,500 AM stations and 2,800 FM stations broadcast in large cities and small towns throughout the United States. Many are affiliated with the NBC, CBS, and ABC radio networks and get much of their news and feature programming from them. Compared with television, most radio programming is local. Radio survived partly because Americans want to hear news, music, and sports when they are in places that television cannot reach: in their cars, at work, at the beach, or in the backyard. Most automobiles are equipped with a radio, and 98 percent of households have at least one radio. On the average, people listen to twenty hours of radio a week. A small segment of the radio stations is publicly owned. Some two hundred noncommercial FM stations are part of National Public Radio (NPR), the radio equivalent of PBS.

MAGAZINES. Ranking fourth as a source of news and information, magazines also survived the arrival of television. Some ten thousand magazines are published in the United States each year. Many of these are highly specialized trade publications, such as *Morbidity and Morbundity,* or special interest magazines, such as *Master Swimmer.* The most popular magazines in the United States, led by *TV Guide, Reader's Digest,* and *National Geographic,* reach 10 to 20 million household addresses a year. Three of the top twenty are national newsmagazines: *Time, Newsweek,* and *U.S. News and World Report.* With a total circulation of more than 9 million a week, they have become important sources of political news. The average American looks at two magazines a week and spends thirty minutes a week reading them.

MEDIA OWNERSHIP

The mass media in the United States are unique in their degree of private ownership. From small local entrepreneurs to huge multinational corporations, the media are predominantly profit-making ventures. Who owns the media? Who decides what we will hear, see, and read? The trend today is toward concentration of ownership. One pattern is *independent ownership,* where an individual or company runs a single radio station or a newspaper and is engaged in no other business enterprise. Independents are becoming increasingly rare.[9] A second pattern is *multiple ownership* of a single type of media, such as a chain of newspapers or a group of several television stations. Even more common today is the third pattern of **cross-media ownership,** where a company controls some combination of newspapers, magazines, publishing houses, and radio or television stations. Although restricted by law under this arrangement, an individual or company can have a virtual monopoly on all the major information sources in smaller areas. The fourth pattern of ownership is *conglomerates:* large, diverse corporations that own various media as well as a host of other businesses.

Media ownership affects the content of news and programming. Increasing concentration of the mass media has raised concerns about the reduced competition among information sources and the enhanced possibilities for control and domination. CBS Inc. owns the CBS national network, five television stations, fourteen radio stations, twenty-two magazines, and several large publishing houses. The New York Times Company owns fifteen newspapers, radio, and television stations. The Washington Post company owns *Newsweek* and five television stations. Time Inc. publishes *People, Fortune,* and *Sports Illustrated* and owns television and cable television stations (Home Box Office) and publishing companies. Single owners exist only in the smallest, most minor markets. The mass media are increasingly dominated by large corporations with multiple holdings inside and outside the communications industry.

ECONOMIC CONSTRAINTS ON THE MASS MEDIA

A tension exists in the mass media between the need for profitability as privately held entities and the demands of objectivity and accountability to the public. The media largely determine what information is received by the public and have a corresponding obligation to objectivity, fairness, and relevance. Countering these political obligations are the commercial requisites of television, radio, magazine, and newspaper production. Audience size and makeup determine how time and space can be sold to advertisers. The major media compete for ratings and circulation—the larger the audience, the greater the revenue from advertising. A single one-minute commercial for the Super Bowl costs more than $1.5 million.

Critics complain that commercialism dominates other values, affecting content adversely. Commercialism affects coverage of politics, emphasizing conflict, personalities, and scandals over more careful analysis of institutions and processes. Election coverage tends to play up the game aspects of the race over issues. Finally, commercialism affects what is considered news. Critics charge that in the race for profits, trivia and fluff have edged out hard news.

The Impact of the Mass Media on Politics

Three main political functions of the mass media have been identified:[10]

1. Surveillance—news-gathering and newsmaking; observing the world, reporting on events, and agenda-setting; calling attention to certain public problems and possible solutions
2. Interpretation—providing an analysis of the meaning and relevance of the events that occur and the people involved
3. Socialization and persuasion—acculturation of the public into the prevailing social norms and efforts to affect public attitudes and behavior

Social scientists have had difficulty in precisely measuring the effect of the media on politics. Many studies have concluded that the media have a negligible effect on public attitudes and political behavior compared with other factors. But these conclusions seem unsatisfactory in the face of the barrage of information and political images that permeate modern life. In this part of the chapter, we first look at the effect of the media on public attitudes and the conduct of elections, then consider the relationship between the media and public officials, and finally examine newsmaking and how the media affect the policy agenda of the United States through both surveillance and interpretation.

THE EFFECT OF MEDIA ON PUBLIC OPINION

Initial fears that television would brainwash a generation of Americans proved to be unfounded. Studies show that political and social attitudes have stability and depth. Media messages are received by people with established attitude structures, not "blank slates." Human beings possess certain cognitive traits that limit the influence of media messages. One is **selective perception**—people tend to see and hear what they want to see and hear. For example, people watching a presidential debate who already have a strong preference tend to give higher evaluations to the candidate of their choice. Viewers tend to screen out or discredit negative messages received about their candidate. A corollary of selective perception is **reinforcement.** Viewers are receptive to messages that tend to reinforce the beliefs and attitudes they already hold. A person is more likely to watch the political speech of the favored candidate than the opponent's. The Nixon-Kennedy debates had an important impact on the election of 1960, not because Republicans switched from Nixon to Kennedy, but because Kennedy's performance reinforced many voters leaning Democratic who had some reservations about Kennedy's maturity and ability.[11] The type of media coverage can make a difference. A majority who watched the 1960 debates on television thought Kennedy had won, while most people

POLITICAL INSIGHT 10–1

THE IRAN-CONTRA HEARINGS AND PUBLIC OPINION

In November 1986, the American public began to learn of a Reagan administration policy of selling arms to the nation of Iran in hopes of winning the release of American hostages held in Lebanon. Some profits from those arms sales were diverted to help the Contra rebels in Nicaragua, despite a congressional prohibition on military aid to the Contras. The Iran-Contra scandal became one of the top stories of 1987, and a select committee of Congress began televised hearings on the affair that lasted through the summer. Millions of Americans were glued to their television sets as the drama and personalities unfolded.

The people behind the arms-for-hostages deal and the diversion of funds to the Contras included the late CIA director William Casey, National Security Advisor John Poindexter, and perhaps the most well-known of the group, Lieutenant Colonel Oliver North, an employee of the National Security Council. The testimony of North, Poindexter, and other administration officials replaced daytime soap operas as the public listened and judged the witnesses, the administration, and the congressional investigators themselves. Members of Congress were distressed about the deceit and duplicity exposed. One noted that it represented nothing less than a "junta" that had seized power in the White House and pursued its own secret foreign policy outside the law. Most on the

(Continued on next page)

The Iran-Contra Hearings.

listening to the debates on the radio thought Nixon had won. In this case, visual impact favored Kennedy.

The effect of the media on attitudes is limited by the strength of opinions. When the public is not aware of a problem or does not hold opinions with much intensity, the impact of the media is greater. For this reason, the media play a more important role in setting the policy agenda than they do in manipulating public attitudes about existing issues. For example, media coverage played a major role in alerting the public to the famine in Africa, spurring private and public relief efforts. Over time, media messages can cause shifts in public attitudes. Original reporting of the events of Watergate resulted in the predictable pattern of reinforcement and selective perception. Those who disliked Nixon were quick to suspect the worse. Those who supported Nixon simply shrugged off the reports as another attempt by the Democrats and the media to get the president. As the evidence unfolded and the wrongdoing became more and more obvious, some Nixon supporters began to change their attitudes. By the time of his resignation in August 1974, following revelation of the infamous tape proving he had knowledge of the cover-up, Nixon's support had dwindled. There remained, however, a hard core of supporters—perhaps 15 percent of the public—who refused to believe any of it. Because they held their convictions so fiercely, no

POLITICAL INSIGHT 10–1

committee agreed that there was no evidence of any direct involvement or cover-up by President Reagan. The American people however, expressed their own judgment, as the hearings had a profound effect on the political landscape.

When the scandal was revealed in late 1986, President Reagan's popularity slipped nearly 20 percent. While he did recover some public support through 1987 and 1988, his popularity did not regain its high-water mark. Oliver North was the most controversial figure in the hearings, turning tables on the congressional investigators. Eloquent, self-effacing at times, tough and combative at others, North emerged as a sort of national folk hero to some Americans. "Ollie-mania" swept the nation, complete with T-shirts proclaiming. "Ollie for president."

Washington Post-ABC News polls conducted in late summer 1987 revealed some startling public reactions to the scandal and the hearings. By a ratio of 63 to 32 percent, the American people believed that Reagan knew about and approved the diversion of funds to the Contras, but only 40 percent believed that the president had made "major mistakes." Only one-third said they would have been bothered "a great deal" if the president had known.

Oliver North was initially believed by the American people. Even though his testimony was contradicted by many other witnesses, 80 percent of Americans polled believed he was telling the truth. Perhaps more impressive was the impact of North's testimony on support for the Contras. Before he testified, Americans opposed Contra aid 67 to 29 percent. Immediately afterward, it was opposed by only 49 to 41 percent. A majority also favored a pardon for North by a 2-to-1 majority.

The effects of the Iran-Contra hearings were dramatic and unexpected, but they were short-lived. Surveys taken several months after the hearings revealed that support for North had dwindled and that public opinion about aid to the Contras had declined to levels near the prehearing period. The televised hearings demonstrated the power of the media but also its great unpredictability for public officials trying to harness that power. In addition, the hearings showed that much of the immediate impact of the media may be short in duration and that the American public is not easily manipulated or influenced over the long haul.

information could dissuade them from their conviction that Nixon was innocent.[12] Political Insight 10–1 examines the effect of the 1987 Iran-Contra hearings on public opinion.

The stability of public attitudes is a protection against the most blatant forms of demagoguery and manipulation. But the impact of the mass media is more subtle and sophisticated. The media socialize citizens to American values and culture through entertainment as well as through news and educational programming. Although the media are much more important in transmitting information than in shaping attitudes, the information is rarely neutral and may result in long-term attitude and cultural change. Television provides diverse images of America, of wealth and poverty, of changing sexual mores, of ethics and values. Most media messages are not explicitly political, but they contain scores of implicit messages about the social order and the legitimacy of the political system. Despite the reluctance of social science to ascribe a critical role to the media, some observers find their influence through socialization and agenda-setting to be powerful and problematic:

> Much of what most adults learn about government—its institutions and members, their activities, decisions, defects, strengths, capabilities—stems from the mass media. The self-same media have the power to decide which issues will be brought before the public, the terms in which they will be presented, and who

will participate, under what conditions, in the presentation. By dint of the subjects they cover (and do not cover) and the ways they structure them, the mass media tell Americans what to think about, how to think about it, sometimes even what to think. This coverage can help or hurt both the public who rely on it, and the powerful who need the media to attain or retain office and enhance their power.[13]

Is this too strong a conclusion? Examining the impact of the media on elections, media relationships with politicians, and the process of newsmaking can further clarify this question.

THE MEDIA AGE AND ELECTIONS

Television has revolutionized the way presidential campaigns are conducted. We now have **media campaigns.** One observer suggests:

> Indeed it is no exaggeration to claim that "the campaign" exists only as a construct of the media: they give to the disconnected though more or less coordinated activities of the participants a kind of scrapbook tidiness, laying out the pieces in patterns, with prominence to some while others are tucked away.[14]

The media do not tell voters whom to choose, but they condition and create the environment in which voters think about the campaign. Television, accompanied by the increasing number of presidential primaries, has changed the way candidates are selected and the factors making for candidate success. The media's role as kingmaker in presidential politics is greatest during the primaries, when a multitude of candidates is in the race. Candidate "image" and overt attacks on the image of opponents through negative campaigns have become two of the most important determinants of the outcome of elections. Television also has changed the kinds of candidates that have emerged. Ronald Reagan is frequently cited as the quintessential media candidate, whose success is largely due to his ability to exploit the media's resources. The media age has also increased the costs of campaigns. Races for the presidency and the U.S. Senate are centered around media exposure and media budgets. Crucial campaign decisions concern the content and timing of television commercials—when to saturate the airwaves and what approach to take. Candidates' behavior has changed. They base their strategy,

Media coverage has changed electoral strategies around the world. Nicaragua's Daniel Ortega adopted "American style" campaign tactics during his unsuccessful campaign for the nation's presidency.

particularly if they are not the incumbent, on making news. The purpose of meetings with factory workers at the plant gates is as much to create an image for the television cameras as to gain the workers' votes.[15]

With the 1988 presidential nominations up for grabs in both parties, new records were set for televised debates between presidential contenders. Between May 29, 1987, and February 14, 1988, thirty-two public debates among all or most of the candidates of one party or the other were held across the nation. Because there were as many as seven Democrats and six Republicans involved at the early stages of the campaign, the debates were often confusing affairs. In one, candidates from both parties were all on the stage, although questioning was divided into separate segments for Republicans and Democrats. Formats varied. Candidates sometimes asked each other questions. Frequently a journalist or invited guest asked questions of the candidates. In many cases, when the candidates had similar positions on issues, contenders attempted to stress character, image, and leadership qualities.

The debates were skewed toward the beginning of the process, particularly before the Iowa caucuses, the New Hampshire primary, and Super Tuesday. Ten debates were held in January 1988 alone. After getting a lock on the Republican nomination by March 1988, George Bush refused Robert Dole's last-gasp challenge to engage in an old-fashioned face-to-face Lincoln-Douglas style debate before the Illinois primary. Despite the large number of televised debates during the caucuses and primaries, relatively few viewers watched them. Only two were televised by the major networks, and many were broadcast to limited areas. While the debates gave voters some opportunity to learn more about the candidates, they appeared to be less important than candidate's paid television advertisements or media coverage of the front-runners. Debates between the two major party nominees in 1988 continued the trend toward such debates constituting a regular and expected part of the general election campaign for president. Political Insight 10–2 looks at the history of televised presidential election debates in the United States.

THE CONTENT OF CAMPAIGN COVERAGE

What do the media convey about the candidates, the parties, the issues? Research was scarce until the last decade, when social scientists began taking a more systematic look at media coverage. Election stories make up around 15 percent of all political news during an election year.[16] One of the most noticeable characteristics of the election coverage is **pack journalism:** television, newspaper, and magazine reporters seem to pick up the same stories, choose the same angles, emphasize the same points.[17] Why? Some suggest it is because reporters have been socialized in the same norms. They seem to have a shared mentality, common incentives in reporting certain aspects of the campaign, and a common perception of the ebb and flow of the campaign. Pack journalism results in a sameness that may reinforce weaknesses or biases in the coverage. It tends to magnify certain factors—like the result of a single primary or a candidate's misstatement—and make it difficult to gain a balanced perspective on the campaign.

The media tend to emphasize the "horse race" aspects of the campaign at the expense of substantive issues.[18] Table 10–1 shows the content of presidential election news on the three major television networks in the period leading up to the 1988 conventions. "Horse race" stories concern those who are leading, ahead, falling behind, tactics, strategies, forecasts, and analysis of poll results. "Policy issue" stories include in-depth or brief coverage of issues, candidates' policy advisers, and attacks on opponents over issues.

Table 10–1 leaves little doubt that television loves the "horse race" and campaign strategy aspect of the election compared to hard issues. In 1987 and 1988, only 215 of the 1,338 election stories broadcast on the three major networks dealt with policy issues. More than 500 stories dealt with the "horse race" aspect of the campaign, and nearly 600 dealt with campaign issues or strategies and tactics. Yet this emphasis on the "horse race" and day-to-day campaign politics did not completely eliminate coverage of policy issues.[19] Table 10–1 also shows the top ten issues mentioned on television news through the end of the primary season in 1988. The

POLITICAL INSIGHT 10–2

AMERICAN PRESIDENTIAL DEBATES

Since the famous Lincoln-Douglas debates in the late 1850s, face-to-face confrontations between political candidates have held a special place in the lore of American politics. But not until the era of television could an entire nation witness the candidates for the highest office in the land square off against each other. Here is a brief summary of the five presidential elections that included televised face-to-face debates between the candidates.

1960. The first televised presidential debates, held in 1960 between Kennedy and Nixon, are legendary. In what was an extremely close race, the first meeting between the two was pivotal in convincing those leaning toward Kennedy that the youthful senator was articulate and knowledgeable. He was also handsome and self-assured. Nixon, in contrast, looked bad. He appeared pale, in need of a shave, and sweating heavily. More people remember what he looked like than what he actually said. Because of the narrowness of his victory, the debates were seen as a critical element in Kennedy's election.

1976. Sixteen years passed before the next debate. Johnson, somewhat insecure about his public image, saw nothing to gain and much to lose by debating Barry Goldwater, who was far behind in the polls in 1964. Nixon, who partially blamed his 1960 loss on the debates, never seriously considered a debate in either 1968, another close election, or 1972 when he was far ahead. But when incumbent Gerald Ford found himself trailing Jimmy Carter, Ford agreed to a series of three debates. In the first, the sound system failed and the candidates stood in silence for twenty-seven minutes. In the second debate, Ford made the much-feared gaffe, stating that Poland was not under the domination of the Soviet Union. Most of the commentary focused on this statement. But there is little evidence that the debate had much impact on Carter's election.

1980. Four years later, incumbent Carter found himself involved in a close race with Reagan. Having acquitted himself adequately in the 1976 debates with Ford, he agreed to meet challenger Reagan in a single debate. Carter seemed more hostile and aggressive than usual, and Reagan struck a responsive note when he asked Americans if they were better off than they were four years ago. Carter, attempting to strike a homey note, discussed his conversation with his daughter Amy about nuclear weapons. Reagan is generally considered to have come out ahead in the debate, which helped foster a marked swing to him in the final days of the campaign.

1984. For the first time an incumbent with a comfortable lead agreed to debate a challenger. Although Reagan had little to gain, his confidence before the cameras, and his 1980 performance, led to his decision to make 1984 the third consecutive campaign to include a face-to-face debate. Reagan met Mondale in a pair of debates—one on domestic policy, the other on foreign policy. The president's worst fears seemed to come true during the first debate. Reagan seemed old and confused, stumbling over answers. Mondale, who had failed to generate much excitement during the primary season and campaign, appeared competent and capable.

(Continued on next page.)

Iran-Contra affair, especially the role of Vice-President George Bush, topped the list. Among the top ten were five economic issues including taxes, trade, and the budget deficit.

Media expert S. Robert Lichter acknowledges the emphasis of television news on the "horse race" aspect of the campaign but adds a word in defense of the major networks.

> The deeper problem with complaints about "horse race" coverage is that the critics are asking the media to do just what they criticize it for doing otherwise—to shape the campaign agenda by forcing the

POLITICAL INSIGHT 10–2

Early surveys showed that a slim majority believed Mondale had won the debate. Given the selective perception and the twenty-point lead in the polls enjoyed by the president, it was a clear sign that Reagan had stumbled. Yet the impact of the media was the most dramatic in the days following the debate. A few days after the debate, the conservative *Wall Street Journal* ran a front-page article on the age issue, questioning the fitness of the president. What followed was a barrage of coverage of such things as the president falling asleep during a meeting with the Pope and other negative images. By the end of the week, the proportion of Americans who believed Mondale had won the debate had doubled! Even Reagan's own campaign staff admitted he had not done well. By the next week, polls showed that Mondale had cut Reagan's lead to eight to ten points.

The impact of the debate was fleeting. The second debate was judged about even, as Reagan appeared more relaxed and in control. The media and the electorate seemed to forget the first debate. Within another week, Reagan's lead was back to the 18-to-20-point margin by which he eventually won the election.

1988. Three debates were held in the fall of 1988, two between presidential candidates George Bush and Michael Dukakis and one between vice-presidential candidates Lloyd Bentsen and Dan Quayle.

The first presidential debate was held in September. Both Bush and Dukakis were well coached, and many of the answers were scripted and thoroughly practiced. The candidates avoided major mistakes, although Bush was caught off guard when asked, "If abortions were outlawed, what criminal penalties would he impose on women who had an abortion?" Dukakis was calm and competent, Bush somewhat less composed. Public opinion polls revealed that Dukakis was the "winner" of the first debate by a narrow but symbolically important margin. The race seemed to be tightening up.

The most dramatic moment in the 1988 campaign came in the vice-presidential debate when Lloyd Bentsen took exception to Dan Quayle's comparison of himself to John F. Kennedy. "Senator, you're no Jack Kennedy," the former friend and congressional colleague of the slain president said to Quayle. Delighted Democrats saw this as the best sound bite of the debates, while the Republican spin doctors called it a cheap shot. By better than a two-to-one margin, the public believed that Bentsen had won the debate and was far more qualified to assume the presidency than Quayle. The race became even tighter. The third and final debate would be Dukakis's chance to regain the lead.

It proved to be a squandered opportunity. Even though some of the questions were dubious, Dukakis failed to change the impression that he was a cold, mechanical technocrat. Bush, in contrast, was more aggressive but more personable; traits that were as important to voters as issues. Bush continued to hammer on the point that Dukakis was too liberal for the American people. Snap polls indicated that a majority thought Bush had won the debate, and within days his slim lead over Dukakis surged with only a few weeks left in the campaign.

candidates to march to the media's tune. The media don't discuss policy issues in greater depth at least partly because the candidates don't, and the candidates don't because it's frequently counterproductive. Policy debates can even backfire on journalists, as Dan Rather learned when he tried to force a reluctant George Bush to dicuss Iran-Contra policy.[20]

Two other main criticisms surround media coverage of presidential elections: that the media are able to anoint the winners by favoring some candidates over others, and that there is a systematic bias in the news. These questions of favoritism and bias in the 1988 television news coverage of the

TABLE 10–1

CONTENT OF TELEVISION NEWS COVERAGE OF THE 1988 PRIMARIES AND CAUCUSES

Main Focus of Story

	Number of Stories
Horse race	537
Campaign issues	312
Strategy and tactics	280
Policy issues	215
Candidate politics	88

Top Ten Issues in Policy Stories

	Number of Mentions
Iran-Contra	114
Taxes	97
Unemployment	85
Economy	83
Central America	78
Trade	73
Drugs	68
Education	58
Civil rights	57
Budget deficit	55

SOURCE: Content analysis of television-election coverage on ABC, CBS, and NBC evening newscasts between February 1987 and June 7, 1988, conducted by the Center for Media and Public Affairs. Reported in S. Robert Lichter, "How the Press Covered the Primaries," *Public Opionion*, July-August 1988, p. 45.

road to the presidential nomination are examined later in the chapter. Although the impact of the mass media may be most dramatic on nominations and elections, the media have important effects on other aspects of politics.

A Difficult Marriage: The Media and Public Officials

A "love-hate relationship" may be the best way to characterize the relationship between politicians and the media. Although they need each other, at the same time they are natural adversaries. Elections do not last forever, and political reporters have to have news. The media tend to be cynical about politicians, while public officials view reporters as arbitrary critics of government, snooping around for some splashy story. Yet officials need the media to communicate their positions, their policies, and their programs to the public. So back and forth it goes with mutual dependence, different objectives, and an undercurrent of suspicion.

THE PRESIDENT AND THE MEDIA

Part of Franklin D. Roosevelt's genius in dealing with the media was his appreciation of the needs of the reporters. Roosevelt was able to fill their unending need for stories and political news—he often held press conferences twice a week—while enhancing the reputation of his administration and manipulating the news as much as possible. Roosevelt was good copy and good listening. Radio stations clamored for more airtime. Roosevelt seemed genuinely to like the media people—the White House press corps—who surrounded him. Today, this pattern seems more the exception than the rule. Although president and media need each other more than ever, there seems to be more latent hostility in the relationship.

Animosity is the fault of both. In Franklin Roosevelt's day, the press was much more deferential. It never made reference to the fact that Roosevelt was in a wheelchair much of the time or photographed him as such. His press secretary, Steven Early, asked the press corps not to, and they obliged. By the Nixon administration, deference seemed to be out. Much of this was the result of Nixon's mistrust of the media and his administration's public attack on their credibility. Nixon sent Vice President Spiro T. Agnew out on the hustings to verbally horsewhip the press, and Agnew obliged by characterizing the press as "nattering nabobs of negativism" and "effete intellectual snobs." According to his former speechwriter William Safire, Nixon changed the name of his meetings with the media from "press conferences" to "news conferences," to shift emphasis from the media to the president as newsmaker. Reporters, editors, and publishers were alienated. The Watergate investigation, pursued vigorously by the media, was seen as a vindication of the media's new aggressiveness. It confirmed the importance of their role as government watchdog. Students streamed into journalism schools hoping to be like Bob Woodward and Carl Bernstein, the *Washington Post* reporters who helped uncover the Watergate story.

Although the relationship between the press and the president changes with each individual who occupies the White House, the differing perspectives of the president and the media can be characterized. Reporters often have a jaundiced view of politicians, seeing them as self-serving and power-seeking.[21] In their search for entertainment and action in the news, journalists are interested in corruption and conflict more than in dry policy debates or political consensus. Presidents see the media as lying in wait for their administration to make a mistake. Presidents often view individual journalists as either friendly or hostile.[22] President Reagan, one of the most effective users of the media, successfully appealed to the public to support his economic program on the eve of key congressional votes in 1981. President Bush was less effective and less successful. His televised appeal to Congress and the nation to support the bipartisan budget summit agreement in October, 1990, failed to prevent the House from defeating the proposal two days later.

Presidents use different devices to control the content of news. News conferences are scheduled at the president's discretion, and under Reagan, they were more structured and orderly. At his earliest news conferences, forty anxious reporters would jump in the air and yell "Mr. President." Reagan required that they stay in their seats and raise their hands. Presidents and their aides sometimes provide **backgrounders**—briefings where the media may not quote the source. Backgrounders and planned leaks allow the president to send up so-called "trial balloons" and escape identification if proposals evoke strong negative reactions. Journalists, anxious for a scoop, play along. Presidents also create "media events," often timed to make the evening news. Presidents may reward sympathetic journalists by granting exclusive interviews—a kind of star system. Ford averaged seven special interviews a year, and Carter averaged three.

Presidential relations with the media run in cycles. The honeymoon period of a new administration, when the media are particularly cooperative and supportive in their interpretation and analysis, lasts about six months. The second stage

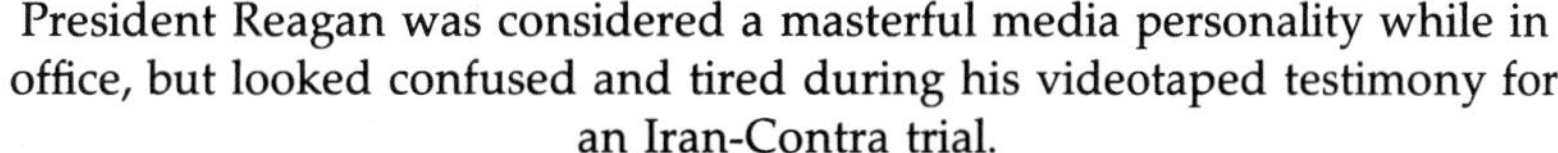

President Reagan was considered a masterful media personality while in office, but looked confused and tired during his videotaped testimony for an Iran-Contra trial.

usually follows the first major controversy and begins a period of adverse coverage. The administration at this point usually steps up efforts to manipulate the media. If conflict continues to escalate, the third stage may become a standoff. A truce usually occurs about the time of a reelection campaign.

When public support falls, presidents have a tendency to blame the media for their failures. Truman lashed out at the media viciously after the failure of the offensive in Korea in 1951.[23] Kennedy blamed the media for the disaster of the Bay of Pigs invasion in 1961, even though he had one of the best relationships with the media of any recent president. Presidential attacks reinforce public doubts about the credibility of the media and heighten media cynicism about politicians.

Hodding Carter III, who was President Carter's State Department spokesman and played a key role during the Iran hostage crisis, summed up the relationship: "Government is not in the truth business. It is the presumed duty of an administration to govern, not to do reporters' work for them."[24] Attempting to influence media coverage is part of governing. Not that presidents intentionally lie to the media, but when they have arrived at a policy, they attempt to convince the media and the public that it is the best course of action. The public relations apparatus of the federal government now costs over $1 billion, more than is spent by the media on covering it! As a result, the relationship between the media, the president, and other components of American government has become more conflictual in recent years. The adversarial element of the relationship should not obscure how much each needs the other to succeed.

MEDIA COVERAGE OF CONGRESS, THE BUREAUCRACY, AND THE COURTS

The presidency dominates the national news far more than other national institutions do, although some studies have shown that the media spend as much time covering Congress as the presidency in a nonelection year.[25] Congress is more difficult for the media to cover; no single personality can be focused on to dramatize the institution. Films of the president relaxing at Camp David have no congressional equivalent. The legislative process is complicated and often difficult to portray accurately in short broadcasts or stories. An important change was the start of televised sessions of the House of Representatives in 1979. A cable channel—C-SPAN—now provides gavel-to-gavel coverage of the House. Although it does not challenge "Monday Night Football" or "L.A. Law," more than 20 million viewers watch C-SPAN at some time during the year.

C-SPAN's regular viewers are loyal, and some of the young Republican mavericks in the House decided to play to this audience. Led by Representatives Newt Gingrich (Ga.) and Robert Walker (Pa.), a small group of Republicans would take the floor late at night after legislative business was completed to lambaste the Democrats and Speaker Tip O'Neill. Tempers flared in early 1984 as the attacks grew particularly harsh in the election year. Under strict House control, the television cameras normally never stray from the center podium and the member who is speaking. One night, however, on O'Neill's order, the cameras suddenly turned to show the Republicans talking to a completely empty chamber. O'Neill wanted the C-SPAN viewers to see that the grandstanding was strictly for show. The Republicans were furious, even the Republican leaders who had previously not been particularly supportive of the mavericks. The great TV-scan controversy left hard feelings on both sides.

Because so much happens in Congress in a given week, and most of it in committee, relatively few congressional activities will make the news. The media choose stories for their entertainment value as well as for their importance. Highly technical debates or hearings are passed over in favor of the appearance of celebrities (like Howard Cosell testifying about boxing), scandals, or key foreign policy issues. State and local media are used by the 535 members of Congress to heighten their visibility and enhance the value of their incumbency. Hearings held in their home town are usually covered, especially if the local representatives can convince a well-known national figure to appear with them. Recording in the congressional television studio, senators and representatives feed their local media a steady diet of prerecorded interviews, tapes, and news releases. Some even have their own weekly television and radio spots. Larger papers and stations resist using this spoon-fed "news" and attempt to develop their own sources. Smaller ones cannot and fill their pages and broadcasts with it.

In the 1980s, attacks on the credibility of the media came from certain members of Congress rather than from the White House. Senator Jesse Helms (R-N.C.) picked up Spiro Agnew's themes and tone in denouncing what he saw as liberal bias in the national news. But Helms, who formerly had his own television program in North Carolina, wanted to go further to promote his views in the news. Early in 1985, he led a group of wealthy conservative investors in an attempt to buy a controlling interest in CBS, promising to shake up all facets of the network when he got control. At the same time, while the prospect was sending chills up the spines of CBS employees, CBS was also battling to prevent a takeover by Atlanta's cable television magnate, millionaire Ted Turner. The attempt by an ideological U.S. senator to gain control of one of the three major networks was seen as an ominous development by many. But as the media plays an increasingly important role in American politics, they may be subject to further such pressures in the future.

Courts receive far less coverage than the other two branches of government. Federal judges and justices do not need the media. Appointed for life, judges meet in private and rarely make speeches. Covering the courts is difficult for reporters, very few of whom have legal training. As a result, much of the reporting that does occur is imprecise and inaccurate. For example, studies have found that the reporting of the *Baker v. Carr* ("one person, one vote") decision and the school prayer cases was misleading and sketchy. Coverage of the courts often concentrates on public *reaction* to a decision more than on the details of the decision itself. Local school desegregation cases have often been the subject of inflammatory and emotional reports fostering public fears, rather than constructive discussions of alternatives or reasonable implementation.

The bureaucracy has it worst of all when it comes to media attention. Most reporters find the vast federal establishment unfathomable and not very entertaining. To a reporter from the glamorous world of the media, a bureaucrat is a bore. What stories do appear often concern a newsworthy cabinet member with an attractive or controversial personality. A few regulatory decisions, such as the banning of saccharin, will make news; day-to-day operations of an agency do not. There is no centralized focus for the media in the bureaucracy. As a result, coverage of the bureaucracy tends to feature blunders, waste, inefficiency, and foul-ups, and this disproportionate emphasis on bureaucratic inefficiency perpetuates a negative public image of the bureaucracy. The importance or overall impact of the bureaucracy on public policy is mostly ignored.

News-Gathering, News-Making, and News Bias

News is what the media, using their own particular criteria, decide to present. Many observers note it is far better that the news media decide what is news than the government, as occurs in many nations. At the same time, many are disturbed by the great power exercised through the media's **gatekeeper role** in determining what the public see and hear and what they do not.

Criteria for determining the news are related to competition for ratings and circulation. The news divisions of the major networks, no less than the entertainment divisions, are in fierce competition. Should high ratings be the factor that determines what is news? Many think not. Pulitzer prize-winning journalist and former television anchorman Ron Powers is a harsh critic:

> The biggest heist of the 1970s never made it on the five o'clock news. The biggest heist of the 1970s *was* the five o'clock news. The salesmen took it.... An extravagant proportion of television news answered less to the description of "journalism" than to that of "show business." ...
>
> An insidious hoax is being perpetrated on American viewers. The hoax is made more insidious by the fact that very few TV news-watchers are aware of what information is *left out* of a newscast in order to make room for the audience-building gimmicks.[26]

How do the Media Select News?

The simplest view of news reporting is that journalists simply gather the facts that are out there and choose the most important ones to present. Such a view is unrealistic. Most would probably agree that some events are automatically news: major elections, assassinations, catastrophes, such as earthquakes and wars. Beyond this, discretion is exercised by the media. The content of news is a function of the world events, media perception of audience interest, competition with other media, and the particular preferences and orientations of reporters, publishers, and producers.

Richard Nixon, not a great fan of the news media, claimed: "For the press, progress is not news—trouble is news."[27] There is some truth to that statement. The media seem to gravitate toward disasters. Responding to this charge, many media now include such things as "good morning news," upbeat coverage of nondisaster, nonscandal, nonconflict news. But sometimes the media can't win; critics attack this kind of story as trivia and fluff. Here are the criteria for inclusion of a story on the "ABC Evening News":

> The Evening News, as you know, works on elimination. We can't include everything. As criteria for what we do include I suggest the following for a satisfied viewer: (1) "Is my world, nation, and city safe?" (2) "Is my home and family safe?" (3) "If they are safe, then what has happened in the past 24 hours to help make that world better?" (4) "What has happened in the past 24 hours to help us cope better?"[28]

News is often concerned with *threats,* whether from plane crashes, rowdy demonstrators, criminals, or communists. Coverage of threats is often followed by *reassurance* that help is on the way, that governments are doing something to counter the threats.[29] The threat-reassurance theme underlies much of the news, whether in stories about the nation's relations with other nations or human interest stories, where personal suffering is followed by some kind of help.

Newscasters themselves become part of the reassurance. Walter Cronkite, longtime anchor of the "CBS Evening News," epitomized the fatherly, trustworthy figure on whom all could rely. A kind of benediction was given at the end of the news as Cronkite reassuringly said, "And that's the way it is, Tuesday, January 23, 19—." Trust and reassurance and a certain kind of glamour are also part of a marketing strategy by network executives, who are constantly seeking the right anchorperson.

Sometimes news anchors become part of the news itself, not just part of the coverage. During a live interview with Vice-President George Bush in early 1988, "CBS Evening News" anchor Dan Rather aggressively questioned—some say attacked—Bush about his role in the Iran-Contra affair. Bush fired back, noting an embarrassing incident in which Rather had walked off the set during a newscast. The confrontation was front-page news across the nation. Most concluded that Bush had "won" the exchange, but others believed it was an intentional ploy by the vice-president to shed his "wimp" image. The line between reporting news and making news is often a fine one.

WHAT KINDS OF STORIES ARE NEWSWORTHY?

Relatively few people are consistently newsworthy—perhaps only fifty are in the news regularly, and they appear in 75 percent of all news stories.[30] This heightens the sense that certain people are powerful (usually politicians) and may detract attention from others who *are* powerful (such as corporation presidents) but who are rarely on the news. Stories deemed newsworthy often emphasize entertainment and novelty, eliminating other more important stories from being considered. Newsworthy stories are also often about familiar things. Foreign news is risky for the media unless it has some direct impact on the United States. Important social problems are rarely newsworthy unless a tragedy occurs. Conflict is more newsworthy than consensus. Reporting of Congress highlights partisan battles rather than bipartisan cooperation, the more normal state of affairs. But despite the frequent emphasis on problems, conflict, and scandals, the media create a context that is strongly rooted in the dominant American political and economic values. The media rarely act as a source of new ideas or a catalyst for social change.

Television news coverage is brief and often superficial. Newspapers can provide longer, more detailed analysis of stories, but today, most people get their news from television. In recent years, the networks have added news programming that deals with single issues in greater depth. One of the first shows to do this successfully was "The MacNeil-Lehrer Report" on PBS. ABC's "Nightline" with Ted Koppel proved highly successful both commercially and critically. Television news has responded to criticism by attempting to improve the content of news programming. Around-the-clock cable news and C-SPAN have added new options for television news watchers and public affairs "junkies." Although economic pressures have a significant impact on what is presented as news, raw commercialism is balanced by professionalism and the commitment to playing a watchdog role. In its overall effect, is the news fair and unbiased?

Bias or Favoritism in the News: Coverage of the 1988 Primaries and Caucuses

Conservatives such as Spiro Agnew, Jesse Helms, and others have long accused the major national media in the United States of a liberal bias. Charges were intensified after a study found that a whopping 81 percent of the media elite had voted for George McGovern in 1972.[31] Although the authors were circumspect in their conclusions, many conservative media critics were not. Liberal media provide liberal news, they concluded.

Media expert Michael Robinson's analysis of the 1980 election coverage led him to disagree.[32] Reviewing some six thousand stories covering the Carter-Reagan battle, Robinson found relatively little bias in the news one way or another. "Issue bias on the network news proved to be more scarce than electoral votes for Jimmy Carter," he concluded. But of the bias that existed, he found that 19 percent of the news stories covering the incumbent Carter were negative, compared with only 14 percent for the challenger Reagan.

The year 1984 was a different story altogether. Robinson, his co-investigator Maura Clancey, and a team of observers pored over tapes of the evening news broadcasts of all three major networks from Labor Day through the election.[33] They scored each piece for "spin"—bias both in terms of content and tone—rating the positive or negative implications about the candidates in the reporters' words. What they found was lopsidedly negative coverage of incumbent Reagan—a negative "spin" ratio of better than ten to one. Was this strong confirmation of a liberal bias in the news?

Robinson and Clancey argued that the explanation for coverage of the 1984 election campaign was more complicated than simply liberal bias. Despite the harsh treatment of Reagan, the researchers found no evidence of a liberal bias in stories about policy issues. They believed that

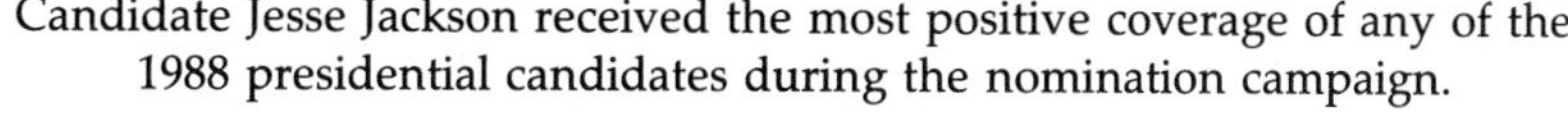
Candidate Jesse Jackson received the most positive coverage of any of the 1988 presidential candidates during the nomination campaign.

Reagan's big lead and media frustration in covering him explained the nature of network coverage of the election campaign.

How did television news cover the multitude of candidates for the 1988 Republican and Democratic nominations for president? Did the media "anoint" the eventual nominees, George Bush and Michael Dukakis, with more favorable coverage? Did the media cover Democrats more favorably than Republicans? S. Robert Lichter analyzed the content of election coverage in 1988 by coding each story for its positive, negative, mixed, or neutral assessment of candidates. An example of good press was when CBS's reporter Bruce Morton said of Jesse Jackson, "He's neon and fireworks. All the rest this week have been pastel." An example of bad press was NBC's political analyst Kevin Phillips calling George Bush, "an overstuffed résumé."[34]

Table 10–2 compares the number of stories and the proportion of favorable spin each candidate received, excluding mixed or neutral stories. George Bush was the subject of the most stories, followed by Jesse Jackson and Michael Dukakis. Jesse Jackson clearly received the most positive coverage from television news, with 74 percent "good press." Coverage of Robert Dole was much more favorable—64 percent positive—than that of his rival George Bush. In contrast to Jackson and Dole, Dukakis received 55 percent favorable spin and George Bush 50 percent. The two eventual nominees received only average coverage among all candidates, casting doubt on the proposition that media favoritism played a key role in their success. Bruce Babbitt was a media darling during the early days of the campaign with 89 percent favorable coverage, but as the subject of only 37 of over 1,000 stories about Democratic candidates, he was quickly forgotten after his withdrawal. Gary Hart's scandal-ridden candidacy received the most negative coverage of any contender with only 38 percent favorable.

What about the media's ability to give early primary and caucus winners the momentum needed to win the nomination? Coverage in 1988 was heavily front-loaded. More stories were broadcast

TABLE 10–2

POSITIVE AND NEGATIVE TELEVISION NEWS COVERAGE OF THE 1988 PRESIDENTIAL CANDIDATES

Candidates	Total Number of News Stories	% Positive Coverage
Jesse Jackson	250	74
Michael Dukakis	249	55
Gary Hart	188	38
Richard Gephardt	164	48
Joseph Biden	61	54
Paul Simon	57	53
Albert Gore	56	54
Bruce Babbitt	37	89
All Democrats	1062	56
George Bush	379	50
Robert Dole	181	64
Pat Robertson	122	49
Jack Kemp	50	58
Alexander Haig	15	67
Pierre du Pont	14	50
All Republicans	781	53

NOTE: Mixed and neutral news stories excluded.

SOURCE: S. Robert Lichter, "How the Press Covered the Primaries," *Public Opionion*, July-August 1988, p. 48.

about the Iowa caucuses and the New Hampshire primary than all the other primaries combined, even though those two states only selected 2 percent of all delegates! But Iowa caucus winners Dick Gephardt and Bob Dole did not receive the "bounce" needed to propel them to victory in New Hampshire or to win the nomination. It appears that other factors, such as the regional advantages Dukakis and Bush enjoyed in New Hampshire, more than compensated for media-induced momentum. In addition, what television bestows it can take away. Gephardt received the most negative coverage before Super Tuesday, and Dole's comments on the evening of the New Hampshire primary spurred more stories about his "meanness." Despite the important role of the media in today's nomination politics, many other factors limit the media's ability to determine the eventual winners.

Were liberal Democratic candidates favored over conservative Republicans? While the liberal Jesse Jackson was favorably covered, conservative Pat Robertson had a positive spin ratio of only 49 percent. Yet other conservatives such as Jack Kemp and Alexander Haig received much more favorable treatment on the evening news. In comparing the ratio of favorable coverage to unfavorable coverage between the two parties, the Democrats had an edge of 56 percent to 53 percent. Lichter concludes, "After extensive coverage of fourteen candidates over more than a year of campaigning, a partisan difference of only 3 percent looks more like balance than bias."[35]

The media cannot make people believe what they do not want to believe. The media are at best in a standoff with the president or other institutions of government unless significant wrongdoing is uncovered. The ability of the media to select what will be news—their gatekeeper function—translates into a powerful agenda-setting role in the policy process. Yet in many other areas, the political impact of the media is limited. The latter may not be for want of trying. The distinction between straight news and opinion is often blurred, particularly on television. Many stories reflect the spin of the reporter. Although there is little evidence of a conspiracy to slant the news in a particular direction, the objectivity of the media will remain a subject for a hot political controversy for many years to come.

Government Regulation of the Media

GOVERNMENT RESTRICTIONS ON THE PRINT MEDIA

According to the First Amendment to the Constitution, "Congress shall pass no law abridging freedom of the press." Strong protection has resulted in a newspaper and magazine industry with open access and wide latitude to print anything it wants to. Yet even with this clear constitutional guarantee there are some limits on the print media.

LIBEL. Individuals are protected by **libel laws** from the publication of malicious, untrue statements that can have a detrimental effect on their reputations. Historically, the United States has had much looser libel laws than other nations, such as Great Britain. It is often difficult to prove libel in American courts. The Supreme Court made it even more difficult to prove libel in cases dealing with public officials in the decision of ***New York Times v. Sullivan*** (1964). A decision that recognized the importance of "political speech" above other forms of free speech, it gives investigative reporters greater protection against libel suits from public officials. The latter may still sue for libel, but they must prove not only that a story is false and that their reputation is damaged but also that it was done maliciously. Even the more conservative Rehnquist Court has made it extremely difficult to prove libel in cases dealing with public affairs and political figures. "Moral Majority" leader Jerry Falwell brought a multimillion-dollar libel suit against *Hustler* magazine publisher Larry Flynt for a harsh parody about Falwell. In 1988, the Court ruled 8 to 0 that, even if the satire was in poor taste, Flynt's right to ridicule Falwell and his political viewpoints was protected under the First Amendment of the Constitution.

Although the print media have the fewest regulations and the greatest latitude for reporting, the bounds are not unlimited. Over the years, the courts and legislatures have seen fit to limit access to and the content of a publication when it is determined to be more in the public interest than unlimited freedom of the press.

LIMITING MEDIA ACCESS TO DOCUMENTS. Like most governments, the United States prohibits the publication of certain materials when national security is threatened. Certain documents are sealed for a specified period of time. Despite strict prohibitions against prior restraint, *The Progressive* was prevented from publishing an article based on materials in the public domain on how to make a hydrogen bomb for more than six months.

GAG RULES. Both the print media and the electronic media are restricted in their ability to cover trials. Judges may limit coverage of a trial without showing why it may be damaging. This is known as a **gag rule.** Nonetheless, American journalists enjoy much greater access to criminal procedures than in Great Britain, where arrests, indictments, and trials are kept under careful wrap.

CONFIDENTIALITY OF SOURCES. Reporters may not always keep their sources secret. If in the course of an investigation reporters learn of a crime, they are not protected (as lawyers or doctors would be) and may go to jail if they fail to reveal their sources. However, some jurisdictions have passed "shield laws," which protect reporters from having to reveal their sources in court.

RESTRICTIONS ON THE BROADCAST MEDIA

From the development of radio in the early twentieth century through the advent of television, the government has played an active role in regulating and restricting the activities of the broadcast media. Access to the electronic media is limited, and as a result the government has taken steps to assure fair public use and access to the airwaves.

Regulation of the broadcast media arose out of necessity. When the first radio stations began to broadcast at any frequencies they chose, the secretary of commerce established restrictions on what frequencies could be used. The Supreme Court struck down the regulations, and chaos ensued as broadcasts by one station interfered with broadcasts of another. Under pressure from the radio industry, Congress passed the Radio Act of 1927, creating the Federal Radio Commission, forerunner to the **Federal Communications Commission** (FCC), formed in 1934. The commission was charged with developing regulations that would create a "fair, efficient, and equitable" system of broadcasting.

The Federal Communications Act of 1934 set up the seven-member FCC to regulate the broadcast industry.[36] To protect public interest and access to the electronic media, the commission restricts the number of television and radio stations an owner may control. The FCC can theoretically change the pattern of ownership through the licensing process that takes place every three years. At this time, the commission examines the mix of programming and overall performance of the station. The public may comment on whether the station license should be renewed. Although such review powers may sound awesome, the FCC exercises little real control over stations. Over the years, very few station licenses have been denied, and the FCC has not used this power aggressively.

In addition to controlling which stations may broadcast through licensing requirements, the FCC has attempted to regulate both the content of and access to the broadcast media. In the 1970s, the commission issued regulations specifying minimum amounts of news and public affairs programming for television and radio, but by 1984, such requirements were abandoned under pressure from broadcasters and a political climate in favor of deregulation.

The FCC came up with two rules governing access to the broadcast media.[37] The **equal time rule** requires stations to sell commercial time to a party's candidate if they sell time to any other party's candidate. Broadcasters opposed this requirement, however, and some responded by refusing to sell time to any candidates. A 1983 amendment to the rule permits broadcasters to exclude minor-party candidates from the equal time requirement. A second FCC requirement, known as the **fairness**

doctrine, required broadcasters to air both sides of controversial issues. In addition, a rebuttal provision allowed people to respond on the air to an attack, free of charge. Under continued pressure from broadcasters, the Reagan administration, and the federal courts, the FCC in 1987 repealed the fairness doctrine. The FCC reasoned that the fairness doctrine had a "chilling effect" on broadcasters, leading them to avoid controversial editorials, and therefore violated the First Amendment. Critics claimed that elimination of the rule would lead stations to disregard opposing views and present one-sided, biased coverage. Supporters of the fairness doctrine in Congress who attempted to enact a version of the rule into law were thwarted by a presidential veto.

As competition among the broadcast media has increased, particularly with the advent of cable television, the large number of rules and regulations placed on broadcasters have declined. Some observers remain concerned about the power of the broadcast media and believe some continued government regulation of both content and access is necessary to protect the free flow of ideas in American democracy.

Campaigns, the Media, and Governing

Can anything be done to reduce the growing chasm between the process of getting elected and the process of governing the nation? As we saw in the conclusion to Chapter 9, reformers have suggested limiting spending, providing free television time, and restricting negative campaigns. But some journalists, disgusted with the trends in campaigns, believe that the media cannot wait for elected officials to reform a system that keeps them in office. *Washington Post* columnist David Broder exclaims, "Today, winning seems an end in itself, by whatever means it takes. After the election, the consultants who masterminded the campaigns collect their checks and get ready for the next round of battles. Only then do the individuals who've been elected try to figure out how to govern."[38]

Broder says that the media should work harder to keep campaigns clean and offers a five-point strategy:

- **Preemption:** Challenge the assumption that the candidates and their consultants have the right to set the campaign agenda. Find out what issues are most important to voters and keep candidates focused on those issues.
- **Innoculation:** Remind people of how they have been manipulated in recent elections by showing some of the more distasteful negative ads before the next round of elections.
- **Interrogation:** Make sure that candidates are personally available to respond to questions about every commercial and piece of direct mail rather than directing questions to campaign staff.
- **Investigation:** Treat every ad as if it were a personal speech by the candidate, weighing its fairness and accuracy and getting independent information or rebuttal by the opponent if necessary.
- **Denunciation:** Columnists, commentators, and editorial writers should denounce candidates who sabotage the electoral process with paid-media demagoguery.

Would Broder's strategy work? Could it help focus campaigns on the issues that must be faced when winning candidates set about on the difficult task of governing? Possibly, but it raises other questions. Should the media alone be responsible for reforming the electoral process? While responsible journalists like Broder might succeed, many other reporters, producers, and corporate media owners have their own political and ideological agenda. Who is to watch the watchdogs? Even with the help of better coverage of elections—more emphasis on issues than who's winning—only the voters can bridge the gap between elections and governing by rejecting candidates who wage negative, trivial campaigns.

SUMMARY AND CONCLUSIONS

1. The mass media in the United States evolved from pamphlets and party presses, with long delays in communication between the states, to electronic journalism and instantaneous communication.
2. Authoritarian governments recognize the importance of the mass media for governing in their extensive regulation and control of the media. In the United States, controls are relatively slight, even compared with other democratic nations. Broadcast media are subject to more controls than print media.
3. The mass media in the United States comprise national television stations and their local affiliates, newspapers, radio stations, magazines, books, motion pictures, and recordings. Television has been America's major source of news since 1962, when it passed newspapers for that honor.
4. Economic considerations have a significant impact on media programming decisions. As profit-making ventures, the media must compete for ratings and circulation, affecting public affairs and news as well as entertainment.
5. The media have an impact on politics in three broad ways: surveillance (news-gathering, observing, reporting, agenda-setting), interpretation of events, and socialization and persuasion of the public.
6. The media cannot control people's minds, as some early observers feared. The impact of the media on public attitudes is limited by selective perception and reinforcement.
7. The media have significantly changed the conduct of elections, becoming a focus of candidate efforts and a major factor in determining which candidates are chosen. Campaign coverage deals more with style and the game aspects of the race than with substantive issues.
8. The relationship between the media and public officials can be characterized as adversarial but mutually necessary. The president in particular is the focus of media attention. He in turn uses the media to help foster his own political and policy objectives.
9. The media play an important role in determining what is news, serving as gatekeepers to what the public sees and hears. Candidates who receive the most favorable news coverage are not necessarily the eventual nominees or election winners.
10. The government regulates the operation of the electronic media through the FCC. The FCC establishes rules for content and public access to radio and television stations, although the fairness doctrine was eliminated in 1987.

The growing influence of the mass media is a fact of life, but its effects are complex. It increasingly shapes the way we think about politics. It is the most critical aspect of the national electoral process. It can be both a tool for governing and a limitation. Former President Ronald Reagan was direct in his 1980 campaign, talking about issues and telling voters what he would do in office. He was masterful in his use of television to govern the country, promoting his policy agenda and denouncing his opponents. Conversely, poor media skills or overly aggressive media can cripple the governing process. Nixon, Ford, Carter, Bush, and even Reagan, at times, all suffered. Effective use of the media in the United States is more essential to policy-making—in getting government to act—than in most other democracies around the world. That means the media will become even more important for understanding American politics in coming decades.

KEY TERMS

backgrounders
cross-media ownership
equal time rule
fairness doctrine
Federal Communications Commission (FCC)
gag rule
gatekeeper role
interpretation
libel laws
mass media
media campaigns
medium of communication
New York Times v. Sullivan
pack journalism
reinforcement
selective perception
socialization and persuasion
surveillance

SELF-REVIEW

1. Describe the evolution of journalism and the mass media.
2. How does the independence of the media differ across nations?
3. Name the major communications media in the United States.
4. What are the patterns of ownership of the media?
5. What are the economic constraints on the mass media?
6. How do the media influence public attitudes?
7. How have the media changed the nature of elections?
8. What aspects of campaigns are most heavily covered by the media?
9. Describe the relationship between the president and the media.
10. How do the media cover the Congress, the bureaucracy, and the courts?
11. What factors affect the content of news?
12. How did television news cover the 1988 presidential candidates?
13. What are government restrictions on the print media?
14. What are some restrictions on the electronic media?
15. How does the media affect governing?

SUGGESTED READINGS

Berkman, Ronald, and Laura Kitch. *Politics in the Media Age.* 1986.
A good introduction to politics and the media.

Crouse, Anthony. *The Boys on the Bus.* 1973.
A highly entertaining look at the media corps as it followed the candidates in the 1972 election.

Graber, Doris. *Mass Media and American Politics.* 1989.
A comprehensive analysis of the importance of the mass media to contemporary politics.

Halberstam, David. *The Powers That Be.* 1979.
Powerfully written account by an award-winning journalist, tracing the personalities and maneuvering behind the *Washington Post,* the *Los Angeles Times,* CBS, and Time Inc.

Paletz, David L., and Robert M. Entman. *Media, Power, Politics.* 1981.
A provocative polemic on the power of the media and its subtle use to manipulate the public.

NOTES

1. An Associated Press story reported in the *St. Louis Post Dispatch, 12 December 1989, pp. 1, 12.*
2. Doris Graber, *Mass Media and American Politics* (Washington, D.C.: Congressional Quarterly Press, 1989), 4.
3. Allen R. Pred, *Urban Growth and the Circulation of Information* (Princeton: Princeton University Press, 1973), 37.
4. F. L. Mott, *American Journalism, 1690–1960* (New York: Macmillan, 1962), 529.
5. David Halberstam, *The Powers That Be* (New York: Knopf, 1979), 16.
6. Graber, *Mass Media,* 21.
7. Ibid., 22.
8. Ibid., 28.
9. Ibid., 41–47.
10. Harold D. Lasswell, "The Structure and Function of Communication in Society," in Wilbur Schramm, *Mass Communications* (Urbana: University of Illinois Press, 1949), 103.
11. Kurt Lang and Gladys Lang, *Politics and Television* (Chicago: Quadrangle, 1968), 212–49.
12. David L. Paletz and Robert M. Entman, *Media , Power, Politics* (New York: Free Press, 1981), 158–65.
13. Ibid., 5–6.
14. Colin Seymour-Ure, *The Political Impact of the Mass Media* (Beverly Hills: Sage, 1974), 38.
15. Graber, *Mass Media,* 205.
16. Ibid., 207.
17. John Carey, "How Media Shape Campaigns," *Journal of Communication* 26 (Spring 1976):50–57.
18. Thomas Patterson, *The Mass Media Election* (New York: Praeger, 1980), 24–25.
19. S. Robert Lichter, "How the Press Covered the Primaries," *Public Opinion,* July–August 1988, pp. 45–49.
20. Ibid., p. 46.
21. Paul H. Weaver, "Is Television News Biased?" *Public Interest* 26 (Winter 1972):57–74.
22. Terry F. Buss and C. Richard Hofstetter, "The President and the News Media," in Steven A. Shull and Lance T. LeLoup, eds., *The Presidency: Studies in Public Policy* (Brunswick, Ohio: Kings Court, 1979), 25.
23. Irving Janis, *Victims of Groupthink* (Boston: Houghton Mifflin, 1972), 67.

24. Hodding Carter III, Remarks made at Washington University in St. Louis, 23 March 1988.
25. Graber, *Mass Media,* 254.
26. Ron Powers, *The Newscasters* (New York: St. Martin's Press, 1977), 234.
27. William Safire, "The Press Is the Enemy: Nixon and the Media," *New York Times,* 27 January 1975, p. 44.
28. A. Westin, ABC News, quoted in Paletz and Entman, *Media,* 17.
29. Paletz and Entman, *Media, Power, Politics,* 18.
30. Graber, *Mass Media,* 78.
31. S. Robert Lichter and Stanley Rothman, "Media and Business Elites," *Public Opinion,* October–November 1981, pp. 42–46, 59–60.
32. Michael Robinson, "Just How Liberal Is the News? 1980 Revisited," *Public Opinion,* February–March 1983, pp. 55–60.
33. Maura Clancey and Michael J. Robinson, "General Election Coverage: Part I," *Public Opinion,* December-January 1985, pp. 49–59.
34. Lichter, "How the Press Covered the Primaries," p.48.
35. Ibid., p. 49.
36. Erwin Krasnow and Laurence Longley, *The Politics of Broadcast Regulation* (New York: St. Martin's Press, 1978).
37. Ronald Berkman and Laura Kitch, *Politics in the Media Age* (New York: McGraw-Hill, 1986), 50–59.
38. David S. Broder, "How to Stop a Political Mudbath in Five Easy Steps," *Washington Post National Weekly Edition,* 22–28 January 1990, pp. 23–24.

CHAPTER 11

INTEREST GROUPS

POLITICAL CLOSE-UP

WORKING THE HILL: A DAY IN THE LIFE OF A LOBBYIST

In 1987, faced with massive budget deficits, Congress looked for ways to raise federal revenues. A proposal to increase excise taxes on beer and wine received serious attention. This was an unpleasant prospect for the two thousand members of the National Beer Wholesalers, which dispatched its lobbyist, Jack Lewis, to work against the tax. Lewis, a former journalist and political science professor, had also once been legislative director for Missouri Senator Thomas Eagleton. Lewis's extensive contacts on Capitol Hill proved invaluable for his career as a lobbyist and his client's success. A reporter followed Jack Lewis through one of his busy days of "working the Hill."

8:00 A.M. Breakfast with a dozen other lobbyists sponsored by the American Trucking Association. Lewis's main objective here is to meet the new senator from Nevada, Democrat Harry M. Reid. Over four cups of coffee, Lewis explains, "You get together with other lobbyists, you exchange ideas, information. You see the senator, get a measure of the

man. One thing you've got to do is build in a 'comfort factor' with them."
9:10 A.M. Lewis convinces a Capitol policeman he has known for years to let him park in a reserved space. Lacking any office of his own, he borrows a telephone in one Senate office to make some calls. Next is a stop by the Appropriations Subcommittee on Transportation to check on another project he is working on.
10:30 A.M. Senator Don Reigle (D-Mich.) invites the lobbyist into his office to talk about the excise tax and its impact. Lewis's strategy is to profile the average beer wholesaler as a small businessman, not a beer baron. He discovers that one of Reigle's best friends is a beer wholesaler. The senator is willing to help but tells Lewis to get him some information on other alternatives for raising revenues.
11:15 A.M. A "social call" to the office of Senator Christopher Bond (R-Mo.) is next. A conversation with Bond's administrative assistant that begins with chat about dalmatian puppies turns to the excise tax on beer. The senator, Lewis is assured, will keep an open mind.
Noon. Lunch at the fashionable French restaurant La Colline with the chief counsel to the Republican whip, Alan Simpson of Wyoming. Casual conversation touches only briefly on the tax issue, but Lewis's recognition and standing in the important senator's office is nudged up a notch.
3:30 P.M. A meeting with Senator John Danforth produces the most tangible results of the day. "Terrible idea," the Missouri Republican says of the excise tax. "I don't smoke, but I drink beer," says Danforth with a smile. "You've got my vote."
3:34 P.M. Senator John D. Rockefeller IV, Democrat of West Virginia, ushers Lewis into his office. Rockefeller tells Lewis that when he was governor, he raised some excise taxes, but he parts by promising he will keep an open mind.

4:45 P.M. The last appointment of the day is short. A member of the key Senate Finance Committee, William Roth (R-Del.), tells Lewis that he opposes any tax increases in the budget. "Some of 'em [beer wholesalers] have already been in here," says Roth—good news to Lewis, who has planned a grassroots campaign to supplement his direct efforts.

5:30 P.M. Lewis walks out of the Capitol to the 116 Club to attend a fund-raiser for North Dakota Democrat Quentin Burdick. In his pocket is a check for $1,000 from SIXPAC, the beer wholesalers' political action committee. At the door, he delivers the check and receives a lapel pin with a silver gavel ($5,000 earns a gold pin). When Burdick appears, Lewis pumps the senator's hand. Later, as Lewis heads for the door, he greets Senator Reid walking in, adding some symmetry to this particular day in the life of a Washington lobbyist.

The excise tax on beer was not adopted in 1987 but was once again proposed in 1990.

SOURCE: *St. Louis Post-Dispatch,* 12 April, 1987, p. E1.

CHAPTER OUTLINE

INTRODUCTION AND OVERVIEW

Today, members of Congress spend as much time raising money for the next election as they do on legislative work. The cost of an average Senate campaign climbed to nearly $4 million in 1988, while the cost of the average House race was nearly $400,000. But contested races in the bigger states can easily cost over $10 million. One senator estimated that he needed to raise $15,000 every day for six years to have enough for his reelection campaign. Senators and representatives make the rounds of evening fund-raisers that take place on a daily basis in Washington and around the country. Many evenings, they make personal telephone appeals for money, what the members call "dialing for dollars." While under the rules, members themselves may not talk about or directly take money in their offices, lobbyists often stop by the desk of a top aide on the way out to drop off campaign contributions of as much as $10,000.[1]

Is growing interest-group influence in policy-making and elections undermining the ability to govern in the public interest? Many fear it is. Although most members claim that money is given with no strings attached, many admit in private that PAC contributions influence their vote. Policymaking based on accommodation between interest groups and public officials can subvert democracy, and government is rendered impotent when powerful interests have a veto over policy decisions.[2] Yet interest groups have their defenders. For many years, political scientists portrayed representation through organized groups as one of the most important links between the people and the government. Many questions about interest groups remain unanswered: Are they essentially good forces or bad forces in politics? Can the public interest be served by the competition among private interests to set the policy agenda? Do interest groups stack the political deck in favor of the haves against the have-nots?[3]

Whether they are called "special interests," "factions," "pressure groups," or "lobbies," **interest groups** play an important role in contemporary American politics. An interest group is an association of people with a common interest, organized to pursue their policy goals in the political process. Interest groups make campaign contributions through their political action committees or PACs. They differ from political parties in their specificity of concern. They usually focus on a narrow range of policy, sometimes a single issue, and the narrowness of their concern is often positively related to how politically effective they are. Political parties, in contrast, aggregate interests. They cut across a broad range of issues and attempt to unite large segments of the population. Parties are policy generalists. Interest groups are policy specialists.

Interest groups are most often concerned with economic benefits. Political economy helps explain not only the goals of interest groups but also why groups form and what groups are most likely to be effective. The analysis of interest groups in American politics examines the following questions:

1. Is group politics merely economic self-interest, or is it an important method of representation in a democracy?
2. How do economic motivations help explain the goals and formation of interest groups? Why do individuals join groups?
3. What are public interest groups, and how are they different?
4. What are the major interest groups in American politics?
5. What is lobbying and how does it affect public policy?
6. What are PACs and how do they affect elections?
7. What are the targets of group influence? What stages of the policy process are most accessible to them?
8. Do interest groups undermine governing processes? Should there be more control over their operation and influence?

The Political Economy of Interest Groups

Group Politics: Economic Self-Interest or the National Interest?

Americans have been called a nation of joiners. Since colonial days, citizens have banded together in associations to pursue political and economic objectives. The Founders, as they feared political parties, also worried about interest groups, another form of faction. James Madison believed it was unfortunate but natural for people to form groups in a democratic regime: "The causes of faction . . . are sown in the nature of man." Madison explained:

> By a faction I understand a number of citizens, whether amounting to a majority or a minority of the whole, who are united and actuated by some common impulse of passion, or of interest, adverse to the rights of other citizens, or to the permanent and aggregate interests of the community.[4]

Adverse to the rights of other citizens! What was feared in interest groups was their "selfishness," which was seen as contrary to the broader national interest. But Madison's warnings went unheeded. Political parties and interest groups soon formed to pursue economic and political goals.

Around 1910, political scientist Arthur Bentley claimed that groups were the key to understanding American government. They were, as he put it, "the raw material of politics."[5] Forty years later, another political scientist, David Truman, picked up Bentley's theme.[6] Bentley's and Truman's view of group politics is positive, emphasizing the representative nature of interest groups over their attempts to pursue narrow economic interests. They believe that group politics build consensus and represent even the average citizen. Rejecting the possibility of identifying a truly national interest, Bentley and Truman hold that the competition among self-interested groups produces policies that are fair and just. Through "mutual adjustment" of goals and bargaining, consensus is achieved.

Their ideas form a theory of politics called **pluralism** – the view that democracy operates best through the competition of diverse groups pursuing their own political and economic interests. From the pluralist vantage point, the role of lobbyists is important and constructive. One writer laments the negative image of lobbyists and interest groups, claiming, "The press plays up the unsavory and sensational aspects of lobbying, printing very few stories about the ordinary, honest lobbyist and his workaday activities."[7]

Critics find the pluralist view too simple, believing that the interest-group system favors the economic elite in the United States and that average citizens are not represented.[8] The *elitist theory* of American politics claims that groups pursuing narrow economic interests do not produce good public policy, but instead result in policies that help the wealthy and the powerful. How can we assess the importance of groups and judge their role in politics? We begin by examining the relationship between economic change and interest-group formation. Next we consider the economic incentives for joining interest groups and some of the surprising implications for interest-group strategies and behavior.

INTEREST-GROUP FORMATION

Changes in American political economy stimulated the formation of interest groups. Industrialization led to the creation of both producer organizations and labor organizations. When farmers changed from producing mostly their own food to selling their food to others, they formed organizations to help achieve their goals in the marketplace, beginning with the Grange in 1867. In the late nineteenth and early twentieth centuries, a multitude of familiar groups were formed, including the National Association for the Advancement of Colored People, the Women's Christian Temperance Union, the American Federation of Labor, and the National Association of Manufacturers. Since World War II there has been a veritable explosion of groups. The 1960s witnessed a sudden proliferation of civil rights, women's rights, consumer, and environmental groups. As factory jobs have declined and the service sector has increased, organizations of workers have changed. Today, more white-collar and professional associations are forming than traditional blue-collar unions.

Government policy itself can lead to the creation of new interest groups. The increase in social welfare programs in the United States since the 1930s has given life to two new types of groups: recipients and service deliverers.[9] As Social Security expenditures have increased, groups such as the American Association of Retired Persons have become active lobbyists to protect Social Security and promote the economic well-being of the elderly. Service deliverers, such as postal workers, social workers, mental health employees, and teachers, have all developed stronger, more active national interest groups.

The formation of one group may lead to the formation of an opposing group. When local business people organize to redevelop a section of a large city, groups such as neighborhood associations, preservationists, and environmentalists may spring up in opposition. The creation of business and labor groups in the nineteenth century followed the same pattern.

The decentralized structure of American government and the relative weakness of the political parties invite the creation of interest groups. With federalism and separation of powers, interest groups have many opportunities to influence policy. From city hall and the state capitol to Congress, the bureaucracy, the White House, and the courts, many access points are available to groups in American politics. Interest-group development in

American politics is tied to national political and economic trends. But the answer to why groups form must also consider individual incentives for membership.

ECONOMIC INCENTIVES FOR GROUP MEMBERSHIP

The pluralist view of interest groups was premised on the notion that groups formed automatically to protect some shared interest.[10] Even if no organized group was in existence, people with shared interests constituted potential groups ready to spring into existence if threatened in some way. The work of economist Mancur Olson challenged this view. In his 1965 book, *The Logic of Collective Action,* Olson pointed out that if individuals behave rationally—that is, act to get the most for the least—they will *not* voluntarily join an association:

> If the members of a large group rationally seek to maximize their personal welfare, they will not act to advance their common or group objectives unless there is coercion to force them to do so, or unless some separate incentive, distinct from the achievement of the common or group interest, is offered to the members of the group individually on the condition that they help bear the costs or burdens involved in the achievement of the group objectives.[11]

The key element in Olson's theory of group action is the type of goal the group desires. He distinguishes between **collective goods,** which must be shared by all group members equally, and **private goods,** which can be divided between some individuals, excluding others. National defense is an example of a collective good—once it is provided by the government, its benefits cannot be excluded from specific individuals. Private goods, such as subscription to a journal or magazine, special discounts, or free insurance, can be limited to only those who join an association. Since most interest groups seek collective goods, they have problems providing economic incentives for members to join. This defines the **free rider problem.** Potential members who choose not to join may still enjoy all the benefits if the group achieves its goal and the collective good is provided. Labor unions have recognized this problem for many years and have solved it in many states by requiring union shops. When a majority of employees vote to be represented by a bargaining agent, all employees must join because they will all enjoy the benefits of collective bargaining.

Although it is easier for producer groups, such as insurance companies, to organize, consumers occasionally vent their anger and frustration.

Other groups have not been able to solve the free rider problem and as a result have a membership that is only a small fraction of the potential membership.

Size is also a critical variable in Olson's theory. Small groups have an advantage over large groups for two reasons. First, the smaller the group, the larger share of the collective good each member receives. If the collective good sought is, for example, tariffs on imported steel and there are ten steel manufacturers, each one stands to benefit substantially (millions of dollars). But for a large potential group, like steel consumers, with millions of possible members, the economic return from joining an organization to fight steel tariffs is infinitesimal (a few cents). Second, the smaller the group, the easier it is to communicate, and the cheaper it is in resource expenditure to organize. If there are ten large steel producers and one refuses to join, it is easier to coerce that firm. Small groups have significant advantages over large groups in getting organized. Therefore, producers are usually better organized than consumers. For example, the Air Transport Association of America (the airlines) is better organized than the Air Passengers Association. But why do so many large membership groups form in spite of the lack of economic advantage?

Motivations other than economic benefit lead individuals to join a group. Important factors that affect group formation and membership include ideological, philanthropic, and organizational motives, which act in concert with the economic motive.[12] Large groups retain the advantage of sheer numbers if they can be effectively mobilized. The role of leadership is also important in group formation. A political organizer, or "entrepreneur," can convince potential members of the benefits of group membership.[13]

Interest groups have formed in response to changes in the American economy, and the generally open nature of American politics has been hospitable to this process. Interest-group formation is also related to the size of the group, the potential membership, and the nature of the good they are seeking in the political system. Some of the most important interest groups are familiar to observers of American politics.

Groups: A Panoply of Interests

Recent Trends in Interest-Group Politics

The tens of thousands of interest groups active in politics range from enormous to tiny, well-known to obscure, heavy hitters to benchwarmers. One of the most notable recent developments has been the emergence of "public interest" groups. Concerned with environmental protection, animal rights, disarmament, and consumer issues, they are less concerned with providing their members with tangible economic benefits.

In the 1990s, new groups are on the rise and some old ones are on the decline. New occupational groups, incorporating the emerging professional-managerial-technical elite, are increasing.[14] Traditional blue-collar unions are on the decline. Civil rights and women's groups are strong, reflecting the new awareness of minorities and women, their new role, and their political clout. Consumer and environmental groups have emerged as the new opponents to business groups in the political process.

Rapid social change produces not only economic dislocations but social uncertainty as well. Suspicious of changing morals and values, fundamentalist, religious groups such as the Moral Majority have emerged as a potent political force. The narrowness and intensity of group politics have increased in recent years, as reflected in the growing number of **single-issue groups.** With extremely limited objectives, these groups devote their energy and resources to but a tiny slice of the policy agenda. Gun control and antiabortion groups are two obvious examples. An inhospitable attitude to compromise by many of the single-issue groups has increased political conflict and made negotiation more difficult.

Group strategies and tactics have changed.[15] Computerization, direct mail, and data-processing advances have refined the ability to mount timely, effective, grassroots lobbying campaigns. Nearly every interest group has moved to Washington, changing headquarters from cities such as

New York to the nation's capital, where the action is. One of the most controversial changes is the rapid increase in the number and influence of political action committees, discussed later in the chapter.

Interest groups have increasingly become a formal part of policy-making. Official status confirms them as legitimate actors in the policy process. Groups enjoy formal representation through bureaucratic advisory committees, group representatives in the White House, and a growing number of special interest "caucuses" in Congress (such as the "coal caucus"). Although interest groups have been on the scene since the early days, they have never had greater influence on American politics than they do today.

PUBLIC INTEREST GROUPS

In the 1960s, a new kind of interest group emerged. Angry at the concentration of power and perceived corporate bias in the traditional interest system, countergroups formed. **Public interest groups** attempted to define larger national interests rather than narrowly defined economic interests and to organize citizens who lack the economic incentive of a big steel producer or agribusiness. In some ways, public interest groups have been remarkably successful. In other ways, they are not yet a match for the better organized, specialized economic interests.

A public interest group has been defined by political scientist Jeffrey Berry as "one that seeks a collective good, the achievement of which will not selectively and materially benefit the membership or activists of the organization."[16] Although there are economic implications for many public interest groups, a fundamental difference exists between, say, Common Cause and the American Medical Association.

Claiming to be a public interest group may be a bit presumptuous. After all, political theorists have struggled for centuries to define just what the public interest is. Conservatives and business groups see many public interest groups as a bunch of young, liberal, environmentally crazed activists acting counter to the real public interest. Part of this image may spring from such prominent public interest group leaders as Ralph Nader.

Ralph Nader became a national figure with the 1965 publication of his book *Unsafe at Any Speed,* a one-man crusade for auto safety, and soon became a symbol of a new consumer activism against the corporate establishment. He was joined by many young people, known as "Nader's Raiders," who pursued research on a variety of consumer issues and lobbied their findings. Nader-backed organizations devoted to these activities grew in number. A hero to some, Nader represents the enemy to others in the corporate world, particularly the auto industry.

Another well-known public interest group is **Common Cause,** founded by a Republican, former Secretary of Health, Education, and Welfare, John Gardner. Common Cause has around 200,000 members who tend to be politically liberal and relatively affluent. Common Cause has focused on "process" issues, particularly campaign finance reform. As a result, the group has not always been popular with politicians. It has been successful in attracting a large membership willing to support the organization to promote "good government."

What are the other public interest groups? Berry identified the largest category as environmental organizations (25 percent), followed by groups concerned with peace and arms control (19 percent), consumer issues (16 percent), general politics (13 percent), church groups (11 percent), and civil rights (6 percent).[17] One-third of these groups are not real membership organizations but consist of a handful of activists, often lawyers, supported by grants from private foundations. Some church-related organizations have no separate membership from the entire denomination membership. Other groups, such as the Audubon Society, Consumer's Union, and the National Wildlife Federation, have large mass memberships. Environmental groups have become more important than ever and "green politics" promise to be a critical part of policy-making in the 1990s. Political Insight 11-1 looks at the "group of ten," the environmental movement's mainstream.

Why do people join public interest groups? Berry found that tangible benefits, such as receiving a magazine, cannot explain group membership.[18]

POLITICAL INSIGHT 11-1

THE GROUP OF TEN: THE ENVIRONMENTAL MOVEMENT'S MAINSTREAM

NATURAL RESOURCES DEFENSE COUNCIL

Annual budget: $16 million
Membership: 130,000
Executive director: John H. Adams

The movements's largest and most aggressive legal advocate, the NRDC seeks enforcement and interpretation of a wide range of environmental statutes in the courts and executive branch. Its large staff of scientists and lawyers is often called for advice in shaping legislation in Congress. In 1989, the NRDC entered the era of mass media campaigning for the first time to publicize its findings on Alar.

SIERRA CLUB

Annual budget: $32 million
Membership: 553,000
Chairman: J. Michael McCloskey

As the only member of the "Group of Ten" without tax-deductible status, the Sierra Club has the most freewheeling lobbying and political apparatus of any of the groups. Founded ninety-eight years ago by naturalist John Muir, it has members in local chapters across the nation and focuses on legislation on the state as well as national level. The club addresses the full range of environmental issues, from wilderness protection to public health to the environmental practices of international lending agencies.

SIERRA CLUB LEGAL DEFENSE FUND

Annual budget: $8.3 million
Contributors: 120,000
Director: Frederick P. Sutherland

Independent of the Sierra Club, this so-called law firm of the environmental movement was formed in 1971 as environmentalists became more confrontational and concerned with stopping pollution. It provides legal services to the environmental community but, unlike NRDC, usually represents other organizations.

NATIONAL WILDLIFE FEDERATION

Annual budget: 85.6 million
Membership: 3 million
President: Jay D. Hair

The federation's advocacy of hunting and fishing issues has resulted in the largest membership of any conservation group and a generally conservative agenda. But under Hair's leadership, the group has widened its focus beyond protecting wildlife habitats and become more aggressive in lobbying on a wide range of environmental issues, including global warming.

WILDERNESS SOCIETY

Annual budget: $20 million
Membership: 360,000
President: George T. Frampton Jr.

The only mainstream group to focus exclusively on protecting the nation's public lands, the society lobbies aggressively to expand wilderness areas and safeguard biological diversity in the United States. Its membership has more than doubled since Frampton became president in 1986.

NATIONAL PARKS AND CONSERVATION ASSOCIATION

Budget: $3.82 million
Membership: 125,000
President: Paul C. Pritchard

Founded in 1919 by Stephen Mather, the first director of the National Park Service, NPCA focuses exclusively on preserving and enhancing the national park system. The group has traditionally favored a low-key approach, but lately, it has become more outspoken as parks have become vulnerable to new threats such as acid rain. Membership in the group has doubled in the last two years.

(Continued on next page.)

POLITICAL INSIGHT 11–1

NATIONAL AUDUBON SOCIETY

Annual budget: $35 million
Membership: 580,000
President: Peter A. A. Berle

Founded in 1905, Audubon grew out of a protest movement by women seeking to stop the slaughter of Florida wading birds, whose plumes were used to decorate hats. It traditionally focuses on preservation of wildlife and natural resources and has a reputation for being politically moderate. More recently, it has taken up clean air as a major objective along with its efforts to preserve the Arctic National Wildlife Refuge, wetlands, and old-growth forests.

IZAAK WALTON LEAGUE

Annual budget: $1.64 million
Membership: 50,000
Executive director: Jack Lorenz

Founded in 1922, the conservative organization named after the eighteenth-century English writer and conservationist is composed primarily of hunters and anglers. It focuses on public education programs promoting responsible use of forests and other natural resources.

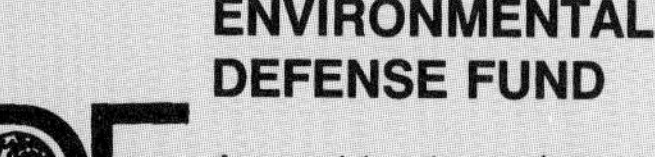

ENVIRONMENTAL DEFENSE FUND

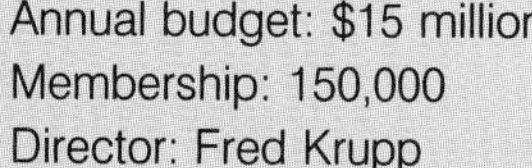

Annual budget: $15 million
Membership: 150,000
Director: Fred Krupp

Founded in 1967 by scientists and lawyers, EDF is best known in recent years for its analysis and sponsorship of novel solutions to environmental problems. Its advocacy of market-based principles to combat acid rain became the centerpiece of the Bush administration's clean air package in 1989.

FRIENDS OF THE EARTH

Annual budget: $2.5 million
Membership: 50,000
Executive director: Mike Clark

Traditionally concerned with international environmental issues, FOE dramatically expanded its scope in its January 1989 merger with the Environmental Policy Institute, a think tank devoted to domestic issues, and the Oceanic Society, which had focused on ocean pollution. Known as the furthest to the political left of mainstream groups, it works closely with grass-roots organizations and aggressively represents their interests in Washington.

SOURCE: *Washington Post National Weekly Edition* April 30-May 6, 1990.

Instead, the incentives are *purposive*—ideological, philanthropic, and policy-oriented factors explain membership in public interest groups. But numbers can be deceiving. Although some groups appear to have relatively large memberships, they still constitute only a small segment of the total population that is unusually attentive and politically concerned.

Imitation is the sincerest form of flattery. The relative success and influence of public interest groups have been copied in recent years by the new right. Conservatives have formed their own organizations and public interest law firms to further their views and counter environmental and consumer groups. James Watt, controversial former interior secretary in the Reagan administration, first became prominent as head of the Mountain States Legal Foundation. With funding from business people, such as the owners of the Coors Brewing Company, this organization fights environmentalists and antinuclear groups in the courts and legislatures over the development of wilderness

FIGURE 11-1

CHANGES IN LABOR UNION MEMBERSHIP, 1970–1986

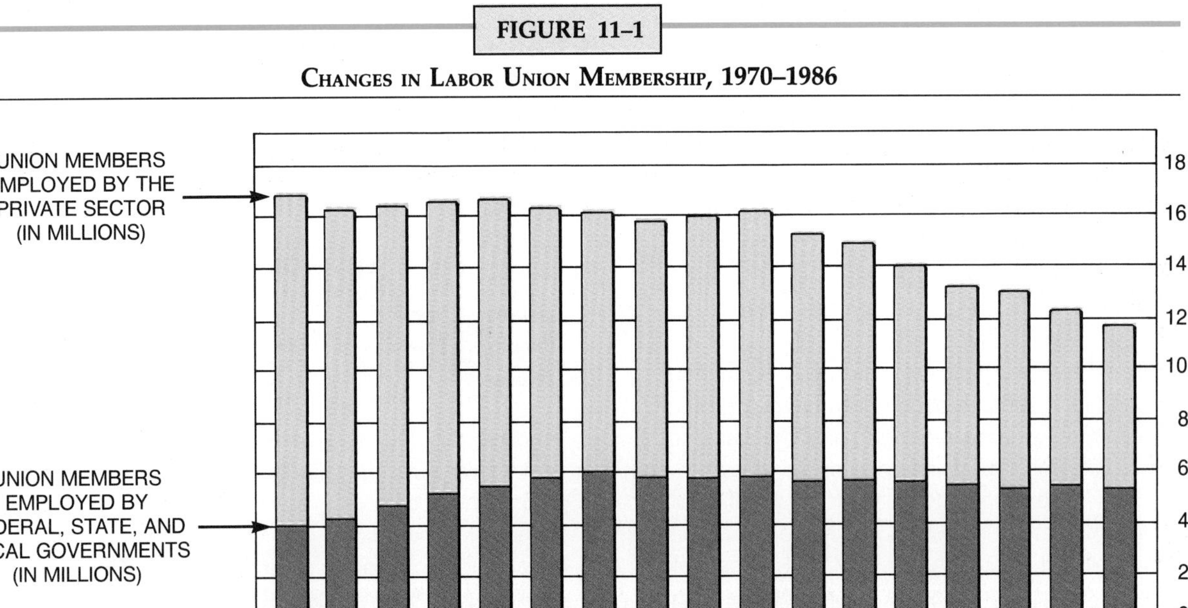

SOURCE: Union Sourcebook, 1987.

and, mining and mineral rights, pollution control, and nuclear power.

PRIVATE INTEREST GROUPS

Despite the proliferation of public interest groups since the 1960s, they still make up only a small proportion of interest groups in the nation. A recent study sampling 564 groups found that 80 percent of interest groups were occupational, professional, or industrial organizations.[19] Although many of the groups are new, the major players in interest-group politics still reflect traditional economic concerns.

LABOR UNIONS. Organized labor has been on the decline since the 1950s. Today, fewer unions command membership from a smaller percentage of the work force. The absolute decline would be even greater had it not been for the increase in public employee unions. Figure 11-1 shows the change in union membership since 1970. The unions' influence in Congress, as measured by their own support score, decreased in the 1970s, and 1980s. Although their contributions to political candidates have risen, the growth of competing political action committees has resulted in a decline in labor's overall proportion of contribution from 50 percent to around 25 percent of all PAC campaign dollars.

The American Federation of Labor–Congress of Industrial Organizations (**AFL-CIO**) is a confederation of unions, the largest in the country. Decision-making authority is shared between local unions and the AFL-CIO national board. Other influential unions include the United Auto Workers and the Teamsters. The composition of the AFL-CIO board reflects underlying shifts in the work force. Now included on the board are the leaders of the American Federation of Teachers, the American Federation of Government Employees, and the American Federation of State, County, and Municipal Employees. In recent years, the policy agenda of labor has shifted from purely economic concerns to issues such as the Equal Rights Amendment and the Voting Rights Act extension.

Labor's scorecard on legislation is mixed. Although it has won some victories in Congress, it has had notable defeats. Labor's continued strength is its numbers and organization, but even though labor leaders have never controlled the voting behavior of the rank and file, defections to Reagan in 1980 and 1984 revealed serious erosion in labor's ability to deliver votes. One weakness may be the scope of its agenda. As one observer of Congress noted, "Labor lobbyists ask for so much that a lawmaker can turn them down one week, knowing there will be an opportunity to make amends on another issue the following week."[20]

Labor is struggling to hold its own in the political arena in the 1990s. Unions are most successful when they ally themselves with business on issues like tariffs and the Chrysler bailout. In terms of innovation and new strategies, however, labor has not kept pace with business.

BUSINESS. Of the 15,000 or so interest groups in the United States, the largest number are business groups. Business is represented by hundreds of associations. The U.S. Chamber of Commerce has been the main organization of small- to medium-sized businesses across the country. Operating through local chapters, the Chamber of Commerce traditionally has lobbied for conservative economic policies favorable to business, although in recent years it has become less doctrinaire in its economic stance and more pragmatic. In recent years, it has grown in size and political importance, despite its advanced age as an organization. The chamber has concentrated on exploiting its large membership, perfecting grassroots mobilization that can produce many thousands of pieces of mail in Washington in a matter of days. The Chamber of Commerce lobbied hard in 1990 against the family leave bill in Congress, which would allow a parent twelve weeks of unpaid leave to deal with a sick child or parent or a birth or adoption.

The National Association of Manufacturers (NAM) is the traditional representative of big business—the Fortune 500 corporations. The NAM was the focal point of opposition of business to New Deal legislation in the 1930s, particularly such labor legislation as the Wagner Act (1935) and the National Labor Relations Act. One of its great successes was the passage of the Taft-Hartley Act (1947) rolling back some of labor's gains from the previous decade.

A major national business interest group is the Business Roundtable, formed in 1974. Consisting of the chief executive officers of two hundred of the largest American corporations, its strategy is quite different from the grassroots techniques of the Chamber of Commerce. Members of this elite group of corporate "heavies" attempt to bring their collective power, prestige, and access to politicians to bear on issues affecting business. Coordinated

Business lobbyists are among the most influential in Washington.

grassroots efforts with the Chamber of Commerce have also been effective.

Big corporations are represented in Washington through multiple channels. Exxon Corporation, for example, is represented by its own Washington office, by such industry associations as the American Petroleum Institute, and by five different law firms and consultants.[21] Business is not a monolithic interest, despite the existence of several national organizations and multiple interest groups and lobbyists. The interests of large corporations and smaller businesses are often at odds. Large corporations today have an increasing stake in continued government regulation and in many cases support the status quo more than the reduction of government. In recent years, one issue uniting different business groups was the huge budget deficits, which they have consistently urged be cut.

Business gained the most from the changes in campaign finance laws that made it easier to form political action committees. Growth in PACs has come primarily from corporate political action committees. Business has also been innovative in its use of think tanks to promote the market system and conservative policies. Heritage Foundation, with a budget of more than $10 million, has attracted notable scholars who produce policy analysis with a pro-business flavor.

AGRICULTURE. At one time, farmers were considered to be more a people's lobby than an economic interest group. But as American agriculture changed and family farms become huge agribusinesses, so did their organization and lobbying. Farmers are represented by a variety of groups, including the National Grange, the American Farm Bureau Federation, and the National Farmers Union. Rarely in the past did these groups work effectively together. Then in 1973, a coalition of twenty farm groups formed to oppose a Nixon administration agriculture bill, one of the farmers' first coordinated efforts.

The activities of agriculture interest groups took on new drama in the late 1970s with the emergence of the American Agriculture Movement (AAM). More militant than the older farm groups, the AAM, formed in 1977, sponsored highly publicized demonstrations in Washington for higher government subsidies and guaranteed prices. In February 1979, more than two thousand tractors festooned with banners snarled traffic throughout the nation's capital. By the 1980s, the AAM had essentially changed from a protest group to an interest group. It opened an office in Washington, hired consultants, and formed a PAC.[22]

The plight of the farmers once again gained the national spotlight in 1985. A debt crisis threatened to bankrupt thousands of American farmers. In a novel lobbying move, the entire South Dakota legislature descended on Congress to push for emergency credit legislation. Throughout the Midwest, farmers held protests and demonstrations to dramatize their situation. In the U.S. Senate, the confirmation of Edwin Meese as attorney general was held up by a filibuster by farm state senators. Congress responded by passing a $1.8 billion loan guarantee program.

In addition to the well-known economic groups, there are literally thousands of other interest groups in Washington trying to affect public policy. What are their goals? What are their strategies?

Techniques of Influence: Lobbying

THE ORIGINS OF LOBBYING

Although interest groups existed at the founding of the United States, the term "lobby" first appeared in 1808 in the Annals of the Tenth Congress. Agents seeking favors from legislators occasionally congregated in the lobby of the New York state capitol in Albany and were soon dubbed **lobbyists.** The term was in common use by the 1830s.[23] The right to lobby, although that word was not used, is encompassed under the First Amendment's protection of free speech and the right to assemble and petition the government.

By the late nineteenth century, lobbying had become a major part of the legislative process. Compared with today, methods were crude and direct. Bribes and payoffs for favorable actions were much more common, and interests were particularly "special." As early as 1833, Daniel Webster complained to the National Bank that his support for the renewal of the bank would not continue unless his "retainer" was "renewed or refreshed." During the Grant administration in the

1870s, twelve members of Congress received stock in a company called Credit Mobilier in return for construction grants for the Union Pacific Railroad, which controlled the company. In 1913, the lobbyist for the National Association of Manufacturers paid a regular fee to receive inside information on legislation. The association also paid bribes to legislators on key committees to keep them favorable to NAM interests. Such revelations led to a series of investigations into the techniques and influence of lobbyists. Pressure mounted on Congress for corrective legislation, while political cartoonists depicted the lobbyist as an overweight, red-nosed fat cat with cash bulging from his pockets. But despite reform attempts in the 1920s and 1930s, lobbying was not regulated until the passage of the **Lobby Registration Act** in 1946, a relatively weak piece of legislation. The regulation of lobbying activities remains quite limited, primarily because of First Amendment guarantees.

Lobbying has changed radically since the 1800s, evolving to the sophisticated practices of today. Interests no longer restrict their activities to Congress and the legislatures. They also focus attention on the White House, the bureaucracy, and the courts in an effort to influence policy.

HOW DO LOBBYISTS ATTEMPT TO INFLUENCE PUBLIC POLICY?

The name of the game in lobbying is *access* and *persuasion.* Since no secret formula for success exists, the most effective interest groups pursue flexible strategies at all the stages of the policy process. A few simple principles help explain the effectiveness of lobbying efforts. First, lobbyists try to gain access to decision-making at the most critical point. If they fail, they must be ready to fall back and try again at another stage. For example, if a group wants new legislation, it should begin with the executive branch. Getting its bill included in an agency's agenda, or better yet, in the president's agenda, is a good start. Congress is the next logical access point, whether to push for new legislation or to block unfriendly bills. Failing here, lobbying shifts back to the executive branch to the implementation stage. Influence on the regulatory process or rule-making stage can recoup earlier losses. Finally, the courts can be used to snatch victory from the jaws of defeat. Interest groups increasingly use litigation to block or delay unfavorable policies or to achieve new, favorable rulings.

A second principle of lobbying is that it is easier to block policies than to enact them. To get a favorable change in policy, such as a clean-air act, requires a sustained effort through the many stages of policy-making. To succeed, each battle must be won. Blocking legislation, such as gun control, means fighting a holding action. To succeed, only one battle in the war must be won. There are many stages where policies can be defeated or subverted. The **National Rifle Association (NRA)** is a model of an effective "veto" lobby. Using a variety of techniques, it has been able to fend off congressional gun control legislation for more than two decades. A third principle is, that the more specific the goals, the more likely is success, and the more limited the goal, the greater the concentration of resources devoted to it.

Lobbying strategies can be characterized by three basic approaches:[24]

1. *Lobbying from the top down*—direct lobbying of key public officials in the decision-making process.
2. *Lobbying from the bottom up*—indirect lobbying through mobilization of a grass-roots campaign, including the use of publicity and the media.
3. *Lobbying by alliances*—working in concert with other interest groups to concentrate resources and efforts.

DIRECT CONTACT OF PUBLIC OFFICIALS. One of the most important roles of lobbyists is to provide information. Even with the growth of congressional staffs, lobbyists are often a main source of information for legislators on certain issues. One ITT lobbyist explained:

> When you work with these politicians, remember you have to prepare the whole goddamned smear. Write the letters, the "off the cuff" comments, the press releases, everything. Believe me, they use most of our stuff; some don't even proofread what we write. . . . The responsibility we accept is to keep them out of trouble.[25]

The information that a lobbyist furnishes can range from straightforward facts through subjective arguments to veiled threats of the lobby's political strength and grassroots support. The NRA uses all three kinds of information. It gives legislators fact

James Baker, Director of Federal Affairs for the NRA Institute for Legislative Action, testifies before Congress. The National Rifle Association uses various pressure techniques to keep gun control issues off the policy agenda.

sheets on gun ownership, crime rates, and the difficulties of enforcing gun legislation. It provides subjective legal and constitutional arguments against gun control. Finally, it may politely remind a legislator of its concerted electoral efforts against "misguided" legislators who voted for gun control.

Direct techniques are best employed when the lobbyist has immediate access to the official. Lobbyists attempt to be available and useful, but instant access is often a luxury reserved only to the most powerful lobbyists. Direct access is expensive. Top lobbyists are often former members of Congress, top legislative staff, or executive branch officials. Former Wisconsin senator Gaylord Nelson became the lobbyist for a coalition of environmental groups, hoping to cash in on his environmental expertise and his contacts with senators and representatives. Other former officials are employed by defense industries and business groups. As we saw in the Political Close-up at the start of this chapter, social contacts can be an effective form of "climate control"; cocktail parties, barbecues, and cruises help create a favorable environment for influence when it is needed. Interest groups want to maintain access even when nothing urgent is happening. But when a crucial issue arises, they want to be right there to explain their position.

Lobbyists first make contact with their natural allies—officials who already have some sympathy with their goals. There is no point in wasting time with those who are already opponents. Direct contact concentrates on persuasion, not pressure. Threats can be counterproductive. One close observer of the persuasion game summarized the rules of conduct:

> Be pleasant and inoffensive, be well-prepared and informed, be personally convinced of your arguments, use the soft sell, convince the official of the issue's importance to him in his constituency or in terms of the public interest, and leave a written summary behind. . . . Do not carry a briefcase to a meeting since the official may think it contains a tape recorder; do not lobby at a party until coffee is being served; eat where the lawmakers eat; smile till your face aches.[26]

MOBILIZATION OF GRASSROOTS SUPPORT. Groups unable to enjoy direct access to top officials may try to exert influence through sheer numbers. The objective of **grassroots mobilization** is to create the impression of massive, widespread support for your position and to actually sway public opinion in the desired direction. Indirect mobilization techniques can range from small rallies to expensive advertising and direct mail appeals. From a full-page advertisement in the *New York Times* to bumper stickers (such as the NRA's "Guns Don't Kill—People Do"), mobilization techniques can take many forms.

Despite their unreliability as a measure of public opinion, letters, telegrams, and telephone calls from constituents remain an effective lobbying technique. With computer mail and automated telephone calling, mass appeals have grown by leaps and bounds in recent years. Legislators know that such appeals may not be a heartfelt outpouring of sentiment, but these campaigns can still work. A classic grassroots mobilization campaign was waged in 1982-83 by American banks. Part of President Reagan's 1981 tax package included a provision calling for a 10-percent withholding of interest on savings accounts. The Internal Revenue Service (IRS) had evidence that large amounts of taxes were escaping collection and believed that the new requirement would significantly increase tax revenues. Scant attention was paid to the withholding provisions during the legislative debate. Banks opposed it but did not have time to get organized before the measure passed. But then they went to work. Millions of bank statements across the country included little brochures with warnings about the new provisions to take effect on July 1, 1983. Savers were urged to write to their representatives and senators to repeal the law. Letters poured in by the bagful, and pressure mounted. Many people erroneously believed that the IRS would be keeping part of their interest. Banks did little to correct this misperception. An outraged Senator Robert Dole (R-Kan.), then chair of the Senate Finance Committee, denounced the massive "propaganda campaign" of the banks in a speech on the Senate floor. Nonetheless, the Senate repealed the provision by a vote of 91 to 7, reversing its decision of less than two years earlier. Grassroots mobilization had done the trick.

BUILDING ALLIANCES WITH OTHER GROUPS. Strength in numbers also applies to lobbying efforts. Some of the most effective lobbying campaigns have been the result of coalitions of interest groups united over a single issue. The battles over the Alaska pipeline bill in the early 1970s are still remembered as one of the greatest lobbying "wars" of all time. On one side was a coalition of environmental groups seeking to protect the Alaskan wilderness from the effects of the pipeline. Several dozen environmental groups joined forces for both direct contact and grassroots efforts. On the other side was an alliance of the big oil companies. Operating under an umbrella organization, they waged a massive information and pressure campaign in Congress. In the end, the pipeline was approved but with guarantees for protecting the wildlife and wilderness land in Alaska.

Some issues are not conducive to interest-group alliances. Even though a formidable array of interest groups geared up to oppose tax reform in 1986, each group wanted to protect its own tax preferences without appearing to oppose all reforms. The result was as much a subtle competition among interests as it was the presentation of a united opposition front.

Lobbying is a growth industry. Washington has blossomed with new consulting firms, law firms devoted to lobbying, and individual lobbyists-for-hire. It is a tough and sophisticated business. As more and more lobbyists crowd the nation's capital, access is at even more of a premium.

Techniques of Influence: Money and Elections

Interest groups want influence, and lobbying is only one way to get it. Money is another. More accurately, money provides *access* that can lead to influence. For that reason, interest groups play an active role in electoral politics and financing candidates for public office. The biggest change in financing American elections in the past fifteen years is the proliferation of **Political Action Committees (PACs),** an acronym that spells money. Figure 11-2 shows the dramatic increase in PACs, particularly corporate PACs. From around 600 in

FIGURE 11–2

GROWTH OF POLITICAL ACTION COMMITTEES, 1974–1989

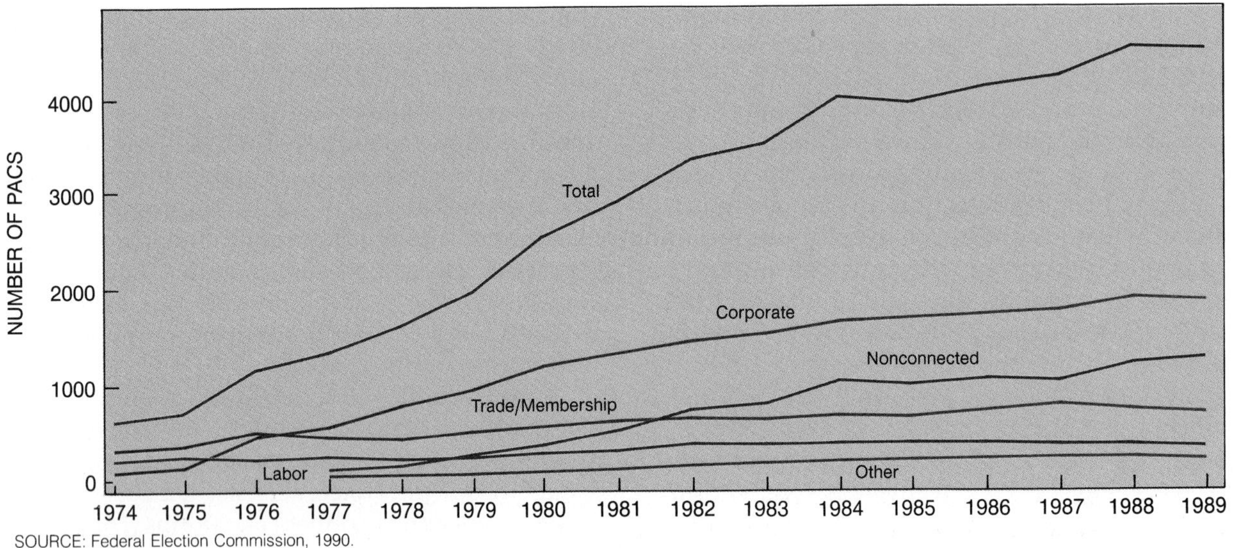

SOURCE: Federal Election Commission, 1990.

1974, the number of PACs had burgeoned to more than 4,200 by 1989.

THE RAPID GROWTH OF PACS

The 1988 congressional elections cost $458 mil-lion, and political action committees gave nearly $150 million, an increase of 250 percent in justeight years. PACs are important because of their influence on elections, and more ominous say the critics, their influence *after* the election. Political action committees arose to fill the vacuum created by the federal law that prohibited unions, businesses, and other interest groups from donating directly to election campaigns. Those organizations, however, were allowed to form political action committees and receive voluntary contributions from members or employees. The PAC, not the company, trade association, or union, then makes the contributions.

Today, political action committees come in every shape and size to support political candidates favored by a variety of diverse groups. Among the food industry one finds the American Bakers' Association BREADPAC, the Peanut Butter and Nut Processors Association's NUTPAC, the United Egg Producers' EGGPAC, the Whataburger Restaurant's WHATAPAC, the National Fisheries Institute FISH-PAC, and to wash it all down, either the Beer Wholesalers' SIXPAC or the nonalcoholic DR.PEPPER-PAC.[27]

The rapid growth of political action committees has come about through change in federal law. PACs are governed by the Federal Election Campaign Act of 1971 with amendments in 1974, 1976, and 1979, and by the Revenue Act of 1971.[28] Individuals and PACs are limited in the amounts they can donate to federal candidates in a given year: $1,000 a candidate, $5,000 to other political committees, and $20,000 per political party. However, if a PAC donates to more than five candidates, the direct limits rise to $5,000 a candidate. An even bigger loophole exists. A PAC may spend as much as it wants on behalf of a candidate so long as it does not donate it directly or coordinate activities with the campaign staff.[29] The Supreme Court affirmed the constitutionality of these so-called "independent" contributions in 1985. Each state has its own campaign finance laws, and significant variations exist across the nation.

The 1974 amendments to the campaign finance act opened the door to scores of new PACs. For the first time, it allowed government contractors to form political action committees. Suddenly, thousands of groups previously forbidden to make political contributions were permitted this kind of campaign activity. Political action committees can be divided into four types: corporate PACs, labor PACs, trade association PACs, and ideological PACs. Ideological, or "nonconnected," PACs are a recent addition to the roster of PACs whose main interest is more partisan and philosophical than economic. As a result, their political strategies are somewhat different from the other three types.

WHO GETS PAC MONEY?

PAC money now accounts for nearly 40 percent of all campaign contributions. The leading source of money remains contributions from individuals, including the candidates' own money. The Supreme Court, in the 1976 case of *Buckley v. Valeo,* struck down limits to what a candidate could contribute to his or her own campaign, once again opening the door to self-financed campaigns by millionaires. Prospective candidates have three options for financing a campaign: to use their own funds if they are wealthy; to pursue the time-consuming task of getting small, individual contributions; or to rely on PACs. Many have done the latter.

Overwhelmingly, the beneficiaries of PAC money are incumbents. Table 11-1 shows how PACs distribute money. Notice that almost 70 percent of all PAC contributions go to incumbents. Challengers get only 14 percent and even less from corporate and trade association PACs. Interest groups that PACs represent want access, and the safest bet is to give to those already in office. As a result, PACs are blamed for making it even more difficult for congressional challengers to defeat sitting members of Congress. Ideological PACs are less likely to give to incumbents than other PACs, but even they give nearly half to incumbents.

Because the Republican party is better funded than the Democratic party, Democrats rely on PAC money more than Republicans. The result is uncomfortable for a number of Democrats who fear the effects of PAC money but who are unwilling to eliminate a method that allows them to compete with the better-funded Republicans. Among PACs, different contribution patterns can be observed. By and large, labor unions give almost all their campaign dollars to Democrats—95 percent of it from the AFL-CIO. Business PACs, on the other hand, are more evenhanded. About two-thirds of their contributions go to Republicans, one-third to Democrats. Business plays both sides of the aisle and recognizes the importance of currying favor with moderate Democrats.

Most PACs give money to those who sympathize with their point of view or are in a position of authority over policies that most affect their interest group. Members of certain congressional committees are more likely to receive contributions than others. The House Committee on Energy and Commerce, which deals with issues of great concern to labor, industry, and environmentalists, has

TABLE 11–1

PAC CONTRIBUTIONS (IN %) TO INCUMBENT CHALLENGER AND OPEN SEAT CANDIDATES FOR CONGRESS, BY PARTY AFFILIATION, 1986

Type of Pac	Incumbent		Challenger		Open Seat	
	Democrat	Republican	Democrat	Republican	Democrat	Republican
Corporate	31.8%	44.5%	3.6%	4.3%	3.5%	12.3%
Labor	50.7	6.9	24.4	.1	17.4	.4
Association	37.9	39.2	5.5	3.0	5.3	9.0
Nonconnected	27.0	23.6	17.2	7.8	13.5	10.8
Other*	42.4	37.9	6.3	2.6	4.9	5.9
Total of all PACs	37.3	31.7	10.7	3.5	8.5	8.4

*Includes PACs of cooperatives and corporations without stock.

SOURCE: Federal Election Commission.

become the new darling of the PACs and one of the most requested committee assignments in the House. Average PAC contributions for the 1988 election were more than $100,000 per member. Several years ago, the first political action committee went over the $1 million mark. In 1986, sixteen gave more than $1 million!

IDEOLOGICAL PACs AND NEGATIVE CAMPAIGNS

One of the more ominous developments surrounding PACs is the smear campaigns waged by "nonconnected" PACs such as the **National Conservative Political Action Committee (NCPAC)**. NCPAC is an ideological group whose aim is not material gain but promoting a certain political philosophy. First emerging as a major force in the 1980 election, NCPAC with its "kamikaze" approach to campaigning became a feared symbol of the aggressive "new right." NCPAC's tactic was to spend millions of dollars mounting its own independent campaign (not given directly to the challenger) to defeat an incumbent whom it perceived as an ideological enemy. In 1980, NCPAC chose Senator Paul Sarbanes of Maryland as a target for defeat. It financed a massive media campaign against Sarbanes, stressing his support for "forced busing," even though he had opposed it on a number of occasions.[30] The NCPAC campaign attracted considerable national attention and provoked a strong reaction against its tactics. Even Sarbanes's Republican opponent denounced the campaign supposedly mounted on his behalf. The voters reacted with sympathy toward the incumbent, who was returned to office with 63 percent of the vote. In 1982, of the twenty-three members of Congress targeted by NCPAC in the election, only one was defeated. Nonetheless, the NCPAC attack alarmed many members, and its style has caught on.

Ideological PACs, which originated in 1977, expanded to more than 1,000 by 1988, growing faster than even corporate PACs. Some, such as Americans for Democratic Action and the Committee for an Effective Congress, support liberal candidates and issues. In general, they are not as well funded as conservative groups. Most of the nonconnected PACs—both liberal and conservative—take a more positive approach to politics than NCPAC.[31] Nonetheless, the sharp increase in negative campaigning pioneered by NCPAC provided impetus for serious campaign finance reform efforts in the 1990s.

Targets of Influence: Interest Groups and the Policy Process

We have looked at why groups form, some of the major interest groups, and their main techniques for influence—lobbying and campaign money. In this part of the chapter, we turn the relationship around by examining interest-group politics from the perspective of the target.

INTEREST GROUPS AND THE POLICY AGENDA

Agenda-setting—determining what becomes a public issue and what remains a private concern—is critical to the policy process. Interest groups play a critical role in determining the government's agenda. The most important targets in agenda-setting are the public at large and government officials. The creation of public issues is a complicated and fascinating aspect of politics. Why did environmental protection and ecology become an issue in the 1960s but not in the 1950s? Why was there sharp pressure for antitrust legislation in the 1890s, but not in the 1870s? The answer is a mix of public opinion, leadership, and timeliness.

Groups that enjoy direct access to the halls of government have the easiest time getting an issue on the policy agenda. Emerging interest groups, outside the mainstream of politics, do not have direct access. As a result, they are able to place issues on the policy agenda only by creating public sympathy, getting the attention of the media, or dramatically gaining the attention of government officials. Methods range from protest and direct action—such as sit-ins, marches, and demonstrations—to staging "media events." Educating the public to new dangers and new problems can be the key to moving an issue onto the policy agenda. The media play a crucial role in this process. Environmental quality, product safety, hunger, civil rights, and poverty were incorporated into the policy agenda through efforts of interests outside government. More recently, the anti-abortion movement, farmers, and religious groups have used similar techniques to move their issues to the public agenda. Getting on the agenda is only the first step. After that, the real work begins.

THE RESPONSE TO GROUP PRESSURE

How does interest-group pressure feel to the pressured? Is it viewed as helpful or harmful? Are decision-makers resistant or compliant? The answer depends on one's institutional vantage point.

CONGRESS. Lobbying used to be synonymous with legislative lobbying. Today, Congress shares interestgroup attention with the other branches. Yet in some ways, Congress remains the most vulnerable and receptive to interest-group pressure. The image of a weak legislature enslaved by powerful lobbyists is incorrect, but so is the view of an independent Congress resistent to lobbying. The truth lies in between. Although "Abscam," "Koreagate," and other scandals are a reminder that bribery still takes place, today's member of Congress is generally not susceptible to blatant nineteenth-century-style influence-peddling. Members of Congress are generally strong-willed individuals who respond poorly to threatening pressure. Instead, lobbyists are very deferential, stressing service and expertise. Legislators, in turn, view them as "harmless," more helpful than threatening, and their concerns as fitting nicely with members' own policy interests and reelection strategies. "What's wrong with PAC money?" many ask. "It reflects legitimate representation of various interests in the state or district."

Congress is open to interest-group influence for several reasons. First, it is a decentralized institution where power is dispersed. Specialization in Congress—more than 135 subcommittees in the House, for example—meshes with the specialization of interest groups. Second, members of Congress today are more like individual political entrepreneurs than loyal party members, and voting patterns reflect shifting coalitions. Third, strongly motivated by reelection needs, members emphasize tangible benefits to the district and serving constituents and groups. Interest groups are influential in Congress because group goals are often compatible with legislators' goals. From time to time, interest-group pressure creates difficult dilemmas. In many more cases, however, it is a mutually beneficial relationship. This, more than anything, explains interest-group success.

Sometimes, the relationship becomes too mutually beneficial. Five members of the U.S. Senate came under heavy criticism in 1989 for their alleged role in intervening with federal bank regulators on behalf of a wealthy contributor, Thomas Keating, owner of the Lincoln Savings and Loan. Senators Alan Cranston (D-Calif.), Dennis DeConcini (D-Ariz.), John Glenn (D-Ohio), John McCain (R-Ariz.), and Don Riegle (D-Mich.) received a total of $1.3 million in campaign contributions from Keating. The so-called "Keating Five" met with bank regulators in 1987. Later, the probe and possible takeover of Lincoln was delayed. Two years later, regulators finally seized Lincoln, but by then, it would cost taxpayers over $2 billion to bail out the mismanaged savings and loan. All five senators found nothing unusual about intervening with federal bureaucrats on behalf of a constituent and denied any undue influence because of Keating's contributions. Nonetheless, appearances of impropriety were obvious, and all five found themselves in deep political trouble.

THE PRESIDENCY. The president and the White House staff take a broader perspective on interest groups than Congress. While much of the interaction on Capitol Hill is between members and specific lobbyists, such as cotton farmers or beer wholesalers, the White House looks at groups more broadly in terms of popular support or potential opposition. The president is concerned with such diffuse groups as women, blacks, or the elderly. Group politics in the White House is conducted as much at a symbolic level as at a material level. Although interest-group appeals to the White House usually include some specific material "gestures," the intention is to create a general image of sympathy and concern. The president's goal is similarly broad: support for his policies and administration. Cabinet appointments may be made with a view to their symbolic importance to interest groups. Special messages to Congress may also be as much public relations for group support as policy-making. Interest-group politics in the White House, despite the existence of formal group liaisons, remain more general and symbolic than in Congress.

Charles Keating.

Despite this general orientation of the White House to broad societal groups, many lobbyists pressure specific individuals in the administration for favors. This became a problem for several former members of the Reagan administration who left their government posts to become lobbyists. Former top Reagan advisers Michael Deaver and Lyn Nofziger were convicted of illegally lobbying their former White House colleagues, although Nofziger's conviction was later overturned. Allegations of influence-peddling connected to his role in helping to place government contracts with groups friendly to the administration continued to plague Attorney General Edwin Meese until his resignation in mid-1988.

THE BUREAUCRACY. Because bureaucrats are not elected and do not need contributions from PACs, one might imagine the bureaucracy to be immune from interest-group pressure. Nothing could be further from the truth. Agencies are in competition with each other for scarce resources, budget dollars, and new programs. They too need political support. Interest groups and clients often form the foundation of agency political support that can be called on to promote the agencies' goals and programs. Because the bureaucracy is specialized, it shares specific goals with interest groups. The cozy arrangements of subgovernments allow all participants to minimize conflict, to engage in informal bargaining over details, and to dominate policymaking to their mutual benefit.

Interest groups play an important role in both the bureaucratic formulation and implementation stages of the policy process. Group opposition at the implementation stage can subvert an agency's goals. Bureaucrats are more likely to work with the interests than to fight them. Although there are numerous examples of unsuccessful group lobbying efforts in the bureaucracy, the more normal pattern is one of bargaining and cooperation.

THE COURTS. The rules of the game in court demand different interest-group tactics and strategies. Federal judges and justices are the most autonomous of national decision-makers, and pressure tactics to sway a decision are perceived as less legitimate.

Interest groups use the court system to pursue litigation. Groups use the advocacy system to seek both specific decisions and more sweeping declarations of judicial policy. Since the civil rights decisions in the 1930s began to chip away at segregation, public interest lawyers have turned to the courts to achieve their aims. The judicial strategy pursued by interest groups has loaded the dockets of American courts. Class action suits allow cases to be brought to court on behalf of entire groups, not just individuals, strengthening the ability of large groups that have difficulty organizing to press claims.

Interest groups sometimes attempt to influence a decision through **amicus briefs**—"friend of the court" position papers providing legal arguments and analysis of the facts of the case. Groups such as the American Civil Liberties Union (ACLU) have effectively used this device. Iran-Contra defendant Oliver North was the unlikely beneficiary of such a brief filed on his behalf by the ACLU in 1988. Interest groups lobby the White House for and against the appointment of judges and justices. Civil rights groups and women's groups were particularly active in the successful campaign to block the nomination of Robert Bork to the Supreme Court in 1987.

Courts are more immune from interest-group pressure than the other institutions of government, but it is a myth that the courts are apolitical or above group influence. Groups play a key role in determining the agenda of the courts. Judges read public opinion polls too. They are mindful of the support and coalitions behind the different sides in a case and may anticipate problems with the enforcement of decisions in the face of significant group opposition. Lacking their own enforcement powers, courts can be undermined if they totally ignore the competing interests along with the legal and constitutional arguments in a case.

Interest Groups and Governing

One of the most pervasive complaints about American politics is that it is dominated by special interests. Throughout history, many have argued that a government dominated by private interests cannot produce policies in the broader national interest. Critics claim that the power of interest groups cripples the ability to govern and undermines democracy. Instead of establishing national policies through representative institutions, governing becomes a series of private agreements between entrepreneurial interest groups and officials. According to Theodore Lowi, the free reign of interest groups "corrupts democratic government because it deranges and confuses expectations about

Are interest group politics and lobbying detrimental to the public interest or critical means through which groups such as these disabled demonstrators get their message across?

democratic institutions . . . and reveals a basic disrespect for democracy."[32]

Interest-group influence may be as much a result as a cause of governing problems. In a system of separate institutions sharing powers, without strong political parties, a vacuum of sorts is created. Interest groups have moved into the void, aggressively and effectively pursuing their goals. A government in awe of powerful interests will be timid and cautious in making policy. Because of the shifting interest-group alignments on major issues, elected leaders must spend more time building support for policies than devising good policies. Issues are considered in local and group perspectives rather than from a broad national perspective. Interest-group cross-pressures further fragment an already decentralized Congress, and stalemate is often the result.

The ability to govern is not the same as big or expansive government. In many cases, weak governments, vulnerable to interest groups, expand more rapidly than those able to govern effectively. Powerful interest groups can result in growth in the public sector, even when there is no national consensus to do so. Ronald Reagan, opponent of big government, also actively pursued political strategies to reduce the power of interest groups, which he believed contributed to the growth of government spending and stood in the way of policies more in the national interest.[33] His campaign for budget and tax cuts in 1981 and for tax reform in 1986 depended on overcoming interest-group opposition. He may have succeeded initially, but stalemate in the late 1980s over key issues left many groups more powerful than ever.

Americans are ambivalent about interest groups. Many recognize that interest groups provide important avenues of representation, but they deplore the special advantages, bribery, and corruption associated with them. Political action committees especially have aroused suspicion and led to calls for reform. Should something be done?

SHOULD LOBBYING BE MORE CLOSELY REGULATED?

Lobbying is currently governed by the Lobbying Registration Act of 1946, passed after decades of controversy over the power of interest groups. The legislation actually did little to limit the activities of groups. In the belief that public scrutiny would make lobbyists (and members of Congress) more accountable to the people, the law provides only for registration and disclosure.[34] Any group spending money with the "principal purpose" of influencing Congress must register and state its general objectives. Groups are also required to file reports with the Congress revealing how much they spent in their lobbying activities.

In 1954, the Supreme Court acted to narrow the applicability and focus of the act in its ruling on the definition of "principal purpose." Groups that performed "other functions" were exempted. Huge loopholes in the law were created because most groups claimed objectives other than influencing Congress. The Court further ruled that individuals spending their own money to lobby were exempt as well. Groups have great flexibility in reporting spending, leading to official reports of ridiculously low figures from some of the biggest lobbyists. Spending for grass-roots mobilization does not have to be reported at all. Only money spent for direct contact with legislators is subject to reporting, and contact between lobbyists and professional staff is ignored as well. The combination of a weak act and a further narrowing by the Court has left the practice of lobbying with few restrictions or limits.

In the ensuing forty years, numerous attempts have been made to strengthen the law or to pass a more comprehensive act. Following the Watergate investigation, with its revelations of abuses, Congress made a serious attempt to pass new legislation. In 1976, the Senate passed a lobbying disclosure bill by an overwhelming margin. Across the Capitol, despite the vigorous opposition of most lobbyists, the House passed a bill after fourteen days of heated debate. But conferees could not reach agreement before the end of the session, and the legislation died. In 1977, advocates of reform again worked hard to report a new bill. Opponents from virtually every interest group in the country made the task difficult, and ultimately no bill was passed. After those two failures, momentum for reform faded, and to date no legislation has been passed to replace the weak 1946 act.

Political scientist Norman Ornstein summarizes the major issues about regulation of lobbying:[35]

1. Which groups should be required to register?
2. Should indirect, grassroots lobbying be included?
3. Should lobbying of the executive branch be regulated?
4. How specific should the reporting requirements be?
5. Should contributors names be disclosed?
6. How could the law be enforced?
7. How much regulation is constitutional under the First Amendment?

These remain very controversial questions. Public interest groups such as Common Cause and Nader's Congress Watch have pushed hard to reform lobbying. Yet even these groups do not agree on the specific provisions of a new law. There is a contradictory element to lobbying reform. Most people believe Congress is too vulnerable to special interest influence, yet they increasingly use the group system to have their own interests represented.[36] While calls for greater control of lobbying continue, much more momentum was building to limit PACs and reform campaign financing.

SHOULD PACS BE RESTRICTED?

Congress and the states created political action committees, and they could restrict them. The seemingly innocent 1974 amendments to the Campaign Finance Act turned out to be a Pandora's box leading to the rapid growth of PACs. With increasing influence obvious in both total numbers of PACs and their proportion of contributions to campaign spending, many have misgivings about the influence of PACs. But will Congress kill the goose that laid the golden egg?

Reformers in Congress have submitted legislation to curb the influence of PACs. Several years ago, more than 140 House members co-sponsored a bill that would limit PAC contributions and encourage small, individual contributions. Advocated by Common Cause, H.R. 4428 in the Ninety-eighth Congress would have permitted House candidates who agreed to limit total spending to $240,000 in the general election to offer individuals a 100 percent tax credit on contributions up to $100. Candidates who participated would be prohibited from contributing more than $20,000 of their own money and from accepting more than $90,000 from PACs. Senators in the 100th Congress struggled with a campaign finance reform bill for two years. The bill, S.2, sponsored by David Boren (D-Okla.) and forty-three co-sponsors, would have placed limits on PAC contributions to Senate candidates, set overall spending limits depending on the population of the state, and provided for some public financing for candidates who voluntarily agreed to accept the restrictions. The bill met stiff opposition not only from interest groups but also from Senate Republicans, who filibustered the bill during debate. Throughout 1987 and 1988, the Democratic majority in the Senate fell short of the sixty votes needed to break the filibuster and pass the bill.

Are interest groups too powerful in American politics? The question continues to stir controversy and debate. Pluralists argue that groups are the basis of democracy, whereas others claim that groups subvert democracy. Some see interest groups as the key to representation; others see them as a barrier to governing. The difficulty reformers have had in regulating lobbying practices and PAC financing of campaigns demonstrates both the public ambivalence about interest groups and the power of the groups who oppose restrictions.

SUMMARY AND CONCLUSIONS

1. Groups have always been an important part of American politics, although their role is controversial. Pluralists claim that groups are the most essential element to understanding how politics works.

2. Groups form to pursue a common interest. Small groups are more likely to form than large groups, because it is not in an individual's material interest to voluntarily join a large organization. Group formation is fostered by economic change, government policy, and the decline of political parties.

3. Recent trends in group politics include the rapid increase in the number of groups, the growth of new public interest groups, the growing importance of PACs, the rise of single-issue groups, and the increasing sophistication of grass-roots lobbying methods.
4. Public interest groups do not seek direct material benefits for their members. Environmental, consumer, women's groups, and groups like Common Cause are examples of public interest groups that have grown rapidly since the 1960s.
5. The major private interests in politics are generally organized for economic reasons. The traditional groups include business, labor, agriculture, and many others. Business groups have taken the lead in developing new, more sophisticated lobbying techniques.
6. The major techniques of influence are lobbying and financing election campaigns. Lobbying techniques can be focused on direct contact with public officials, mobilization of grassroots support, or the building of alliances with other groups. Campaign contributions are made primarily through political action committees (PACs); their purpose is to gain access to Congress.
7. One primary purpose of interest groups is to get their issues on the policy agenda. The targets of interest-group influence are the Congress, the presidency, the bureaucracy, and the courts. The key to understanding interest-group influence is the nature of decision-making in the different institutions and the commonality of goals between policy-makers and interest groups.
8. Critics argue that special interests are creating a crisis of governing and that lobbying and PACs should be restricted. Defenders suggest interest groups are one of the best means of representation in the political system.

Despite the growth of public interest groups, most interests in the United States are organized to pursue the material economic benefit of some segment of society. Interest groups spend millions of dollars in lobbying and campaigns because there are billions of dollars at stake! Pressure from special interests strains the decision-making capability of the legislature. As we shall see in the next chapter, the ability of Congress to govern is severely tested by economic interests and reelection pressures operating in a fragmented policy process.

KEY TERMS

AFL-CIO
amicus briefs
collective goods
Common Cause
elitist theory
free rider problem
grassroots mobilization
interest groups
lobbyists
Lobby Registration Act
Ralph Nader
National Conservative Political Action Committee (NCPAC)
National Rifle Association (NRA)
pluralism
political action committees (PACs)
private goods
public interest groups
single-issue groups

SELF-REVIEW

1. What functions do interest groups play in American politics?
2. Why do groups form?
3. What is the climate for interest-group formation in the United States?
4. Describe some recent trends in group politics.
5. What are the differences between public interest groups and private interest groups?
6. What are the origins of lobbying?
7. How do lobbyists attempt to influence public policy?
8. Why has the importance of PACs grown so rapidly?
9. How do interest groups affect elections?
10. How do interest groups try to affect the policy agenda?
11. Why is Congress open to group pressure?
12. Describe some tactics used by interest groups to secure their goals through the courts.
13. What are some arguments for regulating lobbying? for restricting PACs?

SUGGESTED READINGS

Berry, Jeffrey. *The Interest Group Society.* 1989.
A good study of interest groups, their organization, motivation, and impact on politics.

Cigler, Allan J., and Burdett A. Loomis, eds. *Interest Group Politics.* 2nd ed. 1986.
An excellent collection of readings dealing with the most recent developments in interest groups, including PACs, single-issue groups, and changing techniques of influence.

Olson, Mancur. *The Logic of Collective Action.* 1965.
A difficult but extremely important book that has changed our fundamental understanding of interest-group formation and membership.

Sorauf, Frank J. *Money in American Elections.* 1988.
A study of the history, sources, and effect of money on American elections at all levels.

Bernbaum, Jeffrey and Allen Murray. *Showdown at Gucci Gulch.* 1987.
A lively story of the Tax Reform Act of 1986 as a clash of lobbyists dressed in their expensive Italian shoes.

Notes

1. *New York Times,* 20 March, 1990, p. 1.
2. Theodore Lowi, *The End of Liberalism* (New York: Norton, 1979).
3. See Norman J. Ornstein and Shirley Elder, *Interest Groups, Lobbying, and Policymaking* (Washington, D.C.: Congressional Quarterly Press, 1978), 7-8.
4. James Madison, "Federalist No. 10," in *The Federalist* (New York: New American Library, 1960).
5. Arthur F. Bentley, *The Process of Government* (San Antonio, Tex.: Principia, 1949; Originally published in 1908).
6. David Truman, *The Governmental Process* (New York: Knopf, 1951).
7. Lester Milbrath, *The Washington Lobbyists* (Chicago: Rand McNally, 1963), 298.
8. See E. E. Schattschneider, *The Semisovereign People* (New York: Holt, Rinehart and Winston, 1960).
9. Allan J. Cigler and Burdett A. Loomis, eds., *Interest Group Politics,* 2nd ed. (Washington, D.C.: Congressional Quarterly Press, 1986), 1-26.
10. Ibid., 21.
11. Mancur Olson, *The Logic of Collective Action* (Cambridge, Mass.: Harvard University Press, 1965), 2.
12. See Terry M. Moe, *The Organization of Interests* (Chicago: University of Chicago Press, 1980).
13. Robert H. Salisbury, "An Exchange Theory of Interest Groups," *Midwest Journal of Political Science* 12 (February 1969): 1-32.
14. Cigler and Loomis, *Interest Group Politics,* 19.
15. Ibid., 1-28.
16. Jeffrey Berry, *Lobbying for the People* (Princeton: Princeton University Press, 1977), 7.
17. Ibid., 14.
18. Ibid., 40-42.
19. Jack Walker, "The Origins and Maintenance of Interest Groups" (Paper presented at the annual meeting of the American Political Science Association, New York, September 2-4, 1981).
20. *Congressional Quarterly Weekly Reports,* 28 August, 1982, p. 2115.
21. Robert H. Salisbury, "Interest Groups: Toward a New Understanding," in Cigler and Loomis, *Interest Group Politics* (1982 ed.), 361.
22. Allan J. Cigler, "From Protest Group to Interest Group: The Making of American Agricultural Movement, Inc.," in Cigler and Loomis, *Interest Group Politics,* 46-49.
23. Douglas Cater, *Power in Washington* (New York: Random House, 1964), 206.
24. Carol Greenwald, *Group Power* (New York: Praeger, 1977), 68-70.
25. Thomas Burns, *Tales of I.T.T.: An Insider's Story* (Boston: Houghton Mifflin, 1974), 107-108.
26. Greenwald, *Group Power,* 70.
27. Larry Sabato, *PAC Power* (New York: Norton, 1984), 25.
28. Herbert Alexander, *Financing Politics* (Washington, D.C.: Congressional Quarterly Press, 1980).
29. M. Margaret Conway, "PACs, the New Politics, and Congressional Campaigns," in Cigler and Loomis, *Interest Group Politics,* 127.
30. Ibid., 135.
31. Margaret Ann Latus, "Assessing Ideological PACs: From Outrage to Understanding," in Michael Malbin, *Money and Politics in the United States* (Chatham, N.J.: Chatham House, 1984), 142–71.
32. Lowi, *End of Liberalism,* 296.
33. Harold Wolman and Fred Teitelbaum, "Interest Groups and the Reagan Presidency," in Lester M. Salamon and Michael S. Lund, eds., *The Reagan Presidency and the Governing of America* (Washington, D.C.: Urban Institute, 1985), 297-330.
34. Ornstein and Elder, *Interest Groups,* 102.
35. Ibid., 110.
36. Ibid., 113.

SECTION THREE

National Institutions and Policy-Making

Section III focuses on the key decision-making institutions of American politics—the Congress, the presidency, the bureaucracy, and the judicial system—which work together to govern the nation. Chapter 12 looks at Congress, created by the Founders as the "first branch" of government. In recent years, conflict between serving the needs of local constituents and functioning as a national lawmaker has left Congress with a governing crisis of its own. The presidency, the most visible feature in the political landscape of the nation, is the subject of Chapter 13. Expanding presidential roles and responsibilities, the organization of the White House, and the mobilization of political resources to govern are examined. Chapter 14 confronts perhaps the most important relationship in determining the governing ability of the political system, that between Congress and the president. Executive-legislative relations continue to be one of the most interesting, if frustrating, elements of American politics. Not to be overlooked among policy-making institutions and processes, the highly political federal bureaucracy is analyzed in Chapter 15. The bureaucracy does much more than administer the laws. Through implementation, regulation, and the formation of alliances with interest groups and congressional subcommittees, the bureaucracy affects governing ability. Finally, the judicial system is considered in Chapter 16. The federal courts, headed by the Supreme Court, have been involved in some of the most controversial policy decisions of this generation. The major institutions of national government operate on a daily basis within their own sphere. But the policy-making process and the ability to govern ultimately depend on how well they work together.

CHAPTER 12

Congress

POLITICAL CLOSE-UP

The Fall of a Speaker

A hush came over the packed chamber of the House of Representatives as Speaker Jim Wright of Texas walked to the podium. It was 4 P.M. on the afternoon of May 31, 1989. Anticipation hung in the air. "Let this be a final payment," Wright spoke with emotion in his voice. "Let me give you back this job as a propitiation for all of this season of bad will that has grown among us." His voice tailed off to a whisper, "Give it back to you." The Speaker of the House had given up his post and resigned from Congress. The most powerful member of Congress, third in line for the presidency, was driven from office as a result of alleged ethics violations.

Wright had assumed the speakership in January 1987, only a little more than two years earlier, following the retirement of Tip O'Neill. In those years, Congress had enjoyed one of its most productive legislative sessions. Wright was first elected to Congress in 1954, the year the Democrats recaptured the House from the Republicans. It had been a good year for Texas Democrats as Sam Rayburn became Speaker and Lyndon Johnson became Senate majority leader. Over the next three and a half decades, the Democrats would never lose control of the House. Wright climbed up the leadership ladder slowly, first becoming majority whip, then majority leader, and finally Speaker. In the 100th Congress, his only full term as presiding officer, Wright was acknowledged to be the most powerful and effective Speaker since the legendary Rayburn in the 1950s. But after a year of investigations by the House Ethics Committee, even many Democrats were relieved by Wright's departure.

The drama had begun a year earlier when Wright's archenemy, Republican Newt Gingrich of Georgia, filed ethics charges against him. The credibility of the charges were enhanced when the nonpartisan watchdog-group Common Cause also called for an investigation. The charges centered on two main complaints: first, that Wright had accepted money from long-time friend George Mallick and had intervened to influence legislation that affected Mallick; and second, that Wright had used royalties on a book he had written to evade outside income limitations. The book scheme was centered on *Confessions of a Public Man,* a 117-page paperback that had been published by a friend and paid Wright an astronomical 55 percent royalty. Instead of giving Wright honoraria for making speeches before them, groups would buy as many as several thousand copies of his book. Since outside honoraria are limited, the Ethics Committee accused Wright of using book sales to avoid normal income limits.

The Speaker appeared to be politically strong enough to weather the storm of controversy over the charges as 1989 began. But pressure mounted when several Democrats on the Ethics Committee agreed that as many as sixty-nine violations had occurred. Wright's fate was sealed when he appeared personally before the Ethics Committee in televised hearings to defend himself on technical and legal points, which only contributed to the perception that the charges were correct. The growing controversy created even more tension and ill will between Republicans and Democrats. Countercharges were filed by angry Democrats against Gingrich for a book scheme of his own. But in the end, even Wright's allies realized that his political support had so eroded that the Democrat's ability to run the House was in jeopardy.

In his emotional speech on May 31, Wright spent most of the forty-five minutes refuting the accusations point by point. He angrily defended his wife's role in the affair. He portrayed himself as the victim of "self-appointed vigilantes" but ended with the admonition to all House members that "all of us, in both political parties, must resolve to bring this period of mindless cannibalism to an end."

CHAPTER OUTLINE

INTRODUCTION AND OVERVIEW

The U.S. Congress is almost unique in the world; it is a national legislature with an important, independent impact on public policy. Article I of the Constitution established Congress as the "first branch" of government. The popularly elected House of Representatives was the Founders' most democratic creation, and Congress, the "repository of public will," was the basis for popular democracy. Although relative power has periodically swung between Congress and the president, Congress has always maintained a meaningful role in policy-making. Today, the future is in doubt as Congress faces its own crisis of governing. Despite its influence, Congress has developed a singularly bad reputation among the public it serves. Except during Watergate, the American people have rated Congress far below the president in performance.

Congress plays two increasingly disparate roles. One role is lawmaker, making public policies that govern the nation. The other role is local representative, articulating the viewpoints of various interests in society and securing tangible benefits for individual districts. The two roles clash, and the former seems to be losing. Mounting evidence indicates that members are emphasizing the role of local representative in the interest of securing reelection. As a consequence, Congress' ability to act collectively—to govern—is suffering. Much of the public dissatisfaction with Congress arises in response to its dubious performance as a national policy-maker.

There is an interesting twist to the low evaluations of Congress. The same public that rates Congress poorly as an institution rates its own individual members highly and returns incumbents to office with remarkable regularity. Why does the public love its own members of Congress so much more than it loves Congress? This chapter tries to explain that dichotomy and the governing problems facing Congress by exploring the following questions:

1. How do congressional elections shape the membership of Congress and create the conflict between the roles of national lawmaker and local representative?
2. What explains the phenomenal success of incumbents in their efforts to get reelected? Why has electoral competition declined, and what are the implications?
3. What is the nature of representation in Congress? Should a representative follow the instructions of his or her district or vote on the basis of conscience and personal convictions?
4. How does the legislative process in Congress operate? How does it determine Congress' role in national policy-making?
5. What part does the committee system play in the legislative process? Why did subcommittees increase in number and influence until recently? power?
6. How is party leadership organized, and how do leaders attempt to overcome the decentralization and fragmentation of Congress?
7. How have party leaders and key committees been strengthened in recent years to help Congress make policy?

Elections, Incumbency, and Governing

CAREERISM AND THE MODERNIZATION OF CONGRESS

In the 1800s, Congress was a "citizen legislature," not a "professional legislature" made up of permanent, career politicians. Being a member of Congress was a part-time job with important responsibilities but unattractive features: the long trip to Washington, low pay, separation from families, homes, and jobs, and notoriously hot and humid summers in the District of Columbia.

The high rate of turnover began to decline after the Civil War. More and more members ran for reelection and returned to serve for several terms. The average length of service in the House of Representatives remained at two years (one term) until the 1870s. By the turn of the century, the average stay had increased to two terms, and by 1970, after a century of increase, the average member of the House stayed for five terms, or nearly ten years. Many stayed much longer than that. Representative Carl Hayden was elected to the House in 1912, the year his state of Arizona entered the Union. He later was elected and reelected to the Senate for continuous service in Congress of more than fifty years. In the 1960s, Hayden was only one of several members in their eighties and nineties. A seat in Congress had become a real career, and members fought hard to keep it. As turnover declined, Congress became a much more stable institution with more established rules, norms, and patterns of behavior.

Electoral stability accompanied other changes.[1] Workloads and the length of sessions increased. While Congress met less than six months a year in the nineteenth century, since the 1940s, Congress has been in almost continuous session. Rules to expedite legislative business and general orderliness increased. With less turnover, membership on committees stabilized. Longevity and careerism were rewarded by the **seniority system.** Continuous service on a committee became the sole criterion for determining which member of the majority party would become chair. Committees

Henry Clay addressing the Senate in 1850; turnover of membership was high in this era.

came to dominate, becoming the "little legislatures," where Congress did most of its work. By 1900, party leadership organizations had emerged to keep the House and Senate running smoothly.

THE LOCALIZATION OF CONGRESSIONAL ELECTIONS

Elections played a major role in determining what went on inside Congress when turnover was high. Recent changes in elections hold the key to understanding Congress today. Tied to the decline of political parties and the increased clout of interest groups and PACs, congressional elections are now dominated by individual candidates and their campaign organizations. A congressional election today is less a national election than a set of local contests for 435 House seats and 34 Senate seats. Political scientist Gary Jacobsen describes the ascendancy of the individual:

> Congressional campaigns are overwhelmingly candidate centered. Although national parties have recently expanded their efforts to recruit and finance candidates, most serious congressional aspirants operate, of choice and necessity, as individual political entrepreneurs. The risks, rewards, and pains of mounting a campaign are largely theirs. Most instigate their own candidacies, raise their own resources, and put together their own campaign organizations.[2]

Candidate-centered local elections contrast with the more typical system of party-centered national elections. In a parliamentary system, such as Great Britain's, the party controls access of candidates to the legislative body. A candidate not reselected by the party to run would face certain defeat. The same is true in most democracies, where often the names and symbols of parties, not the names of individual candidates, appear on the ballot. In the United States, the local party needs the member of Congress, not vice versa. When Congressman Phil Gramm of Texas was thrown off the Budget Committee by the House Democrats for his active support of President Reagan, he resigned, switched parties, and won overwhelming reelection as a Republican. Elections that are centered on local candidates rather than on national parties produce members who are independent and individualistic. Not only do the candidates have control of their own electoral destinies, but they also are phenomenally successful at it.

THE PERMANENT CONGRESS?

In the 1982, 1984, 1986, and 1988 congressional elections, a combined total of only fifty House seats in the country changed party hands. Despite the decline of party as a cohesive bond between legislative and executive branches, electoral competition has fallen off significantly. Table 12-1 shows the reelection rates for incumbents since 1946. Congressional elections in 1986 and 1988 produced record success rates for incumbents. In 1988, only nine House seats switched party control, and 402 incumbents were reelected, both a record.[3] Only six incumbents were defeated for a record reelection rate of 98.4 percent, breaking the record of 98 percent set two years earlier. Incumbents won by larger margins than ever. Only 36 of 435 winners received less than 55 percent of the vote in 1988. In the 1954 elections, by comparison, over 100 members won by less than 55 percent of the vote.

Of those incumbents who did manage to lose, the majority were defeated because of some sort of personal scandal or indiscretion, rather than by party or policy factors. For example, Georgia Republican Pat Swindall, one of the six incumbents defeated in 1988, was indicted just weeks before the election for laundering drug money. The picture of the House of Representatives is an institution insulated from electoral change, what some have called the "permanent Congress."

In recent years, Senate elections have proven more responsive to national voting trends than House elections. In the past decade, incumbency reelection rates have varied from a low of 55 percent in 1980 to a high of 93 percent in 1982. It is ironic

TABLE 12–1

REELECTION RATES OF HOUSE AND SENATE INCUMBENTS, 1946–1988

Year	% Reelected of Those Seeking Reelection	Year	% Reelected of Those Seeking Reelection
House		Senate	
1946	82	1946	57
1948	79	1948	60
1950	91	1950	69
1952	91	1952	65
1954	93	1954	75
1956	95	1956	86
1958	90	1958	64
1960	93	1960	97
1962	92	1962	83
1964	87	1964	85
1966	88	1966	88
1968	97	1968	71
1970	95	1970	77
1972	94	1972	74
1974	88	1974	85
1976	96	1976	64
1978	94	1978	60
1980	91	1980	55
1982	90	1982	93
1984	95	1984	90
1986	98	1986	77
1988	98	1988	85

SOURCE: Randall B. Ripley, *Congress: Process and Policy* (New York: Norton, 1983). Updated for 1984, 1986, and 1988.

that the Senate now provides greater measure of electoral responsiveness than the House, given the Founders' intention that the Senate and bicameralism protect against impulsive electoral swings in the House. Yet even in the Senate, incumbency remains a potent force. In three of the past five elections, an average of 85 percent of Senate incumbents were returned to office.

In the past half century, the Democrats have held an average of 254 seats in the House.[4] Since 1982, when the Republican gains of the 1980 election were wiped out, House Democrats have been close to this equilibrium level with 253, 258, and 260 seats respectively. Until some powerful, short-term political forces change the composition of the House from this historical norm, as occurred in 1980, incumbency success and low turnover are likely to remain.

"Declining Marginals?"

Political scientist David Mayhew first brought attention to the phenomenon of **"declining marginals"** in 1974, noting the reduction in the number of marginal election victories in the House of Representatives since the late 1940s.[5] Defining marginality as winning by 55 percent or less, he observed that these marginal swing seats had declined from one in five districts in 1948 to one in thirteen in 1970. But had the marginals really declined? Gary Jacobsen argued that members of the House were no less vulnerable to electoral defeat than they were forty years ago.[6] While incumbents' average margin of victory increased, he observed, their electoral safety did not. In the 1950s, 55 to 60 percent of the vote was needed in an election to virtually assure reelection two years later. In the 1980s, to achieve the same statistical probability of reelection two years hence, a member had to garner 60 to 65 percent of the vote. With the decline of political parties, voters proved to be more volatile than in earlier decades.

Recent analysis suggests that, despite the increased volatility of voters, marginal districts and electoral competition have declined significantly. Once losers who were involved in some sort of scandal are removed from the calculations, the proportion of vote needed to win the next election is identical to what it was in the 1950s.[7] Today, the chances of a scandal-free, unredistricted incumbent losing is practically nil. Freshmen legislators in particular have benefited. In the 1950s, some 15 percent of freshmen members were defeated at the next election, compared to only 4.4 percent of more senior members.[8] By the 1970s, only 6.1 percent of freshmen were defeated in their first reelection bid.

Incumbency Advantages

Congressional incumbents have become immune from defeat for a multitude of reasons. With weakening party ties, voters increasingly respond to cues from incumbents who have the perquisites of office. Mayhew explains,

> If a group of planners sat down and tried to design a pair of American national assemblies with the goal of serving members' reelection needs year in and year out, they would be hard pressed to improve on what exists.[9]

The combination of salary, staff in Washington and in the district, travel allowances, office allowances, and other perks is worth millions of dollars. Members sell themselves using sophisticated marketing techniques that keep their names in front of the public. In one recent year, four billion pieces of franked mail were sent out.[10]

Incumbents are also able to remain in office because of the shortage of strong challengers—well-financed, experienced politicians willing to run. Keeping strong challengers out of the race is a key element to remaining in office and is closely tied to fund-raising and PACs. The 1988 Senate race in New York was an example of the politics of "preclusion." Democratic incumbent Senator Daniel Patrick Moynihan, with millions already collected over the previous five years, began running television commercials in early 1988. Coincidentally or not, about this time, the most viable Republican challengers—who were popular office holders—announced they would not file for the Senate race. Six months before the balloting, Moynihan's seat was secured. This pattern is even more prevalent today in House races. In 1988, eighty-one members—nearly one-fifth of the House—had no opponent at all. Political action committees contribute around 40 percent of congressional campaign funds. As we have seen, this PAC money overwhelmingly goes to incumbents, which serves to further stifle electoral competition.

SARGENT Copyright 1990 Austin American-Statesman. Reprinted with permission of UNIVERSAL PRESS SYNDICATE. All rights reserved.

Consequences for Governing and Public Policy

Declining competition in congressional elections has many consequences. As part of their strategy to get reelected, incumbents emphasize the delivery of benefits—pork-barrel and services—to the district. Such activities are noncontroversial and likely win more votes than they lose. At the same time, more and more candidates shy away from controversial national issues for fear of offending large numbers of voters. Political Insight 12-1 takes a humorous look at how a legislator can straddle the fence on any controversial issue. While incumbents are more secure, congressional campaigns are less substantive and relevant, focusing on credit-taking rather than major national issues. The legislative process is affected as members hunt for political cover when called on to deal with controversial issues. Policies have become more particularized; every member wants a small piece of the pie, making it difficult to target resources where they are most needed.

The insulation of Congress from electoral change is pervasive but not complete. Periodically, in elections such as occurred in 1964, 1974, and 1980, important changes in the composition of Congress take place. Even a small change in the partisan makeup of Congress can have important effects on ideology and policy. Table 12-2 shows party control of Congress, incumbents defeated, and open seats lost since 1954. In years in which the economy is performing poorly, stronger challengers are likely to file against incumbents of the president's party, increasing the probability of some turnover.[11] But this is a tenuous link at best. The overwhelming trend is toward congressional elections "decoupled" from presidential elections, isolated from

TABLE 12–2

CONTROL OF CONGRESS, BY PARTY, 1954–1988

House

Year	Before Election D	Before Election R	Incumbents Lost by D	Incumbents Lost by R	Open Seats Lost by D	Open Seats Lost by R	After Election D	After Election R
1954	213	218	3	18	2	3	232	203
1956	230	201	7	7	2	4	234	201
1958	232	195	1	35	0	14	283	153
1960	281	153	23	2	6	6	262	175
1962	263	174	9	5	2	3	259	176
1964	254	176	5	39	5	8	295	140
1966	294	139	39	1	4	3	248	187
1968	245	187	5	0	2	4	243	192
1970	243	187	2	9	6	8	255	180
1972	256	176	6	3	9	5	244	191
1974	248	187	4	36	2	13	291	144
1976	286	145	7	5	3	7	292	143
1978	285	146	14	5	8	6	276	159
1980	273	159	27	3	10	1	243	192
1982	241	192	1	22	4	6	269	166
1984	267	168	14	3	5	1	253	182
1986	253	182	1	5	8	7	258	177
1988	255	177	2	4	1	2	260	175

Senate

Year	Before Election D	Before Election R	Incumbents Lost by D	Incumbents Lost by R	Open Seats Lost by D	Open Seats Lost by R	After Election D	After Election R
1954	47	49	2	4	1	1	49	47
1956	49	47	1	3	3	1	49	47
1958	51	47	0	11	0	2	64	34
1960	66	34	1	0	1	0	64	36
1962	64	36	2	3	0	3	68	32
1964	66	34	1	3	0	0	68	32
1966	67	33	1	0	2	0	64	36
1968	63	37	4	0	3	2	58	42
1970	57	43	3	2	1	0	55	45
1972	55	45	1	4	3	2	57	43
1974	58	42	0	2	1	3	62	38
1976	62	38	5	4	2	3	62	38
1978	62	38	5	2	3	3	59	41
1980	59	41	9	0	3	0	47	53
1982	46	54	1	1	1	1	46	54
1984	45	55	1	2	0	1	47	53
1986	47	53	0	7	1	2	55	45
1988	54	46	1	3	2	1	55	45

NOTE: The table lists seats held by Democrats (D) and Republicans (R) in the House and Senate just before each election since 1954 and just after the election. Seats that changed control as the result of a vacancy (caused by death or resignation) or when two incumbents faced each other are not included. Independents are included with the party they joined for committee assignments.

SOURCE: *National Journal*, 29 October 1983, p. 2261. Updated for 1984, 1986, and 1988 results.

POLITICAL INSIGHT 12–1

DEAR MR. CONGRESSMAN, WHAT IS YOUR POSITION ON BOOZE?

A well-traveled letter supplied by former Congressman William Hungate pokes some fun at the tendency of many members of Congress to make "strongly neutral" replies to constituents.

Dear Friend,

I had not intended to make a statement or take a position on this controversial subject at this time. However, I am not afraid of controversy, and I am willing to make my position clear on any question.

If, when you say "booze," you mean the devil's brew, the poison scourge, the bloody monster that defiles innocence, dethrones reason, destroys the home, creates misery and poverty—yea, literally takes the bread from the mouths of little children; if you mean the evil drink that topples good men and women from the pinnacles of righteous living into the bottomless pit of degradation and despair, shame and helplessness and hopelessness, then certainly I am against it.

But, if when you say "booze," you mean the oil of conversation, the philosophic wine, the ale that is consumed when good fellows get together, that puts a song in their hearts, and laughter on their lips and the warm glow of contentment in their eyes; if you mean Christmas cheer, the stimulating drink that puts the spring in the old gentleman's step on a frosty morning; if you mean the drink that enables a man to magnify his joy and his happiness and to forget, if only for a little while, life's great tragedies and heartbreaks; if you mean that which brings into our treasuries untold millions of dollars which are used to provide tender care for our little crippled children, our blind, our deaf, our dumb, our pitiful aged and infirm, to build highways, hospitals and schools, then certainly I am for it.

This is my position, sir, and I will not compromise.

Sincerely,

Your Member of Congress

national trends, soft on issues, and providing little impetus for governing.

The resulting independence and autonomy of legislators make it difficult to build coalitions in Congress. Alignments rarely last for more than a single set of votes. These factors also make it difficult for the political parties to impose discipline. How can the Speaker or majority leader get members to go along with the party when the party had little to do with their election in the first place? Interest groups compete for legislators' attention, and interests with lots of money and lots of members tend to get heard. Reelection pressures affect the kind of legislation Congress passes. What kind of members survive and thrive in this altered political world? Who are the legislators, and how well do they represent the public?

Legislators

THE MEMBERS OF CONGRESS

Who are the 100 senators and 435 representatives elected to serve in Congress? Senators, appointed by state legislatures until 1912, are now elected to six-year terms by the voters of each state. Representatives run for reelection every two years; campaigns are never too far away. A profile of members of the 101st Congress (1989-90) is presented in Table 12-3. The average member of Congress is a white Protestant male lawyer around fifty years of age who has already served several terms in Congress. Less than 5 percent are women, and a slightly smaller number are black. The youngest member was twenty-six years old, the oldest was eighty-three.

TABLE 12–3

PROFILE OF MEMBERS OF THE 101ST CONGRESS (1989–90)

	No. of Members	% of Congress
Gender		
Male	508	95%
Female	27	5
Race		
Black	24	4
Hispanic	12	2
White, other	499	93
Age (given in years)		
Average for House	52.1 (years old)	
Average for Senate	55.6 (yrs. old)	
Education		
Attended college	525	98
No college	10	2
Religion		
Protestant	353	66
Catholic	139	27
Jewish	39	7
Other	4	1
Occupation[a]		
Law	247	46
Business	166	32
Professional politician	114	21
Education	53	9
Journalism	25	5
Farming	23	5
Professional sports/ entertaiment	5	1

[a]Multiple responses allowed.

SOURCE: *Congressional Quarterly Weekly Report,* 12 November 1988, pp. 3293–95.

Does the membership represent the American people? Can blacks be properly represented by whites? Are women well represented by men? Are college students well represented by people who are seventy years old? **Representation** is a concept with several meanings.[12] One dimension, called *descriptive representation,* is based on the degree to which the membership of Congress reflects the general population. Table 12-3 shows that Congress does not profile the general population very well.

Imagine what a perfectly representative Congress (in a descriptive sense) would look like. It would be 52 percent female, 12 percent black, 8 percent Hispanic. The average age would be twenty-eight instead of fifty. Only 1 percent, not half, would be attorneys. In their places we would see plumbers, auto workers, full-time housewives, and elementary school teachers.

Taken to this extreme, descriptive representation seems silly. But it is very important in American politics, particularly for women, blacks, and Hispanics. Legislators are role models to others and provide visible evidence of whether the halls of government are equally open to all citizens, regardless of gender, race, or national origin. But legislators do not always act on the basis of their race, gender, age, occupation, or socioeconomic background. For example, liberal white male voters who support abortion rights and cuts in national defense would be better represented by Illinois

POLITICAL INSIGHT 12–2

TWO HUNDRED YEARS OF THE LEGISLATORS' DILEMMA

THE DILEMMA:

Do I follow the wishes of the majority of my constituents [delegate role] or do I vote my conscience using my best judgment [trustee role]?

RESPONSES: WHAT ROLES DID THE FOLLOWING LEGISLATORS ADOPT?

1774 **Edmund Burke's** speech to the Electors of Bristol: "Parliament is a deliberative assembly of one nation, with one interest, that of the whole; where not local purposes, not local prejudices ought to guide but the general good, resulting from the general reason of the whole." A legislator must be guided by "his unbiased opinion, his mature judgment, his enlightened conscience."

1789 **Elbridge Gerry** of Massachusetts and **James Madison** of Virginia, debating a proposed amendment to the Constitution that would give the people the right to "instruct" their representatives:

MR. GERRY: "I think the people have a right both to instruct and bind [their representatives]. . . . To say the sovereignty vests in the people, and that they have not a right to instruct and control their representatives, is absurd to the last degree."

MR. MADISON: "To say that the people have a right to instruct their representatives in such a sense as that the delegates are obliged to conform to those instructions, the declaration is not true. Suppose they instruct a representative, by his vote, to violate the Constitution; is he at liberty to obey such instructions?"

1817 **Lewis Williams** of North Carolina and **John C. Calhoun** of South Carolina, in a speech to the House of Representatives on a bill concerning congressional compensation:

MR. CALHOUN: "Have the people of this country snatched the power of deliberation from this body? Are we a body of individual agents and not a deliberative one, without the power but possessing the form of legislation? If such be the fact, let gentlemen produce their instructions, properly authenticated."

MR. WILLIAMS: "The people are the sovereign power in this country. Hence I lay down the broad principle that they can do nothing wrong and ought to be obeyed."

1978 Senate Majority Leader **Robert Byrd** (D-W.Va.) during the debate over the Panama Canal treaties: "There's no political mileage in voting for the treaties. I know what my constituents are saying. But I have a responsibility not only to follow them but to inform them and lead them. I'm not going to betray my responsibility to my constituents. I owe them not only my industry but my judgment. That's why they sent me here."

SOURCE: Heinz Eulau, John C. Walke, William Buchanan, and Leroy C. Ferguson, "The Role of the Representative: Some Empirical Observations on the Theory of Edmund Burke," *American Political Science Review* 53 (September 1959):742; Charles S. Hyneman and George Carey, *A Second Federalist* (New York: Appleton-Century-Crofts, 1967), 236-38, 240-43; David Vogler, *The Politics of Congress*, 3rd ed. (Boston: Allyn and Bacon, 1980), 82.

Congresswoman Cardiss Collins, a liberal black woman, than by North Carolina Senator Jesse Helms, a conservative white male. An equally important dimension of representation is *policy representation*—how well a legislator reflects the substantive views of a constituency.

REPRESENTATIVES' ROLES

Are legislators bound to follow the wishes of their constituents, even if legislators are personally opposed to these wishes or have moral objections? What would a legislator do if asked to vote on a death penalty bill supported by constituents that he

Congressman Newt Gingrich, the Republican Whip, has a slashing, partisan style both on the House floor and back in his home district in Georgia.

or she found morally abhorrent? How they respond defines their **representational role.** Those who feel compelled to follow the wishes of their constituents adopt the *delegate role.* A "delegate" believes that a legislator is bound to act as the mouthpiece of the district. In contrast, those who feel they were entrusted to exercise their own wisdom and best judgment adopt the *trustee role.* A "trustee" believes that constituents send a legislator to study problems and to make independent decisions on how to vote. Political Insight 12-2 reveals that the dilemma of trustee versus delegate is an old one but still very relevant.

Even when confronted with the dilemma, a legislator may not always react the same way each time. Legislators who switch from a delegate role to a trustee role, depending on the issue, are called "politicos." Fortunately for legislators, the conflict is not an everyday one. Because of the relatively low interest in politics and the multitude of issues before Congress, legislators often cannot determine what the public opinion of the district is, if indeed it exists. Nonetheless, on a number of very important, well-publicized, and controversial issues, such as abortion, the death penalty, tax cuts, school prayer, or international treaties, legislators may face a difficult choice between what the voters in their district want and what they believe is right.

A study of representational roles by Roger Davidson, based on interviews with members of the House of Representatives, found that 46 percent chose the politico role, 28 percent chose the trustee role, and 23 percent chose the delegate role.[13] He also found that the role adopted by members was related to the nature of the district. Members from relatively safe districts were much more likely to adopt the trustee role, whereas members from marginal-competitive districts—who have to worry more about getting reelected—were more likely to adopt the delegate role.

Members of Congress represent their districts in different ways. No single style or role will fit congressional districts as diverse as the entire state of Alaska to a few blocks of New York City. Elected representatives all worry to some extent about reelection. They make choices that must fit their personalities and abilities. How will they present themselves to their district? What role will they play in the legislative process?

HOME STYLE. "Home style" is the way members of Congress present themselves to the district.[14] Home style increasingly helps ensure that the member is reelected to Congress. A typical trip home to the district usually begins with a late Thursday night flight out of Washington's National Airport, rushing to make the plane, hoping for a moment to call the office one last time. Members from the East usually go back to the district every weekend. Midwesterners return about every other weekend, and members from the West, at least every three or four weeks. Time on the flight is not wasted; the legislative aide or secretary in the next seat helps as the work continues.

The member at home has little time for himself or herself. The trip may include any or all of the following: party meetings, prayer breakfasts, public hearings, coffees, teas, fund-raisers, testimonials, or "roasts" for political friends, football games, baseball games, hockey matches, visits to the district offices, radio interviews, appearances on local television, press conferences, dinners, luncheons, strategy meetings, ribbon cuttings, dedications, award presentations, and speeches—lots of speeches, and not much time for casual reading, unless you include the president's budget or staff reports.

One member of Congress called his activities at home "taking care of his people." Richard Fenno, who carefully examined home style, identified key groups of supporters in the district.[15] Despite the wide variety of people members are likely to encounter at home, they usually spend the most time with supporters and potential supporters. The liberal Democrat is more likely to meet with labor unions, senior citizens, teachers, and environmentalists than the conservative Republican, who is more likely to see business leaders, church groups, bankers, and defense contractors. In talking with these groups, members use their characteristic style—whether friendly and relaxed or aggressive and tense—which presumably got them to Congress in the first place. Back in the district, a member tries to keep a finger on the pulse of the constituents.

WASHINGTON STYLE. If Congress is in session the next week, senators and representatives can be seen arriving back in the District of Columbia late Sunday night or Monday morning, often as tired as when they left. They may go directly to a hearing or to the office to check the calendar for the week.

Visitors to Congress are often surprised at their first view of a session of the House or Senate to find only a handful of members on the floor—perhaps one member talking, one listening, and the others whispering to one another. Congress is working, but most of the important legislative work is conducted in committee and subcommittee sessions. Suddenly the bells ring and the lights on the clocks all over Capitol Hill start flashing. An elaborate system of lights and bells signal a quorum call or a vote. The chamber fills with people. Toward the end of the year, more and more time is spent on the floor, debating amendments, casting votes. As adjournment approaches, the House and Senate may be in session into the wee hours of the morning. Bleary-eyed senators and representatives vote on a seemingly endless list of last-minute but critical legislative business.

Long days on the Hill are spent in meetings and attending hearings, interrupted by breaks to return to the floor to vote, then back to meet with constituents visiting Washington. This routine may be punctuated by a series of breakfasts, luncheons, or dinners with lots of chicken salad and soggy peas. Members of a congressional staff sometimes wonder when they will have a few minutes with their boss.

A member generally divides time between the House or Senate chamber, hearing rooms, the congressional office, other locations in Washington, and travel to and from all of them. An important part of a legislator's life in Congress today depends on the assistance of professional staff. Most members divide their staff between district or state offices and congressional offices. More than 20,000 people now work on Capitol Hill. Members have from eighteen to forty people on their personal staff, and committee and subcommittee chairs control committee staff as well. The key staff positions in a congressional office include an administrative assistant, legislative assistants, media and press adviser, appointments secretary, case workers, secretaries, and typists. In addition, members of the House and Senate have available to them the research facilities of congressional support agencies, such as the Congressional ResearchService, the Congressional Budget Office, the Legislative Counsel's Office, the Office of Technology Assessment, and the General Accounting Office. Staff have become tremendously important to both the lawmaking and local representative roles of members.

LEGISLATIVE NORMS

Members' home styles are their own, but their actions in Washington are partly shaped by congressional traditions and the expectations of others. Norms—unwritten rules—are important for understanding the life of a legislator as well as the congressional policy-making process. Norms within an organization are fostered by socialization and enforced with rewards and sanctions that encourage compliance.

Some legislators are more competent and work harder than others. Some focus on publicity and personal glory—"showhorses," as they are disparagingly called. Others concentrate on behind-the-scenes work and the hard negotiations necessary to get legislation passed—these are the "workhorses." Washington style determines the effectiveness and influence of individual legislators. At the same time, as incumbents have become increasingly concerned with reelection, fewer members are actually involved in hard legislating. The work of a legislative insider pays few dividends back home. Time spent legislating could be spent cultivating support in the district.

One of the unwritten rules of Congress is that members should not try to be experts at everything. Instead, specialize. The reward for **specialization** is greater influence and respect for expertise in a particular policy area. Specialization reinforces the committee and subcommittee system and is complimented by **reciprocity**—the recognition of someone else's expertise in return for his or her recognition of yours. As the emphasis of some legislators has shifted away from lawmaking, specialization and reciprocity have declined.

Seniority and apprenticeship norms have also declined in Congress. Thirty years ago, one could find a greater respect for experience and longevity. The notion that a new member of Congress should be seen but not heard while serving an apprenticeship has died out.[16] Today, a member of Congress wants to secure an electoral base and play a role in the legislative process immediately.

Members are loyal to their own chamber and usually courteous to one another. They address one another on the floor as "the distinguished senator from . . .," never by name. Unlike the House of Commons in Great Britain, where catcalls, booing, jeering, and disruptions are an accepted practice, personal attacks are extremely rare on the House and Senate floor. This courtesy of address is sometimes comical. Senator Edward Brooke of Massachusetts once suggested that if the word "distinguished" were removed from floor speeches, legislators could save about 10 percent of their time. Senate Majority Leader Mike Mansfield, unable to break the habit, replied, "I appreciate the remarks of the distinguished senator from Massachusetts."[17] Institutional loyalty creates a strong bond among members, regardless of party. When a House member criticizes the Senate, or vice versa, a sharp rebuke will be forthcoming. Some observers believe that loyalty to the chamber is sometimes stronger than party loyalty.

Congress is an amalgam of 535 individuals with different ideas, ambitions, and personal strengths and weaknesses, representing vastly different states and districts. Members present themselves to their states and districts in the way they believe is best. But in Washington, they must somehow cooperate with one another. Legislative norms are like institutional glue, supplementing the formal rules of the legislative process. In recent decades, norms have weakened as power has become more decentralized and members more individualistic. How has this affected the way Congress makes public policy?

The Legislative Process

The legislative process is long and complex. Figure 12-1 shows in simplified form the stages of the legislative process. What goes on within these boxes are the dynamics of how Congress makes policy.

INTRODUCING BILLS

Only members of Congress may introduce legislation. Some members submit hundreds of **bills** in a session; others may introduce only a few bills in their entire congressional career. The legislative process begins when a House member drops a bill

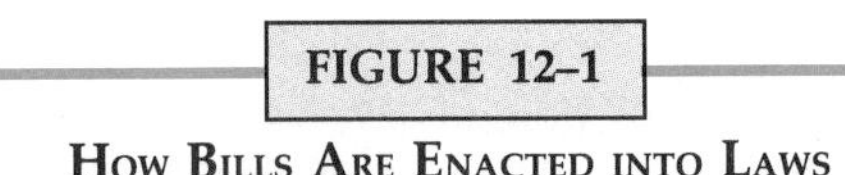

HOW BILLS ARE ENACTED INTO LAWS

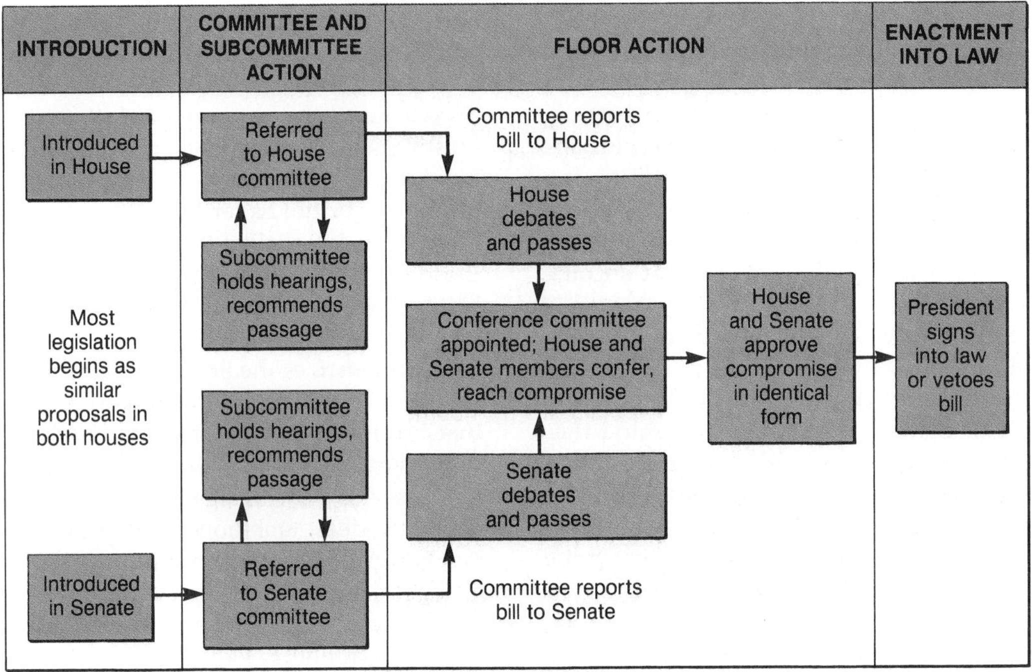

in the "hopper," a wooden box at the front of the chamber. Senators hand their bills to the clerk.

Only in unusual circumstances does a member actually write a bill. Ideas for legislation come from the executive branch, the congressional staff, constituents, and other sources. The Office of Legislative Counsel helps put the bill in correct legal form for introduction. Most bills are *public bills,* dealing with some kind of national program. Members may also introduce *private bills,* concerning pensions, citizenship, and minor problems that affect only one or a few individuals. Congress also passes **resolutions.** A *simple resolution* expresses the sentiment of either the House or the Senate—for example, congratulating the U.S. Olympic gymnastics team. A *concurrent resolution* must be passed in identical form by both houses. Its most important application is in the budget process, and its advantage is that it binds the House and Senate without the signature of the president. A *joint resolution* must be passed in identical form by both houses, but, like a bill, requires the signature of the president before it becomes law.

CONSIDERATION IN COMMITTEE

Once a bill is submitted, it is referred to a committee. Occasionally, referral can be crucial to the life or death of a bill. Before referral became more routine, the presiding officer could send the bill to any committee, including one that would certainly kill it. Today, referral is usually automatic; Congress relies primarily on the parliamentarian to determine which committee gets a bill. If questions remain, the Speaker of the House or the majority leader of the Senate decides. Occasionally a bill is referred to two committees, making the task of final approval twice as hard. Once in committee, a bill is referred to subcommittee.

Many bills are introduced with no expectation of passing. They serve primarily as publicity for the sponsor or to dramatize a certain issue that

Congress is unwilling to deal with. In 1975-76, a total of 24,283 bills were introduced, 2,870 were reported by committees, and 588 were passed. In 1981, with Congress concentrating on President Reagan's economic program, only 13,240 bills were introduced, 1,877 reported, and 473 passed.[18] Because there are so many bills, most never get a hearing. Even if the subcommittee chair schedules a hearing, the bill faces many more obstacles. Hearings serve to clarify the issues, demonstrate the need for the legislation, and give opponents an opportunity to object. Hearings are often held primarily for publicity, with testimony structured to favor one side or the other. Proponents must build a case to help natural allies support the bill and defend their vote back home in the district.

FLOOR CONSIDERATION OF A BILL

In the House of Representatives, a bill reported favorably by a standing (permanent) committee is sent to the Rules Committee. If the Rules Committee refuses to schedule the bill for floor action, it is almost certainly dead. Supporters can resort to the use of a **discharge petition** with the signatures of 218 members of the House, which forces the bill to the floor for consideration within a few legislative days. Discharge petitions rarely succeed. Of the 800 attempts since 1900, only about 25 bills have been brought out, and only *one* of those bills ultimately passed.

The House Rules Committee places the bill on one of the **calendars,** which are lists of bills awaiting floor consideration. The bill must also be given a "rule" that specifies the amount of time allowed for debate and the kind of amendments that will be allowed. Ten hours of debate divided evenly between opponents and proponents would not be unusual for an important measure. Amendments can be limited by a **"closed rule,"** which prohibits any amendments, or a "modified closed rule," which severely restricts amendments. The Senate schedules legislation through **unanimous consent agreements** worked out by the majority and minority leaders. No time limits are placed on debate.

A bill "on the floor" has been taken up by one of the houses and is being debated. On the House side, rules and procedures are stricter than in the Senate. Debate is limited, and amendments are supposed to be germane (relevant) to the measure under consideration. The House usually operates as a committee of the whole, allowing a quorum of 100 members (instead of the normal 218). In the Senate, dilatory tactics, such as the **filibuster** are still allowed (see Political Insight 12-3). Although the Senate has a "germaneness" rule, it is largely ignored. A senator may, for example, offer an anti-abortion amendment to a bill authorizing the MX missile. The Senate does not operate as a committee of the whole.

Few members of Congress decide how to vote based on what is said during floor debate. Not many of them even hear the debate in person (members can listen to the debate on closed-circuit television in their offices). Floor debate can be important, however. It articulates the main issues at stake and allows both opponents and proponents to establish a public record. The debate also helps create the legislative history of a bill, which may be used later by agency officials implementing the law or courts trying to interpret the law. Amendments offered on the floor often make critical changes in a bill before it passes or goes down to defeat.

VOTING PROCEDURES

Votes in Congress are taken in several ways. Many noncontroversial measures are passed by a voice vote. In a "division" vote, members stand up and are counted. Votes on important and controversial legislation are recorded: Members are accountable for their vote. A "teller" vote occurs when the members pass between two tellers who record which way the members vote. The most common vote is the "roll call." The clerk of the Senate still calls the roll, starting with Senator Adams (D-Wash.) and ending with Senator Warner (R-Va.). Since 1973, members of the House have voted by electronic device. Members take their personalized vote-ID card and insert it in one of the slots marked "yea," "nay," "present," or "open" (open is used only when a vote period is in progress). Representatives usually have fifteen minutes to vote.

If a bill is passed, it is sent to the other chamber. If the House or Senate passes a version of the bill in a different form, it must go to a "conference committee" to work out the differences. If the conferences agree on a bill, it must be passed in

POLITICAL INSIGHT 12–3

THE FILIBUSTER: TALKING A BILL TO DEATH

The democratic tradition, so the argument goes, is built on a foundation of free and unlimited debate. The House disposed of unlimited debate in the nineteenth century, but the Senate clings to the filibuster.

Filibusteros were nineteenth-century Caribbean pirates. Somehow the term came to be applied to raids by the minority members on the rest of the Senate using hot air as their rapier. The first filibuster occurred in 1841, when after ten days of tireless debate, the rest of the Senate gave up on the idea of hiring their own printers. Not until 1917 did the Senate adopt Rule 22, allowing a cloture motion to cut off debate.

Rule 22 required two-thirds of those present and voting to approve a cloture motion, and it was difficult to achieve. For philosophical reasons, many southern senators would never vote to cut off debate, even if they favored the bill being strangled. Filibusters became longer and longer. In the 1950s, Senator Wayne Morse put a rose on his desk and claimed it would wilt before he did. Twenty-two hours later the rose had wilted when he quit talking. Senator Strom Thurmond broke the record by two hours a few years later.

In 1975, Rule 22, a continuing focus of controversy, was changed to make it easier to cut off debate, when the Senate rewrote the rule so a constitutional majority of three-fifths, or 60, of its members could stop debate.

But after a century of use by southerners and conservatives, liberals discovered the filibuster. Instead of civil rights bills being subjected to verbal death, the natural-gas deregulation bill faced the peril. There was even a new innovation: the postcloture filibuster. By offering an endless string of procedural amendments and quorum calls, a filibuster was continued in 1977 *after* cloture was invoked. Vice-President Walter Mondale, presiding in the Senate, was able to break that filibuster by ruling all the amendments out of order. In 1979, the rule was again changed to limit to one hour the number of procedural motions that could be debated.

Unless some dramatic change occurs in the 1990s the senate filibuster looks like it will make it to the twenty-first century.

exactly that form (no amendments are allowed) in both the House and Senate. The bill is then "enrolled" (corrected, checked, and signed by the presiding officers of the House and Senate) and sent to the president for signature.

In general, House and Senate procedural differences reflect differences in size (100 versus 435), term (six years versus two years), and historical evolution of the two chambers. The Senate, as the upper chamber that was until the early 1900s an appointed body, is characterized by looser rules, a more even distribution of power, relatively higher prestige, and greater media coverage.[19] The House of Representatives, the lower chamber, has tighter rules and procedures, greater variation in the powers of members, and a more specialized body. Bill referrals may be challenged in the Senate but not in the House. Committees are stronger in the House than in the Senate. In general, floor action is more important in the Senate than the House. But despite the differences, the problems of governing in both chambers center on collective decision-making.

Committees and Subcommittees

Committees are semi-independent islands of legislative power. They are often able to withstand winds blowing from the White House or the Speaker's rostrum. Under the seniority system, even in its weakened form, committee chairs are relatively secure. To a chair who has served in Congress for twenty or thirty years or who can look forward to doing so, the occupant of the White House for four or eight years is a mere transient.

Perhaps the most important trend in the 1970s was the shift in legislative activity from committee to subcommittee. The number of subcommittees expanded, further decentralizing the House and Senate. In the 101st Congress (1989-90) the House had 22 standing committees with 138 subcommittees. The Senate was divided into 16 standing committees with 86 subcommittees (nearly one for each member!). By his or her third term, a majority member of the House can expect to chair a subcommittee. In the eternal quest for electoral security, nothing is more valuable than a subcommittee. It provides a forum, a basis for holding hearings, an enhanced ability to control legislation, and an opportunity to get good publicity, additional staff, and prestige. The proliferation of subcommittees divided power among the members more equally and made coalition building an even more arduous task.

TYPES OF COMMITTEES

Standing committees are permanent committees that exist from one Congress to the next. Their stable membership and jurisdiction make them the most important type of committee. The House Ways and Means Committee, which deals with taxes, has been in continuous operation since the 1790s. Table 12-4 lists the standing committees in the 101st Congress for both the House and the Senate. The standing committees and their subcommittees "mark up" bills—legislators and their staff amend, revise, write, and rewrite the legislation line by line.

Special and select committees are temporary committees appointed for a particular purpose. They usually do not continue from one Congress to the next unless they deal with housekeeping matters, such as the Select Committee on the House Beauty Parlor. Select committees can be critically important. The Senate Select Committee on Watergate conducted televised hearings on the emerging scandal in the Nixon administration. During the Carter administration, the House Select Committee on Energy was formed to deal with the energy proposals of the president and to avoid jurisdictional disputes among standing committees. In 1987, select committees of the House and the Senate conducted joint televised hearings of the Iran-Contra affair. The Senate in 1989-90 had three select and one special committee; the House had five select committees.

One of the senate Judiciary Committee's most important functions is to hold confirmation hearings for presidential nominees to the federal courts. In 1987, they recommended against the confirmation of Judge Robert Bork.

TABLE 12–4

STANDING COMMITTEES OF THE HOUSE AND SENATE, 101ST CONGRESS (1989–90)

Committee	No. of Members	No. of Subcommittees
House of Representatives		
1. Agriculture	45	8
2. Appropriations	57	13
3. Armed Services	52	7
4. Banking, Finance, and Urban Affairs	51	8
5. Budget	35	6
6. District of Columbia	11	3
7. Education and Labor	34	8
8. Energy and Commerce	43	6
9. Foreign Affairs	43	8
10. Government Operations	39	7
11. House Administration	21	6
12. Interior and Insular Affairs	37	6
13. Judiciary	35	7
14. Merchant Marine and Fisheries	43	6
15. Post Office and Civil Service	23	7
16. Public Works and Transportation	50	6
17. Rules	13	2
18. Science, Space and Technology	49	7
19. Small Business	44	6
20. Standards of Official Conduct	12	0
21. Veterans' Affairs	34	5
22. Ways and Means	36	6
	Subcommittee total	138
Senate		
1. Agriculture, Nutrition, and Forestry	19	7
2. Appropriations	29	13
3. Armed Services	20	6
4. Banking, Housing, and Urban Affairs	21	4
5. Budget	23	0
6. Commerce, Science, and Transportation	20	8
7. Energy and Natural Resources	19	5
8. Environment and Public Works	16	5
9. Finance	20	8
10. Foreign Relations	19	7
11. Government Affairs	14	5
12. Judiciary	14	6
13. Labor and Human Resources	16	6
14. Rules and Administration	16	0
15. Small Business	19	6
16. Veterans' Affairs	11	0
	Subcommitee total	86

SOURCE: *Congressional Quarterly Weekly Reports*, 6 May 1989.

Joint committees are committees made up of members of both the House and Senate. There are relatively few joint committees, and they tend to study issues rather than actually legislate. The most important joint committee is the Joint Economic Committee. The right to chair this committee rotates between the House and Senate. When the need for a budget committee became apparent, serious consideration was given in 1973 to the formation of a joint budget committee, rather than separate House and Senate committees. But the historical weakness of joint committees, combined with the desire of each chamber to control its own committees, led to the creation of standing budget committees in both houses.

Conference committees are appointed when the House and Senate pass different versions of a bill. Legislation must be passed in identical form before it can be sent to the president for signature. The Speaker of the House and majority leader of the Senate name "managers" to work out differences. Conference committees become increasingly important when the House and Senate are controlled by different parties, as in 1981-87.

Committee Power and Prestige

All committees are not created equal. They differ in their relative influence, workload, reputation, control of money, and desirability. In both the House and Senate, "money committees" that control the federal purse strings have traditionally been the most powerful and desirable committees. In the House, the Appropriations Committee and the Ways and Means Committee have jurisdiction over most of the revenue and spending decisions. The Budget Committee takes an overview of national spending priorities and fiscal policy and sets the broad parameters of congressional action. In the Senate, the Finance Committee is equivalent to the House Ways and Means Committee. Along with the Budget and Appropriations committees, they form the most important money committees in the Senate. Chapter 17 examines the complicated congressional budget process and the relationship among the money committees.

Money is important, but it is not everything. Reflecting its own constitutional superiority over the House in the field of foreign affairs (through the ratification of treaties and confirmation of ambassadors, secretaries of state, and so on), the Foreign Relations Committee has been the committee most desired by senators. The Finance, Commerce, Judiciary, and Appropriations committees rank just behind, based on the number of requests to transfer.[20] The committees most preferred by House members from the 1950s to 1970 were the Rules Committee, the Ways and Means Committee, and the Appropriations Committee. But by the late 1970s, as the focus of legislators shifted toward serving constituents, the pattern of committee preferences changed as well.

Change was less visible in the Senate, where the Foreign Relations Committee remained extremely popular and money committees were increasingly sought. Changes in committee preferences in the House, however, were more dramatic. The Rules Committee, for two decades the most desired committee, had to be cut in 1983 from thirteen to eleven members because not enough senior members could be found to fill the vacancies![21] This occurred even though the Rules Committee is as important as ever in the legislative process, controlling the flow of legislation to the House. In the past, House "insiders" would seek an assignment on the Rules Committee so they could exert maximum leverage and enhance their influence over lawmaking. Today, fewer members seem interested in playing the role of legislative insider or "broker." Members are not very interested in a committee assignment that does little to help their reelection efforts.

Preferences for committee assignments in recent congresses document some of the changes. Two of the most desired committees were the Energy and Commerce Committee and the Banking, Finance, and Urban Affairs Committee. Competition is fierce to win a seat on the Energy and Commerce Committee, where many new members want to serve. This committee serves the constituent needs of members well while encompassing some of the most important policy issues of the day. One observer noted, "It deals in everything that can be bought, sold, bartered or traded."[22] The Energy and Commerce Committee is the favorite of the PACs. In just one year, the forty-two members of the committee received a total of nearly $5 million from political action committees, an average of more than $100,000 per member.[23]

PARTY RATIOS AND COMMITTEE ASSIGNMENTS

The ratio of Republicans to Democrats on committees is determined by the majority party. They operate within the bounds of "fairness" but are free to set any ratio they wish. In 1981, for example, shaken by the Republican takeover of the Senate, the House Democrats decided to "overrepresent" themselves on certain important committees. On the Rules Committee, the Ways and Means Committee, and the Budget Committee, they established ratios as high as 11 to 5, even though the ratio of Democrats to Republicans was approximately 5 to 4. When they controlled the Senate from 1981 to 1987, the Republicans in the Senate had ratios no greater than 7 to 5 in their committees. Most of the committees are divided between the two parties in a ratio that gives the majority party a slight advantage.

How does a member of Congress go about getting on a desirable committee? Back in the days of "to get along, go along," someone penned the following ditty:

> I love Speaker Rayburn, his heart is so warm
> And if I love him, he'll do me no harm
> So I shan't sass the Speaker one little bitty
> And then I'll wind up on a major committee.[24]

The Democratic members of the House receive their committee assignments from the Democratic Policy and Steering Committee. Selections must be approved by a vote in the caucus (that is, all House Democrats). The House Republican Conference names House Republicans to committees once the majority party has informed them of how many seats they have altogether. In the Senate, the Democratic Steering Committee must approve assignments made by the leader. The Senate Republican Committee on Committees makes its committee assignments.

One of the most important steps in a congressional career is the initial appointment to a committee. Self-selection is an important factor in committee assignment. Newly elected members lobby hard for the prized assignment. One freshman member went to work lobbying for a seat on the Energy and Commerce Committee the day after he was elected.[25] Most members are able to get at least one of the committees they desire, but many have to settle for second or third choice. In the case of the Energy and Commerce, Banking, Budget, Appropriations, and Ways and Means committees in the House, members engage in intense competition. Other criteria are then brought to bear. One criterion is loyalty. The Speaker and other party leaders who play an important role in the Policy and Steering Committee reward Democrats who have higher party support scores. Another criterion is seniority. Other things being equal, a senior member will be given preference over a junior member. Regional considerations sometimes come into play, particularly in the Senate, where some states may lay claim to a seat on a certain committee because the committee deals with matters of particular importance to them. Professional background is sometimes a factor: All the members of the Judiciary committees are lawyers, for example, and many of the members of the Agriculture committees are farmers.

SUBCOMMITTEE GOVERNMENT

The distribution of power within Congress between committees, subcommittees, and party leaders has important consequences for how effectively Congress makes decisions. Beginning in the late 1960s, members adopted a number of reforms to democratize Congress, improve ethics, and provide greater openness.[26] While these goals were achieved to some extent, many of the reforms made policy-making more difficult by weakening committees and once-powerful committee chairs. The enactment of the "subcommittee bill of rights" in 1973 devolved power from committees to subcommittees, further fragmenting decision-making.[27] The 1974 post-Watergate elections that brought ninety freshmen members into the House were a prelude to serious challenges of the seniority system. Three senior committee chairs were voted out of their positions by the House Democratic caucus. As subcommittees grew more powerful and committees weaker, Congress was no longer dominated by a few powerful "whales" but by a large school of "minnows." The benefits for individual members were immense, significantly helping reelection chances.

Greater democracy and subcommittee government gave the rank and file more power, but at the same time, they weakened the ability of Congress to make collective decisions. Dodd and Oppenheimer summarize the effect:

> Subcommittee government created a crisis of interest aggregation. It largely removed committees as arenas in which interests would be compromised, brokered, and mediated; and it led to increasing dominance of committee decision-making by clientele groups, to narrowly focused policy leadership, and to confusion in policy jurisdictions.[28]

Ethics reforms designed to polish Congress's tarnished image with the public also affected governing capacity. Open meeting requirements—so-called "sunshine laws"—required Congress to do more of its business in public. While reforms that promise greater democracy, ethics, and openness are easy to favor, they can inadvertently harm policy-making. Rather than making citizens more attentive, interest groups, PACs, and the media were the prime beneficiaries. Greater accessibility to congressional decision-making made the job of leaders more difficult. Members were less likely to openly trade votes or to publicly take a position against the interest of the district in support of the broader national interest. But by the 1980s, subcommittee government and the growing deadlock between executive and legislative branches created a governing crisis in Congress, particularly over the budget. In response, by the late 1980s, a number of measures were adopted to strengthen committee chairs, party leaders, and foster collective decision-making. Before considering this recent trend away from subcommittee government, let us first look at party leadership and voting patterns in Congress.

Party and Party Leadership

Members of Congress who want to be able to "go their own way" and "vote the district" still need the party leaders to facilitate the legislative process. The party leaders must somehow create coalitions to pass necessary legislation. How can they do it?

Party discipline is weak in the U.S. Congress, particularly compared with parliamentary democracies. In Great Britain, for example, it is a newsworthy story when a few members of the governing party desert the prime minister on an important vote. If the party in power loses an important vote, it must resign and call for new elections. In Congress, it is news if the members of the majority party all vote together on a bill! Fewer than 1 percent of all recorded votes in Congress are straight party-line votes. If presidents could depend on support from their majorities in Congress, Jimmy Carter would have been phenomenally successful. But even with these limitations, party and party leadership remain an important element in Congress.

Even in the absence of party discipline in Congress, the outward signs of party organization are everywhere. The House and Senate are divided by an aisle, with Republicans on one side and Democrats on the other. The two parties have their own cloakrooms, doorkeepers, committee staff, and caucuses. When the Congressional baseball game is played, it is Republicans versus Democrats. (The Republicans usually win.)

House Leadership

The **Speaker of the House of Representatives,** the presiding officer of the House, is the only leadership position specified in the Constitution. Unlike the speaker of the British House of Commons, who maintains neutrality, the U.S. Speaker is also the partisan head of the majority party, but not necessarily the senior member. In the early 1800s, Henry Clay was elected Speaker his first term in Congress. Today, the Speaker will have served many terms in Congress before being selected and will probably have come up through the leadership ranks, first serving as majority leader. Jim Wright (D-Tex.), elected Speaker in 1987, had served in the House since 1955. But as we saw in the Political Close-up that opened the chapter, Wright was forced to resign in June 1989.

As the Congress modernized, the growth of the Speaker's powers helped streamline the legislative process. But the concentration of influence became too great for a majority of members. In 1910, the rank and file revolted against Speaker "Uncle Joe" Cannon, stripping him of many powers. Today, the Speaker remains the most influential member of the House through the use of formal and informal powers. Sam Rayburn, Speaker for sixteen years

The Democratic leaders of Congress: Senate Majority Leader George Mitchell (left) and House Speaker Thomas Foley.

from 1940 to his death in 1961, had a favorite saying: "To get along, go along." Certainly, those who go along with the Speaker are more likely to get the favors he has to give.

The leader of the minority party—the losing candidate for Speaker—becomes the *minority floor leader.* Lacking the resources of the Speaker, the minority leader works with members to cooperate with or oppose the majority, whichever is deemed appropriate.

Second in command in the majority party is the *majority floor leader.* The majority leader is responsible for managing legislation on the floor, scheduling and lining up votes on controversial measures. He is assisted by the *majority whip* and deputy whips, who help the leader get a head count and "whip" up support for legislation that is favored by the party. On the minority side, the whip organization performs a similar function. The final arbiter in many disputes over committee assignments, chairs, procedures, and policy disputes within the party is the *House Democratic caucus.* Significant changes in House leadership occurred for both parties at the beginning of the Bush administration.

REPUBLICAN LEADERSHIP CHANGE

When nominated as secretary of defense by President Bush in 1989, Richard Cheney (R-Wyo.) held the post of minority whip, the number two House Republican leadership position. His confirmation set off a conflict within the House Republican caucus over both ideology and leadership style. Minority leader Robert Michel had come under increasing attack from the "young turks" in the Republican party who were dissatisfied with Michel's conciliatory, collaborative approach to working with the majority party. A leader of these dissidents was Newt Gingrich of Georgia who, frustrated with thirty-five years of uninterrupted minority status in the House, wanted more confrontation with the Democrats.

Gingrich became a candidate for the vacant whip position. He was the antiestablishment candidate with a reputation as a partisan provocateur. He was opposed by Edward Madigan, a legislative insider like Michel. Madigan, who had served as chief deputy whip, was endorsed by Michel and many of the senior Republicans. Gingrich, hated by Democrats for years, had brought the charges against Speaker Jim Wright that ultimately ended his speakership. When the votes in the Republican caucus were counted, Gingrich prevailed by a narrow 87-to-85 majority. He received the votes of younger and more conservative members but had widespread support. The message was for more aggressive, confrontational Republican leadership in the House. To congratulate the new whip, Speaker Wright sent Gingrich an autographed copy of his book, *Confessions of a Public Man*—the subject of his ethics charges. Following his election, Gingrich named another antiestablishment Republican—Robert Walker of Pennsylvania—as his chief deputy whip.

DEMOCRATIC LEADERSHIP CHANGES

The shake-up on the Democratic side of the House was more pervasive. Even before Wright finally resigned as Speaker, House Democrats quickly lined up behind majority leader Thomas Foley (D-Wash.). On June 6, 1989, Foley was elected to succeed Wright as Speaker by the House Democratic caucus. Foley's ascension promised a significant change in leadership style. Contrary to the changes on the Republican side, Foley was more conciliatory and less partisan than Wright, leading some to expect conflict to ease. But partisanship remained high. Minority Leader Michel made a harsh speech following Wright's resignation, infuriating Democrats. The Republican National Committee issued a memo containing innuendos that Foley was a homosexual. President Bush and most congressional Republicans disavowed the memo, and its author was fired, but the damage was done.

The unprecedented resignation of Wright was accompanied by the surprise resignation of the number three Democrat, Majority Whip Tony Coehlo of California. Coehlo—who had been seen as one of the up-and-coming stars of the party—ran into ethical problems of his own concerning financial dealings. Unlike Wright, Coehlo immediately resigned rather than face a prolonged investigation that could damage the party. His departure left an additional vacancy in the Democratic leadership. The number two leadership position that had been held by Foley was won by Richard Gephardt of Missouri. Gephardt had taken himself off of the leadership ladder to run for president in 1988. Renouncing another presidential bid in 1992, the moderate and "squeaky clean" Gephardt quickly became front-runner to become majority leader. An effective insider and visible party spokesman, he easily defeated Ed Jenkins of Georgia, 181-to-76. William Gray of Pennsylvania was elected majority whip on the first ballot, becoming the first black person to hold one of the top leadership positions in the House. The new leadership team was completed when Steny Hoyer was elected caucus chairman, and Vic Fazio was elected caucus vice chairman. The House leadership posts and the leaders in the 101st Congress are shown in Table 12-5.

SENATE LEADERSHIP

Under the Constitution, the vice-president is president (or presiding officer) of the Senate. The vice-president rarely performs this task, but it can occasionally be critically important. Nixon's first vice-president, Spiro Agnew, cast several deciding votes when a Senate roll call ended in a tie. Vice-President Nelson Rockefeller made an important ruling on Senate Rule 22 (cloture and filibuster; see Political Insight 12-3). On a key budget vote in 1985, the Republicans wheeled one member in on a hospital gurney to tie the vote, while Vice-President George Bush was flown in on Air Force One to cast the tie-breaking vote. Normally, the vice-president spends little time in the Senate and even less time actually presiding.

TABLE 12–5

PARTY LEADERSHIP IN THE HOUSE OF REPRESENTATIVES, 101ST CONGRESS

Majority Party (Democrats)

Speaker: Thomas Foley (Wash.)
Majority Leader: Richard Gephardt (Mo.)
Whip: William Gray (Pa.)
Caucus Chairman: Steny Hoyer (Md.)
Caucus Vice Chairman: Vic Fazio (Calif.)
Chief Deputy Whip: David Bonior (Mich.)

Minority Party (Republicans)

Minority Leader: Robert Michel (Ill.)
Whip: Newt Gingrich (Ga.)
Conference Chairman: Jerry Lewis (Calif.)
Chief Deputy Whips: Robert Walker (Pa.), Steve Gunderson (Wis.)
Conference Vice Chairman: Bill McCollum (Fla.)

The "president pro tempore" of the Senate is a ceremonial position given to the senior member of the majority party. Under current succession law, the president pro tempore is third in line for the presidency, after the vice-president and the Speaker of the House.

The real leader of the Senate is the **majority leader.** Although comparable to the Speaker in controlling floor proceedings, the position is not that of a constitutional officer or a presiding officer. The majority leader is aided by the *party whip,* who assists in vote counting, information distributing, and coalition-building activities. The *minority leader* and *minority whip* are the equivalent positions on the other side of the aisle.

While party leaders are not as powerful in the Senate as the House, they play important roles in agenda-setting and as spokespersons for the party. Four men held the post of majority leader of the Senate since 1981. Howard Baker (R-Tenn.) was the first Republican majority leader in a quarter century after the Republicans took control in the 1980 elections. Baker played an important role in the adoption of Reagan's economic and budget proposals in 1981 and presided over a Republican majority anxious to govern after so many years in the minority. When Baker decided not to seek reelection in 1984, Robert Dole (R-Kans.) was elected majority leader. Dole served as majority leader only in the 99th Congress as the Democrats recaptured control in the 1986 elections. Robert Byrd (D-W.Va.) resumed the position of majority leader that he had lost in 1981 (he had become minority leader from 1981-87). Byrd, a consummate manipulator of Senate rules, presided over an increasingly partisan Senate during President Reagan's last two years in office. Byrd decided to step down as majority leader in 1989 but remained in the Senate as chairman of the powerful Appropriations Committee. The Democrats selected George Mitchell of Maine as majority leader at the beginning of the 101st Congress. Mitchell proved to be an articulate and capable leader, helping shepherd through a number of controversial bills in 1990. Table 12-6 shows the Senate leadership positions and leaders in the 101st Congress.

In the 1950s, Lyndon Johnson was a legendary majority leader, probably the last really forceful Senate leader. The days when an inner club dominated by southern Democrats largely ran the Senate are gone. Senators are even more individualistic than House members. National figures in their own right, many are running for thepresidency and more interested in leading than being led. How do party leaders in the House and Senate convince legislators to "go along"?

TABLE 12–6

PARTY LEADERSHIP IN THE SENATE, 101ST CONGRESS

President of the Senate
Vice President Dan Quayle
President Pro Tempore (Ceremonial)
Robert Byrd (D.–W.Va.)
Majority Party (Democrats)
Majority Leader: George Mitchell (Maine) *Majority Whip:* Alan Cranston (Calif.) *Secretary of the Conference:* David Pryor (Ark.) *Chief Deputy Whip:* Alan Dixon (Ill.) *Chair of Steering Committee:* Daniel Inouye (Hawaii)
Minority Party (Republicans)
Minority Leader: Robert Dole (Kans.) *Assistant Minority Leader:* Alan Simpson (Wyo,) *Chair of the Policy Committee:* William Armstrong (Colo.) *Chair of the Conference:* John Chafee (R.I.) *Secretary of the Conference: Thad Cochran (Miss.)*

TECHNIQUES OF PERSUASION

Party leaders in the House and Senate may not be as powerful as they were in the days of Speaker Cannon or Majority Leader Johnson, but they still command resources that make them more powerful than the rank-and-file members.[29] The Speaker presides over the House and recognizes members to speak during debate. He has an important voice in committee assignments, occasionally influences the assignment of bills to committees, and largely controls the timetable and agenda of the House. Since 1974, the Speaker has had the power to appoint all members and the chair of the Rules Committee, subject to final approval by the caucus. Informally, rewards and sanctions can be dispensed. The Speaker and other party leaders influence who gets gifts from the campaign committee, determine who goes on attractive foreign trips, decide who serves on conference committees, and can do many other little things either to smooth a member's political path or to make it rough. Leaders have the power to use the rules and procedures to achieve desired results. The Speaker, for example, can reward a loyal party member by placing a minor bill that the member supports on the consent calendar, guaranteeing its passage. Conversely, he can block such a bill to punish disloyalty.

Leaders help determine a member's reputation within the Congress and can enhance or undermine it. They may even apply stronger sanctions in some cases, such as when Phil Gramm was stripped of his committee assignment by the Democratic caucus. The same message was relayed to Congressman Sonny Montgomery (D-Miss.), who nearly lost his post as chair of the House Veterans Affairs Committee for supporting President Reagan against the Democratic leadership. Montgomery saved his job by "repenting" and campaigning hard for Democratic candidates before the 1982 elections.[30] Speaker Jim Wright angered Republicans by his aggressive partisan leadership in 1987 and 1988. On one occasion, he extended the fifteen-minute electronic voting period so that a party loyalist could change his vote and give the Speaker a narrow one-vote victory on a budget measure.[31]

House and Senate leaders control an extensive information network, including sending "whip notices" that indicate the importance of certain bills and the leadership position. But overall, the most important resources of party leaders in Congress are their own personal skills of persuasion. The "Johnson treatment" was Lyndon Johnson's handshaking, backslapping, subtle threatening, cautiously encouraging style of convincing the member to "go along."[32] In the fractious Senate, persuasion is still, but not always, the key tool.

Majority Leader Robert Byrd was a consummate legislative insider, a master of the folkways of the Senate, but he also demonstrated a willingness to play hardball. Frustrated by the Republican filibuster of the campaign finance reform bill in early 1988, Byrd invoked an obscure Senate rule that had not been used since 1942. He ordered the Senate sergeant at arms to arrest Republican senators for refusing to answer a quorum call. Keeping the Senate in session around the clock in an effort to break the filibuster, Byrd was short one senator to make a quorum (50 percent plus one). The sergeant at arms and his assistants set out in search of Republican senators. One escaped by running down the corridor at full speed. Senator Robert Packwood (R-Ore.) locked himself in his office but, tipped off by a cleaning woman, the sergeant at arms used a passkey to gain entrance. A struggle ensued, in which Packwood injured his shoulder, but he was overpowered and carried by his ankles and arms by three policemen onto the Senate floor. Packwood kept his sense of humor about the whole incident, but the next day other Republicans were furious. Byrd was accused of using police-state tactics of "Nazi Germany and communist Russia" and "banana republic" tactics.[33] Democrats countered that the Republicans should be ashamed of "flaunting the Constitution" and having to be pursued like a "headmaster chasing schoolchildren." The majority leader got his quorum that night, but he was still unable to break the Republican filibuster.

In more normal times, the techniques of congressional leadership include personal contacts, using the rules, making public pronouncements, disbursing favors, lining up interest groups, granting concessions, getting tough, and manipulating people and information. But there are limits to persuasion. Every day, party leaders confront the tension between individual goals and the need to act collectively. Party leaders recognize the importance of constituent demands and are tolerant of members' efforts to meet them. Only in the most extreme cases are firm actions taken. Members of Congress realize that if their institution is to survive as a viable policy-maker, they must be able to act collectively. Party leadership is still the main vehicle for doing so.

PARTY VOTING PATTERNS

Party discipline in the U.S. Congress may be weak compared with parliaments around the democratic world, but party remains the most important factor in explaining voting alignments. The patterns established in hundreds of recorded roll-call votes tell a great deal about congressional voting behavior.[34] In general, the importance of party in congressional voting has declined in the twentieth century, but significant variation in partisanship has occurred in the 1980s as a result of differing levels of presidential effectiveness and divided control of the House, the Senate, and the presidency.

Partisanship in voting patterns can be measured in different ways, depending on how large a proportion of one party opposes the other party.[35] At one extreme are straight-party-line votes, where all members of one party oppose all members of the other party. These remain relatively rare in Congress, occurring on only a handful of votes. A strict definition of party voting is when 90 percent of one party oppose the other. A less strict but firm indication of partisanship is when 75 percent of the members of one party oppose the other party. The least stringent definition of party voting is when a majority of one party (50 percent) votes against a majority of another.

Table 12-7 compares party voting, using the 50 percent definition, from 1975 to 1989. Even by this standard, in many years less than half of all votes in Congress can be considered party votes. But note the increase in partisanship after 1982, particularly in the House. In 1987, almost two-thirds of all votes pitted the two parties against each other—the most partisanship in more than thirty years. Party voting dipped in the House in 1988 but returned to 55 percent in 1989, President Bush's first year in office. In the Senate, however, party voting under Bush declined to barely one vote in three, the least partisanship in fifteen years. Party voting in the House of Representatives also increased in the later years of the Reagan administration under more rigorous standards. Some 32 percent of all House votes were party votes in 1987, using the firmer 75 percent definition of partisanship. This compares with only 12 percent in 1981. The Senate has averaged around 20 percent party votes in the 1980s, under the 75 percent standard. Using the 90 percent criteria, 10 percent of House votes and 9 precent of Senate votes in 1987 were strict party votes.

What issues tended to divide members along party lines? In the 1980s, the budget was the subject of the most divisive partisan voting patterns.[36] Since 1980, the budget has become critical in representing party philosophy and in determining whether the Republican White House or Democratic House would set the nation's policy agenda. Procedural questions and rules were also responsible for party voting in Congress. Other domestic issues were sometimes partisan but not as consistently as rules or budget questions. And although some issues, such as aid to the Nicaraguan Contras, occasionally resulted in party voting, national security and foreign policy issues tended to generate the fewest party coalitions and votes.

TABLE 12–7

PARTY VOTES IN CONGRESS

Year	House (%)	Senate (%)
1989	55	35
1988	47	42
1987	64	41
1986	57	52
1985	61	50
1984	47	40
1983	56	44
1982	36	43
1981	37	48
1980	38	46
1979	47	47
1978	33	45
1977	42	42
1976	36	37
1975	48	48

NOTE: Percentage of votes where at least 50% of Democrats oppose at least 50% of Republicans.

SOURCE: *Congressional Quarterly.*

Congress and Governing

As a deliberative, legislative body, Congress more often waltzes than marches decisively ahead. The legislative process is messy, chaotic, and conflictual and looks disorganized. Yet for all its institutional faults, Congress remains the most powerful, independent legislature in the world—one that has played a leading role in guaranteeing civil rights, in protecting the environment, and in providing greater security for the elderly.[37] In response to the severe budget problems and conflict with the presidency, Congress has continued to adapt. In recent years, power has shifted back from subcommittees toward party leaders and a few key committees.

DISSATISFACTION WITH GOVERNING CAPABILITIES

Ironically, subcommittee government and democratization made policy influence more difficult for members in some ways. The workload increased substantially and staff assumed more power and responsibility. Members became prisoners of their own success: the constancy of fund-raising and courting PACs made members more vulnerable to interest groups and less effective legislators. At the same time, the deficits constrained spending, making it more difficult for subcommittees to deliver benefits as effectively. Members were increasingly fed up with the way Congress was working.

A survey of over one hundred members released in early 1988 by the nonpartisan Center for Responsible Politics provided some startling findings.[38] Without further reforms, the Center concluded, "legislative gridlock will become the norm of congressional life." Specific findings included the following:

- 56 percent favored a formal legislative schedule set by the leadership for the year with departures from it subject to procedural hurdles;
- 86 percent favored a two-year budget cycle;
- three-quarters of senators favored further limitations on filibusters;
- a remarkable 50 percent favored abolishing the appropriations committees and transferring their role to the authorizing committees;
- 43 percent felt PACs exerted a negative influence and supported limitations on them.

While members remain reluctant to relinquish advantages allowing them to serve local constituencies and foster reelection, there was surprisingly strong sentiment to strengthen collective decision-making capabilities.

STRENGTHENING LEADERS AND KEY COMMITTEES

By the late 1980s, there was an apparent reversal of the decentralizing trends of the 1970s and the emergence of a "new committee oligarchy." Committees of growing importance in the House included the money committees that control "must pass" legislation, such as tax bills, spending bills, and bills that allow the government to borrow. These committees include the Budget Committee, the Appropriations Committee, and the Ways and Means Committee. Also increasingly powerful are the Armed Services Committee and the Energy and Commerce Committee, given their important policy jurisdictions.[39]

Party leaders also assumed more power in the late 1980s to get the legislative process moving. One technique was greater use of bills written by the leadership that had not gone through regular committee channels. Critics complained that one-third of the bills passed by the House in 1988 had never been reported by committee. The Rules Committee, firmly controlled by the Speaker and Democratic leadership, has increasingly sent bills to the floor with closed or modified closed rules that limit amendments. The proportion of legislation with open rules (allowing unlimited amendments) dropped from 85 percent in the 94th Congress to 55 percent in the 100th Congress.[40] Omnibus legislation—mega-bills including a wide range of legislative initiatives—also increased. Leaders recognize that since certain budget bills must pass, they can package other legislation with them, further controlling what members may vote on. Rank and file members resent procedures that limit their ability to amend legislation in order to serve their individual interests. But the changes that fragmented power and made them more vulnerable to interest groups and adverse media coverage created the need for counterveiling institutional arrangements for Congress to function as an effective national policy-maker.

Congress remains in a critical period of transition. An overly decentralized Congress dominated by subcommittees could not function effectively under conditions of divided government and fiscal stress. However, power relationships within Congress remain fluid. Even if power has swung back toward party leaders and the "new committee oligarchy," the changes may not be permanent. If Congress is to function more effectively as a policy-maker, members must balance their desire to get reelected with the collective needs of the institution to participate in governing the nation.

Summary and Conclusions

1. The two main functions of Congress are lawmaking and serving the needs of local constituencies. More often than not, these critical functions clash. Members seem increasingly to focus on constituency and reelection concerns.

2. Incumbents have become nearly invincible in congressional elections by creating an array of advantages and resources to help them stay in office, making Congress less sensitive to national electoral trends.

3. The gradual shift in orientation toward constituency concerns has had implications for the committee system, the party leaders, PACs and interest groups, and the nature of congressional policy-making.

4. Congress' membership is not descriptively representative of American society. Because members of Congress emphasize constituent service, the public tends to approve of the performance of its individual members of Congress while disapproving of the overall performance of Congress.

5. Traditional norms of congressional behavior, such as specialization and reciprocity, seniority and apprenticeship, are weaker than they were a generation ago.

6. The complicated legislative process has many stages where the outcome can be influenced: submission, referral, subcommittee and committee hearing, markup, floor consideration, and final passage.

7. The major development in congressional committees in the 1970s and early 1980s was the increase in the number and the influence of subcommittees, further fragmenting power in the House and Senate. This trend was partially reversed by the 1990s.

8. The main force for overcoming decentralization in Congress is party and party leaders. Voting became more partisan in the late 1980s and party leaders more powerful.

9. Although different approaches to governing may be taken, tighter rules and procedures and more powerful committees and leaders help the House and Senate act collectively to govern.

Congress remains a constitutionally powerful partner in governing the United States. But as we have seen in this chapter, it is often a difficult challenge to perform this role effectively. Congressional elections are more likely to be contested over local concerns and the reputation of incumbents than on national issues. Electoral competition remains stifled, while negative campaigns make incumbents more cautious about dealing with controversial issues and tough choices. Many reforms of the 1970s, while making Congress more open and democratic, also made governing more difficult. But the House and Senate have proven to be adaptable political institutions. In recent years, changes have taken place that have strengthened key committees and party leaders. Future success in policy-making will depend on factors both inside and outside of Congress, particularly within the presidency. In the next two chapters, we examine the presidency and the critical relationship between the legislative and executive branches.

Key Terms

bills
calendars
closed rule
cloture motion
conference committees
declining marginals
discharge petition
filibuster
joint committees
reciprocity
representation
representational role
resolutions
Senate majority leader
seniority system
Speaker of the House of Representatives
special and select committees
specialization
standing committees
unanimous consent agreements

Self-Review

1. What are some differences between the nineteenth-century Congresses and the twentieth-century Congresses?

2. Describe the two main functions of Congress.

3. Who are the legislators, and in what way do they represent their constituents?

4. Describe "declining marginals," their relationship to electoral vulnerability, and the responsiveness of Congress to national trends.

5. Why are incumbents so successful at getting reelected?

6. Explain some of the unwritten rules of congressional behavior.

7. Describe the legislative process from introduction of a bill to the signing of an act by the president.

8. What are the procedures for voting?

9. What are the major organizational and procedural differences between the House and Senate?

10. How does the subcommittee system tend to disperse power within Congress?

11. What are the different kinds of committees in Congress, and which are the most powerful?

12. How are party ratios and assignments to committees determined?

13. How is the House and Senate leadership organized?

14. What techniques do party leaders use to convince legislators to conform to party actions?

15. How have party leaders played a more important role in recent years?

SUGGESTED READINGS

Deering, Christopher. *Congressional Politics.* 1989.
A selection of readings looking at Congress on the individual, institutional, and system levels.

Dodd, Lawrence and Bruce Oppenheimer, eds. *Congress Reconsidered.* 4th ed. 1989.
A collection of articles on recent developments in Congress.

Jacobsen, Gary. *Congressional Elections.* 2nd ed. 1987.
A work compiling recent research on congressional elections and its implications for Congress.

Mayhew, David. *The Electoral Connection.* 1974.
Influential analysis of the trends of congressional elections through the early 1970s.

Oleszek, Walter. *Congressional Procedures and the Policy Process.* 3rd ed. 1989.
A good explanation of congressional rules and procedures and their impact on public policy.

NOTES

1. See Randall B. Ripley, *Congress: Process and Policy* (New York: Norton, 1983), 41-75.
2. Gary Jacobsen, *The Politics of Congressional Elections* (Boston: Little, Brown, 1987), 7.
3. Gary Jacobsen, "Congress A Singular Continuity," in Michael Nelson, ed. *The Elections of 1988* (Washington, D.C.: Congressional Quarterly Press, 1989), 128.
4. *Congressional Quarterly Weekly Reports,* 6 May 1989, p. 1060.
5. David Mayhew, *The Electoral Connection,* (New Haven: Yale University Press, 1974).
6. Jacobsen, *Politics,* 30-39.
7. Monica Bauer and John Hibbing, "Which Incumbents Lose in House Elections?" *American Journal of Political Science* 33 (February 1989):262.
8. Jacobsen, *Politics,* 43-44.
9. Mayhew, *Electoral Connection,* 81-82.
10. Roger Davidson and Walter Oleszek, *Congress and Its Members* (Washington, D.C.: Congressional Quarterly Press, 1981), 124.
11. See Gary C. Jacobsen and Samuel Kernell, *Strategy and Choice in Congressional Elections* (New Haven: Yale University Press, 1981).
12. See Hannah Pitkin, *The Concept of Representation* (Berkeley: University of California Press, 1967), 209-10.
13. Roger Davidson, *The Role of the Congressman* (New York: Pegasus, 1969), 117.
14. See Richard C. Fenno, *Home Style: House Members in Their Districts* (Boston: Little, Brown, 1978).
15. Ibid., chaps. 3 and 4.
16. See Norman Ornstein, Robert Peabody, and David Rohde, "The Changing Senate: From the 1950s to the 1970s," in Lawrence Dodd and Bruce Oppenheimer, eds., *Congress Reconsidered* (New York: Praeger, 1977), 3-21.
17. Quoted in David Volger, *The Politics of Congress* (Boston: Allyn and Bacon, 1974), 236.
18. Walter Oleszek, *Congressional Procedures and the Policy Process,* 2nd ed. (Washington, D.C.: Congressional Quarterly Press, 1984), 74.
19. Ibid., 22, 94.
20. William L. Morrow, *Congressional Committees* (New York: Scribners, 1969), 42-43.
21. *Congressional Quarterly Weekly Reports,* 15 January 1983, p. 151.
22. Ibid., 12 March 1983, pp. 501-6.
23. Ibid.
24. Barbara Hinckley, *Stability and Change in Congress* (New York: Harper and Row, 1978).
25. *Congressional Quarterly Weekly Reports,* 12 March 1983, p. 501.
26. Leroy Reiselbach, *Congressional Reform* (Washington, D.C.: Congressional Quarterly Press, 1986).
27. Norman J. Ornstein, "Causes and Consequences of Congressional Change: Subcommittee Reforms in the House of Representatives," in Norman J. Ornstein,

ed. *Congress in Change* (New York: Praeger, 1975), 88-114.

28. Lawrence Dodd and Bruce Oppenheimer, *Congress Reconsiderd* (Washington, D.C.: Congressional Quarterly Press, 1989) 47.
29. Ripley, *Congress,* 215-21.
30. *Congressional Quarterly Weekly Reports,* 8 January 1983, 4-6.
31. *Congressional Quarterly Weekly Reports,* 31 October 1987, p. 2653.
32. Ralph K. Huitt, "Democratic Party Leadership in the Senate," *American Political Science Review* 55 (June 1961):331-44.
33. *St. Louis Post-Dispatch,* 26 February 1988, p. 1.
34. For two early studies that influenced others, see David B. Truman, *The Congressional Party* (New York: Wiley, 1959), and Duncan MacRae, *Dimensions of Congressional Voting* (Berkeley: University of California Press, 1958).
35. See *Congressional Quarterly Weekly Reports,* 16 January 1988, pp. 101-6, for a discussion of standards of party voting and party unity.
36. Ibid., 102-3.
37. See Steven A. Shull, *Domestic Policy Formation: Presidential-Congressional Partnerships?* (Westport, Conn.: Greenwood Press, 1983), chaps. 4, 5.
38. *Congressional Quarterly Weekly Reports,* 16 January 1988, p. 126.
39. Dodd and Oppenheimer, *Congress Reconsidered* (1989), 48-50.
40. Steven Smith, "Taking It to the Floor," in ibid., 339.

CHAPTER 13

The Presidency

POLITICAL CLOSE-UP

The President Earns His Pay, by Harry S. Truman

Three months after the 1948 election, Congress raised the president's salary from $50,000 to $100,000 and provided him with an expense fund of $50,000. Frank Kent, a newspaper columnist for the Washington Star, wrote an article protesting this generosity. President Harry Truman fired off a personal reply the same day, making it clear to Kent just what the president does to earn that money!

February 12, 1949

My Dear Mr. Kent:

Today I read your piece in the *Washington Star* of this date on the salary and expense account of the President of the United States. That piece is a most interesting and astonishing document, to say the least that can be said about it.

Your President is responsible for the administration and management of the greatest, most complicated and most *expensive* organization in the history of the world.

When, on April 12, 1945, *your* President was inducted into that greatest office in the world, by a simple ceremony in the Cabinet Room at the White House at 7:09 P.M., he inherited *two* wars. As Chairman of a Senate Committee, he had furnished co-operative help to President Roosevelt which, according to reliable authority, had saved for the taxpayers some fifteen billions of dollars and which service prevented scandal and corruption in sales to and contracts with the Government.

Your President was forced into becoming a candidate for Vice President by President Roosevelt, who made a personal and national and also a party appeal to the then Senator in charge of the Special Committee referred to, to become the candidate.

Your President knew what he faced. Just eight days short of three months after he became vice president, the blow fell.

He found himself in the top position of responsibility in all the world. Two wars going at top pace. Both ended within five months—a year and a half ahead of the best guess of the "experts." A budget of 103 billions of dollars had been voted for the fiscal year 1945–46. Sixty-five billions of that authorization were cut off—by the President. Expenditures that year were about 45 billions. The next year's expenditures ('46–'47) were 33 billions. Twenty-five billions of dollars were paid on the national debt of 277 billions.

Attempts were made for efficiency and economy by sending reorganization plans to the Congress. All were rejected but one of minor importance.

An attempt was made to utilize wartime experience to reorganize the military establishment. Same result as the reorganization plans—it was bungled by *your* 80th Congress.

For working eighteen hours a day *every* day in the year and for assuming the responsibility, greater than any other dozen men in the *world*, your President received *net* pay of $42,000.00 per year! A most liberal and munificent salary! Probably what you receive for one month's blurbs! From that most liberal salary your president must clothe [himself], and meet regular family expenses—he can't put his wife on the payroll as his secretary as he did in the Senate to meet the "rent" payments.

So the Congress votes certain pay and allowances, to meet this extraordinary situation—and you, of all people, have a spasm about it. I'm really surprised because I've always thought you intellectually honest. From Dave Lawrence, Pegler, Pearson, Winchell, I'd expect just such statements as you made—but we know that they are all liars, and intellectually dishonest.

I'm sorry you joined them.

Sincerely,

Harry S. Truman

SOURCE: Robert H. Ferrell, ed., *Off the Record: The Private Papers of Harry S. Truman* (New York: Penguin, 1980), 155-56.

CHAPTER OUTLINE

INTRODUCTON AND OVERVIEW

Is the president of the United States an awesome czar or a helpless giant? The office is often portrayed as the most powerful position of authority in the world and the president as head of the greatest nation, possessor of massive powers, the driving force of American and world politics. Yet the president seems to be constantly frustrated, blocked at every turn by Congress, the courts, the media, or the bureaucracy. Which is the real American presidency?

The presidency is the most dominant feature of the American political landscape. In its moments of greatness, the presidency has displayed stirring leadership, exceeding all public expectations. In lesser moments, the presidency has left disillusionment and disappointment in its wake. The presidency is the institution of government most able to act decisively, to centralize political authority, to govern. In times of crisis—the Civil War, World War I, the Great Depression, and World War II—the scope of the presidency has expanded, enabling the government to move with dispatch and energy. Of all the institutions of American government, the presidency has demonstrated the greatest range of governing ability. But what enabled the American political system to survive and prosper in extraordinary times may have created unrealistic expectations for performance in normal times.

The presidency has undergone dramatic changes over the past two centuries. The **traditional presidency**, created in Article II of the Constitution, was intended to have limited and checked power, a result of the Founder's fears of monarchy. Except during wartime crises, the traditional presidency had little to do and operated with a relatively small number of people. As late as the 1920s, President Calvin Coolidge often only worked in his office several hours a day (while sleeping as many as fourteen hours)! The presidency changed dramatically after the inauguration of Franklin D. Roosevelt in 1933. Most scholars use this date as the beginning of the **modern presidency**, which was characterized by a more activist, visible, and powerful chief executive. Roosevelt and his successors played a commanding role in both domestic politics and international affairs as the presidency grew in size and power. Political scientist Richard Rose suggests that with the dramatic changes in international political economy, the era of the **postmodern presidency** has arrived.[1]

> The difference between the modern and the postmodern Presidency is that a postmodern President can no longer dominate the international system. . . . While the White House is accustomed to influencing foreign nations, the postmodern president must accept something less appealing: Other nations can now influence what the White House achieves. Whereas the Constitution made Congress and the Supreme Court the chief checks on the traditional and the modern President, the chief constraints on the postmodern President are found in other nations.[2]

Four primary factors shape the presidency and determine its impact.[3]

Powers and roles: The American presidency, based on constitutional powers established in Article II, has expanded dramatically in scope and influence in two hundred years. The presidency depends on both the formal and the informal powers of the presidency and how skillfully they are exercised. The president plays a number of important roles in American politics but rarely acts alone.

The political environment: The presidency exists in a changing environment, both in the world outside the United States and in public expectations at home. The climate for presidential leadership depends on public opinion, the media, Congress, the courts, the bureaucracy, and state and local government. The environment can create expectations for and obstacles to leadership.

The office: The American presidency has become an institution that shapes the incumbent as much as the incumbent shapes the office. The performance of the presidency today is affected by the presidential office: the White House staff, the Executive Office of the President, and presidential advisers. Presidential effectiveness is related to the president's ability to manage the office and to mobilize political resources to govern.

The person: The man or, perhaps in the not-too-distant future, the woman who occupies the White House obviously shapes the presidency. His sense of power, personality, management, and selling abilities play a large role in determining the effectiveness of the presidency.

Each of these factors can be critical, but the overall performance of the presidency is a combination of all four. This chapter considers these factors and asks the following questions:

1. What are presidential powers and presidential roles, and how have they evolved?

2. What does the public expect of the president? What are the key elements of the political environment, and what determines presidential popularity?

3. What is the presidency, and how has the office expanded over the years? What is the role of the White House staff and the cabinet? Who are the president's closest advisers?

4. How does the president mobilize to make public policy? What are the different styles of presidential management and public relations? What are some of the particular problems associated

with foreign policy and economic policy?
5. How do a president's personality and skills affect his ability to govern? What personal skills are essential to effective leadership?

The Powers and Roles of the Presidency

TRADITIONAL CONSTITUTIONAL POWERS

Imagine their amazement if somehow the Founders could spend a few days with the president of the United States today. Although the modern presidency still rests on the constitutional foundations laid two centuries ago, the office has grown dramatically. Recall from Chapter 2 that some of the key decisions made in establishing the presidency were the creation of a single executive, the choice of an indirect method of selection, the rejection of an official cabinet or council, and the attempt to balance and share powers with Congress. Under the specific powers granted in **Article II** of the Constitution, the president—

- Commands the armed forces
- Receives ambassadors
- Commissions military officers
- Wields the "executive power" of the United States
- Grants reprieves and pardons
- May call Congress into session
- Appoints federal officials
- Nominates judges, ambassadors, and other high officials
- Negotiates treaties
- Approves or vetoes legislation
- "Faithfully executes" the laws

The list of formal powers is not very impressive, even though the advocates of a strong presidency had to bargain hard to get even this much. The constitutional basis of the presidency is largely unaltered, but the presidency has been transformed. In the 1840s, James Polk used to complain that he spent too much time correcting the grammar in State Department correspondence. That day seems light years away. The powers of the presidency have expanded into a complex set of political roles.

MODERN PRESIDENTIAL ROLES

Just as George Washington was the model for Article II, so Franklin Roosevelt was the model for those who wrote about the modern presidency after 1945. One classic work of this era was a book written in 1956 by political scientist Clinton Rossiter. His list of presidential roles, described as the different "hats" the president wears, reflects an expansive and heroic image of the president.[4]

- Chief of State
- Chief Executive
- Chief Diplomat
- Commander in Chief
- Chief Legislator
- Party Chief
- Voice of the People
- Protector of the Peace
- Manager of Prosperity
- Leader of the Free World

Although Rossiter left out "protector of animals and small children," his description of presidential roles would almost have fit Superman or Wonder Woman. This was a "heroic" conceptualization of the presidency.[5] Richard Neustadt added a note of realism by focusing on the limitations of presidential power in the American political system.[6] He pointed out that presidents rarely have the power to command. Instead, he wrote, presidential power is the power to persuade, to bargain. Presidents succeed by consolidating and maximizing personal political power by managing political resources skillfully. Through the 1950s and early 1960s, an expansion of presidential power was a desirable end. No one questioned the assumption that a more powerful presidency was a better presidency that would make good public policy.

By the late 1960s and early 1970s, a serious reappraisal of presidential power and the president's role in the political system took place. The divisive war in Vietnam, a presidential war undeclared by Congress, had cast long shadows on the presidency. In its aftermath came evidence of presidential lying and duplicity. Revelations through the publication of once-secret documents tarnished the reputations and credibility of Presidents Johnson and Nixon and even dimmed the posthumous glow of John Kennedy. Vietnam brought on a national identity crisis and a reevaluation of the presidency. Excessive power and isolation from accountability created the "imperial" presidency.[7]

The Watergate scandal went even further in damaging the office of the president. "Enemies" lists, illegal wiretapping, "plumbers" squads, misuse of federal agencies, secret foreign bank accounts, and an obvious contempt for Congress revealed a disrespect for constitutional and democratic principles. The public reacted against the imperial presidency. As the undesirable side of presidential power became apparent, support for a powerful presidency with an increasingly prominent role in policy-making dropped precipitously. The imperial presidency was insulated from reality. Presidential power was too great, too concentrated, too isolated, and too unaccountable. Vietnam and Watergate helped balance the presidency and the other components of the political system, especially Congress, but it also weakened the presidency. At the same time, economic and geopolitical changes were creating new constraints on the presidency.

POSTMODERN PRESIDENTIAL CONSTRAINTS

In recent years, changes in the international environment have had important consequences for the presidency. The United States dominated the international economy and geopolitical system in the decades after World War II. Presidential power was enhanced by the nuclear arms race and the Cold War, as well as by America's leading economic position. But economic balances shifted quickly in the late 1970s and early 1980s. The rapid growth of Europe and Japan and increasing economic interdependence among the nations of the world have changed the nature of the presidency. Rose argues that the resources of the postmodern presidency are often insufficient to meet new international challenges and responsibilities.[8] While the United States has not necessarily declined as a great power, other nations have grown stronger.

Presidents must work collaboratively with world leaders, and their opinions and reactions have become much more important. Competitiveness in international markets is increasingly necessary for the success of the U.S. economy. Issues concerning U.S. trade and international debt are influenced by decisions in Bonn and Tokyo, as well as Washington. The democratization of Eastern Europe and the rapid changes in the Soviet Union have accelerated the shift to the postmodern presidency by removing the containment of communism as the dominant goal of U.S. foreign policy and a source of presidential power.

The crisis in the Mideast in 1990 provided a view of how postmodern presidents handle international aggression in the post-Cold War era. President George Bush and his Cabinet carefully used the United Nations and diplomatic means to forge an international coalition to oppose Iraq's invasion of Kuwait. He lobbied not only for troops and military support from other nations but also for aid from Germany and Japan to help finance America's military action in the Gulf.

As international cooperation becomes a more essential element of the presidency, governing problems related to separation of powers and divided government at home become more serious. While most prime ministers and heads of state can deal authoritatively in negotiations with other world leaders, the president cannot always deliver what is promised. Governing has become more challenging for postmodern presidents because popularity at home is no guarantee of effectiveness abroad. Traditional presidents avoided entanglement with other nations while modern presidents dominated them. Postmodern presidents must have the skills to cooperate and compete.

THE JOB OF THE PRESIDENT

While these changes in the world may have made it more difficult, they have not diminished the need for effective presidential leadership in governing the nation. The president continues to play a variety of essential roles.

HEAD OF STATE AND SYMBOLIC LEADER. With no king queen, or crown prince, it has fallen to the president to represent the nation and its government. In Great Britain, for example, the queen performs the ceremonial duties of head of state, leaving political functions to the prime minister. The American people look to the president first as a symbol of the nation. The president acts as a symbolic leader in both the foreign realm and the domestic realm. The president's role as symbolic head of state can have an important impact on governing by affecting the president's popularity and support for specific policy proposals.

The American president also plays the symbolic role of goal-setter and communicator of national priorities and values. With the growing importance of the mass media, the president's rhetorical and selling skills have become essential to this role. Presidents strive to set broad priorities for the nation, above and beyond their more specific policy proposals. Tough talk about terrorists or emphasizing the traditional values of American political economy is common for presidents as they function as symbolic leader. General goal-setting can be critical to the ability to govern because it can pave the way for specific, substantive proposals.

CRISIS MANAGER. The power of the presidency is greatest during a crisis. At such times, normal competition and opposition give way to acquiescence as both formal and informal powers are increased. The assumption and exercise of presidential authority in a crisis has served almost like a safety valve for the American political system. The power of the presidency has been greatest during wartime, particularly during the Civil War and World War II, and during national security crises. Severe economic crises, such as the Great Depression, have also been characterized by crisis management. The president may be called on to serve as crisis manager in other domestic areas, with varying degrees of effectiveness. For example, in natural calamities, the president can act to declare a disaster and take certain emergency measures. In times of civil crisis, the president may use the National Guard, as President Eisenhower did when he sent troops into Little Rock, Arkansas, in 1957 to uphold the Supreme Court's integration decision.

Just as normal political obstacles diminish during a crisis, so also may the president assume rather awesome formal powers over people, property, and communications when an emergency is declared. But even these powers are checked. Congress is

President Bush with former Republican presidents Ford, Nixon, and Reagan.

usually responsible for granting **emergency powers.** The Supreme Court has occasionally limited presidential exercise of emergency powers, such as it did when Truman took over the steel mills in 1950.[9] Consistent with its general reassertion of power in the 1970s, Congress passed the National Emergencies Act in 1976, terminating many past emergency declarations and limiting how the president could use emergency powers.[10] Although the president's role as crisis manager clearly enhances the ability to govern, it also creates expectations that the president can somehow centralize power and solve problems in noncrisis times.

LEGISLATOR AND COALITION-BUILDER. One of the most important roles of the president is that of legislator and coalition-builder. Presidents assemble a legislative program, consolidate proposals from the bureaucracy, and through their congressional liaison office act as a major lobbyist on Capitol Hill. Congress today is more independent than ever. Party coalitions are more difficult to forge and more fragile when they occur. Jimmy Carter's success in gaining Senate approval for the controversial Panama Canal treaties in 1978 was an extremely skillful job of coalition-building, particularly because two-thirds of the senators were needed to approve. In the economic domain, Reagan's 1981 budget and tax cut program was one of the more dramatic presidential successes in coalition-building in recent years.

EXECUTIVE AND ADMINISTRATOR. Another of the president's important roles is the role of chief executive, where the president functions to execute the laws and to exert some control over the massive federal bureaucracy. But in many ways, the bureaucracy is as much of a constraint on the president as the Congress. When Eisenhower succeeded Truman to the presidency, Truman ridiculed the idea of Eisenhower trying to run the bureaucracy as he did the military: "He'll sit there and he'll say, 'Do this! Do that!,' and nothing will happen. Poor Ike—it won't be a bit like the army."[11] Other presidents have had their troubles with the bureaucracy. Kennedy discovered during the Cuban missile crisis that his direct order to remove missiles from Turkey eighteen months earlier had never been carried out. One of his aides later commented, "Everyone believes in democracy until he gets to the White House and then you begin to believe in dictatorship, because it's so hard to get things done."[12]

Despite their complaints, presidents are far from impotent in shaping bureaucratic policies. One of the most important ways in which they shape policy is through the power of executive appointment. The president controls around three thousand appointments to the top levels of the U.S. government. Although this may seem to be a large number, political appointees are usually less than 1 percent of agency personnel! Presidents Bush and Reagan were extremely careful about making executive appointments, often taking many months to fill high-level positions.

The presidency has expanded far beyond the Article II outline of presidential powers, but the postmodern president is far from an all-powerful force. The president is faced with many limitations in authority, competitors for power, and obstacles to leadership. One obstacle is high public expectations of performance. What do the American people expect of the president? How can presidents maintain the public support and popularity that is so essential to their role in governing?

The President and the Public

PUBLIC EXPECTATIONS OF THE PRESIDENT

The relationship between the American people and their president is often mystifying. Ambivalence about presidential power evidenced at the Constitutional Convention still prevails in different forms. The American public has high expectations of the president. He or she is to be of impeccable personal character. Table 13-1 suggests some of the parameters of behavior—no smoking marijuana, no ethnic jokes, and no atheism. A majority of Americans expect their president to be intelligent, competent, ethical, funny, imaginative, and charming.[13] Policy expectations are also high. Fairly or unfairly, the people hold the president responsible for such things as the performance of the economy, the readiness of national defense, energy prices, and the achievement of social

TABLE 13–1

WHAT THE AMERICAN PEOPLE EXPECT OF THE PRESIDENT

Personal Characteristics of Presidents

Characteristic	% Who Feel It's Important
Intelligence	82
Sound judgment in a crisis	81
Competence, ability to get job done	74
High ethical standards	66
Sense of humor	50
Imagination	42
Personal charm, style, charisma	33

Private Behaviors of Presidents

Behavior	% Who Would Strongly Object
If he smoked marijuana occasionally	70
If he told ethnic or racial jokes in private	43
If he were not a member of a church	38
If he used tranquilizers occasionally	36
If he used profane language in private	33
If he had seen a psychiatrist	30
If he wore blue jeans occasionally in the Oval Office	21
If he were divorced	17
If he had a cocktail before dinner each night	14

SOURCE: Gallup poll, Fall 1979.

justice.[14] Two-thirds of the people blamed President Carter for high energy prices and gasoline shortages during his administration.

Americans are aware that their expectations are high and that it is difficult for presidents to live up to them. More than 75 percent of the public agreed that, compared with an earlier time, the job of president is tougher, Congress is more difficult to deal with, the press is more critical, and public expectations are higher.[15] Can the president meet these expectations?

PRESIDENTIAL POPULARITY

Figure 13-1 shows the pattern of support in the postwar period from the Truman administration to the Bush administration. What factors determine public support for the president? Political scientists have studied the patterns of support and arrived at some explanations for variations.[16] First, presidents gain in popularity during an international crisis or when they act as symbol of the United States (such as at a summit conference). This "rally around the flag" phenomenon does not depend on how successful the operation is. Kennedy gained in popularity even after the disastrous Bay of Pigs invasion in 1961. Second, poor economic performance tends to reduce presidential popularity. President Reagan's decline in popularity to its lowest point corresponded closely to economic downturn and unemployment reaching 10.5 percent. But a president's popularity usually declines over time, no matter what he does. The public (particularly people not of the president's party) appears to grow more disenchanted with an administration the longer it is

FIGURE 13–1

BUSH APPROVAL/DISAPPROVAL

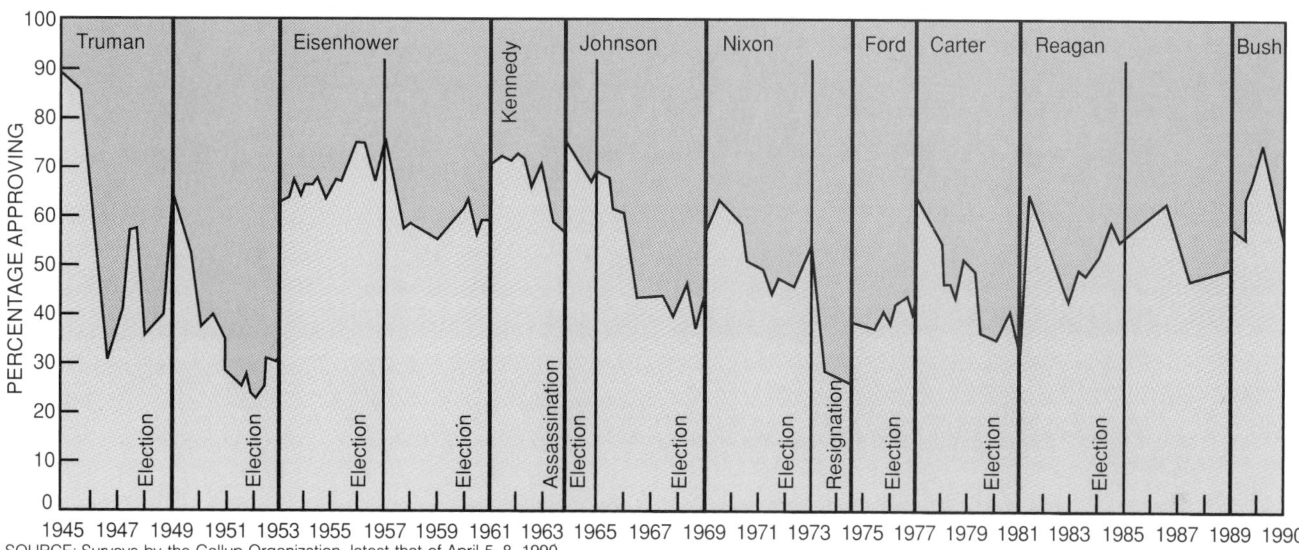

SOURCE: Surveys by the Gallup Organization, latest that of April 5–8, 1990.

in office. Both Republicans and Democrats have suffered this decline.

Public support for President Reagan during his presidency (Figure 13-2) demonstrates some of these historic patterns. Reagan took office in January 1981 with high popularity (68 percent). The failed assassination attempt three months into his first term bumped his approval rating to a record 74 percent. His popularity remained over 60 percent as his economic and budget plan was adopted. With the specter of a growing recession and burgeoning budget deficits in 1982, however, Reagan's popularity declined to its low point close to the time unemployment peaked at over 10 percent. As the economy improved, Reagan's popularity began a steady rise, up to his landslide reelection in 1984. The invasion of Grenada pro-vided a short-term jump in 1983. His popularity remained high through his second term—over 60 percent—with another short jump around the time of the air raid on Libya. The Iran-Contra revelations precipitated a major decline of almost 20 percent beginning in the fall of 1986. He partially recovered into the mid-50-percent-approval range through 1988. Like Eisenhower, Ronald Reagan did not suffer as much of a long-term decline in popularity as most of the other recent presidents.

George Bush enjoyed near record popularity during his first eighteen months in office. While his approval rating at the time of his inauguration was only 51 percent, his popularity with the American people rose steadily. Throughout the first half of 1989, around 60 percent approved of his performance as president, but by midsummer, his ratings were over 70 percent. The numbers would climb even higher. The invasion of Panama in December 1989 demonstrated that the president still receives a boost in ratings when the United States is involved in an armed conflict. The rally-around-the-flag phenomenon catapulted President Bush to a record-breaking approval rating of 80 percent as measured by the Gallup poll in January 1990. Only 11 percent disapproved of his performance. While this level of popularity did not last, Bush continued to be approved by seven of ten Americans through early 1990. His approval ratings once again rose after he sent troops to Saudi Arabia in August of 1990 to confront Saddam Hussein. But the failure of the budget summit agreement and growing impatience over the

FIGURE 13–2

PRESIDENT REAGAN'S PUBLIC APPROVAL RATINGS, 1981–1988

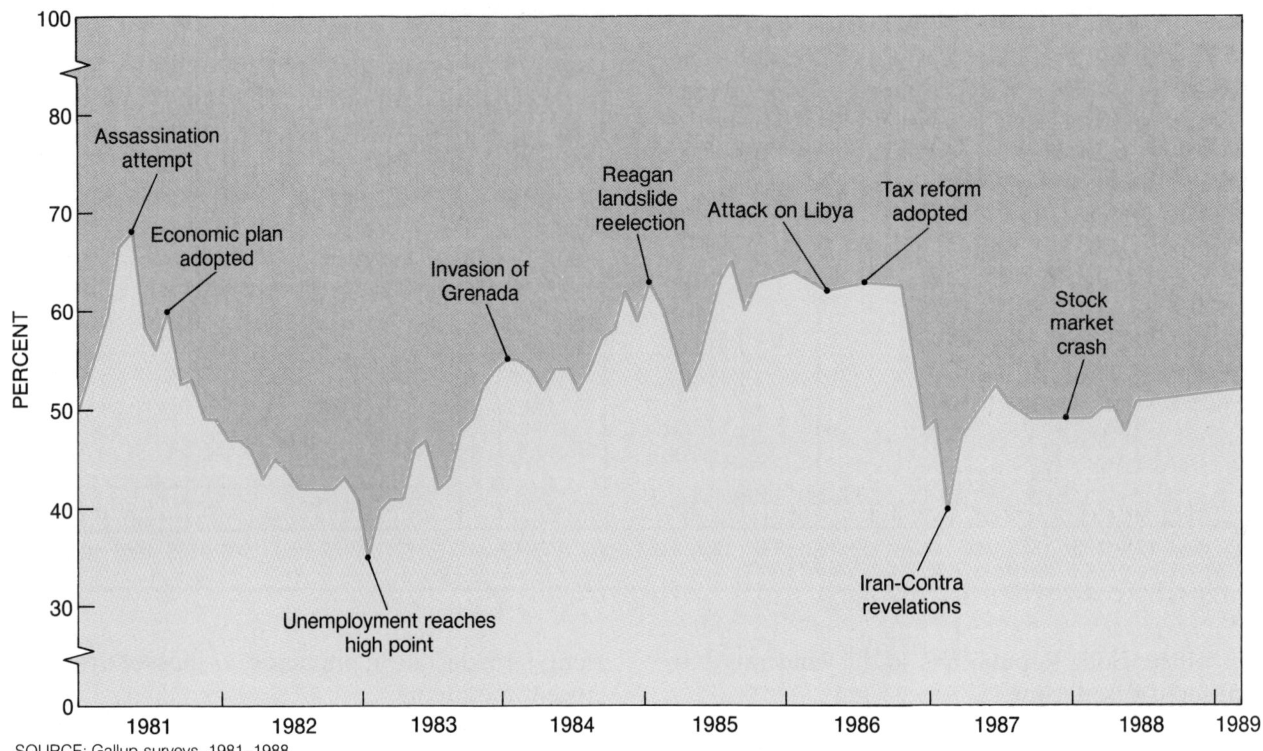

SOURCE: Gallup surveys, 1981–1988.

standoff in the Middle East plunged his approval to 55 percent in October, 1990.

There are hundreds of reasons that people approve or disapprove of a president's performance, and we have mentioned a few patterns. Yet much about presidential popularity remains mysterious, a blending of personality and events. Of course, far from being a helpless pawn, the president constantly works to gain and maintain popular support.

SHAPING PUBLIC OPINION

The president has an array of methods to help shape public opinion, including news conferences, televised addresses, and using the presidential press secretary and other spokespersons who filter the president's views and polish the president's image. Less positive aspects of presidential molding of public opinion also exist. Presidents sometimes withhold negative or damaging information from the public, such as the Pentagon Papers revelations about the Vietnam War.[17] In domestic affairs as well, unfavorable facts and figures may never see the light of day, or may be manipulated.[18] Presidents like to deemphasize bad news and point instead to something that makes them look better. An administration may change the way certain economic indicators are collected. Presidential budget directors may use certain accounting tricks or make unrealistic assumptions to make the budget totals look smaller than they really are. In addition, the White House times the release of information to serve its purposes. A good news item will be released before deadlines of the network news, whereas less desirable news may be released right after the evening news, as the White House did with the resignation of Anne Burford, Reagan's Environmental Protection Agency (EPA) administrator in 1983.

Presidents often are evasive and ambiguous. President Reagan frequently responded that amatter was "still under consideration," even when some decisions were known to have been reached. Direct lies by American presidents to the people are not unknown. Eisenhower, Kennedy, and Johnson all lied about various covert activities by the United States: the U-2 spy plane, the coup in Vietnam, the invasion of the Dominican Republic. President Bush tried to remain vague about his "no new taxes" pledge when agreeing to a budget summit with Congress where all issues were to be on the table. He faced a delicate situation in trying to maintain his popularity while facing tough, unpopular choices. By mid-1990, Bush acknowledged that new revenues were needed.

The modern presidency has become oriented to the media. Has it become more important simply to look presidential than actually to exert meaningful leadership? Marketing the president and his programs to maintain popularity and support seems inevitable today. One danger, however, is that the public will be victims of expedient, shortsighted, and dubious public policies. Another danger is that expectations far beyond what the limited presidency can realistically accomplish will be established.

Is there any way to maintain public support while avoiding the temptation to engage in "feel-good" politics? The answer, in part, depends on how the office of the president is organized and managed.

The Presidential Office

"The president needs help," concluded the Brownlow Report in 1937 after looking over the organization of the White House and the staff support available to the president. When the world was a simpler place and the traditional presidency an easier job, there were few organizational problems. Presidents from Washington to Hoover had fared well enough using cabinet officers and personal secretaries and assistants and assigning a few political appointees to the White House.

These ad hoc arrangements proved insufficient for the modern presidency when the scope of government increased. Social Security, public welfare, regulatory activities, government jobs programs, and a host of other new activities became national policy. Dissatisfied with the available staff, Roosevelt commissioned Brownlow's group to recommend changes to improve the organization and capabilities of his office. The changes that were adopted in the late 1930s and 1940s permanently altered the American presidency.

THE PRESIDENCY

Just what is meant by the term the ***presidency?*** One image of the presidency is the president sitting on top of the entire federal branch. Such a view fails to distinguish between the organization directly surrounding the president and the rest of the bureaucracy. At the other extreme, the presidency is sometimes represented as a single individual carrying great burdens, sitting alone, making decisions for the whole country. Neither image of the presidency is adequate.

The presidency is more than one individual, but it is far less than the entire executive branch. The presidency is the president and those who work directly for him: the inner circle of White House staff and presidential "agencies" that play a regular and important role in decision-making. Although the president is technically the head of the executive branch, presidents have as much trouble with the bureaucracy as they do with Congress. The presidency includes the White House staff, the Executive Office of the President (EOP), and the cabinet. The White House staff and the EOP were created by Franklin Roosevelt in 1939. The cabinet dates back to George Washington's first year in office. Together, these people and institutions form the modern presidency.

THE WHITE HOUSE STAFF

From domestics who cook and clean to domestic policy advisers, the **White House staff** are the president's personal troops. Working in close proximity to the president, they are likely to run into him in the corridors of the White House. The exact titles may change from administration to administration, but the top advisers—the inner circle—usually include the chief and deputy chief of staff, the press secretary, the domestic affairs adviser, the national security adviser, the political affairs adviser, the communications director, the appointments secretary, and various counselors and special assistants. They are housed in the West Wing of the White House near the president's Oval Office. Although vice-presidents have not always enjoyed close relationships with the president, in recent administrations they have been given positions close to the center of power.

The White House staff is made up of the lofty and the lowly. Henry Kissinger largely ran U.S. foreign policy from his White House office during Nixon's first term. Less prominent aides come and go without much notice. Staff members compete for access and proximity to the president, and the location of offices suggests a hierarchy of political importance. Senior staff in the White House are very much the president's men and women. The president sees them daily, grumbles at them when he is in a bad mood, may come to them for advice in times of crisis.

White House staff members serve two critical functions. First, they are the president's ambassadors to key groups and elements of the political system. As ambassadors, the staff links the president to Congress, the bureaucracy, foreign nations, political parties, the media, state and local governments, and the public. Second, they constitute important decision-making groups within the presidency. Figure 13-3 shows some of the most important staff offices and related constituencies. The White House staff grew from fifty during the Roosevelt administration to more than five hundred during the Nixon and Ford years. Under Carter, Reagan, and Bush, the number has stabilized at about four hundred.

The Executive Office of the President

Individuals in the **Executive Office of the President** form a second circle of presidential advisers. Most employees are located outside the White House, usually in the Executive Office Building next door. The EOP was created in 1939, following the report of the Brownlow Commission, and evolved in the post-World War II years. One of its first agencies was the Bureau of the Budget—now named the Office of Management and Budget (OMB). The president's budget office has become a key element

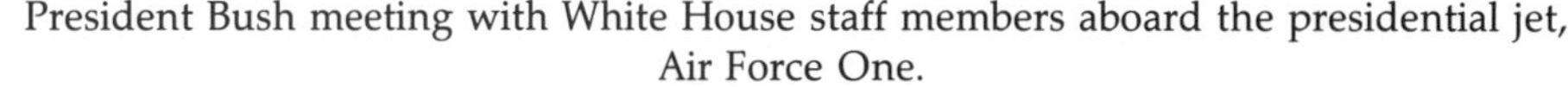

President Bush meeting with White House staff members aboard the presidential jet, Air Force One.

FIGURE 13-3

Presidential Advisers as Decision-Makers and Ambassadors

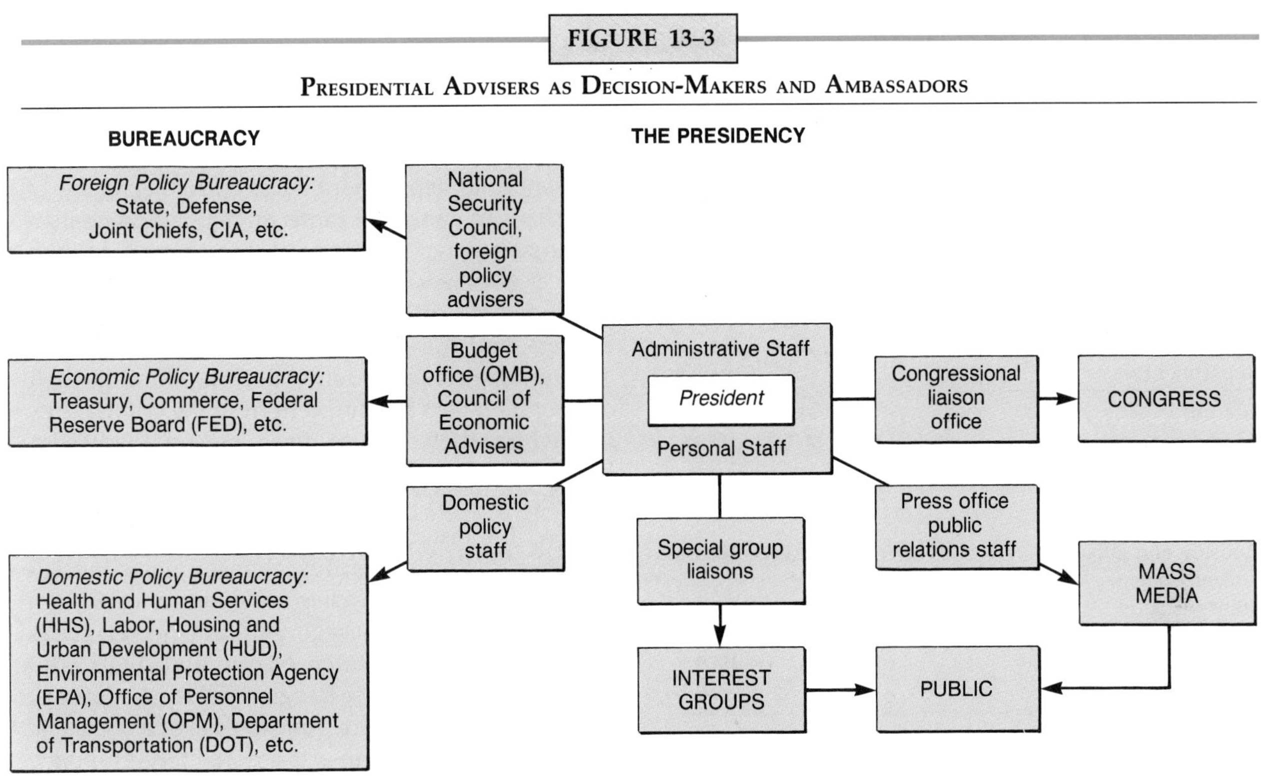

of the presidency through its preparation of the budget, its coordination of the president's legislative program, and its role as liaison with the agencies in money matters.

In 1946, Congress legitimized government management of the economy with the passage of the Employment Act.[19] In addition to defining goals, the act provided the president with staff economists and required him to report annually to Congress on economic policy. The Council of Economic Advisers became an integral part of the EOP and the presidency.

In 1947, Congress used the government's wartime experience to improve national security decision-making when it passed the National Security Act. The act merged the War Department and the separate branches of the services, creating the Defense Department. It designed the National Security Council, making it part of the White House staff, to help the president respond to foreign crises. Finally, it consolidated U.S. intelligence-gathering activities in the Central Intelligence Agency.

Is the Executive Office as efficient as the preceding descriptions would make it appear? Unfortunately, no. The neat organization chart of the White House staff and EOP masks the variation and frequent confusion in staffing arrangements. Two former EOP administrators noted, "EOP's many chiefs and indians spend most of their time and energy maneuvering with, around, and against each other rather than providing coherence and strategy to the rest of government."[20]

The Cabinet

The trend in presidential staffing toward a corps of close, trusted advisers helped foster the decline of the cabinet as an important presidential advisory body. The **cabinet** is made up of the heads of the fourteen executive departments, shown in order of creation (Table 13-2). All cabinet departments are not created equal. There is an "inner" cabinet and an "outer" cabinet.[21] Inner cabinet secretaries—State, Defense, Treasury, and Justice—tend to be more prominent and influential than outer cabinet

TABLE 13–2

THE CABINET DEPARTMENTS

Department	Created
Inner Cabinet	
State	1789
Treasury	1789
Defense (previously War)	1789
Justice	1789
Outer Cabinet	
Interior	1849
Agriculture	1889
Commerce	1913
Labor	1913
Health and Human Services	1953
Housing and Urban Development	1965
Transportation	1966
Energy	1977
Education	1979
Veterans Affairs	1988

secretaries. Presidents tend to appoint professionals with general experience in government to the inner cabinet posts, while leaning toward client-oriented and policy specialist appointments in the outer cabinet. Although a number of blacks and women have been appointed to cabinet positions in recent years, none has ever been appointed to the inner cabinet posts.[22]

Cabinet members occasionally are close to the president, but some are far removed from the center of power. John Kennedy's brother Robert, attorney general of the United States, was one of the president's confidants. Secretary of State James Baker III was a long-time friend of George Bush and a close political adviser. Several of Nixon's cabinet members, in contrast, could not get an appointment to see the president for months at a time. The president is free to choose how he will use or not use the cabinet as a decision-making institution.

Despite two centuries of problems with their cabinets, before taking office almost every president talks about reviving the cabinet. The cabinet was the president's main source of support for a long time. Yet even under George Washington there were constant feuds between Hamilton and Jefferson, his two most important advisers. Presidents initially pledge to use the cabinet because of tradition and the appeal of using department heads to get a hold on the vast federal bureaucracy. That, of course, is the problem. Cabinet members are both presidential advisers and department heads. The secretary of defense is in charge of more than a million civilian employees. The secretary of health and human services oversees 130,000. Cabinet secretaries have divided loyalties. They must answer the call of two masters, and the president knows it.

The criteria presidents use in naming their cabinet members are different from the criteria they use when they choose their personal advisers. Department heads are public figures who give a sometimes vivid public impression of the administration, like Eisenhower's "nine millionaires and a plumber."[23] Presidents must choose among specialists, generalists, and client-oriented individuals. Generalists such as George Shultz, who served as treasury secretary under Nixon and Ford and secretary of state under Reagan, follow the lines of British cabinet members. An example of a specialist is Henry Kissinger, who was a noted foreign policy expert before entering government. Other individuals became cabinet officers because they are associated with clientele groups. Presidents usually choose a combination of the three types, but the balance of one over the others may influence the way a president will be able to make use of the cabinet. For example, a cabinet that includes women, blacks, or Hispanics symbolizes an administration's sensitivity to minority and women's concerns. Cabinet officers may run into trouble when their need to do the president's bidding conflicts with a more independent view of their role. Secretary of Health, Education, and Welfare (now Health and Human Services) Joseph Califano, a prominent figure around Washington from his days in the Johnson administration, became increasingly outspoken in his criticism of President Carter. When he continued to complain about Carter's policies and priorities, he was removed.

Presidents learn through experience whether or not the cabinet is valuable for them. At the outset, Jimmy Carter was committed to making the cabinet a meaningful part of his administration. His declining use of the cabinet reflected a growing disenchantment. In 1977, the cabinet met weekly; in 1978, it met every two weeks; by 1979, it met only once a month on the average; and in 1980, it ceased to meet altogether. President Reagan upgraded the status of the cabinet in his administration and tried to develop a system for enhancing its advisory role. Reagan divided the cabinet into cabinet councils—the equivalent of subcommittees—which also included EOP officials and top White House staffers. By reducing the size of the decision-making groups and increasing specialization, cabinet members worked more closely with the other elements of the presidency.

President George Bush relies on members of his cabinet as a source of consultation and advice more than his recent predecessors. While the White House staff has frequently been more influential than the cabinet, Bush chose to give his most trusted advisers cabinet posts. The cabinet and cabinet-level appointees reflected a blend of old friends, individuals with experience in the last three Republican administrations, and some high-powered newcomers. Table 13-4 shows the original Bush cabinet and other high-level appointees.

At an informal meeting of the cabinet a week before the inauguration, George Bush pulled a handwritten note out of his pocket and read what he called "the marching orders."

"Think big. Challenge the system. Adhere to the highest ethical standards. Be on the record as much as possible. Be frank. Fight hard for your position. When I make a call, we move as a team. Work with Congress. Represent the United States with dignity."[24] Through Bush's first two years in office, his cabinet seemed to be working well together, avoiding some of the internal struggles and backstabbing that had characterized some previous administrations. On the other hand, some felt that the president's emphasis on cooperation and unanimity eliminated creative tension that can produce policy innovation. Three noncabinet members sat at

TABLE 13-4

THE ORIGINAL BUSH CABINET, 1989–90

Cabinet Appointees

Secretary of Defense: Richard Cheney
Secretary of Veteran Affairs: Edward Derwinski
Attorney General: Richard Thornburgh
Secretary of Education: Lauro Cavazos
Secretary of Agriculture: Clayton Yeutter
Secretary of Energy: James D. Watkins
Secretary of Commerce: Robert Mosbacher
Secretary of Transportation: Samuel Skinner
Secretary of Labor: Elizabeth Dole
Secretary of the Treasury: Nicholas Brady
Secretary of State: James A. Baker III
Secretary of Interior: Manuel Lujan
Secretary of Housing and Urban Development: Jack Kemp
Secretary of Health and Human Services: Louis Sullivan

Other High-Level Appointees

Chief of Staff: John Sununu
U.S. Trade Representative: Carla Hills
Budget Director: Richard Darman
Council of Economic Advisers Chair: Michael Boskin
National Security Adviser: Brent Scowcroft
EPA Administrator: William Reilly
Ambassador to the United Nations: Thomas Pickering
CIA Director: William Webster
Drug Czar: William Bennett
White House Spokesman: Marlin Fitzwater

the table with Bush and his fourteen cabinet members: Chief of Staff John Sununu, OMB Director Richard Darman, and Vice-President Dan Quayle. The insiders who dominated the group included Baker—who always sat at the president's right, Darman, and Sununu. As we will see shortly, Bush developed a management style that used the cabinet and the White House staff differently than either Presidents Reagan or Carter.

THE VICE-PRESIDENCY

After almost two hundred years of jokes and wisecracks about the **vice-presidency,** the office has become an important part of the presidency. Walter Mondale and George Bush were the first vice-presidents given important responsibilities that enabled them to contribute positively and consistently to the running of the country. Before this, the vice-presidency was largely ignored. John Nance Garner, Franklin Roosevelt's first vice-president, suggested that the office amounted to little more than a "pitcher of warm spit" (that is the cleaned-up version of what he said). Some of the higher-ups in the Kennedy White House privately ridiculed Vice-President Johnson, calling him "Uncle Cornpone." The vice-presidency has been likened to a spare tire or the raven of death, reminding the president of his own mortality. But for all its drawbacks, fourteen vice-presidents (including George Bush) have succeeded to the presidency, nine as the result of the death or resignation of the president.

The office itself was almost an afterthought, a consolation prize for the loser in the electoral college balloting to reduce any temptation to mount a coup d'état. The Twelfth Amendment required that votes for president and vice-president be cast on the same ballot, making the vice-president a second-class citizen. The vice-president's formal powers are limited to presiding over the Senate and casting a vote in the case of a tie. The vice-presidency is a strange hybrid in the constitutional system of separation of powers, the only office given a role in both the legislative branch and the executive branch. Vice-presidents have been excluded from influence not only because of their lack of constitutional power but also because they often were carelessly chosen and poorly qualified. Remember Spiro T. Agnew? Even capable people who would later prove themselves in office were shut out as vice-president: Nixon and Johnson were underused and frustrated throughout their terms. When Franklin Roosevelt died in 1945, Harry Truman had no idea what was going on in the White House. He was unaware even of the existence of the project to build the atom bomb.

Walter Mondale and George Bush broke the past pattern. In each case, the president allowed the vice-president to assume major responsibilities. Both Mondale and Bush were careful not to upstage the president or to appear to be building their own bases of political support. After the 1980 elections, Mondale made a number of apparently helpful suggestions to George Bush before he assumed office, and Bush later earned respect by the delicate way he handled his responsibilities after President Reagan was shot, assuming many important duties without appearing anxious to take over.

Vice-President Dan Quayle was the source of considerable controversy from the moment he was named to the ticket in 1988 (see the Political Close-up in Chapter 9). In terms of public perception, his tenure was reminiscent of the days of Spiro T. Agnew, when the vice-president was the constant butt of jokes by comedians and late-night talk show hosts. The Bush administration tried hard to counter the negative public image of the vice-president and include him in the inner circle of the White House. In cabinet meetings, Quayle sat opposite the president and on a number of occasions represented the president around the world.

While not an insider, Quayle has had some influence within the administration. His support of the space program apparently helped forestall major budget cuts. He received a vote of support from the president when Bush announced his early decision to retain Quayle on the ticket in 1992. Quayle continued to create public relations problems for himself through an ongoing series of gaffes and misstatements. Overall, however, Quayle appeared to reflect the trend towards an enhanced role for the vice-president.

THE PRESIDENT'S PEOPLE

The presidency is not just councils and task forces; it is also people. Who are the men and women behind the president? One observer described them as a group that includes "buddies, brains, bootlickers and some yahoos."[25]

The perfect presidential adviser, according to the Brownlow Report, would "shun personal power, be highly competent, possess great physical vigor, and have a passion for anonymity." [26] Some presidential advisers have been anything but anonymous. Carter's aide Hamilton Jordan made headlines with his overheard comment about the similarity of the Egyptian ambassador's wife's chest to the pyramids and by spitting a drink on a young woman in a Washington nightclub. But despite the escapades of a few, most presidential confidants have remained largely behind the scenes.

Franklin D. Roosevelt expanded the size and scope of the White House staff. One of his closest personal aides was Louis Howe, who helped organize Roosevelt's growing White House staff. After Howe's death in 1936, Harry Hopkins emerged as the president's closest adviser. Some of Roosevelt's aides remained on the job after his death to help Harry Truman, who found himself suddenly thrust into the Oval Office. Soon Truman replaced them with the "Missouri gang," a group of loyal political friends. Their penchant for a little graft and the occasional kickback caused political embarrassment for Truman on several occasions. Although he was not a member of the "gang," Clark Clifford emerged as one of the most capable and important advisers to Truman and helped shape both domestic policies and the miraculous election victory of 1948.

Dwight Eisenhower believed in delegation of authority. Secretary of State John Foster Dulles ran foreign policy while Eisenhower's old political friend Sherman Adams ran the White House. Adams carefully guarded Eisenhower from unwanted interference and interruptions. Reacting to the highly structured system under Eisenhower, Kennedy adopted a more open White House administration, similar to Roosevelt's. His brother Robert Kennedy was attorney general as well as a close confidant and personal adviser. Lyndon Johnson was a difficult president to work for, and as a result, there was a great deal of staff turnover. Bill Moyers was probably Johnson's closest adviser from 1965 to 1967. Although he was officially press secretary, his responsibilities and influence were greater than the title implies.

Presidential advisers became the center of controversy during the Nixon administration. The power of presidential aides reached its apogee under H. R. Haldeman and John Ehrlichman. Haldeman, an advertising executive, exemplified the Nixon-era adviser—tough and loyal, yet ruthless in his quest for control. As the Watergate scandal unfolded, Nixon sadly accepted Haldeman's resignation in 1973, blaming a hostile press and administration enemies for his downfall. Ford inherited a White House staff and had little time in two years to make much of a mark on the presidency. Although Ford declared that no single person would dominate the White House, his former congressional colleague Donald Rumsfeld emerged as the first among equals.

Jimmy Carter, like Ford, reacted to Nixon's staffing problems and declared that the president's door would be open to many. His close friends from Georgia Jody Powell and Hamilton Jordan dominated the Carter White House. As self-proclaimed outsiders to the Washington establishment, the Carter staff ran into severe problems trying to deal with Washington insiders.

Ronald Reagan installed his former chief of staff from California, Edwin Meese, in the same position in the White House. But the first Reagan administration was run by a triumvirate. James Baker and Michael Deaver joined Meese to orchestrate the political strategies and policies of the administration. In 1985, the trio disbanded, and Secretary of the Treasury Donald Regan moved in as chief of staff for the second term. Regan came under heavy pressure to resign, particularly from First Lady Nancy Reagan, after two years as a powerful chief of staff. Former Senate Majority Leader Howard Baker dropped out of the presidential race in early 1987 to become the new chief of staff and help President Reagan through the Iran-Contra scandal.

The two dominant figures during the first two years of the Bush administration were Secretary of State James Baker III and Chief of Staff John Sununu. Baker and Bush were old political allies in Texas and remained close personal friends, fishing together during leisure moments. Bush and Baker collaborated closely on foreign policy issues, with Baker working with others inside the administration, such as Secretary of Defense Richard Cheney and National Security Advisor Brent Scowcroft. As former White House insider and secretary of the treasury under Reagan, Baker had insight and influence on economic and domestic policies as well.

The other key figure in the first two years of the Bush presidency was Sununu, the former governor of New Hampshire and 1988 campaign strategist. More aggressive and partisan than Bush or Baker, Sununu often played the tough disciplinarian for the president. Sununu acknowledged his job: "I know it means I'm going to be perceived as the guy who has to say no and the president as the guy who . . . might say yes."[27] Working for a president less ideological than Ronald Reagan, Sununu was particularly important to conservatives. His strident partisanship, however, occasionally undercut Bush's efforts to negotiate and cooperate with Congress.

People and institutions are two of the key ingredients of the presidency. But effectiveness in governing also depends on the president's style of management and leadership skills.

Mobilizing to Govern

Although the basic structure of the presidency continues from one administration to the next, presidents have an opportunity to tailor decision-making to their own personal style. Two basic patterns have emerged since Franklin Roosevelt.

Hub-of-the-Wheel Presidents

Franklin D. Roosevelt was a "**hub-of-the-wheel president,**" a president who wanted a finger in every pie. He was the first modern president to put himself in the center of the organization, allowing easy access to a number of people and maintaining a large number of direct contacts with advisers and bureaucrats.[28] Political scientist Frank Kessler describes Roosevelt's system:

> Roosevelt developed a strong aversion to going through channels. . . . Instead, he opted for a wide-open, free-wheeling, conflict-riddled system. . . . There was not the slightest doubt as to who was in charge at the White House; below the president, however, the line of authority was left purposely unclear.[29]

Although difficult to work under, such staff arrangements allowed Roosevelt maximum influence and organizational power. If staff members suspected that Roosevelt had assigned someone else to undertake the same task, they were sure to perform it as faithfully and accurately as possible. Hub-of-the-wheel presidents tend not to have a chief of staff who acts as a gatekeeper to the president.

John F. Kennedy also organized his staff so that he was at the hub of the wheel. Believing that formal channels of communication were often overly restrictive and could hamper policy-making, Kennedy had no chief of staff and appointed trusted allies to key subcabinet-level positions in the departments as private agents who would report directly to him.[30] Kennedy occasionally would surprise the desk officer in an overseas embassy with a direct call, announcing, "This is President Kennedy—what's going on over there?" Although this kind of contact frustrated State Department officials who were concerned about going through channels, it furnished the president with information he felt was less biased. It also kept people on their toes. Kennedy and Roosevelt were the best examples of hub-of-the-wheel styles, but Presidents Truman, Johnson, Ford, and Carter also fit this category.

Pyramid Presidents

Other presidents have opted for a more formal, hierarchical organization, with the president on top of a defined chain of command. These can be called "**pyramid presidents.**" Directly below the president sits a powerful chief of staff who controls the access of people and information to the president. Former General Dwight D. Eisenhower best exemplifies the pyramid style. Eisenhower wanted a presidency that was as much like a military command as possible. Sherman Adams, his chief of staff, acted like a deputy president.[31] It was Adams's job (Eisenhower called him "the governor") to summarize and approve reports and memos coming across the president's desk. The president liked memos no longer than one page, and Adams's initials had to be on the bottom for Ike to read it. Secretary of State John Foster Dulles had direct access to the president, but other cabinet members had to schedule an appointment through Adams to see the president.

Although the president tends to be more isolated in a pyramid system, it frees him from the palace-guard politics that often dominate the White House. Many have been critical of Eisenhower's formal system, but recent analysis of the Eisenhower presidency suggests that the system was consistent with his policy objectives and was sensitive to the political demands of the office.[32]

Richard Nixon also established a hierarchical system within the White House and employed a protective chief of staff. As Eisenhower's vice-president, Nixon appreciated the advantages of this kind of approach and put it into practice when he became president. H. R. Haldeman, the crew-cut, hard-nosed chief of staff, stood between Nixon and the rest of the political world. As Haldeman put it, "Every president needs a son-of-a-bitch, and I'm Nixon's."[33]

Both Nixon and Eisenhower shied away from the personal contact with underlings that so fascinated Roosevelt and Kennedy. Nixon was more comfortable making a decision based on briefing papers, rather than hashing out a decision in an open discussion, as his successor Gerald Ford did.

Pyramid presidents carefully guard their time and accessibility. The danger is that the president may become isolated from reality and lose contact with people and problems. Although there are many explanations for the Watergate scandal that eventually toppled the Nixon administration, it was fostered by the kind of organization and staffing system Nixon employed.

Both the pyramid and hub-of-the-wheel styles of presidential management have their advantages and disadvantages. Presidential time is enormously valuable. It is not humanly possible to solve all the problems alone or to see all the people who crave an audience. At the same time, it is essential to have input, including constructive criticism, from a variety of sources. Presidents sometimes alter their philosophy as they gain experience in running the presidency. Jimmy Carter, reacting to the isolation of previous administrations, entered the office promising to have an open, accessible White House with no chief of staff. By his third year in office, however, he realized the limits of mixed and overlapping responsibility. Carter named Hamilton Jordan as chief of staff in a White House shake-up, moving toward a pyramid system.

THE REAGAN MANAGEMENT STYLE

In February 1987, the Tower Commission investigating the Iran-Contra affair concluded that President Reagan's detached management style was partially responsible for the failed policy. The panel, appointed by Reagan himself, observed, "President Reagan's personal management style places an especially heavy responsibility on his key advisers."[34] "Nevertheless," the report continued, "with . . . so much at stake, the president should have ensured that the . . . system did not fail him."

Ronald Reagan's management style did not initially fit either the pyramid model or the hub-of-the-wheel model. On the one hand, Reagan shared Franklin Roosevelt's and John Kennedy's affinity for politics and personal contact. On the other hand, he was more removed from day-to-day decisions and he delegated more authority to subordinates than his predecessors. From the start of his administration in 1981, critics claimed that Reagan was not in charge and did not know what was going on in the White House. But the adoption of his economic and budget plan, the defense buildup, the emphasis on appointing conservatives in key administrative positions, and other successes were accomplished in spite of his detached management style. During his first term, no single chief of staff ran the show. The trio of Edwin Meese, Michael Deaver, and James Baker III, guided the operations of the White House.

Initially, the administration's clearly defined ideological agenda made it possible for Reagan's management style to work. The EOP and the White House staff were used less to formulate policy than to enforce a fixed agenda.[35] This was in contrast to former presidencies. Franklin Roosevelt assembled the "brain trust" to devise new solutions to the devastating economic depression. Lyndon Johnson gathered leading policy experts to formulate his Great Society programs in the "war on poverty." In Reagan's first term, the executive budget process became the driving force behind domestic policy. Budget Director David Stockman and the Office of Management and Budget were instrumental in mobilizing the administration to govern.

The management style that seemed to work during Reagan's first term failed the president in important ways during the second. In 1985, Donald

President Ronald Reagan's detached management style was one of the factors behind the Iran-Contra scandal.

Regan was made chief of staff. At that time, the organization of the White House more closely paralleled the pyramid model. But as Chief of Staff Regan began to assert increased authority, criticism of his heavy-handed methods began to mount. President Reagan was reluctant to remove Regan, despite the well-publicized feud between the chief of staff and the First Lady. The Iran-Contra revelations dramatically unmasked the negative consequences of Reagan's detached management style. Subordinates, apparently without the knowledge of the president, engaged in a series of illegal and ill-fated covert activities. Promising to "get to the bottom" of things, President Reagan was nonetheless reluctant to acknowledge blame or to change his style. Heavily criticized by the Tower Commission report, Donald Regan submitted his resignation and it was accepted; Howard Baker took over as chief of staff.

THE BUSH MANAGEMENT STYLE

George Bush took a very different approach to managing the presidency than his predecessor, partially because of a different agenda and political environment. A competent set of senior officials, more openness with the media, a conciliatory philosophy, and a calm political environment allowed Bush to enjoy an extended honeymoon in the White House. His style and approach to managing the presidency reflected his conscious efforts to avoid either the excessive micromanagement of Carter or the overly detached macromanagement of Reagan.

Bush attempted to develop a hands-on approach to the presidency without being swallowed up in detail.[36] To strike that happy medium, he avoided dominating his team while still making it clear that he was in charge. For example, in reaching a compromise budget package and deal with Congress on the issue of the Nicaraguan Contras in 1989, Bush provided the overall parameters but allowed Secretary of State Baker and Budget Director Darman to negotiate the details of the agreements. Bush demonstrated his policy involvement and hands-on knowledge of issues by meeting frequently with the news media.

Cabinet members were given wide latitude to make policy decisions for their departments, but Bush was not trying to achieve "cabinet government." As a collective decision-making group, the Bush cabinet has been little different than other recent cabinets. Instead, Bush relied on a small group of senior officials with whom he had a long friendship. Domestic policy has been dominated by Chief of Staff Sununu and Budget Director Darman. Baker initially met with the president several times a day, reflecting not only his importance but also Bush's heavy emphasis on foreign affairs.

President Bush adopted a system that more closely resembles a "hub-of-the-wheel" rather than a pyramid style of management, even though he used a single, powerful chief of staff. Bush operated with an open-door policy, encouraging his aides and cabinet members to keep in contact with him. Bush encouraged his advisers to be pragmatic in their approach to problem solving and in working with Congress. One big difference from the Reagan administration was the lack of a fixed agenda; there was no master plan or overarching strategy. The Bush presidency was more concerned with day-to-day tactics and issues.

In some ways, Bush served as his own chief of staff, calling on the phone, making arrangements, talking directly to members of Congress. Nonetheless, from the outset, Bush decided that he wanted a hard-nosed operator to run the White House. While Bush did not use Sununu to isolate and protect him, Sununu exercised considerable power as chief of staff. As one aide described Sununu, "He is not so much a gatekeeper as much as he is the funnel into which everything is poured."[37] They started the day together, with Sununu presenting a binder of information for Bush that he had compiled from the cabinet and the staff. They met again at the end of the day to review what had been accomplished.

The Bush management style reflected the president's personality and philosophy. He was less ideological than Reagan, hence more willing to be pragmatic and to compromise. With extensive experience in government, Bush was at ease with the specifics of complex policy issues and comfortable discussing them. Lacking an aggressive, confrontational style, Bush appreciated the benefits of a tough chief of staff who can handle much of the administrative and political dirty work. Like his predecessors in the White House, his management style influenced both foreign and domestic policy results.

John Sununu.

MAKING NATIONAL SECURITY DECISIONS

The president has greater ability to govern during a national security crisis than at any other time. Even in normal times, despite the ongoing struggle with the Congress for control of foreign policy, the president remains dominant. Presidents are able to dominate national security policy in four ways: through recognizing foreign governments, by making international agreements, by appointing key personnel to conduct foreign policy, and by using military force when deemed necessary.[38]

How do presidents make decisions in a foreign policy crisis? Although the National Security Council (NSC) has been in place since 1947, in most cases presidents use ad hoc decision-making in a crisis through a temporary informal group of their closest advisers. Kennedy's advisory group during the Cuban missile crisis in 1962 included the secretaries of defense, state, and treasury, the national security adviser, the attorney general, the Vice-President, the chairman of the joint chiefs of staff, the CIA Director, and a close White House aide.[39] These were people whom the president trusted and who controlled the major instruments of foreign policy and defense. Kennedy called this group the "executive committee" of the National Security Council, but it included several members outside the NSC.

The president's dominance of national security decisions can lead to disaster if important options and alternatives are ignored. Political psychologist Irving Janis found that many crisis decisions are made on the basis of what he calls **groupthink**.[40] Members of the small advisory group may be reluctant to dissent from the preferred position of the leader or the majority of the group. At a time when a thorough consideration of alternatives is essential, fewer than usual may be discussed. Janis believes that groupthink was partially responsible for such foreign policy fiascoes as the invasion of North Korea in 1950, the Bay of Pigs invasion in 1961, and the escalation of the war in Vietnam. He suggests that groupthink can be minimized if the president stresses the search for new information, remains impartial at the start of deliberations, and divides up the group from time to time.[40]

Aside from avoiding foreign policy fiascoes, coordination is perhaps the most serious problem for presidents. Authority is divided between the Defense Department, the Central Intelligence Agency, the State Department, the NSC, and the president's other top advisers. President Nixon had problems in his first term when National Security Adviser Henry Kissinger overrode both the secretary of state and the secretary of defense. In the Iran-Contra affair, both Secretary of State George Shultz and Defense Secretary Caspar Weinberger were aware of the policy, but they remained aloof from it because they did not support it. CIA Director William Casey, on the other hand, was deeply involved in arranging the covert operations through Oliver North.

President Bush weighed many factors in deciding to launch a full-scale military invasion of Panama to oust Manuel Noriega in December 1989. As the Panamanian dictator who was under federal indictment for drug dealing became an increasing problem, Bush considered many options for getting him out of office. The administration was criticized for its inaction in October during a failed coup attempt. Immediately afterwards, however, Pentagon officials designed a detailed invasion plan to be ready if needed. The plans were developed by the chairman of the Joint Chiefs of Staff, General Colin Powell, and approved by the joint chiefs. The killing of a U.S. Marine, the beating of a Navy officer, and the sexual harassment of the officer's wife provided the final impetus for the president.

The invasion was plotted with great secrecy. On Sunday, December 17, 1989, less than three days before the invasion, Bush met with his national security advisers. Powell detailed the plan and justified the amount of force that would be employed. Bush wanted to be sure that the invasion would work and not end up like the failed mission to release the hostages in Iran approved by Jimmy Carter in 1979. The group included Bush, Powell, Secretary of State Baker, Vice-President Quayle, CIA Director Webster, Secretary of Defense Cheney, and National Security Adviser Brent Scowcroft. Convinced that all other options had been tried, Bush gave the go-ahead.

The president met with this group again Tuesday afternoon, only hours before the invasion was to begin, in which he was given an hour-by-hour preview of the attack by Scowcroft. Shortly after midnight on December 20, as the invasion was launched, the deputies committee of the NSC met to monitor the progress of the military action. Members of Congress were informed as the operation began. Although not initially captured, Noriega later sought asylum in the Vatican Embassy and eventually surrendered to American authorities.

A similar process characterized President Bush's decision to send U.S. troops into Saudi Arabia following Iraq's invasion of Kuwait on August 2, 1990. Despite some advanced intelligence warnings and ominous Iraqui troop movements in prior days, the administration was taken by surprise by Hussein's invasion. The pivotal decision to deploy troops immediately in Saudi Arabia was made at Camp David only hours after the invasion by a group that included Scowcroft, Cheney, Baker, Powell, and the president. Congressional leaders were scattered around the country because of the August recess and only Sentor Sam Nunn (D-Ga) was consulted in advance. The president embarked upon the largest troop deployment since Vietnam and the most rapid large deployment of troops and materiel in history. As the crisis progressed, Bush went ahead with his scheduled August vacation in Kennebunkport, Maine, where his home on Walker Point became an unlikely command post for the buildup. Although criticized by some for playing golf and fishing while thousands of U.S. troops landed in the Middle East, Bush refused to be "Carterized" by the crisis, a reference to the fact that Jimmy Carter became a hostage of sorts in the White House during the Iranian crisis in 1979-80.

The problem for American presidents in national security policy is not as much one of governing ability as one of assuring the quality of decision-making. In contrast, the problem in economic policy-making is being able to govern at all.

Making Economic Policy

In the economic realm, the president has limited control over a fragmented system of national policy-making. The independent Federal Reserve Board (the Fed), which controls monetary policy, may or may not follow the wishes of the White House. Congress retains significant influence over taxing, spending, and other economic policies. The bureaucracy has much to say about regulation. The presidential role is largely to provide guidance and coherence to national economic policy.

The institutions for doing so constitute the **economic subpresidency**—all those involved in making, defining, communicating, and implementing economic decisions.[41] The economic subpresidency includes the Treasury Department, the Council of Economic Advisers (CEA), the OMB, and the Fed. The president's task is complicated by the fact that each component has slightly different interests, and a competition for supremacy often ensues. Presidents have tried a variety of means to coordinate subpresidency activities. Perhaps the most important development was the formation of the economic **troika** as a policy-making group by John F. Kennedy in 1961. This group is comprised of the secretary of the treasury, the OMB director, and the CEA chair. In terms of broad policy responsibilities, the Treasury Department supplies revenue estimates, the OMB makes expenditure forecasts, and the CEA provides the baseline assumptions of what the economy will do over the coming months.[42] But each wants to play the leading role in defining administration economic policy.

Recent presidents have all tried to create organizational arrangements that would increase their ability to make economic policy. Under Johnson, the economic troika was the most important source of economic policy proposals. Nixon tried to establish a more formal process, creating a cabinet committee on economic policy. Dissatisfied with this group, Nixon later designated Treasury Secretary John Connally as the administration's "economic czar," with primary responsibility for economic proposals. Gerald Ford established the Economic Policy Board to coordinate economic policy. Carter established the Economic Policy Group, which included the troika and the secretaries of commerce, labor, housing and urban development, and state. Reagan used a cabinet council on economic affairs to coordinate policy.

The Reagan administration was characterized by considerable internal dissension after the adoption of the major components of the president's program in 1981. In 1981, OMB Director David Stockman dominated largely because of his superior understanding of the budget and Congress. His fall from grace following ill-considered remarks about the Reagan economic program allowed Treasury Secretary Donald Regan to assume leadership. Internal disputes over the record-high deficits became public in 1983 and 1984. CEA chair Martin Feldstein publicly criticized the administration's lack of attention to the deficits and urged immediate action. Meanwhile, Secretary Regan told Congress that Feldstein's figures were "not worth the paper they were printed on." Feldstein resigned in 1984 amid talk by some White House insiders that the CEA should be abolished! Budget Director Stockman and Defense Secretary Weinberger mounted thinly veiled publicity campaigns against each other over the Pentagon's budget. President Reagan did little to prevent the public bickering.

Economic policy-making in the first two years of the Bush administration was dominated by Richard Darman, with John Sununu often playing an important role as chief of staff. The budget director usually prevailed in disputes with cabinet members over budget and economic questions, although Sununu sometimes intervened to make compromises. The most difficult economic problem for the Bush administration remained the chronic budget deficits, which reached crisis proportions in September, 1990. The administration agreed to a five year, $500 billion deficit reduction plan including large tax increases. President Bush suffered a major defeat, despite a televised appeal, when House Republicans refused to back the plan. Weeks of chaos and indecision followed before an agreement was reached.

Although he did not know Bush well when he was named chief economic advisor, Michael Boskin quickly won the president's trust.[43] Boskin, an economics professor from Stanford University, had no previous experience in government but proved influential in the areas of trade policy and environmental legislation. Boskin, a strong advocate of free trade, fought to cut back imported steel quotas and reduce the list of countries cited for questionable trade practices. In helping formulate the administration's position on the Clean Air Act revision, Boskin worked to minimize elements of the legislation that would have the most damaging effects on the economy. Boskin helped spur a resurgence of the Council of Economic Advisers after it had declined in importance during the Reagan years.

Even if presidents can gain consensus and formulate coherent economic policy, implementation remains a problem. To a great extent, the budget is locked in, and Congress must concur before major changes can be made. Interest rates and the money supply are out of the president's direct control. Economic estimates are often inaccurate, and the impact of proposed economic actions is often unclear. Many economic factors, such as the supply and cost of oil, are largely beyond the president's control as well. Ford and Carter served during the massive oil price increases of the mid-1970s, while Reagan was the beneficiary of a worldwide oil glut and price decline. Oil prices fluctuated wildly after Iraq's invasion of Kuwait, compounding Bush's economic problems. Despite these limitations, the presidency is the institution most capable of giving coherence to national economic policy.

Presidential Personality and Leadership Skills

Presidential Character

How much difference does it make who is in the White House? Some argue that the office—the presidential establishment—and the current political climate primarily determine a president's effectiveness. Political psychologist James David Barber argues that a president's personality has a significant impact on public policy. Barber's studies of the psychological development of presidents led him to several interesting conclusions.[44] He suggests that two important elements of a president's personality emerge in early life and have a significant impact on performance in office. *Character*—emotional security and attitude toward life—generally emerges in childhood. A happy, secure home like Franklin Roosevelt enjoyed can lead to a positive outlook on life. The trials and unhappiness of an orphan shuffled around to relatives, such as Herbert Hoover experienced,

Political Insight 13-1

Presidential Personality

CHARACTER
Emotional rewards derived from activity: happiness, satisfaction

PRESIDENTIAL STYLE
Method of working, activity levels, and emphases

	POSITIVE	**NEGATIVE**
ACTIVE	I. ACTIVE–POSITIVE Confident, flexible, emphasizes results, makes best president Examples: Roosevelt, Truman, Kennedy, Ford, Carter	II. ACTIVE–NEGATIVE Ambitious, striving; high energy levels but low psychic reward; struggles for power in hostile environment Examples: Wilson, Hoover, Johnson, Nixon
PASSIVE	III. PASSIVE–POSITIVE Receptive, compliant, other-directed; desire to be liked makes inner doubts Examples: Taft, Harding, Reagan	IV. PASSIVE–NEGATIVE Withdraws from conflict; drawn by duty, patriotism, sense of responsibility Examples: Coolidge, Eisenhower

SOURCE: Adapted from James David Barber: *The Presidential Character,* 3rd ed. (Englewood Cliffs, N.J.: Prentice-Hall, 1985).

can lead to a more negative, pessimistic outlook. The second element of personality is *style,* a person's general mode of activity, which emerges in early adulthood. A person can develop a relatively passive style, as did Calvin Coolidge, who slept fourteen hours a day, or a compulsively active style, such as that of Lyndon Johnson, who watched three television sets simultaneously (on different channels) and gave dictation while he was on the toilet.

Barber's biographical research into the twentieth-century presidents led him to conclude that the combination of style and character produces four personality types (Political Insight 13-1) and that a number of significant policy failures are directly attributable to certain personality flaws. Perhaps the most dangerous personality is the **active-negative type.** Wilson, Hoover, Johnson, and Nixon are all placed in this category. Active-negatives represent a contradiction between style and character. Their extremely hard work and drive does not bring happiness, only frustration. They see life as a struggle and the world as hostile. Each of these active-negatives fixed on a disastrous course and because of his personality was unable to turn back. Barber's classification of the most recent presidents is more tentative. He placed Ford and Carter in the active-positive category. Barber felt that Reagan's "laid-back" approach to the presidency made him a passive-positive.

Barber's study has received a great deal of criticism. Some accuse Barber of engaging in second-rate amateur psychology. Others claim he puts the presidents he admires in a more favorable light. Still others argue that the many different possible variations in presidential personality cannot possibly be captured in four categories. Although his analysis of earlier presidents has provided some interesting insights, Barber's statements about more recent presidents have been found lacking. The variation in effectiveness of recent presidents suggests that much more is needed in order to gauge how personality affects leadership. But Barber's basic point is important if elusive: Presidential personality does affect presidential performance.

PRESIDENTIAL LEADERSHIP SKILLS

A study by Marcia Whicker and Raymond Moore attempted to clarify the personal skills of presidents that tend to result in effective leadership. Concerned about the relationship between the presidency and governing, they call presidential leadership "that energizing, elusive enigma that makes the United States governmental system work when it is present and falter and stumble when it is not."[45] They believe that, to be effective, modern presidents must have managerial and selling skills. The president who is an excellent manager can set priorities, assemble qualified people, and take steps to achieve goals. The president who is a good salesperson can communicate, motivate, or even manipulate other leaders, the media, and the public.

To compare recent presidents, Whicker and Moore developed a typology of presidential leadership based on these two dimensions—management skills and selling skills. Instead of examining psychological motivations, they focused on the personal skills needed to perform well. Using a variety of qualitative measures and judgments, the authors developed scores for presidential management skills and selling skills. The result was the four categories of presidential leadership shown in Figure 13-4: great leadership, operational leadership, political leadership, and ineffective leadership.[46]

FIGURE 13-4

PRESIDENTIAL PERSONAL LEADERSHIP RATINGS

		SELLING SKILLS	
		Low	High
MANAGEMENT SKILLS	High	OPERATIONAL LEADERSHIP Nixon	GREAT LEADERSHIP Roosevelt Kennedy Truman Eisenhower
	Low	INEFFECTIVE LEADERSHIP Ford Carter Hoover	POLITICAL LEADERSHIP Johnson Reagan

SOURCE: Adapted from Marcia Whicker and Raymond Moore, *When Presidents Are Great* (Englewood Cliffs, N.J.: Prentice-Hall, 1988), 173.

President Bush with Soviet President Mikhail Gorbachev.

GREAT LEADERSHIP. Presidents possessing a high level of both selling skills and management skills are the most effective presidents. They fall into the category of "great leadership." Great presidents can both persuade key audiences to follow their initiatives and devise strategies to implement and manage those policies. According to the measures of Whicker and Moore, the great presidents were Roosevelt, Kennedy, Truman, and Eisenhower. One surprise may be the inclusion of Eisenhower, who has benefited from revisionist scholarship and the availability of new historical sources in recent years. Kennedy, even though he had limited success with Congress in his short three-year presidency, had the sales and management skills needed to succeed. Roosevelt had the highest combined scores on the two dimensions, confirming his reputation as a great leader.

OPERATIONAL LEADERSHIP. Presidents who are good managers but poor communicators lacking effective sales skills provide operational leadership. Among the recent presidents, only Richard Nixon was placed in this category. How can someone with poor communication skills be elected? In the era of modern campaign technology, candidates can be packaged and marketed to the public, but once they take office, their lack of communication skills with Congress, the media, and the public has a detrimental effect on the achievement of their policy goals, even if they are good managers.

POLITICAL LEADERSHIP. Political leadership is provided by presidents who have great oratorical skills and powers of verbal communication but who rate poorly as managers. Such presidents are good campaigners and can inspire important constituencies through television. However, because they lack strong management skills, they are often unable to translate their personal charisma into coherent, well-managed programs. Lyndon Johnson and Ronald Reagan fall into this category. While Reagan seems to be a good fit here, the authors' ratings of President Johnson may be the most controversial. Johnson had tremendous success in getting Congress to enact his legislative program, but he seemed to suffer image problems with the public because he followed the charismatic Kennedy into the White House.

INEFFECTIVE LEADERSHIP. Presidents who rate low on both selling and management skills fall into the category of ineffective leaders. Presidents Hoover, Ford, and Carter are in this category. According to

Whicker and Moore, unusual circumstances may accompany their entry into the presidency. Some, such as Ford, were thrust into the presidency from the vice-presidency. Others, such as Carter, may have benefited from the weaknesses of their opponent and the sins of the previous administration. The problems of ineffective leadership are obvious. When a president lacks two of the skills necessary for success in the presidency, he is unable to govern effectively.

How does George Bush rate in terms of leadership skills and abilities? While it is too soon to adequately judge, the administration clearly has demonstrated marked differences from its recent predecessors. Bush brought much more experience in national government into the presidency than either Carter or Reagan. A competent manager of the White House, he surrounded himself with other experienced insiders, avoiding the political mistakes and slow learning process that characterized the Carter administration. With a more hands-on style, he appeared more in control of the White House than Reagan. Aided by the reduction in international tensions and relative prosperity at home, his selling skills were sufficient to achieve record approval ratings well into his second year in office.

The international political environment was reshaped in the late 1980s, providing new challenges and constraints. The limits of the postmodern-presidency to control international events and the growing dependence on other nations became particularly clear in the Bush administration. Bush took a much more conciliatory approach to governing than Reagan but had a much less ambitious political agenda to pursue. Lacking the congressional support and the dramatic electoral victory that boosted Reagan in 1981, Bush of necessity followed a more prudent and modest course. Interbranch cooperation seemed more constructive than confrontation and deadlock but did not necessarily resolve the tough policy choices that had proven so difficult in the 1980s. President Bush's growing problems in dealing with Congress to govern the nation is explored in the next chapter.

★

SUMMARY AND CONCLUSIONS

1. The American presidency has evolved from the traditional presidency to the modern presidency to the postmodern presidency, where dominance of the international system is no longer possible.

2. The effectiveness of the American presidency is shaped by the powers and duties, the presidential office, the nature of the political environment, and the person who occupies the office.

3. The most important roles of the presidency are head of state and symbolic leader, crisis manager, legislator and coalition-builder, and executive and administrator.

4. The public has high expectations of the president both in terms of character and in terms of policy responsibilities. Presidential popularity is related to foreign policy crises, length of time in office, the performance of the economy, personality, and media skills.

5. The presidential office is the formal, institutionalized organization that has developed around the president to help perform various roles. Closest to the president is the White House staff.

6. The Executive Office of the President (EOP) is a presidential bureaucracy of agencies directly responsible to the president. The Office of Management and Budget is the most important agency in the EOP.

7. The cabinet remains important to presidents but not as a policy-making body. The cabinet is more important for its symbolic dimensions, for communication and consensus-building, and for the few influential individuals it contains. Cabinet officers inevitably divide their loyalty between the president and their department.

8. Within the formal structure of the presidency, presidents surround themselves with people of their own choosing and mobilize to govern according to their own style. Two of the most common organizational arrangements of the White House are described as "pyramid," where the president is on top in a defined chain of command, and "hub-of-the-wheel," where the president is at the center of the organization and has direct contacts with many staff members.

9. Although separate organizations and processes for making national security and economic decisions exist, presidents often use informal arrangements.

10. Presidential personality can have an important effect on performance. In today's political world, presidents need personal management and selling skills to provide effective leadership.

Will postmodern presidents be able to tackle the governing challenges of the 1990s? It seems clear that a vigorous, competent presidency is necessary to make the American political system work. Although the president alone cannot do this, the presidency is still more capable than any other institution of making the American political system govern effectively. The president is in a better position to develop a coherent foreign policy and to coordinate economic policy with the help and concurrence of Congress. But what if there is no cooperation? Do separation of powers, divided government, weak political parties, and strong interest groups threaten a governing crisis? That question is taken up in the next chapter as the ongoing struggle between Congress and the presidency is examined in more detail.

SELF-REVIEW

1. How has the presidency changed from the 1790s to the present?

2. What four main factors shape the presidency and determine its impact?

3. Describe the president's constitutional powers.

4. When is the president's ability to govern the greatest? the least?

5. How do presidents attempt to influence and control the bureaucracy?

6. What does the public expect of the president?

7. What factors account for the rise and fall of presidential popularity?

8. How do presidents attempt to shape public opinion?

9. How is the White House organized?

10. What role do the EOP agencies play?

11. Why has the cabinet declined as a decision-making body?

12. How has the role of the vice-presidency changed since 1977?

13. What are the two most common ways to organize and manage the White House? What elements of each has George Bush used?

14. How do presidents make national security and economic policy? What are the different problems in each area?

15. How are presidential management skills and selling skills related to leadership effectiveness?

KEY TERMS

active-negative personality type
Article II
cabinet
economic subpresidency
emergency powers
Executive Office of the President (EOP)
groupthink
"hub-of-the-wheel" presidents
modern presidency
postmodern presidency
"pyramid" presidents
traditional presidency
troika
vice-presidency
White House staff

SUGGESTED READINGS

Barber, James David. *The Presidential Character.* 1985.
A classic work on the impact of personality on presidential performance.

Lowi, Theodore. *The Personal President: Promise Invested, Promise Unfulfilled.* 1985.
A critical examination of the ability of the American presidency to govern, and a consideration of changes that might make the presidency more effective.

Rose, Richard. *The Postmodern Presidency.* 1988.
How world political and economic changes have changed the possibilities of presidential leadership.

Whicker, Marcia, and Raymond Moore. *When Presidents Are Great.* 1988.
A provocative attempt to categorize leadership effectiveness based on the personal skills of the president.

NOTES

1. Richard Rose, *The Postmodern President* (Chatham, N.J.: Chatham House, 1988).
2. *Ibid.,* 3.
3. Richard A. Watson and Norman C. Thomas, *The Politics of the Presidency* (New York: Wiley, 1983), 8-10.
4. Clinton Rossiter, *The American Presidency* (New York: New American Library, 1956), 3-24.
5. Watson and Thomas, *Politics* 1-18.
6. See Richard Neustadt, *Presidential Power* (New York: Wiley, 1960).
7. Arthur Schlesinger, *The Imperial Presidency* (Boston: Houghton Mifflin, 1973).
8. Rose, *Postmodern President,* 25.
9. *Youngstown Sheet and Tube Company v. Sawyer* (1950).
10. Robert E. DiClerico, *The American President* (Englewood Cliffs, N.J.: Prentice-Hall, 1983), 277-78.
11. Quoted in Neustadt, *Presidential Power,* 9.
12. Thomas Cronin, *The State of the Presidency* (Boston: Little, Brown, 1975), 233.
13. George C. Edwards, *The Public Presidency* (New York: St. Martin's Press, 1983), 190.
14. See Steven Wayne, "Great Expectations: What the People Want from Presidents," in Thomas Cronin, ed., *Rethinking the Presidency* (Boston: Little, Brown, 1982), 186-99.
15. Edwards, *Public Presidency,* 191.
16. John Mueller, *War, Presidents, and Public Opinion* (New York: Wiley, 1973).
17. See David Wise, *The Politics of Lying* (New York: Vintage, 1973).
18. Edwards, *Public Presidency,* 56.
19. See Steven K. Bailey, *Congress Makes a Law* (New York: Columbia University Press, 1950).
20. *National Journal,* 3 April 1982, p. 588.
21. Cronin, *State,* 199.
22. James King and James Riddlesberger, "Patterns of Presidential Cabinet Recruitment from Truman to Reagan" (Paper presented at the annual meeting of the Southwestern Social Science Association, Houston, Texas, 16-19 March 1983).
23. Nelson Polsby, "Presidential Cabinet Making: Lessons for the Political System," in Steven A. Shull and Lance T. LeLoup, eds., *The Presidency: Studies inPublic Policy* (Brunswick, Ohio: Kings Court, 1979), 83.
24. William Safire, "Bush's Cabinet," *New York Times Magazine,* 25 March 1990, p. 32.
25. Frank Kessler, *The Dilemma of Presidential Leadership* (Englewood Cliffs, N.J.: Prentice-Hall, 1982), 53.
26. Quoted in ibid., 4.
27. *Washington Post National Weekly Edition,* 5-11 February 1990, p. 6.
28. See Steven Hess, *Organizing the Presidency* (Washington, D.C.: Brookings, 1976).
29. Kessler, *Dilemma,* 59.
30. Hess, *Organizing,* 78.
31. Kessler, *Dilemma,* 59.
32. Fred Greenstein, "Eisenhower as an Activist President: A New Look at the Evidence," *Political Science Quarterly,* Winter 1979-80, pp. 575-96.
33. Quoted in Joseph Califano, *A Presidential Nation* (New York: Norton, 1976), 192.
34. "The Tower Commission Report," excerpted in *Congressional Quarterly Weekly Reports,* 28 February 1987.
35. Chester A. Newland, "Executive Office Policy Apparatus: Enforcing the Reagan Agenda," in Lester M. Salamon and Michael S. Lund, *The Reagan Presidency and the Governing of America* (Washington, D.C.: Urban Institute, 1985), 135-68.
36. Safire, "Bush's Cabinet," p. 31.
37. *Washington Post National Weekly Edition,* 5-11 February 1990, p. 6.
38. Watson and Thomas, *Politics,* 334.
39. Irving Janis, *Victims of Groupthink* (Boston: Houghton Mifflin, 1972), 140.
40. Ibid.
41. James Anderson, "Managing the Economy: The Johnson Administration Experience" (Paper presented at the annual meeting of the American Political Science Association, Washington, D.C., 27-30 August 1980), 6.
42. Ibid., 20.
43. *Wall Street Journal,* Aug 3, 1989, A16.
44. James David Barber, *The Presidential Character* (Englewood Cliffs, N.J.: Prentice-Hall, 1985).
45. Marcia Whicker and Raymond Moore, *When Presidents Are Great* (Englewood Cliffs, N.J.: Prentice-Hall, 1988).
46. Ibid., 167-83.

CHAPTER 14

The Struggle to Govern: Congress versus the President

POLITICAL CLOSE-UP

"In Crucial Things, Unity": From the Inaugural Address of George Bush, January 20, 1989

I have just repeated word for word the oath taken by George Washington two hundred years ago; and the Bible on which I placed my hand is the Bible on which he placed his.

It is right that the memory of Washington be with us today, not only because this is our Bicentennial Inauguration, but because Washington remains the father of our country. And he would, I think, be gladdened by this day. For today is the concrete expression of a stunning fact: Our continuity these two hundred years since our government began.

We meet on democracy's front porch. A good place to talk as neighbors, and as friends. For this is a day when our nation is made whole, when our differences, for a moment, are suspended . . . .

The challenges before us will be thrashed out with the House and Senate. We must bring the federal budget into balance. And we must

ensure that America stands before the world united; strong, at peace, and fiscally sound. But, of course, things may be difficult.

We need compromise; we've had dissension. We need harmony; we've had a chorus of discordant voices.

For Congress, too, has changed in our time. There has grown a certain divisiveness. We have seen the hard looks and heard the statements in which not each other's ideas are challenged, but each other's motives. And our great parties have too often been far apart and untrusting of each other.

It's been this way since Vietnam. That war cleaves us still. But, friends, that war began in earnest a quarter of a century ago; and surely the statute of limitations has been reached. This is a fact: The final lesson of Vietnam is that no great nation can long afford to be sundered by a memory.

A new breeze is blowing—and the old bipartisanship must be made new again.

To my friends—and yes, I do mean friends—in the loyal opposition—and yes, I mean loyal; I put out my hand.

I am putting out my hand to you, Mr. Speaker.

I am putting out my hand to you, Mr. Majority Leader.

For this is the thing: This is the age of the offered hand.

And we can't turn back clocks, and I don't want to. But when our fathers were young, Mr. Speaker, our differences ended at the water's edge. And we don't wish to turn back time, but when our mothers were young, Mr. Majority Leader, the Congress and the Executive were capable of working together to produce a budget on which this nation could live. Let us negotiate soon—and hard. But in the end, let us produce.

The American people await action. They didn't send us here to bicker.

They ask us to rise above the merely partisan. "In crucial things, unity"—and this, my friends, is crucial. . . .

And so, there is much to do; and tomorrow, the work begins.

And I do not mistrust the future; I do not fear what is ahead. For our problems are large, but our heart is larger. Our challenges are great, but our will is greater. And if our flaws are endless, God's love is truly boundless.

Some see leadership as high drama, and the sound of trumpets calling. And sometimes it is that. But I see history as a book with many pages—and each day we fill a page with acts of hopefulness and meaning.

The new breeze blows, a page turns, the story unfolds—and so today a chapter begins; a small and stately story of unity, diversity, and generosity—shared, and written, together.

CHAPTER OUTLINE

INTRODUCTION AND OVERVIEW

Although the average tourist could walk it in thirty minutes, the mile and a half between the White House and the U.S. Capitol is often a long way in political distance.[1] Governing in the American political system often depends on the relationship between the president and Congress. When they are in relative harmony, each exerting responsible leadership, the system works well. When they clash, the policy-making process can become a war of attrition with stalemate the result. If either branch bogs down, the whole system sputters along. Madison's system of separation of powers and checks and balances is still a dominant feature of American national politics, and it is still creating obstacles to governing. With the growing prevalence of divided government, harsh media campaigns, and powerful interest groups, the relationship between the two branches may be more difficult than ever before.

Congress changed in the 1970s and 1980s. Earlier chapters have noted the fragmentation of power, the decline of marginal seats with the increasing electoral security of incumbents, and the deemphasis of national policy-making for the sake of safe, constituency-oriented activities. Congress has become more difficult to lead by any measure.

The postmodern presidency has changed as well, as we have seen in the growth and subsequent decline of presidential government and the contradiction between high expectations and limited ability to deliver on promises. As he acknowledged in his inaugural address, one of George Bush's greatest political challenges was to work constructively with an independent Congress that was assertive in both domestic and foreign policy.

This chapter examines the relationship between the president and Congress and their struggle to govern the United States. What makes the system work? What gums up the works? Our inquiry explores the following:

1. How has the balance of power swung back and forth between Congress and the president from the days of George Washington to the present? What is the history of conflict and cooperation between the branches? What techniques did early presidents use to sway Congress?
2. What specific abuses of the war-making power, executive privilege, and separation of powers emerged during the Vietnam War and Watergate? How did the impeachment proceedings in Congress ultimately lead to Nixon's resignation?
3. In the aftermath of the Vietnam War and Watergate, how did Congress attempt to correct the imbalance between the executive and legislative branches? What was the effect of a resurgent Congress in the 1970s? Will the end of the cold war alter the balance in the 1990s?
4. How does the president attempt to lead Congress? How does the president assemble a legislative program, and what were the legislative priorities of recent presidents? What are the resources and strategies that presidents have?
5. How does Congress respond to presidential leadership? What are the legislative records of recent presidents? What are a president's options once a bill has passed? What are the keys to presidential legislative success?
6. What are some suggestions for improving ties between Congress and the president to foster more effective governing? What are the problems and prospects for effective policy-making within the present structure of government?

The Pendulum of Legislative-Executive Power

The relationship between Congress and the president has been likened to the swing of a pendulum: periods of presidential dominance followed by congressional resurgence and back again. Although this metaphor is limited, it captures an ebb and flow of influence observed in national politics over the decades. A review of the fortunes of early presidents and their dealings with Congress helps set the stage for a discussion of the struggle to govern today.

The Early Presidents and Congress

George Washington knew many of the people elected to the first Congress. They were together before and during the war and at the drafting of the Constitution. James Madison served as an important legislative adviser to Washington as a member of the House of Representatives from Virginia.[2]

Washington actively sought the advice of the Senate on nominations *before* they were made, but when he made a trip to Congress in person to consult with the Senate on an Indian treaty being negotiated, he was generally rebuffed. Unhappy at his reception, Washington swore he would never go to Congress in person again, although he continued to seek advice in writing.[3] The Senate's response to Washington over the Indian treaty led early presidents to emphasize "consent" rather than "advice" in the matters of treaties and nominations.

Secretary of the Treasury Alexander Hamilton viewed himself as sort of a prime minister of the Washington administration—an agent both of Congress and of the president. He envisioned the post of treasury secretary as a link between branches and personally led Congress in matters of economic policy for three years. The House finally moved toward greater separation of the branches when they denied him entry to the floor.[4] President Washington made modest efforts to establish informal ties with Congress, initiating the custom of White House dinners for legislators. One legislator noted, "The president is a cold, formal man; but I must declare that he treated me with great attention."[5]

Washington's overall record with Congress was good, compared with that of his successor, John Adams. Adams lacked Washington's status or skills, and he presided over an increasingly partisan government divided into Federalist and Anti-Federalist camps (see Chapter 8). Adams was the only president of the first five not to serve two full terms. Although Jefferson as founder of the Democratic party opposed the Federalists, he soon adopted a viewpoint favoring a strong national government, becoming the first president to use political parties and the party caucus as a way to lead Congress. Under the party system in Congress, which also nominated presidential candidates, Jefferson could submit legislation through friendly members. By today's standards, the traditional president was extremely deferential to Congress. Congress, not the president, was the first branch of government. Jefferson, too, wined and dined legislators. One observer noted, "Food and wine were standard accessories of political persuasion [and] the secret of Jefferson's influence."[6]

JACKSON AND LINCOLN

From 1789 to the late 1820s, Congress remained the dominant branch of government. Aside from Washington and Jefferson, presidents often had minimal influence on Congress. The national government had little to do, and Congress could do most of it. The veto was used sparingly. Washington used it twice, while neither Adams nor Jefferson vetoed a bill. The first major expansion of the presidency occurred under Andrew Jackson, not incidentally because the American electorate also expanded dramatically during this time. (See Chapter 9.) Jackson was the first president to claim coequality with Congress in the governing of the nation. "King Andrew the First," as opponents called him, justified his aggressive stance on the basis of his election by universal suffrage. He was a popular president, and he used his popularity to challenge Congress. Jackson was the first to use the veto for political rather than constitutional reasons. He vetoed twelve bills, more than all the previous presidents combined. Jackson saw himself as the "tribune of the people," more truly representative of the nation than the parochial Congress. Neither Congress nor the courts had any right to instruct the president, according to Jackson.[7] Suddenly the language of Article II seemed more flexible than originally recognized. It provided the opportunity for a more expansive view of presidential power. For the first time in history, the pendulum swung toward the presidency. But not for long.

Of the forty-one American presidents, Jackson's successors were particularly weak. Presidents Van Buren, Tyler, Taylor, Pierce, and Buchanan had no desire to challenge Congress, and each only served one term. Not until Abraham Lincoln was inaugurated on the eve of the Civil War did a president again expand the powers of the office.

Lincoln, elected with only 40 percent of the popular vote in a four-way race, assumed great powers to preserve the Union. The sectional conflicts over slavery and commerce that smoldered during the first half of the nineteenth century erupted after his election. Acting as commander in chief to ensure that the laws were "faithfully executed," Lincoln moved swiftly and decisively to preserve the Union. Without the approval of Congress, he instituted a draft, appropriated money, blockaded southern ports, temporarily closed the post office, and suspended the writ of habeas corpus (the right not to be held indefinitely without charge). As a courtesy, he submitted some of the actions to Congress for approval *after* they had already been undertaken. Lincoln based his actions on "popular demand and public necessity" and an expansive view of the "inherent" powers of the presidency.[8]

FROM RECONSTRUCTION TO THE MODERN PRESIDENCY

When the crisis was over, Congress once again assumed dominance in national politics. The Reconstruction Congresses were particularly assertive.

Controlled by the Radical Republicans, who were determined to punish the South, Congress ignored the more conciliatory policies of Lincoln and his successor, Andrew Johnson. When the incompetent Johnson continued to prove meddlesome to Congress, he was impeached by the House and nearly convicted by the Senate on largely trumped-up charges. Johnson survived conviction by a single vote, but the presidency was left in a weakened state. Congress dominated national politics throughout the rest of the nineteenth century. Although Grover Cleveland was more forceful than most presidents of that period, he was left to battle the initiatives of Congress by using the veto. He cast 583 vetoes during his eight years in office; only seven were overridden. Table 14-1 shows presidential vetoes and congressional overrides from President Washington through Bush.

During the last half of the nineteenth century, a number of reforms were proposed to improve relationships between the legislative and executive branches. In the 1860s and 1870s, George Pendleton of Ohio introduced bills to permit cabinet officials to "occupy seats on the floor of the House of Representatives" and to respond to direct questions during sessions on a regularly scheduled basis.[9] None of these proposals was approved.

Congress underwent internal changes of its own during this time. In the House, the Speaker began to consolidate power and was increasingly able to dominate the legislative process. Stable committees and the seniority system began to emerge. Although Republicans dominated the presidency, competition between the parties was very strong in Congress. Majorities were often held by only a few votes.

By the early twentieth century, Congress began to acknowledge a greater legislative role for the president. Teddy Roosevelt and Woodrow Wilson both endorsed the notion of a strong presidency and acted accordingly. Congress approved travel expenses for the president for the first time and began to expect more presidential input into the legislative process. Wilson's power was enhanced by the onset of World War I, but his partisanship in dealing with Congress proved to be his undoing.

TABLE 14–1

PRESIDENTIAL VETOES AND OVERRIDES, 1789–1990

	Total Vetoes	No. Vetoes Overridden		Total Vetoes	No. Vetoes Overridden
Washington	2	0	McKinley	42	0
Madison	7	0	T. Roosevelt	82	1
Monroe	1	0	Taft	39	1
Jackson	12	0	Wilson	44	6
Tyler	9	1	Harding	6	0
Polk	3	0	Coolidge	50	4
Pierce	9	5	Hoover	37	3
Buchanan	7	0	F. Roosevelt	635	9
Lincoln	6	0	Truman	250	12
A. Johnson	29	15	Eisenhower	181	2
Grant	94	4	Kennedy	21	0
Hayes	13	1	L. Johnson	30	0
Arthur	12	1	Nixon	42	6
Cleveland	413	2	Ford	72	12
Harrison	44	1	Carter	31	2
Cleveland	170	5	Reagan	78	9
			Bush	16	0

Presidents not listed vetoed no bills.

SOURCES: *Statistical Abstract of the United States, 1981,* p. 490; and Senate Library, *Presidential Vetoes* (Washington, D.C.: Government Printing Office, 1960), 199. Updated for Bush administration through October. 1990.

The Senate blocked his proposal for U.S. participation in the League of Nations, and Wilson died a broken man.

As government grew, sentiment in Congress also grew to create a national budget. The Budget and Accounting Act of 1921 mandated that the president assemble all executive spending requests into a single package. Although Congress retained full power to appropriate funds, the creation of a national budget and a presidential budget office would later allow the president to develop a leading role in economic policy-making.

The modern presidency emerged under Franklin D. Roosevelt, and the structure and responsibilities of the office were forever altered. Acknowledging permanent changes in the role of the president, the pendulum image still seems appropriate to characterize the post-Vietnam War and Watergate years. Impeachment proceedings against Nixon, efforts to limit the war powers of the presidency, and other examples of congressional resurgence suggest that the balance between Congress and the president continues to shift.

The Vietnam War, Watergate, and Impeachment

THE WAR-MAKING POWER

The Vietnam War was not the first presidential war. President Polk ordered troops into Mexico in the 1840s. McKinley precipitated war with Spain in 1898. Franklin Roosevelt played an active role on the side of the allies before the United States officially entered World War II. Congress never authorized Truman to send troops into Korea in 1950. By the time Lyndon Johnson and Richard Nixon held office, the view that the president had the power to make war without congressional approval seemed to have taken root.

Johnson and Nixon concealed facts about the war in Southeast Asia from Congress and the public. Nixon had authorized secret bombing raids in Cambodia at the same time he was telling the public that the United States would not intervene there. Yet neither president conducted military actions in Southeast Asia over the objections of Congress. On

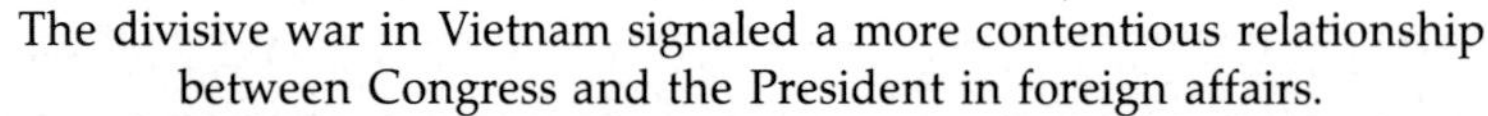
The divisive war in Vietnam signaled a more contentious relationship between Congress and the President in foreign affairs.

the contrary, Congress approved appropriations for the war every year until the fall of South Vietnam in 1975. Even though by the late 1960s serious congressional efforts were being made to stop the war, most members of Congress felt compelled to support the president in even an unpopular foreign military operation.

Undeclared presidential wars were not the only problem. Presidents steadily moved away from treaties (which require Senate approval) toward **executive agreements** (which do not require approval) as the main vehicles of international diplomacy. In the 1960s and 1970s, presidents used executive agreements for the most controversial foreign policy dealings, sending only the most trivial matters to the Senate in the form of treaties—an expedient reversal.

Presidents also used national security claims to legitimize increased government secrecy. The doctrine of executive privilege, dating back to Washington, justifies withholding information from Congress, the press, and the public when the president believes it is in the national interest. Many of these issues came to a head in the most notorious scandal of the American presidency.

Watergate

On June 17, 1972, a group of burglars broke into the Democratic National Committee Headquarters, which was housed in Washington, D.C.'s exclusive **Watergate** hotel and apartment complex.[10] A security guard noticed a door taped open, called police, and five men were arrested. Two years and two months later, on August 9, 1974, Richard Nixon became the first president to resign from office. Facing certain impeachment by the House and conviction in the Senate, Nixon lost the presidency because of his part in the Watergate cover-up.

The investigation of the Watergate break-in led down a winding and often obscure path to the Oval Office of the White House. The investigation uncovered secret, covert units operating out of the White House and a systematic cover-up of the White House involvement in these activities, by the president as well as by others. But from just a clumsy cover-up of a "third-rate burglary," as the White House first called it, it soon became clear that the actions represented a pervasive attack on American democratic institutions.

Claiming executive privilege, President Nixon refused to cooperate with Congress in its investigation and lied to investigators. When Archibald Cox, whom Nixon had named special prosecutor in an effort to show White House backing for an investigation, continued to insist that the White House release a number of tapes of meetings between Nixon and his aides, Nixon fired him. The event, dubbed the "Saturday Night Massacre," represented a crucial turning point as public opinion shifted against the president. The battle over Nixon's tapes continued throughout the rest of 1973 and early 1974. The House of Representatives began hearings on articles of impeachment against the president. More and more facts damaging to Nixon were revealed. Finally, the next special prosecutor, Leon Jaworski, went to the Supreme Court, arguing that Nixon's claim of executive privilege in withholding the tapes was invalid. On June 24, 1974, the U.S. Supreme Court ruled unanimously in *U.S. v. Nixon* that executive privilege was valid in some cases but not to the degree used by the president. Nixon was ordered to turn over the tapes. The decision marked the beginning of the end because the tapes contained the so-called "smoking gun"—evidence that President Nixon knew about the White House involvement with the break-in days after it occurred and participated in the cover-up. When even his diehard conservative Republican support in the House and Senate evaporated, Nixon resigned rather than face impeachment and conviction. Nixon has never acknowledged guilt, noting only that he had lost his "base of support in Congress."

One of the most disturbing aspects of the Watergate scandal was not so much the accumulation of presidential power it revealed as the abuse of that power. President Nixon and his aides had used the power of the presidency not to pursue public policy objectives but to secure personal political advantage. Advocates of a strong presidency had always assumed that presidents would be true to their public trust. The Watergate affair shattered this naive conception and reminded Americans of the Founders' worries about excessive concentration of power. Nixon tried to put his presidency above the

POLITICAL INSIGHT 14-1

THE ARTICLES OF IMPEACHMENT AGAINST RICHARD M. NIXON

RESOLUTION

Impeaching Richard M. Nixon, President of the United States, of high crimes and misdemeanors.

Resolved, That Richard M. Nixon, President of the United States, is impeached for high crimes and misdemeanors, and that the following articles of impeachment be exhibited to the Senate.

ARTICLE I

In his conduct of the office of President of the United States, Richard M. Nixon, in violation of his constitutional oath faithfully to execute the office of President of the United States and, to the best of his ability, preserve, protect, and defend the Constitution of the United States, and in violation of his constitutional duty to take care that the laws be faithfully executed, has prevented, obstructed, and impeded the administration of justice, in that:

On June 17, 1972, and prior thereto, agents of the Committee for the Re-election of the President committed unlawful entry of the headquarters of the Democratic National Committee in Washington, District, of Columbia, for the purpose of securing political intelligence. Subsequent thereto, Richard M. Nixon, using the powers of his high office, engaged personally and through his subordinates and agents, in a course of conduct or plan designed to delay, impede, and obstruct the investigation of such unlawful entry; to cover up, conceal and protect those responsible; and to conceal the existence and scope of other unlawful covert activities.

ARTICLE II

Using the powers of the office of President of the United States, Richard M. Nixon, in violation of his constitutional oath faithfully to execute the office of President of the United States and, to the best of his ability, preserve, protect, and defend the Constitution of the United States, and in disregard of his constitutional duty to take care that the laws be faithfully executed, has repeatedly engaged in conduct violating the constitutional rights of citizens, impairing the due and proper administration of justice and the conduct of lawful inquiries, or contravening the laws governing agencies of the executive branch and the purposes of these agencies.

ARTICLE III

In his conduct of the office of President of the United States, Richard M. Nixon, contrary to his oath faithfully to execute the office of President of the United States and, to the best of his ability, preserve, protect, and defend the Constitution of the United States, and in violation of his constitutional duty to take care that the laws be faithfully executed, has failed without lawful cause or excuse to produce papers and things as directed by duly authorized subpoenas issued by the Committee on the Judiciary of the House of Representatives. . . . In refusing to produce these papers and things, Richard M. Nixon, substituting his judgment as to what materials were necessary for the inquiry, interposed the powers of the Presidency against the lawful subpoenas of the House of Representatives, thereby assuming to himself functions and judgments necessary to the exercise of the sole power of impeachment vested by the Constitution in the House of Representatives.

In all of this, Richard M. Nixon has acted in a manner contrary to his trust as President and subversive of constitutional government, to the great prejudice of the cause of law and justice, and to the manifest injury of the people of the United States.

Wherefore Richard M. Nixon, by such conduct, warrants impeachment and trial, and removal from office.

accountability of democratic politics but did not succeed. The ultimate constitutional sanction given to the Congress to use against the president worked, however slowly and painfully.

Impeachment

The Founders believed Congress should be able to remove the president from office in case of an "emergency" and so devised the **impeachment** process that could be used to depose the president for "treason, bribery, or other high crimes and misdemeanors." Exact definitions of these transgressions were left vague. The removal process itself consists of a majority vote by the House to impeach (a process like indictment), followed by a trial in the Senate. A two-thirds vote is required to convict and remove the president. If a president were removed, he would be forever barred from holding other public office and would be subject to criminal prosecution in the court system.

Political Insight 14-1 examines the three articles of impeachment accepted by the House of Representatives against President Nixon. His resignation eliminated the need to impeach formally—and also protected his pension and other benefits. When Gerald Ford became president, he took the unprecedented step of pardoning the former president, even though Nixon had not formally been accused of any crimes. Historians will long debate the moral and legal consequences of this action, as well as the long-term implications of the Watergate scandal and impeachment proceedings.

Observers still disagree about how well the impeachment proceedings in Congress worked. Some charge that impeachment was incredibly slow, allowing Nixon to remain in office, a crippled incumbent, many months after he should have been removed or should have resigned. A parliamentary system would have moved much more quickly, through action either by the cabinet or by the parliament. Impeachment is a laborious process that hampers the ability of the system to govern while it goes on. If Nixon had stood trial in the Senate, some argue, the situation would have been worse, leaving the United States dangerously weak and vulnerable.

Others believe that the slowness and deliberateness of the impeachment process helped maintain the credibility of the American political system. In the end, all but a small minority were convinced of Nixon's guilt. If the president had been forced out of office sooner, Congress and the press might have been blamed for hounding him out of office. Too fast a process might have been damaging to the ability to govern as well. What happens if the president resigns, dies, is removed, or is disabled? Who is in charge? Political Insight 14-2 looks at those questions in light of **succession laws** and the **Twenty-fifth Amendment.**

Whatever one's judgment about impeachment, the threat of it eventually forced Nixon from office. Congress, already anxious to clip the president's wings in foreign policy, was ready to assume new leadership in government. The Iran-Contra scandal in 1986 and 1987 rekindled the debate once again, raising complex constitutional and political issues.

The Iran-Contra Scandal

Two administration initiatives became entwined to create the **Iran-Contra affair.** The first was a decision authorized by President Ronald Reagan to sell arms to Iran in hopes that certain individuals in the Iranian government would facilitate the release of the American hostages in Lebanon. While some within the administration opposed this move, the president proceeded with it. This covert operation was undertaken without getting the approval of Congress or even notifying it.

The second Reagan administration policy was to provide assistance to the Contra rebels in Nicaragua, who were attempting to topple the Sandinista government. Congressional responses to administrative initiatives was mixed—approving aid to the Contras on several occasions, defeating it on others. Administration critics contend that this inconsistency undermined the coherence of U.S. policy and left the Contras in a vulnerable position. The controversy focused on a series of prohibitions on aid to the Contras enacted by Congress—the Boland Amendments. The initiatives became linked when National Security Adviser John Poindexter, Lieutenant Colonel Oliver L. North, CIA Director William Casey, and others decided to divert profits from the Iranian arms sale to the Contras, despite the Boland Amendments. North and Poindexter

POLITICAL INSIGHT 14-2

PRESIDENTIAL SUCCESSION AND DISABILITY

Although the Constitution specifies that the vice-president is next in line for the presidency, it is silent on further succession. There have been three different succession laws in American history. In drafting the first succession law in 1792, Congress placed its own officers—the Speaker and president pro tempore—next in line. In 1886, Congress decided to place the cabinet next in line for the presidency, beginning with the secretary of state and proceeding in order of the seniority of departments. In 1947, the Congress once again changed the order of succession, returning to the earlier principle of placing congressional leaders in line to succeed the vice-president. Under current law, if both the president and the vice-president leave office through death, resignation, or impeachment, the Speaker of the House and the president pro tempore of the Senate are next in line for the presidency, then followed by the secretary of state and cabinet officers.

Even with a succession law, the Constitution left many unanswered questions that could prove dangerous for the political system. Article II was little help on the question of who would govern if the president were sick or disabled. The Twenty-fifth Amendment, approved in 1967, attempted to clarify this problem. American presidents have on several occasions been seriously incapacitated. In 1881, after being struck by an assassin's bullet, President Garfield managed to live two months with the bullet lodged in his spine. In 1919, President Wilson suffered a serious stroke, which left his side paralyzed. During both of these times, it was unclear whether the vice-president had any power, and the president's personal staff jealously guarded the president's prerogatives, preventing the vice-president from taking over. More recently, President Eisenhower suffered a heart attack in 1955. Once again the White House staff, rather than the vice-president, kept the government going. If President Reagan had been more seriously injured when he was shot by John Hinckley in 1981, he could have been declared "disabled" by the cabinet. The Twenty-fifth Amendment provides:

> The vice-president shall become president following the death or resignation of the president.
>
> The president shall nominate a new vice-president when there is a vacancy in that office, subject to confirmation by majority vote of the House and the Senate.The president may declare himself in writing to be unable to discharge his duties, and in this case the vice-president becomes "acting president" until the president notifies Congress in writing to the contrary.
>
> If the president is unable (or unwilling) to notify Congress himself of disability, a majority of the cabinet may declare the president disabled. The president may resume his duties unless the vice-president and a majority of the cabinet indicate to Congress he is not fit to return. In this case, Congress has forty-eight hours to decide who is president.

The disability provisions raise some interesting possibilities for palace intrigue. What kind of politics might arise in Congress if the president claimed to be able to govern, but the cabinet claimed he was not? Only a few years after its ratification, the Twenty-fifth Amendment was used in naming two new vice-presidents. After the resignation of Spiro Agnew (who pleaded "no contest" to corruption charges), Gerald Ford was named vice-president. Shortly after Nixon's resignation, Ford named Nelson Rockefeller vice-president.

On July 13, 1985, President Ronald Reagan had a malignant polyp removed from his large intestine. Before anesthesia was administered, Reagan signed a letter to the Speaker and president pro tempore of the Senate, informing them that Vice-President George Bush would assume his duties and serve as acting president during surgery. Reagan claimed in the letter *not* to be setting a precedent under the Twenty-fifth Amendment, but he clearly is the first president to use its disability provisions. Seven hours and fifty-four minutes after relinquishing power, Reagan informed Congress that he had resumed his duties as president.

claimed in congressional hearings that the president had not authorized the diversion.

When the diversion of funds to the Contras was discovered, President Reagan appointed a commission headed by Former Texas Senator John Tower to investigate. The Justice Department appointed a special counsel to see whether there had been any criminal violations. Poindexter and North were later convicted on some of the charges. The Tower Commission report, issued early in 1987, was critical of the foreign-policy-making organization in the White House and the role of the National Security Council.

Following the Vietnam War and the Watergate scandal, Congress took steps to increase its influence in both foreign and domestic policy-making.

The Resurgent Congress

INCREASING FOREIGN POLICY PREROGATIVES

Congress moved on several fronts to restore its influence in foreign affairs and national security policy.

THE WAR POWERS ACT (1973). Many members of Congress in the early 1970s were determined to prevent future Vietnams. No more undeclared presidential wars, they pledged. After years of debate and conflict within Congress on defining its proper role, Congress passed the War Powers Act in 1973 and overrode a veto by President Nixon. The **War Powers Act** stated that the president can commit U.S. troops overseas only following a declaration of war from Congress or in the case of a "national emergency." Congress must be consulted before the deployment of troops in "every possible instance." The president must inform Congress within forty-eight hours of any such commitment of troops, and the troops may not remain abroad longer than sixty days without congressional authorization. Finally, Congress may order the president to remove the troops at any time by passing a concurrent resolution that the president may not veto. We shall see below that this final provision was placed in jeopardy by the 1983 Supreme Court decision against the legislative veto.

Every president since Nixon has opposed the War Powers Act, but all have grudgingly complied with most of its requirements. Little prior consultation with Congress has taken place, but Congress has been informed of military actions within the forty-eight-hour time limit. President Reagan, although claiming the act was unconstitutional, successfully appealed to Congress for authorization to keep troops in Lebanon beyond sixty days in the fall of 1983. But the terrorist bombing that took the lives of more than two hundred American marines shortly afterward soured both branches on continued U.S. presence in Lebanon. Reagan also notified Congress immediately after the 1983 Grenada invasion, although the administration continued to claim that the act should not apply. Bush notified Congress of the 1989 Panama invasion and of his decision to send U.S. troops to Saudi Arabia in 1990.

In 1987 President Reagan refused to invoke the War Powers Act over the issue of flying the American flag on oil tankers from Kuwait to protect them from attack by Iran. One hundred members of Congress filed suit in federal court, claiming that the president had violated the War Powers Act. They argued that the decision to reflag Kuwaiti tankers placed U.S. forces in a dangerous region where hostilities were imminent. The lower court refused to rule, however, arguing that it was a political question that had to be settled between Congress and the president. Meanwhile, President Reagan announced that he would not observe the sixty-day limitation because it was an unconstitutional intrusion on his power as commander-in-chief. The future of the War Powers Act remains in question, with neither branch happy with its effects.

Experts differ in their assessment of the real effect of the War Powers Act. Some believe it has actually strengthened the presidency by legitimizing the commitment of troops without a declaration of war.[11] Most believe that, for better or for worse, it has increased congressional involvement in overseas military operations.

THE CASE ACT (1972). The year before the War Powers Act, Congress moved to limit presidential autonomy in making executive agreements, hoping by doing so to increase both congressional scrutiny of and actual input into U.S. foreign policy. The 1972 **Case Act** requires that all executive agreements be reported to Congress within sixty days. It also states that Congress can object to an agreement or mandate separate congressional approval for certain agreements.[12]

OVERSIGHT OF INTELLIGENCE AGENCIES. The reputations of the Central Intelligence Agency and other U.S. intelligence-gathering agencies were badly tarnished during the Vietnam War and Watergate periods. For years, the operations of the intelligence community had been completely secret. Its budget was hidden, and even the heads of the appropriations committees did not know how much money went into covert activities.[13] In an attempt to increase the accountability of the CIA, Congress increased oversight of the intelligence agencies by creating a new select committee in the Senate in 1975.

THE NATIONAL EMERGENCIES ACT (1976). Congress moved in 1976 to limit the president's extensive emergency powers, in force since the 1930s, by passing the **National Emergencies Act.** The president is required to specify which laws will be used when a national emergency is declared. All such emergencies must now end after six months, although the president can declare another emergency. This gives Congress an automatic opportunity to review emergency powers.

INCREASING DOMESTIC POLICY IMPACT

Congress attempted to reestablish a constitutional balance in domestic policy as well as in foreign policy. One area where Congress had clearly fallen behind the executive branch was in budgeting and economic policy-making. Another area where it could assert greater control was administrative oversight.

THE BUDGET AND IMPOUNDMENT CONTROL ACT (1974). Fifty years after the beginning of the executive budget in 1921, Congress was still approving taxing and spending bills in pieces, never considering the budget as a whole.[14] As processes grew more unworkable and Congress seemed less able to control spending growth, President Nixon began to "impound" funds—he simply did not spend monies appropriated by Congress. Previous presidents had impounded monies, but to a more limited extent. Nixon impounded funds at will, striking at the heart of congressional spending power.

In 1974, Congress responded by limiting impoundment and by creating a new budget process of its own in the **Budget and Impoundment Control Act.**[15] (Chapter 17 examines the operation of the congressional budget process in more detail.) The main innovations were new budget committees to recommend resolutions setting revenue and spending totals to guide the actions of other committees. The procedure gave Congress a chance to vote on the entire budget, considering fiscal implications as well as national priorities. To help Congress in this task, the law created the Congressional Budget Office (CBO), which gave Congress more accurate and independent information on taxing and spending questions. Impoundment was made illegal. The Gramm-Rudman mandatory deficit reduction law of 1985 revised the congressional budget process in an attempt to strengthen enforcement procedures. Its deficit targets limited congressional options, but also the president's discretion.

ADMINISTRATIVE OVERSIGHT AND CONFIRMATION. The restoration of congressional checks on the president appeared in other ways too, as Congress conducted more investigations of agencies and departments and into the administration of programs.[16] Over the years, Congress used a number of informal techniques to direct administrative action. But since the 1970s, Congress has increasingly turned to formal, statutory means to increase its control of the bureaucracy. The most effective control it has is over money. Congress has limited the discretion that agencies may exercise in "reprogramming" money within their budget from one account to another. Also, Congress has challenged personnel ceilings imposed by the Office of Management and Budget when legislators wanted to increase spending in a certain program.

Confirmation politics seems to have heated up since the mid-1970s, a further indication of the tension between the two branches. Beginning with the rejection of two consecutive Supreme Court appointments by President Nixon in 1970, Congress has been tougher on presidential nominees. Senators have been particularly concerned with financial disclosure and conflict of interest. Nixon, Ford, Carter, and Reagan all lost some high-level appointments on financial grounds.

Despite his conciliatory inaugural message, President Bush soon found himself engaged in a bitter confirmation fight with the Senate over his nomination of John Tower to become secretary of defense. Tower's critics accused him of alcoholism and womanizing and of only marginal competence to run the Pentagon. Bush fought hard for his old Texas political ally, arguing that a newly elected president ought to have the opportunity to begin with the cabinet of his choice. Senators defended their constitutional right to advise and consent to presidential appointments. Even before the vote, it was clear that Tower would lose when more than fifty senators publicly announced their intention to oppose him. Bush insisted on bringing the nomination to a vote, anyway, rather than withdrawing it. The failure to confirm Tower was a stunning defeat and ignominious "first" for the president: None of Bush's forty predecessors had ever had a cabinet nominee turned down at the start of his first term.

The Senate failed to confirm John Tower as President Bush's Secretary of Defense in 1989, the first time in history that an initial cabinet appointment was rejected.

THE LEGISLATIVE VETO. One of the most potent practices of congressional control of the executive came to an end in 1983. The legislative veto was struck down by the Supreme Court in the case of ***Immigration and Naturalization Service v. Chadha*** (1983), a decision in which more acts of Congress were declared unconstitutional in a single decision than in the entire history of the Court!

The **legislative veto** was an arrangement whereby Congress delegated powers to the executive branch but gave itself an opportunity to block certain agency actions without the approval of the president. During the 1970s, at least one hundred new legislative vetoes were enacted, taking three forms: one-house vetoes, two-house vetoes, and committee vetoes.[17] Depending on the legislation, the House, the Senate, both houses, or a single committee could veto an administrative action. The objective was to give Congress greater control of the regulatory process and public policy administration. But the Court said that Congress had strayed too far over the boundaries of separation of powers.

Writing for a 7-to-2 majority in the *Chadha* case, Chief Justice Warren Burger explained that the power of one branch must not be eroded by the other branch. Because the legislative veto bypassed the president, it was judged to violate the Constitution. If Congress wanted to exercise greater control over the bureaucracy, the Court said, it needed to go through the regular legislative process of passing a law that the president could sign or veto.

The strict interpretation of separation of powers used in the *Chadha* decision was employed by the Supreme Court in 1986 to overturn part of the Gramm-Rudman law. As originally enacted, the law provided that if deficit targets were not met, across-the-board budget cuts would be ordered by the comptroller general, who headed Congress's General Accounting Office. In the case of *Bowsher v. Synar* (1986), the Court struck down this automatic trigger mechanism on the grounds that it was unconstitutional for an officer of the legislative branch to order the president to make budget cuts.[18] The constitutional flaw was repaired when Congress revised the Gramm-Rudman law in 1987 to give the Office of Management and Budget the power to determine mandatory cuts.

THE INDEPENDENT COUNSEL LAW

Another reassertion of congressional authority came to the forefront during the Iran-Contra scandal and reopened questions about separation of powers. In 1978, believing that executive branch officials could not be trusted to investigate their own wrongdoings, Congress enacted a statute to allow the appointment of a special prosecutor to pursue cases of misconduct. The law was revised in 1982 and 1987, passing Congress by large margins. A number of prominent executive branch officials were investigated over a decade, including Hamilton Jordan and Tim Kraft of the Carter administration and Michael Deaver, Lyn Nofziger, Edwin Meese, Oliver North, and John Poindexter of the Reagan administration. The constitutionality of the independent counsel statute was challenged by several of those under investigation, and a case was heard by the Supreme Court in 1988. The Reagan administration claimed that prosecution was strictly an executive branch function. Administration lawyers argued that the law was an unconstitutional violation of separation of powers because it allowed a judicial panel to appoint a special prosecutor and determine the scope of the investigation.

The Supreme Court ruled in the case of *Morrison v. Olson* (1988) that the law was constitutional. For the first time in a decade of legal confrontations between legislative and executive branches, the Court sided with Congress. Writing for a 7-to-1 majority, Chief Justice William Rehnquist observed that Congress had not usurped the president's power. Following the restrictive *Chadha* and *Bowsher* decisions, it appeared that the Court recognized some limits to the absolute separation of branches.

THE BUSH ADMINISTRATION'S RESISTANCE TO CONGRESSIONAL INTRUSIONS

Critical of the expansion of congressional power at the expense of the presidency, President George Bush made a concerted effort to reverse recent trends. He not only challenged the constitutionality of the War Powers Act but also attempted to recapture presidential prerogatives in a number of areas:[19]

Pocket veto: Bush asserted that the president may pocket veto a bill (veto it by not signing it, in effect, "keeping it in his pocket") any time Congress recesses for more than three days, not only at the end of the session. The administration was looking for an opportunity to exercise the pocket veto under these circumstances and set up a court test.

Line-item veto: The Bush administration suggested on several occasions that the president already has the ability to veto specific items in legislation—an ability long sought by President Reagan. Administration lawyers scrutinized British common law history for a legal justification and were considering looking for a bill on which to test their theory.

Executive privilege: Bush asserted that the presidency has greater powers to withhold information from Congress. For example, the administration held that inspectors general are not required to provide information concerning open criminal investigations. Covert activities may be concealed if the president deems it is necessary for national security. Bush successfully negotiated with Congress over deleting a provision requiring forty-eight hour notification of covert activities by clarifying his notification procedures.

Disregarding committee instructions: Bush argued that instructions to agencies contained in committee reports (but not the legislation itself) have no legal basis and can be ignored. He also asserted that Congress cannot interfere with the internal affairs of the executive branch by telling it how to deliberate or whom to consult with. Bush particularly contested congressional requirements to earmark funds for certain purposes or obtain congressional approval to transfer monies. The president equated these instructions with the unconstitutional legislative veto. Congress can put requirements into actual statutes that the president has the opportunity to veto.

Not enforcing unconstitutional laws: Bush has asserted that in certain cases, the administration does not have to enforce laws it believes to be unconstitutional until there is a judicial ruling. Bush began the practice of issuing a constitutional interpretation when he signed a bill, giving instructions to agencies. He declared that one provision of a defense spending bill, for example, had "no legal force."

While Bush was not the first president to reassert presidential prerogatives, his was a more coordinated and systematic campaign than in the past. Attorney General Thornburg, Chief of Staff Sununu, and presidential counselors were charged with finding every opportunity to protect and reassert presidential prerogatives, particularly in foreign affairs. Yet the desire for constitutional power sometimes conflicts with immediate political goals. Bush was accused of weakening the presidency in 1989 when his compromise with Congress on aid to the Contras included an informal congressional veto. Columnist David Broder wrote, "This evasion of the Constitution was so smelly it had to be accomplished through a side agreement, embodied in a letter from the Secretary of State. But that does not lessen the corrosive quality of Bush's capitulation."[20]

Has Bush's resistance to congressional intrusions restored a healthy balance or further heightened tensions between branches? Has the basis for governing become further eroded? While these questions remain unresolved, the next section looks at how presidents attempt to lead Congress.

Presidential Leadership in Congress

Expectations of presidential leadership have changed. In the early days of the Republic, presidents would have been overstepping their bounds to present an annual legislative program. Today, Congress and the American public expect it.

The President's Legislative Program

The first step in assembling the president's program is to sift through the legislative requests of the agencies and departments. This process, called **central clearance,** is conducted by the Office of Management and Budget. Legislative requests are circulated to any other agency that might be affected, so in theory internal disputes can be worked out in advance, before they "go public." Major legislative initiatives are coordinated inside the White House. The president's final legislative program is a statement of priorities and requests for legislation. The experiences of recent presidents suggest how important it is that the president make legislative priorities clear. Better still, the White House must try to capture the imagination of the media and the public. Carter's energy programs, Reagan's economic program, and Bush's drug proposals were all sent to Capitol Hill with high hopes and ambitions. Some fared better than others. Why?

Presidential Success on Capitol Hill

How often do presidents get legislation they submitted approved by Congress? A few highly publicized victories or defeats can create a reputation of success or the aura of failure. Often the media focus only on the most dramatic battles on Capitol Hill; presidents may have a different record on less visible bills they send to "the Hill."

Presidents are most successful in the area of foreign affairs and national defense, with a congressional approval rating of around 55 percent.[21] Although still the highest, the approval rate declined markedly after 1965. From 1948 to 1965, Congress approved nearly 70 percent of the president's requests in foreign policy. After the war in Vietnam and the assumption of greater powers by Congress, the success rate declined to just over half.[22] Social welfare proposals are adopted at the second highest rate—50 percent. Agriculture is right behind, at 49 percent. Economic bills dealing with government management are approved at a 37-percent rate, and bills in the area of natural resources are adopted around 35 percent of the time. At the other end of the scale are presidential initiatives in civil rights. Included in this policy area are the controversial civil rights and voting rights proposals described in Chapter 6, as well as other issues on rights for minorities and women. Only one in four (26 percent) of the presidents' requests were enacted into law in this period.

Success on Congressonal Votes

Identifying presidential initiatives to Congress and determining whether they are approved as the president wished are extremely difficult because of the extensive changes made by Congress.[23] A more reliable indicator of presidential success is based on opposition or support for bills and resolutions in final form before action by Congress. Some measures are proposals the president submitted, and others originated in Congress. Figure 14-1 shows the percentage of times the president's position was upheld by Congress from the Eisenhower to the Bush administrations. Most presidents enjoy their greatest success with Congress in their first year in office before seeing a general decline, although several presidents proved to be exceptions to this pattern.

Eisenhower began his term with a high 90-percent success rate in 1953, his first year, when both the House and Senate were controlled by the Republican party. His support had declined steadily by the late 1950s before he rebounded in his last year in office. Kennedy, an exception to the normal trend, began with a success rate of 80 percent, which climbed past 85 percent in 1963. Johnson, like Eisenhower, had a 90-percent success rate in his first year in office followed by a gradual decline. Nixon and Ford were noticeably less successful than their predecessors. Nixon's congressional support dropped to 50 percent in 1973—his last full year in office—in the midst of the Watergate investigation. Despite his problems with Congress, Jimmy Carter had a success rate of around 75 percent that remained relatively stable during his four years in office. In contrast, Ronald Reagan was supported by Congress 82 percent of the time he took positions on legislation in 1981 but suffered a precipitous decline throughout the rest of his presidency.

The Reagan administration began on a high note in 1981, blitzing through Congress the most radical revision of economic and budget priorities in a generation. But as a recession hit in 1982 and budget deficits increased, Reagan's support on Capitol Hill steadily eroded. Reagan's success rate of only 43.5 percent in 1987, after the Iran-Contra scandal and the Democrats recaptured the Senate, is a record low. Looking only at the most important votes—the fifteen or so key congressional votes each year—Reagan's plummeting success is even more obvious.[24] From a high of 87-percent success in 1981 on these measures, his success dropped to only 12 percent in 1987. Confrontations became more common as Congress overrode several vetoes of key bills. The president also lost the bitter struggle with Congress over the appointment of Robert Bork to the Supreme Court.

Bob Gorrell in the Richmond News Leader.

FIGURE 14–1

PRESIDENTIAL SUCCESS ON VOTES, 1953–89*

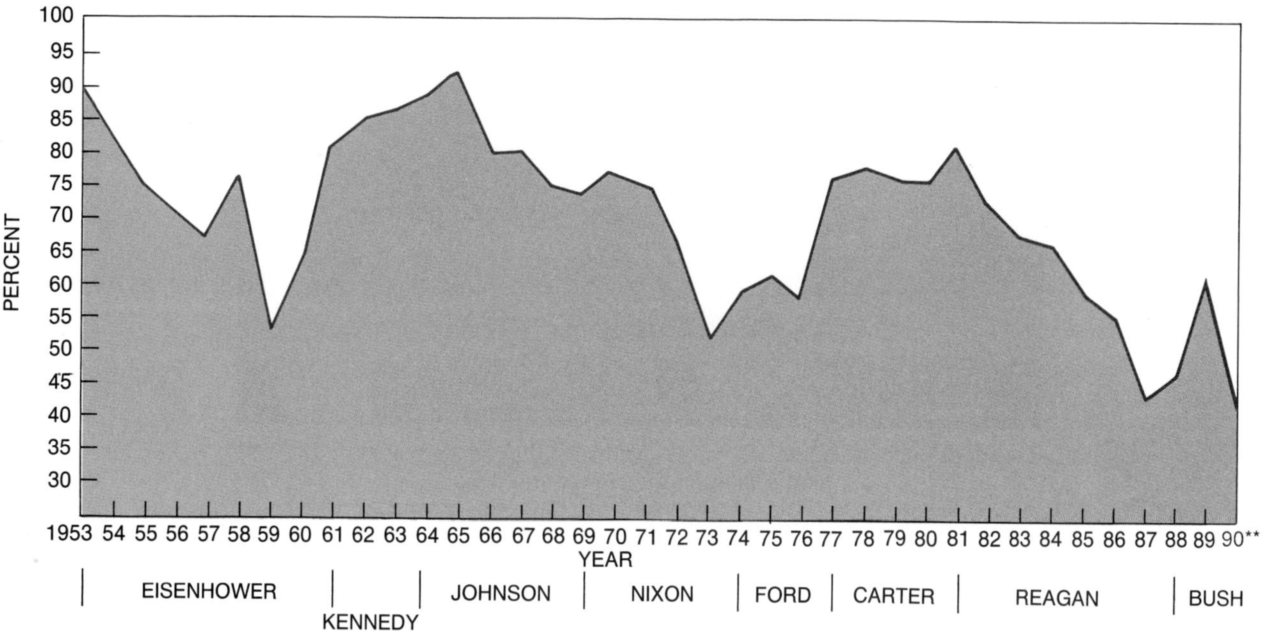

NOTE: *Percentages based on votes on which presidents took a position. **Bush through Oct 10, 1990.
First year of president's administration.
Source: *Congressional Quarterly Weekly Reports*

BUSH AND CONGRESS

Bush began his presidency in 1989 with Congress supporting his position only 63 percent of the time, the lowest success rate for a first-year president since Gerald Ford's 58 percent in the last half of 1974. Like Nixon and Ford, Bush began his presidency with both houses of Congress controlled by the opposition party. With the lowest percentage of members of his own political party holding seats in Congress of any president in history, a more conciliatory approach was a political necessity. As we saw in the Political Close-up that opened this chapter, Bush made overtures to Congress and tried to set a different tone than Reagan. The Tower defeat, however, left many observers doubting whether the new approach would make any difference.

Bush recovered and set out to negotiate deals with Congress over two of the most divisive issues of the 1980s: aid to the Contras and the budget deficit. In March 1989, the administration reached agreement over a package of nonmilitary aid for the Contras. In return, the administration promised not to seek military aid and to make diplomatic overtures to the Sandinista government. This issue became moot in 1990 when Nicaragua held free elections and the Sandinista government was voted out of office. A budget agreement was reached in April 1989, the first time in a decade that legislative and executive branch officials had reached agreement so early.

Leery of appearing to capitulate excessively to the Democratic Congress, the administration confronted Congress on a number of issues. The president vetoed a minimum wage bill from Air Force One in a carefully orchestrated manner designed to show his willingness to oppose Congress when necessary. Bush prevailed on a number of issues, such as blocking congressional efforts to cut aid to El Salvador and to halt development of the Stealth bomber. Bush's political clout with Congress declined further in 1990. While the defeat of the budget summit agreement was the most dramatic loss, his overall success rate was only 43.6 percent

President Bush attempted to sway congressional opinion in a speech before a joint session of the House and Senate.

through October, 1990. The House was particularly resistant to leadership from President Bush, approving his position only 28 percent of the time. Congress failed to approve a constitutional amendment to ban flag burning or to approve further restrictions on federal funding for abortion that the president sought. In issues where Congress enacted legislation over his opposition, he exercised the veto power. None of his first sixteen vetoes were overridden.

Despite the president's attempt to develop a more constructive engagement with the Congress, the two branches were increasingly at odds with each other. How can the patterns of presidential success and failure on Capitol Hill in recent decades be explained?

ACCRUING POLITICAL CAPITAL

Presidents seem to have a finite pool of influence to draw on in their dealings with Congress. Whether it is called "pull," "muscle," "clout," or "naked influence," it refers to presidential resources. These resources make up **political capital;** presidents have only a limited supply and when it is gone, it is gone. In early 1965, Lyndon Johnson alluded to this phenomenon after his landslide election over Barry Goldwater:

> I was just elected president by the biggest popular margin in the history of the country—16 million votes. Just by the way people naturally think and because Barry Goldwater simply scared the hell out of them, I've already lost about three of those sixteen. After a fight with Congress or anything else, I'll lose another couple of million. I could be down to 8 million in a couple of months.[25]

The president's ability to govern depends on the amount of political capital he has and how effectively he spends it. What are the president's political resources?[26] Election results, as President Johnson suggested, are among the most important. In 1961, Kennedy had difficulty getting passed many of the same programs that sailed through for Johnson in 1965, partly because Kennedy won a cliffhanger election over Nixon in 1960 and had less of a mandate to call on. Nixon won a landslide in 1972 but did not effectively translate it into political capital. Reagan's victory in 1980, although less convincing than Nixon's, was much more effectively converted into political capital. Bush's 1988 victory, although substantial in the Electoral College, was not as overwhelming as Reagan's 1980 and 1984 victories.

Majorities in Congress are a second element of presidential capital. Kennedy's majorities in 1961 were slim, compared with the huge Democratic majorities in the House and Senate in 1965. Nixon did not carry large numbers of Republicans into Congress in 1972, and he faced Democratic majorities in both houses. Carter faced large but independent Democratic majorities. His experience demonstrates that majorities alone do not ensure presidential success. After the 1980 elections, Ronald Reagan was able to turn the Republican victory in the Senate and the better showing in the House into real political advantage. Bush clearly lacked this political capital with record-low numbers of party supporters in the House and Senate. Election mandate and congressional majorities can be thought of as presidential "fuel," as one observer in the Office of Management and Budget put it:

> You ought to think of the presidency as an engine. Each president enters office facing the same model—the horse-power is generally stable and the gears are all there. What differs is the fuel. Different presidents enter with different fuel. Lyndon Johnson entered office with a full tank, while Ford entered on empty.[27]

Another critical presidential resource is *popularity.* Studies have shown that the more popular a president is with the public, the more successful he is with Congress.[28] Chapter 13 examined some of the correlates of presidential popularity and how presidents attempt to maintain and enhance popular support. The more successful a president is at maintaining popularity, the more effective are his appeals to Congress. On this dimension, Bush excelled. Some suggested that without his record levels of popularity in 1989 and 1990, his support in Congress would have been even lower. Presidential *reputation* is also an element in political capital. Reputations are often difficult to change once imprinted in the minds of the media and the public. Nixon was always seen as a brooding, somewhat enigmatic character. Ford, a former college athlete, managed to achieve a reputation as a clumsy bumbler, tripping over his own feet physically and politically. Carter kept the reputation he promoted for himself: the rank amateur. When his image should have been changing to political pro, he was still considered an apprentice. Reagan's reputation and popularity suffered greatly because of the Iran-Contra scandal. All these factors combine to create a pool of presidential political capital. How do presidents use it?

LOBBYING AND THE CONGRESSIONAL LIAISON OFFICE

In the day-to-day relations with Congress, success flows from a combination of public relations and lobbying. Presidents and their lieutenants armtwist, cajole, threaten, promise, wine and dine, call, write, try to impress, invoke patriotism, call on party loyalty, urge bipartisanship, logroll, backscratch, and offer pork barrel—all in an effort to get 50 percent plus one of the members of both the House and Senate to vote the way the president wants. It is a difficult job. Victory today means little tomorrow. To help them organize their lobbying efforts better, presidents have a **congressional liaison office** as part of the White House staff.

The model of the modern congressional liaison was developed by Larry O'Brien under Presidents Kennedy and Johnson.[29] The liaison office coordinates the legislative efforts of the president, conveying information and carrying messages between "the Hill" and the White House. Presidents Kennedy and Johnson emphasized the importance of congressional relations and made O'Brien an important part of the operation. President Nixon, in contrast, found pampering Congress distasteful. Although he brought in Bryce Harlow, Eisenhower's former congressional liaison, to head his liaison office, the office was not as active or as effective as its predecessors.[30] The Carter liaison office, headed by Frank Moore, was highly criticized in the early months of the Carter administration. Carter's people were considered inexperienced in the workings of Capitol Hill and incompetent on legislative matters. Moore's office did little to smooth the ruffled feathers of Speaker O'Neill, who was angered at slights by the president and Hamilton Jordan (whom O'Neill referred to as "Hannibal Jerkin"). During Reagan's first term, his congressional liaison staff, under the direction of Max Friersdorf, received high marks. With a much more modest policy agenda and an assertive Congress, the Bush liaison team often conentrated on preventing a veto override.

PRESIDENTIAL REWARDS AND PUNISHMENTS

What can presidents offer to members of Congress who are increasingly concerned with tangible benefits and reelection? Not as much as one might think. The president controls several thousand jobs in the executive branch, judgeships, attorneys, and members of boards and commissions, but there are limits to what a president can do with these appointments.[31] In some cases, efforts to pay off political friends backfire. As Lincoln said, "Filling a patronage job creates nine enemies and one ingrate."

The White House can use its influence to direct federal dollars—pork barrel—to the states and districts of friendly members for a multitude of federal projects that help the economy and prosperity of a region. Every military base, installation, dam, park, recreation area, federal building, or navy yard is fiercely sought by members of Congress. Assistance from the White House can be very helpful.

Presidents may share a little of the glamour of the White House with members of Congress. President Carter downplayed the "regal" dimensions of the presidency in reaction to the "imperial presidency" of the 1960s and 1970s. Johnson, in contrast, used the trappings of the office to the hilt. He raised his Oval Office desk a few inches and had the White House carpenter cut a few inches *off* the chairs in the room, making a visitor to the president's office feel even smaller. As Johnson put it, "It's hard to bargain from your knees." Johnson used to invite members down to the LBJ ranch for barbecues and drive them around in his jeep. President Reagan used presidential glitter to great effect. Entertainment of members at White House dinners, picnics on the lawn, teas, trips to Camp David, photo sessions—all helped create a strong feeling of loyalty to the president. Although many members may be immune to this kind of flattery, it makes more friends than enemies. Presidents who avoid this kind of politicking lose opportunities for influence.

Presidents sometimes try go over the heads of Congress and take their appeal to the people. A major address in prime time can be a boon to his efforts. Kennedy, Johnson, Carter, Nixon, Ford and Bush, all made televised appeals for support with varying success. Ronald Reagan, the "great communicator," used his media effectiveness to complement the other techniques. His televised speeches urging citizens to lobby their legislators to support his economic program produced a flood of mail on Capitol Hill.

Along with the carrot, presidents sometimes try the stick. In early 1985, President Reagan let it be known that he might withhold campaign support from Republican senators up for reelection in 1986 who had been "disloyal."[32] Although campaign support is not always effective or even desired (some Democrats in 1978 believed that an appearance by Carter would hurt rather than help them), a boost from a popular president can be important in a close race. The president can help with fund-raising by appearing in campaign commercials, issuing invitations to the White House, appointing incumbents up for reelection to special committees, and making campaign stops in a candidate's district. But in 1986, President Reagan's campaign efforts on behalf of Republican senators were futile, as seven incumbents went down to defeat. President Bush helped Republican candidates around the country raise money in 1990, but his declining popularity reduced his political clout.

STRATEGIES WITH CONGRESS

Varying results flow from a president's management and selling skills, from the political environment, and from different amounts of political capital. Nonetheless, some dos and don'ts of presidential leadership can be offered.[33]

Move it or lose it. With declining levels of congressional support over time, an agreed-on lesson of recent years is the need for presidents to move quickly if they hope to achieve their legislative goals. Lyndon Johnson recognized this, according to one of his top aides:

> You've got to give it all you can that first year. Doesn't matter what kind of majority you come in with. You've got just about one year when they treat you right and before they start worrying about themselves. . . . You can't put anything through when half of the Congress is thinking about how to beat you. So you've got one year.[34]

Despite the impressive showing of the Reagan administration in its first eight months, looking back on it Budget Director David Stockman felt the administration should have gone for even more that first year. Carter's advisers realized too late they had squandered that fleeting period of presidential influence. As political scientist Paul Light concluded, "Presidents cannot wait for a comprehensive review of domestic issues and alternatives. There is not enough time, information, or energy. If presidents are to take advantage of what little resources they have, the domestic agenda must move quickly."[35] Obviously, this strategy has some potentially negative consequences, particularly the danger of ill-advised, poorly designed legislation.

Set clear priorities. Limitations in presidential resources make it increasingly necessary for the president to focus congressional attention on a small set of concrete legislative proposals. A far-reaching wish-list is unlikely to garner results. Carter's chief adviser, Hamilton Jordan, reflected on their failure to set clear goals:

> If I look back at one thing, I would say that we made a mistake in the first two or three years . . . by not establishing public priorities for three or four major issues. Instead we came to Washington and we jumped on all the issues that were . . . important to our people.[36]

Hire experts, not amateurs. The effectiveness of the legislative liaison staff and other components of the White House staff plays a tremendous role in determining the success of the president's program in Congress. Immediate, successful action is important because of the rapid depletion of the president's political capital; inexperienced staff have no opportunity to learn what they are doing. By the time amateurs learn their job, the opportunity for influence will probably have passed.

Understand Congress. Effective presidents understand what motivates members of Congress and base their appeals on that knowledge. That means negotiation and compromise are almost always necessary. The president and the White House staff must deal with Congress the way they really are—oriented to reelection and the district as much as to national policy—not the way they think Congress should be. Former members do not automatically understand the needs of Congress or make successful presidents.

Effective strategies for presidential success with Congress in the 1990s must be more pragmatic than

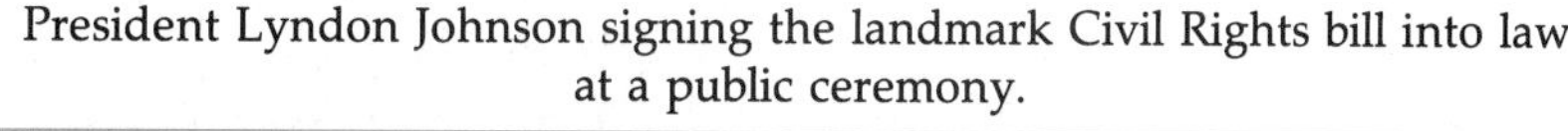

President Lyndon Johnson signing the landmark Civil Rights bill into law at a public ceremony.

idealistic. They must reflect the changes in Congress in the past quarter century and the increasing difficulty in building legislative coalitions. Today's strategies reflect governing problems—the decline of party and party leadership, the limits of power in the postmodern presidency, and the decline of presidential influence as the term advances.

THE VETO POWER

The Founders argued over whether to give the chief executive any power to veto legislation. Some wanted an absolute veto without any possibility for reversal. Others wanted the president to share the veto with a cabinet council. Constitutional architects settled on a veto that could be overridden by two-thirds of both houses. How does the president decide to say yes or no to what Congress has passed?

Vetoes were used sparingly in the early years of the Republic—only when a measure was considered unconstitutional did early presidents believe a veto was justified. Andrew Jackson changed all that, although his 12 vetoes look insignificant compared with Franklin Roosevelt's 635. The president today uses a formalized process to decide whether he will sign or veto a bill. The **enrolled bill process,** like central clearance, is coordinated by the Office of Management and Budget. A bill is "enrolled" when it is passed in identical form and signed by presiding officers of both houses of Congress. Advice and opinions are solicited from the agencies and departments. The OMB assembles the results and makes a recommendation to the president. The president takes the OMB's recommendation most of the time when it recommends signing the bill but follows its suggestion to veto less frequently.[37] The president, who is subject to greater political pressures than the bureaucracy and the OMB, is often more reluctant to veto than they are to recommend a veto.

The list of presidential vetoes and overrides since 1789 in Table 14-1 reveals that several of the early presidents did not veto a single bill. Does a high number of vetoes mean that relations between the legislature and executive were on the rocks? Such was the case for Cleveland, Truman, Nixon, and Ford, but Franklin Roosevelt is the exception. His expansive view of presidential power and occasional troubles with Congress during his twelve years in office help explain his record total. Truman faced a Republican Congress after the 1946 elections and used the veto to stave off a resurgent opposition. Similarly, Eisenhower faced a Democratic Congress for six years of his eight-year term and also used the veto frequently.

Kennedy and Johnson used the veto sparingly. In fifty-one combined vetoes, neither was overridden. Nixon and Ford used the veto more frequently, and Ford has the dubious distinction of being second only to the impeached and nearly removed Andrew Johnson in the percentage of his vetoes that were overridden by Congress. The threat of a presidential veto is often as effective as the actual exercise of the power. Nixon and Ford vetoed spending bills because they were "budget busters," and Reagan often did the same thing. George Bush used the veto power in foreign and domestic policies. In a number of cases, such as the minimum wage, Congress ultimately adopted the president's position after unsuccessfully trying to override the veto.

The president's choices on bills that pass Congress are more diverse than the decision to sign or not sign. Table 14-2 summarizes the president's options, procedures to be followed, and results. The presidency has come a long way in expanding the scope of its legislative relations since the Framers debated the veto power. Nonetheless, the veto remains an important if negative presidential prerogative in attempting to influence Congress and the course of public policy.

Congress, the President, and Governing

CHANGING THE CONSTITUTION?

Can a system devised in the 1780s serve the governing needs of a political system in the 1990s? In the critiques of governing presented in Chapter 1, critics complained that, except in very unusual periods, American politics are too often characterized by stalemate. Numerous critics point to the inaction and inability to govern resulting from separation of powers. Is it time to make fundamental reforms in the Constitution to improve the ability to govern? Chapter 2 suggested general

TABLE 14–2

TO SIGN OR NOT TO SIGN? THE PRESIDENT'S OPTIONS WITH A BILL

Option	Procedure	Purpose	Effect
Sign	President affixes signature within ten days of receipt.	To approve the legislation	Bill becomes law.
Not to sign during the session.	Bill remains on desk for more than ten days.	To disassociate the president from the bill while letting Congress have its way.	Bill becomes law without president's signature.
Simple veto	President vetoes bill and sends message to Congress with explanation.	To indicate the president opposes bill; bill is unconstitutional; Congress is requested to correct the bill.	Bill is returned to Congress for vote on override. If two-thirds of both houses fail to override, veto is sustained.
Pocket veto	President does not sign bill submitted with *fewer* than ten days left in the session.	To kill bill with no explanation from president; cannot be overridden.	No vote to override is taken because Congress is out of session. Must be resubmitted next year and go through each step in the legislative process.

approaches to constitutional change to enhance governing. Let us look at some specific constitutional amendments that have been proposed.[38]

Vote for president, vice-president, and member of Congress as a team. This change is intended to increase the dependence of legislators on the president and to eliminate split-ticket voting (a voter, for example, selecting a Democrat for Congress but a Republican for president). Terms for members of Congress would be made the same as the president's so that the president and legislators would be more interdependent and have greater protection against the pressures of interest groups.

Allow the president to select some of the cabinet from the House and Senate while having them retain their seats in Congress. Eliminating the strict separation between legislative and executive branches would require an amendment to Article I, section 6, which prohibits any member of Congress from holding a position in the executive branch. The proposal is intended to increase the intimacy between Congress and the president, allowing them to develop a sense of collective responsibility.

Allow the president, once each term, to dissolve Congress and call for new elections. If the president dissolved Congress, Congress could simultaneously call for new presidential elections. All congressional candidates would be nominated within 60 days, the presidential candidates within 90 days, and the national elections would occur within 120 days. Congress could stay in session and the president remain in office until after the new elections. With this change, if a complete stalemate resulted between Congress and the president the public would be able to break it by voting for a new government. A constitutional amendment to this effect would move American government toward a parliamentary model, where a prime minister can dissolve parliament or a no-confidence vote by parliament results in new elections if the government is defeated.

Increase the term of the president, vice-president, senators, and representatives to six years elected simultaneously. The six-year term for the president is intended to enhance the president's objectivity and acceptance of programs offered in the public interest. If at the same time the president retained the ability to dissolve Congress, he or she would not have to operate as a "lame duck." Six-year terms for legislators would enable them to resist the power of special interest groups and would make elections more national in scope.

GOVERNING UNDER SEPARATION OF POWERS

Proposals to change the Constitution to promote more effective governing processes in the United States are intriguing but unrealistic. The Constitution has proven extremely difficult to amend, and there is clearly no set of proposals that a majority could yet agree on. Separation of powers is here to stay. What approaches to governing are possible under these constraints?

Even with the decline of political parties, something approaching **party government** occurred under Ronald Reagan in 1981. With the help of three dozen conservative Democrats, the president was able to maintain a working majority on economic and budget issues for about eight months, long enough to enact his program. Before that, party government last appeared in 1965 following Johnson's landslide victory in the presidency and the election of large numbers of new Democrats to Congress. Under current political conditions, however, party government simply cannot work. Partisanship under divided government increases the chances for deadlock when controversial issues become politicized. Both Social Security and taxes are good examples of issues where governing has become nearly impossible.

Another approach to governing under separation of powers would depend on changing the executive-legislative balance. **Presidential government** occurred under Roosevelt in the 1930s and to some extent lasted through the 1960s. In the face of a national crisis or a complete breakdown of Congress's ability to reach decisions, a stronger president could once again emerge. But the trend seems to be running in the other direction. The postmodern presidency faces greater constraints than presidents did two generations ago at the same time that Congress has staked out an even greater policy-making role. With the easing of tensions after the cold war and less need for the president to protect the nation from nuclear war, the balance may shift even more.

Although not seen for a century or more, **congressional government** is another possibility. If congressional power increases in comparison to presidential power, and the House and Senate improve collective decision-making, Congress could assume the leading role in policy-making. The president may take on more ceremonial duties, while the "new oligarchy" of party leaders and key committee chairs centralizes authority in Congress. Something like the French system might evolve with an independently elected president exercising certain powers while the government is formed based on legislative majorities.

None of these approaches seems much more feasible than amending the Constitution. Even with substantial majorities, Congress has not been able to assert its own agenda, and President Bush tried to expand the legal authority of the presidency. Under divided party control and separation of powers, the only real options are some degree of bipartisan cooperation, the appointment of independent commissions to make the politically unpalatable decisions, or stalemate. Bipartisanship and **coalition government** can work, as we saw in the case of the Tax Reform Act of 1986 in Chapter 1. But both parties must agree to change the rules of political engagement by not seeking partisan electoral advantage. Independent commissions can be used to help provide "political cover" for Congress and the president. Facing bankruptcy in the Social Security trust fund, the 1983 bailout plan was formulated by a special commission and then approved as quickly and quietly as possible. Legislative-executive summits are another device to break deadlocks and try to govern responsibly. But the failure of the five-month budget summit in 1990, when both the president and congressional leaders were rebuffed, casts doubts on this approach, too.

Coalition government is not always popular or effective. Partisans in both parties criticize legislative-executive accommodation for blurring party differences. Governing through commissions or summits often reduces the ability of rank-and-file members to influence policy when compromise packages are considered under closed rules that restrict or prohibit amendments. Nor does bipartisan accommodation necessarily face up to tough policy choices or settle underlying differences: they may become an exercise in "lowest common denominator" bipartisanship where differences are papered over, each side takes political cover, and real responsibility is avoided.

Yet under existing political conditions, there seem to be few alternatives. As one Democratic senator noted, "We have a coalition government now. It only works when both sides are on board."[39] Short of constitutional amendment, a dramatic change in national electoral results, or a significant shift in the balance between Congress and the president, governing with some degree of bipartisan cooperation seems to be the only viable means to avoid deadlock.

SUMMARY AND CONCLUSIONS

1. Throughout most of the nation's first century, national politics was dominated by Congress. Occasionally, the pendulum swung toward the presidency, as in the era of Jackson and Lincoln.

2. The balance of power between the president and Congress permanently changed after the administration of Franklin Roosevelt, architect of the modern presidency.

3. Reacting to the "imperial presidency" and to abuses of presidential power, Congress took a number of steps in the 1970s and 1980s to increase its power. The War Powers Act and the Budget and Impoundment Control Act were two of the most important.

4. Reacting to the continued assertion of congressional power, George Bush has attempted to expand the prerogatives of the presidency on a number of fronts.

5. As much as at any time in history, the ability of the American political system to govern depends on relations between Congress and the president. Presidents today are expected to present a legislative program to Congress and to work for its passage.

6. Presidential success on Capitol Hill depends on the president's political capital and how effectively it is used. Presidential resources include popularity, congressional majorities, perception of a mandate to govern, and professional reputation. The White House congressional liaison office contributes to presidential effectiveness.

7. Presidents have been most successful in securing congressional approval in the areas of foreign affairs and national defense, followed by social welfare and agriculture. Presidents have been least successful in getting Congress to approve their proposals in civil rights.

8. Presidents experience declining influence with Congress through their term. This was particularly true of Ronald Reagan. As a result, presidents must use their limited resources carefully. They must move quickly in the first year, set clear legislative priorities, hire experienced staff, and understand the needs of Congress.

9. As a last resort in battles with Congress, the president may use the veto power. Active use of the veto hampers the ability of the political system to work effectively.

10. Short of amendments to the Constitution, dramatic changes in national election results, or a significant shift in the balance of power between Congress and the president, governing through bipartisan coalitions seems to be the only viable alternative.

The American political system remains unique. In few other nations are executive and legislative branches so independent. What concerns many observers is the demise of arrangements and practices that used to bind the Congress and the president together. The Founders labored to create a system that would both preserve liberty and be able to govern, separating Congress and the president so they could check and balance each other. The resulting arrangements still shape politics today. The most critical issues facing the nation today cannot be solved without some agreement issuing from both ends of Pennsylvania Avenue. The struggle of the president and the Congress to govern has been going on for two hundred years and will continue to be a dominant feature of politics in America's third century.

KEY TERMS

Budget and Impoundment Control Act
Case Act
central clearance
coalition government
congressional government
congressional liaison office
enrolled bill process
executive agreements
Immigration and Naturalization Service v. Chadha
impeachment
Iran-Contra affair
legislative veto
National Emergencies Act
party government
presidential government
political capital
succession laws
Twenty-fifth Amendment
War Powers Act
Watergate

SELF-REVIEW

1. How has the balance of legislative-executive power varied over the past two hundred years?
2. What specific powers did Congress feel were abused by presidents during the war in Vietnam?
3. How did Nixon abuse presidential power?
4. What are the disadvantages of the impeachment process?
5. What steps did Congress take in the 1970s and 1980s to alter the balance of power between the legislative and executive branches?
6. How did President Bush attempt to strengthen the presidency?
7. How does the president assemble a legislative program?
8. What is presidential political capital? How is it used effectively?
9. List some rules of thumb for presidents who want to get a program through Congress.
10. What are a president's options with an enrolled bill?
11. What are some constitutional reforms that aim to establish parliamentary links between the legislative and executive branches?
12. Describe the main differences between the party government approach and the bipartisan approach to governing.

SUGGESTED READINGS

Burns, James MacGregor. *The Power to Lead.* 1984.
Burns, long a critic of the limitations of governing in American politics, analyzes the problem and makes some structural proposals for improvement.

Crabb, Cecil V., Jr., and Pat M. Holt. *Invitation to Struggle: Congress, the President, and Foreign Policy.* 2nd ed. 1989.
An analysis of the role of Congress and the president in foreign affairs, including some detailed case studies of the recent past.

Light, Paul. *The President's Agenda: Domestic Policy Choice from Kennedy to Carter.* 1983.
A book based on the author's interviews of former White House staff on the source, management, and strategies of domestic policy-making in the presidency.

Pfiffner, James P. *The Strategic Presidency.* 1988.
A study of presidential transitions and how a newly elected president can "hit the ground running."

NOTES

1. See Anthony King, "A Mile and a Half Is a Long Way," in Anthony King, ed., *Both Ends of the Avenue* (Washington, D.C.: American Enterprise Institute, 1983), 246-72.
2. Louis Fisher, *The Politics of Shared Power: Congress and the Executive* (Washington, D.C.: Congressional Quarterly Press, 1981), 33.
3. James D. Richardson, ed., *A Compilation of Messages and Papers of the Presidents,* vol. 1, pp. 64-115, cited in ibid., 33.
4. Fisher, *Politics,* 33.

5. William Maclay, *Sketches of Debate in the First Senate of the United States* (New York: Ungar, 1965), 135, 172, quoted in Fisher, *Politics,* 36.
6. James S. Young, *The Washington Community, 1800-1828* (New York: Columbia University Press, 1966), 168.
7. Edward S. Corwin, *The President: Office and Powers* (New York: New York University Press, 1957), 19.
8. J. G. Randall, *Constitutional Problems under Lincoln* (Magnolia, Mass.: Smith, 1964), 58.
9. Fisher, *Politics,* 37.
10. For a complete review of the Watergate scandal, see *Watergate: Chronology of a Crisis* (Washington, D.C.: Congressional Quarterly Press, 1975).
11. See Charles Black, "The President and Congress," *Washington and Lee Law Review* 32 (Fall 1975):850; and Stuart Darling and D. Craig Mense, "Rethinking the War Powers Act," *Presidential Studies Quarterly* 7 (Spring 1977):126-36.
12. Loch Johnson and James McCormick, "Foreign Policy by Executive Fiat," *Foreign Policy* 28 (Fall 1977): 117.
13. See House Select Committee on Intelligence, *U.S. Intelligence Agencies and Activities: Intelligence Costs and Fiscal Procedures Hearings,* 31 July-8 August 1975.
14. Lance T. LeLoup, *The Fiscal Congress* (Westport, Conn.: Greenwood Press, 1980).
15. See Allen Schick, *Congress and Money* (Washington, D.C.: Urban Institute, 1980).
16. See Fisher, *Politics,* chap. 3.
17. Louis Fisher, "Legislative Vetoes, Phoenix Style," in the *Carl Albert Center Extensions,* Spring 1984, p. 2.
18. *Bowsher v. Synar* 106 S.Ct. 3181 (1986).
19. *Congressional Quaterly Weekly Reports,* Feb 3, 1990, pp. 291-95.
20. *Washington Post National Weekly Edition,* May 15, 1989, p. 4.
21. See Lance T. LeLoup and Steven A. Shull, "Congress versus the Executive: The 'Two Presidencies' Revisited," *Social Science Quarterly* (1979).
22. See Aaron Wildavsky, "The Two Presidencies," *Transaction* 4 (December 1966).
23. For a good explanation of the difficulties and methods of determining the presidents' success in Congress, see Steven A. Shull, *Domestic Policy Formation: Presidential-Congressional Partnership?* (Westport, Conn.: Greenwood Press, 1983), 183-99.
24. For an explanation of the key votes, see *Congressional Quarterly Weekly Reports,* 2 January 1988, pp. 24-41.
25. Doris Kearns, *Lyndon Johnson and the American Dream* (New York: Harper and Row, 1976), 226.
26. Paul Light, *The President's Agenda* (Baltimore: Johns Hopkins University Press, 1983), 26-34.
27. Quoted in Charles Jones, "Presidential Negotiations with Congress," in King, *Both Ends,* 102.
28. See George C. Edwards, *Presidential Influence in Congress* (San Francisco: Freeman, 1980), 86-115.
29. See Steven Wayne, *The Legislative Presidency* (New York: Harper and Row, 1978).
30. Ibid.
31. Frank Kessler, *The Dilemmas of Presidential Leadership* (Englewood Cliffs, N.J.: Prentice-Hall, 1982), 151.
32. *New York Times,* 15 March 1985, p. 1.
33. See Light, *Agenda,* 217-25.
34. Harry McPherson, *A Political Education* (Boston: Little, Brown, 1972), 268.
35. Light, *Agenda,* 218.
36. Hamilton Jordan, "Meet the Press," 23 November 1980, quoted in ibid., 230.
37. See Wayne, *Legislative Presidency.*
38. Donald Robinson, ed., *Reforming American Government* (Boulder, Colo.: Westview, 1985).
39. *Congressional Quarterly Weekly Reports,* 30 December 1989, p. 354.

CHAPTER 15

The Bureaucracy

POLITICAL CLOSE-UP

Bureaucratic Doublespeak

Bureaucrats have often been accused of making up a special language related to their field that results more in confusion than in clarity. While lawyers, academics, and politicians also use jargon all too often, bureaucrats seem to be the worst offenders. A group of English teachers formed a "Committee on Public Doublespeak" in an attempt to prevent "dishonest and inhumane uses of the English language" and to monitor "grossly deceptive, confusing remarks with potentially pernicious social and political consequences." Their "Doublespeak Awards" are designed to call public attention to the problem. Competition among the Defense Department, the attorney general, and the National Aeronautics and Space Administration (NASA) for first place recently was fierce.

Third prize for doublespeak went to the Department of Defense for the following gems:

> Marine Corps expeditionary soft shelter system; a frame-supported tension structure (a tent)

> An emergency exit light (a flashlight)
>
> A hexiform rotatable surface compression unit (a steel nut)
>
> A manually powered fastener-driving impact device (a hammer)
>
> An aluminum transfer case (a temporary coffin)

Second prize went to Attorney General Edwin Meese for his comments on the Supreme Court's *Miranda* ruling, which requires police officers to read a suspect his or her constitutional rights. Meese was asked whether people who were innocent benefit from the ruling:

> Suspects who are innocent of a crime should, but the thing is, you don't have many suspects who are innocent of a crime. That's contradictory. If a person is innocent of a crime, then he is not a suspect. . . . [The decision's] practical effect is to prevent the police from talking to a person who knows the most about the crime—namely the perpetrator. . . . *Miranda* only helps guilty defendants. Most innocent people are glad to talk to the police. They want to establish their innocence so that they're no longer a suspect.

First place went to NASA for its muddled account of the tragic launch of the space shuttle *Challenger:*

> The normal process during countdown is that the countdown proceeds, assuming we are in a go posture, and at various points during the countdown we tag up the operational loops and face to face in the firing room to ascertain the facts that project elements that are monitoring the data and that are understanding the situation as we proceed are still in the go direction.

SOURCE: *St. Louis Post-Dispatch,* 24 November 1986, p. 14a.

Chapter Outline

Introduction and Overview

Bureaucracy is an inevitable result of complex social, economic, and political activities. From the large private corporation to the grant-giving foundation, the church, and the state, bureaucratic organization is an inescapable element of modern society. The term "bureaucracy" dates back to eighteenth-century France; its definition was "rule by autocratic public officials." Today, **bureaucracy** generally refers to large-scale formal organizations, structured in a hierarchical fashion, with a division of labor often based on technical expertise. The following analysis concentrates on public bureaucracy in the United States, but many generalizations apply to other bureaucracies as well.

Bureaucracy is involved with many aspects of the policy process and governing. Although linked to the formulation of policy proposals for both the presidency and the Congress, the main function of a bureaucracy is to administer policies. As such, bureaucracies are deeply involved with policy implementation and regulation. In making and implementing policy, the federal bureaucracy is closely linked to congressional subcommittees and interest groups. These important policy networks are called "subgovernments" or "iron triangles."

Despite its critical role in American politics, bureaucracy is not well understood, or well liked. In the following pages, we examine how citizens evaluate their experiences with bureaucrats and what is myth and reality about bureaucracy. Bureaucracy also affects the ability of the system to govern. Does bureaucracy provide a means for efficient policy implementation or a series of obstacles to innovation and effectiveness? Has the bureaucracy become more powerful in determining public policy as the ability of Congress and the presidency to cooperate has declined? In developing a realistic view of American bureaucracy and the federal executive branch, the following questions are considered:

1. How did American bureaucracy evolve and develop from early patronage and the spoils system to the modern civil service?
2. What is the bureaucracy, and who are the bureaucrats?

3. How does the bureaucracy make public policy? What is its role in administration, implementation, and regulation?
4. If bureaucracies are relatively influential, what are the sources of their power? What is their relationship with interest groups, Congress, and **clientele groups?**
5. Do laws of bureaucratic behavior exist? What is "bureaucratic politics"?
6. How do the president and Congress attempt to control and manage the federal bureaucracy?
7. What are the cases for and against bureaucracy? What happens to the role of bureaucracy in American politics when other institutions are suffering governing problems?

The Evolution of the Bureaucracy

THE ORIGINS OF THE FEDERAL BUREAUCRACY

At the Constitutional Convention, the Founders concentrated on the president's powers and duties and paid little attention to how he would run the executive branch. The four original departments—State, War, Treasury, and Justice—were created by the first Congress. A conflict soon arose between the legislative and executive branches over the power of removing department officials. Did the president or the Congress have ultimate control of the bureaucracy? Still suspicious of the powers of the presidency, some members of Congress wanted to have the right to remove officials as well as to confirm their appointment.[1] Arguing strongly against this view, James Madison exclaimed, "If any power whatsoever is in its nature Executive, it is the power of appointing, overseeing, and controlling those who execute the laws."[2] The Congress in a very close vote affirmed Madison's position, and the first four departments were created with secretaries removable only by the president.

The debate over the removal power was not resolved in the first Congress but became an issue once again after the Civil War. Congress was determined to limit the power of President Andrew Johnson and passed the Tenure of Office Act, prohibiting the president from removing officials without congressional approval. Johnson, believing the act to be unconstitutional, removed Secretary of War Edwin M. Stanton. Stanton's removal became the main grounds for the impeachment and trial of Johnson. Presidential versus congressional control of the executive branch is still in conflict today, as the *Chadha* decision overturning the legislative veto revealed (see Chapter 14).

The early bureaucracy was tiny by today's standards; there were less than a dozen employees in the State Department, less than one hundred in the War Department. The few available federal appointments were fiercely sought after. The largest government agency was the Post Office: Delivering the mail was one of the national government's most important functions in the early years. By 1816, some four thousand federal employees were on the rolls. Fifteen years later, in the administration of Andrew Jackson, the number had tripled.[3] As the presidency expanded, so did the president's desire to use the bureaucracy as a source of political power, a means of assuring loyalty and rewarding friends and supporters. *Patronage*—political favoritism in making appointments—became the main criterion for appointment.

THE SPOILS SYSTEM

The **spoils system**—from the maxim "To the victors belong the spoils"—was the culmination of patronage. It not only embraced new appointments but under Jackson also included removing officials from the previous administration. Jackson was not the first president to use the spoils system, but he did so far more extensively than any previous chief executive, in spite of the harsh criticism he incurred. Jackson's impact on the bureaucracy went beyond the spoils system, however. In an attempt to gain greater control, he reshuffled the departments and rotated employees, inadvertently modernizing the bureaucracy.[4] By separating the *job description* from the *individual* who held that job, the bureaucracy began to take on the more formal, impersonal characteristics now associated with large organizations.

The spoils system operated until the 1880s. During the Civil War, inadequacies in the executive branch became evident. The need to hire new officials to run the government during the war, and the rapid industrialization that followed, led to significant growth in the bureaucracy (see Table 15–1). As bureaucracy grew, so did demands for reform of the spoils system.

THE CIVIL SERVICE SYSTEM

In 1881, President Garfield was gunned down by a disgruntled office-seeker. Public horror over a system of political favoritism that led to corruption and violence resulted in proposals for reform of the spoils system. A system based on merit, not political favoritism, was demanded. In 1883, the **Pendleton Act** created a permanent U.S. **civil service** based on merit. Government employees were protected from firing because of political party affiliation.

The merit system of the civil service was radically different from the old spoils system. Jobs were classified by the nature of the skills involved, and hiring was done on the basis of competitive examination rather than political connections. Those with the highest scores and the greatest skills got the jobs. Job tenure insulated bureaucrats from blatant political threats. Civil service created greater stability in government employment and fostered a body of expertise and experience.

One hundred years later, the civil service remains an established part of American national government, but it is not without its critics. Some even wonder if the United States should not go back to something like the old spoils system.[5] Why? Critics complain that executive-branch employees today are too entrenched, too difficult to move, and unresponsive to the president and Congress.

TABLE 15–1

CIVILIAN EMPLOYEES, FEDERAL EXECUTIVE BRANCH, 1818–1990

Year	Number of Employees	Year	Number of Employees	Year	Number of Employees
1818	4,837	1949	2,102,109	1970	2,981,574
1821	6,914	1950	1,960,708	1971	2,860,000
1831	11,491	1951	2,482,666	1972	2,815,000
1841	18,038	1952	2,600,612	1973	2,788,000
1851	26,274	1953	2,558,416	1974	2,866,000
1861	36,672	1954	2,407,676	1975	2,857,000
1871	51,020	1955	2,397,309	1976	2,842,000
1881	100,020	1956	2,398,736	1977	2,848,000
1891	157,442	1957	2,417,565	1978	2,885,000
1901	239,476	1958	2,382,491	1979	2,869,000
1911	395,905	1959	2,382,804	1980	2,847,000
1921	561,142	1960	2,398,704	1981	2,800,000
1931	609,746	1961	2,435,804	1982	2,760,000
1941	1,437,682	1962	2,514,197	1983	2,722,000
1942	2,296,384	1963	2,527,960	1984	2,758,000
1943	3,299,414	1964	2,500,503	1985	2,775,000
1944	3,332,356	1965	2,527,915	1986	2,785,000
1945	3,816,310	1966	2,759,019	1987	2,878,000
1946	2,696,529	1967	3,002,461	1988	2,899,211
1947	2,111,011	1968	3,055,212	1989	2,904,852
1948	2,071,009	1969	3,076,414	1990	2,955,328

SOURCES: *Historical Statistics, Colonial Times to 1970* (Washington, D.C.: Census Bureau, 1976); *Statistical Abstract of the United States* (Washington, D.C.: Census Bureau, 1981); Budget of the United States, FY 86, FY 87, FY 88, FY 89, FY 90.

Today, the president of the United States has *fewer* appointments at his disposal when he enters office than Andrew Jackson did in 1829. Of the 2.9 million civilian federal employees, more than 99 percent are covered by some kind of merit system. It is extremely difficult to fire a civil servant, and only a few hundred employees a year are dismissed for incompetence. Despite some complaints, a wholesale return to the spoils system would be impossible. The Supreme Court sounded the final death knell of the patronage system in 1990 by barring most hirings and promotions based on party affiliation. Political leaders must seek other ways to harness the bureaucracy.

The federal bureaucracy continued to grow after the Pendleton Act was passed. Until the 1880s, federal agencies had been primarily service organizations. Most employees worked for the military or delivered the mail. The creation of the Interstate Commerce Commission (ICC) in 1887 marked an important change in the role and power of the bureaucracy, beginning federal regulation of economic activity. Although the major expansion of regulation would not occur until the 1930s, the formation of the ICC foreshadowed a new role for the bureaucracy.

The most dramatic growth in the federal executive branch occurred during the administration of Franklin D. Roosevelt. Federal employees increased from around 600,000 when he took office to 3.8 million at the end of World War II. Perhaps even more important than the rapid growth, the 1930s marked the beginning of a shift in lawmaking power from Congress to the bureaucracy. As the government became more involved with regulating the economy, health, safety, welfare, energy, and communications, Congress found it increasingly difficult to develop specific policies in complex new areas. As a result, Congress delegated direct lawmaking authority to the executive branch. When Congress delegates authority, it does not necessarily abrogate its constitutional responsibilities. Rather, legislators attempt to rely on more specialized experts to develop the fine details—the rules and regulations—of how laws will be applied. Agencies administering congressional legislation must act in accordance with *legislative intent*—the goals and objectives of Congress. **Delegation of authority** has been controversial since the 1930s, and antibureaucratic forces in the 1980s continued to debate the question.[6] For many years, the Supreme Court ruled that delegation of authority to agencies by Congress was unconstitutional. Threatened by an angry Franklin Roosevelt, who suggested expanding the Court, the justices finally upheld delegation of authority to the bureaucracy.

RECENT CHANGES IN CIVIL SERVICE

Efforts to reform the bureaucracy continue. President Richard Nixon, convinced that the bureaucracy was filled with liberal Democrats who were unresponsive to his leadership, tried to restructure the departments into four "superdepartments." Congress did not go along with his proposal.[7] Recent presidents applied new budget systems to improve bureaucratic management and efficiency. Johnson implemented planning programming budgeting, Nixon tried management by objective, and Carter mandated zero-base budgeting for the federal bureaucracy. The Carter administration made other important changes in restructuring the civil service: Congress created the **Office of Personnel Management (OPM)** to oversee the civil service system (formerly run by the Civil Service Commission) and developed a **Senior Executive Service (SES).**

The Senior Executive Service was designed as a cadre of high-level civil servants—more generpalists than specialists—who could be transferred from agency to agency. The system was modeled in part on the British civil service, which has traditionally emphasized general training and mobility over technical expertise. The SES consists of eight thousand federal managers throughout the bureaucracy. In theory, they are more responsive and responsible because the president and cabinet secretaries have more discretion in rewarding, transferring, or removing them. These ambitious reforms have only been modestly successful. Many eligible executives did not join the SES, and only a small increase in mobility has occurred among the group. Very few have been fired. The president is still limited in his ability to make appointments and force transfers. Presidents continue to rely on the appointment of *political executives* to enforce administration priorities on the vast federal bureaucracy.

The Federal Bureaucracy

HOW BIG IS THE BUREAUCRACY?

Critics disparage bureaucrats as "pointy-headed," "briefcase-toting," and "faceless." Bureaucracies are described as "huge," "bloated," and "fat." How big is the bureaucracy? Table 15–1 documents the growth in federal employees over the years and the relative stability in numbers over the past twenty years. However, as a percentage of total U.S. population, the size of the bureaucracy has actually declined in recent decades, partly as a result of a sharp increase in government contracting for services with private firms. Planning, management, evaluation, research, development, design, and construction are increasingly contracted out. Work is paid for with federal dollars, but the employees are not counted as part of the bureaucracy.

Bureaucratic "bigness" can also be measured by what employees actually do. In the 1960s and 1970s, expenditures and the number of rules and regulations increased much faster than the number of employees. The same number of employees were doing more. This trend was reversed during the Reagan administration. Between 1981 and 1987, the annual number of final and proposed federal regulations declined from 10,300 to 8,000.[8] Budget cuts, particularly for domestic agencies, additional review of all new rules and regulations by the OMB, and political appointees oriented to reducing the scope of regulatory activity all limited the growth of bureaucratic activity. In terms of its size, U.S. public sector employment is comparable to other countries. It was estimated that in the 1980s, the United States had 8.1 public employees for every 100 citizens, about average for industrial democracies.[9] Japan is lower, with 4.5 per 100 citizens; Great Britain is higher, with 10.9 per 100; France and Germany have 7.5 and 8.3 public employees per 100 citizens, respectively.

Bureaucracies can change in shape as well as size. The federal bureaucracy has begun to swell at the top and shrink at the bottom. Even though the total number of employees has remained stable, more layers of middle and upper management have been added. In 1930, the Department of Labor was headed by the secretary of labor and two assistant secretaries. Today, the department has three deputy undersecretaries and six assistant secretaries. Similar trends can be found in other departments.

COMPONENTS OF THE BUREAUCRACY

The bureaucracy consists of departments, agencies, bureaus, and governmental corporations.

DEPARTMENTS. The heads of the fourteen federal departments form the president's cabinet (see Chapter 13). Figure 15–1 shows the classic, schematic view of the executive branch: the president sitting atop scores of departments, agencies, boards, and bureaus. In reality, the White House struggles to control and manage the bureaucracy. Cabinet secretaries also face formidable challenges in taking over the reins of a huge department. Table 15–2 compares departments by age, personnel, and budget. In addition to the differences, each department has its own particular character and political clout.

AGENCIES. One way that departments differ is in their agencies and subunits, which have different loyalties, tasks, and motivations. A department secretary's task is often a microcosm of the president's—controlling and coordinating the activities, policies, and priorities of a complex organization. Two kinds of agencies are found in the bureaucracy: independent agencies and departmental agencies. Departmental agencies are part of a larger cabinet department. Figure 15–2 shows the agencies and offices of the Department of Health and Human Services. Under that department's huge umbrella are a variety of units that administer many of the major social welfare programs of the federal government.

Independent agencies are semiautonomous and not part of any department. Two important independent agencies are the National Aeronautics and Space Administration and the Environmental Protection Agency (EPA). Their independence is a result of the historical circumstances of their formation. Although important, they lack the clout of a separate department. One reason for creating an independent agency is the desire to keep new mission-oriented agencies from the bureaucratic inertia of older, established departments. For

FIGURE 15–1

THE GOVERNMENT OF THE UNITED STATES

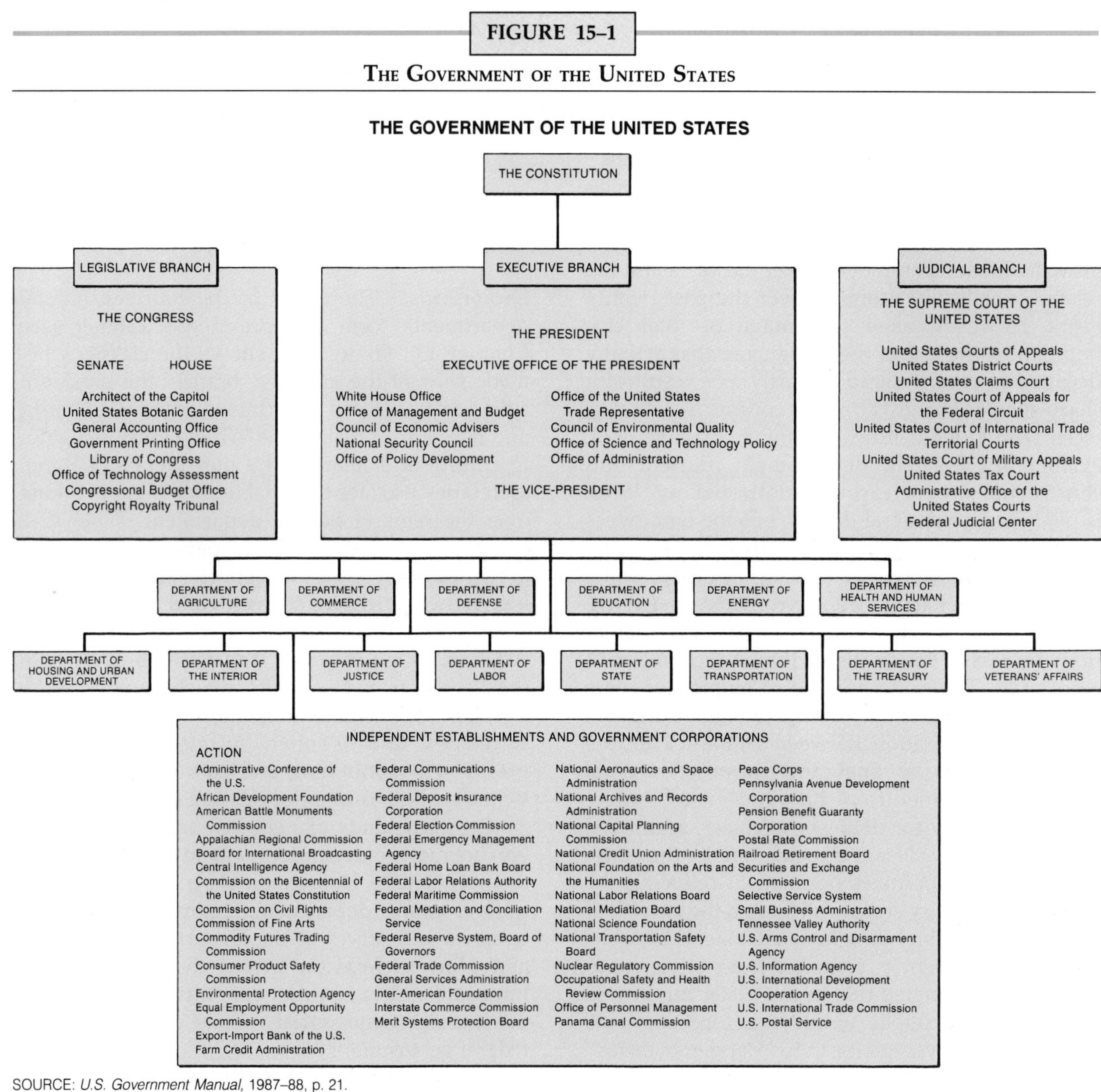

SOURCE: *U.S. Government Manual*, 1987–88, p. 21.

example, in 1964, the Office of Economic Opportunity (OEO) was created to implement Lyndon Johnson's Great Society programs. To maximize White House control, planners located the OEO in the Executive Office of the President. NASA and the EPA too were goal-oriented agencies set up to move rapidly toward achieving their objectives unimpeded by the rest of the bureaucracy. Both agencies developed quickly.

Sometimes being an independent agency is not enough to satisfy the demands of clientele groups. During the 100th Congress, veterans groups pursued an extensive lobbying campaign to elevate the Veterans Administration (VA) into a cabinet-level

TABLE 15–2

COMPARING THE FEDERAL DEPARTMENTS

Department	Seniority (Year Created)	Personnel (No. of Employees, 1990)	Budget (1990 Outlays, $ Billions)
State	1789	25,800	3.9
Treasury	1789	155,500	235.7
Defense (War)	1789	1,017,300	293.8
Justice	1789	80,000	6.8
Interior	1849	68,500	3.1
Agriculture	1889	104,200	42.4
Commerce	1913	86,500	3.5
Labor	1913	18,500	23.0
Health and Human Services (Health, Education, and Welfare)	1953	114,000	424.4
Housing and Urban Development	1965	13,000	22.6
Transportation	1966	64,300	27.3
Energy	1977	15,700	11.0
Education	1979	28,100	24.5
Veterans Affairs	1988	206,000	29.8

SOURCE: *Budget of the United States*, FY 90.

department. While neither veterans programs nor the number of veterans had greatly changed in the late 1980s, the campaign paid off. The House passed the bill in late 1987 by a wide margin, and the Senate passed it in 1988. President Reagan signed the bill into law and the Department of Veterans Affairs became the fourteenth cabinet department. Proponents successfully argued that the VA deserved department status because of its clientele (27 million veterans and their dependents) and size (ranking below only the Defense Department and the Postal Service).

Two years later, a similar move was made to elevate the EPA to departmental status. Advocates argued that the creation of a Department of Environmental Protection would give the new secretary greater authority to develop environmental policies at home and abroad and elevate the importance of environmental issues within the president's cabinet. The House passed a bill creating the new department in March 1990 by a substantial margin. The Bush administration originally favored the creation of the new department but opposed the House bill. The point of contention concerned the creation of a new Bureau of Environmental Statistics that would be an independent arm of the department charged with gathering data on environmental quality. Democratic sponsors wanted this bureau to be free of OMB manipulation of data to conform to administration policy. White House officials argued that the bill undermined the president's authority and restricted oversight of the new bureau.

The federal bureaucracy also includes **regulatory agencies,** which administer federal law and police certain practices, professions, and policy areas. They may be independent or part of a department. Independent regulatory agencies, such as the Securities and Exchange Commission, the Federal Trade Commission, and the Federal Communications Commission, are usually governed by boards whose members are appointed by the president for fixed terms. Both independent and department regulatory agencies, such as the Occupational Safety and Health Administration (OSHA), are often involved in political controversies. They make sensitive political decisions and are heavily lobbied from all sides. OSHA was one of the most controversial regulators of the 1970s and 1980s.

GOVERNMENT CORPORATIONS. The U.S. government is engaged in a variety of activities run by public

FIGURE 15–2

THE DEPARTMENT OF HEALTH AND HUMAN SERVICES

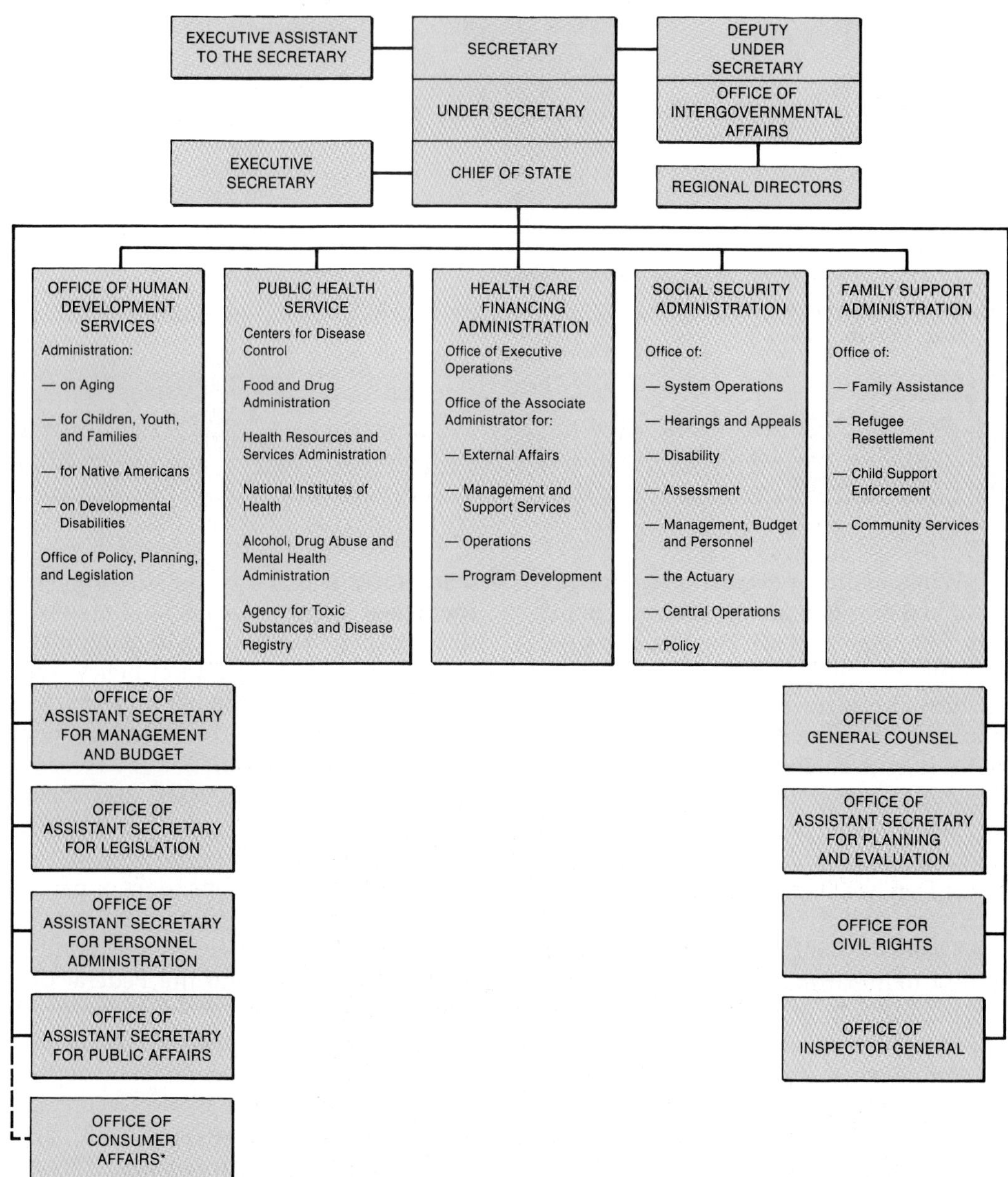

*Located administratively in the HHS but reports to the president.

SOURCE: *U.S. Government Manual*, 1987–88, p. 291.

corporations. One of the best-known **government corporations** is the Tennessee Valley Authority (TVA). Originally established in the 1930s as the first of what was to be a vast network of federally owned power companies, the TVA is a classic example of government ownership and management. Other important government corporations include the Commodity Credit Corporation, which purchases surplus commodities to maintain government crop subsidy programs; Amtrak, the U.S. passenger rail system; Comsat, which owns communications satellites; and the Post Office, now a government corporation called the U.S. Postal Service.

If the organization of the federal bureaucracy seems a little arbitrary, it is. Is there a compelling logic to fourteen departments instead of six or twenty? The Post Office used to be a cabinet department—now it is a government corporation. OSHA is part of the Labor Department because its proponents in Congress, in organized labor, and in the department itself decided that is where it would best suit their needs. The shape of the bureaucracy reflects the growth in the policy agenda of government and the power of interest groups. The Departments of Education and Veterans Affairs won cabinet rank because of the influence of their clients in national politics. Once in existence, agencies fiercely resist being put out of business. President Reagan pledged to eliminate both the Education Department and the Energy Department during the 1980 campaign, but he learned how quickly departments can become entrenched. He left office with fourteen departments rather than the eleven he promised in 1980.

Bureaucratic Fragmentation: The War on Drugs

Many complaints about the bureaucracy concern its overlap, duplication, and fragmentation of authority. Built piece by piece as public needs and demands change, there is little rationality to its shape. Bureaucracy often expands when policymakers are particularly anxious to solve problems, but solutions are complex and difficult. In a time of fiscal scarcity, existing agencies are often anxious to make sure that they get some of the action. This can lead to inefficient expenditure of resources and severe problems of coordination. The Bush

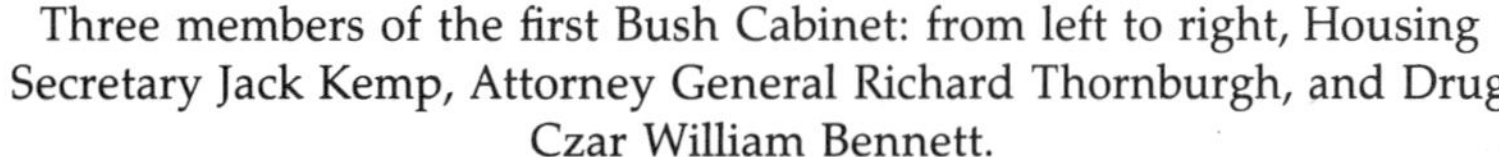
Three members of the first Bush Cabinet: from left to right, Housing Secretary Jack Kemp, Attorney General Richard Thornburgh, and Drug Czar William Bennett.

Bureaucracy is a necessary if complicating factor in the War on Drugs because of all the federal, state, and local agencies involved.

administration's war on drugs is a good example of these phenomena.

Bush announced his antidrug program in September 1989 to a public increasingly concerned with the scourge of drugs in society. With the growing national frenzy over drugs, Congress and the president significantly boosted federal funds for the effort, despite continuing deficit problems. Congress approved spending of nearly $9 billion in 1990, a billion more than the president requested and an 800 percent increase since 1981. This is a different governing problem. Even when the two branches agree, successful policy-making takes more than money; it takes knowledge of a problem and effective strategies to deal with it. Because policy-makers are not sure how best to solve the drug problem, the tendency has been towards a shotgun approach. Four main elements are involved in the war on drugs. Prevention of greater drug use focuses on education and awareness to reduce the demand for narcotics. The strategy of interdiction attempts to block the importation of drugs and to confiscate drugs already in the country. Investigation and prosecution involves identifying, finding, arresting, and convicting drug dealers and users. Finally, treatment programs attempt to provide counseling and rehabilitation for drug addicts.

Each of these strategies involves different departments, bureaus, and agencies in the federal bureaucracy as well as thousands of state and local officials. Table 15–3 lists some of the dozens of federal departments, agencies, and programs enlisted into the war on drugs. As the amount of money, the different approaches to the problem, and the number of agencies increased, problems of coordination became overwhelming. This ultimately led to the creation of another part of the bureaucracy—a national "drug czar" heading up the newly created Office of National Drug Control Policy. President Bush named former Secretary of Education William Bennett to head the office and attempt to coordinate the war on drugs.

PEOPLE IN BUREAUCRACY

Behind the caricatures of bureaucrats are men and women. Where do they come from? How do they get their jobs? Where do they work? What do they do? About 14 million people are public employees in the United States, most of them state and local employees. Half of all state and local employees are teachers and school administrators. Police and firefighters are also primarily hired at the state and local level. In contrast, more than half of all federal employees work for the Defense Department or the Postal Service.

Federal departments and agencies are headed by **political executives** appointed by the president. The best political jobs in Washington are listed in a congressional publication called the "plum book." The favored individuals obtain positions as assistant secretaries and undersecretaries in the agencies and are often put into positions of authority over high-ranking career civil servants. This naturally creates tension between career civil servants and what one observer has called "a government of strangers"—political executives who do not know the agency or its practices.[10] Compared with the "lifers," political appointees are transients who come and go like the seasons.

TABLE 15–3

DEPARTMENTS, AGENCIES, AND PROGRAMS INVOLVED IN THE WAR ON DRUGS

Justice Department
- Drug Enforcement Administration
- Federal Bureau of Investigation
- Federal prison system
- Criminal and tax divisions
- U.S. Attorneys and marshalls
- Immigration and Naturalization Service
- Interpol
- Federal court system

Department of Housing and Urban Development

Department of the Interior
- Bureau of Land Management
- U.S. Park Service
- Bureau of Indian Affairs
- Fish and Wildlife Service

Department of Defense
- Interdiction and demand reduction

Health and Human Services
- Alcohol, Drug Abuse, and Mental Health
- Family Support Administration
- Human Development Services

Department of Education

Department of Labor

State Department
- Agency for International Development
- U.S. Information Agency

Department of Transportation
- Federal Aviation Administration
- Coast Guard

Department of the Treasury
- Internal Revenue Service
- U.S. Customs Service
- Bureau of Alcohol, Tobacco, and Firearms

Department of Veterans Affairs

Executive Office of the President
- Office of National Drug Control Policy

Civil service applicants, in contrast, often begin by taking a competitive exam. (Professionals such as lawyers, economists, and engineers are given scores based on their application but need not take an exam.) Candidates are hired through the Office of Personnel Management (OPM), which sends to the agency the names of three people they may hire. If hired, a person is then assigned a GS (general schedule) rating that ranges from GS1 to GS18. Corresponding salaries are from $11,000 to more than $80,000. "Middle grade" refers to employees in the GS13–15 range. "Supergrades" are usually GS16–18. Employees not covered by the OPM follow a similar procedure of job classification under their own personnel system. Contrary to popular belief, only 13 percent of federal employees actually work in the District of Columbia. The rest are scattered across the nation, close to the people they serve.

Once hired, and having successfully completed a probationary period, civil servants are secure in their jobs. Procedures established by the OPM and work rules negotiated by public-employee unions protect workers from arbitrary dismissal. The government finds it very difficult to fire someone for incompetence, and it can take as long as three years to exhaust all avenues of review and appeal. Should public employees have the right to strike? Federal air traffic controllers thought they did in 1981, but President Reagan took a hard line against the strike and dismissed all the Professional Air Traffic Controllers Organization members two days later. His action had a chilling effect on other unions and was generally seen as a major setback for the labor movement within the public sector.

This brief sketch provides an overview of the bureaucratic establishment of the United States, a vast network of departments, agencies, corporations, boards, and commissions, hiring millions of people scattered across the nation. The key questions about the bureaucracy involve politics and governing. What role does the bureaucrat play in making public policy?

Bureaucratic Policy-Making

Implementation

Implementation is the process of clarifying legislative intent and carrying out the goals and objectives of policies. Some policies tend to be self-executing—as soon as the president, Congress, or the courts speak, the action occurs. For example, in 1957, President Eisenhower ordered troops into Little Rock, Arkansas, to assure the integration of Little Rock's public schools. In 1951, President Truman ordered federal officers to seize and operate the steel mills, which were threatened by a strike. Both actions were taken immediately with no question or delay. Most policies, however, are not self-executing; they must be implemented by the bureaucracy. According to political scientist Robert Lineberry, three components of implementation can be described: (1) assigning responsibility to an existing agency or creating a new one; (2) translating legislation into operational rules, guidelines, and regulations; and (3) making decisions about the allocation of time and money to achieve the objective.[11]

For a long time, implementation was largely ignored. It is now clear that one of the most important aspects of a policy is how it affects people and whether it works. In the 1964 Civil Rights Act, implementation of the provisions prohibiting discrimination in restaurants, hotels, and other public accommodations was accomplished successfully. Discrimination was visible, and compliance was in the economic interest of southern business people.[12] In contrast, civil rights laws dealing with housing discrimination resulted in little progress. How does the bureaucracy foster compliance? Money and grants can be withheld from those who do not comply. Litigation through the courts is another device that is used by the bureaucracy.

Public policy is most effective when implementation is taken into account during the formulation stage. But too often controversies that cannot be solved because of deadlock or governing problems in the legislative process are simply dumped onto the bureaucracy. Two problems result. Effective administration is hampered because the bureaucracy is given little guidance. Second, the power and discretion of bureaucrats inadvertently increase.

Routine Administration and Discretionary Power

Once major issues are resolved in the implementation of policy, a more routine process of administration begins. For example, officials responsible for Social Security have elaborate routines for processing claims, hearing appeals, and paying benefits. But the existence of routine administration does not mean the absence of bureaucratic power. Instead of shaping rules, regulations, and policies, bureaucratic power may be exercised through administrative discretion.

No set of laws, regulations, rules, or procedures can anticipate every case or exception. In this lies the considerable discretionary power that bureaucrats often have over their clients. Public employees who have direct and frequent contact with the citizenry are what scholar Michael Lipsky calls "street-level bureaucrats."[13] They are the cops on the beat, the social worker in the welfare office, the admitting nurse in the public hospital, the Internal Revenue Service agent auditing taxes, the parole officer, or the EPA official measuring the level of dioxin in someone's backyard. Most Americans have contact with their government at the street level, not in the White House or State House or on Capitol Hill.

THE COSTS AND BENEFITS OF REGULATION

When Congress delegates authority to the bureaucracy, implementation often includes the promulgation of rules and regulations. The regulatory process is the development of rules to carry out the intent of Congress. In the executive branch, the process is called rule-making rather than lawmaking, but regulations carry the full force of law.

As noted earlier, regulation began with the Interstate Commerce Commission (ICC) in 1887. Regulation increased greatly in the 1930s as the activities of broadcasters, stock traders, food and drug producers, and many other groups were brought under government scrutiny. Another major expansion of regulation occurred in the 1960s, when government intervened to protect the environment, occupational health and safety, and consumers. Increased regulation stems from more aggressive implementation by the bureaucracy as well as from additional legislation from Congress. But regulation imposes certain costs, and those paying the costs began to complain. Businesses argued that regulation was too costly, tended to increase inflation, and represented unwarranted government interference. Deregulation and general antipathy to "big government" became a key element of Reagan's successful bid for the White House in 1980.

How pervasive is government regulation? Regulation critic Murray Weidenbaum describes how government regulations affect a "typical" couple as they go through their day.[14] John and Mary are awakened by an alarm clock powered by electricity regulated by the Federal Energy Regulatory Commission. The toothpaste and mouthwash they use were approved by the Food and Drug Administration. Their breakfast cereal is approved by the Department of Agriculture and labeled according to the regulations of the Federal Trade Commission. As they pull out of their driveway, the automatic seat-belt in their car mandated by the National Highway Traffic Safety Administration is fastened. A light on the dash indicates that the catalytic converter required by the Environmental Protection Agency needs repair. While at the service station, they fill up with EPA-required unleaded gasoline.

Mary's job was secured thanks to protection by the Equal Employment Opportunity Commission. During the day, she furnishes information on her firm's finances for the Securities and Exchange Commission and fills out statistical forms for the Census Bureau. Her retirement plan at the company is overseen by the Department of Labor. At lunch, she checks on a home loan application at a bank regulated by the Federal Home Loan Bank Board. The loan itself it provided at more favorable interest rates by the Federal Housing Administration.

John works in a factory and belongs to a union. The right to bargain collectively is protected by the National Labor Relations Board. Safety in the factory is the concern of the Occupational Safety and Health Administration, whose regulations have had a profound impact on the layout of the plant, rest rooms, exits, sound levels, goggles, headwear, and the like. The material the factory produces will be shipped according to regulations of the ICC for truck and rail transport, the Civil Aeronautics Board for air transport, and the Federal Maritime Commission for shipping by sea.

At home that night, the television programs the family watches are guided by the Federal Communications Commission. John reads the health warning on his package of cigarettes from the surgeon general of the United States. The mattress they sleep on is filled with government-approved materials.

Are the lives of Americans too regulated? Weidenbaum thinks that regulation costs too much for the benefits it delivers. He argues, for example, that auto safety requirements have done little more than make cars more expensive. But Joan Claybrook, former head of the National Highway Safety Administration, estimates that the delay in requiring passive restraints in passenger cars between 1985 and 1990 alone cost 40,000 lives. Political Insight 15–1 shows the ups and downs and politics of the seat belt and air bag controversy.

Are the improvements in health and safety resulting from regulation worth the cost? Like other elements of American politics, what benefits one group may impose costs on another. People's perspective on the EEOC or OSHA may depend on whether they are employers or employees. Steven Kelman, who has studied the impact of regulation, concludes that regulation simply reflects the legitimate interests of the public over dominant business interests:

> A series of laws in areas like environmental protection, occupational safety and health, consumer product safety, and equal opportunity has restricted the prerogatives of business firms to pursue production, hiring, and marketing practices. . . . Business and conservatives have now launched a counterattack against these changes. New regulatory programs neither threaten freedom nor contribute significantly to inflation. . . . The harms that social regulations of the last decade were intended to curb were not insignificant. Frequently, the harm was borne disproportionately by the more disadvantaged members of society, while the more advantaged produced the harm. The social regulation of the past decade grew largely, then, out of a sense of fairness.[15]

Kelman concludes that regulation has had impressive results. Racial and sexual discrimination have been reduced. Consumers have more and better information about products and their safety. Workers are now exposed to fewer toxic chemicals such as asbestos and lead, and occupational deaths have been reduced. Both air and water are cleaner today than ten years ago. Childproof container caps have dramatically cut child-poisoning deaths. Government-mandated mileage requirements have resulted in startling improvements in the efficiency of domestic autos, even though the manufacturers said originally that it could not be done. The result has been a significant reduction in energy consumption and oil imports.

THE COSTS AND BENEFITS OF DEREGULATION

Although President Bush remained an advocate of continued deregulation, the fervor for reducing or eliminating federal regulations cooled noticeably by the early 1990s. Critics pointed to increasingly high costs and severe consequences of deregulation. Airline deregulation had mixed consequences around the country. While larger cities often benefited in terms of more flights at lower costs, smaller cities were burdened with fewer flights at higher costs. Cities with "hub" airports dominated by a single airline faced higher average fares. Lack of regulation of the securities markets was partially blamed for the stock market crash in 1987. But the most costly result of deregulation was the financial collapse of substantial numbers of the nation's savings and loan institutions.

Deregulation of the thrift industry had allowed managers of savings and loans to make a number of risky investments. When the price of oil dropped in the early 1980s, a number of thrifts in oil states such as Texas and Oklahoma went bankrupt. But the severity of the savings and loan crisis did not become apparent until the Bush administration took office. By then, thousands of thrifts were insolvent, and the president was forced to propose a massive bailout plan that was adopted in the summer of 1989. Only six months later, because of higher interest rates, the slow pace of thrift closures, and more savings and loan failures, the cost to the taxpayers grew to mammoth proportions. By 1990, estimates for the total cost of the bailout had ballooned to $300 billion, with some suggesting the total would be more than half a trillion dollars.[16] These costs would have to be paid by taxpayers, worsening the real budget deficit, even though much of the bailout costs were kept "off budget."

Regulation, one of the most important aspects of bureaucratic policy-making, involves questions of political economy. The antagonists in the battle over regulation have both material economic interests and certain political values to protect (such as the free market). Increasingly, policymakers are using cost-benefit analysis to judge the merits of regulation. Although such analysis can help make more sound decisions, it cannot eliminate the competing political values and economic interests underlying the debate. After a decade, the proponents of deregulation found themselves facing growing support to strengthen government regulations in a number of sensitive areas.

Political Insight 15-1

The Politics of Regulation: The Saga of Seat Belts and Air Bags

1967. Manual seat belts (active restraint) are required on all new passenger cars beginning with the 1968 models.

1969. Government proposes air bags (passive restraint) in new cars and asks for comments.

1970. Government issues a rule requiring passive restraint system in passenger cars beginning with 1974 models.

General Motors says it plans to provide air bags, first as options and then as standard equipment, on all its cars by 1975. Eventually, about 10,000 cars are so equipped.

1971. Nixon administration grants a two-year delay in passive restraint requirement, fearful of its economic effect on auto industry.

Government proposes an interlock system that prevents a car from starting without the manual belt fastened as alternative to air bags.

1972. Federal rule requires an interlock system in cars.

1974. Amid loud protests from motorists and the auto industry, Congress prohibits interlock system, and the rule is rescinded.

Government proposes a revised passive restraint system.

GM puts air bags in about 10,000 luxury cars in 1974-76.

1976. Ford administration defers the passive restraint system one year.

Volkswagen offers passive belts in some models and has continued to do so.

Transportation Department scraps the restraint requirement and orders a "demonstration program" beginning with 1980 model cars, calling for 500,000 cars to be equipped with air bags. Ford, GM, Mercedes-Benz, and Volkswagen agree to take part.

1977. Carter administration abandons the demonstration program and reopens rule-making. Final rule is approved calling for passive restraints to be phased in over three years, beginning with 1982.

GM offers passive automatic belts in 1978 through 1980 model Chevettes but then abandons idea.

1981. Reagan administration rescinds passive restraint rule, arguing that passive belts would be disconnected and that the auto industry has decided against air bags.

Insurance companies file suit asking that the requirement be reinstated.

1982. Rescinding of the rule is overruled by a federal court of appeals.

1983. Supreme Court upholds the lower court ruling and orders the Transportation Department to reexamine issue.

Transportation Secretary Elizabeth Dole issues new proposal and says she wants to examine the issue from the beginning. She sets an April 1984 deadline for a decision.

1984. Mercedes-Benz begins in May to offer a driver-side air bag on a limited number of vehicles. The cost is $880.

1985. Secretary Dole announces rule that gives states the choice of mandatory seat-belt laws or regulations requiring air bags by 1989.

1986. According to Gallup rolls, seat-belt usage doubled between 1984 and 1986, with 52 percent saying they used seat belts, compared with only 25 percent in 1984.

1989. Although thirty-three states and the District of Columbia passed mandatory seatbelt laws, that is not enough. Automatic passive restraints—air bags or seat belts—are required on all 1990 cars.

1990. Lee Iacocca, once an ardent opponent, praises air bags. First head-on collision between two cars with air bags occurs—both drivers live.

SOURCES: From *St. Louis Post-Dispatch,* 11 July 1984 (supplied by United Press International) Gallup Report, April 1986, p. 29, *Washington Post National Weekly Edition,* 5-11 March 1990, p. 12.

Health and Human Services Secretary Louis Sullivan. Regulations protecting health and safety but resulting in significantly greater costs are a controversial aspect of bureaucratic policy-making.

Bureaucratic Power and Politics

Agencies and bureaus are political actors, some relatively powerful, others weak. Conflicts and competition among bureaucracies are often based on their position, interests, and relative power, giving rise to bureaucratic politics, which in turn helps shape foreign and domestic policies. At the same time, regular and observable patterns of action by bureaucrats have led scholars to specify certain laws of bureaucratic behavior. Such behavior also has important consequences for public policy. Bureaucratic power arises from two main sources: expertise and support from clientele groups.[17]

EXPERTISE

German sociologist Max Weber is the originator of modern theories about bureaucracy. Emphasizing the efficiency of hierarchical bureaucratic organizations, Weber noted that bureaucratic power was rooted in technical skills that distinguished bureaucrats from average politicians.[18] Bureaucratic expansion is partly an outgrowth of the technological revolution that occurred in the nineteenth century. As scientific and technological developments have continued to change the nature of social life, the need for experts has increased. Most of the government's experts are part of the bureaucracy.

Guy Benveniste describes the situation: "This is the age of experts: the briefings, the flip chart, facts and figures from computer output, forecasts and trend analysis. . . . The environment is being changed not so much by factors outside the control of man—weather, earthquakes, or new diseases—as by man-made inventions."[19] Technical problems need a bureaucrat with highly tuned technical skills to solve them—this is the **technocrat.** Bureaucracies are populated with technocrats and experts. What is the result?

Knowledge becomes power. If only one person in a group understands something, that person has power over the rest. As a result, some technocrats try to foster their power by making their knowledge inaccessible. They want to make politicians dependent on them rather than the reverse. For their part, politicians are leery of relying on experts and jealously guard their right to final decision-making authority. Technical experts often have a very narrow focus and are not used to balancing a multitude of values. Politicians need the advice of experts but try to avoid being captured by them.

CLIENTELE GROUPS

Despite their emphasis on expertise, agencies behave strategically in the political arena. Interested in self-preservation and growth, they devise appropriate strategies, strive for control, and attempt to create and cultivate political support. Like Congress or the presidency, bureaucrats engage in actions that will build public support and clients. In addition to legal authority and expertise, bureaucrats have political allies.

When programs for agriculture were threatened with cuts, farmers showed up in Washington driving their tractors around the White House and the Capitol. Teachers lobbied to preserve the threatened Department of Education. Agencies rely on groups like these as a source of support and power. Agencies not only need a clientele but also have to be able to mobilize them at crucial times. **Clientele groups** can help through letter-writing, strikes, testimony at congressional hearings, and demonstrations. Such departments as Agriculture and Education have an easier time mobilizing their clientele than other agencies, such as the Bureau of Prisons. Foreign aid programs and such agencies as the U.S. Weather Service have a more difficult time identifying and mobilizing client groups.

Agencies with significant clientele groups often find their interests are closer to Congress than to the White House. The result is a set of dominant alliances in American politics that link agencies, congressional subcommittees, and interest groups—subgovernments.

SUBGOVERNMENTS

Bureaucratic power in the United States is related to the dominance of interest groups in certain arenas and the fragmentation in Congress. The resulting coalitions, alternately called "triple alliances," "subgovernments," or "iron triangles," reflect mutual interests that cut across institutional boundaries. **Subgovernments** are specialized alliances that often are able to dominate the policy process within

TABLE 15–4

AGRICULTURE SUBGOVERNMENTS

Commodity	Congressional Subcommittee	Agency	Interest Group
Cotton	House Cotton Subcommittee	Agricultural Stabilization and Conservation Service (ASCS) cotton program	National Cotton Council
Oilseeds and rice	House Oilseeds and Rice Subcommittee	ASCS programs for peanuts, rice, tungnuts, flaxseed, soybeans, dry edible beans, and crude pinegum	Soybean Council of America
Tobacco	House Tobacco Subcommittee	ASCS tobacco program	Tobacco Institute
Dairy and poultry products	House Dairy and Poultry Subcommittee	ASCS milk program	National Milk Producers Federation; National Broiler Council
Livestock and grains	House Livestock and Grains Subcommittee	ASCS programs for wheat, corn, barley, oats, grain sorghum, rye, wool, and mohair	National Association of Wheat Growers; National Wool Growers Association

SOURCE: Randall B. Ripley and Grace A. Franklin, *Congress, the Bureaucracy, and Public Policy*, 4th ed. (Homewood, Ill.: Dorsey, 1987), 103, Table 4–3. Reprinted with permission from the Dorsey Press.

particular area of concern. Table 15–4 lists the powerful subgovernments in agriculture, and Figure 15–3 diagrams one of them—the "tobacco" subgovernment.

Agriculture has long been dominated by subgovernments.[20] Price supports are administered by the Agricultural Stabilization and Conservation Service (ASCS) of the Department of Agriculture. The tobacco subgovernment includes the ASCS, the industry interest group (the Tobacco Institute), and the House Agriculture Subcommittee on Tobacco. The three units work together to maintain maximum tobacco price levels and acreage allotments for tobacco. The system is maintained in Washington, but its influence reaches into many states and counties. The congressional subcommittee supports the programs and maintains the budget of the agency, while the agency may help committee members with constituent problems. The Tobacco Institute provides information to both the agency and the subcommittee, as well as campaign contributions through their PAC for the members of the committee. The institute is a loyal client, testifying on behalf of the agency in congressional hearings. All in all, subgovernments are often cozy, semiautonomous arrangements of mutual benefit.

Subgovernment dominance may be challenged by outside forces. Pressure from nonsmoking groups and the secretary of health and human services is a threat to the security of the tobacco subgovernment. Other commodity subgovernments, such as cotton, are more secure. Some subgovernments are in competition with each other and must share influence. For example, the "health research" and "cancer" subgovernments go after the same money and prerogatives within government. The Patent Office and the Antitrust Division of the Justice Department are also competitive subgovernments.

Subgovernments can disintegrate. Although they often quietly control a policy area to their own mutual benefit, their dominance can be challenged by other subgovernments, consumers, or other participants in the political process. The "sugar" subgovernment collapsed in 1974 after the House defeated the proposed Sugar Act. The soaring world price of sugar had created unfavorable publicity and pressure from consumer groups.

FIGURE 15–3

THE TOBACCO SUBGOVERNMENT

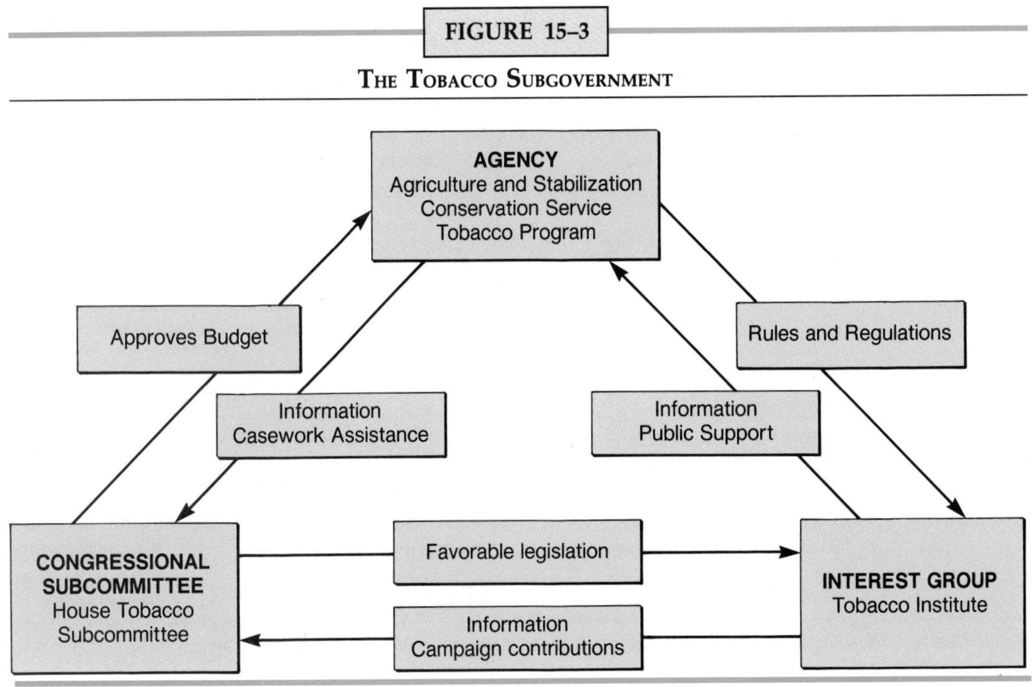

Dominance of certain spheres of public policy by these iron triangles has important consequences for governing. Interest groups, congressional subcommittees, and agencies all tend to fragment political power. Agencies are a critical element in the arrangement, arriving at mutually beneficial bargains with interest groups rather than establishing more broadly based national policies. Subgovernments tend to increase government spending and make cutbacks even more difficult. Agencies' emphasis on their own political interests renders the bureaucracy more of an obstacle to effective governance by Congress or the president than a vehicle to administer national policy uniformly. By examining the motivations of individual bureaucrats, it is possible to develop generalizations about bureaucratic behavior.

LAWS OF BUREAUCRATIC BEHAVIOR

Some of the "laws" of bureaucratic behavior are given tongue-in-cheek—such as Murphy's law, which says, "If anything can go wrong, it will." Old Murphy was a pessimist. After all, American bureaucrats landed a man on the moon in a decade, just as they said they would. Then there are Parkinson's laws: "Work expands to fill the available time" and "Expenditures increase to meet income." These sound a little more plausible.

Political economist Anthony Downs tried to summarize the behavior of agencies by looking at the collective effects of rational, self-interested behavior by individual bureaucrats and formulated some of the patterns into general laws.[21] Let us look at a few:

The law of increasing conservatism. As agencies and their employees grow older, they tend to become more cautious, more conservative, and concerned more with self-preservation than with the tasks or missions of their agency. Younger agencies, dominated by zealots and action-oriented bureaucrats, tend to be more aggressive and goal-oriented.

The law of diminishing control. The bigger an organization, the more difficult it is for the people at the top—including politicians—to control the actions of the organization.

The law of shifting power. The more conflict that exists within an organization, the greater the tendency for power to shift to those at the top of the organization.

The law of duplication. The greater the controls exercised on one organization, the more likely it is that a new organization will be generated to accomplish its goals.

The law of progress through imperialism. Bureaus like to expand and take over the turf of others, which often results in surprising innovation by doing things differently and better.

The law of information distortion. Communication within organizations occurs through both formal channels and informal means (such as lunchroom conversations). The more steps in the bureaucratic organization that information has to pass through, the more distortion occurs.

The law of free goods and nonmoney pricing. Requests for free services expand to meet the capacity of the agency to produce the good. Therefore, an agency must find some way to impose "charges" to ration its product. Some examples would be making reservations to stay at national park campgrounds, long waiting lines, slow service, difficult application procedures.

Bureaucracies are territorial, go through life cycles, and differ in aggressiveness and assertiveness. The characteristics of bureaucratic behavior, along with technical expertise and clientele groups, help explain the phenomenon of bureaucratic politics.

BUREAUCRATIC POLITICS AND GOVERNING

Early political scientists believed that politics could be separated from administration. This rather naïve view of bureaucratic power and behavior was based on a reformist desire to keep agencies out of the political fray. Public policy today is strongly influenced by bureaucratic politics, which Francis Rourke defines as "the competitive struggle among organizations and officials in the executive branch to determine what policy decisions will be made and who will carry them out."[22] Bureaucratic politics stem from competition among agencies—a desire to expand turf and protect their own self-interest. Bureaucratic politics are also related to the political support of agencies and their clientele groups and the differing policy objectives held by bureaucrats.

When Congress and the president are unable to govern, bureaucratic politics increasingly determines the content of public policy decisions. A study by Evelyn Brodkin asks, "If we can't govern, can we manage?"[23] She argues that when policy conflicts are not resolved legislatively, they reemerge in administrative form and are resolved by bureaucratic politics. Brodkin's study of welfare policy in the 1970s and 1980s shows this process in action. While Congress and the president were not able to agree on any major changes in the system, administrative decisions had substantial policy consequences that went largely unnoticed.

The bureaucracy has other implications for governing. The ability to make sound public policy on major national issues is often limited by entrenched subgovernments, bureaucratic self-interest, and the independent political power of agencies. The mandates of Congress and the president are not always faithfully carried out. Broader national interests are often caught up in bureaucratic infighting or political stalemate. Recognizing these potential barriers to governing, Congress and the presidency devote a great deal of energy to bureaucratic oversight, to reducing the bureaucracy's independent tendencies, and to making the bureaucracy more responsive to political leaders.

Keeping Bureaucracy Accountable in a Democracy

The problems of bureaucracy, which appear to be universal, are even greater in such countries as the Soviet Union, where, until recently, virtually every aspect of life and commerce was administered by a state bureaucracy. General Secretary Mikhail Gorbachev's attempts to reform the Soviet economy have run into an entrenched Soviet bureaucracy. In the more limited bureaucratic environment of the United States, political leaders strive for democratic control of bureaucracy. Officials attempt to assure that as bureaucracy grows larger, it remains accountable to the political institutions of the nation and ultimately to the people. Interest groups, even with subgovernments, are not always satisfied with the bureaucracy. Along with Congress and the presidency, they attempt to keep bureaucracy accountable.

The President and the Bureaucracy

Presidents have always had their troubles with the bureaucracy. Franklin Roosevelt had the following conversation with one of his advisers:

> When I woke up this morning, the first thing I saw was a headline in the *New York Times* to the effect that our Navy was going to spend two billion dollars on a shipbuilding program. Here I am, the Commander in Chief of the Navy, having to read about that for the first time in the press.
>
> The Treasury . . . is so large and far-flung and ingrained in its practices that I find it is almost impossible to get the actions and results I want—even with Henry [Morgenthau] there. But the Treasury is not to be compared with the State Department. You should go through the experience of trying to get any changes in the thinking, policy, and action of the career diplomats and then you'd know what a real problem was. But the Treasury and the State Department put together are nothing as compared with the Na-a-vy.[24]

Roosevelt sounded humorously despairing about his ability to lead the bureaucracy along the paths the White House wanted it to go, but presidents are not helpless in these attempts. Two means of control available to presidents are appointment and staff coordination and monitoring.

Appointment of Political Executives. Presidents attempt to make bureaucracies loyal to the White House by appointing political executives to head the departments and agencies. Although the Pendleton Act created a civil service system based on merit, the president has several thousand positions to fill in the departments and agencies. Political executives are supposed to be loyal to the president, but there are limits to presidential control. Political executives, appointed at the start of an administration, may be seen as temporary visitors by career civil servants. Career bureaucrats sometimes can obstruct the actions of political appointees and blunt their effectiveness in the agency.

The Reagan administration, perhaps more than any other recent administration, made an overt effort to influence the bureaucracy by naming appointees who shared the president's conservative

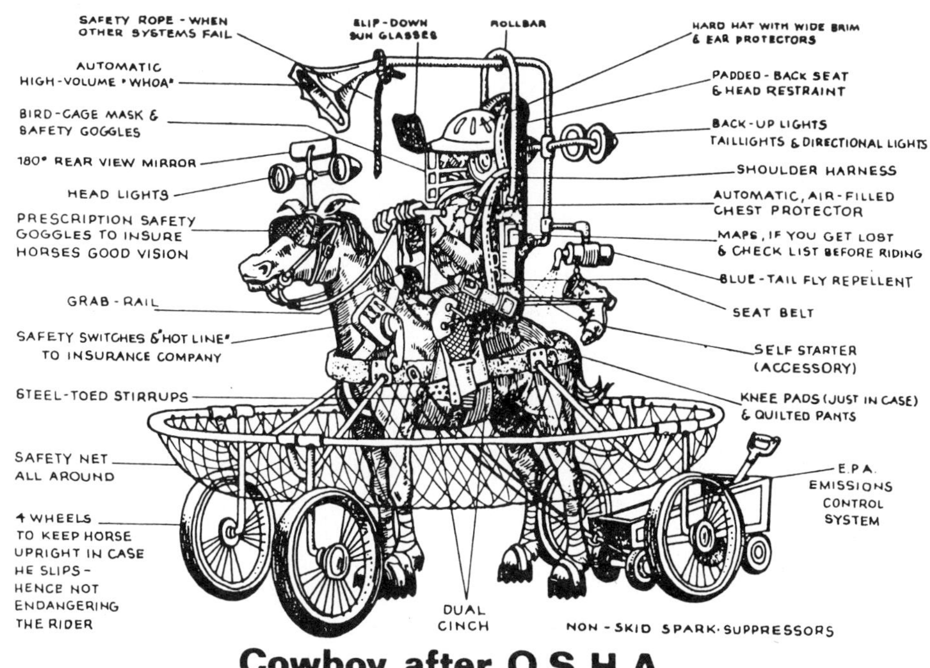

Congressional Quarterly Weekly Reports, 26 March 1988, p. 783. Copyright © 1988 by Congressional Quarterly Inc. Reprinted by permission.

philosophy and would carry the message to the front lines of the bureaucracy. As a careful, slower screening process was required, leaving a large number of the appointments unfilled during the first months of the administration, vacancies in political appointments initially enhanced the power of the top civil servants left to run the agency. But Reagan's political appointees had a considerable impact on public policy and the direction of the agency when they arrived. In civil rights policy, for example, Reagan administration appointments to the Equal Employment Opportunity Commission and the Civil Rights Division of the Justice Department slowed the pace of enforcement. A number of outstanding suits were settled, and a number of others were dropped.

The activities of the Occupational Safety and Health Administration, a regulatory villain to conservatives, were dramatically slowed by its top administrator. Refusing to use emergency provisions, he required all OSHA employees to follow the more cumbersome process of rulemaking. Once ridiculed by business groups for its excessive zeal in making safety regulations (see the accompanying cartoon of the "OSHA Cowboy"), OSHA was criticized in the 1980s forits laxity in enforcing safety regulations. A reduced budget further curbed what the agency could do. OSHA enforcement activities—fines, inspections, and violations—were substantially reduced in the 1980s. There was a change in tone as well. Political Insight 15–2 compares OSHA inspector ID cards before and after Reagan as the administration sought to make the bureaucracy less intrusive.

The policy direction of the Environmental Protection Agency was also influenced by Reagan appointees, who were given the mission to reduce EPA aggressiveness and to settle more complaints against polluters. A political scandal erupted, however, when it was discovered that top political appointees collaborated with polluters. In the face of public and congressional pressure, Reagan was forced to remove the EPA director, Anne Burford, and half a dozen other political appointees in the agency. Still, despite the independence of the bureaucracy and the potential pitfalls of overzealous appointees, presidential appointments provide considerable opportunity to shape actions of the bureaucracy.

POLITICAL INSIGHT 15-2

MAKING REGULATORS MORE POLITE?

THE ID CARD OF THE OSHA INSPECTOR USED TO READ:

Occupational Safety and Health Administration officials are authorized to carry out any special duties assigned by the secretary of labor and to enter without delay, inspect and investigate during working hours and at other reasonable times any factory, plant, establishment, construction site or other area, work place or environment where work is performed including all pertinent conditions, structures, machines, apparatus, devices, equipment and materials therein and to question privately any such employer, owner, operator, agent or employee.

The bearer of this credential is a duly authorized representative of the U.S. secretary of labor entrusted with the responsibility of carrying out in a courteous and professional manner inspections under Section 8 and certain other provisions of the Occupational Safety and Health Act of 1970.

UNDER THE REAGAN ADMINISTRATION, IT READ:

The central purposes of the visit are to assure compliance and to assist employers and employees in finding and reducing or eliminating hazards in the work place that threaten safety or health.

A related purpose of the visit is to describe the many programs available from a variety of sources to assist you in carrying out an effective safety and health program. Your comments and suggestions on how we might be more effective in assisting employers and employees are welcomed.

SOURCE: *St. Louis Post-Dispatch*, 9 April 1984.

In other ways, presidential control is limited. Certain agencies were purposely established to be independent of the White House. The president may nominate members of the board and the chair but may not remove them once in office. Most such appointments serve fixed terms of office and can be removed only by impeachment. Such agencies include the Federal Reserve Board, the Federal Maritime Commission, and the National Science Foundation.

THE OMB AND WHITE HOUSE STAFF CONTROL. Attempts by the presidency to control the bureaucracy extend beyond the appointment power. The Office of Management and Budget (OMB) and the White House staff attempt to coordinate policy-making in the bureaucracy and monitor implementation. Bureaucratic independence, self-interest, and imperialist tendencies make implementation an ongoing problem. Central clearance and the enrolled bill process are designed to promote continuity within the executive branch both on legislative requests and on the decision to sign or veto a bill (see Chapters 13 and 14).

Budget formulation gives the OMB an opportunity to monitor the activities of the agencies—hence the management part of the OMB's title. Budget examiners—OMB professionals assigned to particular departments and agencies—perform this task. An examiner's job is to know everything possible about an agency and its programs. When the agency submits its budget requests each year, the examiner formulates a series of questions and inquiries for the review process, looking carefully to see if the programs are being administered in accordance with White House policy.

One of the most important developments during the Reagan administration was assigning the Office of Management and Budget a "regulatory veto" in an attempt to reduce the regulatory activity of the bureaucracy. In 1981, President Reagan issued Executive Order No. 12291, prohibiting agencies from issuing rules until the OMB had decided the benefits exceeded the costs. The result was a number of bitter controversies. The OMB quashed rules concerning asbestos, nuclear waste, infant formula, and toxic substances. The OMB's power over federal rule-making was extended in 1985 by another executive order requiring OMB approval of any agency activity that could lead to rule-making.

In February 1990, the U.S. Supreme Court issued a ruling that limited the power of the OMB to quash agency regulations. The Court ruled that the OMB lacked statutory authority to block certain regulations issued by other agencies.[25] Interpreting the 1980 Paperwork Reduction Act for the first time, the Court ruled that the OMB had overstepped its authority and the ruling restricted its regulatory veto over other agencies. This change was not welcomed by the administration since it would limit President Bush's activities in deregulation. Congress attempted to further rein in the OMB's power in regulatory review while reauthorizing the Paperwork Reduction Act, but the administration threatened a veto.

The Senior Executive Service was in part a reform designed to give the president more flexibility and influence over the top layer of civil servants. The 1978 civil service reform also created "inspectors general" to be assigned to twelve major agencies. The goal of these "bureaucratic police" was to ferret out waste and fraud within government and to act "meaner than junkyard dogs" in their pursuit of wrongdoing. The program was not enthusiastically greeted in the bureaucracy.[26] Some departments left the positions vacant for more than a year, and most observers conclude the program has had little impact.

Congress and the Bureaucracy

Attempts to make bureaucracy accountable are not limited to the president. Congress plays an important role in the battle to maintain bureaucratic responsiveness. The relationship between Congress and the bureaucracy is ambivalent. Subgovernments linking congressional subcommittees, interest groups, and agencies protect congressional influence. Members do *not* view bureaucrats as the enemy and want to assure the continued flow of certain benefits. Some have argued that Congress purposely expanded the bureaucracy to enhance its own reelection chances.[27] In doing so, legislators become necessary intermediaries in citizens' confrontations and problems with the bureaucracy.

If the relationship between Congress and the bureaucracy is not a war, it is not all friendship either. Members of Congress constantly complain about bloated bureaucracies wasting the taxpayers' dollars. Besides rhetoric, members exert some other methods of control. While many critics complain that Congress neglects its oversight role, Mathew McCubbins and Thomas Schwartz suggest that this is not the case. They distinguish between two kinds of congressional oversight. **Police-patrol oversight** is the more traditional view of oversight, involving a systematic sampling of agency activities by Congress to detect any violations of legislative goals. Less well recognized is what they call **fire-alarm oversight,** which involves procedures that enable citizens and interest groups to "sound the alarm" if agencies are violating legislative goals. "Instead of sniffing for fires," they write, "Congress places fire alarm boxes on street corners, builds neighborhood fire houses, and sometimes dispatches its own hook-and-ladder in response to an alarm.[28]" Members of Congress actually prefer fire-alarm oversight to regular police-patrol oversight because it serves their interests at little cost. Supporters sound the alarm, and the member gains credit by eliminating the cause of the complaint. Furthermore, fire-alarm oversight is often more effective because it can reveal the most glaring violations by the bureaucracy. Congress has passed a number of laws making it easier for constituents and interest groups to press grievances against the federal government. While bureaucratic power in policy-making has increased because of delegation of authority, McCubbins and Schwartz argue that the growing emphasis on fire-alarm oversight has allowed Congress to maintain a relatively effective method of bureaucratic control.

The budget affords Congress an opportunity to perform police-patrol oversight both through the authorization process and through the appropriation processes (see Chapter 17), which entail hearings on agency programs and operations. Questions can be tough, especially if the agency officials seem to be wasting money.

Despite the 1983 *Chadha* decision, which overturned the legislative veto, Congress continues to exercise control through formal and informal arrangements with agencies (see Chapter 14). Formal statutory limits, amendments in appropriations bills, and other legal restrictions have been passed since 1983. What Congress cannot do since *Chadha* is bypass the president in creating a veto power for itself. Informal agreements with agencies have become more important.

Congress has its own watchdog agency, the General Accounting Office (GAO), to audit executive-branch agencies. Headed by the comptroller general of the United States, the GAO looks for mismanagement, abuses, illegal activities, and general misuse of funds. Audits, performed on a selective basis, have helped Congress discover many agency irregularities over the years. But despite the GAO's generally good record, it too is limited in how much of the vast executive branch it can oversee.

INTEREST GROUPS, CITIZENS, AND THE BUREAUCRACY

Congress and the president are joined by interest groups and citizens in wanting to keep the bureaucracy accountable. Subgovernment dominance can work well if the interest group has sufficient influence. But in other cases, interest groups fight the bureaucracy and use all means at their disposal to limit its actions. The growing preference of Congress for fire-alarm oversight has given both groups and citizens more formal and informal opportunities to "sound the alarm."

Although numerous economic interests have learned to prosper under regulation, many groups attempt to escape regulation, particularly rules dealing with civil rights, environmental protection, and consumer issues. In contrast, some interests fight to *keep* regulations when they are perceived to be in their interest. Many airlines and airports fought airline deregulation, and railroads and certain trucking interests have opposed deregulation in the Interstate Commerce Commission.

The **Freedom of Information Act** allows individuals and groups to penetrate the bureaucracy. Passed in 1966 and revised in 1983, the law permits access to information in government records (although access in matters dealing with national security and other sensitive areas is restricted). People can find out if agencies have a file on them and what it contains, for example. When the bill was up for extension, the Reagan administration supported Senator Orrin Hatch's (R-Utah) attempts to curtail access to information, but a coalition of media people and research scholars fought successfully to prevent new limits.[29] The Freedom of Information Act is an important tool for individuals and groups to monitor the bureaucracy and protect their own rights.

Bureaucracy: For and Against

The word "bureaucrat" often has a negative connotation. Bureaucrats are the butt of jokes and criticized and demeaned in public forums, including academic literature. Why? Is it a fair assessment or a pervasive bias?

THE CASE AGAINST BUREAUCRACY

Max Weber's pioneering work on bureaucracies did not paint a pretty picture. He called bureaucrats "specialists without spirit, sensualists without a heart."[30] A recent article by a bureaucracy observer began with a list of horror stories about the performance of bureaucracies:[31]

> A doctor in Illinois received \$2.7 million in Medicare payments over the past five years.
> The Pentagon owns a luxury hotel in Hawaii toentertain military people on twenty-seven acres worth \$351 million.
> A cancer patient who applied for Medicare was sent a letter saying she was ineligible because she had died last April.[32]
> The Department of Energy declassified a

number of documents, including eight that showed how to construct an atomic bomb.

A terminally ill woman was denied Medicaid to help pay her huge medical bills because her welfare payments were $10.80 too much to qualify.

Stories like these appear in the papers every day, but the criticism of bureaucracy is more widespread. Scholar Ralph Hummel presents a broad-based attack suggesting bureaucracy is a threat to personal freedom: (1) Bureaucrats deal with cases, not people. (2) Bureaucrats care about control and efficiency, not humanistic values. (3) Bureaucrats find it in their interest to shape and inform rather than communicate what shall take place; they create their own secret language. (4) Public bureaucracies are control institutions increasingly ruling society.[33] Is this true, or have bureaucrats simply done a poor job at public relations?

THE CASE FOR BUREAUCRACY

Political scientist Charles Goodsell suggests that the case against bureaucracy is based mostly on myths.[34] National surveys reveal citizens generally have favorable perceptions about their encounters with bureaucrats. Table 15–5 shows the results of several surveys by the University of Michigan,[35] and these results have been replicated in other studies. Citizens in the great majority of cases are satisfied, responding that bureaucrats are mostly helpful and efficient and that they have been treated fairly.

Citizens of other countries evaluate their encounters with bureaucrats less favorably than Americans. Respondents in the United States overwhelmingly believe they receive equal treatment from bureaucrats—a higher proportion than in Germany, Italy, or Mexico.[36] Comparisons are even

TABLE 15–5

CITIZEN SATISFACTION WITH BUREAUCRACY

1. How satisfied were you with the way the office handled your problem?	
Very satisfied	43%
Fairly well satisfied	26
Somewhat dissatisfied	12
Very dissatisfied	14
Don't know, no answer	5
2. How much effort did the people at the office make to help you?	
More than they had to	16%
About right	57
Less than should have	12
No effort	9
Don't know, no answer	6
3. How efficient did you think the office was in handling your problem?	
Very efficient	43%
Fairly efficient	31
Rather inefficient	9
Very inefficient	11
Don't know, no answer	6
4. Do you feel you were treated fairly or unfairly by the office?	
Fairly	76%
Unfairly	12
Mixed	5
Don't know, no answer	7

SOURCE: Daniel Katz et al., *Bureaucratic Encounters* (Ann Arbor: Institute for Social Research, University of Michigan, 1975), 64–69, 221. Reprinted with permission from the Institute for Social Research.

Protecting and cleaning up the environment will become an increasingly important function of the bureaucracy in coming years.

more dramatic with less developed nations, where graft and corruption are rampant and most people believe all officials are corrupt. Americans give the bureaucracy high marks for integrity.

Many popular beliefs about bureaucrats are incorrect. Studies of the demographic characteristics of public employees reveal that measured by education, religion, income, and party affiliation, civil servants are generally typical of the public at large.[37] Like Congress, the courts, the presidency, and large corporations, the top echelon of the civil service is dominated by white males of high socioeconomic status. But because the bureaucracy is so large, its overall membership is actually more typical of the American public than any other branch of government.

Is there really a bureaucratic mentality leading to dehumanizing behavior, a lack of caring about human values? Once again, evidence suggests the contrary.[38] Surveys of bureaucrats reveal considerable concern for clients, strong advocacy for more benefits, and support for the dignity and rights of people. Of course, the actions of one uncaring bureaucrat can leave a lasting impression that erases the memory of many caring officials. Also, work in the bureaucracy, far from being debilitating and dehumanizing, is evaluated highly by public employees themselves. Although they have their share of frustrations, a large proportion express high job satisfaction.

Another myth about bureaucracy is the belief that the bigger the bureaucracy, the less efficient it is. Bigger can be more efficient. For example, studies have shown that larger fire departments have considerably faster response times than smaller departments.[39]

Assessing the bureaucracy is difficult, but clearly many popular beliefs are more myth than reality. At times it can be unresponsive, pursuing its own values and self-interest rather than trying to respond to presidents, parties, or the public. When this occurs, however, Congress, the presidency, interest groups, and citizens have means at their disposal to keep the bureaucracy accountable. Overall, public agencies and their employees do a good job providing public services, supplying needed technical expertise to the problems of government, and carrying out the laws of the land. But the bureaucracy does have a public-image problem. The media pay scant attention to the bureaucracy except to publicize mistakes and slipups. Effective and courteous administration is not news.

No single judgment can fairly assess the bureaucracy's strengths and weaknesses. Bureaucracy is essential, but it poses political problems. It may grow too powerful if Congress and the president are unable to govern. Even if most public employees are doing a good job, the sheer size, complexity, and fragmentation of the bureaucracy create obstacles to governing.

Summary and Conclusions

1. The federal bureaucracy grew from a few hundred employees to nearly 3 million in two hundred years. Jobs were originally given to the party faithful as patronage under the old spoils system. The Pendleton Act in 1883 created the modern civil service based on merit.
2. Recent reforms of the civil service system include the creation of the Office of Personnel Management, the Senior Executive Service, and inspectors general to ferret out waste and fraud.
3. The federal bureaucracy is a complex maze of departments, agencies, bureaus, boards, and commissions that developed as the policy agenda of government expanded. Although the number of federal employees has not increased in recent years, the total impact of the bureaucracy is greater.
4. The bureaucracy does not simply carry out the law but actually makes policy by translating legislation into operating rules and regulations. Federal regulatory activities were constrained in the 1980s, but the costs of deregulation are becoming more obvious in the 1990s.
5. Bureaucracies are powerful because of their control of technical expertise. Large organizations are highly political, and public policy decisions are often affected by bureaucratic politics. Bureaucratic alliances with interest groups and congressional subcommittees create unique subgovernments capable of dominating policy-making in certain areas
6. Congress, the presidency, citizens, and interest groups all help keep the bureaucracy accountable and responsive.
7. Many of the more scathing criticisms of rigid bureaucratic mentality and inefficiency seem to be based more on popular myth than on fact..

The political mood of the 1980s swung against big government and the bureaucrats that administer it and toward deregulation. But the mood may be at least partially swinging the other way in the 1990s. The savings and loan collapse is an expensive disaster related to deregulation. Despite cutbacks and deregulation, a national consensus supports continued domestic and social programs and a host of other regulatory activities. Liberal or conservative, Republican or Democrat, public officials will continue to strive for greater responsiveness and effectiveness in the administration of public policy. Bureaucracy is an easy target. The more difficult challenge is to make it work better.

Key Terms

bureaucracy
civil service
clientele groups
delegation of authority
fire-alarm oversight
Freedom of Information Act
government corporations
implementation
independent agencies
Office of Personnel Management (OPM)
Pendleton Act
police-patrol oversight
political executives
regulatory agencies
Senior Executive Service (SES)
spoils system
subgovernments
technocrat

Self-Review

1. What was the spoils system?
2. How did the civil service system develop?
3. What are the most recent changes in the civil service?

4. How is the executive branch organized?
5. What is delegation of authority?
6. Describe policy implementation.
7. How are regulations developed, and what are their costs and benefits?
8. What are the sources of bureaucratic power?
9. Describe the structure of subgovernments and how they work.
10. Define "bureaucratic politics."
11. How does the presidency attempt to control the bureaucracy? Congress? Interest groups?
12. Compare police-patrol oversight with fire-alarm oversight.
13. How do citizens feel about their encounters with bureaucrats?
14. What are some bureaucratic myths?

SUGGESTED READINGS

Benveniste, Guy. *The Politics of Expertise.* 2nd ed. 1983.
An examination of the role of experts in modern bureaucracies and the problems of control by leaders.

Downs, Anthony. *Inside Bureaucracy.* 1967.
A systematic examination of bureaucratic behavior based on assumptions of the rationality and self-interested behavior of bureaucrats.

Goodsell, Charles. *The Case for Bureaucracy.* 1982.
A self-proclaimed polemic in defense of bureaucracy, attempting to refute various charges against agencies and public officials.

Heclo, Hugh. *A Government of Strangers.* 1977.
A study of the problems of political executives—the "strangers"—dealing with career civil servants in the federal bureaucracy.

Ripley, Randall B., and Grace Franklin. *Congress, Bureaucracy, and Public Policy.* 5th ed. 1990.
A thorough review of the relationships between members of Congress and executive-branch officials, focusing on subgovernments.

NOTES

1. Charles Hyneman and George Carey, *A Second Federalist* (New York: Appleton-Century-Crofts, 1967), 167; the comments of Representative Jackson of Georgia.
2. Ibid., 164.
3. See *Historical Statistics, Colonial Times to 1970* (Washington, D.C.: Census Bureau, 1976).
4. See Mathew Crenson, *The Federal Machine: Beginnings of a Bureaucracy in Jacksonian America* (Baltimore: Johns Hopkins University Press, 1975).
5. See Charles Peters, "A Kind Word for the Spoils System," *Washington Monthly,* September 1976.
6. See Theodore Lowi, *The End of Liberalism* (New York: Norton, 1979).
7. See Richard Nathan, *The Administrative Presidency* (New York: Wiley, 1983).
8. Computed from regulations printed in the *Federal Register,* reported in the *National Journal,* 14 May 1988, p. 1254.
9. Charles Goodsell, *The Case for Bureaucracy* (Chatham, N.J.: Chatham House, 1982), 111.
10. Hugh Heclo, *A Government of Strangers* (Washington, D.C.: Brookings, 1977).
11. Robert Lineberry, *American Public Policy* (New York: Harper and Row, 1977), 70–71.
12. See Harrell Rodgers and Charles Bulloch, *Law and Social Change* (New York: McGraw-Hill, 1972).
13. Michael Lipsky, "Toward a Theory of Street-Level Bureaucracy," in Willis Hawley et al., eds., *Theoretical Perspectives in Urban Politics* (Englewood Cliffs, N.J.: Prentice-Hall, 1976), chap. 8.
14. Murray Weidenbaum, *The Future of Business Regulation* (New York: AMACON, 1979), 1–13.
15. Steven Kelman, "Regulation That Works," *New Republic,* 25 November 1978.
16. *Congressional Quarterly Weekly Reports,* 7 April 1990, p. 1056.
17. See Francis E. Rourke, ed., *Bureaucratic Power in National Politics* (Boston: Little, Brown, 1978), 1.
18. Max Weber, "Essay on Bureaucracy," in ibid., 85.
19. Guy Benveniste, *The Politics of Expertise* (San Francisco: Boyd and Fraser, 1977), 4.
20. Randall B. Ripley and Grace Franklin, *Congress, Bureaucracy, and Public Policy* (Homewood, Ill.: Dorsey, 1976), 76–79. The following section relies on their analysis.
21. Anthony Downs, *Inside Bureaucracy* (Boston: Little, Brown, 1967), 261–80.
22. Rourke, *Bureaucratic Power,* 159.
23. Evelyn Z. Brodkin, "Policy Politics: If We Can't Govern, Can We Manage?" *Political Science Quarterly* 102 (Winter 1987–88):571–87.
24. Martin S. Eccles recalled the conversation with Roosevelt, reported in Peter Woll, *American Bureaucracy* (New York: Norton, 1977), 207.
25. *New York Times,* 22 February 1990, p. A1.
26. See Timothy B. Clark, "Meaner Than Junkyard Dogs," *Washingtonian,* June 1982.

27. Morris Fiorina, *Congress: Keystone of the Washington Establishment* (New Haven: Yale University Press, 1977).
28. Mathew McCubbins and Thomas Schwartz, "Congressional Oversight Overlooked: Police Patrols versus Fire Alarms," in Mathew McCubbins and Terry Sullivan, eds., *Congress: Structure and Policy* (Cambridge: Cambridge University Press, 1987), 426–41.
29. *Congressional Quarterly Weekly Report,* 22 May 1982, pp. 1229–30.
30. Max Weber, *The Protestant Ethic and the Spirit of Capitalism,* trans. Talcott Parsons (New York: Scribners, 1958), 182.
31. Clark, "Meaner."
32. Goodsell, *Case,* 3.
33. Ralph Hummel, *The Bureaucratic Experience* (New York: St. Martin's Press, 1982), 3.
34. Goodsell, *Case.*
35. Daniel Katz et al., *Bureaucratic Encounters* (Ann Arbor: Institute for Social Research, University of Michigan, 1975), 121–26, 186–87.
36. Gabriel Almond and Sidney Verba, *The Civic Culture* (Boston: Little, Brown, 1963), 70–72.
37. Goodsell, *Case,* 84–85.
38. Ibid., 92–100.
39. Ibid., 121.

CHAPTER 16

THE JUDICIARY

POLITICAL CLOSE-UP

INSIDE THE SUPREME COURT: THE ABORTION DECISION

It is just called the conference room, but few have ever been inside this secret abode of the Supreme Court. The room is spacious, with a thick carpet, walls paneled in oak. In the center of the room is a twelve-foot-long table, covered with green felt, surrounded by nine dark leather swivel chairs. On October 12, 1972, Chief Justice Warren Burger sat at the end of the table in his usual place. William O. Douglas, the senior associate justice, was at the other end. The other seven justices were seated around the table. On the back of each chair was a brass nameplate: Burger, Douglas, Marshall, White, Stewart, Blackmun, Brennan, Rehnquist, and Powell. No clerks or lawyers were in the room, just the justices. It was a conference on the upcoming abortion decision.

The justices were considering an appeal on two cases: *Roe v. Wade* and *Doe v. Bolton.* Justice William O. Douglas, on the Court since his appointment by President Franklin D. Roosevelt in the 1930s, had long been in favor of striking down restrictive abortion laws. Continuing hard feelings between Douglas and Burger

included the issue of who would write the majority abortion opinion. Harry Blackmun of Minnesota was asked to write the opinion by Burger, an assignment Douglas believed he had the right to make as the senior associate justice on the majority side. But the legal and moral issues that previous spring were too complex to determine which view commanded a majority.

Blackmun had spent the summer researching the abortion question in the library at the Mayo Clinic. The questions were incredibly difficult. When did life start? How pervasive was a woman's right to privacy? When did the state's interest in the fetus intercede over privacy rights? What guidance did the Constitution provide? At the meeting on October 12, Blackmun presented the outline of his opinion strongly arguing to strike down the abortion laws. What had seemed a shaky majority at best in the previous session of the Court had become a solid 6-to-3 majority.

In the weeks after the conference, more drafts of the decision circulated among the justices. The essence of the decision was based on the concept of "viability" of the fetus. Medically, gestation was divided into three trimesters, and the state's interest was different in each. In the first trimester the state had no interest and abortion could not be restricted. In the second, the state had an interest and abortions could be regulated to protect the mother's health. In the third trimester, when the fetus was viable, the state's interest was in protecting the life of the fetus and abortion could be restricted.

The justices considered medical, legal, and constitutional issues and disagreed on all three. Rehnquist and White argued that the Court should not take up the issue at all. Douglas and Stewart, although favoring the decision, disagreed on the legal basis of the opinion.

The final draft of the opinion was finished in December. Rehnquist and White had submitted their own dissenting opinions. Stewart's and Douglas's concurring opinions were completed, but there was still no word from the chief justice. He was stalling until after Nixon's inauguration. Only days before the final decision, Burger decided to vote with the majority, making the decision 7-to-2, and submitted a brief concurrence. The decisions were announced on January 22, 1973.

From the quiet confines of the conference room came one of the most controversial decisions in the history of the Supreme Court. The *Roe* decision, and its companion *Doe* decision, culminated decades of work by pro-abortion activists determined that women must retain the right to control their own bodies. But the decisions set off a chain reaction among anti-abortion forces dedicated to protecting the life of the unborn child. In the 1990s, amid the bombings of abortion clinics and a shot fired into Justice Blackmun's home, political controversy over the Supreme Court's 1973 decision raged on.

SOURCE: Bob Woodward and Scott Armstrong, *The Brethren* (New York: Simon and Schuster, 1979), 27, 29, 193-207, 215-23, 271-84.

CHAPTER OUTLINE

Introduction and Overview

The Evolution of the Court System
Establishment of the Federal Court System
Judicial Review: *Marbury v. Madison* (1803)
Early Policy Concerns of the Supreme Court
Economic Liberty and the Court
Judicial Activism and Political Philosophy: The Warren, Burger, and Rehnquist Courts

The Judiciary: A Dual Court System
State Courts
Federal Courts
Federal District Courts
U.S. Circuit Courts of Appeals
The U.S. Supreme Court
Jurisdiction of the Federal Courts
Judges and Justices
The Judicial Selection Process
Appointment to the Supreme Court
Rejection of Supreme Court Nominees
Appointment of Lower Federal Court Judges
Selection of State Judges
Removal of Judges

The Judicial Process: Policy-Making in the Courts
What Do the Courts Do?
Getting a Case to the Supreme Court
Trials in the Supreme Court
Making Decisions: Court Politics

Governing Through the Courts
Characteristics of Judicial Policies
Judicial Activism: Are Courts Too Powerful?
Is Judicial Self-Restraint Enough?

Assessing the Courts: Problems and Prospects
Has the United States Become Too Litigious?
Public Evaluations of the Court System

Summary and Conclusions

INTRODUCTION AND OVERVIEW

The abortion decision is only one of the political hornet's nests the Supreme Court has stirred up in recent years. Decisions on school prayer, busing, pornography, and the rights of the accused have placed the Court in the center of a political firestorm. The problem of the Supreme Court is quite different from that of the presidency, Congress, or the bureaucracy. Few complaints are heard about the weak or "do-nothing" courts. On the contrary, most of the concern is with a high court that is too powerful. On the surface the Court seems very different. It lacks the commanding presence of the presidency, the rough-and-tumble fragmentation of the Congress, the imposing scope and impersonality of the bureaucracy. The U.S. Supreme Court today, to most eyes, is eight men and one woman making critical political decisions behind closed doors.

There are two distinct views of the Supreme Court and its role in the governing process. The first holds that the Court governs too easily and that its power should be reduced. Appointed for life, with few checks on their actions, some see the justices as autonomous political actors, actively involved in policy-making that should be left to the executive and legislature. A handful of justices are in a position to dictate policy to a nation without fear of reprisal. The second view notes the strict limits on the Court's ability to govern and sees it as an essential guardian of the Constitution. The Court makes policy only when other branches of government fail to act or cannot act. As a national decision-maker, the Supreme Court has more severe limitations than any other branch. It does not control its own policy agenda. Justices can react only to cases brought before them by others; they cannot choose the issues or problems. Justices cannot implement their own decisions but must instead rely on others to carry out their orders. The second view sees the Court as democratic, despite the justices' elite status.

The Supreme Court is the top echelon of a complex judicial system in the United States. The federal judiciary consists of courts, justices, and judges that interpret the law, resolve conflicts, and make policy. The U.S. Supreme Court is one of the most powerful national courts in the world. How can we judge the role played by the courts in American politics and assess their effect on the ability of the political system to govern? The following questions guide the analysis:

1. How has the American court system evolved? How did the Supreme Court develop the power of judicial review? How have the focus and influence of the Court changed over the years?
2. What is the judiciary? Who are the judges and justices, and how are they selected?
3. How do courts make policy? How do cases get to court, and what actions may the courts take?
4. Are the courts too powerful? What are some of the checks on courts?
5. What are the problems and prospects of the courts? How does the public assess the court system? How can the system's ability to govern be judged?

★

The Evolution of the Court System

ESTABLISHMENT OF THE FEDERAL COURT SYSTEM

When the first Congress of the United States convened in 1789, one of its tasks was to create a judicial system. The Constitution specified that the judicial power would be vested in the Supreme Court and "in such inferior courts as the Congress may from time to time ordain and establish." The Supreme Court was to have **original jurisdiction** (the court that is the first to hear a case) only in limited instances, such as disputes between states. In most cases, the Supreme Court would have **appellate jurisdiction** (the court that reviews the decisions of a lower court).

The most important power of federal courts is the power of **judicial review**—the ability to determine whether an action by another branch of government is constitutional and, if not, to declare it null and void. Judicial review is the ground on which the courts have expanded their influence in policy-making and the main reason that courts in the United States play a more important role than courts in other nations. Judicial review is not granted to the courts in the Constitution. It is a precedent established in the case of ***Marbury v. Madison*** (1803), although one that had been practiced in some colonial courts. Despite this tradition, most of the Founders and early members of Congress did not expect the courts to become as influential as they are today.[1] Hamilton, writing in *Federalist paper* No. 78, noted that the judicial branch was the branch "least dangerous" to the rights of citizens.

The Judiciary Act of 1789 created a **dual court system**—a set of federal courts operating side by side with state courts. During the debate on the

Judiciary Act, some members of Congress argued that a complete set of federal courts was not needed. Congressman Samuel Livermore of New Hampshire complained that federal courts were duplicative and would "fill every state in the Union with two kinds of courts, [which will be] unnecessary, expensive, and disagreeable to our constituents."[2] The majority in Congress disagreed, creating both federal district courts with original jurisdiction and federal appeals courts. The Supreme Court remained the final arbiter. A dual court system is the natural outgrowth of federalism, producing a set of national laws and fifty different sets of state laws.

JUDICIAL REVIEW: *MARBURY V. MADISON* (1803)

Thomas Jefferson defeated John Adams in the election of 1800. Adams, fearing that the new president and his supporters would weaken the national government, tried to load the courts with loyal Federalists as one of his last acts. The newly created judgeships and last-minute appointments became known as the "midnight judges." In the waning hours of the morning, as Jefferson's inauguration approached, John Marshall, Adam's secretary of state, attempted to deliver the commissions. He was able to dispense all but seventeen of them. Marshall himself became chief justice of the Supreme Court. Jefferson's new secretary of state, James Madison, refused (on Jefferson's orders) to make the rest of the appointments to Federalist candidates. When William Marbury, one of the unlucky seventeen, sued to get his appointment, Marshall presided over the court that would decide the case.

A very delicate political situation existed. The Supreme Court was still new and relatively untried. Like other American political institutions, its power and legitimacy were not yet established. If Marshall ordered Jefferson and Madison to make the appointments, there was no way to be sure the order would be enforced. Open defiance by the president would have dealt a severe and permanent blow to the Court and created a constitutional crisis.

Marshall successfully avoided a direct confrontation, giving up an immediate advantage while securing the future power of the Court. The Court unanimously ruled that Madison was wrong but that the Supreme Court did not have the power to compel him to deliver the commissions. Although the Judiciary Act of 1789 specifically gave the courts the power to do so, Marshall shrewdly ruled that Congress had erred. In giving the Court this power, he stated, Congress had violated the original jurisdiction provisions of Article III of the Constitution, and he declared those provisions of the Judiciary Act unconstitutional. "A law repugnant to the Constitution is void," his opinion declared, and both Congress and the president are bound by the Court's decision. Marbury and the other sixteen did not get their judgeships, but Marshall established judicial review and changed the future course of the Supreme Court.

Marshall could have come up with many less radical solutions, but he went out of his way to establish this dramatic precedent. Even so, many questions about the scope of judicial review remained. Should the Court be limited to interpreting its own powers, or could the Court declare any act of Congress or the president unconstitutional? Succeeding generations followed the broader interpretation of judicial review. John Marshall's impact on American government was far more significant than that of many of the early presidents. He promoted not only a strong Court but also a strong national government during his thirty-four years on the Court.

EARLY POLICY CONCERNS OF THE SUPREME COURT

The power of the national government and slavery were the major issues for the early Supreme Court. The case of *Martin v. Hunter's Lessee* (1816) established the Court's power to declare a state law void if it was in conflict with federal law. In 1824, the Court expanded the national government's ability to regulate interstate commerce in the case of *Gibbons v. Ogden,* which involved Robert Fulton and his steamboat lines. As slavery came to dominate American politics, the Court turned its attention in that direction. President Andrew Jackson chose Roger Taney, a strong states' rights advocate, to succeed Marshall in 1835. Taney presided over the

Court when it exercised the power of judicial review for the second time in the infamous *Dred Scott* case of 1857 (see Chapter 6).

Dred Scott v. Sanford was probably the low point in the Supreme Court's history, preceding the bloody Civil War by four years. The Court attempted to settle the most important political dispute of the century in a single, arbitrary decision that was clearly out of tune with growing national sentiment against slavery. The decision was overturned by the Emancipation Proclamation in 1863 and by the Thirteenth, Fourteenth, and Fifteenth Amendments to the Constitution after the Civil War.

ECONOMIC LIBERTY AND THE COURT

In the decades that followed, the Supreme Court began to focus on business and the economy. From the 1860s to the 1930s, the Court made a number of decisions that protected and sanctified the institution of private property and protected the rights of businesses, corporations, and property holders. The Court's application of the Fourteenth Amendment, which guarantees that no state shall deprive persons of "due process" or "equal protection" of the law, to the civil rights of blacks was extremely narrow. Yet the Court acted broadly to protect economic rights under the same amendment. The Civil Rights cases of the 1880s upheld state laws segregating schools, railroad passenger cars, and public accommodations and sanctified exclusionary voting laws. In contrast, the Court interpreted "person" to include corporations and was generous in protecting the rights of business against the interests of labor and government. In a number of "economic due process" cases, the Court struck down laws permitting labor strikes, invalidated the federal income tax, and overturned child labor laws and other restrictions on working hours and conditions.

The period from 1870 to 1930 was an era of judicial activism from a conservative perspective. Between 1789 and 1865, only two laws were declared unconstitutional. In the next seventy-five years, more than seventy laws were struck down to protect "economic freedom." By the 1930s, with the advent of Franklin Roosevelt and the New Deal, the Court found itself out of step with the other branches of the national government. The justices, appointed by Republican presidents, continued to declare key portions of the New Deal unconstitutional. One of the most important pieces of legislation was the National Recovery Act, which the Court overruled in *Schechter Poultry Corporation v. U.S.* (1935). Frustrated and upset at what he considered the Court's intransigence, Roosevelt devised a plan ostensibly to help the "nine old men" on the bench cope with the Court's busy agenda. The president submitted a bill to add justices to the Court to "ease their heavy workload." Roosevelt's proposal was a transparent attempt to appoint justices of his choosing and gain a favorable majority on the Court. His "Court-packing" plan was roundly criticized and was never adopted. Nonetheless, after *Schechter* and the Court-packing plan, no other New Deal legislation was overturned. Some have called this change in philosophy by the Court "the switch in time that saved nine."

JUDICIAL ACTIVISM AND POLITICAL PHILOSOPHY: THE WARREN, BURGER, AND REHNQUIST COURTS

After the 1930s, the thrust of the Supreme Court changed once again. The appointment of Chief Justice Earl Warren in 1953 by President Eisenhower initiated another era of judicial activism, but this time in a liberal rather than a conservative direction. Since the 1930s, the Court has not interfered with the ability of the federal government and state governments to regulate economic activity. It has moved instead toward the protection of individual liberties. The Warren Court began by handing down the landmark *Brown v. Topeka Board of Education* (1954) decision declaring segregation in public schools unconstitutional. Some of its most controversial decisions came in extending rights to the criminally accused—rights at time of arrest, the right to counsel, rights against self-incrimination, and protections from unreasonable search and seizure. The Warren Court also announced the "one person, one vote" rule in drawing up legislative boundaries and mandated a round of redistricting in the 1960s.

Earl Warren stepped down in 1969. Unhappy with the direction of the Warren Court, President Nixon repeated his desire to appoint conservatives and so-called "strict constructionists" who would tone down the activism of the Warren Court. In describing his preferences for Supreme Court appointments, Nixon made the common error of linking judicial activism with the political philosophy of that particular Court—in the 1960s, the liberalism that extended individual rights and liberties. Nixon named Warren Burger to replace Warren.

Under Chief Justice Burger, the Supreme Court initially continued the emphasis on the protection of individual rights. The abortion decisions announced in 1973 were perhaps the most important rulings of the decade. But by the 1980s, with additional appointments by Nixon, Ford, and Reagan (Jimmy Carter had no vacancies to fill during his four-year term), the Court had clearly taken on a more conservative hue. In several key areas, the Burger Court of the 1980s scaled back rights extended by the Warren Court of the 1960s. As the Court has become more conservative, has it become less activist? The *Chadha* decision of 1983, striking down the legislative veto (see Chapter 14), ruled more federal laws unconstitutional in a single decision than in the entire history of the Supreme Court. One of the justices, John Paul Stevens, believes that in recent years, his colleagues on the Court have gone out of their way to express broad, sweeping opinions in cases that could have been decided on narrower grounds.[3]

Chief Justice Burger resigned in 1986 after seventeen years to devote full time to planning the celebration of the Constitution's bicentennial. President Reagan nominated Associate Justice **William Rehnquist** to become chief justice and Antonin Scalia to take Rehnquist's place. Because Rehnquist was one of the most conservative members of the Court, observers expected to see a further tilt to the right. While the Court did become more conservative in the 1980s under Rehnquist, moderate justices still commanded a majority on a number of decisions. Two important decisions for the Court's conservative wing were the rejection of the contention that the death penalty was racially biased and the upholding of a lower court decision allowing judges to refuse to set bail for accused criminals who may pose a threat to society.

The early Rehnquist Court, however, did not roll back many of the decisions of the Warren and Burger Courts, and it even extended civil rights and liberties in some areas. Decisions extended the rights of women, expanded the legal foundation for affirmative action, broadened protection for free speech, and continued to support a clear separation between church and state.[4] In a number of cases, such as the 7-to-2 decision to overturn Louisiana's law requiring the teaching of creationism, Rehnquist and Scalia found themselves dissenting from the majority decisions.

A key turning point in determining the philosophy of the Court came with the Senate's refusal to confirm President Reagan's nomination of Robert Bork to the Supreme Court in 1987 (this is discussed in more detail below). Reagan's second choice, Judge Douglas H. Ginsburg, had to withdraw when he revealed he had smoked marijuana. Instead, Reagan's third choice, Anthony Kennedy, was confirmed in 1988. At the time of their appointments, Rehnquist was sixty-one years old, Scalia was fifty, and Kennedy was fifty-one, meaning that the impact of Reagan's appointments is likely to be felt well into the twenty-first century.

The addition of Justice Anthony Kennedy created a conservative majority that rendered dramatic rulings in a number of key areas. The Court issued rulings that upheld a restrictive state abortion law, severely limited the applicability of affirmative action, refused to clarify ambiguous legislative intent, and upheld actions of law enforcement officials against criminal defendants. The Court appeared to look much like Ronald Reagan intended when he took office: placing greater emphasis on states, anti-abortion, recalcitrant on civil rights, and tough on crime.

Kennedy, Reagan's third and final appointment to the Court, provided the crucial fifth vote in a number of cases, joining Chief Justice Rehnquist and Justices O'Connor, Scalia, and White. Kennedy voted with Rehnquist, the most conservative member of the Court, 90 percent of the time. The minority of Justices Stevens, Marshall, Brennan, and Blackmun often wrote bitter, stinging dissenting opinions, challenging the constitutional interpretation and motives of the majority. Kennedy's most surprising vote was to affirm the decision declaring flag-desecration laws unconstitutional (see the Political Close-up in Chapter five). This decision, along with one allowing "dial-a-porn" operations, upheld First Amendment rights and suggested a libertarian vein in the majority's philosophy. The new majority reflected a different direction for the Court than was followed in the 1970s and 1980s. When Justice Brennan resigned in 1990, President George Bush nominated David Souter to take his place on the high court. Souter's confirmation and possible impact are examined in Political Insight 16–1. (See page 429).

Clearly, in two hundred years, the powers and the focus of the Supreme Court have changed. In the first seventy years, the Court concentrated on the powers of the national government versus those of the states, which included the slavery question. For the next seventy years, the Court protected the rights of business by limiting economic regulation. In recent years, the Court has focused on individual rights. Throughout its history, the Court has undergone subtle political swings in ideology as well as in judicial activism. It has shown a willingness to engage highly controversial issues and to make sweeping, broad-based decisions. What is the proper balance? Is the Court too political? Before examining these questions, we need to look at the court system that extends below the lofty pinnacle of the Supreme Court.

The Judiciary: A Dual Court System

STATE COURTS

Federal courts and state courts exist side by side in the United States. The two systems meet only on those rare occasions where state cases are heard on appeal by the U.S. Supreme Court. In one sense, the United States has fifty-one court systems. Acknowledging variations in state courts, however, the courts are commonly thought of as a dual system.[5] At the bottom of the state court system are the minor courts, often called justices of the peace in rural areas and municipal courts in the cities. Their jurisdiction is usually limited to civil functions, traffic violations, and criminal offenses—everything from getting married to spitting in public.

Next up the ladder are county courts, which have broader jurisdiction. (They have different names in many states but are approximately equivalent in function.) Included are common pleas courts, juvenile courts, domestic relations courts, and probate courts. The main courts of original jurisdiction at the state level are trial courts, where juries hear cases. Twenty-six states have appeals courts above the county courts. In the other twenty-four states, appeals from the county-level courts go directly to the state supreme court. In the great majority of cases, the decision in the state's highest court is final. Rarely are appeals from state courts taken to the Supreme Court of the United States. The Supreme Court will take a state case on appeal only under special circumstances or if a substantial federal question is involved. A state case taken on appeal does not start over at the bottom of the federal court system but goes directly to the U.S. Supreme Court. However, state laws can be challenged in lower federal courts.

FEDERAL COURTS

Federal courts are either legislative courts or the more familiar constitutional courts.[6] **Legislative courts** administer a particular body of law and perform legislative as well as judicial tasks. The customs court, the tax court, and the court of military justice are examples of legislative courts. Unlike constitutional courts, legislative courts may issue *advisory opinions*—that is, they may offer opinions without having a specific case at hand.

Constitutional courts—federal district courts, federal appeals courts, and the U.S. Supreme Court—are the heart of the federal judiciary. Figure 16–1 shows the structure of the federal court system.

FEDERAL DISTRICT COURTS. Like the county courts at the state level, the district courts are the trial courts of the federal judiciary. Here civil and criminal cases are tried and justice is dispensed. As courts of original jurisdiction, they first hear a case and usually make the final disposition of the case. Across the United States are 94 district courts employing 575 judges. Federal district judge is an important and exclusive job in the United States. Here is where the action is in federal courtrooms. Cases range from school desegregation to kidnapping and

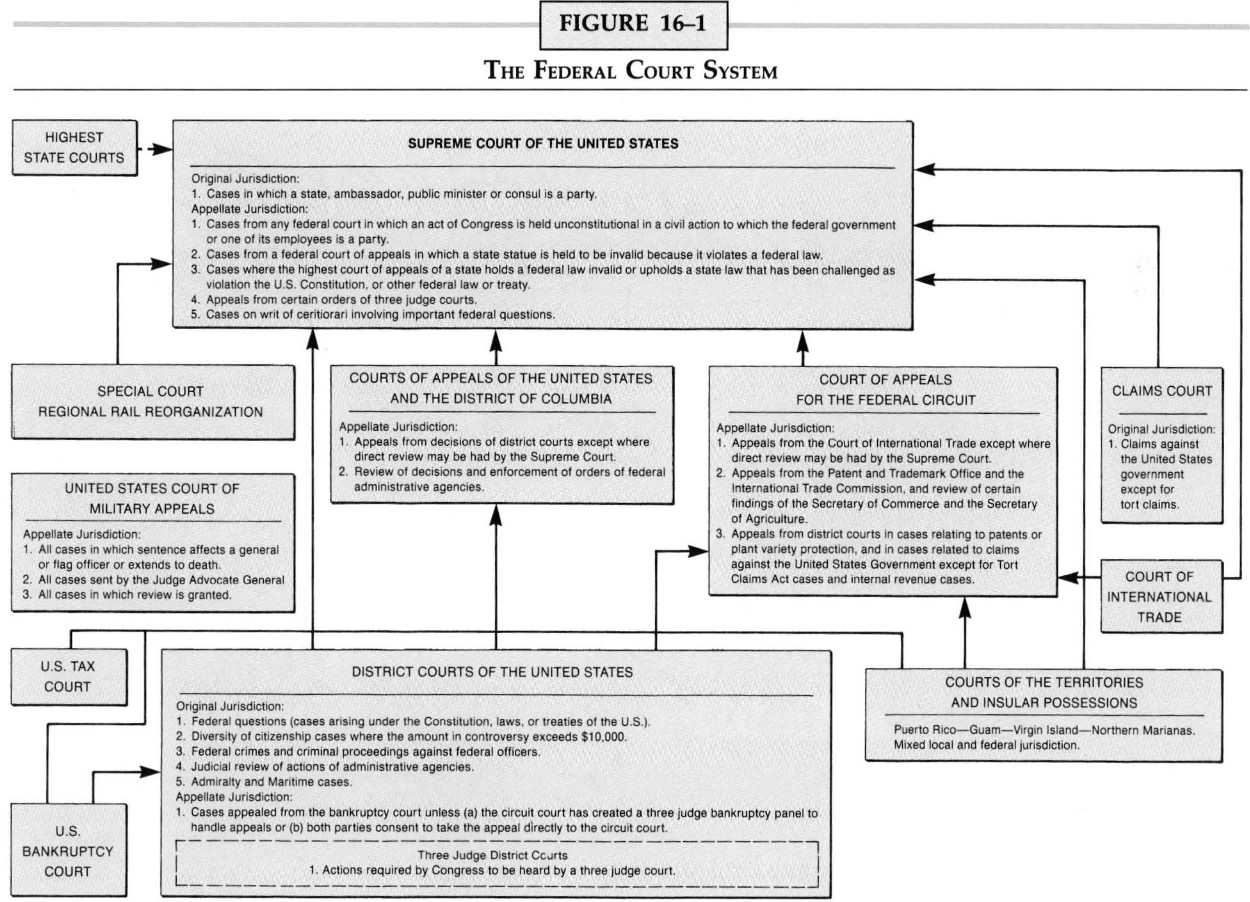

FIGURE 16–1
THE FEDERAL COURT SYSTEM

attempts to assassinate the president. Trials can be held without juries if all parties agree, but if a jury trial is demanded, twelve jurors must serve, and their decision must be unanimous.

U.S. CIRCUIT COURTS OF APPEALS. Cases heard in the federal district courts may be appealed to the federal appeals court. Unlike the lower courts, the court of appeals has only appellate jurisdiction; it considers cases that have already been tried in district court. The United States has twelve courts of appeals (called "circuit courts" from the days when judges used to ride from town to town on horseback) employing 168 judges.[7] A chief judge presides in each of the twelve circuits. Cases appealed from the district courts are not retried by juries but are usually argued in front of three-judge panels. A winnowing process results in only a small percentage of all cases being heard by the appeals courts (around seven thousand a year). Occasionally, appeals from legislative courts are heard. In some districts, cases are decided strictly on the basis of written arguments. Other districts, such as the second, preserve oral argument in virtually all cases. Figure 16–2 is a map of the twelve circuits and the ninety-four districts in the United States.

FIGURE 16–2

U.S. CIRCUIT COURTS OF APPEALS AND U.S. DISTRICT COURTS

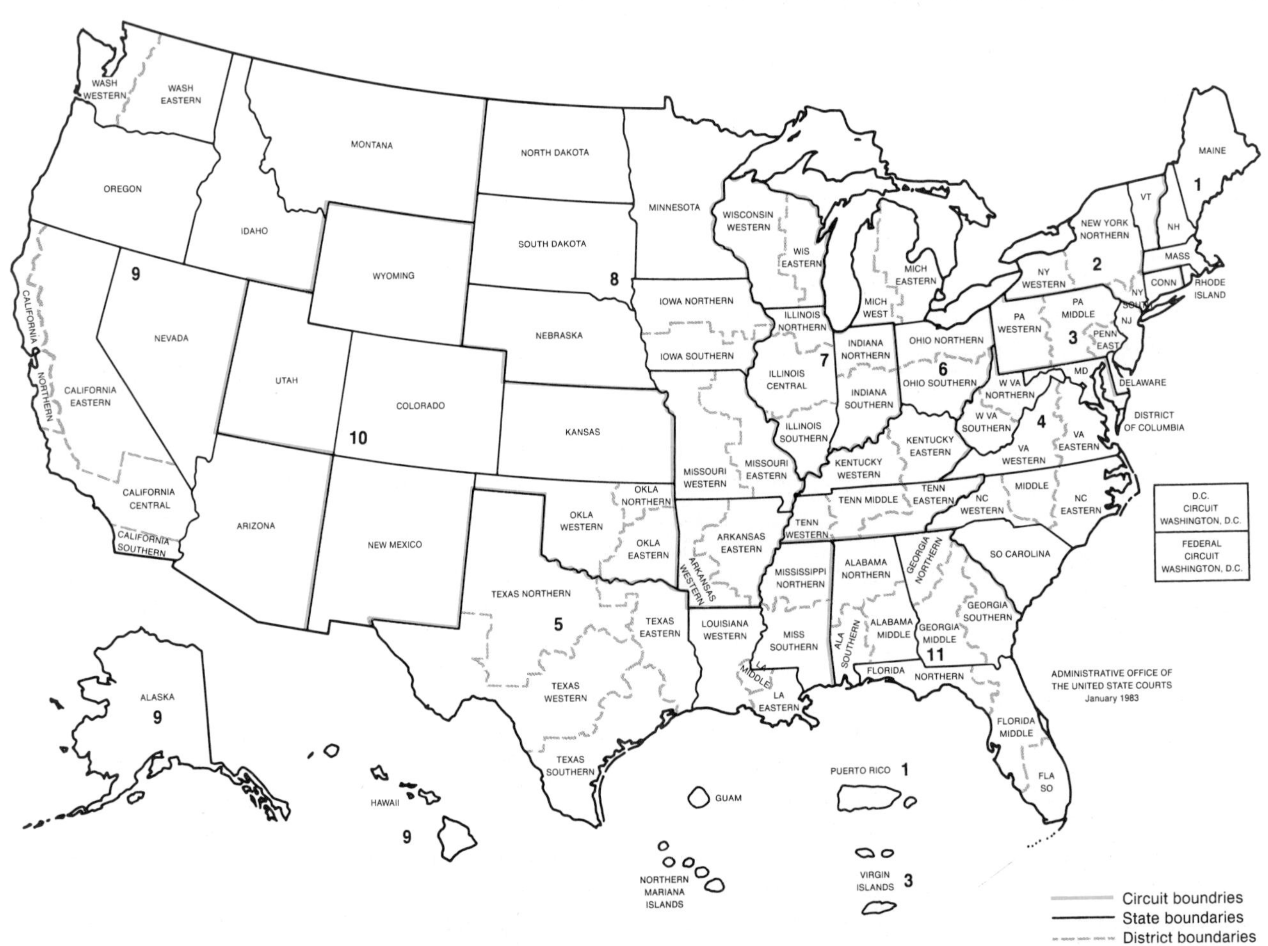

TABLE 16–1

CHIEF JUSTICES OF THE UNITED STATES

Chief Justice	Appointed by President	Year Appointed
John Jay	Washington	1789
Oliver Ellsworth	Washington*	1796
John Marshall	Adams	1801
Roger B. Taney	Jackson	1836
Salmon P. Chase	Lincoln	1864
Morrison R. Waite	Grant	1874
Melville W. Fuller	Cleveland	1888
Edward D. White	Taft	1910
William Howard Taft	Harding	1921
Charles Evans Hughes	Hoover	1930
Harlan Fiske Stone	Roosevelt	1941
Frederick M. Vinson	Truman	1946
Earl Warren	Eisenhower	1953
Warren E. Burger	Nixon	1969
William H. Rehnquist	Reagan	1986

*Washington appointed John Rutledge, who served as chief justice for a few months but was never confirmed by the Senate.

THE U.S. SUPREME COURT. As prescribed in the Constitution, the Supreme Court is the highest court in the land. It is primarily an appeals court but, as we saw in the *Marbury* case, it has some original jurisdiction as specified in Article III. Congress may establish the number of justices on the Court. For the past century, the Court has had nine justices, but it has had as few as five and as many as ten in its history. The chief justice of the United States is the first among equals and has an important impact on the direction of the Court. The key post of chief justice does not necessarily go to the associate justice with the most seniority. The president may appoint an associate justice (as in the case of Rehnquist) or someone off the Court (as in the case of Burger) to be chief justice when a vacancy occurs. The opportunity to name a chief justice is one of the most important appointments a president can make, and only thirteen of the forty-one U.S. presidents have had the chance. Like other federal judges, chief justices serve for life and can be removed only through impeachment. Table 16–1 lists the chief justices of the Supreme Court, one of the most elite positions in American politics. William Howard Taft, the only man to hold both the presidency and the job of chief justice, considered heading the Court to be the more desirable job of the two.

JURISDICTION OF THE FEDERAL COURTS

Courts cannot initiate policy; they can only respond to controversies brought before them. Federal courts consider two kinds of law. *Civil law* consists of rules governing relationships between private citizens, embodied in statutes and established in previous court decisions (common law). *Criminal law* consists of the rules that define offenses of one person against another and that are punishable by the state.

Federal courts have jurisdiction in both civil cases and criminal cases. Figure 16–1 contains definitions of original jurisdiction and appellate jurisdiction of the courts. District courts have jurisdiction over all crimes against the United States, for civil cases of more than $10,000, and for any other category prescribed by Congress. The courts of appeals have appellate jurisdiction over almost all federal courts of original jurisdiction—constitutional and legislative courts, territorial

Supreme Court of the United States as of June, 1990, before the resignation of William Brennan and nomination of David Souter.

courts, District of Columbia courts, independent regulatory commissions, and some bureaucratic agencies. The Supreme Court has original jurisdiction in only a few cases that involve the states, foreign ambassadors, or other nations. It has appellate jurisdiction over all federal courts and state courts if a federal question is involved.

JUDGES AND JUSTICES

The judicial system includes the courts, court reporters, court administrators, clerks of the court, lawyers on both sides, and the public. But perhaps the most crucial participants in the judiciary are judges and justices, the men and women dressed in black robes who preside over the courtrooms. Who are they? Where do they come from? How do they get their jobs?

Federal judges are a special group. Like other key national institutions, courts were long the sole province of white males from high social status backgrounds.[8] Until only recently, women and minorities were excluded. Today, the Court can no longer be described as nine old (white) men. The first black Supreme Court justice, Thurgood Marshall, was appointed by President Johnson in 1967. The first woman justice, Sandra Day O'Connor, was appointed by President Reagan in 1981. She is profiled in the accompanying People in Politics. Table 16–2 lists the current justices of the Supreme Court, date of appointment, date of birth, and background.

Until recently, racial and sexual barriers were equally strong in the federal courts below the Supreme Court. President Jimmy Carter made a concerted effort to achieve greater diversity in the composition of the federal judiciary. Table 16–3 compares the number of blacks, women, and Hispanics appointed to the federal bench by President Bush and his five predecessors.

THE JUDICIAL SELECTION PROCESS

Federal judges are appointed by the president with the "advice and consent" of the Senate. It sounds simple but, behind each appointment, politics is in full swing.

TABLE 16–2

THE JUSTICES OF THE SUPREME COURT OF THE UNITED STATES (BY SENIORITY)

Name	Home State	Prior Experience	Appointed By	Year of Appointment	Date of Birth
Byron R. White	Colorado	Deputy attorney general	Kennedy	1962	June 8, 1917
Thurgood Marshall	Maryland	Counsel to NAACP, federal judge	Johnson	1967	July 2, 1908
Harry A. Blackmun	Minnesota	Federal judge	Nixon	1970	Nov. 12, 1908
William H. Rehnquist (Chief Justice)	Arizona	Assistant attorney general, associate justice	Nixon, Reagan	1972, 1986	Oct 1, 1924
John Paul Stevens III	Illinois	Federal judge	Ford	1975	April 20, 1920
Sandra Day O'Connor	Arizona	State judge	Reagan	1981	March 26, 1930
Antonin Scalia	New Jersey	Federal judge	Reagan	1986	March 11, 1936
Anthony Kennedy	California	Federal judge	Reagan	1987	July 23, 1936
David Souter	New Hampshire	State attorney general and judge	Bush	1990	Sept. 17, 1939

On Capitol Hill, the Senate Judiciary Committee conducts its own background checks and holds hearings on the nominee's record and fitness for the job. The committee then recommends to the full Senate to confirm or reject the nomination. In the twentieth century, presidents have had most of their nominees confirmed by the Senate. But in a classic confrontation between Congress and the president, Ronald Reagan had a key nomination to the Supreme Court rejected by the Senate in 1987.

APPOINTMENT TO THE SUPREME COURT. Only 104 individuals have served on the U.S. Supreme Court in two hundred years. Table 16–4 shows the number

TABLE 16–3

APPOINTMENT OF MINORITIES TO THE FEDERAL JUDICIARY (IN PERCENTS)

U.S. Court of Appeals

	Women	Blacks	Hispanics
Johnson	2.5	5.0	Not available
Nixon	0.0	0.0	Not available
Ford	0.0	0.0	Not available
Carter	9.6	16.1	3.6
Reagan	7.2	1.2	1.2
Bush	20.0	0	20.0

U.S. District Court

	Women	Blacks	Hispanics
Johnson	1.6	3.3	2.5
Nixon	0.6	2.8	1.1
Ford	1.9	5.8	1.9
Carter	15.5	14.3	6.2
Reagan	8.2	2.0	4.8
Bush	20.0	0	0

NOTE: SOURCES: Based on figures compiled by Sheldon Goldman, University of Massachusetts, and the Justice Department. Reported in *Congressional Quarterly Weekly Reports*, 6 January 1990, p. 39.

TABLE 16–4

PRESIDENTS' APPOINTMENTS TO THE U.S. SUPREME COURT

President	No. of Appointments
George Washington	10
John Adams	3
Thomas Jefferson	3
James Madison	2
James Monroe	1
John Quincy Adams	1
Andrew Jackson	6
Martin Van Buren	2
William H. Harrison	0
John Tyler	1
James Polk	2
Zachary Taylor	0
Millard Fillmore	1
Franklin Pierce	1
James Buchanan	1
Abraham Lincoln	5
Andrew Johnson	0
Ulysses Grant	4
Rutherford Hayes	2
James Garfield	1
Chester Arthur	2
Grover Cleveland	4
Benjamin Harrison	4
Grover Cleveland	0
William McKinley	1
Theodore Roosevelt	3
William Howard Taft	5
Woodrow Wilson	3
Warren Harding	4
Calvin Coolidge	1
Herbert Hoover	3
Franklin Roosevelt	8
Harry Truman	4
Dwight Eisenhower	5
John Kennedy	2
Lyndon Johnson	2
Richard Nixon	4
Gerald Ford	1
Jimmy Carter	0
Ronald Reagan	4
George Bush*	1

NOTE: *through 1990

of appointments to the Supreme Court by each president. Jimmy Carter and four other presidents had no appointments during their term. The selection of a Supreme Court justice gives a president an opportunity to influence policy long after his or her term in office is over. President Adams's appointment of John Marshall is still the most dramatic example. Although he appoints a justice for life "during good behavior," a president has no guarantee of what a justice will do once on the Court. Eisenhower's appointee, Chief Justice Earl Warren, led the Court in several surprising directions in the 1960s. In most cases, however, presidents have a pretty good idea of the judicial philosophy of nominees. Based on their previous record as judges, it is usually possible to predict their general policy orientation.[9]

When a vacancy on the Court occurs through death or resignation, a complex screening process begins. Two important participants in the process are the Justice Department and the American Bar Association (ABA). Consulting with the president's advisers, the attorney general and his staff prepare a list of top candidates for the position. They look for potential nominees whose political party affiliation and political philosophy correspond with the president's. The FBI then conducts extensive background checks. A list of potential candidates is submitted to the ABA, which rates the candidates. Finally, the president selects a name and submits it to the Senate.[10]

REJECTION OF SUPREME COURT NOMINEES. On October 23, 1987, by a vote of 42 to 58, the U.S. Senate refused to confirm President Reagan's nomination of **Robert H. Bork** to become an associate justice of the Supreme Court. The outcome was no surprise. Two weeks before the Senate debate had even begun, fifty-three senators had announced their intention to oppose Judge Bork. The debate was intense and bitter, if anticlimactic.

Senator William Armstrong (R-Colo.) charged that opponents had made vicious personal attacks on Judge Bork and that outside interest groups had played a major role in orchestrating the campaign against him. Senator Gordon Humphrey (R-N.H.) accused opponents of trying to intimidate pro-Bork witnesses and of using Ku Klux Klan tactics. Supporters claimed that a nominee had never before been subjected to as much scrutiny or to such a concerted campaign to oppose the nomination. Opponents defended the confirmation process and, more basically, the Senate's constitutional right to "advise and consent" on the president's nominees to the high court. During the debate, Senate

Judiciary Chair Joseph Biden (D-Del.) disputed the claim that they had politicized the process. "Any politicizing has been driven by President Reagan's single-minded pursuit of a judiciary packed with those who are his ideological allies," he argued. How unusual was the Bork confirmation process, and how can the defeat of the nomination be explained? Some historical perspective is essential to answer that question.

Judge Bork was the twenty-seventh presidential nominee to the Supreme Court who failed to win Senate confirmation. In addition to Bork, the nominations of eleven others had been formally rejected, while another fifteen nominations were withdrawn or never came to a vote because of lack of support. A large number of the unconfirmed nominations occurred with lame-duck presidents late in an administration, or who were simply weak politically. Opposition to these unsuccessful nominees was frequently based on their judicial philosophy, on ideological issues, or on purely political considerations. While the strategies and tactics in the case of Bork may have been more advanced, and Judge Bork had a larger published record to examine, the Bork nomination was similar to other cases.

President John Tyler holds the record of five unconfirmed nominations, but even the revered George Washington lost a Supreme Court nominee. In 1795, President Washington nominated John Rutledge of South Carolina, a former delegate to the Constitutional Convention and a former associate justice of the U.S. Supreme Court, to be chief justice. Political opposition to Rutledge, which proved decisive, centered on his outspoken criticism of the Jay Treaty with England. Presidents since Washington have argued that Congress should give the chief executive considerable leeway in appointments to the Court. But senators often remind presidents that in the original draft of the Constitution, it was the Senate, not the president, that nominated Supreme Court justices. They believe that the Founders clearly intended the Senate to play an active and meaningful role in confirmation. When significant opposition arises, the president must dig in and muster political resources just as in any other legislative battle with Congress.

Recent cases reflect controversy and politicized Supreme Court nominations. President Nixon had two consecutive nominations rejected by the Senate. In 1969, he nominated Clement Haynesworth, who was attacked by labor and civil rights groups. Ethical improprieties eventually combined with the policy opposition to doom the nomination. Nixon next nominated Harold G. Carswell. Critics pointed to Carswell's support of segregation early in his career and to his poor record in decisions overturned on appeal. In one of the most infamous lines in American politics, Nebraska Senator Roman Hruska admitted that Carswell was not a great legal mind, but he claimed that "mediocre people are entitled to representation too." Carswell was also rejected.

Republicans attacked Democratic nominees during the Johnson administration. In 1968, the lame-duck President Johnson nominated Associate Justice Abe Fortas as chief justice. Senator Strom Thurmond (a Judge Bork defender in 1987) led an attack against the liberal ideology and judicial philosophy of Fortas. Ethical questions were also raised. Opponents filibustered against the nomination, and supporters were unable to muster the votes to invoke cloture. Fortas finally asked the president to withdraw his name from nomination.

Racial and religious factors have occasionally been related to opposition to Supreme Court nominees. In 1967, conservative southerners opposed President Johnson's nomination of Thurgood Marshall, the first black named to the Court. Opponents claimed that Marshall would be too liberal, but a then politically stronger Johnson was able to win approval for Marshall. Fifty years earlier, when Woodrow Wilson nominated Louis Brandeis, the first Jewish justice, critics claimed that Brandeis had radical political views. Wilson, however, had enough political strength to win confirmation of Brandeis in 1916.

For two centuries, questions of judicial philosophy and political views have played a prominent role in battles over Supreme Court appointments. Most nominees win easy approval in the Senate, but in the case of nominees who are controversial—for whatever reason—the political standing of the president and his influence in Congress play a key role in whether the nominee is confirmed or defeated. Judge Bork was only the most recent nominee to learn this lesson. President Bush had an easier time gaining confirmation of his nominee, David Souter, in 1990, as Political Insight 16–1 reveals.

PEOPLE IN POLITICS

SUPREME COURT JUSTICE SANDRA DAY O'CONNOR

As the Supreme Court prepared to hear oral arguments in the controversial case of *Webster v. Reproductive Health Services* (1989), national attention focused on Justice Sandra Day O'Connor. Her views on abortion and the 1973 *Roe v. Wade* decision had never been completely clear to activists on either side. Through an accident of history, the first woman in two hundred years to serve on the U.S. Supreme Court was in a pivotal position to help decide the most controversial women's issue of the era.

The daughter of affluent sheep and cattle ranchers, Sandra Day was born in El Paso, Texas, in 1930 and grew up on a ranch in New Mexico. She studied economics and then law at Stanford University. At the age of 22, she graduated at the top of her law school class. In December 1952, she married fellow attorney John Jay O'Connor III. Anxious to start her career, she discovered that the blue-chip California law firms were not interested in hiring a woman, whatever her class rank. Disappointed but not discouraged, Sandra O'Connor became an attorney for San Mateo County before taking a position in Germany for three years.

O'Connor and her husband settled in Arizona upon their return, and she entered private practice. Although she had personally felt the discrimination against women, she was not an ardent feminist. In 1959, she took five years off to start her family and became the mother of three sons. She was president of her local Junior League and contributed many hours of volunteer work. When she returned to work in the mid-1960s, O'Connor became an assistant attorney general in Arizona. She was elected to the state senate in 1968, where she served for six years. During her tenure in the legislature, she voted several times to repeal the state's restrictive abortion laws, votes she would later disavow.

Her judicial career began in 1975, when she was named to the superior court in Arizona, where she made her reputation as a tough, hard-nosed judge. O'Connor was demanding and often unpopular. A 79-year-old former Arizona Supreme Court judge practicing before her was blasted by Judge O'Connor for sloppy work. She later recommended that he be disbarred. Over the next six years, she became known as a solid, conservative judge. But her career would take a meteoric rise soon after U.S. Supreme Court Justice Potter Stewart announced his retirement in 1981.

President Ronald Reagan wanted to make good on his campaign promise to appoint a judicial conservative and opponent of abortion. The political benefits of achieving those goals and naming the first woman to the Court was appealing to the president. It would undercut critics who felt the administration's anti-abortion position violated women's rights if its view was articulated by a woman. O'Connor reassured the administration that she found abortion offensive, and her nomination to the Court was announced by the White House. Those reassurances did not satisfy many anti-abortion activists, however. Picketers protesting her nomination and her votes in the Arizona Senate marched outside the building where her confirmation hearings were being held.

Her nomination was easily approved by the U.S. Senate, and O'Connor was sworn in as an associate justice. Throughout the 1980s, she generally sided with the conservatives on the Court but was not confronted with an opportunity to rule on the *Roe* decision until 1989. By then, she had been joined by two other Reagan appointees as the *Webster* case was heard. With Brennan, Marshall, Blackmun, and Stevens supporting the 1972 abortion decision and Rehnquist, White, Scalia, and Kennedy widely seen as opponents, O'Connor appeared to be the critical swing vote. She voted with the anti-abortion justices in allowing greater state restrictions on abortion in the *Webster* decision, but it was a narrow ruling. Attempting to find some middle ground, O'Connor did not join those arguing for the reversal of *Roe.* That difficult decision still awaited when and if the Court took a case that directly challenged the constitutionality of *Roe v. Wade.*

POLITICAL INSIGHT 16-1

THE NOMINATION OF DAVID SOUTER TO THE SUPREME COURT

A year and a half into his presidency, George Bush was presented the opportunity to make his first appointment to the U.S. Supreme Court. The resignation of Justice William Brennan in July of 1990 gave Bush a chance to strengthen the conservative majority on the Court by appointing a justice who shared the president's views. The bruising battle and eventual rejection of Robert Bork in 1987 was fresh in the memories of both the administration and the Senate. But Bush had already shown a tendency to appoint less ideological judges than Reagan had to lower federal court vacancies, and all had been confirmed by the Senate. He continued this approach in naming his choice for the high Court – Judge David H. Souter of New Hampshire.

Souter, a 50-year-old bachelor, was a judge on the U.S. Court of Appeals, having been confirmed by the Senate for that position only a few months earlier. Educated at Harvard and Oxford, Souter had served as Attorney General in New Hampshire and as a justice on the New Hampshire Supreme Court. He had lived in the same house in Weare, New Hampshire since he was 11. The quiet, reticent man who had not published widely was a stark contrast to the forceful and controversial Bork. As reporters and Senate staff scuried to investigate his background and views, he remained somewhat of a mystery. The question on the minds of most observers concerned his view on abortion. Would he be the crucial vote to overturn *Roe V. Wade?*

With Congress out of session in August, Souter and the administration had ample time to prepare for his confirmation hearings before the Senate Judiciary Committee. Chairman Joseph Biden opened hearings on September 13, 1990 and Souter testified for three days. His calm, low-key testimony was dissatisfying to some Senators who pressed Souter to be more specific on his views, but his approach was clearly successful.

Souter repeatedly refused to clarify his views on abortion, stating that it would be improper to indicate how he would rule without the specific facts of a case. This position was disappointing to activists on both sides of the abortion dispute. The National Abortion Rights' Action League (NARAL) came out against confirmation, fearing he would vote to overturn *Roe*. On the other side, Howard Phillips of the Conservative Caucus oppposed Souter because he had served as a trustee of a hospital that permitted abortions. After his testimony, neither side knew for sure how David Souter would rule on the abortion controversy. However, he had clearly made a positive impression on Republicans and Democrats alike, who praised his fairness and open-mindedness. Biden, despite lingering doubts, called Souter's testimony a "tour de force."

On September 27, the Judiciary Committee voted 13-1 to approve Souter and send the nomination to the full Senate. Only Senator Edward Kennedy voted against the nominee, fearing he would erode abortion rights. But other liberal Democrats who might have been expected to oppose his nomination voted to confirm Souter. Senator Howard Metzenbaum said that, despite some personal doubts, his instincts were that Souter was a fair jurist who understood the weight of responsibilities that confronted him. The nomination went to the full Senate on October 2 where the debate paralleled committee deliberations.

Eight Democratic senators joined Kennedy in opposing Souter, but Majority Leader George Mitchell argued that the nominee had demonstrated a reasoned approach and sound understanding of the Constitution. By a vote of 90-9, Souter was easily confirmed. Souter was sworn in as the 105th justice of the U.S. Supreme Court on October 9, and immediately took his seat to hear cases in the second week of the Court's 1990-91 term. Despite the intense scrutiny of the nomination and confirmation process, David H. Souter's future impact on law and public policy remained as uncertain to President George Bush as it did to rest of the country.

Appointment of Lower Federal Court Judges. Although federal district judges serve the national government, they are appointed from the states in which they reside. As a result, the president is less free to select candidates for the federal district and appeals courts judgeships. Patronage and parochial politics come into play. Lower court appointments are often considered the prerogative of the senator of the president's party in states where the vacancy occurs. Senators make specific recommendations to the president under a practice called **senatorial courtesy.** By mutual agreement, other senators may refuse to approve any judicial appointment if the relevant senator finds the nominee "personally obnoxious." In one famous case, President Kennedy was coerced into appointing a segregationist judge in Mississippi because the two Democratic senators would approve no other nominee.

Jimmy Carter found this process of senatorial courtesy itself "personally obnoxious." In the 1976 campaign, he pledged to make judicial appointments on merit. This was easier said than done. During Carter's administration, the Omnibus Judgeship Act of 1978 was passed. It created 152 new judgeships allowing Carter to appoint more federal judges than any other previous president.[11] At the appeals court level, Carter's merit system was used, but many senators balked at giving up senatorial courtesy, an important source of political patronage. Carter did not force senators to set up merit commissions, but a number of senators voluntarily complied with his request. Others refused. Although not a complete success, Carter's reforms of the judicial selection process had some impact on how senators choose their nominees.

The Reagan administration's judicial selection process was dominated by efforts to name ideological conservatives to the federal bench—a "one-pronged test" for federal judges.[12] Although supporting the merit panels developed by Carter, the Reagan administration showed its respect for senatorial courtesy by indicating its intention to consult with the appropriate Republican senators. The main criterion for selection, however, was ideology. Believing that Carter's appointments had skewed the lower courts, Reagan promised to appoint new judges attuned to "the groundswell of conservatism" evidenced by the 1980 and 1984 elections. Critics claimed that the Reagan administration was going far beyond any of Reagan's predecessors in trying to determine in advance potential nominees' views on specific issues.

The Bush administration took a much slower and purposeful approach to naming federal judges. By the end of his first year in office, President Bush had appointed only fifteen judges in total, about a third of the total that Reagan appointed in 1981.[13] This was also the lowest total number of judges named by a president in a single year in almost thirty years. In addition, the Bush administration did not seek to reshape the underlying philosophy of the federal bench as Reagan had. Members of both political parties criticized the slowness of the Bush administration because of growing backlogs of cases on court dockets around the country. Critics on the right lamented Bush's disinterest in seeking ideological conservatives for vacancies.

Bush also ran into problems within his own party over the issue of senatorial courtesy. The administration wanted to maintain some degree of merit in the appointment system by requiring home state senators to submit more than one name to the Justice Department when vacancies arose. The White House declined to nominate the choice of Senator James Jeffords (R-Vt.) to a judgeship in Vermont, finding his membership in an all-male club unacceptable. With the support of other Republican senators and a number of Democrats, Jeffords blocked action on several other pending nominees as a way to pressure the White House.

What is the judicial appointment process like from the nominee's point of view? First, the nominee must comply with all requests for information about past legal records, personal finances, and political activities and must fill out a pile of forms. (The FBI at the same time asks questions of the nominee's neighbors.) One candidate reported that it took him and his staff weeks to complete the questionnaires. Detailed inquiries include questions on the candidate's background, financial data, past cases, publications, health, and eyeglass prescription! Groups requesting information included the Senate Judiciary Committee (forty-nine pages), the Justice Department (forty-seven pages), the Federation of Women Lawyers, and several other civil rights and women's rights groups. The candidate then becomes a public figure. Interest groups and legislators may question past judicial decisions or other past actions while the candidate was in political life.

Selection of State Judges. Methods of selecting state judges vary from state to state. Some states allow the governor to appoint state judges, but most states use some form of election. Terms of judges vary from several years to life. Arkansas and Alabama directly elect their state judges. South Carolina and Virginia allow the legislature to elect the judges. California and Missouri developed compromise merit systems in the 1930s and 1940s to counter the objections to both election and appointment.[14] After an initial appointment for a brief period, each judge must receive voter approval to keep the job and to serve a longer term. Under both the California and the Missouri systems, the great majority of judges are retained. Nonetheless, each state provides some increased measure of protection against a bad appointment without subjecting judges to the same political pressures and constraints of direct election. Partisan politics can also come into play in the retention process. In California, Judge Rose Bird was not retained by voters after conservative groups spent huge sums in a statewide media blitz, publicizing her controversial rulings.

Removal of Judges. Federal judges, including justices of the Supreme Court, serve for life. They may be removed only by impeachment, following the same process as for the president. This power had been rarely used throughout history, with only eleven federal justices impeached and five removed from office through 1985.[15] Between 1986 and 1990, however, four time-consuming impeachment cases were considered by Congress. District judges Harry Claiborne of Nevada, Alcee Hastings of Florida, and Walter Nixon of Mississippi were impeached by the House, convicted by a two-thirds vote in the Senate, and removed from office. A fourth, Judge Robert Aguilar, faced racketeering charges. With so many demands on its time, Congress considered alternatives to impeachment, such as creating a national commission to study whether it should stay responsible for removing corrupt federal judges. There was sentiment in some quarters for a constitutional amendment to allow judicial panels rather than Congress to remove judges.[16]

In summary, the judicial system of the United States consists of courts in the fifty states that exist parallel to the federal courts. The two systems join only at the highest level—the Supreme Court of the United States. The workhorses of the court systems are the trial courts—the federal district courts and the state county courts. What happens inside the courtrooms? What do courts do, and how do they make policy?

The Judicial Process: Policy-Making in the Courts

What do the Courts Do?

Courts enforce the rules that society chooses to live by. In this way, courts serve as society's umpires or referees. This role of the courts is **norm enforcement,** a function performed in almost all organized societies and political systems.[17] In a primitive tribe, norm enforcement may be performed by the chief. In a dictatorship, the dictator may both make the rules and be the arbiter of whether they have been broken. In the system of separation of powers developed in the U.S. Constitution, an independent judiciary was established to enforce norms by applying statutory law and judicial precedents to a particular set of circumstances. Courts apply previously determined rules to the facts. If a woman slips on a snow-covered sidewalk and is injured because the sidewalk was not cleared, the owner is liable for damages under long-established rules and precedents. If a man burglarizes a house, he is liable under criminal law for the penalties prescribed. One of the important principles of norm enforcement is ***stare decisis,*** which is Latin for "let the decision stand." Courts normally are bound to follow both the statutes and precedents that have been established to deal with similar cases.

If courts only enforced norms, their role would not be controversial. But courts make new norms. They make policy. Problems brought before courts extend far beyond the scope of written statutes and judicial precedent. The judiciary has taken the lead in many of the most hotly debated policies of the current era. The Court made segregation illegal and ruled that schools must be integrated. It decided that legislative districts must be approximately equal in population. The Court ruled that prayer in public schools was in violation of the Constitution. It established rules and procedures for police in apprehending and arresting criminals, and it specified the rights of the accused. It established the right to abortion. The line between norm enforcement and policy-making is often a fine one, but clearly the courts do more than passively apply law and precedent to a set of facts.

Getting a Case to the Supreme Court

The Supreme Court is requested to hear almost five thousand cases a year, but the justices simply decline to review most of them. In the cases they do consider, the lower court decision is usually affirmed or reversed without further comment. Only a few hundred cases a year are really important—the cases that make judicial policy. Cases can get to the Supreme Court in three ways. First, cases can be heard by the Court through *certification*.[18] An unusual method, certification is the process by which the lower court asks the high court for technical instructions. Second, cases may come to the Court on a *writ of appeal*, in which the appellants argue their right to have the Court hear the case. The Court dismisses most of these because the federal question involved is not sufficient. Most cases come to the Supreme Court through a third method: a *writ of certiorari*, a request for the Court to "inform" or "make more certain" a lower court ruling. Under the "rule of four," four justices are needed to grant a writ of certiorari. Around 95 percent of the requests are denied by the Court.

Taking a case to the Supreme Court is an expensive proposition, but indigents may appeal to the Court under a petition, *in forma pauperis*. One of the most famous Court cases filed by a pauper was *Gideon v. Wainwright*, the decision that established the right of criminal defendants to have legal counsel even though they could not afford to hire their own attorney (see People in Politics Chapter 5). Interest groups play an important role getting cases to the courts. The National Association for the Advancement of Colored People (NAACP) was instrumental in bringing civil rights and school desegregation cases to the courts from the 1930s to the 1950s. Supreme Court Justice Thurgood Marshall was the NAACP's attorney in the *Brown* case in 1954. The American Civil Liberties Union takes up cases dealing with First Amendment freedoms, assuming the financial burden of court challenges for people who otherwise could not afford them.

To get a case to the Court, a person must have *standing* to sue: He or she must present a real issue (not a potential one) and must be able to show personal harm. "Standing" is a legal concept used to limit the cases that can get to Court. Recall from the "Political Close-up" at the beginning of this chapter Justice Rehnquist's argument that the plaintiffs in the *Roe* case did not have standing to sue. The majority in that case disagreed. When a large number of people are affected, they can benefit from a suit without actually going to court. **Class action suits** are cases brought on behalf of all people in similar circumstances. The suit leading to the 1954 *Brown* decision was brought on behalf of all black children in schools segregated by law. Consumer groups have been major users of class action suits against manufacturers of defective or unsafe products. However, a tremendous increase in class action suits in the 1960s led the Court to tighten rules governing these cases. In 1974, the Court declared it would not hear cases unless every member of the "class" had been notified of the case. This action made it more difficult and expensive to pursue class action suits, which as a result have declined in the last decade.

Trials in the Supreme Court

The Supreme Court Building is an impressive marble structure located behind the U.S. Capitol, a stone symbol of American justice. Number One, First Street, S.E., has two immense bronze doors (weighing 13,000 pounds) over which are inscribed the famous words "Equal Justice Under Law." Inside the building are the offices of the justices and their clerks and staff, and the courtroom itself. The impressive courtroom has a forty-four-foot dome supported by twenty-four marble columns.[19] Court sessions run from October to June, during which time the Court usually convenes three days a week for four hours a day. The justices sit at the bench in front of a thick, purple curtain. When the session is to begin, the curtain parts and the justices march in clad in their traditional black robes, the Chief Justice first, followed by the associate justices in order of seniority. All stand. "Oyez, Oyez," bellows the clerk. Justices take their places around the chief justice, again in order of seniority.

Before they hear a case, the justices read written briefs, which summarize the history, precedents, facts, and legal arguments of the case. The Court convenes to hear oral arguments, in which the attorneys summarize their case and the justices typically ask questions, often interrupting and grilling the lawyers on a key point. Occasionally oral arguments can be important. Justice William O. Douglas claimed that "oral arguments win or lose the case."[20] In the oral presentations, issues not addressed in the briefs may be discovered, or new perspectives may be gained. During the Court sessions, the U.S. government's lawyer—the solicitor general—is present. The third-ranking official at the Justice Department, the solicitor general is usually a distinguished attorney, often a law professor.

MAKING DECISIONS: COURT POLITICS

Like legislators, justices have records and established positions on issues. Because each set of circumstances is different, justices are theoretically open-minded about their positions. In reality, many justices are relatively predictable. Former Justice Hugo Black held an "absolutist" interpretation of the free speech clause of the First Amendment (see his remarks in Chapter 5, Political Insight 5–2). When a free speech case came before the Supreme Court, it was a near certainty that Black would vote to deny any limits on free speech, even if the subject was unpopular (such as pornography). Chief Justice William Rehnquist, in contrast, has a consistent record for allowing restrictions in free expression cases.

The justices meet in conference to discuss, deliberate, and ultimately to render a decision. Because a key decision was leaked to the press some years ago, not even clerks or secretaries are allowed to join the nine justices in their conference room deliberations. The process is very political. One justice may cautiously attempt to determine the other justices' positions before a tentative vote is taken. Subtle attempts are sometimes made to sway the opinion of others, but most justices jealously guard their independence. On particularly controversial decisions, the chief justice may work to build a unanimous decision or at least a large majority. In Supreme Court politics, a 5-to-4 decision is unsatisfying. It leaves considerable doubt in the minds of the plaintiff, the defendant, the legal community, and the nation.

Discussion of the case proceeds from the chief justice down through the associate justices in order of seniority. When a tentative vote is taken, however, progression is in the other direction, with the chief voting last. If the chief justice is on the majority side, he or she has the right to designate which justice will draft the opinion. If he is in the minority, the most senior justice on the majority has the right to make the assignment. Not until several drafts of the opinion have been discussed and a final draft is agreed on is a final vote taken. Even though a justice may be on the prevailing side, he or she may not completely agree with the reasons for the decision given in the opinion. In this case, a *concurring opinion* may be added to the decision. Justices who oppose the majority have the right to file a *dissenting opinion,* or they may choose simply to vote against the majority opinion. Several justices may jointly submit a dissenting opinion or may write separate dissenting opinions if they are opposed for different reasons.

Landmark decisions need convincing majorities. It is in the Court's interest to have as much agreement as possible to establish the legitimacy of a decision. In the case of *Nixon v. U.S.* (1974), the justices felt it was particularly essential to have a unanimous decision to force the president to relinquish the Watergate tapes. Some 170 years after *Marbury v. Madison,* the Supreme Court was still concerned about its power and the possibility of being ignored by the president.

The Supreme Court announces its decisions in public session. When the Court sets the date for delivering the most critical decisions, the public, the parties in the case, and the press wait in anxious anticipation.

Chief Justice William Rehnquist is the first among equals and has an important influence on court politics and policy decisions.

Governing Through the Courts

CHARACTERISTICS OF JUDICIAL POLICIES

Judicial policy-making does not consider all dimensions of public policy equally.[21] Foreign policy questions, for example, are rarely taken up in a court of law. During the height of controversy over the Vietnam War, the Supreme Court consistently refused to hear cases that would require it to rule on the constitutionality of the war. With few exceptions, the Court rarely becomes involved with taxing and spending decisions. Much of the Court's policy-making in recent decades has focused on individual freedoms and the regulatory activities of government.

Judicial policies are often ambiguous.[22] Because the courts rule on the facts of a specific case, their opinions often leave many unanswered questions about the complete scope and application of the decision. Judicial decisions are often unsatisfactory, raising as many new questions as they answer. Ambiguity is inherent in the judicial process and to some extent distinguishes courts from legislatures. Although judges might want to make policies that are broad in scope, their ability to govern is restricted to ruling on the facts at hand. As a result, it often takes a number of cases with differing situations before the broad outline of a policy becomes clear.

Vagaries of Supreme Court policy-making are exemplified in the death penalty controversies of the 1970s.[23] The Court ruled in 1972 in the case of *Furman v. Georgia* that state death penalty statutes were unconstitutional as written. But the 5-to-4 decision itself presented several contrary views to the state legislators trying to redraft their death penalty statutes. Only two of the five justices (Brennan and Marshall) in the majority ruled that the death penalty per se was unconstitutional. The other three (Douglas, Stewart, and White) found the statutes defective because they allowed unlimited discretion in the imposition of the death penalty. Each wrote a separate opinion. The dissenters (Burger, Blackmun, Powell, and Rehnquist) argued for judicial restraint and deference to the state legislatures. They pointed out to the states that the majority ruling did not prevent capital punishment for specific crimes. Thirty-five states rewrote their statutes in an attempt to conform to the mixed messages of *Furman.*

Four years later, the Court once again reviewed a number of death penalty statutes. In *Gregg v.*

Georgia (1976) and related cases, the Court ruled that Georgia, Florida, and Texas now had constitutional death penalties. Marshall and Brennan reaffirmed the view taken in *Furman* that the death penalty was a cruel and unusual punishment and therefore unconstitutional. Douglas, Stewart, and White joined the four dissenters in *Furman* to create a 7-to-2 majority. At the same time, however, the Court ruled that Louisiana and North Carolina did not have constitutional statutes because their mandatory death penalty laws allowed no discretion at all. Questions persisted, and the Court was forced to clarify its stand on discretion versus mandatory sentencing the next year. In *Harry Roberts v. Louisiana* (1977), the Court ruled in a 5-to-4 decision that while unlimited discretion is unacceptable, mandatory death sentence laws must allow mitigating and aggravating circumstances to be taken into account. Once again the majority changed because of individual justices' views of the facts and the Constitution. The message seemed to be that the Court wanted "guided discretion" but under rules that eliminated arbitrariness and capriciousness.

The confusion over the death penalty cases reveals key characteristics of judicial decisions. Although the Supreme Court attempts to clarify constitutional bounds to other political actors, it does not speak with a single voice. Unlike Congress, the justices do not have to agree on the language of a single bill. A majority of justices need only agree on a decision. They work with a given set of facts rather than a broad range of possibilities. The Court does not give advisory opinions. Death penalty statutes must be enacted into law before they can be reviewed. The justices tried to indicate what kind of death penalty statute would be constitutional, but they could not draft a model.

Despite *stare decisis* and past precedents, courts are free to overrule past decisions. The Court has overruled its own decisions more than 150 times.[24] The Court is a political as well as a legal institution, subject to changing times and social mores. In *Colegrove v. Green* (1947), the Court ruled that malapportionment of legislatures was a political question that the courts could not touch. Fifteen years later, after virtually no progress by state legislatures in solving their own apportionment problems, the Court reversed itself and established the principle of "one person, one vote" in *Baker v. Carr* (1962). The separate-but-equal doctrine stood for fifty-eight years until the Court reversed itself in the *Brown* decision of 1954. Knowing the Court can reverse itself, groups hoping to overturn the Court's position in a close decision may engage in a flurry of lobbying efforts and litigation. Opponents of abortion devoted many of their efforts to overturning the 1972 *Roe* decision and seemed to be getting closer after the 1989 *Webster* decision.

The ability of the courts to govern is also limited because judicial decisions are not self-enforcing. Courts depend on the support of other institutions to implement their decisions. Although most decisions are complied with, the process can take many decades, as have the desegregation decisions.[25] Court decisions are often intertwined with policymaking in Congress and in the executive branch, as well as in state governments. Legislation and bureaucratic rule-making may follow a court decision, which in turn may result in another court case.

Although the focus of courts is limited to certain policy areas and the decisions are often restricted in scope, the remedies prescribed by courts can be sweeping. The nature of judicial remedies has been one of the most controversial aspects of the courts in recent decades. When courts rule, for example, that overcrowded prisons constitute cruel and unusual punishment, the financial effect on state and local government can be staggering. Officials have been confronted with the choice of building expensive new prisons or simply letting criminals go free. Federal court decisions have mandated the merger of school districts and a tax increase for some of the citizens in the new district. A federal judge has taken over a school district, and another has run a large corporation that has been placed in receivership. The outcome of an election can be overturned by a court and a new election ordered. Many people are affected by the willingness of courts to mandate sweeping remedies—and many complain.

JUDICIAL ACTIVISM: ARE COURTS TOO POWERFUL?

Opponents of controversial court decisions accuse the courts of legislating. In recent years, the courts have occasionally stepped in where the legislative and executive branches have failed to act on the most divisive political issues. Yet judicial activism has strong supporters. Proponents argue that only the courts are free enough of political influence to guarantee the rights of the poor and the relatively powerless in society. They note that courts step in only when a relevant case is brought to them after the other branches have been unwilling to act. Opponents of judicial activism criticize the lack of expertise that judges and lawyers have on so many diverse and complex social issues. Opponents resent the fact that judges are appointed, not elected, and therefore immune to popular control. They assail the courts as the least democratic institutions in the U.S. political system.

Judicial activism can be understood partly as a reaction to the problem of governing in legislative and executive institutions. Weak parties, strong interest groups, a fragmented Congress, and limits to presidential leadership often result in stalemate. Policy-making in many areas is controlled by subgovernments—bargaining among a small group of self-interested participants. Vagueness in legislation and increased delegation of authority have increased not only the power of the bureaucracy but also the power of the courts. As government has attacked problems on more and more fronts, a greater need has arisen for clarification and amplification. The result is an enhanced role for the courts.

IS JUDICIAL SELF-RESTRAINT ENOUGH?

Although courts are limited to dealing with cases that are brought to them, the rapid expansion of litigation is reducing the viability of this check. The Supreme Court already hears only a small fraction of the cases requesting review and has an increasingly large number of issues to consider. Perhaps the most important check on the Court is *judicial self-restraint,* which limits the cases it considers.[26] Before a case can be taken up by the Court, standing to sue and the existence of a real controversy must be demonstrated. All remedies in lower courts must have been exhausted. The federal question in the case must be substantial, and the complaint must address the specific provision of the Constitution that is in question. Only questions of law, not fact, are normally the basis for review. The Court still endorses the view that political questions should be left to the legislature. If a law is found to be unconstitutional, the Court will attempt to limit its finding to a very specific section of the law. Finally, the Court operates under the principle that "bad" legislation is not necessarily unconstitutional.

Although less direct and visible, public opinion and politics influence the Court as well as the other institutions of national government.

Is judicial self-restraint enough? Have the self-imposed limits on the Supreme Court's policy-making provided an adequate check on the autonomous exercise of power? The Court in the 1980s and 1990s appears to be taking an activist stance on many issues. The shift to the right reflects the slow but sure process of political response. Although justices are insulated from direct political pressure, the Court does respond to public opinion and the actions of the other branches. Political scientist Robert Dahl concluded that although a time lag of as much as a decade or two may exist, court decisions tend to conform with majority sentiment over time.[27] Congress and the states can check the Supreme Court by amending the Constitution as was done after the *Dred Scott* decision and the ruling that the progressive income tax was unconstitutional. In recent years, the abortion and school prayer decisions have attracted the most congressional attention in proposed constitutional amendments.

Constitutional amendment is the ultimate check on the ability of the Supreme Court to govern, but it is extremely difficult to accomplish. The Founders wanted an independent judiciary and also one that was checked and balanced through separation of powers. They made sure the amendment process was difficult and would not be used every time some political faction was unhappy. Amendment is a last resort—a final safeguard if courts abuse their power and decisions stray too far from the national sentiment.

Assessing the Courts: Problems and Prospects

Has the United States Become Too Litigious?

Webster defines "litigious" as "contentious, prone to lawsuits." Get a lawyer and sue! Has this become the public philosophy? The number of cases filed in federal court continues to climb, and hundreds of thousands of cases are filed at the state level. People sue over an amazingly wide variety of matters. A few years ago, fans of the Philadelphia Eagles football team filed suit, claiming that the owners fraudulently claimed the team was "professional" and provided "entertainment." A college student in Connecticut filed suit against a professor and university claiming that she did not learn anything and had been defrauded of her tuition! Entertainer Johnny Carson sued his neighbors over dog poop on his lawn. Other suits have wider application. In the late 1960s, baseball player Curt Flood of the St. Louis Cardinals challenged the reserve clause, which bound a player to a certain club. Flood lost, but within a few years, subsequent decisions revolutionized sports contracts and led to free agency and multimillion-dollar salaries. Cases like the one involving actor Lee Marvin created "palimony"—the rights of live-in but unmarried partners to assets and support. Malpractice suits have changed the practice of medicine as cautious doctors look over their shoulders at potential liability.

A hallmark of the American judicial system is equal justice under the law. Changes in the last three decades have moved toward more equal *access* to the justice system. It is easier to get to court. Also, more lawyers are available than ever—ten times more per capita in the United States than in France! Is the litigation explosion the fault of the lawyers? Partly, but if the U.S. justice system is being severely challenged, it is also the result of changes by the public, insurance companies, business, and judges. American society has a strong individualist tradition. Litigation, particularly suits against the government, are one expression of that individualism. In addition, the growth of public interest law in the 1960s opened new avenues for the achievement of political goals through the courts by environmentalists, consumer groups, the handicapped, women's rights groups, and other new forces in politics, balancing the courts' use by corporations and other established political interest groups that had existed for years. Greater equality of access to the judicial system may have resulted in excess litigation, but what are unnecessary or nuisance suits for one party are the route to social justice for another.

The court system in the United States is overloaded at all levels. With the increase of lawsuits and more aggressive prosecutions in the war on drugs, dockets are backlogged and swamped with cases. Drug cases represent more than 26 percent of new filings and up to 60 percent in some courts.[28] Cases filed in federal districts courts nearly tripled in the last twenty years, to 280,000 per year. Cases in the appeals courts have quadrupled, while the average case load per judge has doubled. Congress has not approved the creation of new judgeships since 1984, although pressure is mounting. The backlog of cases in the court system has made President Bush's slow pace of filling vacancies subject to even more criticism.

PUBLIC EVALUATIONS OF THE COURT SYSTEM

Judicial activism has made the courts controversial. Permissiveness by the courts is cited by 53 percent of Americans as one of the major causes of the country's problems.[29] More than 90 percent of all respondents believe improvements in administering justice are needed. Of this group, 51 percent believe the system is fundamentally unsound and needs many improvements or a complete over-haul. When the questions concern criminal courts, disapproval is even sharper. Two-thirds are dissatisfied with the way criminal courts are doing their job. In a recent survey, some 83 percent felt that courts were too easy in dealing with criminals, up from 52 percent fifteen years earlier. The public supports reforms to toughen up the system—limit bail, reduce protections of defendants, eliminate the insanity defense. The American public is concerned about the viability of the justice system, and a remarkable consensus of opinion exists that courts have been too soft on criminals and are not doing their job.

Yet the public does not blame the judges.[30] Despite the low evaluation of criminal courts, judges remain among the most respected members of our society, significantly ahead of executive-branch cabinet officers and senators and representatives (see Figure 16–3). The public believes judges are more likely to act in the public interest than any other group.

FIGURE 16–3

JUDGES REMAIN HIGHLY TRUSTED

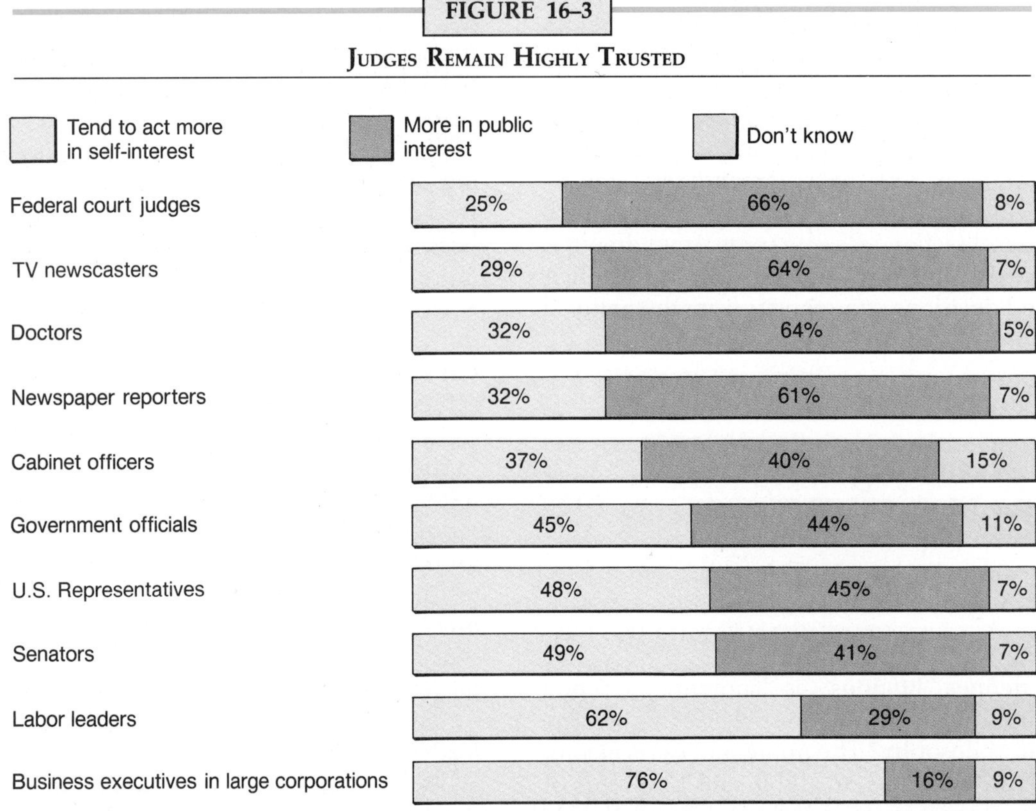

SOURCE: Survey by the Roper Organization (Roper Report 81-8). August 15-22, 1981. Reported in ***Public Opinion,*** August-September 1982, p. 25. Reprinted with permission of American Enterprise Institute for Public Policy Research.

SUMMARY AND CONCLUSIONS

1. The power of the Supreme Court was enhanced early in U.S. history by the assertive leadership of Chief Justice John Marshall, who established judicial review in the case of *Marbury v. Madison* (1803).
2. The substantive focus of the Supreme Court has shifted from concern with the power of the national government through economic due process to concern with individual rights. Judicial activism has varied over time, alternately conservative and liberal in different periods.
3. The judicial establishment in the United States consists of a dual system of state and federal courts made up of trial courts and appellate courts and headed by the U.S. Supreme Court.
4. Federal judges are appointed by the president. Although presidents have discretion in naming members of the Supreme Court, senatorial courtesy gives U.S. senators of the president's party considerable influence over the selection of federal district judges.
5. The main purpose of the courts is norm enforcement—the application of existing law and precedent to particular situations—but they also make important new policies through their decisions.
6. Few cases make it up the judicial ladder to the Supreme Court. Those that do must meet both legal and constitutional criteria. The Court's decisions attempt to balance political interests and protect the Constitution.
7. The ability of the Court to govern is limited by its inability to initiate actions, by self-restraint, and by precedents and legal principles. Nonetheless, the Court has become more active, more powerful, and more involved in political questions, acting when the other branches have been unable to do so.
8. The American public is highly critical of the justice system, especially its perceived permissiveness. However, people still have more faith in the credibility of judges than in any other participants in the political process.

Many problems face the American judiciary. From unpopular decisions of the Supreme Court to the crowded dockets of the criminal courts, people have serious questions about the performance of the courts. Too often assessments of the role and the performance of the Supreme Court are based on current policy preferences. People who see its decisions favorably praise the Court for taking on the tough issues. People who oppose its decisions criticize the Court for being activist, elitist, or undemocratic. A more consistent, balanced view of the role of the Court is needed.

Courts are political. Over time, presidential appointments can change the philosophy of justices and judges and lead to new policy directions. The result is a measure of responsiveness, however slow. The challenge for the courts is to maintain both governing ability and accountability, remaining responsive yet able to take controversial policy actions when government is otherwise paralyzed.

KEY TERMS

appellate jurisdiction
Robert H. Bork
class action suits
constitutional courts
dual court system
judicial review
legislative courts
Marbury v. Madison
norm enforcement
original jurisdiction
William Rehnquist
senatorial courtesy
David Souter
stare decisis

SELF-REVIEW

1. How was judicial review established?
2. Describe the evolution of the powers and focus of the Supreme Court since Marshall.
3. What is the dual court system?
4. Describe the courts in the federal judiciary.
5. What is the jurisdiction of the federal courts?
6. What is norm enforcement?
7. How do the courts make policy?
8. What are the three ways a case can get to the Supreme Court?
9. What is the procedure for trying cases before the Supreme Court? For deciding cases?
10. Why are judicial decisions often ambiguous?
11. What checks exist on the power of the courts?
12. How does the public evaluate the court system?

SUGGESTED READINGS

Abraham, Henry J. *The Judiciary: The Supreme Court in the Governmental Process.* 1983.
A clear and concise summary of the Court in national politics.

Frank, Jerome. *Courts on Trial.* New York: Atheneum. 1967.
Written in 1949, this extremely bright and insightful look at the court system by a federal judge is still relevant.

Goldman, Sheldon, and Thomas P. Jahnige. *The Federal Courts as a Political System.* 1985.
A readable analysis of courts as legal and political institutions.

Schmidhauser, John. *Judges and Justices: The Federal Appellate Judiciary.* 1978.
An examination of federal judges on the appeals courts and how they operate.

NOTES

1. Edward S. Corwin, "The Constitution as Instrument and Symbol," *American Political Science Review,* December 1936, p. 1078.
2. Charles S. Hyneman and George W. Carey, *A Second Federalist* (New York: Appleton-Century-Crofts, 1967), 186–87.
3. *New York Times,* 5 August 1984, p. 1.
4. *Wall Street Journal* 26 June 1987, p. 40.
5. Henry J. Abraham, *The Judiciary: The Supreme Court in the Governmental Process* (Boston: Allyn and Bacon, 1983), 5–6.
6. Ibid., 7.
7. *Congressional Quarterly Weekly Reports,* 6 January 1990, p. 38.
8. See John Schmidhauser, *Judges and Justices: The Federal Appellate Judiciary* (Boston: Little, Brown, 1978), 95–98.
9. See C. Neal Tate, "Personal Attribute Models of the Voting Behavior of U.S. Supreme Court Justices," *American Political Science Review* 75 (1981).
10. Herbert Jacob, *Justice in America* (Boston: Little, Brown, 1978), 102–4.
11. Sheldon Goldman, "Carter's Judicial Appointments: A Lasting Legacy," *Judicature* 64 (1981):344.
12. Stuart Taylor, Jr., "The One-Pronged Test for Federal Judges," *New York Times,* 22 April 1984, p. E5.
13. *Congressional Quarterly Weekly Reports,* 6 January 1990, p. 38.
14. Jacob, *Justice,* 103.
15. Henry J. Abraham, *The Judicial Process: An Introductory Analysis of the Courts of the United States, England, and France* (New York: Oxford University Press, 1980), 45–49.
16. *Congressional Quarterly Weekly Reports,* 3 March 1990, p. 663.
17. Jacob, *Justice,* 23.
18. Abraham, *Judiciary,* 25.
19. Abraham, *Judicial Process,* 200–201.
20. *Philadelphia Inquirer,* 9 April 1963, p. 3., cited in Abraham, *The Judiciary,* 34.
21. Jacob, *Justice,* 39.
22. Ibid., 40.
23. See Lucius Barker and Twiley Barker, *Civil Liberties and the Constitution* (Englewood Cliffs, N.J.: Prentice-Hall, 1982), 307–11.
24. A. P. Blaustein and A. H. Field, "Overruling Opinions in the Supreme Court," *Michigan Law Review* 47 (1958):151.
25. Laurence Baum, *The Supreme Court* (Washington, D.C.: Congressional Quarterly Press, 1981), 181–2.
26. Abraham, *Judicial Process,* 373–97.
27. Robert Dahl, "Decision-Making in a Democracy: The Supreme Court as a National Policy-Maker," *Journal of Public Law* 6 (1958): 279–295.
28. *Congressional Quarterly Weekly Reports,* 6 January 1990, p. 42.
29. *Public Opinion,* August–September 1982, p. 24.
30. Ibid., 25.

USA

SECTION FOUR

Public Policies

This final section of the text considers the results of politics: public policies and their impacts. The test of governing is whether a political system is able to produce timely, responsive policies that solve public problems. In this section, we examine the most important policies and issues in American politics today. Chapter 17 looks at the budget, which is rapidly becoming the most important policy process in national government. First, the politics of the budget are reviewed, showing how the complex parts of government come together to set national priorities. Next, the policy issues in the budget are considered—the deficit dilemma, social spending, defense spending, and taxes. Chapter 18, on economic, energy, and environmental policies, considers the fiscal decisions contained in the budget. In addition to fiscal policy, the chapter explores monetary policy, trade policy, and the issues of energy and the environment. The lack of integration of these attempts to promote national prosperity is a prominent feature of economic policy-making. Chapter 19 explores the dilemma of poverty and social welfare policy, tracing the nation's programs back to the 1930s and discussing the sharp controversies over the impact of the "war on poverty" and the future of Social Security and Medicare. Chapter 20 examines U.S. foreign policy and national defense, beginning with the emergence of the Cold War after World War II and the resulting containment doctrine, which dominated foreign policy until the remarkable changes in Eastern Europe and the Soviet Union. The chapter concludes with current issues in national defense, including the military cutbacks and the peace dividend. The question of the ability to govern and the proper role of Congress and the president in foreign policy and defense provides familiar ground on which to conclude the discussion.

CHAPTER 17

The Federal Budget: The Politics of Taxing and Spending

POLITICAL CLOSE-UP

The 1990 Budget Summit Agreement: "Demonstrating The Will to Govern or Inheriting A Political Turkey?"

After five months of intense negotiations, a small group of White House and congressional leaders reached a tentative budget agreement on September 30, 1990. It was sent to Congress where it received a rude reception. Much of the debate centered on the need to get something passed to keep the country running versus the vehement complaints of both liberal and conservative critics about the specifics of the plan. The following excerpts from the House debate over the proposal took place shortly before it was defeated.

Mr. Traficant (D - OH): But do you know what gets me, Mr. Speaker? The new twist, and this is a real good one, "Call your Congressmen and get them to support this tax. America needs it." Well, they called me—they're still against it.

Count me out. Count me out. We have had TEFRA, ATRA, COBRA,

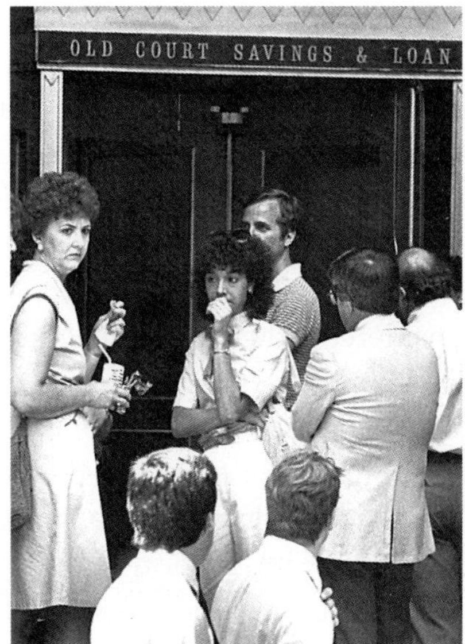

OEFRA, AMRA, All taxes, none vetoed, and now we have UTRO, the Ultimate Tax Rip-off of 1990 Act. I am not for it. Period. And everyone should figure it out. When a bottle of Mogen David wine and Ripple is taxed the same as a $5,000 bottle of champagne, something is wrong.

There is not a cancer in America, there is an elephant pickng our pocket, and he's not even wearing sunglasses anymore. Think about that.

Mr. Clinger (R – PA): Mr. Speaker, this budget crisis reminds me of an old Tarzan movie. At some point in the movie drums would begin to beat meaning the natives were restless.

If you listen you can hear the drums begin to beat outside the beltway.

There is not much that is lovable in this package but the drums I am beginning to hear are saying: "What's wrong with you people? You can't do the most fundamental thing we expect you to do—set the spending priorities of the Nation. Why should we rehire you?" And they are right. So I am going to vote for this agreement because the alternative is worse and I do not just mean sequestration. In my mind failure to pass the budget is an admission of failure—an admission that we do not have the political will to govern.

Mr. Ravenal (R – SC): Mr. Speaker, this morning I went to a meeting, and I was given a copy of an article that appeared yesterday in the Wall Street Journal prepared by the Joint Tax Committee of Congress. What it shows is that the poorest Americans are going to pay in this budget summit agreement, if it is passed, better that three times the amount of increased taxes as the average taxpayer.

Mr. Speaker, this old boy from South Carolina has been in politics for

40 years, and I want to say to my colleagues, Mr. Speaker, that anybody that votes for something like that, with this budget summit agreement, is going to inherit a political turkey that is going to hang around his or her neck for the rest of their political life, and I am not going to do it.

MR. HOUGHTON (R – NY): Mr. Speaker, we are talking about the budget, and it is so easy to criticize anything. Everybody has his own agenda. I can cite for my colleagues figures upon figures which will say this is a terrible deal.

However, as my collegues know, Harry Truman once said that any jackass can kick down a barn. It takes a carpenter to build one.

From the business standpoint there are three things which can be done: Accept this budget, do nothing, or go into sequester. And, if we go into sequester, the shock waves that this will have on our economy, already on the verge of a recession because of the oil problem, are going to be enormous.

Mr. Speaker, I think the Lord Himself could come down and propose a budget, and it would be hacked to pieces within half an hour around here.

The American people want action. They have it in the form of this budget. We ought to enact it.

SOURCE: *Congressional Record,* Wednesday, October 3, 1990, no. 127, H8707 – H8711.

CHAPTER OUTLINE

INTRODUCTION AND OVERVIEW

Peter Finley Dunn's famous Mr. Dooley once quipped, "Those buckos are talkin' economics but they're thinkin' politics," an apt description of Congress and the president trying to make decisions about the federal budget. In recent decades, the budget has embodied the most critical public policy choices facing the nation. The budget is an accounting of the nation's finances—where the money comes from and what it is spent on, who pays and who benefits. It is a statement of national priorities determining how much is spent on Social Security, national defense, AIDS research, health care, education, the arts, agriculture, the war against drugs, transportation, and literally thousands of other national programs. The federal budget also accounts how these programs are paid for, through income taxes, payroll taxes, corporate taxes, excise taxes, or borrowing.

Since 1981, the budget has become the nation's most difficult test of governing ability. Recurring stalemate, confrontation between executive and legislative branches, and eleventh-hour compromises that neither side is happy with have become hallmarks of the budget process. Budgeting has come to dominate policy-making while sharply dividing the political parties. A decade of brinkmanship between Congress and the president brought chronic deficits that required massive borrowing to pay the bills. The resulting numbers are staggering. The national debt tripled from around one trillion dollars to three trillion dollars between 1980 and 1990, requiring interest payments alone of $185 billion per year. The consequences for the future prosperity of the U.S. economy remain uncertain but worrisome.

Perhaps most seriously, the governing crisis over budgeting produced outcomes that no one claimed to want or would take responsibility for. Both parties and both branches decried the deficits. Congress blamed the president, and presidents blamed the Congress, leaving citizens confused and disillusioned. As the opening Political Close-up showed, the budget process is partisan and politicized. Too often each branch pursues its own budget process, followed by confrontation and deadlock, necessitating high-level summits between Congress and the administration to keep the government running.

This chapter examines the federal budget and the budget process. While budgeting may at times seem boring and technical, it boils down to the basic institutions and processes of governing. While deadlock and delay over such issues as campaign finance reform may be unfortunate, budget decisions must be made every year for government to function. To help understand the federal budget and how it is determined, this chapter explores the following questions:

1. How has budgeting evolved into the governing crisis that has dominated the 1980s and early 1990s?
2. What policy choices are contained in the budget? What is the annual cycle of budgeting?
3. How are budgets assembled in the executive branch? What is the role of the president, the Office of Management and Budget, and the agencies and departments?
4. What does Congress do with the president's budget when it is received? How does the congressional budget process attempt to coordinate decisions on the whole budget with decisions on its many parts?
5. What are the major outlays in the budget, the sources of federal revenues, and the issues surrounding the control of deficits?

The Evolution of a Budget Crisis

THE SHIFTING POWER OF THE PURSE

Taxing and spending decisions and who will make them have been controversial since the Constitutional Convention. The Founders very carefully entrusted the power of the purse to Congress, requiring all taxing and spending bills to originate in the popularly elected House of Representatives. For over a century, executive branch agencies sent their requests for funds directly to Congress. By the beginning of the twentieth century, the old system of running the government's finances was clearly outdated. Government programs and activities grew, and there were mounting concerns over how to manage the executive branch. The result was the passage of the **Budget and Accounting Act** of 1921, which created a national budget to be submitted by the president and the Bureau of the Budget (BOB) to assist the president.[1]

The national budget helped swing the balance of budgetary power from Congress toward the president. The shift was even more pronounced in the 1930s and 1940s, when government expanded and the BOB became part of the presidency. As Congress's appropriations committees continued to examine the budget in the old way—agency by agency—presidents became more concerned with budget totals. In the 1950s and 1960s, budget issues became increasingly important, encompassing controversial taxation issues and competing spending needs. Conflict between the branches increased as presidents attacked Congress for overspending and deficit spending. Congress felt its influence slipping, and some members feared losing their constitutional power of the purse altogether.

Budgeting was a favorite target for reform in both legislative and executive branches. Presidents tried to make reforms to improve planning and management. President Johnson tried a planning-programming-budgeting system (PPB). President Nixon implemented a system called management by objective (MBO) and changed the BOB into the Office of Management and Budget (OMB).[2] Jimmy Carter instituted zero-based budgeting (ZBB). But critics dismissed these reforms as bureaucratic "alphabet soup" that had little impact on curbing spending or keeping the budget in balance.

The most critical reform was taken by Congress in a dramatic effort to restore its influence in budgeting. The Budget and Impoundment Control Act of 1974 was specifically intended to curb the president's power and to create a new, more responsible budget process in Congress. This act created new budget committees, a budget timetable, and the Congressional Budget Office (CBO) to provide budget and economic information. Congress, too, could now consider taxing and spending as a whole, rather than on a piecemeal basis.

FROM BLITZKRIEG TO STALEMATE

The full impact of the congressional budget reforms was not felt until 1981, when President Reagan convinced majorities in both houses to adopt his economic and budget plan. Using congressional budget procedures such as budget resolutions and reconciliation (see below), a White House media blitz, and effective lobbying, the administration prevailed. Taxes were slashed by 25 percent over three years, domestic spending and entitlements were cut, and a trillion-dollar-plus defense buildup was begun. The president was able to prevail over the objections of most congressional Democrats. But this was but one year's battle in what would become a prolonged budget war of attrition.

By late 1981, the economy was sinking into recession, lowering government revenues while mandatory spending was automatically expanding. In addition, the changes made in 1981 did not balance out; spending cuts in domestic programs did not nearly compensate for the major tax cuts

President Reagan promised to prune federal spending.

and the defense buildup. The result was the highest budget deficits in peacetime history. The U.S. government was spending $200 billion a year more than it collected in taxes, resulting in massive borrowing. The deficits paralyzed the budget process. Congress refused to accept domestic spending cuts. President Reagan refused to consider raising taxes or slowing the defense buildup. The two branches deadlocked as crucial deadlines were missed. Budget summits sometimes produced agreements but failed to solve underlying problems. In 1985, the Balanced Budget Act, commonly known as the Gramm-Rudman-Hollings law, was enacted to break the political gridlock. Deficits were reduced to the $150-billion range but persisted into the Bush administration.

After two hundred years, the balance of budgetary power between Congress and the president has created a recurring governing crisis. Neither branch can resolve underlying conflicts by itself. Checks and balances prevent one side from imposing its will on the other. At the very time that the U.S. economy faces growing pressures to increase international competitiveness, the political system seems unable to make effective fiscal and budget policies. Let us look in more detail at how budgets are made and what choices they contain.

The Budget Process

Macrobudgeting versus Microbudgeting

Budgets contain literally thousands of decisions, from the great to the miniscule and from the very general to the very specific. Compare wide-ranging decisions, such as how much to spend on defense, with such minor decisions as how many stenographers an agency may hire. **Macrobudgeting** involves high-level decisions on spending, taxes, and the deficit that shape the budget as a whole.[3] How much should defense grow? Is a tax increase needed to reduce the deficit? Can entitlement costs be controlled? Macrobudgeting also involves projections and estimates of the totals and of the relative budget shares going to different functions. Should the United States spend more on space, on health care, on veterans? Macrobudgeting includes the fiscal policy implications of the revenue and spending totals. How will the deficit affect the economy? Key participants in macrobudgeting involve the president, the budget director, top party leaders in Congress, and the congressional budget committees.

While much attention is paid to the budget totals, thousands of individual programs and activities are contained in the budget. **Microbudgeting** involves lower-level decisions concerning agencies, programs, and line items. Should the B-2 bomber or NASA's space station be built? Should funding for day-care centers be increased? Should an agency's allocation for travel be reduced? The budget is composed of thousands of specific activities across a broad spectrum of government agencies and programs. Microbudgeting centers on agency officials, OMB budget examiners, and the appropriations and authorizing committees in Congress.

In the past two decades, budgeting in the United States moved from an emphasis on microbudgeting to an emphasis on macrobudgeting. Basic changes in the nature of the federal budget itself—the growth of entitlements, the increasing inflexibility of outlays, the existence of chronic deficits, and the importance of economic projections and estimates—made changes in the budget process inevitable. How are budgets determined?

The Dynamics of Budget-Making

Microbudgeting and macrobudgeting are fundamentally in conflict with each other. One observer has aptly characterized the budget process as "the war between the whole and the parts." Micro-level choices—decisions on the parts of the budget—are made by agency officials and members of Congress who are program supporters. These advocates want to spend more on health, education, defense, or social services, which creates tremendous pressure for overall spending growth. Those responsible for macro-level choices—decisions on the whole budget—must act to restrain growth in the totals. For example, the president and the budget director must often say no to agency requests for program expansion. In Congress, the budget committees and party leaders enforce budget resolutions that limit what the spending committees can authorize and appropriate. The result is conflict at all stages of budgeting.

Microbudgeting is usually a bottom-up process of summing spending commitments and requests. In the 1960s, political scientists described the budget process as incremental—making small upward adjustments based on last year's spending. **Incrementalism** became the accepted explanation for the stability and regularity of budgeting.[4] But incrementalism applies only to microbudgeting. As macrobudgeting grew more important in the 1970s and 1980s, it became apparent that incrementalism was increasingly irrelevant when it came to the major issues in national budgeting. Macrobudgeting establishes totals, usually from the top down. Congress recognized the necessity of macrobudgeting and created budget committees, the Congressional Budget Office, and a new budget process in 1974. Congress attempted to further strengthen its ability to control the budget and reduce deficits by passing the Gramm-Rudman law in 1985. President Reagan and his budget director, David Stockman shaped the budget from the top down in 1981, when they gained congressional approval of a package of domestic cuts, a defense buildup, and major tax reductions.

The dynamics of budgeting can be best understood as a combination of bottom-up and top-down processes—individual participants creating upward spending pressures and the president and congressional leaders trying to determine the overall needs and costs (Figure 17–1).

FIGURE 17–1

THE DYNAMICS OF BUDGET-MAKING

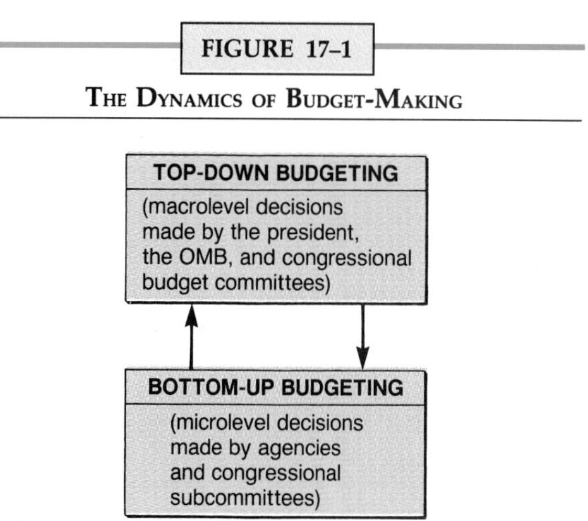

THE ANNUAL BUDGET CYCLE

In addition to being the product of top-down and bottom-up pressures, the national budget is also a repeated series of steps, or a cycle. The budget process is extremely fragmented. Many groups, officials, and participants have a hand in the final result. Figure 17–2 shows the main stages in a budget cycle, the participants, and the timing.

The U.S. government operates on a **fiscal year (FY)** that runs from October 1 through September 30. The accounting period begins three months before the calendar year. On October 1, 1990, FY 1991 began. The entire budget cycle takes more than three years from the time agencies first begin to put together their requests until the **General Accounting Office (GAO)** completes its selected audits.

The budget process is initiated in the offices of agency officials who begin to assemble their requests up to a year and a half before the start of the fiscal year. The president submits the budget in January, a few weeks after Congress starts its session. Congress has nine months to do its part with the budget and tries to get everything completed by late September. If it fails to do that, emergency funding legislation must be approved to prevent the government from shutting down. Once a budget has been enacted, the OMB, the Treasury Department and the agencies work together in the process of spending the money—writing the checks and paying the government's bills. After the fiscal year has been completed and another budget has taken effect, the GAO chooses certain key agency programs to audit to ensure that money is spent legally and efficiently.

The cycle of budgeting is one of the most regularized patterns of national policy-making. But the budget is more than routine annual decisions. Many choices involve the commitment of funds for multiyear periods. It takes many years, for example, to build a nuclear aircraft carrier. And the Social Security legislation passed in 1983 made commitments that extend through the twenty-first century. On the revenue side, the Tax

FIGURE 17–2

THE BUDGET CYCLE

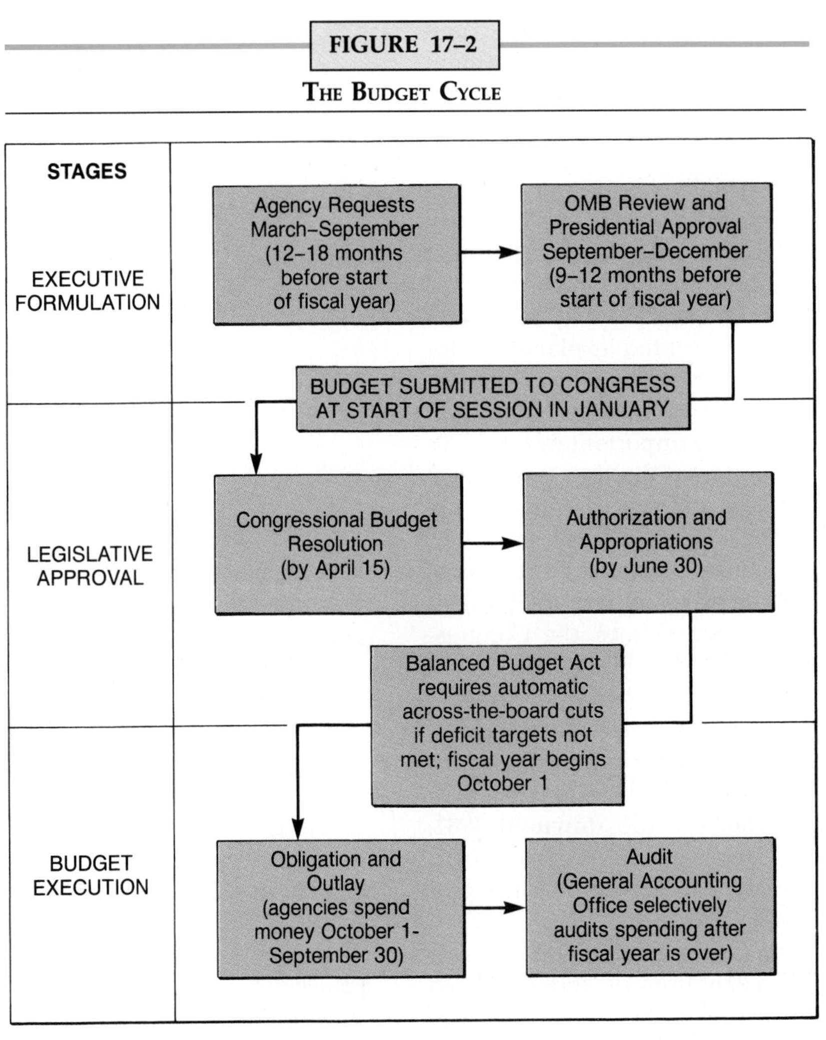

Reform Act of 1986 affected revenue totals for the coming decades. Budgeting is a combination of decisions that commit spending and tax policies for many years.

Budgeting in the Executive Branch

Participants in the budgetary process adopt certain roles defined by their self-interest and responsibilities. Agencies are advocates trying to get more money for their programs. The OMB, in contrast, is a guardian—the heartless budget-cutter of the executive branch. Its job is to say no in order to keep spending down. The president stage-manages the whole process, trying to establish priorities as well as to protect or enhance his personal political record.

AGENCY STRATEGIES

Agencies love to spend money, but they find many potential budget-cutters in their path. One of the first things an agency has to decide is how much to ask for. Is a 50-percent increase too much? Is a 5-percent increase too small? For the most part, agencies act assertively: They request increases as large as they think they can justify.[5] Behavior varies

Political Insight 17-1

How Agencies Succeed at the Budget Game

Call out the troops. Make sure not only that you have a clientele but also, if you are threatened with budget cuts, that you get them organized! Parade them into the congressional hearing room. Sponsor a letter-writing campaign. Get the ear of the president!

Follow the current fashion. Fads in Washington can change as often as skirt lengths or tie widths. The successful agency will be sure to get on the latest bandwagon. In the 1950s, when national prestige was associated with scientific achievement, agencies tried to tie their programs to the space race. In the 1960s, any kind of social program or antipoverty effort would help your chances. In the 1970s, it was energy and conservation. When Carter supported the preservation of landmarks, the Department of Interior was quick to reclassify some of the land it owned as historic sites.

Threaten to cancel the popular program—The "Washington Monument" ploy. The Washington Monument ploy was originated by a creative official in the National Park Service. When faced with a budget cut, he claimed the agency would have to close the monument, one of the most popular tourist attractions in Washington. Knowing that reviewing officials could not tolerate a cut in your popular program, you can shield less attractive alternatives. Of course, this can be a little dangerous—the cut could always go through.

Capture the congressional budgeters' imagination. Don't just provide the same old boring tables and countless pages, do something to get the Appropriations Committee members excited. The officials at NASA are the acknowledged masters at this. Their hearings are a version of "show and tell" complete with model rockets, sections of airplane wings, films, and other gadgets. They knew they had succeeded when one congressman asked them if they could beam people up to space as Scotty did on "Star Trek."

If you can't impress them, confuse them. This is an effective strategy if your agency deals with any highly technical area. Although committee members develop expertise over the years, agency officials have often succeeded in obfuscating issues and inundating members with data. So give them the latest technical jargon and more technical studies and figures than they know what to do with.

Get a foot in the door. Even the most ambitious program can be sold cheaply in the first year. Try to convince budget reviewers in the OMB and Congress that the amount is so modest as to be insignificant. This used to work pretty well, but the "camel's nose" trick has gotten more difficult in recent years. Congress and the CBO may now require the agency to show the full cost of a program.

Try the end run. If OMB cuts are too painfully deep, you can always break the rule of unity of the executive budget. Agency officials are supposed to defend the figures that are in the president's budget, rather than what they really want. However, a cleverly planted question by a friendly member can reveal in a hearing how much more money the agency really needs. But be careful. OMB officials sometimes sit in the audience taking notes.

But whatever you try, don't cheat. For all the budget games and strategies, perhaps the most important thing an agency can trade on is its good name. A lie discovered is a disaster. Even overly aggressive strategies can backfire. Agencies can be innovative within limits, but the basic rule of the game is to play it straight. Well, relatively straight.

with the age, mission, and general personality of the agency (see Chapter 15). If it wants to achieve even modest growth an agency must request increases. Of course, agencies are not free actors in the process. They are subject to instructions from the department, the OMB, and the White House and to oversight by Congress. Yet they are not without their own friends, allies, and power. To succeed in budgeting, an agency must be imaginative as well as aggressive. Political Insight 17–1 looks at some of the creative games and strategies that agencies play.

The budgeting environment is different for each agency. The Department of Health and Human Services, for example, despite its large budget, is relatively poor. It administers programs that largely involve cash transfers, and although it does a lot of check-writing, it has little direct control over the money. Budgets seem to grow in phases. Early in their history, agencies usually experience a period of rapid expenditure growth, which then levels off or declines. At all phases of their existence, they are strategic participants in quest of dollars. The most successful agencies are often the most politically astute, sensitive to the changing political winds in Washington. The 1980s were a difficult time for nondefense agencies, as top-down cuts made serious inroads in agency operations. The 1990s have proven to be difficult for the defense establishment, as officials seek a "peace dividend" by paring military spending.

THE OMB: ASSEMBLING THE BUDGET

The Office of Management and Budget has the reputation of being one of the most powerful agencies in Washington. Its relatively small size (six hundred employees) belies its influence over budgeting and policy-making. In addition to assembling the massive budget documents, the OMB monitors agencies throughout the year and helps formulate national policy. The complexity of government makes the OMB and its analytic tools invaluable to the president and the White House staff.

The budget process begins with the **spring preview,** when the OMB requires agencies to review their broad goals, programs, and activities. At the beginning of the summer, the OMB sends out the director's letter—instructions to the agencies about the submission of their requests. Agencies sometimes do not pay much attention to these instructions, but they must be prepared to justify contrary requests. By the end of the summer, agencies are required to submit formal requests to the OMB. Budget season really starts with the **fall review,** where the OMB takes a careful look at the budget requests and almost routinely cuts back what the agencies have asked for.

The Office of Management and Budget works within the broad guidelines established by the president, but many specific decisions are left to the OMB. By November, the director's review takes place. The OMB director meets with the cabinet secretaries and budget officers to go over the specific amounts that will appear in the president's budget. Conflict is often heated and intense when the budget director confronts powerful cabinet secretaries. James McIntyre, President Carter's budget director, had a particularly tough time with Housing and Urban Development Secretary Patricia Harris. In their first meeting, when McIntyre told her about cuts he was making, she blistered the air with accusations and insults. "She called him a white racist, oppressor, a Fascist, a heartless monster—you name it—and all he said was, 'Now Pat, you know you don't mean all that.'"[6] Under David Stockman, the OMB was more aggressive about imposing top-down cuts on agencies in the early 1980s. Agency officials claimed that their input was completely ignored in the budget process as the administration used a "meat-ax" approach to pare agency requests. Richard Darman, President Bush's powerful budget director, often found himself at odds with cabinet secretaries over cuts in their operations. Darman is profiled in the accompanying People in Politics.

The budget must be completed by January in time to go to the printer. Because of estimation error, changing economic assumptions, or late decisions by the White House, some of the totals are left open until the last possible minute. The OMB has a difficult job, attempting to be both objective *and* loyal to the president, and it is not particularly popular with other agencies or with Congress.

THE PRESIDENT'S ROLE

Because the budget is submitted in the president's name, many people assume the president is deeply involved with budgeting. Such is not always the case. The budget process presents a president with political opportunities, but it also creates some difficult political problems, as George Bush discovered in 1990.

What are the problems of presidential budgeting? All presidents talk like fiscal conservatives.

PEOPLE IN POLITICS

RICHARD DARMAN: PRESIDENT BUSH'S BUDGET DIRECTOR

Soon after his election in November 1988, President-elect George Bush made one of the most important appointments to his leadership team—his budget director. Since the post was first created in 1921, the head of the president's budget office has become one of the most powerful persons in Washington, D.C., often eclipsing cabinet members in influence and importance. To head the OMB, Bush chose Richard Darman, a Republican veteran of budget wars who had served the Reagan administration.

Darman, born in North Carolina in 1943, grew up in a wealthy New England family. He graduated from Harvard Business School and later taught at Harvard's John F. Kennedy School of Government. He entered the federal government and served in the four Republican administrations before Bush. Darman began as an aide to Attorney General Eliot Richardson during the Nixon administration. He became undersecretary of commerce under Gerald Ford, leaving the executive branch after Jimmy Carter's election. Darman returned to government in 1981, where he worked in the White House with James Baker as deputy chief of staff. Darman played a key role in the 1981 budget blitz and was one of the architects of the tax cut. When Baker moved from the White House to the Treasury in 1985, Darman moved with him as deputy secretary.

A noted legislative tactician, Darman was one of the key administration negotiators during the enactment of tax reform in 1985 and 1986. His somewhat abrasive and superior manner and disdain for those less intelligent than himself, however, sometimes caused trouble. During the tense negotiations over tax reform, House Ways and Means Chair Dan Rostenkowski let it be known that he would not deal with Darman. In 1987, Darman left government to join the investment firm of Shearson Lehman Brothers. With the election of George Bush, Darman returned to Washington to become OMB director and the key adviser on budget and economic matters.

Led by Darman, the administration's first encounters with Congress in 1989 were encouraging, with an agreement being reached on the outline of the 1990 budget in April 1989. But the agreement came apart by the fall, and many on Capitol Hill blamed the budget director for stirring partisan controversy and double-dealing. His insistence on the adoption of Bush's capital gains tax reduction and criticism of congressional Democrats raised animosity levels between the two branches. Darman further irritated congressional leaders with his prologue to the FY 1991 budget.

Previous budget directors, in deference to the president, had rarely even had their name mentioned in the budget documents submitted to Congress. But Darman included a cleverly written fifteen-page introduction to the 1991 budget under his own name. Darman's essay chastised Congress for its budget irresponsibility and use of budget tricks. He called the budget "the ultimate Cookie Monster," after the Sesame Street character who can't seem to consume enough cookies. He warned of six "hidden PAC-Men" in the budget that, like their video game counterparts, threaten to gobble up billions more in spending in the coming years. The hidden Pac-Men included health care, Social Security, toxic waste disposal, and credit programs. Darman's broadside at Congress was one of the opening volleys as the budget battles between Bush and Congress were played out in the 1990s.

They cultivate the image of being tightfisted with the public's money. But in reality, presidents love to spend. The political system demands action and progress, and these cost money. Public expectations are fickle: People want limited government and lower spending as long as *their* favorite programs are not cut. The government's response is often a heavy dose of public relations, trying to make the budget all things to all people. If the president wants to cut back, he may emphasize his role as fiscal conservative and note that sacrifice is necessary. If the president wants to increase spending, he is likely to emphasize public necessity and innovative leadership.

The White House is subject to tremendous pressure from interest groups and agencies to increase spending, but even relatively free-spending presidents, such as Lyndon Johnson, have to say no to many requests. (Here is where an effective budget director proves useful.) Perhaps the biggest problem of presidential budgeting is the creation of high expectations and the inevitability of disappointing certain groups and interests. Presidents must focus on macro-level choices. But a major constraint on the president is the inflexibility of budget outlays, limiting the potential of top-down budgeting. A president simply cannot turn the government around quickly. It takes years of consistent effort to make changes in the composition of the budget.[7]

What role does the president actually play? Although the budget is a critical part of presidential policy-making, presidential involvement with the details of the budget is extremely limited. The president sets the broad outlines under which others work, and the OMB puts the budget together. At certain times, the budget has been prepared virtually without the president, as during the months that Nixon was preoccupied by Watergate. When the president is inactive, authority drifts downward to OMB officials and the White House staff. Yet as President Reagan has shown, effective delegation to a powerful budget director and clear priorities can produce results.

In addition to overseeing the preparation of the annual budget, the president has several opportunities to affect taxing and spending. Although impoundment is no longer legal, the president can request a *deferral* (a proposal that the funds not be spent that year) or a *rescission* (a proposal that the funds be returned to the Treasury). Deferrals are automatically accepted unless Congress passes a motion to the contrary; rescissions must be approved by a vote of Congress. Second, the president can also veto appropriations bills. Although Congress passes its budget in the form of **budget resolutions,** which do not need the signature of the president, these do not create spending authority. The resolutions are binding only on the congressional committees that create spending authority through appropriations bills, and these bills are subject to presidential veto. Third, the president can propose emergency spending legislation as President Bush did in 1990 to support the fledgling democracies in Panama and Nicaragua.

The first year of the Reagan administration was a model of presidential manipulation of the budget process to achieve political and economic objectives. Reagan succeeded for several reasons. First, the administration was well organized and got its proposals to Congress extremely quickly. Stockman had already outlined cuts in agencies' budgets before many department heads had even been named. The timing worked to the administration's advantage. Second, the president was able to dominate the policy agenda by focusing attention on a few crucial taxing and spending proposals. Reagan did not swamp Congress with his complete "wish list" based on campaign promises. Third, the administration was innovative in its use of procedures. The use of **reconciliation,** a previously little-used procedure, was the best example. Finally, the president waged an effective lobbying and public relations campaign. Capitalizing on his first-year popularity, his effective use of television, and a professional congressional liaison operation, he was able to change budget trends.

Reagan's 1981 budget success was not repeated throughout the rest of his term. Facing an obstinate Democratic House, the president's budgets were pronounced "dead on arrival" when they reached Congress. Relatively little new was proposed in the president's budget, compared with his budgets before 1983. Worse, serious conflicts over the budget emerged within the administration. Fearing the impact of the $200 billion deficits, the president's economic advisers engaged in unprecedented public criticism of one another and of the budget. It was an unusual display of public dissension from an administration that earlier seemed to have a clearer vision of priorities than previous administrations. President Reagan seemed content to let Congress come up with its own budget, although he warned he would veto any tax increase.

Budgeting in the executive branch takes place in the agencies, the OMB, and the White House. When observers talk about the "president's budget," they are only partly correct. The chief executive has final responsibility, but his influence over the budget is limited in a number of ways. Still, despite the budget inflexibility created by mandatory entitlements such as Social Security, the sensitivity of the budget to inflation, interest rates, and other economic changes and general spending pressure, the president can effectively use the budget as a vehicle for setting national priorities.

Budgeting in Congress

CONGRESSIONAL BUDGET DECISIONS

The new congressional budget process began operation in 1975 with great fanfare. Ten years later, only a few remained enthusiastic.[8] Those who wanted the budget process to be used to cut spending were most disappointed. The budget process has improved the way Congress operates. It has provided more complete and accurate information and has focused congressional attention on budget totals and the longer-term implications of budget decisions. Nonetheless, conflict and stalemate place the budget process in jeopardy.

Congressional budgeting is a series of separate taxing and spending decisions that are only loosely linked. Table 17–1 summarizes the five categories of decisions that Congress makes on the budget. Macrobudgeting takes place by establishing *budget totals.* The House and Senate approve overall spending and revenue totals through *budget resolutions* prepared by the House and Senate budget committees. Resolutions are based on economic and budget projections made by the CBO. **Authorizations** are the legislative authority for a program and must be passed before money can be appropriated. The standing committees in both houses (except the budget and appropriations committees) report authorizations. *Appropriations* are the way Congress actually creates the spending authority that allows the executive branch to operate. Working primarily in highly specialized subcommittees, the House and Senate appropriations committees are responsible for this traditional exercise of the power of the purse. *Revenue decisions* are under the purview of

TABLE 17–1

CONGRESSIONAL BUDGETARY DECISIONS

Type of Congressional Budget Decisions	Key Participants in Congress	Type of Action by Congress
1. Budget totals	CBO, budget committees, and party leaders	Concurrent resolutions on the budget
2. Authorizations	Authorizing committees	Authorizations, entitlements
3. Appropriations	Appropriations committees	Individual appropriations bills
4. Revenues	Ways and Means and Finance committees	Tax bills
5. Oversight and review	Appropriations and authorizing committees; CBO and GAO	Hearings and investigations; special studies, audits

the tax-writing committees: the House Ways and Means Committee and the Senate Finance Committee. They consider tax bills separate from spending legislation. As conflict between the legislative and executive branches over the budget escalated in the 1980s, Congress was frequently forced to enact budget resolutions, authorization appropriations, and revenue bills in a single massive omnibus bill. A variety of congressional efforts to see that money is effectively spent come under the category of *oversight and review.*

AUTHORIZATIONS AND APPROPRIATIONS

Authorizations are statutes that establish the authority for an agency or a program to exist and may set limits on the amount of money that may be appropriated for that purpose.[9] There are three kinds of authorizations. *Annual authorizations,* for such agencies as NASA, the Atomic Energy Commission, and the National Science Foundation, require reapproval every year. Annual authorizations offer the most thorough oversight and program review but are often duplicative and cumbersome because agencies must appear before four committees each year. *Multiyear authorizations* allow a program to exist for a fixed period of time, usually between two and five years. An example was revenue sharing, authorized for four years. The third type of authorization is a *permanent authorization,* which establishes indefinite authority for a program and for funds to be appropriated for it. An example is Medicare. More than 60 percent of authorizations are permanent, 25 percent are multiyear, and only around 15 percent are annual.

Authorizing committees—the standing committees of Congress—play an important role in taxing and spending. Authorizations set boundaries for the appropriations committees. During the 1960s and 1970s, the authorizing committees tried to get around the stingy appropriations committees (which were not approving enough money to suit them) by creating "backdoor spending"—entitlements, loan guarantees, and other devices to circumvent the normal process of review. The Budget Act of 1974 attempted to curtail backdoor spending.

Appropriations are the actual means by which the Congress creates budget authority. It is a process that occurs every year, and much of the work is done by the House and Senate appropriations committees and their subcommittees, which hold extensive hearings into the agencies' activities. As "guardian of the public purse," the House and Senate appropriations committees were among the most powerful and influential panels in Congress. Commenting on the way the committees fulfilled their trust, appropriations expert Richard Fenno noted:

> The action verbs most commonly used are "cut," "carve," "slice," "prune," "whittle," "squeeze," "wring," "trim," "lop," "chop," "slash," "pare," "shave," "whack," and "fry." The tools of the trade are appropriately referred to as "knife," "blade," "meat ax," "scalpel," "meat cleaver," "hatchet," "shears," "wringer," and "fine tooth comb." . . . Budgets are praised when they are "cut to the bone."[10]

By the end of the 1960s, it was clear the appropriations committees were behaving less like guardians and more like advocates of particular programs. The authorization-appropriations process was deteriorating. Spending bills were not passed in time, and some were not passed at all. But rather than eliminate the old system, congressional reformers superimposed a new system on top of it.

THE CONGRESSIONAL BUDGET PROCESS

The Budget and Impoundment Control Act of 1974 established a new congressional budget process and gave legislators a macrobudgeting perspective for the first time. The original timetable was followed for a decade before it was revised by the Gramm-Rudman-Hollings mandatory deficit reduction law (Balanced Budget Act) in 1985. The congressional budget timetable is shown in Table 17–2.

Here is how the revised budget process is supposed to work. When the president's budget is transmitted to Capitol Hill, the House and Senate budget committees begin to hold hearings, taking testimony from administration officials, the Congressional Budget Office, and outside experts. By February 25, the authorizing and appropriations committees must submit their "views and estimates" to the budget committees. These reports project the committees' taxing and spending plans for the coming year. The budget committees in both the House and the Senate each draw up the congressional budget resolution that specifies (1) the total revenues, (2) the total spending, (3) the size of the deficit, (4) the total national debt, and (5) a breakdown of outlays by functional category. Key economic and budget assumptions are developed by the CBO, which issues a series of annual reports containing five-year projections. Congress is supposed to pass the budget resolution containing binding totals by April 15.

While the budget committees and party leaders are shaping the budget totals, the authorizing and

TABLE 17–2

CONGRESSIONAL BUDGET TIMETABLE

Action to Be Completed	On or Before
President submits budget	First Monday after January 3
CBO reports to budget committees	February 15
Committees submit views and estimates	February 25
Congress passes budget resolution (second resolution abolished)	April 15
House appropriations bills reported	June 10
Congress passes reconciliation	June 15
Congress passes all appropriations	June 30
Fiscal year begins	October 1

Senators (left to right) Warren Rudman (R-N.H.), Phil Gramm (R-Tex.), and Fritz Hollings (D-S.C.), the authors of the mandatory deficit reduction law.

appropriations committees are working at the same time on the specific parts of the budget. The president's requests are divided into thirteen separate appropriations bills, each considered by a subcommittee. Appropriations bills are supposed to be reported by June 10 in the House. Differences in the spending bills and the budget resolutions are resolved by a process called *reconciliation.* Originally designed to be used at the end of the process in September, reconciliation was officially moved in 1985 to the beginning of the process. Reconciliation bills are extremely controversial because they specify which programs and spending must be cut back to meet the totals in the budget resolution. The reconciliation bill should be passed by June 15 and the revised appropriations bills by June 30.

In the late 1970s, Congress generally was able to meet the original deadlines, but as conflict over the budget escalated in the 1980s, it began to miss more and more key dates. As deficits grew, the Democratic House, the Republican Senate, and the Reagan administration found themselves deadlocked. Budget resolutions were not being passed until September or later, and in one year, no appropriations bills had been approved by October 1. As the fiscal year approached with no budget enacted, Congress stayed in session nearly through the night. Temporary stopgap bills, lumping together a host of taxing and spending measures, were passed. Members complained about political gridlock. On several occasions federal workers were sent home when not even a temporary budget was adopted. Frustration over growing deficits and an incapacitated budget process exploded in 1985 with the adoption of a radical new approach.

THE BALANCED BUDGET ACT: MANDATORY DEFICIT REDUCTION

On December 11, 1985, Congress enacted the Balanced Budget and Emergency Deficit Control Act. It is more commonly known as the **Gramm-Rudman-Hollings** mandatory deficit reduction law after its leading Senate sponsors, Phil Gramm (R-Tex.), Warren Rudman (R-N.H.) and Fritz Hollings (D-S.C.).[11] Besides revising the congressional budget process, the act set deficit targets for the next five years that would lead to a balanced budget in the final year. If the annual target was not reached, indiscriminate across-the-board cuts would be imposed. Half the cuts would come from defense programs, the other half from domestic programs. The theory behind this meat-ax approach was that the cuts would be so onerous that Congress and the president would be forced to put together their own package to meet the targets. To help Congress reach the deficit limits, Gramm-Rudman-Hollings enhanced macrobudgeting in Congress, beefing up enforcement procedures and strengthening the ability of party leaders to quash "budget-busting" bills from the authorizing and appropriations committees. The bill was extremely controversial and unpopular, but members feared voting against any measure that would reduce the deficit. Although expressing some doubts, President Reagan signed it for the same basic reason.

Automatic cuts, called **sequesters,** were to be ordered through a complicated process involving the Office of Management and Budget, the Congressional Budget Office, and the General Accounting Office. The Supreme Court struck down the provisions for automatic cuts as a violation of separation of powers (see Chapter 14). In 1987, Gramm-Rudman-Hollings was revised to repair the constitutional flaw and to change the deficit targets, which had quickly proved unworkable. The goal of a balanced budget was postponed until 1993. Conflict continued to undermine the budget process despite the changes. Congress continued to miss the deadlines in the timetable and to engage in confrontational politics with the president. Problems continued in the Bush administration, requiring major changes in the FY 1991 budget and the budget process itself.

The budget agreement of 1990 that finally produced a $500 billion deficit reduction package through 1995 also made further changes in the Balanced Budget Act and the budget process. Gramm-Rudman-Hollings deficit targets were revised for the third time in five years, delaying achievement of a balanced budget until 1996. The new targets were $205 billion in FY91, $197 billion in FY92, $169 billion in FY93, $112 billion in FY94, $63 billion in FY95, and a deficit of zero by FY96. The new deficit targets excluded Social Security and the costs of the savings and loan bailout. Several other changes were adopted to protect the discretionary portions of the budget and include entitlements and revenues in the deficit-reduction process. Among discretionary outlays, spending caps for defense, domestic, and international programs were established for three years, 1991-1993. Revenues and entitlements were subjected to "pay as you go" rules, meaning that any changes that lost revenue or increased spending had to be offset within that category. Discretionary spending was also protected from across-the-board cuts because of changes in economic assumptions. The 1990 budget agreement also strengthened enforcement mechanisms within Congress, making it more difficult to approve any changes that would increase the deficit.

The transition of budgeting to macro-level negotiations between Congress and the president to achieve top-down control has altered the nature of budgetary politics in the United States. Partisanship, legislative-executive conflict, and the uncertainty of budget estimates make meeting the timetable difficult. Congressional actions in terms of authorizations, appropriations, and budget resolutions are overlapping and repetitive. The process remains vulnerable to special interest amendments that can quickly unglue a tenuous compromise package. Budget totals are increasingly sensitive to the economy. For example, a one-percent increase in unemployment automatically increases the deficit by $30 billion. Yet the policy consequences of the budget are critical. They affect not only the health of the economy but also the nation's defense and domestic well-being.

The Federal Budget in Perspective

HOW BIG IS THE BUDGET?

Politicians love to dramatize the growth of federal spending by noting that federal outlays in stacked dollar bills would reach to the moon or by estimating how much the government spends per second. Such imagery conveys little useful information about real budget trends. The best measure of the size of the federal budget is relative to the gross national product (GNP), because it allows comparisons of the real growth of the public sector, accounting for both inflation and economic growth. Figure 17–3 shows federal outlays and revenues as a percentage of GNP from 1963 through 1995.

Several important trends are apparent. First, the relative size of the federal budget has increased

FIGURE 17–3

FEDERAL OUTLAYS AND REVENUES AS A PERCENTAGE OF GNP, 1963–1995

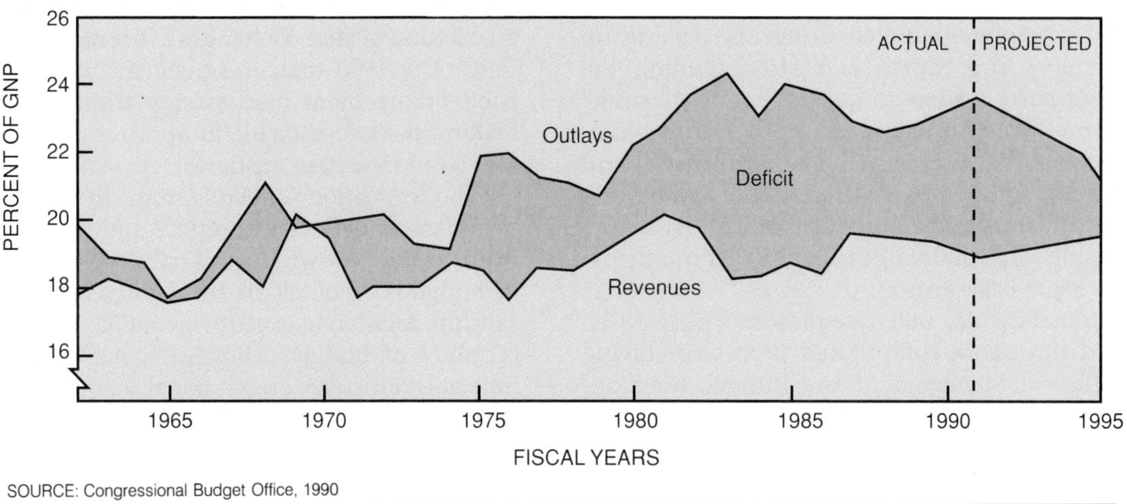

SOURCE: Congressional Budget Office, 1990

from around 17 percent of GNP in 1965 to a high of 25 percent in 1983. With the budget cuts of the 1980s, spending declined to 22 percent by 1991. Second, the growth pattern is irregular, largely owing to the performance of the economy. In a recession, outlays automatically increase while GNP goes down, which tends to increase the relative share of the public sector. Third, revenues have rarely equaled spending, which results in deficits. After the significant tax cut passed in 1981, federal revenues declined as a proportion of GNP from 21 percent in 1980 to 19.6 percent in 1990. The results are deficits substantially larger than any in history.

The scope of budget dollars is staggering. Decisions deal with billions and even trillions of dollars. In FY 1991, federal outlays were approximately $1.25 trillion, with a deficit surpassing $200 billion. It took a painful political exercise of cutting spending and raising taxes in 1990 to put deficits on a declining path.

THE COMPOSITION OF FEDERAL SPENDING

Where do the hundreds of billions of federal dollars go? The largest single spending category is Social Security and other entitlements (Medicare, Medicaid, federal retirement, and income support programs). **Entitlements** are payments mandated under federal law that pay benefits to individuals if they meet eligibility requirements (are "entitled" to them). Payments for these programs are mandatory, unless Congress changes the law. Entitlement and other mandatory spending for 1990 was $584 billion. The second largest component is national defense—$297 billion for 1990. Figure 17–4 compares the composition of federal spending in three time periods: 1970, 1980, and 1990. Between 1970 and 1980, defense spending fell from 42 percent of the budget down to 23 percent. At the same time, social welfare entitlement spending went from 28 percent to 42 percent. The Reagan administration embarked on a budget policy to restore the defense share of the budget while reducing entitlements and other domestic spending. Interest paid on the national debt has grown since 1970, and it continues to grow as the large deficits accumulate, pushing up the cost of interest and the share of the budget it consumes.

Table 17–3 looks at the federal budget by function, beginning with the 1990 base and the projection for 1995. Functional subtotals are used by Congress in its budget resolutions and offer a view of the purposes of spending. Income security, defense, health, and interest on the debt are the big-ticket items. Other functions, such as energy, transportation, education, and agriculture, make up smaller portions of the budget and are projected to decline further relative to the rest of the budget.

SOURCES OF FEDERAL REVENUES

Where does the money come from to pay for these budget items? Figure 17–5 shows the sources of federal revenues as a percentage of GNP. Personal income taxes are the main source, making up 45.9 percent of all monies collected in 1990. Although relatively stable since 1970, personal income tax collections would have been considerably higher without the tax cut of 1981. The Tax Reform Act of 1986 reduced personal income taxes from 47percent of all revenues. Social Security taxes (primarily FICA) are the second highest source of revenue. In 1960, these payroll taxes made up only 15 percent of federal receipts. By 1970, they provided 23 percent of federal revenues, and by 1990, they constituted 36.3 percent. Corporate income taxes, in contrast, have declined as a source of revenue. In 1960, some 23 percent of all tax collections came from corporations. By 1985, this had declined to 6 percent. Tax reform increased corporate taxes up to 9.5 percent of all revenues by 1990. Excise taxes currently make up about 4

FIGURE 17–4

COMPOSITION OF FEDERAL SPENDING 1970, 1980, 1990

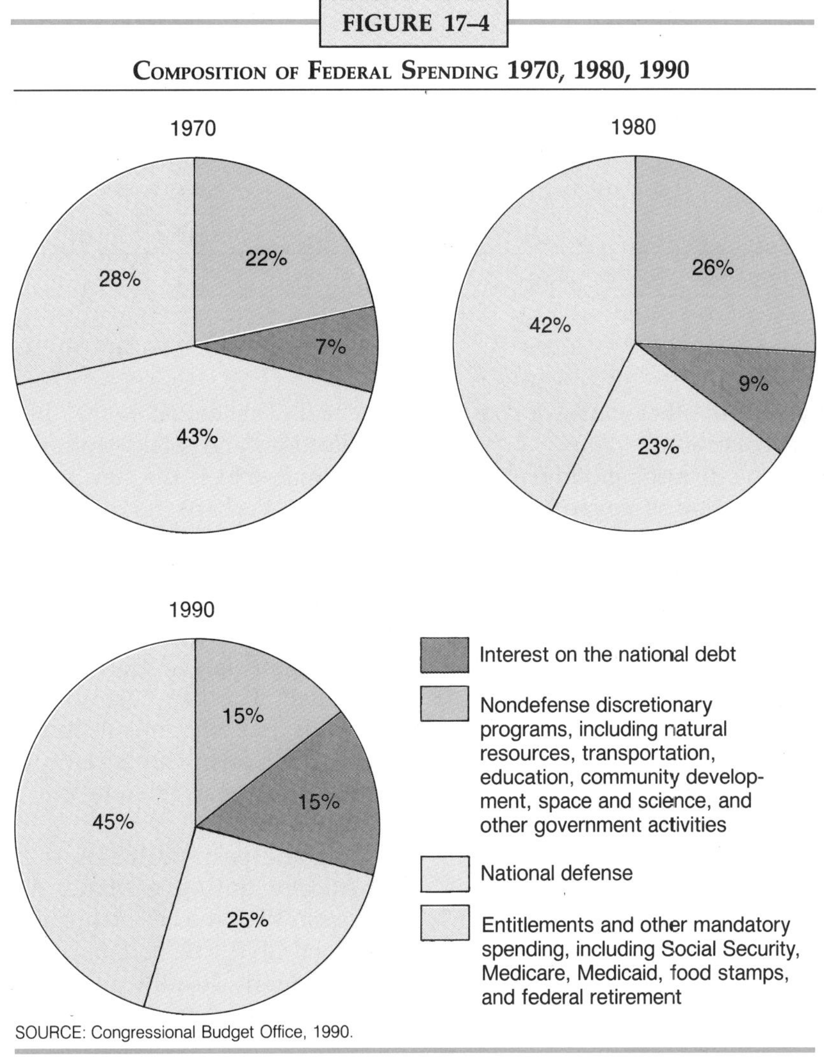

SOURCE: Congressional Budget Office, 1990.

TABLE 17–3

BUDGET OUTLAYS BY FUNCTION, 1990 AND 1995 (IN BILLIONS OF DOLLARS)

Function	1990	1995 (Projected)
National defense	297	355
International affairs	15	19
General science, space, and technology	14	18
Energy	3	5
Natural resources and environment	18	21
Agriculture	13	14
Commerce and housing credit	30	9
Transportation	29	30
Community and regional development	8	9
Education, training, employment, and social services	39	47
Health	57	98
Medical insurance	95	171
Income security	146	189
Social security	249	338
Veterans benefits and services	29	36
Administration of justice	10	16
General government	10	13
Net interest	180	209
(Offsetting receipts)	−37	−47
Total outlays	1,205	1,555

SOURCE: Congressional Budget Office, 1990.

percent of tax revenues. All other sources make up 5 percent of total tax collections.

By the mid-1980s, the disturbing budget trends were the main preoccupation of government. Defense underwent a trillion-dollar buildup, and entitlements and other mandatory spending for social programs also continued to grow. At the same time, the income tax cut of 1981 left revenues lagging far behind. The result was chronic deficits and a burgeoning national debt.

The Deficit Dilemma

DEFICITS AND THE NATIONAL DEBT

Ever since Lord Keynes suggested it was acceptable for governments to spend more than they take in, government deficits have been politically controversial. The **deficit** is the difference between tax collections and total spending in a single year. The **national debt** is the sum total of all the deficits in history. Perhaps no other issue in the postwar period has been as ubiquitous as the "balanced budget" issue. When a conservative Republican president continued to swear allegiance to the concept of a balanced budget while apparently sanctifying large deficits, considerable confusion resulted. The gap between what the government spends and what it collects in taxes must be made up by borrowing. Interest on the total debt must be paid every year, at a total cost of $185 billion a year by 1991.

In the past, the national debt grew most dramatically during wartime. After the end of the Korean War, the U.S. national debt was about equal to total GNP. The national debt, while increasing in dollar terms, steadily decreased relative to GNP, to around 30 percent in the mid-1970s. Since 1981, it is once again on the rise. By 1989, it had risen to nearly 50 percent of GNP.

Two kinds of budget deficits can be distinguished. A *cyclical deficit* is one caused by fluctuations in the economy. If the economy were at its full productive capacity, the budget would be in balance. Cyclical deficits are related to compensatory fiscal policy (see Chapter 18), designed to use the budget to stimulate the economy. A *structural deficit* is a gap between revenues and expenditures that would continue to exist even at full employment. It is a built-in gap that could be changed only by raising taxes or cutting spending. The large deficits of the 1980s were largely structural deficits caused by the 1981 tax cut and defense-spending increases and aggravated by the 1981–82 recession. Deficits are of great concern because of their link to high interest rates, the value of the dollar overseas, the high costs of interest payments, and fears that growing deficits could either stimulate inflation again or dampen further economic recovery.[12]

Deficit reduction continued as one of the major political challenges of the 1990s. Without any policy changes—that is, without tax increases or spending cuts—the deficit would have remained far above the targets of the Balanced Budget Act. President Bush and Congress faced a difficult challenge in putting together a comprehensive deficit-reduction package in 1990.

FIGURE 17–5

REVENUES BY SOURCE AS PERCENTAGE OF GNP, 1965–1993

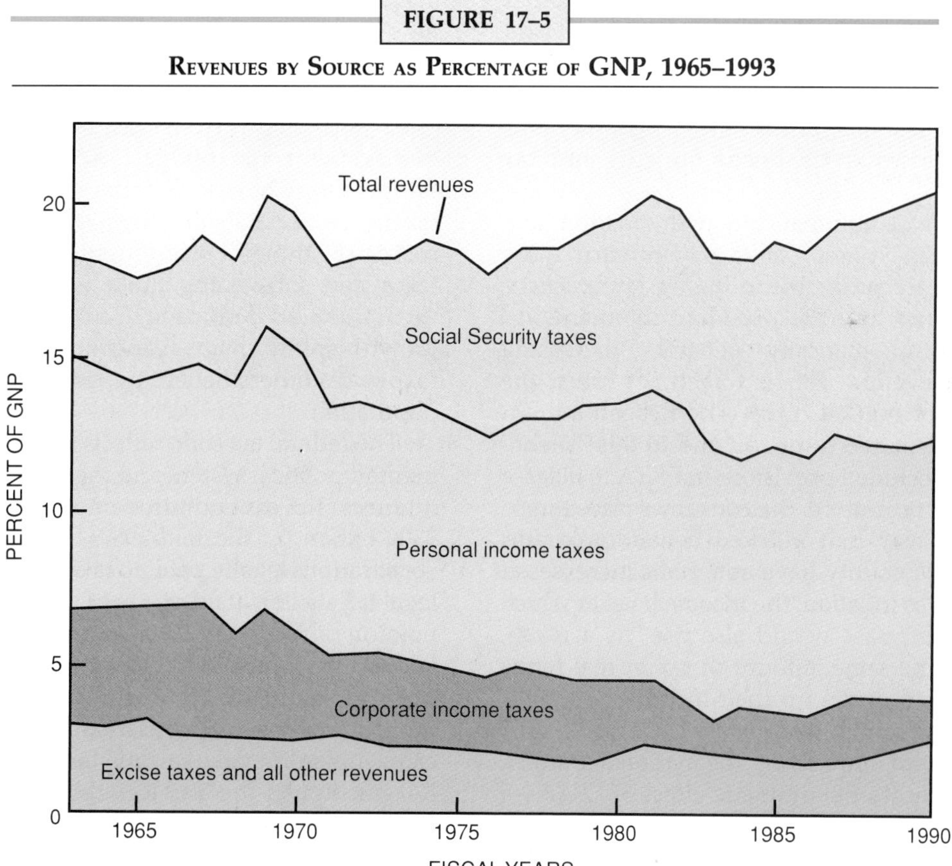

SOURCE: Congressional Budget Office, 1990.

Taxes

THE 1981 TAX CUT

Taxes are a critical element of budget policy. Not only do they supply the funds needed to run government programs and pay beneficiaries, but they also provide incentives to the public to behave in a certain way. The keystone of the Reagan economic plan was an across-the-board cut in personal income taxes and a cut in corporate taxes to stimulate investment. In 1981, Congress adopted the president's program by passing the Economic Recovery Tax Act **(ERTA),** the largest tax cut in American history. ERTA cut tax rates proportionately across the existing tax brackets (then ranging from 11 percent to 50 percent). Recognizing the growing deficit problem, Congress enacted another major tax bill in 1982, the Tax Equity and Fiscal Responsibility Act. This legislation attempted to raise revenue through other taxes and make a small dent in the deficit. It left intact the key components of ERTA—the across-the-board tax cuts and **tax indexing.**

Taxes increase automatically with inflation. In a progressive tax system, as taxpayers earn more money, they are pushed into higher tax brackets. Unless Congress and the president intervene, inflation will automatically generate increasing amounts of revenue. This is sometimes called the inflation tax or bracket creep. The Reagan administration, determined to put an end to this "silent" tax increase, included provisions in ERTA to *index*—that is, to link tax rates to the consumer price index. In the same way that indexed benefit programs such as Social Security have automatic increases at the same rate as inflation, the income level at which rates would increase would also rise. As a result, citizens pay the same amount of tax in real terms even if inflation drives up their income.

The Reagan administration's tax policies in 1981 had a profound impact on the national budget. Figure 17–6 shows the dramatic effect of ERTA—a five-year revenue loss of $732 billion. Looking at personal income taxes as a percentage of GNP, the top dotted line in Figure 17–6 indicates what tax collections would have been without the tax cut. The bottom dotted line shows what tax collections would have been without indexing, which took effect in 1985.

THE TAX REFORM ACT OF 1986

At the same time that decision-makers looked for palatable ways to raise revenues, a number of critics urged massive overhaul of the entire income tax system. Federal income taxes are progressive, taxing higher income categories at higher rates. But ever since the implementation of the progressive income tax, Congress has granted a number of exclusions, exemptions, deductions, deferrals, and other special tax preferences. Some of the most popular and widespread examples of tax preferences are the ability to deduct home mortgage interest, charitable contributions, and state and local taxes from gross income. Others, like the "three-martini lunch" (deductible for business people), were more controversial and gave rise to the term *tax loophole.* Yet one person's tax loophole is another's divine right; it depends on one's perspective. In the last decade, the Office of Management and Budget and the Congressional Budget Office have kept better records of the cost of tax preferences, labeling them *tax expenditures.* Their cost can be thought of as the equivalent of collecting taxes and subsidizing those who qualify for the exemption or deduction. Tax expenditures have grown rapidly, many benefiting small groups of taxpayers, others benefiting large segments of the population.

The federal tax code reflects the impact of a fragmented political system and the influence of special interests. Tax expenditures amounted to more than $300 billion by the mid-1980s. A number of large corporations legally paid no taxes. Millionaires with legal tax shelters paid no tax or very little tax. Public opinion surveys revealed that the federal income tax was perceived by the public as the least fair tax at any level of government! From an unusual coalition of liberals and conservatives in both parties came a plan to make income taxes fairer. President Reagan signed the **Tax Reform Act** in 1986.

Tax reform dramatically changed the nation's income tax system. Historically, the top rates paid by the wealthiest taxpayers have fluctuated according to the prevailing economic and political sentiments of the time. Figure 17–7 shows the maximum

FIGURE 17–6

EFFECT OF 1981 REAGAN TAX CUT AND TAX INDEXING

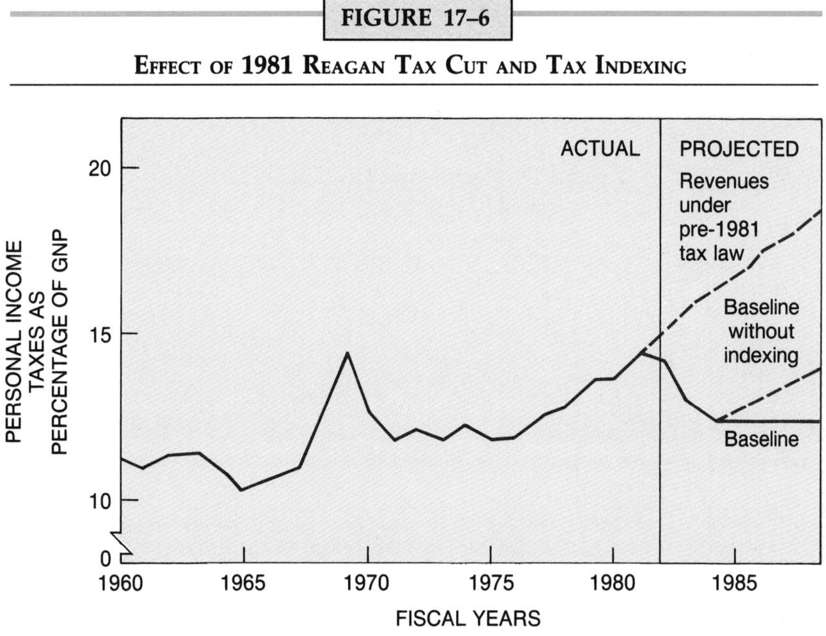

SOURCE: Congressional Budget Office, February 1983.

rate for individuals since the income tax was first adopted in 1913. It reached as high as 90 percent from the end of World War II through the Kennedy administration. The top rate was 70 percent when Ronald Reagan took office. ERTA lowered it to 50 percent, and the Tax Reform Act of 1986 lowered it to 28 percent, a rate comparable to the 1920s.

Tax reformers were able to lower rates by eliminating tax loopholes—abolishing some of the billions of dollars of tax expenditures. But many of the most popular deductions, such as the deduction for home mortgage interest, were retained. The new law reduced the number of tax brackets from fourteen to two, 14 percent and 28 percent. Corporate rates were lowered from 46 percent to 33 percent, but more income was made subject to taxation. Tax reform shifted some of the tax burden from individuals to corporations.

Low-income taxpayers gained significant relief under the law. Tax liability for people earning less than $10,000 was reduced by two-thirds. At the other end of the income scale, tax shelters utilized by the wealthiest taxpayers were sharply curtailed. Overall, it was calculated that under the new system 79 percent of Americans would pay less, while 21 percent would pay more. Despite this, the confusion caused by all the changes in the first few years left the public very unhappy with the new law. The tax law provided little simplification—one of the original goals of tax reformers. Nor did it deal with the problem of the deficit. Despite his "read my lips—no new taxes" pledge, President Bush faced the risky proposition of raising taxes to deal with the deficits.

THE 1990 BUDGET AGREEMENT

Because of the seriousness of the deficit crisis, tax issues were laid back on the table during budget negotiations in 1990. Although many Republicans were upset that President Bush backed away from his "no new taxes" pledge, most analysts agreed that there was simply no alternative if the government was to deal responsibly with the deficits. The tax package in the original summit agreement was one of the main reasons it was voted down by the House, causing a temporary government shutdown. House Democrats felt that plan was unfair, placing an undue burden on lower and middle income taxpayers. House Republicans did not want

FIGURE 17–7

THE MAXIMUM INCOME TAX RATE FOR INDIVIDUALS SINCE 1913

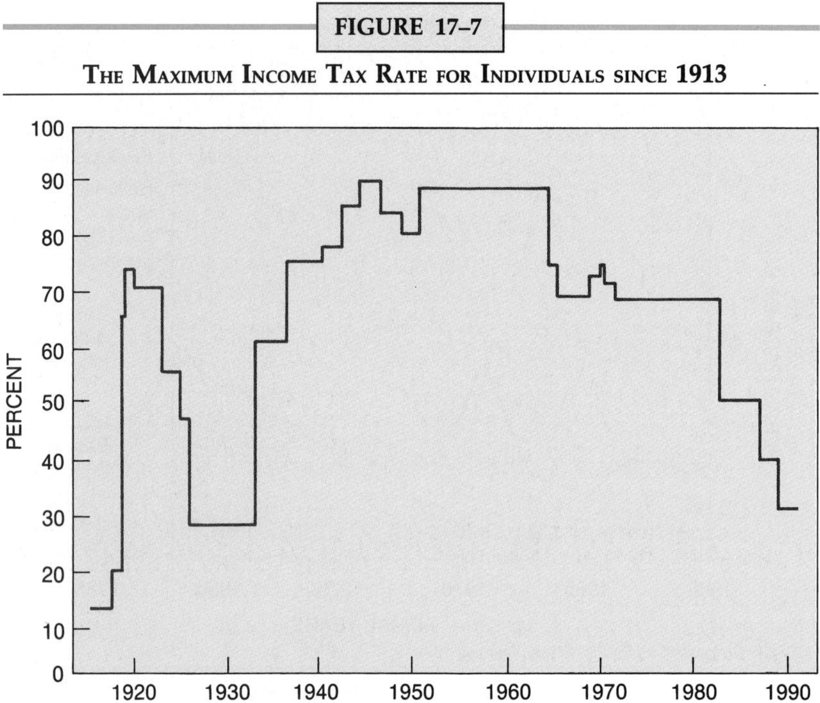

NOTE: The maximum tax rate was raised to 31% in October, 1990
SOURCE: Joint Committee on Taxation

any new taxes at all. As a result, most of the votes for the final agreement had to come from the Democratic side. This political calculus eventually led to an increase in income tax rates despite the Tax Reform Act four years earlier. The controversial budget package finally adopted in 1990 cut spending by approximately $350 billion and raised taxes by approximately $150 billion over five years. Major provisions included:

Income taxes: The top rate for personal income taxes was raised from 28 percent to 31 percent for the wealthiest taxpayers. Itemized deductions were reduced and personal exemptions phased out for households making over $100,000 annually. Capital gains taxes remained at 28 percent. These provisions would raise $40 billion over five years.

Excise taxes: Federal gasoline taxes were raised 5 cents to a total of 14 cents a gallon. Taxes were increased on a pack of cigarettes by 4 cents a pack in 1991 and another 4 cents in 1993. Excise taxes on wine, beer, and liquor were increased. A luxury tax of 10 percent was assessed on expensive cars, boats, furs, and aircraft. Taxes on telephone calls and airline tickets were increased. Combined new excise taxes raised nearly $70 billion over five years.

Social Security and Medicare: Social Security rates were not increased but revenues were enhanced by $9 billion by making coverage mandatory for all state and local employees. Revenues from Medicare were raised by $27 billion over five years by making wages up to $125,000 subject to the 1.45 percent tax.

Corporate taxes: Taxes on corporations were increased by limiting deductions for insurance losses, tightening rules on foreign companies doing business in the United States, increasing interest penalties on companies that owe money to the IRS, and other changes totaling $19 billion in new revenues by 1995.

User fees: The budget agreement also raised $19 billion in new revenues by increasing fees on banks, nuclear power plants, boaters using federal waterways, and increasing fines for safety violations.

When insolvent savings and loan institutions began to fail because of mismanagement, the government was obligated to insure all deposits. This has increased budget deficits in the 1990's by hundreds of billions of dollars.

Domestic spending cuts: Major cuts occurred in Medicare benefits by increasing premiums and deductibles, lowering projected outlays by $12 billion over five years. Reimbursement to doctors and hospitals that provide Medicare coverage was cut by $30 billion during the same period. Other cuts over five years included $15 billion sliced from agriculture price supports paid to farmers, $14 billion less to federal pensioners, and $12 billion cut from other domestic programs.

Defense spending cuts: Discretionary military spending would be cut by a total of $182 billion over five years according to the final package passed by Congress and signed by President Bush.

Despite the dramatic spending cuts and tax increases, the 1990 budget agreement was as notable for what it did not do as for what it did. Congress and the president did not levy a surtax on millionaires as many Democrats wanted. Indexation of tax rates was not repealed or delayed. New consumption taxes, which remain relatively low in the United States compared to other industrialized nations, were not levied. The CBO estimated that a value added tax (VAT) or national sales tax could have raised $75 to $150 billion over five years.[13] Nonetheless, the bitter controversy and governing crisis that preceded the 1990 budget agreement show how difficult budget choices continue to be for Congress and the president.

SUMMARY AND CONCLUSIONS

1. The concept of a comprehensive national budget developed early in the twentieth century, giving the president the responsibility for compiling and presenting it to Congress. One result was a major increase in presidential power.

2. Budget decisions are made at both the micro level and the macro-level. Macrobudgeting has become increasingly important in recent years. Budgets are built simultaneously from the bottom up and the top down. The budget is made in an annual cycle by agencies, the OMB, the president, and Congress.

3. Each participant in the executive branch plays its own special role in budgeting, agencies acting as advocates for greater spending and the OMB trying to cut back on the requests. The president oversees the process and tries to impose broad priorities on the budget.

4. Congress was granted the power of the purse in the Constitution but in practice has had difficulty exercising such power effectively and responsibly. The congressional budget process, a complicated combination of taxing and spending decisions, remains in a flux. In response to the deficit crisis, Congress enacted the Gramm-Rudman-Hollings deficit reduction law in 1985 but amended it in 1987 and 1990.

5. The budget has grown rapidly, to over $1.2 trillion by 1991. In spite of a slowing of entitlement growth, rapid increases in defense spending and a major cut in personal income taxes resulted in historically high deficits in the 1980s that carried into the 1990s.

6. The Tax Reform Act of 1986 closed many tax loopholes and reduced tax rates but caused a great deal of confusion for taxpayers.

7. Despite the bitter controversy of the budget in 1990, Congress and the president finally agreed on a $500 billion deficit-reduction package over 5 years.

Budget controversies have raised serious questions about the ability of the American political system to govern. The issues surrounding the budget seem to push government to its limit. An executive-dominant system, like that found in most parliamentary democracies, would be more able to centralize political authority and impose a solution for a problem like chronic deficits, either through tax increases or severe spending cuts. But even parliamentary systems struggle with budget inflexibility, relative uncontrollability of expenditures, and economic uncertainties. The danger of the American political system in dealing with competing budget priorities is stalemate, an inability to act in the face of a growing crisis. If the agreement reached in 1990 fails to reduce the deficits, the political system may suffer through another paralyzing crisis in the coming years.

Key Terms

appropriations
authorizations
Budget and Accounting Act
budget resolutions
deficit
entitlements
ERTA
fall review
fiscal year (FY)
General Accounting Office (GAO)
Gramm-Rudman-Hollings
incrementalism
macrobudgeting
microbudgeting
national debt
reconciliation
sequesters
spring preview
tax indexing
Tax Reform Act

Self-Review

1. What have been the major developments in budgeting since the 1960s?

2. Compare macrobudgeting and microbudgeting.

3. Describe the annual budget cycle.

4. How does the OMB assemble the budget?

5. What role does the president play in budgeting?

6. What kinds of budget decisions must Congress make?

7. How does the congressional budget process balance budget resolutions with authorizations and appropriations?

8. Describe the issues surrounding deficits and the debt.

9. What categories compose federal spending, and what are the sources of federal revenues?

10. What are some of the main obstacles to reducing spending?

11. Describe the changes made by tax reform and some of the alternatives for revenue increases to reduce the deficit.

12. Describe the tax increases enacted in 1990 as part of the deficit-reduction package.

Suggested Readings

Congressional Budget Office. *Reports to the House and Senate Budget Committees.* Multiple parts. Annual.
Some of the best available budget analysis, including multiyear projections, economic assumptions, and consideration of budget alternatives.

LeLoup, Lance T. *Budgetary Politics.* 4th ed. 1988.
An overview of the federal budget process and the nature of budgetary decisions.

Office of Management and Budget. *The Budget of the United States.* Annual.
The president's statement of policies, priorities, and requests to Congress.

Wildavsky, Aaron. *The New Politics of the Budgetary Process.* 1988.
The originator of incrementalism analyzes changes in the federal budget over twenty years.

Rubin, Irene, *The Politics of Public Budgeting* (1990).
An examination of local, state, and national budgeting processes.

NOTES

1. For the history of the creation and evolution of the Budget Office, see Larry Berman, *The Office of Management and Budget and the Presidency, 1921–1979* (Princeton: Princeton University Press, 1979).
2. See Richard Nathan, *The Plot That Failed: Nixon and the Administrative Presidency* (New York: John Wiley, 1975).
3. See Lance T. LeLoup, "From Microbudgeting to Macrobudgeting: Transition in Theory and Practice," in Irene Rubin, ed., *New Directions in Budget Theory* (Albany: SUNY Press, 1988), 19–42.
4. See Aaron Wildavsky, *The Politics of the Budgetary Process* (Boston: Little, Brown, 1964).
5. Lance T. LeLoup and William Moreland, "Agency Strategies and Executive Review: The Hidden Politics of Budgeting," *Public Administration Review* 38 (May–June 1978).
6. *Newsweek,* 8 January 1979, p. 30.
7. See Allen Schick, "The Budget as an Instrument of Presidential Policy," in Lester M. Salamon and Michael S. Lund, eds., *The Reagan Presidency and the Governing of America* (Washington, D.C.: Urban Institute, 1985), 91–125.
8. For analysis of the congressional budget process, see Lance T. LeLoup, *The Fiscal Congress* (Westport, Conn.: Greenwood Press, 1980); Allen Schick, *Congress and Money* (Washington, D.C.: Urban Institute, 1980); and Dennis Ippolito, *Congressional Spending* (Ithaca, N.Y.: Cornell University Press, 1981).
9. See Lance T. LeLoup, *Budgetary Politics,* 4th ed. (Brunswick, Ohio: Kings Court, 1988), 194–224.
10. Richard Fenno, *The Power of the Purse* (Boston: Little, Brown, 1965).
11. See Lance T. LeLoup, Barbara Graham, and Stacey Barwick, "Deficit Politics and Constitutional Government: The Impact of Gramm-Rudman-Hollings," *Public Budgeting and Finance* (Spring 1987):83–103.
12. Office of Management and Budget, *Budget of the United States, FY 1984,* pp. 2-16–2-19.
13. Congressional Budget Office, *"Reducing the Deficit: Spending and Revenue Options,"* February 1990, p. 417.

CHAPTER 18

Economic Policy, Energy, and the Environment

POLITICAL CLOSE-UP

The Exxon Valdez Oil Spill

On the night of March 24, 1989, the supertanker *Exxon Valdez* was carrying its massive load of crude oil through Alaska's Prince William Sound. The ship had filled its spacious tanks in the port of Valdez, at the end of the Alaska pipeline. Although the ship's captain, Joseph Hazelwood, had his driver's license suspended for drunk driving, he was nonetheless licensed to handle the tanker. Hazelwood had been drinking that day and left the bridge in charge of the third mate. In the darkness, the tanker lurched to an unexpected stop. As it ran aground on a well-marked reef in the sound, a massive hole was torn in its single-hull bottom. In the next few hours and days, nearly 11 million gallons of crude spilled into the sound.

The scope of the world's worst oil spill was soon apparent. The thick slime rolled along one thousand miles of pristine cobblestone beaches from a slick that grew larger than the state of Delaware. Rocks, plants, trees, birds, mammals, fish, and other sea creatures were caught in its relentless

path. The fresh pine scent of the cove gave way to the powerful odor of a refinery. The sound was closed to ship traffic as officials from Alaska, Washington, the Coast Guard, and Exxon tried to assess the damage. The toll measured in oil-fouled carcasses was staggering: 36,000 birds, 1,000 otters, 150 eagles, and countless fish. Once-thriving salmon, herring, and shrimp fishing came to an immediate and perhaps permanent halt.

Officials moved quickly but to little avail. Worst-case plans had prepared for a spill of only 2.5 million gallons, less than one-fourth of what the *Exxon Valdez* spewed into the sound. Exxon immediately sent in teams to contain the oil still gushing out of the ship and begin the cleanup, pouring millions of dollars a day into the effort. Exxon put thousands of Alaskans to work in the cleanup, paying as much as $25 per hour to fishermen whose livelihoods had been destroyed. But two weeks after the accident, President Bush announced that Exxon's efforts were inadequate and the federal government was taking over the effort. Crude was still flowing out of the *Exxon Valdez.* Around the world, nations volunteered help in the cleanup. The Soviet Union sent the world's largest oil-skimming ship to Alaska.

Oil was king in Alaska, the most important industry in the state, supplying much of the United State's growing thirst for petroleum. The Alaska pipeline brought prosperity to the state and needed energy to the rest of the country. But with it came risks—and the growing conflict between economic growth, energy production, and protection of the environment. Exxon, one of the world's largest corporations, could afford the cleanup costs with profits that would reach $3.5 billion in 1989, even after deducting $1.7 billion for the cleanup and possible lawsuit judgments. A nationwide boycott of Exxon organized by consumer activists had little impact on the multinational giant.

The effects of the disastrous spill reverberated throughout Washington. Legislation to permit exploration and drilling in the Arctic National Wildlife Refuge in Northern Alaska was buried. Oil-spill liability legislation, deadlocked in Congress for fifteen years, was revived. Legislation to require double-hulled tankers and tougher ship-licensing procedures and to limit offshore oil leases was introduced. Hazelwood was indicted but later acquitted on the most serious charges. He was sentenced to one thousand hours of service to help clean up Prince William Sound. Ten months after the spill, Exxon was indicted by the Justice Department on charges that could carry fines up to $700 million.

A year after the spill, Prince William Sound looked better but had not returned to normal. Scientists found that oil had penetrated six to twenty-eight inches below the surface of the ground. The future of the fishing industry remained unknown. Meanwhile, the nation's appetite for oil continued to grow as supertankers moved in and out of the harbor, carrying the needed fuel to the lower forty-eight states.

CHAPTER OUTLINE

INTRODUCTION AND OVERVIEW

Around the world, governments often succeed or fail based on their ability to pursue sound economic policies. While President Gorbachev won the Nobel Peace Prize for reducing world tensions, changing domestic economic policy and converting to a market system have proven much more difficult. Even with a sound and stable economy, some of the greatest governing challenges in the United States fall in the economic realm. Some worry that American political institutions are too weak to manage a modern political economy.[1] The challenges are many:

Can fiscal policy help keep inflation low and employment high? Can the nation's trade deficit and international balance of payments be managed more effectively? Can U.S. industry remain competitive in the world marketplace? Can interest rates and monetary decisions be coordinated with other central banks? Can the budget be balanced without causing a recession? Can energy sources be developed without polluting the environment? Can the air and water and toxic dumps around the country be cleaned up without a massive loss of jobs?

Changes in the world economic system have made economic policy-making even more complex for Congress, the president, the bureaucracy, and American business and financial institutions. Concern with questions of economic equity—assuring a decent standard of living for the nation's poor—and environmental protection must be balanced with policies to encourage economic growth. Inherent conflicts between economic goals are apparent in policy disputes over such issues as trade restrictions, clean air, capital gains taxes, the minimum wage, child care, interest rates, incentives to increase national saving, and deficit reduction.

This chapter looks at some of the many aspects of economic policy, energy policy, and environmental policy. Building on the foundation established in Chapter 3, we know that policy-making is grounded in well-established economic traditions and values, even as it attempts to adapt to a rapidly changing international environment. Tradeoffs between competing goals and objectives in economic policy often pose vexing dilemmas for leaders and generate heated political conflicts. The chapter considers the following questions:

1. What is economic policy, and why does it pose such dilemmas for decision-makers?
2. How has fiscal policy evolved in the postwar period, and is it still effective as a tool of economic management?
3. How is monetary policy made, and is it coordinated effectively with other economic policies?
4. What are the conflicts between the desire for free trade and the desire to protect domestic industry from competition? Does the United States need an industrial policy?
5. What are the energy sources that fuel the American economy, and what kind of national strategy is needed to promote growth while protecting the environment?
6. How can the growing sentiment among Americans to protect the natural environment be balanced with the desire for jobs and economic growth?

★

The Dilemma of Economic Policy

WHAT IS ECONOMIC POLICY?

The U.S. government attempts to smooth out the bumps and eliminate politically unacceptable outcomes of the market system in an economy that remains largely in private hands. **Economic policy** describes the actions taken by the government to affect the performance of the national economy. Some of the actions are direct (such as price controls), whereas others are indirect (for example, emission standards, which may increase the cost of automobiles or electric power). Major policy questions and indicators of success and failure include the following:

Employment. How much should the government attempt to reduce unemployment? How much joblessness is tolerable? The most common indicator of joblessness is the unemployment rate—the percentage of people in the work force without a job who are actively seeking employment. Full employment in the United States today is considered to be around 5 percent unemployment.

Price levels. How can inflation be controlled, and what level of price increase is acceptable? Israel has an annual inflation rate of more than 100 percent, but President Carter suffered politically when the U.S. rate went over 10 percent. The standard indicators of inflation are the *consumer price index* (CPI), which measures retail prices, and the *producer price index* (PPI), which measures wholesale prices.

Economic growth. How much should the government do to stimulate the economy? The size of the domestic economy is measured by the **gross national product (GNP),** the sum total of all goods and services produced. Economic growth is measured by percentage change in GNP at an annual rate. When GNP is controlled for inflation, it measures "real" growth.

Interest rates. How high or low should interest rates be to foster economic growth without stimulating inflation? How much may the government do to control interest rates? Interest rates vary from very short terms (rates for money borrowed over the weekend, for example) to extremely long term (rates for twenty-five to thirty years). One of the most well publicized is the *prime rate,* the interest rate large commercial banks charge their most dependable corporate customers.

Balance of trade and international payments. Should the government erect tariffs or establish quotas for the number of Japanese autos or Italian shoes that can be imported into the country? What should be done if the nation buys more than it sells? The *balance of trade* is simply the difference between the goods and services a nation imports and exports. The *balance of payments* is the balance of trade plus all currency, tourist expenditure, foreign and military aid, and capital moving in and out of the country. The value of the dollar compared with other currencies has an effect on these balances.

Policy-makers in Washington look at a host of other economic statistics that tell how well the economy is doing. But economic policy involves highly emotional questions as well as familiar economic indicators. How much reliance should be placed on the market system? When is it legitimate for the government to intervene? How much regulation to protect the environment is acceptable when business complains about its cost and inefficiency?

CHARACTERISTICS OF U.S. ECONOMIC POLICY-MAKING

Managing economic policy to promote the nation's prosperity is a difficult dilemma for political leaders. Three important points help explain it.

Economic goals conflict with one another. The fundamental problem with economic policy is that many desirable goals, such as full employment and low inflation, are often incompatible. Choices must be made. Is inflation a greater problem than unemployment? Is higher spending for national defense more important than high interest rates or large budget deficits? Goals are subject to trade-offs, although their exact nature may be unclear. Economic policy-making establishes some relative ordering of economic goals in the form of concrete policy actions.

Power and responsibility for economic policy is fragmented. Not only does government economic policy have multiple and overlapping dimensions, but it also has a particularly large number of participants making decisions. Besides the presidentdent are the Congress, the Treasury Department, the Office of Management and Budget, the Council of Economic Advisers, the Commerce Department, the Federal Reserve Board, numerous other government agencies, and hundreds of powerful interest groups. In addition, many of the most critical economic decisions are made in the private sector in terms of investment decisions, money spent on research and development, and plant openings and closings. Because of this decentralization, U.S. economic policy tends to be uncoordinated.

Economic policy actions do not always produce the desired result. Economics is an inexact science. A gap often exists between intention and outcome. Even if the varied political actors can come up with some rough agreement on policy actions, the policies they choose will not always have the desired effect. Serious disagreement among professional economists leaves politicians free to follow their political instincts instead of economic principles. Imprecision and inaccuracy in economic estimates foster additional conflict in the process and heighten uncertainty. Yet politicians must continue to seek the best advice possible.

Although many economic policies can be discerned, the following major components are considered: (a) fiscal policy—the manipulation of taxing and spending; (b) monetary policy—the control of the supply and cost of money and credit; (c) trade and industrial policy—exports, imports, and attempts to promote industrial growth and development; (d) energy policy—alternate sources, prices, supply, and conservation; and (e) environmental protection—the use of regulation, subsidy, and controls to protect the environment.

The following analysis looks at economic policy as decision-makers see it, focusing on how economic ideas are translated into public policy through the political process.

Fiscal Policy: Stabilizing the Economy

Fiscal policy applies to decisions about the level of government spending, revenues, and the deficit. Working through the budget process, fiscal decisions are intertwined with decisions on the allocation of resources to defense and domestic

Government economic policy attempts to manage an economy that remains primarily shaped by the actions of private producers and consumers.

needs. Since the late 1930s, the president and Congress have attempted to manipulate taxes and spending to compensate for inadequacies or excesses of private sector economic activity. Generally, fiscal policy tries to smooth out the swings of the business cycle.

THE EMPLOYMENT ACT (1946)

If anything approaching a consensus over economic policy has existed in the last fifty years, it probably occurred immediately after World War II. The nation seemed ready to embrace the goal of full employment as the primary national objective. It appeared as a goal in both the Republican and the Democratic platforms in 1944, although more boldly in the Democratic program. The public strongly supported the goal of full employment. In a 1944 Roper poll, 68 percent of the American people answered yes to the question "Do you think the federal government should provide jobs for everyone able and willing to work but who cannot get a job in private employment?"[2] Such sentiments seem radical by today's standards.

The original full employment bill introduced in Congress in 1945 declared:

> All Americans able to work and seeking work have the right to useful, remunerative, regular, and full-time employment, and it is the policy of the United States to assure the existence at all times of sufficient employment opportunities to enable all Americans . . . to exercise this right.[3]

If not enough jobs were produced by the private sector, it would be the responsibility of the government to provide investments and expenditures sufficient to create jobs. Conservative pressures substantially modified the language of the bill as it worked its way through the legislative process in 1945 and 1946. What emerged from Congress was the **Employment Act** (not the Full Employment Act), establishing as a goal of the United States "to use all practicable means [to promote] maximum employment, production, and purchasing power."[4]

Although Congress did not go as far as it might have, the Employment Act was an important piece of legislation. It established the Council of Economic Advisers (CEA) and required that the president submit an economic report to Congress annually. As Congress and the president turned to the actual problem of making economic policy, the consensus of the immediate postwar period evaporated.

By 1947, the Republican majorities in Congress made cutting taxes their highest priority. Following their takeover of the Eightieth Congress, Republican leaders proposed a 20-percent across-the-board cut in personal taxes.[5] In 1947, President Truman vetoed two Republican tax bills, frustrating congressional leaders. Only a few years after passage of the Employment Act, it was clear that there was no consensus on fiscal policy. Economic goals were in conflict in a very partisan context, a pattern that has often been repeated since. Part of the problem was the disagreement among economists about what tax cuts would achieve.[6] No clear guidance existed for fiscal policy, and in its absence, the process became highly politicized.

The Republicans finally got their tax cut in 1948 after a successful appeal to conservative Democrats. It was probably well timed because the first postwar recession occurred in 1948-49. A **recession** is a period of decline in GNP (usually for at least two consecutive three-month quarters) and is most often characterized by rising unemployment and declining inflation. Eight recessions occurred between World War II and mid-1990.

The Kennedy-Johnson Tax Cut

Three recessions occurred during the Eisenhower administration, but none was deep or long-lasting. Under Kennedy and Johnson in the mid-1960s, the economy grew at a steady pace. Inflation and unemployment remained at relatively low levels, and the budget was in balance. The key fiscal policy action of this period was the 1964 tax cut, championed at the time as a model of Keynesian stabilization policy. First developed during the Kennedy administration, the Revenue Act of 1964 included both personal and corporate tax reductions to lower unemployment and stimulate the economy. It worked. Real output rose without aggravating inflation. With more money to spend and more income to tax, government revenues actually increased, despite the tax cut. An example of **demand-side fiscal policy,** the tax cut focused primarily on increasing the purchasing power of consumers. Most economists agree that the Keynesian prescription of increased expenditures and reduced taxes helped spur economic growth and a reduction in unemployment to below 4 percent from 1966 to 1969.[7] But the celebration was short-lived as the specter of inflation began to loom.

The relationship between inflation and employment was a critical element of the economic debate. In the 1960s, most people believed it was possible to maintain full employment while controlling resulting higher inflation by **incomes policy**—voluntary or mandatory wage and price controls. Their economic advisers convinced Kennedy and Johnson to use voluntary wage and price "guideposts" to keep prices from rising. In one famous confrontation, President Kennedy went on television to oppose a steel price increase that violated the administration's targets. The big steel companies eventually backed down and lowered prices.[8]

The Johnson administration increased the amount of money spent on social welfare programs through the "war on poverty" (see Chapter 19). As the administration escalated the American role in Vietnam, defense outlays also began to expand rapidly. The result was overstimulation of the economy and an increase in inflation. The administration was presented with a difficult economic situation and an unpopular political choice. President Johnson turned to restrictive tax legislation for the first time in more than a decade to try to slow the economy. After a period of protracted negotiations between Congress and the president, a tax surcharge was approved. Despite the tax increase, economic activity and inflation continued to increase.[9] Again economic goals clashed with domestic and defense goals, and national priorities shifted. Economic estimates proved unreliable; outlays consistently exceeded projections. A growing frustration and increased conflict developed over economic policy.

Nixon and Wage-Price Controls

More problems with inflation led the Nixon administration to make a surprise intervention in the economy. With congressional authorization, President Nixon in 1971 imposed direct wage and price controls. Although such controls succeeded in restraining inflation in the short run, their premature removal helped fuel an inflationary surge in 1973. Keynesian economics and the notion of a trade-off between inflation and unemployment was coming under increased attack. Critics of Keynesian fiscal policy, such as economist Milton Friedman, urged greater reliance on **monetary policy**—manipulating the money supply—to combat inflation.[10]

After the wage and price controls of the Nixon administration were lifted in 1973, the world economy suffered a severe shock. Members of the Organization of Petroleum Exporting Countries (OPEC) refused to sell their oil to Western nations that traded with and were sympathetic to Israel. The Arab oil embargo revealed just how vulnerable the U.S. economy was to external factors. Reductions in supplies of oil and poor international food harvests triggered a massive round of price increases that moved rapidly through all sectors of the economy. Food and energy price increases accounted for 62 percent of the increase in the consumer price index in 1973.[11]

FORD, CARTER, AND STAGFLATION

Inflation had taken on a life of its own. The mid-1970s became the era of **stagflation**—simultaneously high levels of unemployment and inflation. Economists and politicians were dismayed to learn that the United States could have double-digit inflation during a recession. Only ten years earlier, when President Kennedy confronted big steel, the combined sum of inflation and unemployment was only 6 or 7 percent. By 1974, the sum eclipsed 20 percent as both figures hit double digits.

Presidents Carter and Ford faced difficult economic choices. Conventional Keynesian economics furnished little guidance on how to fight inflation and unemployment both. During this period, federal spending continued to grow, particularly entitlement programs. In the states, taxpayer revolts were under way by 1978. California voters passed Proposition 13, limiting that state's ability to increase property taxes. Other states followed suit. In Washington, D.C., attention turned from fiscal policy to stimulate the economy to monetary policy to control inflation. But when the Federal Reserve Board attempted to clamp down on the money supply in the late 1970s, the result was historically high interest rates that dampened economic activity. The stage was set for the election of Ronald Reagan in 1980.

REAGAN'S FISCAL POLICIES

As we saw in Chapter 3, economic issues were a dominant factor in the election of Ronald Reagan in 1980.[12] Democrats who felt they were worse off in 1980 than they had been in 1976 deserted Jimmy Carter in droves. Reagan outlined several approaches to fiscal policy based on the view that government spending on domestic programs was too high and out of control, that taxes were too high, restricting the economy's growth potential, and that federal deficits were too large. The most important new spending commitment was to increase national defense. President Reagan mobilized political resources to pass the major components of his economic program in 1981.

Many of Reagan's advisers rejected the notion of a trade-off between inflation and unemployment altogether.[13] The **supply-side** approach generally accepted by the administration stressed the need to provide incentives for society's producers. This meant tax breaks for business to encourage investment and expansion. It meant bigger tax reductions for the higher-income segments of society. The across-the-board nature of the income tax cut was an important feature of the policy. It put proportionately more money back in the hands of the wealthy than in the hands of the poor. Fiscal policy was linked to monetary policy by continuing relatively tight monetary policies, carefully controlling the expansion of the money supply. But the high levels of interest rates threatened to choke off the economic recovery in 1981-82, and the Reagan administration began to pressure the Federal Reserve Board to loosen its grip on the money supply.

In spite of Reagan's campaign speeches against the budget deficit, the goal of a balanced budget was abandoned in favor of other economic and political priorities. Large increases in defense spending, coupled with the largest tax cut in history, created structural deficits—a set of spending commitments greater than the revenue-producing capacity of existing tax policies—causing division within the administration.

Deficits would be the most controversial part of the Reagan economic record. The other news was better. Although unemployment had risen to a high of around 10 percent in 1982, it declined to 5.2 percent by the end of 1988. The recovery that began in 1982 was sustained throughout the Reagan and early Bush presidencies—the longest period without a recession in history. On the inflation front, the administration was also successful. Aided by a glut in the world oil market, which caused declines in the price of petroleum products, inflation in the United States declined from the double-digit range to around 4 percent in the 1980s. Inflation climbed toward 5 pecent under President Bush in 1989 and 1990. Figure 18-1 shows actual and projected inflation, unemployment, and real growth in GNP from 1980 to 1995.

THE EFFECTIVENESS OF FISCAL POLICY

Since the 1930s, fiscal policy has been one of the federal government's most important tools in managing the economy. Yet governing problems have often blunted its effectiveness. A tax cut or increase that might take six weeks for a parliamentary system to adopt might take Congress and the president six months or even as long as two years to enact, or a deadlock might prevent it from ever

FIGURE 18–1

ECONOMIC PERFORMANCE AND PROJECTIONS, 1980–1995

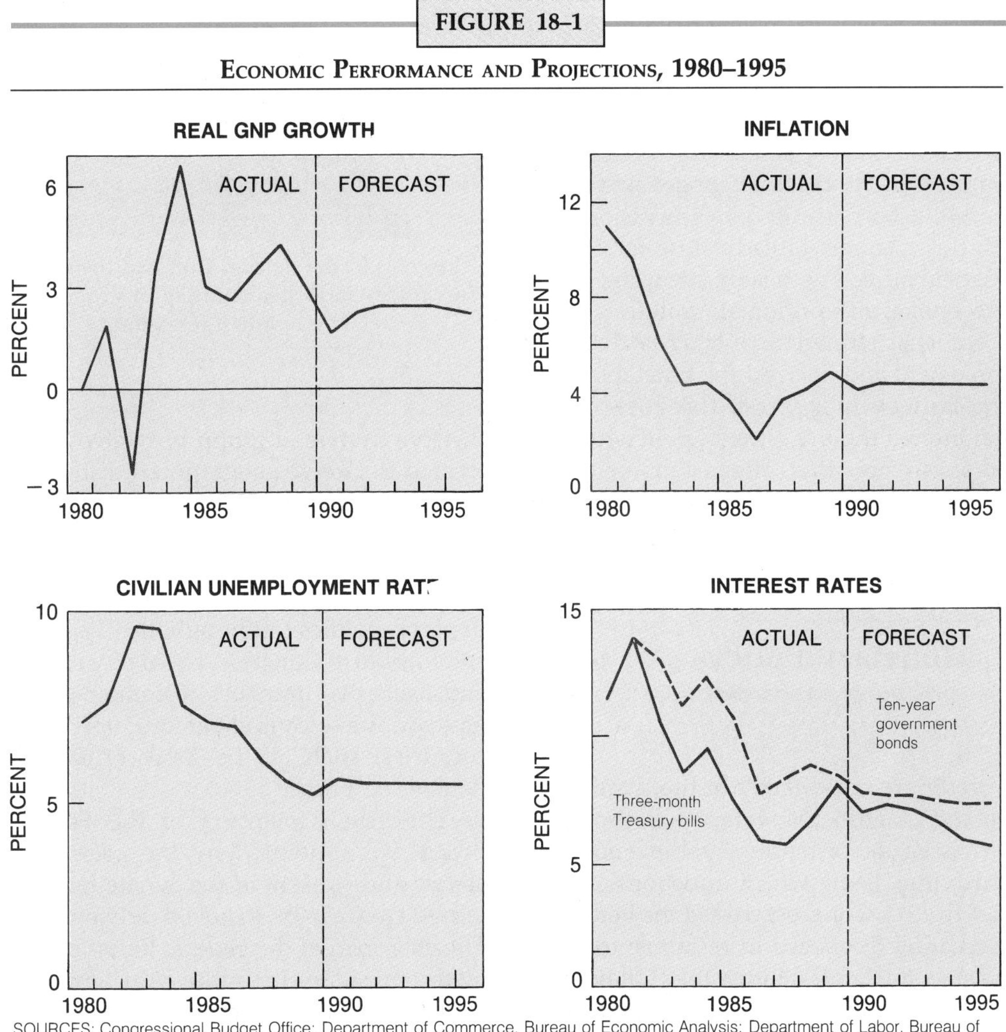

SOURCES: Congressional Budget Office; Department of Commerce, Bureau of Economic Analysis; Department of Labor, Bureau of Labor Statistics; Federal Reserve Board, 1990.

passing at all. A study by the Congressional Research Service found that fiscal policy can help stabilize the economy, but in a number of instances, policies have taken effect too late to be effective.[14]

In recent years, however, paralysis over taxing and spending choices has, in effect, choked off the potential of fiscal policy as a tool of economic management. The recession of 1982 helped reduce the double-digit inflation of the late 1970s, but monetary policy has been the main vehicle for keeping it under control since. While the large budget deficits have acted to stimulate the economy and prevent recession, many remain concerned about the long-term consequences of running substantial deficits during periods of prosperity. As outlays have become more inflexible, and revenues have become extremely politicized, the two basic ingredients of fiscal policy have become nearly impossible to manipulate for economic reasons. The Balanced Budget Act made deficit reduction a higher priority than fiscal policy. This posed a potentially dangerous situation for President Bush and Congress in the 1990s. Oil prices skyrocketed to over $40 a barrel after Iraq's invasion of Kuwait. With the economy already close to recession, tax increases coupled with large spending cuts threatened to choke off continued growth. As a result, both branches struggled to reach a deficit-reduction agreement and delayed the timetable for balancing the budget. In general, the governing problems that limited the use of fiscal policy led to increased emphasis on other dimensions of economic policy, particularly monetary policy.

The crisis in the Persian Gulf had the effect of raising fuel prices and threatening to push the U.S. economy into a recession.

Monetary Policy

THE FEDERAL RESERVE SYSTEM

Money and credit are not directly in the hands of the president and Congress. Monetary policy in the United States is made primarily by the **Federal Reserve Board (the Fed),** which functions as a central bank.[15] In 1913, Congress passed the Federal Reserve Act creating the board in response to the Panic of 1907 and the bank failures that followed. The Federal Reserve Board oversees the Federal Reserve System, a group of twelve member banks located in twelve geographical districts. The Fed is a "bankers' bank," dealing with other large banks, not consumers or corporations. While the Fed operates as a central bank, it still reflects the original mandate to keep its banking operations independent of politics. Although the Fed is ultimately responsible to Congress, the ability of the legislative and executive branches to influence its actions is limited, unlike central banking operations in other countries, such as the Bank of England or the Banque de France.

The seven members of the Federal Reserve Board are appointed by the president with the advice and consent of the Senate for fourteen-year terms. They can be removed only by impeachment. The chairman of the Federal Reserve Board, named by the president for a four-year term, is one of the most influential economic policy-makers in the country. Alan Greenspan was appointed to chair the Fed in 1987, succeeding Paul Volcker, who served under both Carter and Reagan.

One of the key decision-making groups in monetary policy is the **Federal Open Market Committee (FOMC)**, a panel of the seven governors (the official title of board members) and five of the twelve federal reserve member bank presidents. Like the Supreme Court, the FOMC meets in secret, making decisions on the sale and purchase of government securities on the open market. To understand how this affects money and interest, we must look more closely at the monetary system.

Money supply consists of all the currency and bank deposits, vehicles of economic exchange and transaction backed up by the strength of the nation's economy. Currency is no longer backed by silver or gold, but its value is maintained by its limited supply, by trust, and by general convention. The three components of the money supply are as follows:

> M1: the sum of currency and demand deposits (checking accounts), traveler's checks, and money that is likely to be used for current purchases
>
> M2: M1, plus money and assets more likely to be held as long-term financial assets, such as savings accounts, small time deposits, money-market mutual fund shares, and Eurodollar deposits
>
> M3: M2, plus large time deposits and institutional money-market fund balances

Like other economic policies developed in the twentieth century, monetary policy attempts to counter swings in the private sector economy. If the Fed wants to reduce credit, it cuts down the reserves available to member banks and raises interest rates. Operating through the Open Market Committee, the Fed buys or sells government securities. When it sells securities to the banks, it reduces the reserves available to the banks. This operates to restrict the growth of M1 and tends to raise interest rates. High interest rates can also be fostered by the Fed's discount-rate policy. The discount rate is the interest rate at which the central bank loans money to its member banks, which affects the rates they charge their own customers.

Historically, the Fed has been more conservative than other government decision-makers and has often pursued policies that seemed to hold back economic expansion. How can the president and Congress coordinate monetary policy with other economic policies? The president can eventually appoint a new Fed chairman, but he may have to wait several years. Presidents, however, are not totally without other influence over the course of monetary policy. A recent study showed that, despite the frequent complaints of presidents, Fed policy does respond to guidance from the White House.[16] Although the Federal Reserve Board is a creature of Congress and subject to any changes in its organization and operation that Congress may make, most agree that Congress exerts relatively little control over the Fed.

Should Congress and the president have more influence over the money supply and interest rates? Supporters of the current arrangement fear politicizing monetary policy and argue for the continued independence of the Federal Reserve Board. Critics maintain that central banks function just as effectively in parliamentary systems, where the government has more control and produce monetary policy that is more consistent with other economic policies. Although Fed decisions respond indirectly to pressure from the president and Congress, questions about control of monetary policy remain, particularly when Federal Reserve Board policies are unpopular.

U.S. MONETARY POLICY IN THE GLOBAL ECONOMY

The economy of the United States is increasingly intertwined with the world economy.[17] The economic events of 1987, which culminated in the stock market crash, can be traced to U.S. monetary policy and its combined effects with domestic fiscal policy and the economic policies of other industrialized nations.

In response to double-digit inflation and interest rates topping 20 percent, the United States began a period of restrictive monetary policy in 1979. Under Fed Chairman Paul Volcker, growth of the money supply was carefully targeted to reduce domestic inflation. Other nations followed suit but also pursued a less stimulative fiscal policy. While U.S. budget deficits were rising, most other nations were reducing their deficits. Consequently, in 1980 and 1981 inflation-adjusted interest rates in the

FIGURE 18–2

REAL LONG-TERM INTEREST RATES

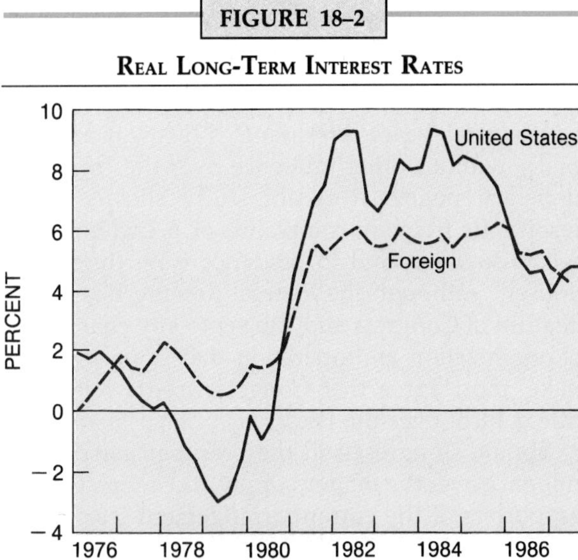

SOURCE: Congressional Budget Office, 1988.

United States rose above those in other countries (see Figure 18-2). As the 1981 tax cut and defense buildup stimulated the economy, the U.S. budget deficit grew to more than 5 percent of GNP. This had two important consequences. The value of the dollar abroad rose to record levels, and significant amounts of foreign capital flowed into the United States. The combined effect of fiscal and monetary policy severely weakened the competitiveness of U.S. industry abroad. As a result, in a remarkably short period of time the United States went from a net creditor to a debtor nation.

With inflation under control, U.S. policy-makers looked with increasing alarm at the growing trade deficit. As a result, restrictive U.S. monetary policy was eased in 1984, reducing the difference between U.S. and foreign real interest rates (see Figure 18-2). Beginning in 1985, the value of the dollar on overseas currency markets began to fall very quickly. By the end of 1986, the value of the dollar had fallen by one-third against the currencies of America's major trading partners. Fears of a collapse of the dollar laid the groundwork for the volatile financial markets and world stock market collapse in 1987.

Financial ministers of the major industrial nations agreed that the dollar had fallen enough and that more stable exchange rates would be desirable. Their efforts failed to stem the decline, however, as private investors continued to unload their dollars. In the United States, interest rates began to rise in response to concern about renewed inflation. Stock market prices continued to climb to record highs. Because foreign governments also allowed their interest rates to rise, the Federal Reserve Board continued to tighten monetary policy to prevent further declines in the dollar. In 1987, the Fed limited growth in the money supply so that it fell below its targeted expansion rate. As a result, U.S. interest rates increased again.

Nervous investors around the world responded on October 19, 1987, when the U.S. stock market registered its largest single decline in history (see Chapter 3). The Federal Reserve Board quickly shifted gears in the wake of the crash, immediately allowing the money supply to expand and interest rates to fall. By 1988, it appeared that the Fed's response had helped avoid the onset of a disastrous depression, such as the one that followed the market crash in 1929. The long-term result, however, was a very difficult challenge for U.S. economic policy-makers. Following the crash, the Federal Reserve Board was faced with the tricky prospect of walking a tightrope between an overly restrictive monetary policy, which could lead to a recession, and an overly expansionist policy, which could increase inflation and lead to further steep declines in the dollar. The Congressional Budget Office concluded:

> The turbulent events of 1987 were global in both their causes and effects. They demonstrated the openness of the U.S. economy, and the degree to which conditions in the United States are influenced not only by domestic economic policy but by foreign fiscal, monetary, and exchange rate politics as well as by foreign private investors operating in global financial markets. The result is increased uncertainty both here and abroad .... It has become more difficult now than at any time in recent past to foresee fundamental economic trends, the responses of policymakers to those trends, and the outcomes of the policies themselves.[18]

The Federal Reserve Board continued to pursue restrictive monetary policy to prevent inflation through 1988 and 1989, slowing real economic growth from 5.5 percent in 1987 to 4 percent in 1988 and to 2 percent in 1989.[19] Economic growth was also reduced by the modest deficit reductions and restrictive monetary policy pursued by the central banks of other industrialized nations. Beginning in the middle of 1989, consistent with the urgings of the Bush administration, the Fed began to loosen restrictions to allow expansion of the money supply and lower interest rates. Yet fears of inflation remained because of high import prices and other factors. With forecasts showing relatively modest growth and continued inflationary pressure in the early 1990s, the Fed continued to walk a careful line in keeping the economy on track. Monetary policy not only affects economic activity in the United States but has important consequences for the balance of trade.

Trade Policy

Since colonial days, American leaders have been concerned about trade with other nations. Should goods be freely exchanged between nations, or do certain domestic industries need protection from cheap foreign imports? Under what circumstances might the government place quotas or impose tariffs on imports? Should the United States retaliate against unfair trade practices abroad or against any nation that has a substantial trade surplus with the United States?

TRADE AND THE U.S. ECONOMY

Economists generally favor a policy of free trade on the basis of the theory of **comparative advantage.** The open exchange of goods between nations allows each nation to export what it produces most efficiently and cheaply and to import goods that other countries produce most efficiently. The net result is higher productivity, lower consumer prices, and more rapid economic growth. So why not leave trading markets completely open? Because political and nationalistic concerns create strong pressures to protect certain domestic industries from cheaper foreign competition. Whether demands for protectionism come from American autoworkers or from French farmers, they can be a potent political force.

In the early years of the Republic, the U.S. economy was primarily based on trade of raw materials, agricultural goods, rum, and other such products. Despite his general support for market capitalism, Secretary of the Treasury Alexander Hamilton's first national economic policies called for **tariffs,** fees or duties placed on imported goods, to protect America's fledgling industries producing manufactured goods. Throughout the nineteenth century, Congress debated the advisability of tariffs on imported products. During the same period, the United States continued to be a net importer of manufactured goods and the recipient of foreign capital.[20] By the beginning of the twentieth century, however, the U.S. economy had been transformed

FIGURE 18–3

THE U.S. TRADE DEFICIT, 1980–1989

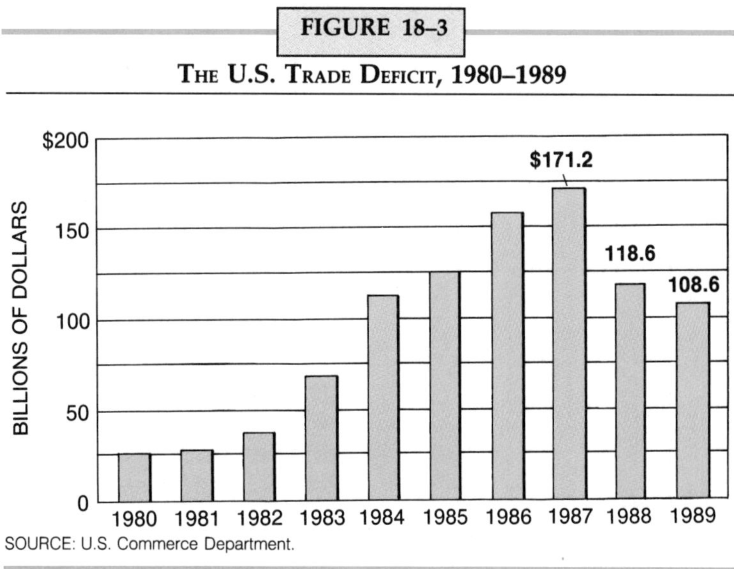

SOURCE: U.S. Commerce Department.

by the industrial revolution. Trade began to account for less and less GNP as the economic system became more self-sufficient.

Protectionism was blamed for the severity of the Great Depression in the 1930s. Following the stock market crash of 1929, the 1930 Smoot-Hawley tariffs set off a round of retaliatory international protectionism that dried up world trade and led to the most devastating world depression in history. When the world economy recovered after World War II, care was taken not to repeat the mistake of the 1930s. In 1947, the world's industrial nations signed a General Agreement on Tariffs and Trade (GATT) to regulate commerce and promote open trade. Nonetheless, even under that agreement some tariffs and protectionist measures were allowed. Dominant and self-sufficient in the postwar economy, U.S. exports and imports declined to 5 percent of GNP by 1960.

As the first signs of the globalization of the economy began to appear in the 1960s, imports and exports once again began to increase. By 1980, their share of GNP had grown to 12.5 percent of GNP. But after 1975, the United States began to import more than it exported. The gap between imports and exports—the trade deficit—began to grow dramatically in the early 1980s as the strong dollar hurt U.S. exporters. Figure 18-3 shows the trade deficit in the 1980s, reaching a peak of $171 billion in 1987. Even though the value of the dollar began to plunge after 1985, the trade deficit continued to grow. American industries were no longer competitive in world markets. The nation that had invented the color television, the microwave oven, and the video recorder was completely shut out of the world market for these goods. Most or all of those products were made overseas and imported into the United States. Americans developed a taste for imported goods—European cars; Japanese cameras, skis, and pianos; clothing from the Far East; and a long list of other consumer goods. Figure 18-4 shows the increasing penetration of foreign goods into the United States in the 1980s, growing to almost 23 percent by 1987. This gave rise to increasingly vocal calls for protective trade legislation.

FIGURE 18–4

FOREIGN GOODS IN U.S. MARKET

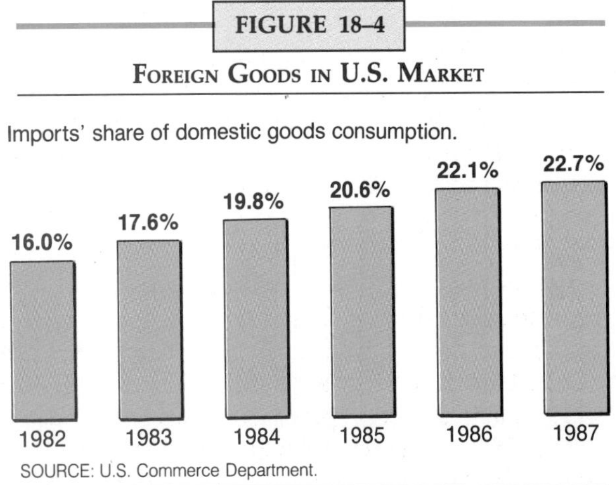

SOURCE: U.S. Commerce Department.

GROWING DEMANDS FOR PROTECTION

As exports dropped and American factories closed their doors, demands for protection for domestic industries escalated. The trade imbalance was particularly acute with Japan, whose goods flooded the American market. Trade imbalances also grew with Europe and the emerging industrial nations of the Pacific Basin. Imported cars, which had been less than 10 percent of the U.S. market in the 1960s, grew to 27 percent by 1980.[21] Sales of American-made cars slumped. Chrysler teetered on the brink of bankruptcy, and only a bailout by the federal government kept the number-three U.S. automaker afloat. A quarter of a million jobs in the auto industry were lost, and in 1980 alone, some 1,500 car dealers went out of business. A coalition of industry and labor demanded government protection from Japanese imports, pressuring Congress and the president to impose quotas on Japanese cars. Fearing legislation, the Japanese adopted their own "voluntary" quotas. The recovery of the domestic auto industry after 1982 helped diffuse some of the pressure temporarily.

The steel industry was also badly hurt; many small and medium firms closed their doors. Foreign steel imports reached 23 percent of total U.S. consumption in 1983.[22] Producers, such as U.S. Steel and Bethlehem Steel, and their employees led the growing demands for restricting the amount of foreign steel sold in the United States to a total of 15 percent. They claimed that overseas producers were "**dumping**"—selling goods for less than they sold them in their own domestic markets in order to establish a market share. Dumping, made possible by government subsidies, is prohibited by U.S. law but is difficult to prove. In 1978, the Carter admin-

The Bush administration accused Korea of "dumping" sweaters and other clothing, made in factories like the one above, by selling them cheaper in the U.S. than in their home market.

istration introduced a "trigger price mechanism" that automatically initiated a dumping investigation when the price of imported steel fell below a certain level. In 1982, European steel producers agreed to a voluntary quota on imports to the United States.

Protection for a nation's industries, whether in the form of tariffs or quotas, may save jobs and even entire industrial sectors, but it does incur a cost. Protectionism insulates industries from competition, discourages increases in efficiency and productivity, and costs consumers billions of dollars. Improvements in the quality control of U.S. automakers were directly linked to the competition from Japan. In the long run, protectionism may reduce imports, but it will not make exports more competitive in the world market. Nonetheless, as jobs were lost and factories closed, demands for protection came from additional sectors of the American economy—for example, shoes, clothing, and electronics. Policy-makers walked a tightrope between a policy of open and free trade and protecting U.S. industries.

THE POLITICS OF TRADE

American leaders, particularly Republicans, have long voiced strong support for free trade, but as economist Herbert Stein observed, "Every American president denies that he is protectionist, but presidents differ in the degree to which they are prepared to make exceptions."[23] Protectionism has increased since 1955. Of all the goods imported into the United States in 1986, some 22 percent were covered by one kind of special protection or another, compared with 12 percent in 1980 and only 8 percent in 1975. Table 18-1 compares imports, the costs to consumers of tariffs and quotas, and the estimated decrease in imports caused by special protection from 1955 to 1985.

The voluntary limits on Japanese imports, according to one estimate, boosted the average cost of each car sold in the United States by $2,500. President Reagan announced in 1985 that he would not press for the curbs to continue, but rumblings in Congress convinced the Japanese to keep them. American automakers lobbied for even harsher restrictions. The steelmakers won restraints in 1983, when a quota for foreign steel of 20 percent of the domestic market was announced. The administration negotiated tough bilateral treaties with Hong Kong, Taiwan, and South Korea on a variety of goods. Higher duties were placed on motorcycles to help America's only producer, Harley-Davidson.

In 1987, a trade war with Europe was threatened when the Reagan administration announced its intention to levy a 200-percent tariff on European wine, cheese, and other foods in retaliation for European Economic Community restrictions on U.S. grain exports. Both sides finally backed down, but the harsh exchanges reflected the growing importance of trade in the world economy and the administration's concern about the U.S. trade deficit. Problems were also encountered with Canada, America's largest trading partner. A bilateral agreement in 1987 helped diffuse some of the tension.

Protectionist sentiments remain strong in Congress and were an important issue in the 1988 presidential election. Of all the candidates, Democrat Richard Gephardt of Missouri took the toughest stance on trade. His controversial proposals called for automatic sanctions against Japan and other countries running a large trade surplus with the United States. Gephardt's campaign commercials claimed that a Korean-made Hyundai automobile would cost $48,000 if the United States had trade barriers comparable to those in Korea. This approach helped him win the Iowa caucuses and thrust him into the race for the Democratic nomination for president. But the tough-trade message did not sell as well in the South on Super Tuesday or in states in the next primaries, and Gephardt eventually withdrew from the race. But although they backed away from Gephardt's more punitive approach, members of Congress were determined to get tough on trade.

Congress passed a trade bill that was vetoed by Reagan in 1988. Included were tougher rules against unfair trade practices, expanded promotion of U.S. exports, authorization for a new round of talks to expand GATT, and training programs for displaced American workers. Congress would have the last word on the trade bill, however, before the election. With several controversial provisions removed, Congress passed the identical bill in August 1988 that President Reagan reluctantly signed into law. The bill extended presidential authority to negotiate trade agreements; required the president to retaliate against unfair trade practices or explain why not; expanded benefits to workers displaced by imports; and strengthened export promotion and training programs. One of the most important elements of trade policy surrounded the sensitive negotiations to revise the General Agreement on Tariffs and Trade. The Uruguay round of GATT, completed in 1990, gave the United States an opportunity to add such items as intellectual property and financial services to the list of products. Although trade deficits have been reduced from the 1987 peak, cutting them further remains an important issue for Congress and President Bush in the 1990s.

TABLE 18–1

GROWTH OF U.S. IMPORTS AFFECTED BY SPECIAL PROTECTION, 1955–1985 (DOLLARS IN BILLIONS)

	Total U.S. Imports	Value of Imports Affected by Special Protection	Cost to Consumers of Special Protection	Estimated Decrease in Imports Caused by Special Protection
1955	$ 11.6	$ 0.577	$ 0.703	$ 0.629
1960	15.1	3.380	6.352	5.917
1965	21.5	4.759	9.627	8.720
1970	40.2	9.655	16.439	14.631
1975	99.3	7.894	13.117	12.424
1980	245.3	28.928	32.749	22.619
1985*	360.0	80.000	65.000	50.000

*Estimate

SOURCE: Institute for International Economics.

DOES THE UNITED STATES NEED AN INDUSTRIAL POLICY?

Some have suggested that one way to reduce the trade deficit is to develop an aggressive national industrial policy to help boost technological innovation, product development, and marketing.

Industrial policy, in general, is any government policy designed to promote or facilitate changes in the structure of the economy.[24] The government of Great Britain in the 1960s and 1970s used industrial policy to save declining heavy industry, infusing money to many ailing industries and partly nationalizing the coal, steel, automobile, and shipbuilding industries. One critic suggests that such policies "seem almost to be devoted to creating an industrial museum."[25] However, defenders note that without government assistance, Great Britain might have lost all domestic steel and auto production, a highly undesirable situation both politically and strategically. An example in the United States was the Chrysler bailout in the late 1970s. Facing bankruptcy and the loss of hundreds of thousands of jobs, the government fashioned a loan and loan guarantee program to keep the giant corporation afloat. Only a few years later, the third largest U.S. auto manufacturer was able to pay off the loans early. Although some still dispute the efficacy of the program, most point to Chrysler as a successful example of an industrial policy that backs older companies in trouble.

An alternate industrial policy strategy of developing new industries was proposed by Robert Reich in his book *The Next American Frontier*.[26] The government, says Reich, should establish policies to promote the new high-tech growth industries, redirecting resources away from older industries on the decline to new fields, such as computers, microchips, aerospace, and other new areas. The Japanese Ministry of International Trade and Industry (MITI), often cited as a model for this approach, created a "miracle by design."[27] Proponents suggest that a similar agency could be created in the United States to help foster economic growth, productivity increases, and the transition of economic resources from noncompetitive areas to new growth areas.

Industrial policy proposals were met with skepticism in many quarters. Former Council of Economic Advisers Chair Charles L. Schultz challenges the potential of industrial policy, arguing that the United States has not been deindustrializing as some claim and that it has in fact made significant progress in industrial growth in the past decade.[28] Schultz also challenges the real impact of MITI in

Japan. He claims not only that it is impossible for a government to pick the proper "mix" of industries for a country but also that to try to do so would be disastrous.

Concerns about the productivity of American industry and declining trade competitiveness have given impetus to the discussion of industrial policy and other ways to boost U.S. exports. The trade deficit and policies designed to reduce it will continue to be a critical element of the economic policy debate in the coming decade. America's use of natural resources and its dependence on imported oil are also a key part of that debate.

Energy

ENERGY IN THE UNITED STATES

The economies of the developed world depend on energy. Without petroleum, coal, nuclear power, or natural gas, factories and cities would grind to a halt. Fears of such an eventuality were sparked in many industrialized nations when the flow of oil from the Middle East was shut off in 1973 and again with the threat of a war in the Persian Gulf in 1990. Since the Arab oil embargo, energy has been a critical policy concern of nations around the world.

FIGURE 18-5

U.S. ENERGY SOURCES, 1986.

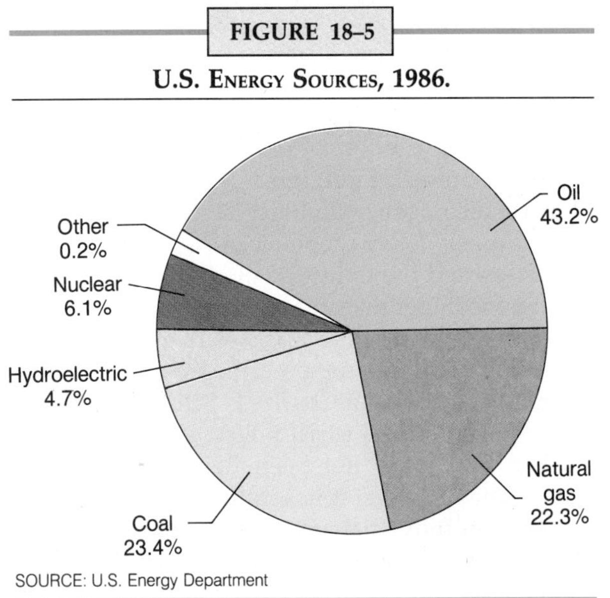

SOURCE: U.S. Energy Department

The United States is blessed with rich natural energy resources that are vast in scope, compared with the size of the population it has to support. The nation has three main sources of energy: oil, coal, and natural gas (see Figure 18-5). Americans became used to cheap and abundant energy as the United States became the leading economic power. Today, the United States is the biggest consumer of energy in the world. With only 2 percent of the world's population, the United States uses 24 percent of the world's energy resources, about double what Europe and Japan use per unit of economic output. China, in contrast, has 20 percent of the world's population but uses only 9 percent of its energy.[29] With the 1973 Arab oil embargo, it became clear that domestic production of oil was unable to meet demand. The United States has declining reserves, and most of the known world oil reserves are in the Middle East. The realization of the nation's energy dependence jolted the American people. Demands for exploitation of new energy resources and for conservation of existing sources grew, and many of these new demands came into sharp conflict with other economic and environmental priorities.

In 1978, the peak year for petroleum consumption, the United States imported half of the oil it consumed. By the mid-1980s, only one-third of domestic consumption was imported, still a substantial amount. Imports from the Organization of Petroleum Exporting Countries declined between 1979 and 1985. However, U.S. energy output is not increasing, and oil exports rose again after 1985. By 1990, imports were back to near 50 percent of all oil consumed. U.S. dependence on foreign oil imports played a role in President Bush's decision to deploy over 250,000 troops in the Middle East in 1990.

Energy is crucial to the economy in two major ways: Economic growth is dependent on continued energy supply, and energy pricing can have severe inflationary effects on prices. In addition, petroleum is a nonrenewable resource. Once consumed, it is gone. Alternative energy sources, such as the sun, wind, water, or wood, are renewable resources, but each has technological, economic, or other limitations. Coal, the most abundant fuel in the United States (there is a seven hundred years supply), is also one of the dirtiest to burn. Public policy on energy aims to ensure a constant supply of energy at relatively stable prices without devastating the environment—a big order to fill.

In addition to the problem of maintaining supply, energy prices have a tremendous effect on overall price levels. The surge of inflation that occurred in the early 1970s was largely triggered by the price increases caused by the oil embargo. Gasoline sold for 27 cents a gallon in 1973. By 1977, it was 62 cents a gallon. Prices hit a peak in 1981, when gasoline cost American consumers $1.32 per gallon, a level unthinkable only a few years earlier. Old gas pumps that were not calibrated for more than 99 cents a gallon had to be altered or junked. Yet the United States still enjoyed fuel prices some 50 to 75 percent cheaper than in many industrialized nations, where a gallon of gas sells for the equivalent of $3.00 to $5.00. Some analysts predicted gasoline prices above $2.00 a gallon after the 1990 crisis in the Gulf.

DECONTROL OF ENERGY PRICES

The energy-pricing problem is directly related to supply. For many years, government policies regulated the price of oil and natural gas, keeping them artificially low. That policy had several advantages. People could heat their homes and drive their cars relatively cheaply. Industries could expand production without heavy additional energy costs. But with low prices, consumers treat energy almost as if it were a free good. Suddenly, when supply shortages appear, the government becomes concerned with cutting consumption.

Artificially cheap prices work against conservation, so in 1979, President Carter decontrolled domestic oil prices, allowing them to rise to the world level. His action had both positive and negative effects. First, it encouraged conservation. People turned down thermostats, bought more fuel-efficient cars, turned off lights, and so on. Second, it encouraged exploration and production. With decontrol, oil and other energy companies could explore for new sources of oil and gas with the promise of high prices and high profits. Reliance on economic market mechanisms, as opposed to government regulation, is typical of the change in approach that characterized public policy in the late 1970s and 1980s. Although deregulation is more traditionally a Republican stance, the Democratic party supported movement in this direction as well. However, direct government intervention also played a major role in reducing energy consumption. Government requirements that automakers produce more fuel-efficient cars resulted in dramatic fuel savings in the last decade, despite initial resistance from manufacturers.

Decontrol also had negative consequences. Price increases were inflationary, although this was a short-term effect. More seriously, the tripling and quadrupling of energy prices severely hurt people on the lower end of the economic ladder. Stories of elderly and poor people huddled in freezing tenements began to appear in the press with alarming regularity. Although some remedial actions were taken, the need to bring U.S. energy pricing into line had serious social costs. In the 1980s, the same procedure took place with natural gas.

NUCLEAR POWER

When the nuclear age dawned at the end of World War II, government promised that the destructive power of the atom would be harnessed for constructive peacetime uses. The Atomic Energy Commission (AEC) was formed to put nuclear energy to work, providing cheap and renewable energy forever. Through the 1950s and 1960s, a few nuclear power plants were licensed by the AEC, but public concern about their safety began to grow. The AEC was merged into the Department of Energy in the 1970s, and the Nuclear Regulatory Commission was charged with ensuring nuclear safety. Despite regulations so strict that it can take a decade to license a plant, the nuclear accident at Three Mile Island nuclear plant in 1979 brought the growing controversy to a head. By the 1980s, it was clear that nuclear power would not provide the alternative energy source for the next century once envisioned. The public, while concerned with economy and fuel efficiency, remains too nervous about nuclear power to make it a viable option. In addition, the unexpectedly high costs of nuclear power have led many experts to revise their initially rosy predictions of nuclear energy as the permanent answer to the nation's energy needs.

ANOTHER ENERGY CRISIS IN THE 1990S?

Could the United States repeat the mistakes of the 1970s twenty years later with a return to lines at gasoline pumps and brownouts? The energy glut of

Nuclear power remains a controversial and expensive source of energy.

the mid-1980s may have lulled the public, business leaders, and public officials into complacency. A number of disturbing trends are apparent, particularly the growing dependence on foreign oil. Since 1985, domestic oil production has steadily declined while imports rose from 5 million barrels a day to 8 million barrels a day in 1989[30]. Figure 18-6 shows these trends, which some forecasts claim could result in imports of 60 percent or more by the end of the 1990s. Electricity production may be insufficient, with no new nuclear plants ordered since 1973 and new restrictions on coal-fired plants because of the 1990 Clean Air Act revision. At the same time, energy consumption continued to increase, with Americans turning back to bigger, less energy-efficient cars.

The Bush administration began developing a national energy strategy that would attempt to balance economic, energy, and environmental needs. Bush departed from the energy policies of the Reagan administration in a number of ways. Reagan promised to eliminate the Department of Energy during the 1980 campaign, believing that energy policy was best left to the private sector. When the elimination of the department became politically impossible, the administration still dropped conservation plans that had been initiated during the Carter administration. Bush, in contrast, supported efforts by Energy Department officials to place more emphasis on environmental and conservation efforts and mandated them to develop a national energy strategy by early 1991.[31]

The process of developing a national energy strategy provoked sharp conflicts between industry and environmentalists, and the president took a cautious approach to proposals that might hurt the economy. Environmentalists urged the development of renewable energy sources, such as solar and wind energy. Although efforts were begun to encourage renewable sources during the Carter administration, they were largely dropped during the 1980s because of the Reagan administration's opposition and falling energy prices. Bush's Energy Secretary, James Watkins, and department officials promised that renewable sources would be part of the national energy strategy.

Concern with growing dependence on foreign oil imports in the 1990s also affected the strategy. The oil industry and oil state legislators proposed increased incentives for domestic exploration and production. But oil drilling in environmentally sensitive areas became extremely unpopular with the public after the disastrous spill off the Alaskan coast by the *Exxon Valdez* in March 1989. Immediately after the accident, Congress stopped action on legislation that would have allowed additional drilling in Alaska wilderness areas. The Bush administration received a task force report that urged that new exploratory drilling off the coasts of Florida and California be postponed. But as energy supplies were threatened because of the conflict in the Mid East, another serious energy crisis faced the United States and her allies in the 1990s.

Energy needed to fuel economic growth often degrades the land, fouls the air, and endangers the health of the population. In spite of continued pressure for energy production and economic

FIGURE 18–6

GROWING DEPENDENCE ON IMPORTED OIL

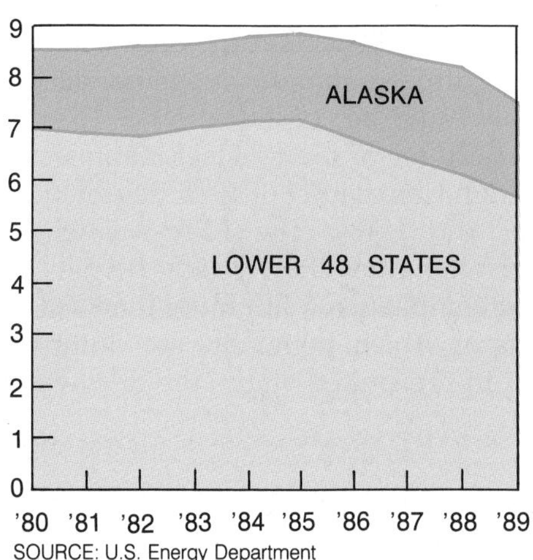

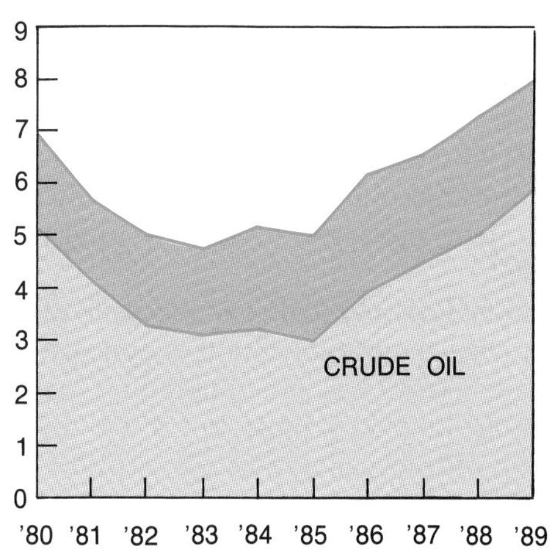

SOURCE: U.S. Energy Department

development, environmental constraints and limitations have been imposed.

The Environment

POLLUTION AND THREATS TO THE EARTH

The United States is a wasteful society. With abundant natural resources, early developers of the American economy disregarded questions of ecological balance or resource depletion. Consider what each American uses in his or her lifetime—more than 20,000 gallons of gasoline, 50 tons of iron and steel, and 13,000 pounds of paper. Much of what is consumed is in turn discarded. In a lifetime, the average American will throw away 125 tons of garbage, including 10,000 throwaway bottles, 17,000 cans, and 27,000 bottle caps. [32] Americans produce over 150 million tons of garbage every year—enough to fill the New Orleans Superdome twice a day. But the problem is more than trash: Today industrial pollution threatens plants, animals, buildings, rivers, oceans, and the land. Air pollution from automobiles and factories presents major health hazards to citizens living in big cities. Syringes and medical waste wash ashore on East Coast beaches. The release of fluorocarbons from aerosol cans is a major factor in the depletion of the ozone layer of the earth's upper atmosphere, increasing the amount of dangerous ultraviolet light reaching the earth. Scientists believe that pollution is causing a "greenhouse" effect that is raising temperatures on earth. Acid rain has damaged the forests in large areas of the Northeast and Canada and polluted lakes and rivers.

Before large-scale industrialization, it was natural to ignore the environment, and throughout most of American history, the environment was most forgiving. Resources seemed inexhaustible. Pollution was regarded as an inevitable by-product of economic progress. But as more Americans bought automobiles, the air grew dirtier and more dangerous. As the factories multiplied and continued to pour their waste into rivers and lakes, fish died and some rivers were so filthy they caught fire. Sentiment to protect the environment grew, but very slowly at first. In 1948, an air pollution emergency over the smokestack town of Denora, Pennsylvania, claimed forty-eight lives.[33] Cities such as Pittsburgh and Los Angeles had frequent smog alerts. Yet until the late 1960s, virtually no significant public policy to curb pollution had emerged.

Despite the deaths at Denora, the federal government did not pass air pollution legislation until 1955. Up to this point, emissions were completely unrestricted. Although Congress was warned about the dangers of pollution in Lake Erie as early as 1912, permanent water pollution legislation was not passed until 1956.[34] By then, Lake Erie was well on its way to becoming an ecologically dead lake. How did the environment suddenly become a public issue in the 1960s?

The environmental movement is an example of how the public policy agenda can change. Concern with environmental issues was precipitated by the emergence of public interest groups, but it was an issue that gained widespread grassroots support. In 1965, some 17 percent of the general public mentioned reducing pollution as one of the three most important issues. By 1970, this figure had tripled, to 53 percent.[35] The combination of elite group leadership and public support led to meaningful legislation.

MAJOR ENVIRONMENTAL LEGISLATION

Legislative efforts came to fruition with the passage of three major bills between 1969 and 1972. The first was the National Environmental Policy Act of 1969. Intended to prevent government agencies and programs from damaging the natural environment, the law required the filing of *environmental impact statements* identifying the effect of a proposed policy on the environment.[36] One of the most famous impact statements concerned a small fish called the snail darter. Protection of this endangered species held up a major federal water project for years. The 1969 act created numerous opportunities for public interest groups to challenge federal projects and delay or prevent their implementation. Cases like that of the snail darter led to criticism from environmental opponents that broader economic interests were being subverted to minor, even frivolous, concerns.

Congress created the **Environmental Protection Agency (EPA)** in 1970 to administer the growing number of environmental programs, giving the EPA power to develop regulations. This awesome task quickly enmeshed the EPA in political controversy. The Clean Air Act of 1970, the second major bill, gave the Department of Transportation some responsibility in reducing auto emissions. First implemented in the 1968 model year, auto emission control requirements were increasingly tightened during the 1970s. Under the Clean Air Act, the EPA was required to monitor industrial air pollution in literally hundreds of industries.

A third major piece of legislation was the Water Pollution Control Act of 1972, designed to clean up rivers and lakes. The EPA was charged with developing guidelines, issuing permits, and monitoring compliance. With more than sixty thousand points at which pollutants are dumped into the water in the United States, the EPA was presented

Beaches on the East Coast had to be closed when syringes and other medical wastes washed upon the shore.

POLITICAL INSIGHT 18-1

MAJOR ENVIRONMENTAL LAWS

1969 **The National Environmental Policy Act** required government agencies to submit environmental impact statements identifying the effect a proposed policy would have on the environment. This act did not apply to the private sector.

1970 **The Clean Air Act** created the Environmental Protection Agency and gave it authority to monitor industry compliance with pollution laws. It also gave the Department of Transportation responsibility for reducing auto emissions.

1972 **The Water Pollution Control Act** charged the EPA with developing guidelines, issuing permits, and monitoring compliance with the cleanup of rivers and lakes.

1975 **The Marine Protection Research Act** allows the EPA to regulate ocean dumping and cleanup.

1976 **The Resource Conservation and Recovery Act** allows the EPA to regulate the dumping and disposal of hazardous wastes. Under this law, the preferred methods of disposal are (1) source reduction, (2) recycling, (3) on-site disposal, (4) incineration, and (5) land fill.

1980 **The Comprehensive Environmental Response, Compensation, and Liability Act (Superfund law)** created a fund, paid into by hazardous-waste-producing companies, that is used to clean up existing hazardous-waste dump sites where blame cannot be determined. The act also contains a "joint and several liability" clause that empowers the EPA to place full responsibility for cleanup on any company found to have illegally dumped at a site, whether or not that company acted alone. The Superfund law also requires all cleanup technologies to meet safety licensing requirements.

1986 **The Safe Drinking Water and Toxic Enforcement Act** prohibits the discharge of any known carcinogen or reproductive toxin that may get into surface water or groundwater. It allows citizens to sue industries and places the burden of proof on the industry.

1987 **The Toxic Substances Control Act** mandates the removal of asbestos and other carcinogenic substances from all buildings and gives the EPA enforcement authority.

1990 **Clean Air Act Amendments** strengthened the EPA and its ability to develop more specific timetables and methods for achieving clean air standards. The act targets auto emissions, toxic industrial emissions, and acid rain.

with a massive task.[37] Industries complained that the EPA was too strict and took the agency to court. Environmentalists claimed that the EPA was too lenient and did the same. The movement to clean up the environment became a protracted series of battles over how fast and how much. The trade-off between protecting the environment and the demands of industry to operate profitably and freely forms the nexus of conflict of environmental politics. Political Insight 18-1 summarizes major environmental legislation of the past two decades.

GROWING ENVIRONMENTAL CONCERNS IN THE 1990S

Despite the considerable progress that had occurred in the 1970s and 1980s, environmental problems around the globe were becoming more severe. While coal-burning utilities emitted 15 percent less sulfur than in 1970, over 150,000 lakes in the United States and Canada were already acidified or seriously threatened. New cars emitted 96 percent less carbon monoxide and hydrocarbons, but with so many additional vehicles, half the nation's population in 1990 lived in counties where the air violated existing standards. While fish had returned to many lakes and streams, their flesh contained toxic chemicals that pose a health risk.[38] The ozone hole and the greenhouse effect grew significantly worse. Tropical rainforests were being lost at a rate of 88,000 square miles per year, compared to half that rate ten years earlier. And by the year 2000, the population of the Earth will exceed 6 billion, compared to 3.7 billion in 1970, further straining the Earth's delicate ecosystem.

Environmental problems are now more global in scope than a generation earlier. If developing areas such as China, Latin America, and Africa adopt consumption and waste patterns like those of the United States, the Earth faces a catastrophe. Some countries of Eastern Europe have already polluted and destroyed natural resources far more seriously than any other place in the world. A growing awareness and concern with environmental issues is apparent among Americans, spurred by desires to preserve the wild and fears of cancer from the growing presence of toxic chemicals. In 1990, surveys revealed that 74 percent of Americans believed that protecting the environment was so important that improvements had to be made regardless of the cost.[39] That compares to only 45 percent who felt so in 1981. Even the chairman of Du Pont, the company that once advertised "better living through chemistry," stated that corporations must be environmentally sensitive to survive. These changing perceptions helped spur Congress and the president to revise the Clean Air Act.

STRENGTHENING THE CLEAN AIR ACT

Growing concern with the environment and a new willingness to compromise moved to break a deadlock that had bottled up clean air legislation in Congress for years. The Bush administration helped spur the process by submitting a proposal to Congress in 1989 and engaging in a period of intense negotiations with Congress over the legislation. After months of efforts, the Senate passed a bill in April 1990 and sent it to the House. The staunchest opposition came from coal-state senators, led by Robert Byrd (D-W.Va.) who feared economic disaster for his state. The battle between competing interests in the House was dramatized by two key members: Energy and Commerce Committee Chairman John Dingell (D-Mich.) and the Environment Subcommittee Chairman Henry Waxman (D-Calif.). Dingell, from Detroit, was a fierce advocate of the auto industry and a long-time opponent of any regulations that would harm it. Waxman, from Los Angeles, represented one of the nation's smoggiest districts. They negotiated a number of agreements that enabled the clean air bill to pass the House by a substantial margin.

The 1990 **Clean Air Act Amendments** included four main titles:[40]

Attainment of air quality standards (smog). Twenty years after the original Clean Air Act, over one hundred cities had never come into compliance. The new law established degrees of air pollution—from moderate to extreme—and specified how cities would meet the new standards. Each state was required to identify specific sources of emissions and to submit an implementation plan. The EPA was empowered to develop a federal implementation plan if the state failed to do so or if compliance was not reached. The states or the EPA could require, for example, vehicle inspections, emissions tests, vapor recovery systems at gas stations, transportation control measures (such as carpooling), curtail woodburning stoves, or various other methods of reducing smog.

Motor vehicles and fuels. The new law would establish new tailpipe emissions limits for cars, trucks, and buses and a program to develop alternate fuels. Separate, more rigorous standards were established for fleets of vehicles. First-round limits on emissions are to be phased in between 1993 and 1995. But if twelve of the nation's smoggiest cities are not in compliance by 2001, more restrictive second-round limits would be imposed. Alternate fuels programs were targeted at the nation's nine smoggiest cities, where compliance will be reached by allowing the sale only of specially reformulated gasoline in those cities after 1994.

Toxic air pollutants. Under the existing law, standards for most carcinogens were never set because doing so would have resulted in the complete shutdown of certain industries. Under the new provisions, the EPA would establish first-round standards for additional pollutants and require the installation of technological pollution controls. Second-round standards for toxic emissions will depend on health standards.

Acid rain. The act established new standards to limit emissions of sulfur dioxide, the chief cause of acid rain, primarily by requiring utilities in the Midwest that burn dirty coal to reduce emissions. Pollution allowances were granted to utilities for emitting sulfur dioxide. Allowances could be bought or sold, allowing some to pollute more but still limiting total emissions. Emission-reduction deadlines were established for 1995 and 2000. Utilities using "scrubbers" in order to keep burning high-sulfur coal would have more time to come into compliance or would receive extra allowances.

ENVIRONMENT VERSUS THE ECONOMY: AN INEVITABLE CONFLICT?

Conflicts between the environment and the economy are inevitable. It costs money to clean up the air and the water, just as it does to make products safer, more clearly labeled, more thoroughly tested. After the initial expansion of environmental legislation and regulation in the early 1970s, the political balance began to swing the other way. The election of Ronald Reagan in 1980 ushered in an era of retrenchment and in some cases the undoing of previous environmental standards. But in the 1990s, environmental concerns appear to be emerging stronger than ever.

Environmental policy-making is increasingly subject to problems of governing, particularly in the area of hazardous-waste disposal. Because many states are now closing their boundaries to the hazardous waste produced by neighboring states, each state has been charged by the federal government with the responsibility of siting its own facilities to treat, incinerate, or bury such waste. Only one state, Arizona, has successfully sited such a facility. Others—New Jersey, for example—are experiencing a phenomenon called **environmental gridlock**—the inability of states to locate and establish facilities to treat or eliminate hazardous wastes. The state's problem involves what land-use planners call "Lulus" (locally undesirable land uses): Most people agree that the facilities are needed, yet no one wants such a facility in his or her community. New Jersey formed a Hazardous Waste Siting Commission to locate and construct two waste incinerators and one aboveground storage facility to meet the state's considerable hazardous waste problem. But citizens groups—called **NIMBYs** (Not In My Back Yard)—organized to oppose any siting or even testing in their communities. These protests greatly frustrated the efforts of the state, and after three years, the commission abandoned its plans. Many other states are now having the same experience.

Economic policy is increasingly subject to concerns about energy sources and supplies and protection of the environment. The era when development always took precedence over ecology is over, but energy production, economic growth, and protection of the environment will continue to clash. How the balance is struck depends on both political and economic forces and the ability of the political system to resolve difficult choices.

SUMMARY AND CONCLUSIONS

1. Economic policies are actions taken by the government to affect the performance of the national economy. They are characterized by competition and conflict among economic goals, the fragmentation of power and responsibility, uncertainty of outcome, and a gap between intention and desired result.

2. Fiscal policy is the manipulation of taxes and spending to manage and stabilize aggregate economic activity. Budget deadlocks have significantly reduced the effectiveness of fiscal policy.

3. Monetary policy affects the growth of the money supply and the level of interest rates, both crucial to the performance of the economy. The Fed is relatively independent of political control, which has occasionally led to policies that are at odds with fiscal policy.

4. Trade is one of the oldest elements of economic

policy. The desire for free trade clashes with demands for protection. Trade deficits continue to be one of the most difficult economic problems facing policy-makers.

5. Energy is essential to the performance of the economy, but its production often presents threats to the natural environment. The United States is once again becoming dependent on foreign oil.

6. Environmental protection is increasingly important to Americans in the 1990s. Despite progress since 1970, environmental problems are becoming more serious on a global basis.

7. The Clean Air Act Amendments of 1990 were the most important environmental legislation in a decade, attempting to strengthen the nation's commitment to clean air.

The nature of economic policy has shifted dramatically since World War II. Fiscal policy, once the dominant tool for maintaining employment and stabilizing economic growth, is now but one of many factors. Governing problems—the recurring deadlock over the budget—have made it difficult for officials to manipulate revenues and outlays to produce a desired economic result. Monetary policy has become more important, particularly in terms of controlling inflation and coordinating policies with other industrialized nations. Although less "democratic" than other economic policy decisions because of the autonomy of the Federal Reserve Board, monetary policy decisions are made and implemented quickly. With the globalization of the economy and the increased importance of imports and exports for domestic prosperity, trade has become more important and more controversial. Such issues as industrial policy reflect growing concern with increasing the competitiveness of U.S. business in the world market. The supply and cost of energy is also more critical to the economic equation. As the burgeoning world population strains the Earth's resources, economic growth and energy consumption must be balanced with protection of the environment.

These changes provide more difficult challenges for government than have been faced at any other time in history. A multitude of economic interests clash, making policy-making more complex and difficult. Economic, energy, and environmental policies are increasingly tied to the actions of other governments, reducing the ability of the U.S. government to act alone. Despite the fragmentation of power in the American political system, the many elements of economic policy need to be coordinated if they are to be effective. All of these changes place further demands on the governing capacity of the political system if the United States is to remain prosperous and successful in the future.

KEY TERMS

Clean Air Act Amendments
comparative advantage
demand-side fiscal policy
dumping
economic policy
Employment Act
environmental gridlock
Environmental Protection Agency (EPA)
Federal Open Market Committee (FOMC)
Federal Reserve Board (the Fed)
fiscal policy
gross national product (GNP)
industrial policy
monetary policy
money supply
NIMBYs
recession
stagflation
supply-side fiscal policy
tariffs

SELF-REVIEW

1. Define "economic policy."

2. What are the main characteristics of U.S. economic policy-making?

3. Describe the major fiscal initiatives of postwar administrations from Kennedy to Bush.

4. Compare demand-side and supply-side fiscal policies.

5. How does the Fed make monetary policy?

6. How did monetary policy in the 1980s affect the U.S. balance of trade?

7. Describe the theory of comparative advantage.

8. What forms may protection of industries take?

9. What are the costs and benefits of protectionism?

10. What are the positive and negative consequences of energy deregulation?

11. Compare energy policy in the Carter, Reagan, and Bush administrations.

12. Describe the major revisions of the 1990 Clean Air Act.

13. Why are environmental protection and economic development in conflict?

SUGGESTED READINGS

Best, Michael, and William Connolly. *The Politicized Economy.* 1982.
A provocative, critical look at American political economy.

Greider, William. *Secrets of the Temple: How the Federal Reserve Runs the Country.* 1987.
An inside look at the Fed, arguing that political leaders should have more control over monetary policy.

Reich, Robert. *The Next American Frontier.* 1983.
A book advocating that the United States formulate industrial policy to help new, high-tech industries get started.

Schick, Allen. *Making Economic Policy in Congress.* 1984.
A collection of articles examining in detail the strengths, weaknesses, and problems Congress has in making national economic policy.

Thurow, Lester C. *The Zero Sum Society.* 1980.
A stimulating analysis of the problems of balancing the pursuit of equality with economic vitality.

NOTES

1. Samuel P. Huntington, "The United States," in M. Crozier et al., *The Crisis of Democracy* (New York: New York University Press, 1975).
2. Elmo Roper, quoted in Herbert Stein, *The Fiscal Revolution in America* (Chicago: University of Chicago Press, 1969), 174.
3. Steven K. Bailey, *Congress Makes a Law* (New York: Columbia University Press, 1950), 41-42.
4. See ibid., chap. 5.
5. Congressional Budget Office, "The Fiscal Policy Response to Inflation," January 1979, p. 208.
6. Ibid., p. 211.
7. See Arthur Okun, "Measuring the Impact of the 1964 Tax Reduction," in Warren Smith and Ronald Teigen, eds., *Readings in Money, National Income, and Stabilization Policy* (Homewood, Ill.: Irwin, 1970), 345-58; Lawrence R. Klein, "Econometric Analysis of the Tax Cut of 1964," in J. S. Duesenberry et al., eds., *The Brookings Model: Some Further Results* (Chicago: Rand McNally, 1969), 459-72.
8. See Grant McConnell, *Steel and the Presidency* (New York: Norton, 1963).
9. See Arthur Okun, "The Personal Tax Surcharge and Consumer Demands, 1968-70," *Brookings Paper on Economic Activity* 1 (1971): 167-217; William L. Springer, "Did the 1968 Surcharge Really Work?" *American Economic Review* 65 (September 1975): 644-59. Lawrence R. Klein, "An Econometric Analysis of the Revenue and Expenditure Control Act of 1968-69," in Warren Smith and John Colbertson, eds., *Public Finance and Stabilization Policy* (Amsterdam: North Holland, 1974), 333-55.
10. Herbert Stein, "Tour d'Horizon: A Calm View of Economic Policy," *AEI Economist,* May 1983, p. 2.
11. Senate Committee on the Budget, *Hearings, First Concurrent Resolution on the Budget, FY 77,* 4 (26 February 1976): 10.
12. See Gerald Pomper, "The 1980 Presidential Election and Its Meaning," in Thomas Cronin, ed., *Rethinking the Presidency* (Boston: Little, Brown, 1982): 3-28.
13. Stein, "Tour d'Horizon," p. 3.
14. Congressional Research Service, *Economic Stabilization Policies: The Historical Record, 1962-1976,* 95th Cong., 2nd sess. (November 1978).
15. See John Woolley, *Monetary Politics* (New York: Cambridge University Press, 1984).
16. Nathaniel Beck, "Presidential Influence on the Federal Reserve in the 1970s," *American Journal of Political Science* 26 (August 1982): 415-45.
17. This section relies on the analysis in Congressional Budget Office, *The Economic and Budget Outlook, FY 89-93,* February 1988, pp. 2-14.
18. Ibid., p. 14.
19. Congressional Budget Office, *The Economic and Budget Outlook FY 1991-95,* February 1990, p. 2-3.
20. Murray Weidenbaum, "Toward a More Open Trade Policy," Center for the Study of American Business, Washington University, St. Louis, no. 53 (January 1983): 34-35.
21. Ibid., p. 3.
22. *Washington Post National Weekly Edition* 1 (December 1983): 20.
23. Herbert Stein, "U.S. Foreign Trade and Trade Policy," *AEI Economist* (July 1983): 3.
24. *National Journal,* 26 February 1983, pp. 416-20.
25. Arthur T. Denzau, "Will an 'Industrial Policy' Work for the United States?" Center for the Study of American Business, Washington University, St. Louis, no. 57 (September 1983): 3.
26. Robert B. Reich, *The Next American Frontier* (New York: Times Books, 1983).
27. Chalmers Johnson, *MITI and the Japanese Miracle: The Growth of Industrial Policy 1925-1975* (Stanford, Calif.: Stanford University Press, 1982).

28. Charles Schultz, "Industrial Policy: A Dissent," *Brookings Review,* Fall 1983, pp. 3-13.
29. *New York Times,* 27 April 1990, p. 17.
30. *Nation's Business,* February 1990, p. 20.
31. *National Journal,* 20 January 1990, pp. 125-28.
32. G. Tyler Miller, *Living in the Environment: Concepts, Problems, and Alternatives* (Belmont, Calif.: Wadsworth, 1975), 15.
33. Walter A. Rosenbaum, *The Politics of Environmental Concern* (New York: Praeger, 1973), 6.
34. Ibid., 10.
35. *Gallup Poll Index,* June 1970, 8.
36. Richard A. Liroff, *A National Policy for the Environment: NEPA and Its Aftermath* (Bloomington: Indiana University Press, 1976).
37. Charles Schultz, *The Public Use of Private Interest* (Washington, D.C.: Brookings, 1977), 52-53.
38. *New York Times,* 27 April 1990, p. 17.
39. Ibid.
40. *Congressional Quarterly Weekly Report,* Special Supplement, 12 May 1990.

CHAPTER 19

Social Welfare Policy

POLITICAL CLOSE-UP

Poverty in America, 1904

Why are there poor people in an affluent society? In nineteenth-century America, most people regarded poverty as strictly a personal problem, the fault of the impoverished, to be dealt with by charity. But in 1904, a book was published that began to open people's eyes to the problem of poverty. Robert Hunter's Poverty, *the result of the author's years in the back-street tenements of New York and Boston, painted a vivid and distressing picture. Poverty was "discovered" during the Progressive era of the early twentieth century, as it would be again in the 1930s and the 1960s. Hunter shocked Americans with his claim that 10 to 20 million out of 80 million Americans—some 12 to 25 percent of the population—lived in destitution. He characterized the poor in these words:*

Did not the Lord say, "The poor always ye have with you?" But those who say this fail to distinguish between the poor who are poor because of their own folly and vice, and the poor who are poor as a result of social wrongs. The sins of men should bring their own punishment, and the poverty which punishes the

vicious and the sinful is good and necessary. Social or industrial institutions that save men from the painful consequences of vice or folly are not productive of the greatest good. There is unquestionably a poverty which men deserve, and by such poverty men are perhaps taught needful lessons. It would be unwise to legislate out of existence, even were it possible to do so, that poverty which penalizes the voluntarily idle and vicious. In other words, there are individual causes of poverty which should be eradicated by the individual himself, with such help as his family, the teachers, and the preachers may give him. For him society may be able to do little or nothing. The poor which are always to be with us, are, it seems to me, in poverty of their own making.

But surely as this is true, there are also the poor which we must not have always with us. The poor of this latter class are, it seems to me, the mass of the poor; they are bred of miserable and unjust social conditions, which punish the good and the pure, the faithful and industrious, the slothful and vicious, all alike. We may not, by going into the homes of the poor, be able to determine which ones are in poverty because of individual causes, or which are in poverty because of social wrongs; but we can see, by looking about us, that men are brought into misery by the action of social and economic forces. And the wrongful action of such social and economic forces is a preventable thing.

From the millions struggling with poverty come the millions who have lost all self-respect and ambition, who hardly, if ever, work, who are aimless and drifting, who like drink, who have no thought for their children, and who live contentedly on rubbish and alms. But a short time before many of them were of that great, splendid mass of producers upon which the material welfare of the nation rests. They were in poverty, but they were self-respecting; they were hard-pressed, but they were ambitious, determined, and hard-working. They were also under-fed, under-clothed, and miserably housed—the fear and dread of want possessed them, they worked sore, but gained nothing, they were isolated, heart-worn, and weary.

SOURCE: Robert Hunter, *Poverty* (New York: Harper and Row, 1965), 62–65.

CHAPTER OUTLINE

INTRODUCTION AND OVERVIEW

Welfare is a dirty word. To millions of Americans, welfare recipients are loafers and deadbeats who drive Cadillacs and rip off the system. Budget-sensitive bureaucrats acknowledged the problems with the word when in 1978, the Department of Health, Education, and Welfare (HEW) changed its name to Health and Human Services (HHS). Yet despite this emotional bias against "welfare," a majority of Americans are compassionate about the problems of the have-nots in society and have special concern for the elderly, the handicapped, and the sick and infirm. Why does such ambivalence exist in the public mind? What are the images and realities of poverty policy in the United States?

Poverty can be seen as an economic phenomenon. It is possible to measure quite precisely the distribution of income and wealth, the amount of transfer payments, and the number of people below some officially designated poverty line. But poverty policy is a function of political values as much as economic concerns. Public ambivalence about social welfare has deep roots in our political culture. Values of individualism, self-reliance, and laissez-faire capitalism all help contribute to current welfare politics.

This chapter examines social welfare in the United States, beginning with the development of the first public assistance programs and continuing through the policies of the Bush administration. We then consider the nature of economic inequality in America. Social welfare policy illuminates the theme of governing. Given the public ambivalence about welfare, policy-makers have engaged in a process of piecemeal policy-making over the years. The result is a patchwork quilt of social programs. Governing processes are also affected by the power of certain groups to defend their programs from cuts. The extreme sensitivity of politicians to Social Security, for example, limits policy options and threatens stalemate. Finally, we consider the costs, impact, and current issues surrounding social welfare programs. The following questions are examined:

1. Why was the United States one of the last developed nations to provide for the poor and elderly through public assistance and Social Security programs?
2. How did the major social welfare programs in the United States evolve?
3. What is the nature of economic inequality in the United States? Who are the poor?
4. What are the costs of the major social welfare programs? How effective have they been in reducing poverty?
5. Is Social Security or Medicare going bankrupt? What are the current problems surrounding these and other social welfare entitlement programs?
6. How did social welfare policy change in the 1980s? What reforms were made?

Characteristics of Social Welfare in America

The United States was one of the last of the developed nations to take some responsibility for the impoverished. Even today, compared with other developed countries, the United States is less of a welfare state and provides fewer benefits and protections to the poor. Most Western capitalist nations have for several generations accepted the need for state intervention to furnish minimum incomes and protect people against such problems as sudden loss of job, serious illness, and old age.[1] The U.S. system of protection is more limited, although it has radically expanded during the past fifty years. These are several reasons for the less than wholehearted acceptance of social welfare programs in the United States, reasons that are deeply rooted in American values.

Americans have traditionally believed poverty was as much the fault of the poor as the fault of society. One of the most pervasive ideas of American political economy is that hard work should be rewarded and idleness punished. The strength of the values of individualism and materialism has meant that those who cannot make it economically are often looked down upon by the rest. Although the elderly and the disabled are seen in a more charitable light, the unemployed and the working poor are often blamed for their plight. Hunter's *Poverty* represented one of the first serious challenges to this view in the Progressive era. Yet this attitude, particularly among conservatives, remains alive and well in American politics today.

Americans reject notions that income should be redistributed from the rich to the poor. The public does not want a "Robin Hood" government. As we saw in Chapter 3, most people are opposed to any significant redistribution of income and wealth. Even liberals who support welfare programs do not believe the rich should be fleeced to give to the poor. Although the personal income tax has been progressive, the total tax system in the United States has not significantly redistributed income from the rich to the poor.[2] Ideologies supporting relative income equality are even more strongly rejected by Americans. Proposals to make taxes more progressive or to increase transfer payments to the poor encounter strong opposition. It takes extraordinary political resources to expand social welfare programs, except when poverty seems to be "rediscovered" about every twenty or thirty years. During these cycles of social concern, the basic resistance to increasing social programs abates temporarily.

Myths about welfare and poverty help perpetuate the status quo, making policy innovation difficult. Different views of who "deserves" assistance help explain why Social Security is an extremely popular program and why **Aid to Families with Dependent Children (AFDC)** is unpopular. A number of myths about welfare and poverty often distort reality. The basis of many such myths is anecdotal evidence: Someone saw a Cadillac parked in front of a shanty. A newspaper ran the story of a "welfare queen" in Chicago who ripped off the system by claiming forty-five fictitious children. Someone used food stamps to buy beer. Stories become generalizations

FIGURE 19–1

VARIATION IN AFDC BENEFIT LEVELS

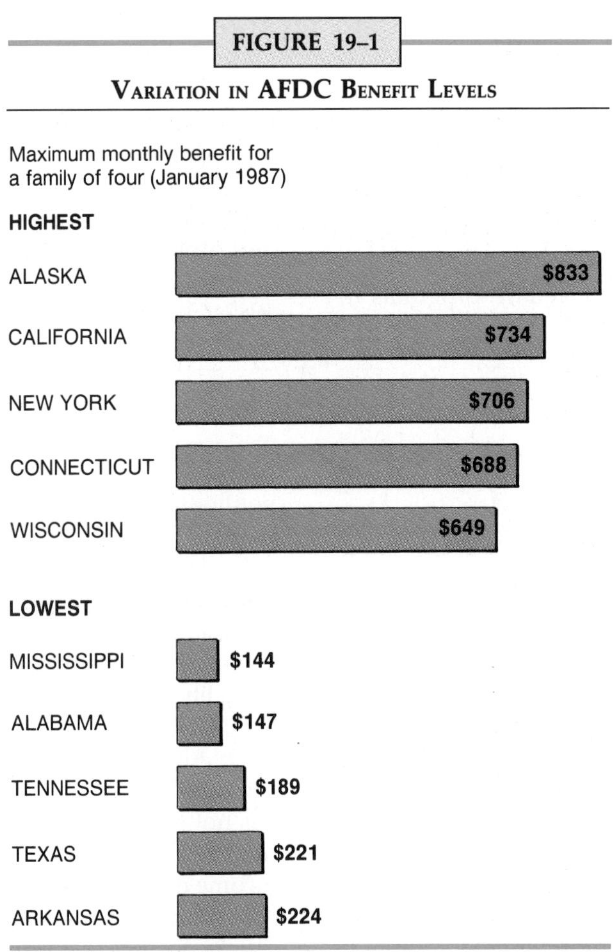

about people getting rich on welfare, women having babies to get bigger assistance checks, people on welfare not wanting to work. Social science attempts to go beyond stories and look at systematic evidence. Although welfare myths do not usually square with the facts, they affect public attitudes and public policy.

Social welfare programs are shared between the state and federal governments, leading to significant variations in coverage. Federalism is a key to understanding American social welfare policy. In most other Western nations, the social welfare policies are centrally coordinated and uniform throughout the nation. The architects of major social welfare legislation in the United States needed to accommodate the various interests of the states. The result is significantly different levels of support, depending on what state a person lives in. Figure 19–1 compares the maximum monthly benefit for a family of four in the highest and lowest-paying states. Although there is more uniformity in medical care for the poor and the elderly, public assistance, education, and housing vary by state and locality. Many of the controversies over federalism in the 1980s surrounded the question of which level of government should take responsibility for social programs. The ability to make effective social welfare policy is also closely tied to divided state and national responsibility.

The United States is one of the richest nations on earth. In the midst of this affluence, large disparities in wealth and income, and a large number of people who live below minimum subsistence levels, can be found. Since 1970, the purchasing power of welfare benefits has declined by one-third. Squalor amid opulence—is it immoral or as American as apple pie? How did we get where we are today?

FDR's New Deal programs provided jobs for some of America's millions of unemployed.

The Evolution of Social Welfare Policies in the United States

HOOVER, THE DEPRESSION, AND THE NEW DEAL

The election of Herbert Hoover in 1928 was actually seen as a victory for the advocates of greater social welfare activity.[3] In his campaign, Hoover promised, "Given a chance to go forward . . . we shall soon with the help of God be within sight of the day when poverty will be banished from this nation."[4] Yet only a few years later, shantytowns housing cold, hungry, and poor people that sprung up around the cities were sarcastically called "Hoovervilles." Hoover became known as the man who sat in the White House while Americans starved. The tragedy of the Hoover administration's failure to respond to the Great Depression reflected the limits of public policy and the American philosophy toward poverty before 1930. It was a philosophy based on volunteerism, self-help, and limited government responsibility. The view of social welfare in the 1920s cast the federal government in the role of facilitator – helping states, cities, individuals, and organizations to direct their efforts. The philosophy did not reflect a lack of caring, but it did reflect a belief that there was little government could legitimately do.

Despite mounting pressure for more direct action from the federal government in the midst of massive unemployment, hunger, and lack of housing, Hoover resisted:

> Economic depression cannot be cured by legislative action or executive pronouncement. Economic wounds must be healed by the action of the cells of the economic body – the producers and consumers themselves. Recovery can be expedited and its effects mitigated by cooperative action. That cooperation requires that every individual should sustain faith and courage; that each should maintain his self reliance.[5]

Hoover's intransigence extended to vetoing relief bills passed by a restive Congress. Increasingly isolated in the White House against a growing tide of criticism, Hoover persevered: "I am opposed to any direct or indirect government dole. Our people are providing against distress in true American fashion."[6]

True American fashion was about to change. Hoover took his case to the people in the 1932 election and was crushed by the Roosevelt landslide. The next four years would not only change the nature of social welfare policies in the United States but also would shift the basic party alignment in the nation. When he took office, Franklin Roosevelt did not have a clear program or specific set of policies. But he represented a willingness to change, to use the resources of government more fully. The New Deal social welfare policy was not to emerge for two years, although a number of short-term remedies were implemented to help those in greatest need. The administration quickly provided additional funds to state and local agencies already established to help the poor. But the more durable changes in public policy were fashioned by Roosevelt's Cabinet Committee on Economic Security.

President Roosevelt's group of international scholars and thinkers examined the experiences of the European nations that were ahead of the United States in implementing social welfare programs. The proposals they considered ranged from the evolutionary to the revolutionary, but the choices they eventually made acknowledged traditional American values. Constitutional questions had to be considered as well. The federal government had possessed the power to levy a progressive income tax for only twenty years. Some feared the Supreme Court might strike down legislation because there was no explicit authorization for a comprehensive social welfare program in the Constitution. But outside pressure was building. In Louisiana, for example, charismatic Governor Huey Long was proposing a more radical "Share the Wealth" plan that would take from the rich and give to the poor. Against this background, Congress passed the Social Security Act of 1935.

THE SOCIAL SECURITY ACT OF 1935

Much of the current "welfare state" in America was created by the **Social Security Act** of 1935. Today, it is supported by the single largest expenditure in the budget, and provisions of the act are still controversial. What were the issues over the Social Security Act fifty years ago? One was state versus federal control. Although the federal government had been aggressive in attacking the worst cases of deprivation, considerable support still existed for the idea that states should administer new welfare programs. Roosevelt's advisers were divided over this question. Labor Secretary Frances Perkins favored state management, while President Roosevelt's close personal adviser Harry Hopkins favored national control.[7] The drafters settled on two kinds of programs. The first was **contributory programs,** in which both employers and employees contributed to a fund and individuals received benefits when they retired or were unemployed. These programs were looked on as a form of insurance. The second type of program established by the act was **noncontributory**—cash transfer or aid programs for elderly people without other means of support, for the blind, and for dependent children. These programs were **means-tested**—that is, eligibility depended on the income level of the family. Not all social welfare programs have means tests, so benefits go to middle- and upper-income groups as well as to the poor. Political Insight 19–1 summarizes the major programs created by the Social Security Act that are still in force today.

The main feature of the Social Security Act of 1935—Social Security **(Old Age Survivors Disability Insurance; OASDI)**—was controversial at first. "Socialism!" cried the critics. Nonetheless, the bill was popular on Capitol Hill and sailed through Congress virtually intact. Determined that Social Security would not be dismantled by a future Republican Congress or president, Roosevelt purposely fostered the notion of Social Security as retirement insurance. Each beneficiary was assigned an account (a Social Security number) in which his or her earning history would be recorded to assure benefits at the time of retirement. President Roosevelt's move was a success. Social Security quickly became popular—so popular that politicians have found it almost impossible to modify.

Other elements of the 1935 act have not fared as well. AFDC, although much smaller and less expensive than Social Security (federal outlays of $13 billion in FY 1991), remains unpopular. It embodies the notion of "giveaway," stirring resentment in the middle class. Such attitudes have hampered attempts to restructure and coordinate cash assistance programs in recent years. Unemployment Compensation, **Supplemental Security Income** (SSI), and the remaining parts of the Social Security Act fall between the extremes of OASDI and AFDC in public acceptance.

Was the Social Security Act a piece of radical legislation? Despite the significant nature of change

POLITICAL INSIGHT 19–1

MAJOR PROVISIONS OF THE SOCIAL SECURITY ACT OF 1935

The Social Security Act of 1935 created the following social welfare programs.

CONTRIBUTORY PROGRAMS

OASDI (Old Age Survivors Disability Insurance). The program, called "Social Security," provides monthly payments to retired workers, to disabled workers and their dependents, and to the widows and children of deceased workers. It is a federal program run by the national government (the Social Security Administration) in Washington and is funded by a payroll tax on employers and employees. Social Security is the most expensive ($264 billion in FY 1991) and the most popular of the social welfare programs. Not really an insurance program (in which money a person pays in is kept and invested and paid back with interest), it is funded on a current financing basis, with a reserve of around six to nine months in the trust fund. Social Security can get in financial trouble if the commitments to pay grow faster than the ability to raise money from those still paying into the fund. It has no means test.

Unemployment Compensation. This is a program to protect workers who suddenly lose their jobs. It provides weekly payments, depending on prior salary, for twenty-six weeks, with occasional extensions by Congress in periods of high unemployment. Recipients need to prove that they are actively seeking a job. The program is run by state governments with benefit levels varying across the states. It is funded by state and federal taxes on employers, although the money goes to the states. No means test is required.

NONCONTRIBUTORY PROGRAMS

AFDC (Aid to Families with Dependent Children). AFDC is a traditional welfare program providing cash assistance to the needy. Benefits may go to children in families with two parents in twenty-seven states, but payments most often go to single female parents of dependent children. The program is administered by the states, which determine benefit levels and eligibility. A family that qualifies in one state may not qualify in another. AFDC is funded jointly by the federal government and the states and is means-tested.

OAA, AB, AD (Old Age Assistance, Aid to the Blind, and Aid to the Disabled; now SSI—Supplemental Security Income). Regular Social Security left the elderly who had not contributed without support. The elderly, along with the blind and disabled, receive straight cash assistance based on need. Since 1974, these programs have been consolidated as Supplemental Security Income, funded exclusively by the federal government. SSI is means-tested.

brought by the Social Security Act and other New Deal programs, political scientist Dorothy James points out that the programs were fully in accord with the values of the American political and economic system. She observes:

> Poverty was considered a temporary condition due to unemployment, agricultural depression or the dependence of youth, or it was considered a condition due to individual problems such as blindness, or old age. Welfare was assumed to be a temporary measure which would end with rising employment and national income.[8]

Poverty was not seen as a result of complex sociological factors or the American economic system. Although the social programs of the New Deal helped protect people at the lower end of the economic scale, they did not fundamentally change how Americans viewed poverty.

MISERY REDISCOVERED: THE 1960S "WAR ON POVERTY"

Extraordinary circumstances prompted the extension of social welfare in the 1930s. An economic crisis of historic proportions led to an expansion of government responsibility. Although Americans retained their fundamental belief in the U.S. economic system and the causes of poverty, they no longer accepted the passive role of government. Officials had an obligation not only to manage the economy to prevent depression but also to protect those in society who suffered economic hardship because of it. World War II finally brought the U.S. economy back to full employment, and the 1940s and 1950s were decades of relative prosperity. Questions of poverty and social welfare were far removed from the public mind. Instead, the Cold War, communists, and nuclear weapons absorbed the minds of Americans. But in the early 1960s, another generation discovered poverty.

During the 1960 presidential campaign, John Kennedy, traveling through West Virginia while campaigning in that state's important primary, was shocked at the rural poverty he observed. He pledged, if elected, to do something about it. Kennedy's experience, plus the extraordinary influence of a book, Michael Harrington's *The Other America,* helped put poverty back on the policy agenda. Harrington alerted people to the squalor that existed amid the affluence of contemporary America. Poverty became tied to the struggle for civil rights, and by 1964, social welfare became a significant national issue once more. Lyndon Johnson declared a "war on poverty." This time public policy was responding not to the economic crisis of depression but to economic inequality. Poverty had suddenly become unacceptable in the face of unprecedented general wealth and prosperity.

The "war on poverty" took shape through several important pieces of legislation. The **Economic Opportunity Act** of 1964 created programs very different from those of the Social Security Act thirty years earlier. Instead of cash transfers through contributory and noncontributory programs, the act established new services and agencies to help the poor directly.

President Johnson had assembled a team of experts to come up with an innovative legislative proposal—such people as Robert Kennedy, Sargent Shriver, and Daniel Patrick Moynihan.[9] The legislation they wrote and sent to Congress included the following programs:

> The *Neighborhood Youth Corps,* to give poor young people actual on-the-job experience
> *Head Start,* to give poor preschool children the same social and educational experiences as more affluent children
> The *Job Corps,* to train or retrain the chronically unemployed
> *Work-study programs* for college students
> *Literacy programs* to help adults compete in the job market

Title II of the economic opportunity bill, creating **community action programs (CAPs),** was to become the most controversial part of the "war on poverty." CAPs were the brainchild of reformers who felt that previous social welfare policy was paternalistic and that poor people should have some say over their own lives. The bill called for "maximum feasible participation" of the poor in community action programs, a concept that was to become embroiled in arguments over its meaning and implementation. Attorney General Robert Kennedy explained the intention of the drafters:

> The institutions which affect the poor—education, welfare, recreation, business, labor—are huge, complex structures, operating far outside their control. They plan programs for the poor, not with them. Part of the sense of helplessness and futility comes from the feeling of powerlessness to affect the operation of these organizations.
>
> The community action programs must basically change these organizations by building into the program real representation for the poor . . . giving them a real voice in their institutions.[10]

Despite the early controversy over CAPs and maximum feasible participation, Congress adopted the Economic Opportunity Act almost exactly as it was submitted by the president.[11] The law created great expectations. Yet unlike Social Security, only a few years later many of its agencies and programs were under attack. The structure and organization of programs were complicated and controversial. In the big cities, elected officials resented poor groups trying to take over CAPs. In Washington, legislators complained about excessive regulation and bureaucracy. In the nation at large, the poor, angry and frustrated, complained they were no better off. Negative experiences were to have a lasting impact on social welfare policy for more than two decades.

HEALTH CARE: MEDICARE AND MEDICAID

Perhaps the most important social welfare program to emerge in the 1960s was the **Medicare Act** of 1965. By this time, most European nations had some form of national health care or government insurance to help pay health-care costs. Great Britain had created the National Health Service under the Labor government in the late 1940s. Although President Truman had proposed national health insurance in the United States at the same time, the mood of Congress and the nation would not support such action for another two decades. Even very limited proposals to have the medical care costs of the elderly or impoverished paid by the government were seen as too hot politically, as they had been in 1935, when the original Social Security bill was being written.

Federal health-care programs had long been opposed by the medical establishment. Fearing that a program like the British National Health Service might be adopted by Congress, the American Medical Association (AMA) and allied health-care providers led a crusade against "socialized" medicine. Although a residue of support had always existed for medical care for the elderly, the election of 1964 gave President Johnson the majorities necessary to marshal support for such a program. Even so, the AMA fought it to the end.[12] House Ways and Means Chair Wilbur Mills (D-Ark.), originally an opponent of Medicare, saw the growing political tide of support. His switch in favor helped lead the Medicare bill to successful passage. The original bill was expanded to include **Medicaid**—assistance to the poor in paying medical bills. The Medicare-Medicaid bill ultimately passed Congress by large majorities. Today, nearly 50 million people receive benefits under the law, but serious questions exist about the programs' financial solvency.

The "war on poverty" was short-lived. As much as anything, it was swept up in the growing national preoccupation with the war in Vietnam. Poverty programs were caught in a budget squeeze when military expenditures demanded a larger share. Also, controversy surrounded many of the poverty programs and the Office of Economic Opportunity, which had been created to administer them. National concern with the plight of the poor faded, and polls showed that citizens wished to slow, but not reverse, the rate of expansion of civil rights and social welfare. The 1968 elections brought a new occupant to the White House and a new approach to social welfare policy.

NIXON AND THE FAMILY ASSISTANCE PLAN

Americans who complained about draft resisters and hippies often linked those groups to "welfare bums and cheaters." AFDC had never been a popular program, and with the election of Richard Nixon, it once again came under heavy fire from both the right and the left. Critics on the left complained that payments were inadequate, leaving many people below even the stingiest definition of poverty. Worse, they claimed, AFDC created perverse incentives, encouraging poor fathers to abandon women and children so the latter could receive benefits. Critics on the right were concerned with the growing costs of welfare and who deserved "handouts." Pointing to evidence of fraud and abuse, they insisted that poor people should work for their government check. No one seemed happy with the "welfare mess."

Enter Richard Nixon. In an administration that would not distinguish itself in domestic policy, Nixon offered a proposal for restructuring the welfare system in the United States.[13] The plan, labeled the **Family Assistance Plan** (FAP), was a kind of guaranteed annual income through a negative income tax. Many reformers in the 1960s had suggested replacing the hodgepodge of programs and the state-controlled AFDC program with a nationally administered guaranteed annual income program. The Family Assistance Plan would have established a minimum level of income below which the government would *pay* families rather than *tax* them. The FAP was a surprisingly radical proposal. Advocates claimed it would eliminate the fraud found in the present system and would increase incentives for welfare recipients to find jobs. But despite some appeal to Democrats, it bogged down in Congress, where Nixon lacked the political clout of Roosevelt or Johnson. Liberals who might have been sympathetic argued that the proposed benefit levels were too low. The president's unpopularity kept some legislators from taking a serious look at the program.

Although the FAP probably would not have passed anyway, the 1972 campaign killed the bill once and for all. Democrat George McGovern made one of his most serious blunders in the campaign when he proposed a widely criticized guaranteed annual income program as a substitute for the FAP. After this, the Nixon administration lost interest in its own program for comprehensive welfare reform. The Watergate scandal helped ensure that it would not reemerge in Nixon's abbreviated second term.

ENTITLEMENT GROWTH IN THE 1970s

The 1970s were relatively quiet on the social welfare policy front. Although no sweeping reforms were proposed to restructure welfare or Social Security, several important trends emerged. The most profound change was the rapid growth of social welfare entitlements through the automatic expansion and indexing of programs. *Entitlements,* which include Social Security, AFDC, Medicare, and Medicaid, are government programs that guarantee payment to any person who qualifies. *Indexing* of programs means tying benefit levels to the cost-of-living index (see Chapter 17).

Entitlements mushroomed during the 1970s. Total spending increased from $65 billion in 1970 to $267 billion in 1980, a 400-percent increase. Part of the growth resulted from inflation and increased prices, but entitlements grew much faster than price levels—7 percent a year *after* controlling for inflation. Entitlements grew from 33 percent of the federal budget to 47 percent during this period. Additional growth was the result of the natural expansion of eligible recipients, but much of it came from liberalization and expansion of programs. Important legislative changes that facilitated growth include the following:[14]

Large increases in Social Security benefits—15 percent in 1970, 10 percent in 1971, and 20 percent in 1972 (an election year)
Expansion of eligibility for Medicare to include the disabled (1972)
Start of the replacement Supplemental Security Income program (1974)
Mandating of the food stamp program for all counties (1974)
Indexing of Social Security, linking benefits to the consumer price index (1975)
Elimination of the food stamp purchase requirement (1979)

The food stamp program is a good example of how entitlements grew. Starting out as a tiny program in the 1960s, the food stamp program had increased its outlays more than tenfold to above $12 billion by the end of the 1970s. Food stamps were favored by welfare reformers because they tended to equalize the sharp variations among states in AFDC payments. Because the price that recipients paid for their food stamps was based on income, food stamps compensated for welfare variations across states. Eligibility for food stamps was broadened. In addition, food programs were popular not only with traditional supporters of poverty programs but also with farmers and the Agriculture Department. It was an easy program to love, improving the nutrition and health of more than 20 million Americans and beefing up the sale of food products. Yet as the costs of the program escalated, it became a target for budget-cutters. Food stamps were high on the hit list of social programs of the Reagan administration in 1981.

REAGAN'S CUTS AND THE "SOCIAL SAFETY NET" OF THE 1980s

The election of Ronald Reagan in 1980 brought the costs of social welfare programs and entitlements into the national spotlight. In whirlwind fashion, Reagan and his advisers prepared a legislative program that would take social welfare spending to the chopping block. Not since the days of Lyndon Johnson and Franklin Roosevelt had there been a comparable flurry of legislative activity. Only a few weeks after his inauguration, Reagan issued revisions for the FY 1982 budget. In it, the administration explained that social programs would be cut under certain criteria:

> The first criterion is the preservation of the social safety net. The social safety net consists of those programs, mostly begun in the 1930s, that now

POLITICAL INSIGHT 19–2

THE REAGAN CUTS IN SOCIAL WELFARE

The first year of the Reagan administration was a year of remarkable legislative and budgetary change. In 1981, the president made significant cuts in the rate of growth of a number of social welfare programs, in addition to passing the largest tax cut in history. Reagan had long contended that the federal government was doing too much in the area of social welfare. Programs were too expensive. Benefits did not go to the truly needy. As part of the reconciliation package in 1981, Congress agreed to some significant cuts in entitlements and other domestic programs. In all, the administration was able to reduce spending levels in domestic programs by $38 billion in 1981. Some of the important changes were as follows:

Food stamps. The administration was successful in getting Congress to limit eligibility of families in the program to less than 130 percent of the poverty line. The effect of this change was to eliminate about 25 percent of the families that had been receiving food stamps and to reduce overall expenditure levels by about $2 billion.

AFDC. Several provisions were approved to tighten up eligibility for welfare payments. Recipients could not have incomes of more than 150 percent of the poverty line. Striking workers were ruled ineligible for AFDC and for food stamps. The limit on personal assets to qualify for assistance was lowered to $1,000, except house and car. Congress also approved a provision counting housing assistance and food stamps in computing recipients' income to determine eligibility.

Unemployment Compensation. The administration succeeded in eliminating the additional thirteen weeks of benefits provided by the states after the initial twenty-six weeks of benefits were exhausted.

Medicare. The reconciliation package increased the amount of deductible expenses that elderly recipients had to pay on their medical and hospital bills. Significant change in the Medicare funding formula would not come until 1983, however.

Medicaid. The administration reduced the amount that the federal government contributed to state Medicaid programs. This program, along with AFDC, was part of the "trade" proposed by the Reagan administration in his New Federalism program.

Social Security. Although benefits were not reduced generally, changes affecting certain groups were made. Benefits for full-time college students and for children sixteen to eighteen years old were phased out. The minimum benefit for new recipients was eliminated.

> constitute an agreed upon core of protection for the elderly, the unemployed, and the poor, and those programs that fulfill our basic commitment to the people who fought for this country in times of war.[15]

Having pledged to protect social programs, the administration listed its goals: (1) revision of entitlements to eliminate unintended benefits, (2) reduction of benefits for those in the middle- and upper-income groups, (3) imposition of fiscal restraint on social programs of "national interest" and elimination of the rest, and (4) consolidation of categorical grants to states and cities into block grants. The administration proposed a three-year $130 billion cut in social welfare programs, a significant reduction below existing levels. Critics were quick to object, claiming that the social safety net under Reagan was filled with holes—the effect of budget cuts would fall most heavily on the poor and the elderly.

In the fierce legislative battles of 1981, where House Republicans were joined by conservative Democrats, the president prevailed in many instances. Political Insight 19–2 summarizes some of the major cuts.

Throughout his administration, Ronald Reagan continued to propose cutbacks in social programs, although they were much less successful after 1983, facing the larger Democratic majorities in Congress. In addition to questions about the efficacy of the social safety net, many asked whether welfare for the poor had not been replaced with welfare for the rich in tax breaks for corporations and wealthy individuals. With the national economy improving, this issue of "fairness" was raised repeatedly by the Democrats. The FY 1986 budget sent to Congress called for another $144 billion in cuts in entitlements over the next five years. Unlike his proposals four years earlier, however, President Reagan seemed content to let Congress come up with its own package of cuts. Resistance in Congress was fierce, even among Republicans. Many members believed that social programs had already absorbed their fair share of budget cuts and that cuts had to be balanced more evenly between defense needs and domestic needs.

BUSH ADMINISTRATION PROPOSALS

The Bush administration took a less antagonistic approach toward social welfare programs but, facing continued budget deficits, proposed a number of cuts. They were counterbalanced by modest new initiatives, such as a proposal to create a tax credit for child-care expenses. In his 1991 budget proposals, President Bush proposed major cuts in the fast-growing Medicare program by reducing reimbursements to hospitals, restricting future increases to doctors and hospitals, and hiking the premiums paid by Medicare beneficiaries. The administration also asked Congress to make reductions in child nutrition programs by eliminating subsidies for school lunches for families well above the poverty line.[16]

Between the 1930s and the 1990s, the politics of social welfare had passed through several distinct stages. Although late in protecting the welfare and security of the elderly and the impoverished, once programs were established they became a permanent fixture in U.S. public policy. Yet poverty and social welfare captured the nation's attention for only limited periods of time. Only in the 1930s and 1960s were major efforts undertaken to broaden social welfare. Before considering some of the major issues confronting policy-makers, let us step back and examine the nature of poverty and the costs and benefits of government programs.

Poverty in America

WHAT IS POVERTY?

There are two approaches to defining poverty. The first is an **absolute** definition of poverty, based on some objective standard of subsistence. The official government poverty line specifies the amount of income necessary to maintain a minimum subsistence. The second is a **relative** definition of poverty, based on a subjective evaluation of the lack of income compared with the dominant standards of the society. John Kenneth Galbraith defined relative poverty in the following way:

> People are poverty-stricken when their income, even if adequate for survival, falls markedly behind that of the community. Then they cannot have what the larger community regards as the minimum necessary for decency; and they cannot wholly escape, therefore, the judgment of the larger community that they are indecent. They are degraded for, in the literal sense, they live outside the grades or categories which the community regards as acceptable.[17]

How do the two definitions affect public policy on poverty? Does society, acting through its government, have an obligation to eradicate either absolute poverty or relative poverty? Is it even possible to eliminate relative poverty short of total income equality? Even formulating an absolute definition of poverty has proved controversial.

The measurement of poverty is important because it often determines who is eligible to participate in government programs.[18] The **poverty line** is a policy instrument that also affects those above the threshold, particularly the working poor. Before 1964, no attempt was made to define poverty. At that time the Social Security Administration developed a poverty formula. Using the assumption that the poor spend one-third of their income on food, the poverty line was set at three times the Department of Agriculture's "economy food plan." In 1964, the official poverty line was determined to be

$3,000 for a family of four. The formula has continued as the basis of the U.S. government's poverty line adjusted by the consumer price index. (In 1989, the official poverty threshold for a family of four was $12,675.) Critics have attacked the formula on a number of grounds, including the fact that the original food budget was nutritionally inadequate and that regional variations in prices and changing spending patterns are not reflected in the formula. Although many alternatives to the poverty formula have been proposed, none has been adopted.

THE POOR AND AMERICA'S UNDERCLASS

Despite the social welfare programs that have been in effect for the past fifty years, poverty still exists in the United States. The devastated sections of inner cities and run-down rural areas provide abundant physical evidence of deprivation and poverty. How many Americans live below the poverty line? Who are they?

In the late 1980s, approximately 35 million Americans lived below the poverty line. Table 19–1 shows the percentage below the official government poverty line since 1959. Some of the effects of the "war on poverty" and the expansion of entitlements in the 1960s and early 1970s can be seen. From 1959 to 1973, the percentage of poor dropped by half—from 22.4 percent to 11.1 percent. After 1973, the trend reversed, rising to 15 percent in 1983. Economic growth in the 1980s moderated the trend but did not substantially reduce the total poverty population. The incidence of poverty is related to race, gender, age, and type of family unit. The poverty rate for blacks is three times the rate for whites, while the rate for Hispanics is twice that for whites. A feminization of poverty has taken place. There has been a sharp increase in the number of households headed by a female that fall below the poverty line, and the poor are disproportionately children.

Figure 19–2 compares the incidence of poverty by type of family unit from 1970 to 1986. The hardest-hit group is single mothers with children; nearly half of all such households are below the poverty line. While the rate has remained high since 1970, there has been an alarming increase in the number of female-headed households. At the other extreme are married couples with children, and nonelderly singles and couples without children. Only 4 to 6 percent of these households are below the poverty line. The most significant change in poverty incidence has taken place with regard to older Americans. Poverty rates for unrelated elderly people and childless elderly households have been cut by two-thirds in fifteen years. Americans over the age of sixty-five are now among the most affluent groups in society.

About one-third of the poor receive AFDC benefits. Of the 11 million Americans on welfare, 50 percent have been on welfare for eight years or more; 66 percent are under the age of eighteen; 28 percent are under six years old; 58 percent are nonwhite; and 58 percent have had less than eleven years of education.[19] Families on AFDC and the

TABLE 19–1

CHANGES IN RATES OF POVERTY, 1959–1988

Year	% of Population Below Poverty Line
1959	22.4
1960	22.2
1965	17.3
1966	14.7
1967	14.2
1968	12.8
1969	12.1
1970	12.6
1971	12.5
1972	11.9
1973	11.1
1974	11.7
1975	12.3
1976	11.8
1977	11.6
1978	11.4
1979	11.7
1980	13.0
1981	14.0
1982	14.7
1983	15.2
1984	14.4
1985	14.0
1986	13.6
1987	13.4
1988	13.1

SOURCE: U.S. Bureau of the Census, 1990.

FIGURE 19–2

INCIDENCE OF POVERTY BY TYPE OF FAMILY UNIT, 1970-1986

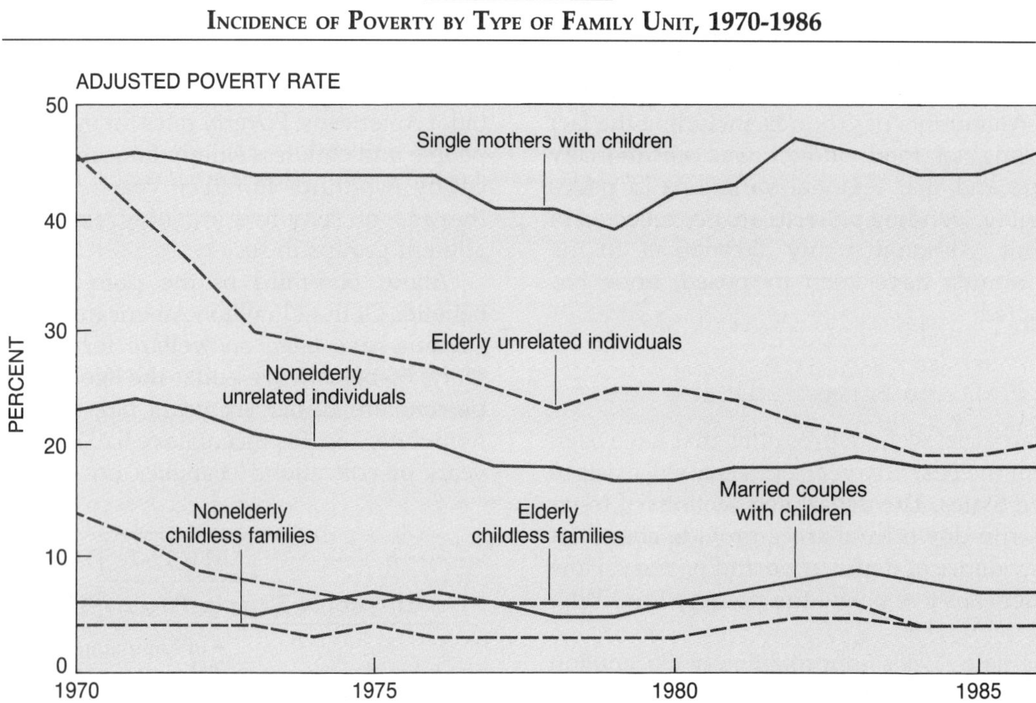

SOURCE: Congressional Budget office (1988) tabulations of Current Population Survey data.

working poor with minimum-wage jobs have fallen farther below the poverty line in the past fifteen years. But even these figures do not paint a complete picture of the culture of poverty.

Social scientists have attempted to go beyond the official definition of poverty and identified a group of hard-core, chronic poor—the **underclass.** Scholars do not agree on an exact definition of the

FIGURE 19–3

THE UNDERCLASS: FOUR CHARACTERISTICS

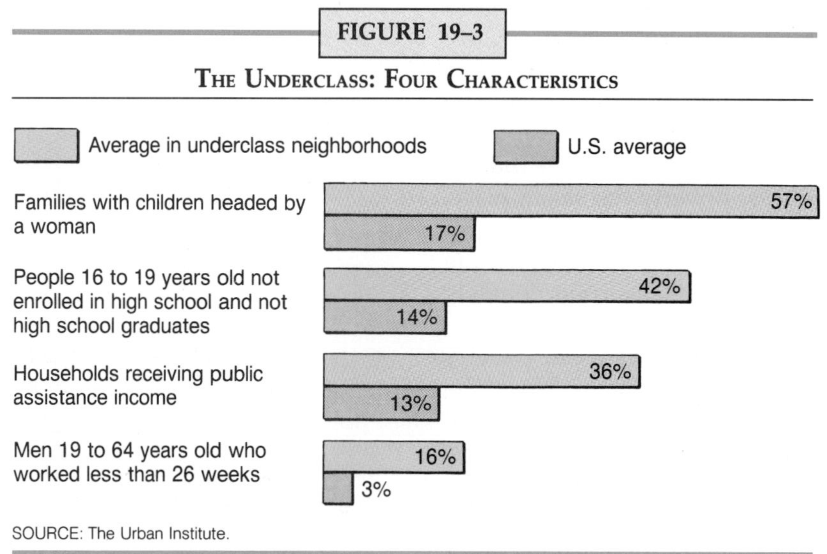

SOURCE: The Urban Institute.

underclass, but they generally recognize that a severely disadvantaged group exists in near-total isolation from mainstream society. Members of the underclass are characterized by more than having incomes below the poverty line. They are concentrated in deteriorating inner-city areas, where not working is the norm and where drugs, teenage pregnancy, prostitution, and crime are a way of life. A 1987 study by the Urban Institute defined an underclass neighborhood as one with an extremely high concentration of:

Families with children headed by a female
High school dropouts
Households on welfare
Unemployed working age males

While the incidence of poverty increased about 5 percent in the 1970s, the size of the underclass, under the above definition, quadrupled in ten years. The underclass neighborhoods are disproportionately populated by nonwhites. Figure 19–3 compares the prevalence of these four categories of people found in underclass neighborhoods with the national average. Scholars believe that a better understanding of the truly disadvantaged is essential if better public policies to eradicate the chain of poverty are to be developed. Examination of the truly disadvantaged has also led to a debate over the success or failure of U.S. social welfare policy in the past two decades.

Do Social Welfare Programs Work?

WHO RECEIVES BENEFITS?

To assess the impact of government programs on poverty, we must first see where the money goes. Means-tested programs, such as AFDC, food stamps, and Medicaid, go predominantly to the poor, as intended. But far more is spent on non-means-tested entitlements (see Figure 19–4). Only one dollar in five spent on non-means-tested entitlements goes to the poor. Social Security, Medicare, Veterans benefits, worker's compensation, unemployment compensation, and education outlays go mostly to Americans who are above the poverty level. Overall, most social welfare expenditures go to middle- and upper-income Americans. Some see this as evidence that not enough resources are directed to the poor. Others are reassured that the middle class, which bears a large share of the federal

FIGURE 19–4

SOCIAL WELFARE SPENDING (BILLIONS OF DOLLARS SPENT IN FY 1991)

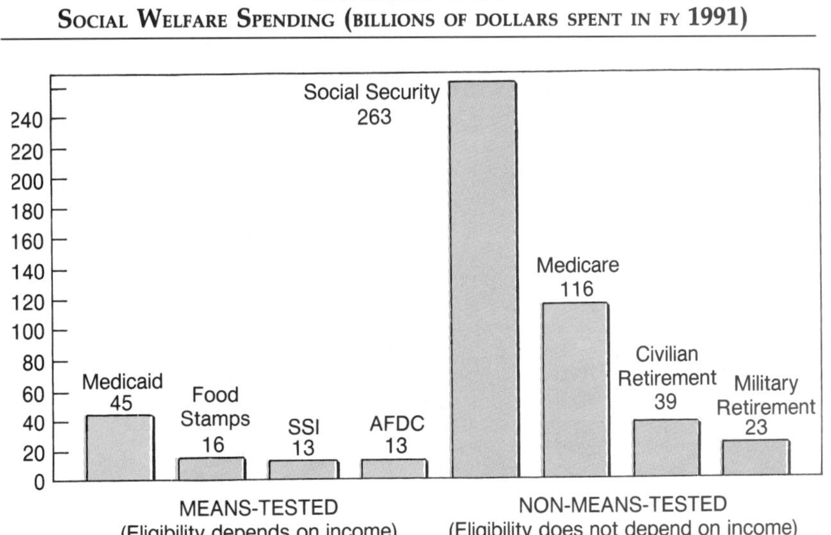

tax burden, is also the recipient of many social welfare outlays.

THE CUMULATIVE EFFECTS OF SOCIAL WELFARE PROGRAMS

Social welfare expenditures lift a number of people above the poverty threshold. According to figures compiled by the Congressional Budget Office, 27 percent of the population would have been below the threshold without any income assistance.[20] Social Security, even though it is not means-tested, is also the most important program in lifting people out of poverty. With Social Security, 9 million families of elderly, disabled, and survivors climbed above the poverty line. The cash transfer payments of AFDC and SSI brought another 2 million families above the poverty line, reducing the total percentage of poor to below 13.5 percent. Food stamps, housing assistance, Medicare, and Medicaid lowered the poverty rate to 8.1 percent. The discrepancies between Congressional Budget Office and Census Bureau figures for the corresponding time period are primarily the result of including Medicare, Medicaid, and housing assistance in computing poverty.

Social welfare programs do have an impact. The data suggest that without these programs, significantly more Americans would live in poverty. Yet the controversy over social welfare programs rages on.

THE "WAR ON POVERTY": WON OR LOST?

In the mid-1980s, social scientist Charles Murray created a national stir with his book *Losing Ground*,[21] which concluded that social programs backfire. Murray contended that the conditions of poor people, particularly blacks, actually worsened during the 1960s and 1970s, despite the rapid increases in federal spending. Citing figures on increases in illegitimacy, youth unemployment, welfare dependency, and crime, Murray concluded that the poverty programs of the 1960s created perverse incentives that encourage idleness and discourage working. The poor, he wrote, would be better off financially if they did not get married, stayed on welfare, and did not take even part-time

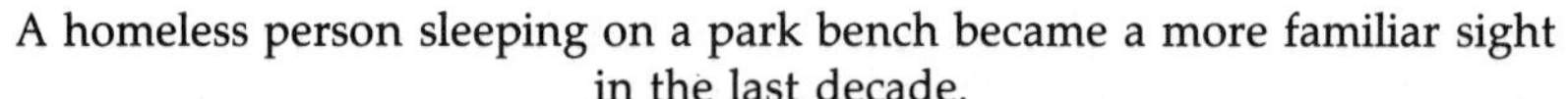

A homeless person sleeping on a park bench became a more familiar sight in the last decade.

work. Such poverty programs have created a permanent class of nonproductive poor. Despite the best intentions of policymakers, poverty actually had increased.

Critics were quick to question both Murray's analysis and his conclusions. Long-time social activist Michael Harrington, who helped launch the "war on poverty," claimed that Murray's own numbers did not support his conclusions.[22] He attacked the simplicity of Murray's analysis and noted that Murray ignored the reduction in poverty among the elderly, improvements in health care of the poor, and gains in nutrition. About the same time that Murray's book appeared, another scholar, John Schwarz, published an extensive study of the impact of Great Society programs, reaching starkly different conclusions.[23] His book, *America's Hidden Success,* concluded that, far from causing more poverty, the effects of social programs have been seriously underestimated:

> The War on Poverty decisively changed the living conditions facing the poor. Programs such as food stamps virtually eliminated serious malnutrition among low-income children and adults in America. Medicaid and Medicare greatly increased the access of low-income Americans to health care. In turn, the enlargement of both nutritional and medical programs led to a decline in the infant mortality rate among minority Americans of 40 percent between 1965 and 1975, a drop that was eight times larger than the decline that had taken place prior to 1965. The expansion of governmental housing programs helped to reduce the proportion of Americans living in overcrowded housing from 12 percent in 1960 to 5 percent in 1980. Such are only a few of the contributions of the 'failed policies of the past.'[24]

Questions about the impact of poverty programs and social welfare expenditures are indeed complex. Different measures and indicators can generate significantly different conclusions. But by the late 1980s, a consensus that the nation needed a new approach to welfare was emerging.

WELFARE REFORM

By the end of the Reagan administration, both liberals and conservatives agreed that a new approach to welfare that would move people from the welfare rolls to payrolls was needed. As we have seen, after the demise of President Nixon's Family Assistance Plan, little significant policy innovation in antipoverty programs took place at the federal level. There were some developments at the state level, however. A number of states implemented "workfare" programs and other education and training programs. **Workfare** programs required recipients to take employment at the minimum wage to remain eligible for benefits. Other states required recipients to enroll in classes to complete their high school education or in training programs to acquire job skills. Massachusetts developed a program to move welfare recipients from dependency to productive labor. Programs like these helped spur Congress to consider welfare reform on the national level.

In October 1988, after two years of intense efforts and complex negotiations, the most sweeping overhaul of the nation's welfare system in fifty years was enacted. President Reagan signed the Family Support Act of 1988 after it passed by overwhelming margins in both houses of Congress. These large margins belied the deep differences that separated Democrats and Republicans throughout the 100th Congress. Both sides claimed the goal of reducing welfare dependency but had differed sharply on how to bring it about. The welfare reform package made the following changes:

Created the Jobs Opportunity and Basic Skills Program (JOBS), which mandated that each of the fifty states develops programs "to assure that needy families with children obtain the education, training, and employment that will help them avoid long-term welfare dependence."[25] States would provide high school equivalency courses, remedial education programs, job training, and other programs aimed at those groups most prone to welfare dependency. Each state must come up with its own JOBS program by 1990 that would be monitored in Washington by the Department of Health and Human Services. All welfare recipients except those with children under three years of age would be required to participate in the program as long as child care services were provided.

An applicant at a county welfare office. Welfare reform adopted in 1988 requires states to develop programs to get people off welfare.

Required each state to provide child care for each welfare recipient participating in the JOBS program. States were allowed to fulfill the child-care requirement in a variety of ways, such as providing day care directly, making cash payments to beneficiaries, or issuing vouchers for child care. The JOBS program and mandatory child-care provisions were financed by a new entitlement where the federal government picked up 90 percent of the costs.

Allowed welfare to be paid to two-parent families. Previously, only 27 states would pay welfare benefits to a mother if a husband or other male were in the household. Critics felt this encouraged abandonment and tended to break up families. Under the new law, both parents could be required to participate in JOBS program activities. It also allowed parents of young children to keep federal medical insurance for up to a year after they found jobs.

Enhanced child support enforcement to reduce the financial burden on government for fathers who abandon children or fail to pay court-ordered support payments. The law provided for immediate wage withholding, nationwide tracking and monitoring systems, and the establishment of an interstate commission on child support.

The Family Support Act, despite the many changes it made in the welfare system, was not a complete revamping of AFDC. It brought in elements of workfare, strongly supported by Republicans, but only if day-care facilities were provided, a provision strongly supported by Democrats. Not all were happy with these provisions, with one opponent calling the JOBS mandatory work requirement "slavefare." Democrats conceded on the workfare provisions because President Reagan pledged to veto any bill without them. The cost of the JOBS program was approximately $6.8 billion over seven years.

Even with the adoption of some reforms, the nature and effectiveness of the nation's welfare programs will continue to be an issue in the 1990s.

Accompanying this controversy are concerns about the larger non-means-tested entitlements—Social Security and health care programs.

Insecurity about Social Security

IS THE SYSTEM FINANCIALLY SOLVENT?

Social Security has taken its place in America right next to motherhood and apple pie—and well it should, according to some. It may be the most expensive program in the federal budget next to defense, but it does more to reduce poverty in the United States than any other program. Yes, say critics, but it also provides tax-free income to wealthy retirees. Will the money be there when it comes time for people now in their twenties and thirties to retire? Many Americans are afraid it will not.

Owing to Franklin Roosevelt's effort to sell Social Security as a retirement program, many Americans do not understand the "current financing" basis of Social Security—that what is paid *out* comes from what is paid *in* that same year. Therefore, the financial soundness of the program depends on demographic and economic factors, not on what people actually contributed to the program. Compared with what they paid in, most beneficiaries today receive five to ten times more than their contributions to the fund, plus compound interest! Leaving aside the question of whether the benefit levels are adequate, from an input-output perspective today's Social Security recipient receives a bonus. But what about tomorrow's recipients?

The Social Security trust fund is currently running a surplus as a result of the 1983 bailout. That surplus is projected to grow until the end of the twentieth century. However, even under the most positive assumptions, the trust fund will run a deficit for some part of the next century. The stability of the Social Security trust fund depends on how fast *wages* grow relative to *prices*. Receipts are derived from a tax on earned income, but benefits

Reprinted with special permission of King Features Syndicate, Inc.

are linked to the consumer price index. Therefore, economic growth combined with relatively low inflation would help increase receipts faster than benefits. However, inflation combined with high unemployment (reducing the wage base) would have the opposite effect. The second determinant of the financial soundness of Social Security has to do with population trends. The baby-boom generation will begin retiring by the year 2015 and largely out of the work force by the year 2030. At this point, based on actual and projected birthrates, there will only be 2.5 workers taxed to pay benefits to every Social Security recipient,[26] compared with about one recipient for every four workers today and one to seven when the system started in the 1930s.

SOCIAL SECURITY AND PROBLEMS OF GOVERNING

When President Reagan and his budget-cutters assumed office in 1981, they decided that curbing government spending could be accomplished only by going after the rapidly expanding social welfare entitlements. At the same time, however, they recognized the politically untouchable status of Social Security. Democrats dared them to cut this popular program, and many Republicans shared their concerns. Therefore, in the first round of domestic budget cuts in 1981, the total of $38 billion included only small reductions in Social Security benefits, and those were targeted at certain groups of recipients. No general benefit reduction was proposed. The savings were modest, but so was the potential political damage.

Feeling confident because of the early success of the administration's economic plan, the White House had floated a trial balloon about certain "reforms" of the Social Security system. The outcry from the Democrats on Capitol Hill was instant. "The president doesn't care about the elderly," they claimed. "Reagan wants to cut Social Security." An angry White House accused Congress of playing politics with a serious political issue and quickly pulled back. The financial problems of the system were obvious to all, but Social Security legislation was dead in 1981–82.

The Social Security deadlock was broken in 1983, when a different political strategy was tried. Recognizing that the government could not deal with the issue in a partisan context, particularly in an election year, Reagan and the congressional Democrats called a truce. The president created a bipartisan commission on Social Security, with half of the members named by Reagan and half by House Speaker Tip O'Neill, which would report in December 1982—*after* the 1982 congressional elections. As the new Congress met in 1983, it was uncertain whether the commission's recommendations would be followed. Although not especially palatable to either side, both sides closed their eyes and swallowed the recommendations without major change. Both credit-taking and finger-pointing were avoided. Politically, it appeared that no other course would have received bipartisan support.

The 1983 Social Security changes were neither popular nor particularly well understood among the general public. The major provisions, adopted by Congress and signed by the president in 1983,

> Delayed the cost-of-living adjustment by six months (saving outlays of $22 billion over five years)
>
> Taxed 50 percent of benefits of recipients earning $20,000 (single) and $25,000 (married), increasing receipts by $22.4 billion over five years
>
> Accelerated the increased payroll tax, increasing receipts $19 billion over five years
>
> Included all nonprofit institutions in the system and all new federal employees, increasing receipts $11.6 billion over five years

The total impact of the Social Security bailout in 1983 was to reduce the shortfall between receipts and benefits in the Social Security trust fund by $114 billion from 1984 to 1988.

SOCIAL SECURITY AND THE DEFICIT

In early 1990, Senator Daniel Moynihan made a proposal to slash Social Security taxes because of the surpluses building up in the trust fund. The New

Senator Daniel Patrick Moynihan.

York Democrat argued that Social Security taxes were regressive, fell heavily on the middle class, and tended to mask the "true" deficit in the operating portion of the federal budget. Moynihan's proposal received heavy play on media talk shows and in the press, raising new questions about the government's finances. The strong reaction caught many off guard, including both the president and Democratic leaders in Congress. President Bush opposed the tax cut idea, claiming it might endanger future benefits. Many Democrats quietly opposed the idea because, unless taxes were raised elsewhere, cutting Social Security taxes would make the deficit even worse.

The Social Security trust fund had a surplus of $159 billion at the start of 1990, which was projected to grow to $700 billion in 1995.[27] These surpluses reduce the deficit in the rest of the budget because they are relinquished to the Treasury in return for government securities. Trust fund surpluses do not cover up the real size of the deficit because they simply reflect transfers within different parts of the budget. Nonetheless, as Social Security taxes rise as a result of the 1983 bailout and the surpluses continue to grow, there may be increasing political pressure to change the law. To prevent this, the budget agreement reached in October, 1990 made it more difficult for legislators to tinker with Social Security.

Costs and Options in Social Welfare Policy

ARE THE COSTS OF ENTITLEMENTS OUT OF CONTROL?

Entitlement programs are blamed for hardening the budgetary arteries, tying the hands of decision-makers, and committing the government to uncontrolled growth in spending. But entitlements also protect beneficiaries and create stability in national policy.

Indexing of Social Security benefits is one example of both positive and negative payoffs of entitlement programs. Although indexing proved costly in the 1970s, it also seemed essential to slow the increases in benefit levels, which before indexing were significantly greater than the inflation rate. Indexing eliminated the practice of election-year increases in benefits but made the spending side of the budget very sensitive to inflation. Entitlements are not completely uncontrollable. Recent experiences have demonstrated that Congress can initiate or be pressured into changing the substantive law that creates entitlements. Because the amount of spending is so great, a slight alteration in an entitlement program can result in more cost savings than the complete elimination of some discretionary domestic programs.

Table 19–2 shows projected entitlement spending through 1995. Leading the pack is Social Security, which with Medicare and Medicaid accounts for two-thirds of entitlements, projected to grow to $335 billion by 1995. Medicare and Medicaid programs costing $161 billion in 1991 are projected to increase by over 50 percent, to $253 billion, by 1995. Health-care costs for the federal government are the most rapidly increasing item in

TABLE 19–2

PROJECTED OUTLAY FOR ENTITLEMENTS, 1991–1995 (IN BILLIONS OF DOLLARS)

Category	1991	1995
Means-Tested Programs		
Medicaid	45	70
Food stamps	16	19
Supplemental Security Income	13	18
Family support (AFDC)	13	16
Veterans pensions	4	4
Child nutrition	5	6
Earned income tax credit	4	5
Guaranteed student loans (Stafford loans)	4	3
Other	2	3
Subtotal Means-tested programs	108	146
Non-Means-Tested Programs		
Social Security	263	335
Medicare	116	183
Subtotal	380	518
Other retirement and disability		
Federal civilian	39	51
Military	23	29
Other	5	6
Subtotal	67	86
Unemployment compensation	16	19
Other programs		
Veterans benefits	15	16
Farm price supports	12	10
Social services	6	5
Other	21	10
Subtotal	54	41
Non-means-tested programs	517	664
Total		
All entitlements and other mandatory spending	624	809

SOURCE: Congressional Budget Office, 1990

FIGURE 19–5

ENTITLEMENT SPENDING AND GROWTH

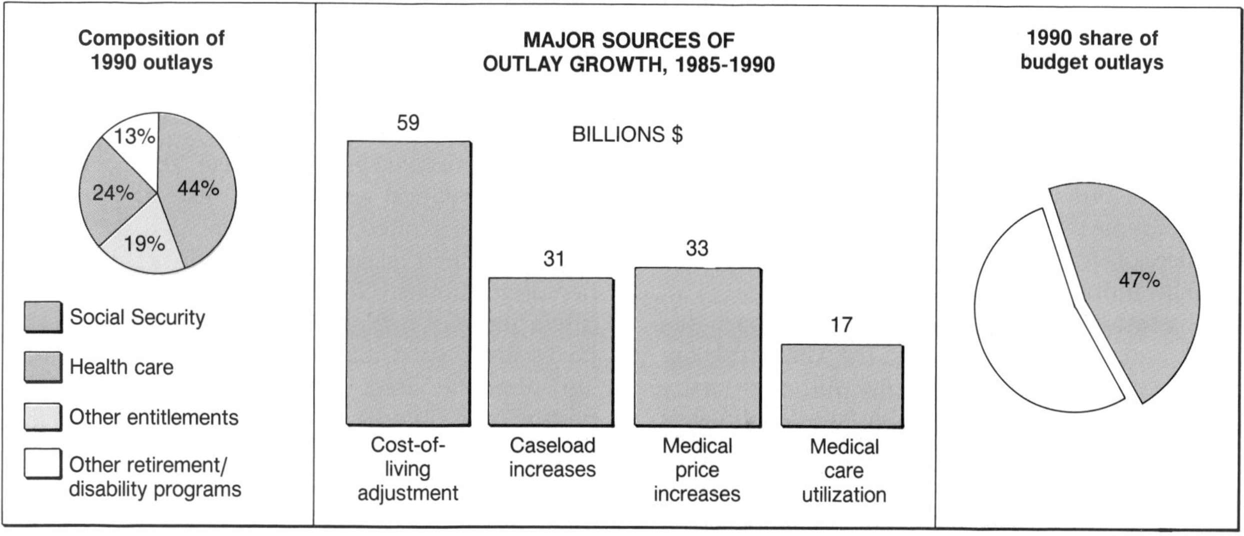

SOURCE: Congressional Budget Office, 1985, 199.

the budget. Medicare and Medicaid became key targets for cuts in the Bush administration, increasing controls on payments to doctors and hospitals. In just twenty-five years, Medicare and Medicaid have grown from small programs to major outlays providing billions of dollars in benefits to more than 50 million Americans. Over the past decade, costs of these two programs have risen by an average of 17 percent a year. Figure 19–5 shows that growth is attributable to four factors: (1) increased program enrollments, meaning that more eligible recipients are taking advantage of benefits, (2) expanding use of medical services by beneficiaries, and (3) rapidly rising health-care costs—hospitalization, doctors' fees, tests, and X-rays, and (4) inflation.

Federal retirement, railroad retirement, military retirement, and disability programs are also a significant part of entitlements. Although such programs do not receive the attention of AFDC and food stamps, they actually constitute a larger portion of the government's cash transfers. Government retirement benefits go primarily to middle- and upper-class recipients and are much less controversial than aid to the poor. But even these popular benefits became targets in the 1980s. Former Budget Director David Stockman called military retirement pensions "a disgrace" and urged cuts. Because of cuts in entitlement growth achieved in the 1980s, spending for AFDC, SSI, food stamps, and veterans pensions is projected to rise only slightly, both in real terms and as a proportion of the federal budget. Finally, unemployment benefits and other entitlements are projected to remain constant in current dollars throughout the early 1990s.

What will be the social welfare agenda in the coming years? Thirty-eight million Americans have no health-care coverage at all, and catastrophic illnesses can wipe out a family's savings, even with some insurance. The gap between rich and poor in America continues to widen. The plight of the homeless seems to be capturing the nation's attention, but continuing budget deficits have made political leaders extremely cost-conscious. Rapidly increasing costs of entitlements concern Republicans and Democrats alike, but the history of social welfare politics has generally been partisan. Since the 1930s, the Democrats have been more aggressive in proposing expansion of coverage and benefits, and Republicans have been more resistant. As a result, particularly under divided government, isssues such as Social Security have tested the ability of the system to govern effectively. Perhaps even sterner tests over such issues as catastrophic health care, Medicare, child care, and family leave policy await in the 1990s.

★

SUMMARY AND CONCLUSIONS

1. The United States was one of the last developed nations to provide public assistance for the poor and retirement programs for the elderly, largely because of traditional American values of self-reliance, individualism, and capitalism.

2. Government responsibility for the poor, disabled, and elderly expanded in the 1930s with the passage of the Social Security Act. Although many social welfare issues are divisive, most politicians now accept the framework of social welfare programs laid down fifty years ago.

3. Poverty was rediscovered in the 1960s—not during a depression but in a time of affluence when poverty seemed inexplicable. Nixon's Family Assistance Plan was the last serious presidential proposal for comprehensive welfare reform.

4. The most important changes in social welfare policy in the 1970s were the rapid expansion and growth of entitlement spending. In reaction to a decade of unprecedented growth, the Reagan and Bush administrations attempted to reduce the growth of social welfare entitlements.

5. The poor in America are increasingly found in households headed by a female with children. Poverty among the elderly has been significantly reduced in the past fifteen years.

6. Social welfare programs have not eliminated poverty, but they have succeeded in lifting millions of Americans above the poverty line. Nonetheless, a heated debate on the overall impact of poverty programs continues.

7. Social Security has become a highly emotional issue, increasingly difficult for politicians to deal with in a responsible fashion. The 1983 changes stabilized the system for the short run, but Social Security remains highly sensitive to both demographic and economic trends.

8. Current social welfare issues include curbing the costs of entitlements, reducing government health-care costs, helping the homeless, and providing health care for the uninsured.

Social welfare politics reflect the values of American political economy. Unlike its European cousins, the United States developed without a highly defined class structure or a system of hereditary nobles. No aristocracy existed to inculcate a sense of noblesse oblige—the view that the haves are responsible for helping the have-nots. Not until the Great Depression engulfed a large portion of the middle class, swelling the ranks of the poor dramatically, did government policy change.

But even with this new national responsibility, many old attitudes lingered. Welfare remains an unpopular program, not because it costs so much but because it is a symbolic handout. In reality, the federal government spends relatively little on public assistance, compared with other programs. Despite some fraud and abuse—often highly publicized—most welfare recipients are "truly needy." The underclass exists in a circle of poverty that is difficult to escape and that remains impervious to government programs.

The ability to govern is sorely tested by social welfare issues. When the fear of even discussing Social Security becomes so great that nothing can be done, a governing crisis exists. In the 1930s, 1960s, and 1980s, significant changes were made in social welfare policy under particular sets of circumstances. But as parties decline, fragmentation increases, interest groups multiply and strengthen, and governing on the toughest issues becomes more difficult.

KEY TERMS

absolute versus relative poverty
AFDC (Aid to Families with Dependent Children)
community action programs (CAPs)
contributory versus noncontributory programs

Economic Opportunity Act (1964)
Family Assistance Plan
means test
Medicaid
Medicare Act
OASDI (Old Age Survivors Disability Insurance)
poverty line
Social Security Act
SSI (Supplemental Security Income)
underclass
workfare

SELF-REVIEW

1. How can poverty be defined?
2. What accounts for the ambivalence of American attitudes toward social welfare?
3. List the major programs created by the Social Security Act of 1935.
4. What was Nixon's Family Assistance Plan?
5. What changes did the Reagan administration make in social welfare programs?
6. Describe the incidence of poverty.
7. What is the underclass?
8. What is the cumulative effect of social welfare programs?
9. What were the features of the Social Security compromise in 1983?

SUGGESTED READINGS

Donovan, John. *The Politics of Poverty.* 1973.
One of the most readable accounts of the "war on poverty," its great promise, and its ultimate disappointment.

Harrington, Michael. *The Other America.* 1963.
Still well worth reading, the book that awakened Americans from their complacency about the "affluent society" by detailing the misery and suffering in the United States and helped begin the "war on poverty."

Murray, Charles. *Losing Ground: American Social Policy, 1950–1980.* 1984.
A provocative analysis concluding that poverty programs have actually increased poverty and created a permanent class of poor.

Schwarz, John E. *America's Hidden Success: A Reassessment of Twenty Years of Public Policy.* 1984.
An analysis that suggests the impact of poverty programs of the 1960s has been substantially underestimated.

NOTES

1. See Dorothy Wedderburn, "Thought and Theories of the Welfare State," in *What Should Be the Role of the Federal Government in Extending Public Assistance . . . ,* Congressional Research Service, 93rd Cong., 1st sess., No. 93–12.
2. Joseph Pechman and Benjamin Okner, *Who Bears the Tax Burden?* (Washington, D.C.: Brookings, 1974), 7.
3. See Edward Berkowitz and Kim McQuaid, *Creating the Welfare State* (New York: Praeger, 1980), chap. 4.
4. Sidney Lens, *Poverty: America's Enduring Paradox* (New York: Crowell, 1971), 4.
5. Harris G. Warren, *Herbert Hoover and the Great Depression* (New York: Norton, 1959), 193.
6. James David Barber, *The Presidential Character* (Englewood Cliffs, N.J.: Prentice-Hall, 1977), 30.
7. Berkowitz and McQuaid, *Creating the Welfare State,* 99.
8. Dorothy Buckton James, *Poverty, Politics, and Change* (Englewood Cliffs, N.J.: Prentice-Hall, 1972), 51.
9. See John Donovan, *The Politics of Poverty* (Indianapolis: Bobbs-Merrill, 1973).
10. Hearings, Subcommittee on War on Poverty Program, *Hearings on the Economic Opportunity Act of 1964 (Part I),* 88th Cong., 2nd sess., 1964, p. 305.
11. Donovan, *Politics,* 35.
12. See Eugene Feingold, *Medicare: Policy and Politics* (San Francisco: Chandler, 1966).
13. See Richard Nathan, *The Administrative Presidency* (New York: Wiley, 1983).
14. Congressional Budget Office, *An Analysis of the President's Budgetary Proposals for FY 84,* February 1983, 95–96.
15. Office of Management and Budget, *FY 82 Budget Revisions,* March 1981, pp. 8–9.
16. Congressional Budget Office, *An Analysis of the President's Budgetary Proposals FY 1991,* March 1990.
17. John Kenneth Galbraith, *The Affluent Society* (New York: New American Library, 1958), 251.
18. League of Women Voters, *Human Needs: Unfinished Business on the Nation's Agenda* (1981), 2.
19. *New York Times,* 22 April 1987, p. E5.
20. See Congressional Budget Office, "Poverty Status of Families," June 1987.
21. Charles Murray, *Losing Ground: American Social Policy, 1950–1980* (New York: Basic Books, 1984).
22. Michael Harrington, "Crunched Numbers," *New Republic,* 28 January 1985, pp. 7–10.

23. John E. Schwarz, *America's Hidden Success: A Reassessment of Twenty Years of Public Policy* (New York: Norton, 1984).
24. John E. Schwarz, "The War We Won," *New Republic,* 18 June 1984, p. 19.
25. *Congressional Quarterly Weekly Reports,* 8 October 1988, p. 2826.
26. See Congressional Budget Office, "*Financing Social Security: Issues and Options for the Long Run,*" November 1982.
27. Congressional Budget Office, *The Economic and Budget Outlook FY 1991–95,* pp. 47–49.

CHAPTER 20

Foreign Policy and National Defense

POLITICAL CLOSE-UP

"The Mask Fell Away So Rapidly . . ."

Excerpts from a speech by Czechoslovakian President Vaclav Havel before a joint session of the U.S. Congress, February 21, 1990.

Havel, by his own admission an intellectual first and a politician second, was Czechoslovakia's leading playwright and political thinker. He was frequently jailed under communist rule for advocating human rights and democracy. Havel was arrested as recently as October 1989, only two months before the old regime collapsed, and he was the consensus choice to become president of the new Czechoslovakia.

"The last time they arrested me, on October 27, of last year, I didn't know whether it was for 2 days or 2 years.

Exactly 1 month later, when the rock musician Michael Kocab told me that I would probably be proposed as a Presidential candidate, I thought it was one of his usual jokes.

On the 10th of December 1989, when my actor friend Jiri Bartoska, in the name of the Civic Forum, nominated me as a candidate for the office of president of the republic, I thought it was out of the question that the

Parliament we had inherited from the previous regime would elect me.

Nineteen days later, when I was unanimously elected President of my country, I had no idea that in 2 months later I would be speaking in front of this famous and powerful assembly, and that what I say would be heard by millions of people who have never heard of me and that hundreds of politicians and political scientists would study every word I say.

When they arrested me on October 27, I was living in a country ruled by the most conservative communist government in Europe, and our society slumbered beneath the pall of a totalitarian system. Today, less than 4 months later, I am speaking to you as the representative of a country that has set out on the road to democracy, a country where there is complete freedom of speech, which is getting ready for free elections, and which wants to create a prosperous market economy and its own foreign policy.

It is all very extraordinary. . . .

And now what is happening is happening: the totalitarian system in the Soviet Union and in most of its satellites is breaking down and our nations are looking for a way to democracy and independence. The first act in this remarkable drama began when Mr. Gorbachev and those around him, faced with the sad reality of their country, initiated their policy of "perestroika." Obviously, they had no idea either what they were setting in motion or how rapidly events would unfold. We knew a lot about the enormous number of growing problems that slumbered beneath the honeyed, unchanging mask of socialism. But I don't think any of us knew how little it would take for these problems to manifest themselves in all their enormity, and for the longings of these nations to emerge in all their strength. The mask fell away so rapidly that, in the flood of work, we have literally no time even to be astonished.

I often hear the question: How can the United States of America help us today? My reply is as paradoxical as the whole of my life has been: You can help us most of all if you help the Soviet Union on its irreversible, but immensely complicated road to democracy. It is far more complicated than the road open to its former European satellites. You yourselves know best how to support, as rapidly as possible, the nonviolent evolution of this enormous, multinational body politic toward democracy and autonomy for all of its peoples. Therefore, it is not fitting for me to offer you any advice. I can only say that the sooner, the more quickly, and the more peacefully the Soviet Union begins to move along the road toward genuine political pluralism, respect for the rights of nations to their own integrity and to a working, that is a market-economy, the better it will be, not just for Czechs and Slovaks, but for the whole world. And the sooner you yourselves will be able to reduce the burden of the military budget borne by the American people. To put it metaphorically: The missions you give to the East today will soon return to you in the form of billions in savings. . . ."

As long as people are people, democracy in the full sense of the word will always be no more than an ideal; one may approach it as one would a horizon, in ways that may be better or worse, but it can never be fully attained. In this sense, you too are merely approaching democracy. You have thousands of problems of all kinds, as other countries do. But you have one great advantage: You have been approaching democracy uninterruptedly for more than two hundred years, and your journey toward the horizon has never been disrupted by a totalitarian system. Czechs and Slovaks, despite their humanistic traditions that go back to the first millennium, have approached democracy for a mere twenty years, between the two world wars, and now for the three and a half months since the seventeenth of November of last year.

CHAPTER OUTLINE

Introduction and Overview

The Cold War and Containment
From Hot War to Cold War
The Truman Doctrine and the Marshall Plan
Containment
The Korean Conflict: An Application of Containment

The Nuclear Threat and Brinkmanship
Eisenhower, Dulles, and "Massive Retaliation"
Kennedy, Cuba, and Communism

Vietnam and Reassessment of American Foreign Policy
Lyndon Johnson and Vietnam
Nixon, Kissinger, and Détente

Beyond Containment and Back Again
Carter and Human Rights
Reagan and a Return to Cold War Rhetoric
An Easing of Tensions during the Gorbachev Era

Democracy Movements and the End of the Cold War
Repression of Democracy in China
Political Change in the Soviet Union and Eastern Europe
Poland
Czechoslovakia
Hungary
East Germany
Romania
Bulgaria

The Defense Budget
Military Spending Trends
The Composition of Defense Spending
Strategic Weapons and SDI
The "Peace Dividend"

The Political Economy of Defense
The Military-Industrial Complex
The Economic Effects of Defense Cuts

Governing in Foreign Affairs

Summary and Conclusions

INTRODUCTION AND OVERVIEW

After forty-five years of tension in a world divided between the United States and its democratic allies in the west and the Soviet Union and its communist allies in the east, the Cold War came to an end. As peoples around the world watched on their televisions, the Berlin Wall—poignant symbol of the Cold War—came tumbling down. First, it opened symbolically as Germans streamed across at Checkpoint Charlie, then brick by brick as jubilant Germans took sledges to it, and finally, bulldozers eradicated it for good. While the democracy movement in China was crushed by tanks in Tienanmen Square in June 1989, by the end of the year, the Iron Curtain in Europe had fallen. The Soviet Union, initial impetus for the transformation, faced perhaps the most difficult transition of all as the economy deteriorated and the union of republics seemed ready to come apart at the seams.

The transition to democracy and market economies would be difficult for the Soviet Union and nations of Eastern Europe. But the end of the Cold War profoundly challenges the United States, as well. The success of democracy represents the fulfillment of forty-five-year-old American policy objectives, yet it presents both opportunities and risks. In the coming years, the United States must evaluate its foreign policy, defense posture, and national security strategies. The transformed international environment will also affect the domestic policy agenda, decision-making institutions, and processes of governing.

Foreign policy involves the relations between one nation and other nations, encompassing actions taken to influence the behavior of other states while adjusting to the international environment.[1] Defense policy is reflected in foreign policy but more specifically refers to decisions regarding the size, shape, and nature of the military and strategies for its use. National security policy includes elements of both foreign and defense policy and, more broadly, aims to keep the nation prosperous and secure. It also involves decisions to intervene militarily, as the United States did in Panama in December 1989 and in the Middle East in August 1990.

Foreign policy and national defense are closely tied to economic issues and questions of legislative-executive relations in governing. Problems of stalemate and inaction have rarely occurred when national security is at stake, since the president has assumed greater power. But with the reduction of the communist threat and world tensions, policy-making in the foreign realm may come to more closely approximate policy-making in the domestic realm. This chapter looks at the following questions:

1. How did the Cold War and containment of communism become the central theme of post World War II foreign policy?
2. What was the posture of the Soviet Union and the United States through the 1940s, 1950s, and 1960s?

Panamanian dictator Manuel Noriega was captured by U.S. forces after the 1989 invasion and brought back to the United States to stand trial.

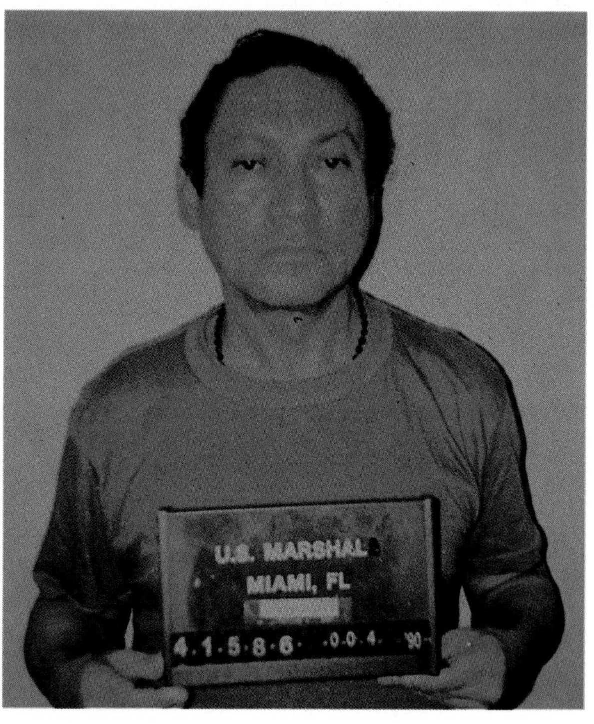

3. How did the Vietnam War affect U.S. foreign policy through the 1970s and 1980s?
4. How did the revolutions in Eastern Europe and the end of the Cold War unfold?
5. What are the patterns of military spending in the post-war era, and how might they be altered in the 1990s?
6. What are the military-industrial complex and the "peace dividend"?
7. How are recent world changes likely to effect legislative-executive relations and the prospects for governing in the 1990s?

The Cold War and Containment

Throughout much of its early history, the United States remained relatively aloof from world affairs. George Washington in his farewell address, warned the country against "entangling alliances." His successors heeded this advice. The United States tried to avoid entanglement in the shifting European alliances, while insisting (through the Monroe Doctrine) that Europeans in turn not meddle in the western hemisphere. However, this "isolationism" was only partial. The United States actually attempted to extend its international influence in numerous ways.[2] Domestic economic interests influenced territorial expansion in the nineteenth century and "gunboat diplomacy" at the turn of the century. But sentiment for isolationism persisted until the bombing of Pearl Harbor in 1941. World War II put an end to any vestiges of neutrality in American foreign policy.

FROM HOT WAR TO COLD WAR

The United States and the Soviet Union fought as allies during World War II, partners in the task of defeating Adolf Hitler and eliminating the Nazi threat to Europe. Despite Americans' distaste for communism and the Bolsheviks, Americans and Russians had an overriding common goal. But after the war, the alliance fell apart. What little real friendship existed had collapsed by the time victory was secure. A new generation of American leaders drew clear "lessons" from World War II: Never again would the United States be a passive bystander in the international arena.[3] As the major world power, the United States became the chief architect of the United Nations, the new world forum. The only threat to U.S. dominance of a new world order was the Soviet Union.

The perspective from the Kremlin in Moscow was far different from that within the White House or Capitol Hill. The Russians had experienced yet another invasion from the west when Hitler followed the path that Napoleon had taken before him. The results were devastating. In World War II, the Russians lost 20 million soldiers and civilians, many times more than U.S. casualties. The Soviets came out of the war with an absolute determination to secure their borders permanently against enemy penetration. As American troops headed to Berlin from the west, the advancing Red Army occupied the devastated countries of Eastern Europe. These states were to form a buffer to the West that the Soviets so badly wanted. The Allies agreed to partition Europe, both because they believed the Russians were entitled to some of the victors' spoils and because, practically, little could be done to remove them from their positions. So Stalin established hegemony (political and economic dominance) over the nations of Eastern Europe. To the Kremlin, it made perfect sense. To the United States, it certified fears of communist expansionism.

In 1946, former Prime Minister Winston Churchill made a speech in the town of Fulton, Missouri. Churchill introduced a new term to the American vocabulary when he warned that the Russians were building an "iron curtain" around Eastern Europe. The American public and their leaders, already skittish about communism, turned their attention to the problem of checking the expansion of communism. The hot war was over, but the level of international tension remained high as U.S.-Soviet relations entered the deep freeze. The Cold War was on.

THE TRUMAN DOCTRINE AND THE MARSHALL PLAN

A civil war in Greece and fighting in Turkey in 1947 provided the first opportunity for shaping postwar American foreign policy. Truman saw the communist forces in Greece as part of a worldwide pattern of communist aggression and warned the Soviets against taking any active role in Greece and Turkey. President Truman announced that the United States would "support free peoples who are resisting attempted subjugation by the armed minorities or by outside pressures."[4] The general policy became known as the **Truman Doctrine.** It was based on a view of the world order as a confrontation between totalitarianism (the Soviet Union) and freedom (the United States). The Truman Doctrine was the forerunner of the broader containment doctrine.

The political economy of postwar Europe was of great concern to American leaders. They believed that economic instability in Europe posed a serious threat for two reasons. First, economic chaos, poverty, and low productivity almost inevitably led to political chaos. The Nazis had come to power in Germany during just such an economic upheaval. Economic instability, reasoned leaders in Washington, would open the door to communist disruption. Second, economically weak nations cannot defend themselves. Although not anxious to rearm Germany, the U.S. leaders wanted economic recovery to head off any threat of Soviet military takeover or domestic communist revolution. The result was Secretary of State George Marshall's plan for economically rebuilding Europe, known as the **Marshall Plan:**

> It is logical that the United States should do whatever it is able to do to assist in the return of normal economic health in the world, without which there can be no political stability and no assured peace. Our policy should be the revival of a working economy in the world so as to permit the emergence of political and social conditions in which free institutions can exist.[5]

Military aid from the United States to directly affected areas such as Greece and Turkey was supplemented with billions of dollars in economic aid to other nations of Western Europe.

CONTAINMENT

Announcement of the Truman Doctrine and the Marshall Plan was followed within weeks by an important article in the journal *Foreign Affairs* signed by "Mr. X," who was later revealed to be a State Department official, noted Soviet affairs expert George Kennan. In his article, Kennan described the nature of the Soviet threat and the basis of the American policy response. Soviet policy, he argued, was designed to ensure that it "filled every nook and cranny available to it in the basin of world power." He went on to articulate the doctrine of **containment:**

> It is clear that the main element of any United States policy toward the Soviet Union must be that of a long-term, vigilant containment of Russian expansive tendencies. . . . Soviet pressure against the free institutions of the western world is something that can be contained by the adroit and vigilant application of counterforce.[6]

The doctrine of containment furnished the intellectual framework to encompass both the Truman Doctrine and the Marshall Plan. It established confrontation of the Soviets as the modus operandi of American foreign policy.

The containment doctrine would soon be tested. In 1948, the United States participated in the establishment of a military alliance with the nations of the North Atlantic, including Germany. Steps were taken to form an independent German government. Fearing a revitalized Germany, the Soviets cut off transportation and communications into the partitioned city of Berlin, which lay within the Soviet sector of Germany. Fear of war gripped both West and East as the United States airlifted food and supplies into the beleaguered city. The Berlin crisis ended when the blockade failed and the Soviets once again opened the road to traffic. But the pattern of the Cold War was set—high tension, action met with reaction, and confrontation.

While the Berlin crisis was ending, the United States finalized agreement on the nation's first peacetime military alliance since the early days of the Republic. The **North Atlantic Treaty Organization (NATO),** formally ratified in 1949, committed the United States to station American troops abroad.[7] The stage was set for a series of multilateral military alliances entered into by the United States, an attempt to extend the protective "nuclear umbrella" to a number of other nations. The Soviets developed nuclear weapons by 1949 and moved quickly to counter the threat of NATO. A mutual defense pact of the nations of Eastern Europe, the **Warsaw Pact,** was formed. Actions by both sides continued to heighten mutual fear and mistrust.

THE KOREAN CONFLICT: AN APPLICATION OF CONTAINMENT

In 1950, Communist North Korea invaded South Korea. Even though Korea had not previously been defined as being within the network of security interests of the United States, America's new global role and the doctrine of containment were brought to bear on the situation. The Truman administration saw North Korea as a puppet of the Soviet Union and resolved to oppose the invasion. Tension over events in Asia was already high because of the success of Mao Tse Tung and his Communist party in taking control of mainland China in 1949.

The United States brought the Korean question to the still fledgling United Nations and its Security Council. With the Soviet delegate absent (protesting the UN refusal to grant a seat to mainland China), the remaining members promptly passed a resolution committing troops to Korea to repel the invasion. Despite fighting under the UN banner, the Korean War was primarily an American operation. The original aims of the war were to push the North Koreans back north of the thirty-eighth parallel, which divided the two Koreas. But after initial military successes, advisers in the White House pressed to expand the war and to reunite Korea under the government of South Korea. China, now firmly under the control of Chairman Mao, was extremely nervous about the presence of foreign troops on its borders and warned the United States not to pursue the invading force back into North Korea.

Chinese warnings were not taken seriously. Decision-makers in Washington questioned the capabilities of the Chinese military after decades of civil war.[8] On November 28, 1950, a force of more than 200,000 Chinese troops surprised American forces, inflicting heavy casualties, trapping entire units, and forcing U.S. troops to beat a hasty retreat. While General Douglas MacArthur lobbied to expand the conflict and invade China, Truman and the joint chiefs of staff thought better of it. MacArthur continued to publicly criticize American restraint. Truman and his advisers attempted to undo their error, avoid further engagement with China, and continue to fight a limited war. In April 1951, Truman finally fired MacArthur for insubordination and for undermining U.S. policy. The Korean War became a bloody stalemate, an inconclusive series of advances and retreats. It also became a political graveyard for the Truman administration. The chairman of the joint chiefs summed it up. America, he said, was involved "in the wrong war, at the wrong place, at the wrong time, and with the wrong enemy."[9]

By the end of the Truman administration, postwar American foreign policy was firm. The containment doctrine spelled out the U.S. commitment to prevent the spread of communism through NATO and other military alliances. Although the American people supported a hard line against communism and the Russians, the nation was weary of war. This weariness paved the way for a new variation of the containment doctrine with the election of President Eisenhower.

The Nuclear Threat and Brinkmanship

EISENHOWER, DULLES, AND "MASSIVE RETALIATION"

Dwight Eisenhower vowed during the 1952 election campaign to go to Korea as a first step in ending the increasingly unpopular war. He eventually gained a settlement on the original border between the North and the South along the thirty-eighth parallel by threatening to use nuclear weapons against China. With his influential secretary of state, John Foster Dulles, Eisenhower developed a variant of containment based on U.S. nuclear superiority and following the strategy employed to end the Korean War—that is, threatening massive retaliation, using nuclear weapons, to counter communist

A Lance missile in Germany, part of the U.S. forces in NATO designed to contain Soviet expansion during the Cold War.

aggression. Dulles articulated the doctrine more fully in 1954, when he announced that the United States would "retaliate instantly, by means and at places of our own choosing."[10] So began the era of "brinkmanship," escalating conflicts to the brink of nuclear war.

Frustration over the success of Mao in China and the events of Korea had a profound impact on domestic American politics in the 1950s. The phenomenon of McCarthyism—named after Wisconsin Senator Joseph McCarthy—had a divisive effect on the nation. McCarthy accused U.S. officials of being "soft on communism." Politicians such as Richard Nixon made their entry into elective office by using McCarthy-like tactics—labeling their opponents "pinko," "communist sympathizers," or "fellow travelers." Matching McCarthy's tirades against communism at home, the foreign policy rhetoric of the Eisenhower administration continued at a high pitch.

The actions of the Eisenhower administration, however, did not match its belligerent words. Nuclear weapons were not used to help the French in Vietnam in 1954 or after the Soviets crushed the Hungarian Revolution in 1956. Meanwhile, inside the Kremlin, Soviet leaders' worst fears of the West were being realized. While Americans saw the Soviet Union as the leader of an international communist conspiracy to rule the world, the Soviets saw the United States rearming Germany, developing a hostile system of alliances, and threatening to blow them off the face of the earth. The result was continued belligerence on both sides, typified by Russian Premier Nikita Khrushchev's threat to "bury" the West and a commitment by the Soviet Union to catch up to the United States militarily. Spending a huge portion of their national resources on defense, the Russians began a military buildup to end U.S. superiority. The effects of the policies followed by each side seemed to be the opposite of what was desired. The arms race spiraled rapidly, each side more firmly convinced that the other had menacing intentions.

Kennedy, Cuba, and Communism

Between 1955 and 1960, the Soviet Union made a number of important strides, increasing American fears. First, they developed their capability to deliver nuclear weapons through strategic bombers and intercontinental ballistic missiles (ICBMs). Second, in 1957, the Russians successfully launched *Sputnik,* the first artificial satellite to orbit the Earth. Although the direct effects of *Sputnik* were negligible, it shocked Americans. The event suggested that Soviet technology was progressing rapidly and that the Russians now had the lead in the space race. Third, the Soviets seemed to be making inroads among Third World countries. Many nations in Africa and Asia had replaced colonial regimes with native governments. Although many of the new governments were officially nonaligned and concerned mainly with economic development, a number were pro-Soviet and anti-American. One of the most troublesome such governments for the United States was Cuba. In 1959, Fidel Castro overthrew the repressive Batista regime and installed a communist government, supported by Moscow, only ninety miles off the U.S. coast.

The international situation was tense when John F. Kennedy was inaugurated as president in 1961. The world seemed more dangerous than ever. During the campaign Kennedy responded to public concern about Soviet nuclear power by criticizing Eisenhower and Nixon for allowing a "missile gap" to develop between the Soviet Union and the United States. It is clear now that no missile gap existed and that the United States still had nuclear superiority. Kennedy did not question the basic assumptions of American foreign policy. He accepted the tenets of containment and the analysis of international communism and was a "cold warrior" in the fashion of Truman and Eisenhower.[11] Kennedy's inaugural address delivered a clear message to the world:

> Let every nation know, whether it wishes us well or ill, that we shall pay any price, bear any burden, meet any hardship, support any friend, oppose any foe to assure the survival and the success of liberty.

Kennedy's stance was quickly tested. In the spring of 1961, only a few months after taking office, he gave approval to the disastrous Bay of Pigs invasion, an operation designed as a clandestine liberation of Cuba from its communist government. The Central Intelligence Agency and other foreign policy advisers convinced Kennedy that the invasion could be carried out by Cuban exiles without American involvement being discovered. The invasion was characterized as a "perfect failure."[12]

Only eighteen months later, a dangerous crisis involving Cuba took place: the Cuban missile crisis in October 1962. Kennedy used the lessons of the Bay of Pigs to redesign decision-making in the White House in an attempt to prevent another fiasco. Most see the missile crisis as Kennedy's finest hour, in which he made a strong but measured response. Foreign policy expert Graham Allison summarizes the importance of the crisis:

> The Cuban missile crisis is a seminal event. For thirteen days of October 1962, there was a higher probability that more human lives would end suddenly than ever before in history. Had the worst occurred, the death of 100 million Americans, over 100 million Russians, and millions of Europeans as well would make previous natural calamities and inhumanities appear insignificant. Given the probability of disaster—which President Kennedy estimated as "between 1 out of 3 and even"—our escape seems awesome. The event symbolizes a central, if only partially thinkable, fact about our existence. That such consequences could follow from the choices and actions of national governments obliges students of government as well as participants in governance to think hard about these problems.[13]

Other crises dotted the one thousand days of the Kennedy administration. In 1961, the Russians erected the Berlin Wall, which became a symbol of Soviet repression and of the barriers between West and East. Kennedy, despite aggressive rhetoric, accepted the wall, which paved the way for formal recognition of two Germanies ten years later.

Despite his continuation of Cold War foreign policy, there is some evidence that in the last year of his life, Kennedy was softening his views. Profoundly influenced by the missile crisis, Kennedy sounded a note of **détente**—a normalization of relations and reduction in tensions—in June 1963. Later that summer, in a televised address, he told the American people about the ongoing nuclear test-ban negotiations and urged, "Let us make the most of this opportunity, and every opportunity, to reduce tension, to slow down the perilous nuclear arms race, and to check the world's slide toward final annihilation."[14] Kennedy did not live to see progress toward this end. His administration committed American advisers to the struggle in Vietnam and sanctioned covert CIA activities there. Whether Kennedy, had he lived, would have taken the nation down the same path in Vietnam as his successor did will be the subject of endless speculation. Whatever might have been, the war in

Vietnam was a logical extension of containment but one that would deal a severe blow to the view that the United States could act alone as world policeman in containing communism.

Vietnam and Reassessment of American Foreign Policy

LYNDON JOHNSON AND VIETNAM

Kennedy's successor was not well versed in foreign policy when he suddenly found himself in the presidency in November 1963. Although he joined in condemning McCarthy as a senator, Johnson accepted the basic tenets of containment. His belief that containment of communism in Asia must preclude victory by North Vietnam in its struggle with South Vietnam came to dominate, and ultimately topple, his presidency. Discussions of U.S. options in Southeast Asia in the 1960s still centered on the monolithic nature of the worldwide communist threat and the "domino theory"—that if one nation fell to communism, its neighbors would as well. Johnson and his key advisers accepted these assumptions. The war in Vietnam was an undeclared war but one that Congress had tacitly approved of through the Gulf of Tonkin resolution in August 1964. Based on a disputed incident between Vietnamese ships and American ships, the resolution gave the president the go-ahead to use military force.

Despite the Gulf of Tonkin resolution, President Johnson campaigned against Barry Goldwater in the 1964 presidential contest as the candidate of peace. Johnson implied that he would not escalate the American role in Vietnam, while portraying his opponent as a dangerous warmonger. Yet only weeks after the election, the American presence in Vietnam began to increase. By 1967, a handful of Green Berets had become an army of 550,000. Although a majority of Americans supported the war effort through the end of the 1960s, domestic opposition to U.S. involvement in Vietnam was widespread. Even proponents of the American presence criticized the handling and strategy of the war. Political scientist Ithiel Pool, a supporter of the Johnson administration's policy goals, concluded afterward:

> It is hard to understand how intelligent men could believe that aerial bombardment, harassment and interdiction artillery fire, defoliation, and population displacement could be effective means to win a population or how moral men could believe them appropriate means of action among the population we are defending.[15]

Much of the information on the planning and implementation of U.S. policy in Vietnam was revealed in the Pentagon Papers when former government official Daniel Ellsberg turned over an array of secret documents to the *New York Times* and other newspapers. The nation was shocked at revelations of covert operations, government lying, cover-ups, plotting of assassinations, and a systematic pattern of deceiving the American public. Rather than admit defeat or pull back, however, the administration continued to buy time, engaging in a series of holding actions because "this is not a good year to lose Vietnam to communism."[16]

By 1968, domestic opposition to the war in Vietnam had grown increasingly vocal and occasionally violent. President Johnson was challenged in the New Hampshire primary by a little known Minnesota senator, Eugene McCarthy (no relation to Senator Joseph McCarthy), who, campaigning on a peace platform, amazed the nation by nearly matching Johnson's vote total. A few weeks later, Senator Robert Kennedy entered the race, posing a real political threat to Johnson's renomination. Tired and frustrated about the mess in Vietnam, Johnson withdrew his candidacy. Richard Nixon completed a dramatic political comeback when he won the presidency in 1968. He would preside over a nation torn apart by the war in Vietnam and would use that experience to set some new directions in American foreign policy.

NIXON, KISSINGER, AND DÉTENTE

Two dimensions were apparent in Richard Nixon's foreign policy. The first conformed to the traditional postwar view of containment and American military action to oppose communism. The second, however, represented a more realistic view of the world and America's role in it.

President Nixon chose Harvard professor Henry Kissinger to serve as his national security adviser, a man whose name would become a household word. Nixon and Kissinger, despite the damage Vietnam had caused to Johnson, continued serious efforts to win the war militarily, even as more responsibility was being turned over to South Vietnam. Such an approach was consistent with the early Nixon, the militant anticommunist. The secret bombing of Cambodia was revealed to the public in the spring of 1970, setting off another torrent of protest and demonstrations across the nation. In Ohio, national guardsmen fired on student demonstrators at Kent State University, killing four young people. All over the country, colleges and universities were closed down as students protested both the shootings and U.S. policy in Southeast Asia.

Based largely on the difficult lessons of Vietnam, the second dimension of President Nixon's foreign policy emerged. Nixon and Kissinger realized that Vietnam was at least a tactical mistake. Although they did not challenge the philosophy of containment, they questioned the strategy to best achieve it. What emerged was the **Nixon Doctrine,** stressing indirect military assistance to friendly governments to resist communist revolutionary movements. Nixon suggested:

> The postwar period in international relations has ended. The United States will participate in the defense and development of allies and friends, but . . . America cannot—and will not—conceive all the plans, design all the programs, execute all the defense of the free nations of the world.[17]

The Vietnam experience resulted in a reassessment of the means of foreign policy if not the proper ends of foreign policy. The United States could no longer protect the world from communist expansion alone.

Another component of the new Nixon-Kissinger foreign policy was the policy of détente. Although hinted at in the 1950s and 1960s, the first real break through in normalizing relations with the Soviet Union and China came in the early 1970s under Nixon. His impeccable anticommunist credentials gave him an opportunity to extend olive branches to both the Russians and the Chinese. Both responded. For the first time, an administration acknowledged divisions in the Eastern bloc, and Kissinger skillfully played on this division. On the one hand, Kissinger and Nixon were willing to bargain with the Soviets, offering them trade concessions in return for restraint in the Third World and acknowledging Soviet parity in nuclear weapons by signing the Strategic Arms Limitation Agreement (SALT I). On the other hand, they pursued the normalization of relations with China, one of the most important innovations of the Nixon-Kissinger years, culminating in President Nixon's visit in 1972.

Despite détente, Nixon and Kissinger did not eliminate the old notion of containment. For example, they orchestrated the overthrow of the communist (although democratically elected) Allende government in Chile. But their changes in the means of achieving goals successfully reduced international tensions. The Nixon Doctrine was finally applied to Vietnam when the United States turned over the fight against Ho Chi Minh and the North Vietnamese to South Vietnam, even though this meant certain defeat. Although the final end for South Vietnam did not come until the Ford administration, its fate was sealed when Nixon began to withdraw the bulk of American troops.

The administration of Gerald Ford did not bring any significant departures in foreign policy. The continuation of Henry Kissinger as secretary of state ensured continuity until the election of Jimmy Carter in 1976. Carter's succession to the presidency seemed to create the first real challenge to the postwar doctrine of containment in thirty years.

Beyond Containment and Back Again

Carter and Human Rights

Jimmy Carter was determined to break out of the straitjacket of containment that had defined American foreign policy for three decades. Several months into his term, Carter articulated the changes he planned for his administration:

> A rapidly changing world . . . requires U.S. foreign policy to be based on a wider framework of international cooperation. Our policy during the [postwar]

> period was guided by two principles: a belief that Soviet expansion must be contained, and the corresponding belief in the importance of an almost exclusive alliance among noncommunist nations on both sides of the Atlantic. . . . That system could not last forever unchanged.[18]

Carter's policy of international cooperation meant that instead of seeking arms ceilings and freezes, Carter would seek reductions and real disarmament. In the area of human rights, the administration would be more evenhanded. The **human rights doctrine** meant that the United States would no longer propagandize against left-wing dictatorships in communist countries while doing business with equally bloody right-wing dictators.

The Carter foreign policy, appearing to be the first real innovation since the end of World War II, seemed to hold great promise. But containment was difficult to banish, and Carter's foreign policy was largely a disappointment. Human rights policy was applied unevenly. Violations by new friends, such as China, and old allies, such as South Korea and Pakistan, were ignored for political reasons, undermining the policy's credibility. The policy of curtailing arms shipments to Third World nations was abandoned when more pragmatic considerations prevailed, such as in Egypt and Saudi Arabia, where the United States had clear interests to protect.

The Carter administration enjoyed some successes in foreign policy, but they were more personal than anything else. The Camp David agreements between Egypt and Israel represented the first real progress in stabilization of the Middle East since 1948. The Panama Canal treaties, although not very popular domestically, were critically important to the future of U.S. relations with Latin America. But in the area of détente and relations with the Soviets, the Carter years were marked by a return to international tension and hostility. Tensions were greatly exacerbated by the Soviet invasion of Afghanistan in 1980. The United States boycotted the summer Olympic games in Moscow later that year and embargoed shipments of American grain, decisions that were extremely unpopular in the towns and villages of the United States.

Despite the inconsistencies of Carter's foreign policy, it might have been judged more of a success, even in the short run, if it had not been for one event. The fall of the shah of Iran, the ascension of the Ayatollah Khomeini, and the capture of hostages at the American embassy in Iran became symbols of American impotence in world affairs. Fifty-two of the U.S. diplomats held as hostages were imprisoned 444 days in all. The hostage crisis was more the fault of poor U.S. intelligence than of Carter's foreign policy. But the national frustration it engendered was accompanied by a feeling that American policy was weak and ineffective. The failed rescue mission in Iran, again not the fault of the president, only increased that frustration. Ronald Reagan and the Republicans capitalized on the negative national mood by portraying foreign policy under Carter as signifying weakness and retreat. Carter lost the 1980 election badly, and the hostages in Iran were not released until just a few hours before the inauguration of Ronald Reagan as the fortieth president of the United States.

REAGAN AND A RETURN TO COLD WAR RHETORIC

Ronald Reagan had spent much of his political career warning about communism and the Russian threat. In many ways, he more closely resembled the politicians of the Eisenhower-Dulles years than politicians of the 1980s. Reagan had campaigned hard against the decline of U.S. defense in the face of significant Soviet military gains. When he assumed office in 1981, harsh rhetoric accusing the Soviets of a desire to dominate the world emanated from the White House. The spirit of détente was dormant, if not dead. Most of the foreign policy pronouncements in the first term attacked the Soviets for seeking military superiority, for engaging in international terrorism, and for seeking to subvert democratic governments in Central America and Africa.

In 1983, the Reagan administration was involved in two military actions. In the fall of 1983, the United States invaded the tiny Caribbean island of Grenada a week after a left-wing coup overthrew an already unfriendly government. Although the U.S. invasion provoked considerable criticism abroad, it was extremely popular at home. As much as anything, it was intended to send a message to the Soviets. Although the United States might no longer threaten to intervene anywhere in the world, Reagan clearly displayed a willingness to use military action in the western hemisphere. A second area of direct military intervention was the troubled nation of Lebanon. There, an international peacekeeping force was caught in an untenable position between a weak domestic government and a sectarian civil war that seemed to defy solution. A terrorist bomb attack cost the lives of more than two hundred American soldiers at the marine headquarters in Beirut. Responding to domestic pressures, Reagan redeployed American troops to ships off the coast of Lebanon in early 1984.

Nearly forty years after the end of World War II, the international posture of the United States showed some remarkable similarities to that of the early postwar years. Although the Reagan administration was not embroiled in the constant crises of the Truman, Eisenhower, or Kennedy years, Reagan's frequently bellicose, hard-line stance recalled his predecessors.

Between 1945 and 1985, American foreign policy accommodated the Truman Doctrine, the Nixon Doctrine, and Carter's human rights doctrine. Yet the dominant feature of American foreign policy over forty years was not change but the resiliance of the containment doctrine. The rapid U.S. military buildup and return to an aggressive Cold War posture under Reagan brought America nearly full circle.

AN EASING OF TENSIONS DURING THE GORBACHEV ERA

While not abandoning the doctrine of containment, President Reagan began to soften his rhetoric toward the Soviet Union following his reelection in 1984 and a major change in Soviet leadership the following year. In March 1985, Mikhail Gorbachev assumed power in the Soviet Union. Three aged and ailing Soviet leaders—Brezhnev, Andropov, and Chernenko—had died within a period of twenty-eight months. Assuming leadership at the age of fifty-four, Gorbachev provided much needed stability and a new direction in Soviet policy.

A new pragmatic approach to both foreign and domestic policy in the Soviet Union was revealed. Gorbachev launched a campaign to reform the Soviet economy called ***perestroika***—a restructuring. Hoping to overcome the entrenched inefficiency of the bureaucratized, centrally managed Soviet economy, Gorbachev wanted to decentralize and introduce some limited elements of markets into the system. A greater tolerance of free expression and a partial relaxation of the harsh treatment of dissidents was observed. ***Glasnost*** was the Soviet leader's term for this new openness. Public demonstrations against the government were tolerated. Letters to the editor disagreeing with some government policies were printed in official government media. Gorbachev demonstrated a more pragmatic attitude in foreign policy. He wanted to halt the still-escalating arms race in order to put more resources into the domestic economy, which had been drained by continued high levels of military spending. Troops were withdrawn from Soviet-occupied Afghanistan in 1988. President Reagan displayed a cautious but supportive attitude toward these changes. Reagan and Gorbachev met in Geneva in 1985 for the first of their five summit conferences. Political Insight 20–1 chronicles the history of superpower summit meetings in the postwar era.

In 1987, the **intermediate nuclear force (INF) treaty** was negotiated and signed in Washington. This represented the first progress in the postwar era of not just limiting the arms race but actually destroying existing nuclear weapons. While additional progress in eliminating long-range nuclear weapons was not made in 1988, the easing of tensions in the late 1980s was one of the most hopeful steps toward a more peaceful world since the dawn of the nuclear age in 1945. That hope would become reality in late 1989.

Democracy Movements and the End of the Cold War

REPRESSION OF DEMOCRACY IN CHINA

A sense of change was in the air in 1989, but it was an ill wind that blew from China for democracy and U.S.-China relations. Following the visit of Henry Kissinger and Richard Nixon to the People's Republic of China, U.S. administrations had followed a policy of steadily normalizing relations. President Bush had been envoy to China in 1974-75 and had strong ties to the nation. But following China's

POLITICAL INSIGHT 20–1

SUPERPOWER SUMMIT MEETINGS

Geneva, 1955. Eisenhower, Khrushchev discuss disarmament, German unification, NATO.
Camp David, 1959. Eisenhower, Khrushchev discuss nuclear test ban, disarmament, Berlin, trade, and credits.
Paris, 1960. Eisenhower, Khrushchev trade charges over U-2 spy plane. Talks collapse.
Vienna, 1961. Kennedy, Khrushchev discuss nuclear test ban, disarmament, Germany, Laos.
Glassboro, N.J., 1967. Johnson, Kosygin discuss the Six-Day War, Vietnam, nonproliferation and the Moscow antiballistic missile (ABM) system.
Moscow, 1972. Nixon, Brezhnev sign ABM and SALT I agreements.
Washington/San Clemente, 1973. Nixon, Brezhnev fail to agree on ceilings for strategic launchers and MIRVs, but sign other agreements.
Moscow, 1974. Nixon, Brezhnev sign protocol agreement on ABM treaty and treaty to limit underground nuclear tests.
Vladivostok, 1974. Ford, Brezhnev discuss strategic arms and European forces; sign joint statement resuming SALT talks.
Vienna, 1979. Carter, Brezhnev sign SALT II treaty and discuss nuclear test ban.
Geneva, 1985. Reagan, Gorbachev discuss SDI (strategic defense initiative), INF, nonproliferation, and chemical weapons, agree to more meetings.
Reykjavik, 1986. Reagan, Gorbachev discuss deep nuclear weapons cuts but fail to agree.
Washington, 1987. Reagan, Gorbachev sign INF treaty.
Moscow, 1988. Reagan, Gorbachev discuss Soviet withdrawal from Afghanistan, reductions in long-range nuclear weapons.
New York,1988. Reagan and Gorbachev say farewell; Gorbachev meets Bush.
Malta, 1989. Bush, Gorbachev sign no major agreements but agree to speed negotiations on arms control and trade issues.
Washington, 1990. Bush, Gorbachev reach significant arms control agreements (including chemical weapons), make progress on U.S.-Soviet trade, but disagree on German reunification.
Helsinki, 1990. Bush and Gorbachev meet on short notice to show their solidarity against Saddam Hussein's annexation of Kuwait.

SOURCE: Adapted and updated from *New York Times*, 6 December 1987.

brutal crackdown against dissenters in 1989, relations were dealt a setback.

In April 1989, hundreds of students began congregating in Beijing's Tienanmen Square. They engaged in peaceful demonstrations for democratic reforms to accompany the economic reforms that had occurred in the preceding years. The numbers of student protesters swelled in Beijing and other cities around China. Hundreds of thousands of marchers occupied Tienanmen Square in an atmosphere that sometimes seemed more like a festival than a confrontation. Soldiers who had moved into positions around the square were often befriended by the protesters. Meanwhile, within the top echelons of China's Communist party, a leadership struggle between reformers and hard-liners was playing itself out. The old guard, led by Deng Xiaoping, emerged victorious and ordered a crackdown. On the night of June 3, army tanks rolled through the square, killing hundreds, perhaps thousands of Chinese students. The democracy movement in China—at least for a while—was through, as the government attempted to jail those who had survived.

The Bush administration suspended military sales to China and visits by military personnel. But critics argued that Bush had not gone far enough and were particularly incensed when it was discovered that Bush had sent National Security Adviser Brent Scowcroft on a secret mission to China later in the year. Bush vetoed a bill passed by Congress to protect Chinese students living in the United States. The veto was upheld in the Senate by the narrowest of margins only after an all-out lobbying blitz by the White House. While democracy was dealt a setback in China, sudden and swift strides were made in Eastern Europe.

POLITICAL CHANGE IN THE SOVIET UNION AND EASTERN EUROPE

Continuing changes within the Soviet Union suddenly altered the military and political calculus within the Warsaw Pact nations. After more than four decades, the Soviet Union could no longer afford to support its massive military commitments. Gorbachev lit the match that would spark the democratic revolutions by opening up political discussions, proposing further economic reforms, and announcing his intention to cut troops in the eastern bloc.[19] By 1989, it had become clear that the Soviet Union would not intervene to prop up the communist regimes of Eastern Europe.

Within the Soviet Union, reforms continued. Gorbachev shifted authority away from the Communist party to government institutions, consolidating power in his own hands as political leader. Elections for the Soviet parliament reflected growing citizen dissatisfaction with the Communist party. Gorbachev tried to make gradual progress from a planned economy to a mixed economy with only limited success. Two factors threatened the stability of the regime in the 1990s. Independence movements in the republics threatened to tear the nation apart, particularly in the Baltic republics of Latvia, Estonia, and Lithuania. Secondly, the reforms failed to prevent a growing economic crisis. Conservatives felt change was coming too fast, while radical reformers urged more sweeping changes. The election of Gorbachev's rival, Boris Yeltsin, as president of the Russian republic in 1990 provided the first real challenge to Gorbachev's leadership. While uncertainty grew about the political future of the Soviet Union, dramatic developments took place throughout Eastern Europe.

POLAND. Democracy came peacefully to Poland. One of the first Eastern European nations to hold elections, the Solidarity party took control of the government in 1989. Solidarity leader Lech Walesa became prime minister, agreeing to share power with the communists. Preparing for local elections for the first time in generations, Polish leaders created local councils and brought thousands of Poles into the political process. Facing a severe economic crisis, Poland adopted radical reforms to transform to a market system. Despite a difficult first winter of shortages and growing unemployment, the stabilization of its currency put Poland ahead of many other Eastern European nations, as well as the Soviet Union.

CZECHOSLOVAKIA. The political revolution in Czechoslovakia occurred quickly after thousands of demonstrators clashed with police in November 1989. Repression by the government enraged the citizenry. Backed by massive demonstrations, Civic Forum, a coalition of opposition groups, forced the communists to step aside a week later. President Vaclav Havel's remarks that open this chapter convey the excitement felt as his nation embraced democracy. With stronger democratic traditions than most of their neighbors, Czechoslovakians began to form political parties. The Czechoslovakian economy was also in better shape, having moved away from central planning several years earlier.

HUNGARY. Much of the largely peaceful political change in Hungary came from within the Communist party, which changed its name and philosophy. In October 1989, parliament abolished the Hungarian People's Republic and established the Republic of Hungary.[20] Elections in 1990 removed most of the former communists from power. Although the nation faced difficult economic problems because of a huge foreign debt, progress was made in privatizing state-owned industries. Leaders also faced growing conflict among different nationalities within the country.

EAST GERMANY. The collapse of communism in East Germany was among the most dramatic as massive demonstrations throughout the country shook the government. Hard-liner Erich Honecker, who had ruled for nearly two decades, fell in October 1989, beginning a rush to reunify with West Germany. A massive exodus of East Germans to the west caused economic strains on both sides of the border, speeding the process of **reunification.** Although reunification divided Bush and Gorbachev on the question of a united Germany's membership in NATO, both sides acknowledged its inevitability. Nonetheless, memories of the two world wars in the twentieth century made many leaders wary of a united Germany. Monetary union was agreed on in 1990, and despite economic problems, the strength of West Germany's economy made the future more promising for East Germans than for many of their neighbors. Only one year after the communist regime fell, East Germany and West Germany officially became one nation again in October, 1990.

ROMANIA. The bloodiest revolution occurred in Romania, as dictator Nicholas Ceaucescu slaughtered citizens to forestall the inevitable. Rebels occupied the national television studios and finally seized power in December 1989. Ceaucescu and his wife were executed by a firing squad a week later. But the road to democracy was particularly rocky in Romania. Elections in May 1990 were frought with irregularities and returned many former communists to power. With an economy devastated by years of mismanagement, thousands of Romanians faced starvation. Continued instability left the possibility of a takeover by the military.

BULGARIA. Following the developments in neighboring countries, the communists kept power in the short run by scheduling elections and loosening restrictions on free expression. Severe economic problems, including shortages of basic staples, plagued the government.

Other positive developments in the world followed on the heels of the upheaval in Eastern Europe. In Nicaragua, the communist Sandinista regime called for free elections in early 1990. In an upset, Sandinista President Daniel Ortega was defeated by reformer Violeta Chamoro and relinquished power, bringing democracy to that Central American nation. The role of the Contra rebels, one of the most divisive U.S. issues of the 1980s and the source of Iran-Contra scandal,

U.S. troops in Saudi Arabia.

POLITICAL INSIGHT 20-2

OPERATION DESERT SHIELD: CRISIS IN THE PERSIAN GULF

On August 2, 1990, Saddam Hussein launched an invasion of neighboring Kuwait and annexed it as part of Iraq. This action was not only a violation of national sovereignty but threatened the world's oil supplies and economies. President Bush launched Operation Desert Shield, a massive deployment of American troops and materiel into Saudi Arabia to confront Iraq. By the end of 1990, over a quarter of a million U.S. troops were deployed in the Persian Gulf. Nonmilitary solutions to the crisis were also pursued. The United Nations' Security Council condemned the invasion and authorized economic sanctions against Iraq to force its withdrawal from Kuwait. Arab and Western governments sent troops to stand beside American soldiers. But would the coalition hold together? A prolonged stalemate would be costly and frustrating but a bloody confrontation would result in thousands of casualties, destabilize the Middle East, and destroy much of the world's oil supplies. The eventual outcome would affect future American foreign policy in several crucial ways.

The importance of world support to U.S. initiative. Unlike military actions in Grenada and Panama in the 1980s, multilateralism was a key element of Operation Desert Shield. U.S. credibility in the future will increasingly depend on working in concert with other nations, including the Soviet Union. Dismissed as largely irrelevant and anti-American a decade ago, the United Nations has taken on enhanced mportance as an internaitonal organization and focal point for U.S. policy initiative.

Defining U.S. international goals and strategies. The eventual resolution of the crisis in the Gulf would help

(*Continued on next page.*)

was favorably resolved. But despite the unprecedented changes that had created new democratic governments and market economies in the world, many questions remained unanswered. How would the United States react to the new international climate? Some of those answers would begin to emerge in the face of the first post-Cold War crisis. Political Insight 20-2 examines the crisis in the Gulf that resulted from Iraq's invasion of Kuwait.

The Defense Budget

MILITARY SPENDING TRENDS

During World War II, by far the largest portion of federal spending was for national defense. One fear of the postwar period was that demilitarization—with its reduction in military spending—would lead to a severe recession. This fear proved groundless, both because of deferred consumer demand and because, with the escalation of Cold War tensions, demilitarization never was completed. From the Korean War through the Vietnam War, defense spending fell from about 75 percent of total outlays to around 45 percent of outlays in 1968. The end of the war in Vietnam was marked by a reduction in the growth in defense spending accompanied by rapid increase in social welfare entitlements. The defense portion of the federal budget shrunk to 23 percent by 1980. The election of Ronald Reagan ushered in an era of renewed military buildup—rapid increases in defense spending to strengthen what Reagan argued was a dangerously weak military. Reagan's plan was that defense spending would compose 30 percent of the budget by the end of the 1980s.

Under the Reagan buildup, defense spending was slated to rise from 5 percent of GNP in 1980 to 8 percent of GNP by 1990. Defense spending surged between 1981 and 1985, but the deficit and Gramm-

POLITICAL INSIGHT 20-2

answer a number of questions about U.S. policy in the 1990s. Under what circumstances would the United States be willing to commit and use military force? As troop levels in Europe were reduced, would the United States establish a permanent presence in the Middle East? To what extent will economic goals, such as protecting energy supplies, become intertwined with counteracting international aggression? How would the costs and burdens of military actions be shared with other nations?

Shaping U.S. Defenses. The outcome of the crisis will also have consequences for the shape of the defense establishment and the military budget in the 1990s. Decisions on force levels, maintaining the technological superiority of weapons systems, the balance between conventional and strategic weapons, and the overall mix of activities in the defense budget will partially depend on the outcome in the Persian Gulf.

Domestic political and economic consequences. The crisis in the Middle East also would have important consequences for President Bush's political support and reelection chances, the balance of power with Congress, and the economy. The president's approval rating increased in August as the preparations for military conflict began, rising to more than 75 percent. Yet only three months later, support had already fallen to 55 percent. The confrontation with Iraq was fraught with risks for the administration and the nation. War would have devastating consequences on the U.S. and world economies. Many members of Congress argued that U.S. military action must be premised on a formal declaration of war. While Bush initially received bipartisan support from Congress, it would not be satisfied to simply stand by and watch.

The outcome of the confrontation with Iraq could have consequences for decades. In a sense, the 1990s resemble the immediate post-War period of the 1940s. As untested strategies are applied, new security interests are defined, different world alignments form, and the full scope of a new world order begins to emerge.

Rudman-Hollings cut short the buildup after 1985. Defense spending had fallen back to 5.4 percent of GNP in 1990. Figure 20–1 shows defense spending since 1945 in constant dollars, controlling for inflation. Real outlays in 1990 still equal or surpass average peacetime expenditures, exceeded only by peaks reached in World War II, the Korean War, the Vietnam War, and the 1985 peak of the Reagan buildup.

THE COMPOSITION OF DEFENSE SPENDING

The political debate over the shape of the U.S. defense budget is conducted at two levels. The first concerns the macro-level—determining the total budget, its proportion of GNP, and the rate of real growth. The second aspect of the debate is at the micro-level, examining particular weapon systems and determining the need for and efficiency of each system.

The defense budget is broken down into its component parts in Figure 20–2. The largest components are procurement; operations and maintenance; salaries, benefits, and other personnel costs; and research and development. Almost half the defense budget goes toward salaries of military personnel and to their maintenance and support. There are two kinds of forces in the American arsenal. Conventional weapons, such as fighter planes, tanks, ships, and all the people and materiel that accompany them are designed to fight nonnuclear engagements. They make up the bulk of outlays. Strategic weapons—the nuclear arsenal that is designed to deter attack—make up only 10 percent of the costs of procurement, operations and maintenance, and personnel. But nuclear weapons and their delivery systems, such as the MX missile and the B-1 bomber, are among the most controversial expenditures.

STRATEGIC WEAPONS AND SDI

If containment was the cornerstone of postwar American foreign policy, then deterrence was the cornerstone of American strategic defense policy. **Deterrence** is based on the view that if one nation has the capability to annihilate the other, the latter nation will be deterred from attacking the former. Strategic weapons—the nuclear arsenal and their delivery systems—are the building blocks of deterrence. In the 1960s and 1970s, deterrence was based on the strategy of **mutually assured destruction (MAD)**—the ability to inflict "unacceptable damage" on the other side if it launched a first strike. The MAD doctrine, by the late 1970s, had garnered many critics who felt it was too inflexible a response.

Beginning with the Nixon administration, mutually assured destruction led the Americans and the Russians to the negotiating table. The first **Strategic Arms Limitation Talks (SALT)** agreement was signed in 1972. SALT negotiations in the 1970s and 1980s were designed to limit the future production and deployment of strategic weapons. The superpowers also initiated negotiations to reduce the nuclear arsenals through the **Strategic Arms Reduction Talks (START).** Progress was miniscule in the 1970s. As a result, the NATO allies agreed to deploy a new generation of American missiles in Europe in the 1980s. Following through on the commitments of the Carter administration, the Reagan administration went ahead with plans to place Cruise and Pershing II missiles in Western Europe.

As concerned as the Soviets were about the deployment of new American missiles in Europe, they perceived the most serious threat from Reagan's Strategic Defense Initiative (SDI), known as "Star Wars." This new approach, based on emerging American technology, was to supplant mutually assured destruction with mutually assured defense. Reagan proposed the development of a highly sophisticated system of satellites and space stations equipped with lasers, rockets, and other devices capable of intercepting and destroying incoming missiles. This protective shield of space-weapon nuclear defenses, the administration claimed, would remove the constant terror of nuclear holocaust and provide a new basis for national security in the twenty-first century.

Would such a system make the world more secure, as the administration claimed, or less secure, as critics claimed? Some doubted the feasibility of

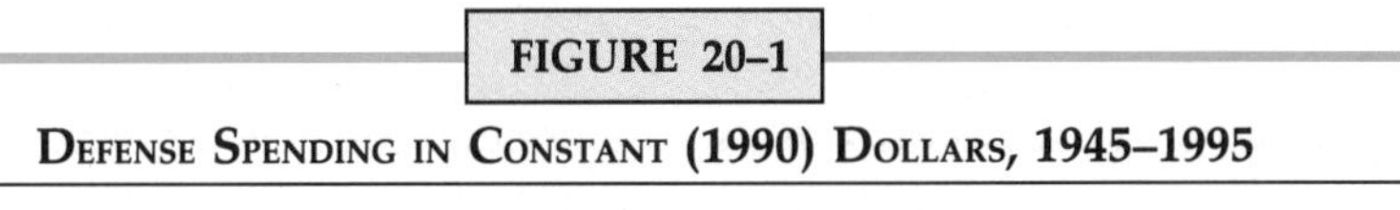

FIGURE 20–1

DEFENSE SPENDING IN CONSTANT (1990) DOLLARS, 1945–1995

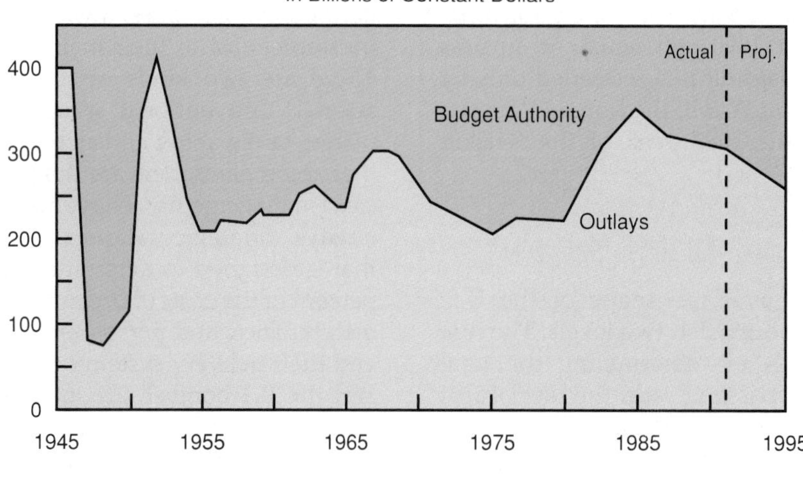

SOURCE: Congressional Budget Office, 1990.

FIGURE 20–2

Composition of the U.S. Defense Budget

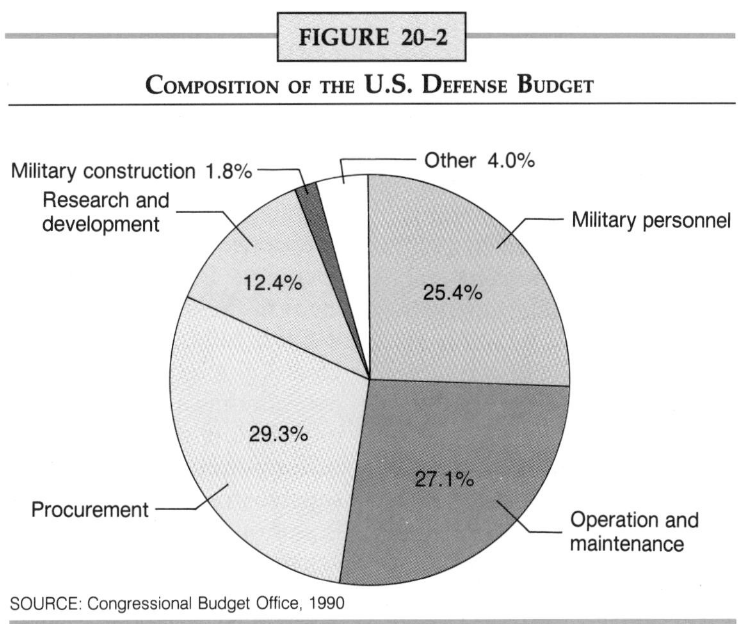

SOURCE: Congressional Budget Office, 1990

developing such advanced weapons. Skeptics noted that even if such weapons were possible, the cost to the American taxpayer would be trillions of dollars. The main attack, however, was on SDI's destabilizing effect. The Soviets would have to embark on a program of their own, expanding the arms race to the heavens, where it might never be controlled. America's allies expressed concern that a nuclear defense would render their missiles obsolete. Although the United States and the Soviet Union would be protected, Europe would not.

The strategic defense initiative was a major topic of conversation during the Reagan-Gorbachev summits held in the late 1980s. The Reagan administration believed that SDI was directly responsible for bringing the Soviets to the bargaining table in the first place and that it remained a key bargaining chip in negotiating levels of nuclear weapons. Opponents in Congress continued to criticize spending precious budget dollars on SDI, particularly in the face of the budget deficits. But while the president's requests for funding were cut, Congress appropriated billions of dollars in new funding each year of Reagan's second term.

Bush and Gorbachev made significant progress in arms control agreements. In 1990, they reached an accord on reducing long-range nuclear missiles, the most significant strategic arms limitation treaty to date. They also agreed that both the United States and the Soviet Union would destroy most of their stocks of chemical weapons and not modernize existing stocks. Nonetheless, differences remained between the two nations and within the U.S. government. President Bush, a supporter of SDI, continued to request funding to maintain development. Operation Desert Shield in Saudi Arabia, combined with the reduction of the Soviet threat, would force decision-makers to shape new foreign and defense strategies for the 1990s.

The "Peace Dividend"

The changes in the international environment have necessitated a rethinking of America's defense posture and strategies. In addition, they have created expectations of a **"peace dividend"**; substantial amounts of spending that could be cut from the defense budget and used to reduce the deficit, address domestic needs, or lower taxes. Some urged caution against moving too quickly to let down the nation's defenses in case of a reversal in the Soviet Union or because of potential troublespots, such as the Middle East and other areas. Bush initially moved cautiously, but with continued deficit worries, many in Congress proposed major cuts in the defense budget. It seems clear that, even with military action against Iraq, the 1990s will be a decade of reexamination of national security needs and of cuts in military spending below current levels.

How much money could the "peace dividend" free up for other purposes? A cut in real spending of 2 percent per year could save $9 billion in 1992 and $30 billion a year by 1995.[21] A 4-percent real reduction per year would save $18 billion in 1992 and $57 billion a year by 1995. With inflation at around 4 percent, this option would in effect freeze the defense budget at current dollars. If used to reduce the deficit rather than for other purposes (thus saving interest on the debt), the savings increase to $68 billion a year by 1995. Some have called for even greater cuts. But there will be fierce resistance to drastic cuts and competition for any resources that result. The "peace dividend" alone will not solve the nation's budget problems.

Many more basic issues are involved in deciding how to cut the defense budget than choosing an overall reduction rate. Congress and the president must reevaluate the nation's role in the world and the level of troops and military hardware needed to maintain it. In operation *Desert Shield,* the United States deployed a massive force of over 250,000 troops into the Gulf region in a matter of weeks—the most rapid large-scale deployment in history. Mobility and flexibility will be more important than deterring the Soviet Union. In 1990, the United States had 2.1 million people in the armed forces. The changing situation in Europe will likely allow reduction in overall levels of the 300,000 U.S. troops stationed in Europe as part of NATO. Reductions in active duty military personnel of 250,000 to 500,000 could save 38 to 70 billion dollars by 1995.[22] Weapons systems are also a major component of defense spending and a source of possible savings by cancelling or delaying the purchase of new systems. Although strategic weapons make up only around 10 percent of the defense budget, numerous proposals have surfaced to reduce the purchase of modernized nuclear weapons and to scrap SDI altogether.

Decisions on the defense budget not only depend on U.S. foreign policy and national security considerations. The choices that are ultimately made will also be influenced by the impact of defense spending on the U.S. economy.

The Political Economy of Defense

THE MILITARY-INDUSTRIAL COMPLEX

Defense involves life-and-death issues of nuclear war and chemical weapons but also more mundane questions, such as who benefits from defense spending. Political economy is an important element of the defense question and may even relate to the broader questions of weapons and strategies. One of the most commonly posited links between the economy and defense is the so-called "military-industrial complex." The first warning about the military-industrial complex came from an unlikely source: President and former General Dwight D. Eisenhower. In his farewell address Eisenhower warned:

> This conjunction of an immense military establishment and a large arms industry is new in the American experience. The total influence—economic, political, even spiritual—is felt in every city, every statehouse, every office of the federal government. We recognize the imperative need for this development. Yet we must not fail to comprehend its grave implications. Our toil, resources, and livelihood are all involved; so is the very structure of our society.
>
> In the councils of government we must guard against the acquisition of unwarranted influence, whether sought or unsought, by the military-industrial complex. The potential for the disastrous rise of misplaced power exists and will persist.[23]

The **military-industrial complex** is an implicit partnership of military officers, managers and owners of defense industries, legislators whose districts benefit from defense spending, and bureaucrats whose careers are tied to military growth.[24] Is this coalition a conspiracy or just a mutually beneficial alliance? Even if the latter, critics complain, one result is dangerously high levels of military spending and the development of unneeded weapons systems. Further, such a coalition militarized American foreign policy and increased Cold War tensions.

Does the military-industrial complex exist? Some evidence is suggestive. Nearly 10 percent of American jobs in the mid-1980s were tied to defense spending. Between reserves, active forces, civilian personnel, and private sector employees, defense spending has a tremendous impact on the economy. On occasion Congress has even appropriated more than the administration requested for certain defense programs and weapons. Cost overruns by defense contractors are notorious, with costs sometimes ending up ten times greater than the contracted cost. Examples of price-gouging by defense contractors include a twelve-cent wrench that cost the government nearly $10,000, a $600 toilet seat, and a $7,000 coffeemaker. Defense contractors are dependent on government spending. The majority do more than 60 percent of their business with the U.S. government.[25] A swinging door operates between the Pentagon and the largest defense contractors. The one hundred largest defense contractors employ more than two thousand retired military officers at the rank of colonel or higher. A major scandal over defense contracting occurred in 1988, when an investigation revealed Pentagon officials were leaking classified information to contractors in return for large payoffs. Military spending offers tangible rewards to bureaucrats anxious to further their careers, profits for defense contractors, security for union leaders who fear layoffs, and pork barrel for members of the House and Senate, who see it as a source of prosperity for their states and districts.

Does this mean that foreign policy and defense policy in the United States are dominated by the military-industrial complex? No. Clearly such a complex is a potent force tending to support defense spending, but it is often countered by other factors. Decision-makers need to be on guard against undue influence and to monitor military planning and weapon procurement carefully. For good or ill, the stability of U.S. foreign policy goals is probably fostered by the existence of the military-industrial complex. Although it may not be able to dominate the policy process, its activity, according to Kegley and Wittkopf, "constrains policy innovation by creating obstacles to alterations in the kinds of foreign policies the United States pursues."[26]

THE ECONOMIC EFFECTS OF DEFENSE CUTS

Defense spending does not have an even impact across the cities and states of the United States. During a debate among Democratic candidates for the U.S. Senate nomination from Illinois, all the contenders lamented the fact that Illinois was low among the fifty states in benefits from defense spending. Each candidate pledged to do something about this, such as target defense spending to the state or compensate with other federal dollars. Defense spending is a critical element of domestic politics.

Issues in national defense are not limited to the crucial questions of war and peace, nuclear deterrence, or foreign policy strategies. National defense

TABLE 20–1

STATES MOST AFFECTED BY DEFENSE SPENDING

Where the Pentagon Spends the Most		Where Military Spending Has the Biggest Impact	
Purchases in 1989, in billions		Percent of 1989 gross output	
California	$90.1	Virginia	10.8%
New York	40.7	Alaska	9.8
Texas	34.8	Washington	9.7
Virginia	25.0	Hawaii	9.5
Florida	22.9	California	8.9
Pennsylvania	20.2	Connecticut	8.7
Ohio	19.7	Maryland	8.7
Massachusetts	17.7	Mississippi	8.2
Illinois	16.6	Missouri	7.2
New Jersey	15.5		

SOURCE: *New York Times*, 15 April 1990. p. 14.

also involves questions of military bases, jobs, billion-dollar contracts, and which states will get those lucrative projects.

Table 20–1 shows the states where military spending was the highest and the states that were most dependent upon defense contracts in 1989. California, New York, and Texas received the most dollars, while defense spending made the largest contributions to the economies of Virginia, Alaska, and Washington. Conversely, these states will be hardest hit by significant cuts in the Pentagon's budget. But despite the importance of defense spending, economists predict that the U.S. economy is capable of absorbing military cuts in the long run.[27] The cuts could leave 100,000 people out of work in the short run following military discharges or the closing of weapons plants. The effects would be more serious in particular cities or regions that are heavily dependent on defense. A positive side effect of the cuts would be the release of skilled technicians and engineers into the civilian sector. Overall, the economic effects of the defense reductions of the 1990s will be significantly less than those that followed World War II and Korea. Cutting back can be an extremely difficult task for members of Congress. One of those most closely involved in the politics of base closings in the 1990s is Representative Pat Schroeder, profiled in the accompanying People in Politics.

Governing in Foreign Affairs

A quarter century ago, during the height of the Cold War, political scientist Aaron Wildavsky concluded:

> The United States has one President, but it has two presidencies; one presidency is for domestic affairs, and the other is concerned with defense and foreign policy. Since World War II, Presidents have had much greater success in controlling the nation's defense and foreign policies than in dominating its domestic policies.[28]

In the midst of a threatening and dangerous Cold War that demanded lightning-quick response, the presidency was on guard to answer the nation's call. Many factors led to increased executive dominance: Expanded political resources gave presidents greater power to act in foreign affairs and allowed them to avoid the political problems normally associated with domestic issues. Congress and other

To a greater degree than leaders of other nations, the president of the United States shares power in foreign affairs with the legislature.

PEOPLE IN POLITICS

REPRESENTATIVE PATRICIA SCHROEDER

Some of the most crucial decisions about national defense involve not sophisticated weapons but military installations and facilities that are worth hundreds of millions to local economies. One of the leading experts in the House of Representatives on defense issues in general and military bases in particular is Congresswoman Pat Schroeder, a Democrat from Colorado. Ranking fifth in seniority on the Armed Services Committee in the 101st Congress, Schroeder chaired the important Military Installations and Facilities Subcommittee. During the Bush administration, Schroeder played a crucial role in one of the most divisive political issues—military base closings.

Schroeder was first elected to the Congress from her district in greater Denver in 1972, despite the disastrous showing of George McGovern on the Democratic party's national ticket. Born in Portland, Oregon, in 1940, she graduated from the University of Minnesota and later received a law degree from Harvard University in 1964, at a time when many dramatic changes were sweeping the country. Long intrigued by public affairs, Schroeder's first job out of law school was working for the National Labor Relations Board. She next pursued an academic career in Colorado but increasingly felt the tug of politics as the antiwar movement gathered momentum around the country. In 1968, she was elected a precinct committeewoman in the Denver County Democratic

Party. Four years later, she became the Democratic nominee for Congress from Colorado's first district.

After nearly two decades in Congress, Schroeder is one of its best-known members. Long a media favorite for her quotability and Will Rogers-style humor, she coined the phrase "the teflon president" to describe Ronald Reagan's ability to avoid blame for problems. But her reputation inside Congress is based on competence and knowledge of complex defense issues. The military base-closing issue was so hot that Congress and President Reagan appointed a bipartisan commission to come up with recommendations. The Bush administration sent proposals for additional base-closings that eventually came to Schroeder's sub committee. The issue became highly partisan when Schroeder accused the administration of axing a disproportionate number of the bases in Democratic districts.

Pat Schroeder has also been outspoken in her call for "burden sharing"—that the United States' allies should pay their fair share for mutual defense. She has also advocated the full participation of women in combat. A number of women were involved in the Panama invasion, and several exchanged gunfire with Noriega's Panama Defense forces during the first hours of action. Schroeder submitted legislation (HR 3868) in the 101st Congress that would allow women to be sent directly into combat throughout a four-year trial period.

Representative Schroeder has become a national figure in her own right from her position in Congress. For a time, she was an active candidate for the 1988 Democratic presidential nomination. Able to raise only one-quarter of the campaign funds she would need, she dropped out before the Iowa primary. A longtime advocate of abortion rights and family planning, she has national support from the pro-choice women's groups. Mentioned as a possible presidential candidate in 1992 or 1996, Schroeder will continue in the interim to help reshape the U.S. armed forces to meet the new international environment of the 1990s.

competitors for power acquiesced, believing that presidential dominance was necessary.

Just as events in the two decades after World War II altered the balance of power between Congress and the president, so are current developments again reshaping it. The view that "domestic policy can only defeat us; foreign policy can kill us" is less relevant now. While the proliferation of atomic weapons into such regions as the Middle East remain a dangerous threat, acid rain and ozone depletion may now be more likely to kill us than a nuclear holocaust. In the 1990s, Wildavsky's description might have to read like this:

> The United States has one President and one presidency for both domestic affairs and defense and foreign policy. Since the end of the Cold War, the already blurred distinctions between the president's powers in foreign policy and domestic policy have nearly vanished. Only in unusual circumstances—when secrecy and direct unilateral military intervention can be politically justified—does the President of the United States retain a clearly enhanced ability to control policy.

The balance of power with Congress has changed since the Vietnam War. Congress now makes significant decisions on virtually every aspect of foreign and defense policy, from diplomacy to defense spending to the intelligence community. And while Congress generally supported the invasion of Panama, only a few weeks later, President George Bush struggled to convince enough senators to uphold his veto of congressional sanctions against China, even with his public approval rating at 80 percent. It is not so much that the presidency has been "carved down to size" by Congress or other rivals for power. Rather, the end of the Cold War and the transformation of the global economy, more than such restrictions as the War Powers Act, are eroding what remains of the president's superiority in foreign affairs.

Today, both the United States and the Soviet Union are adapting to the post-Cold War world, changing both the assumptions and objectives of their foreign and defense policies. Foreign and domestic issues are less distinct than they once were. Domestic prosperity increasingly depends on trade balances and competitiveness in international markets. Global influence increasingly depends on economic strength and fiscal integrity at home. The policy agenda is changing. Consider some of the most critical foreign policy challenges of the next decade: securing and stabilizing world energy sources; providing assistance to emerging democracies of Eastern Europe and Central America; reevaluating the nature and structure of U.S. forces and their deployment around the world including the Mideast; reducing global pollution and protecting the earth's ecosystem; taking actions to reduce Third World poverty and deprivation; expanding the world trading system to include new products and services; breaking international drug cartels; and responding to terrorism. None of these can be solved by the president acting alone; the two branches must work together in order to govern effectively.

As the successful invasion of Panama in 1989 and the deployment of U.S. troops in Saudi Arabia in 1990 showed, situations still remain where the president, as commander and chief, will initially control policy. Secretary of Defense Richard Cheney, responding to questions about the Panama invasion, laid down criteria that needed to be met to justify the president sending in troops:

- "The United States should not commit forces to combat overseas unless the engagement . . . is deemed vital to our national interest."
- If troops are committed, "we should do so wholeheartedly and with the clear intention of winning. If we are unwilling to commit the forces necessary to achieve our objectives, we should not commit them at all."
- "If we do decide to commit forces . . . we should have clearly defined political and military objectives and we should know precisely how our forces can accomplish those objectives."
- "Before the U.S. commits forces, there must be some reasonable assurance we will have the support of the American people and their elected representatives in Congress. This support cannot be achieved unless we are candid in making clear the threats we face; the support cannot be sustained without continuing and close consultation. We cannot fight a battle with the Congress at home while asking our troops to win a war overseas."
- "The commitment of U.S. forces to combat should be a last resort."[29]

Polls continue to indicate that the American public will support the president in such instances, particularly when a Hussein, Ghadafi, Khomeni, or

Noreiga exists. In the long run, however, the constraints imposed by domestic and international opinion are likely to further restrict military intervention as an option. Working multilaterally, building coalitions with other nations, and using the United Nations to establish legitimacy—as Bush did in confronting Iraq—will be essential in military action is to be credible.

Today, a new set of conditions exist, and the international environment exerts growing influence on the performance of American government. Geopolitical changes continue to help shape the policy agenda, presidential power, and executive-legislative relations. The challenge of governing effectively under these new conditions is greater but more essential than ever.

Summary and Conclusions

1. American foreign policy in the postwar era was dominated by the doctrine of containment until the dramatic changes in the world that reduced the threat of communism.
2. Strategies in the immediate postwar period evolved from the Truman Doctrine and the Marshall Plan to the threat of "massive retaliation" under Eisenhower and Dulles. Kennedy continued brinkmanship, coming perilously close to nuclear confrontation in the Cuban missile crisis.
3. The war in Vietnam, more than any other event in the postwar period, resulted in a reassessment of American policy. Important shifts can be seen in détente and the Nixon Doctrine, but the underlying philosophy of containment continued.
4. Détente began to fall apart toward the end of the Carter administration, particularly after the Russian invasion of Afghanistan, paving the way for the Reagan presidency and a return to the rhetoric of the Cold War. Relations with the Soviet Union began to normalize following the assumption of leadership by Mikhail Gorbachev and culminating with the ratification of the INF treaty in 1988.
5. Changes in the Soviet Union helped precipitate democratic revolutions in the nations of Eastern Europe.
6. Deterrence depends on the relative balance of strategic weapons, one of the most controversial aspects of the military buildup. The SDI proposals represent an attempt to move from deterrence to a defensive system protecting the United States from incoming missiles.
7. The political economy of defense is influenced by the military-industrial complex—a loose alliance of military, corporate, and government officials. Although it influences policy and creates pressure for more defense spending, it does not dominate the politics of national defense.
8. Changes in the last two decades have reduced presidential dominance in foreign affairs despite recent actions in Panama and the Mideast.

Key Terms

containment
détente
deterrence
glasnost
human rights doctrine
INF treaty
Marshall Plan
military-industrial complex
mutually assured destruction (MAD)
Nixon Doctrine
North Atlantic Treaty Organization (NATO)
Operation Desert Shield
perestroika
Strategic Arms Limitation Talks (SALT)
Strategic Arms Reduction Talks (START)
Truman Doctrine
Warsaw Pact
"peace dividend"
German reunification
democracy movements

Self-Review

1. Compare the terms "foreign policy," "defense policy," and "national security."
2. Describe the Truman Doctrine and the Marshall Plan.
3. What was the containment doctrine?
4. How was containment applied in Korea?
5. What was the doctrine of "massive retaliation" and what was it based on?

6. How did Kennedy deal differently with Cuba in 1961 and 1962?

7. What are the Nixon Doctrine and détente?

8. Define Carter's human rights doctrine.

9. How did Reagan change American foreign policy in his first and second terms?

10. Describe the normalization of relations between the United States and the Soviet Union and the end of the Cold War in the 1990s.

11. What are the major trends in defense spending?

12. Describe the theory of deterrence, MAD and SDI.

13. What is the military-industrial complex?

14. What is the current balance between legislature and the executive in foreign affairs?

SUGGESTED READINGS

Janis, Irving. *Victims of Groupthink.* 1972.
A fascinating look at foreign policy fiascos with a social-psychological explanation for their occurrence.

Kegley, Charles W., Jr., and Eugene Wittkopf. *American Foreign Policy.* 1985.
A good overview of American foreign policy and its various sources, stressing the continuity of containment in the postwar era.

Mann, Thomas. *A Question of Balance: The President, The Congress, and Foreign Policy (1990).*
A survey of executive-congressional interplay in the changing arena of foreign policy.

NOTES

1. George Modelski, *A Theory of Foreign Policy* (New York: Praeger, 1962).
2. Fredrick Pearson and J. Martin Rochester, *International Relations* (Reading, Mass.: Addison-Wesley, 1984), 117.
3. Steven Ambrose, *American Rise to Globalism: American Foreign Policy, 1938–1980* (New York: Penguin, 1980), 13–14.
4. Harry S Truman, "Special Message to the Congress on Greece and Turkey," *Public Papers of the Presidents* (Washington, D.C.: Government Printing Office, 1963).
5. George C. Marshall, "European Initiative Essential to Economic Recovery," *Department of State Bulletin* 16 (June 1947): 1160.
6. George F. Kennan, "The Sources of Soviet Conduct," *Foreign Affairs* 25 (July 1947): 566–82.
7. See Fredrick Pearson, *The Weak State in International Crisis* (Washington, D.C.: University Press of America, 1981), chap. 3.
8. On the decision to invade North Korea, see Richard Neustadt, *Presidential Power* (New York: Wiley, 1960), and Irving Janis, *Victims of Groupthink* (Boston: Houghton Mifflin, 1972), chap. 3.
9. Janis, *Victims,* 57.
10. John Foster Dulles, "The Goal of Our Foreign Policy," *Department of State Bulletin* 31 (December 1954): 892.
11. See Bruce Miroff, *Pragmatic Illusions* (New York: McKay, 1976), chap. 3.
12. Janis, *Victims,* 14.
13. Graham Allison, "Conceptual Models and the Cuban Missile Crisis," *American Political Science Review* 63 (September 1969): 689.
14. John F. Kennedy, *Public Papers of the President* (Washington, D.C.: U.S. Government Printing Office, 1964), 602–3.
15. Ithiel Pool, *Reprint of Publications on Vietnam, 1966–1970* (Cambridge, Mass.: MIT Press, 1971), 2.
16. See Daniel Ellsberg, "The Quagmire Myth and the Stalemate Machine," *Public Policy* (Spring 1971): 242–64.
17. Richard M. Nixon, *United States Foreign Policy for the 1970s: A New Strategy for Peace* (Washington, D.C.: U.S. Government Printing Office, 1970).
18. Jimmy Carter, in *Department of State Bulletin* 76 (June 1977): 622.
19. *New York Times,* 18 February 1990, p. E2.
20. *Congressional Quarterly Weekly Reports,* 9 December 1989, pp. 3376–77.
21. Congressional Budget Office, *The Economic and Budget Outlook FY 1991–95,* January 1990, p. 66.
22. Congressional Budget Office, *Reducing the Deficit: Spending and Revenue Options,* February 1990, pp. 37–105.
23. Dwight D. Eisenhower, "Farewell Address," reported in Kegley and Wittkopf, *American Foreign Policy,* 254.
24. See C. Wright Mills, *The Power Elite* (New York: Oxford University Press, 1956).
25. Bruce Russett, *What Price Vigilance?* (New Haven: Yale University Press, 1970), 94.
26. Kegley and Wittkopf, *American Foreign Policy,* 259.
27. *New York Times,* 15 April 1990, p. 1.
28. Aaron Wildavsky, "The Two Presidencies," *Trans-Action,* 4 (December 1966).
29. Quoted in *Washington Post National Weekly Edition,* 22–28 January 1990, p. 4.

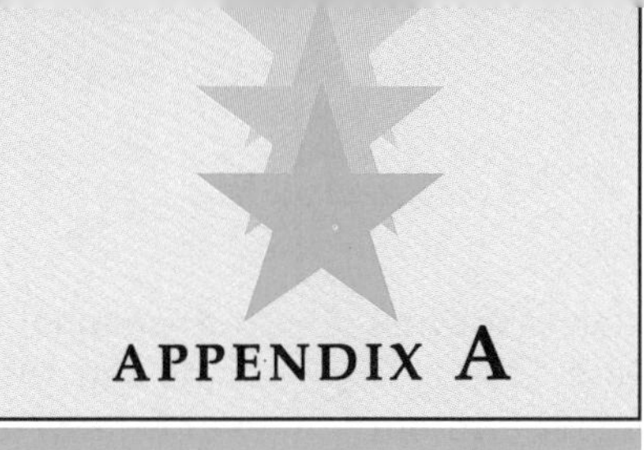

APPENDIX A

Federalist Paper No. 10

James Madison

NOVEMBER 22, 1787

To the People of the State of New York

Among the numerous advantages promised by a well constructed Union, none deserves to be more accurately developed than its tendency to break and control the violence of faction. The friend of popular governments, never finds himself so much alarmed for their character and fate, as when he contemplates their propensity to this dangerous vice. He will not fail therefore to set a due value on any plan which, without violating the principles to which he is attached, provides a proper cure for it. The instability, injustice and confusion introduced into the public councils, have in truth been the mortal diseases under which popular governments have every where perished; as they continue to be the favorite and fruitful topics from which the adversaries to liberty derive their most specious declamations. The valuable improvements made by the American Constitutions on the popular models, both ancient and modern, cannot certainly be too much admired; but it would be an unwarrantable partiality, to contend that they have as effectually obviated the danger on this side as was wished and expected. Complaints are every where heard from our most considerate and virtuous citizens, equally the friends of public and private faith, and of public and personal liberty; that our governments are too unstable; that the public good is disregarded in the conflicts of rival parties; and that measures are too often decided, not according to the rules of justice, and the rights of the minor party; but by the superior force of an interested and over-bearing majority. However anxiously we may wish that these complaints had no foundation, the evidence of known facts will not permit us to deny that they are in some degree true. It will be found indeed, on a candid review of our situation, that some of the distresses under which we labor, have been erroneously charged on the operation of our governments; but it will be found, at the same time, that other causes will not alone account for many of our heaviest misfortunes; and particularly, for that prevailing and increasing distrust of public engagements, and alarm for private rights, which are echoed from one end of the continent to the other. These must be chiefly, if not wholly, effects of the unsteadiness and injustice, with which a factious spirit has tainted our public administrations.

By a faction I understand a number of citizens, whether amounting to a majority or minority of the whole, who are united and actuated by some common impulse of passion, or of interest, adverse to the rights of other citizens, or to the permanent and aggregate interests of the community.

There are two methods of curing the mischiefs of faction: the one, by removing its causes; the other, by controlling its effects.

There are again two methods of removing the causes of faction: the one by destroying the liberty which is essential to its existence; the other, by giving to every citizen the same opinions, the same passions, and the same interests.

It could never be more truly said than of the first remedy, that it is worse than the disease. Liberty is to faction, what air is to fire, an aliment without which it instantly expires. But it could not be a less folly to abolish liberty, which is essential to political life, because it nourishes faction, than it would be wish the annihilation of air, which is essential to animal life, because it imparts to fire its destructive agency.

The second expedient is as impracticable, as the first would be unwise. As long as the reason of man continues fallible, and he is at liberty to exercise it, different opinions will be formed. As long as the connection subsists between his reason and his self-love, his opinions and his passions will have a reciprocal influence on each other; and the former will be objects to which the latter will attach themselves. The diversity in the faculties of men from which the rights of property originate, is not less an insuperable obstacle to a uniformity of interests. The protection of these faculties is the first object of Government. From the protection of different and unequal faculties of acquiring property, the possession of different degrees and kinds of property immediately results: and from the influence of these on the sentiments and views of the respective proprietors, ensues a division of the society into different interests and parties.

The latent causes of faction are thus sown in the nature of man; and we see them every where brought into different degrees of activity, according to the different circumstances of civil society. A zeal for different opinions concerning religion, concerning Government and many other points, as well of speculation as of practice; an attachment to different leaders ambitiously contending for pre-eminence and power; or to persons of other descriptions whose fortunes have been interesting to the human passions, have in turn divided mankind into parties, inflamed them with mutual animosity, and rendered them much more disposed to vex and oppress each other, than to cooperate for their common good. So strong is this propensity of mankind to fall into mutual animosities, that where no substantial occasion presents itself, the most frivolous and fanciful distinctions have been sufficient to kindle their unfriendly passions, and excite their most violent conflicts. But the most common and durable source of factions, has been the various and unequal distribution of property. Those who hold, and those who are without property, have ever formed distinct interests in society. Those who are creditors, and those who are debtors, fall under a like discrimination. A landed interest, a manufacturing interest, a mercantile interest, a monied interest, with many lesser interests, grow up of necessity in civilized nations, and divide them into different classes, actuated by different sentiments and views. The regulation of these various and interfering interests forms the principal task of modern Legislation, and involves the spirit of party and faction in the necessary and ordinary operations of Government.

No man is allowed to be a judge in his own cause; because his interest would certainly bias his judgment, and, not improbably, corrupt his integrity. With equal, nay with greater reason, a body of men, are unfit to be both judges and parties, at the same time; yet, what are many of the most important acts of legislation, but so many judicial determinations, not indeed concerning the rights of single persons, but concerning the rights of large bodies of citizens; and what are the different classes of legislators, but advocates and parties to the causes which they determine? Is a law proposed concerning private debts? It is a question to which the creditors are parties on one side, and the debtors on the other. Justice ought to hold the balance between them. Yet the parties are and must be themselves the judges; and the most numerous party, or, in other words, the most powerful faction must be expected to prevail. Shall domestic manufactures be encouraged, and in what degree, by restrictions on foreign manufactures? Are questions which would be differently decided by the landed and the manufacturing classes; and probably by neither, with a sole regard to justice and the public good. The apportionment of taxes on the various descriptions of property, is an act which seems to require the most exact impartiality; yet, there is perhaps no legislative act in which greater opportunity and temptation are given to a predominant party, to trample on the rules of justice. Every shilling with which they over-burden the inferior number, is a shilling saved to their own pockets.

It is in vain to say, that enlightened statesmen will be able to adjust these clashing interests, and render them all subservient to the public good.

Enlightened statesmen will not always be at the helm: Nor, in many cases, can such an adjustment be made at all, without taking into view indirect and remote considerations, which will rarely prevail over the immediate interest which one party may find in disregarding the rights of another, or the good of the whole.

The inference to which we are brought, is, that the *causes* of faction cannot be removed; and that relief is only to be sought in the mean of controlling its *effects.*

If a faction consists of less than a majority, relief is supplied by the republican principle, which enables the majority to defeat its sinister views by regular vote: It may clog the administrations, it may convulse the society; but it will be unable to execute and mask its violence under the forms of the Constitution. When a majority is included in a faction, the form of popular government on the other hand enables it to sacrifice to its ruling passion or interest, both the public good and the rights of other citizens. To secure the public good, and private rights, against the danger of such a faction, and at the same time to preserve the spirit and the form of popular government, is then the great object to which our enquiries are directed: Let me add that it is the great desideratum, by which alone this form of government can be rescued from the opprobrium under which it has so long labored, and be recommended to the esteem and adoption of mankind.

By what means is this object attainable? Evidently by one of two only. Either the existence of the same passion or interest in a majority at the same time, must be prevented; or the majority, having such coexistent passion or interest, must be rendered, by their number and local situation, unable to concert and carry into effect schemes of oppression. If the impulse and the opportunity be suffered to coincide, we well know that neither moral nor religious motives can be relied on as an adequate control. They are not found to be such on the injustice and violence of individuals, and lose their efficacy in proportion to the number combined together; that is, in proportion as their efficacy becomes needful.

From this view of the subject, it may be concluded, that a pure Democracy, by which I mean, a Society, consisting of a small number of citizens, who assemble and administer the Government in person, can admit of no cure for the mischiefs of faction. A common passion or interest will, in almost every case, be felt by a majority of the whole; a communication and concert results from the form of Government itself; and there is nothing to check the inducements to sacrifice the weaker party, or an obnoxious individual. Hence it is, that such Democracies have ever been spectacles of turbulence and contention; have ever been found incompatible with personal security, or the rights of property; and have in general been as short in their lives, as they have been violent in their deaths. Theoretic politicians, who have patronized this species of Government, have erroneously supposed, that by reducing mankind to a perfect equality in their political rights, they would, at the same time, be perfectly equalized and assimilated in their possessions, their opinions, and their passions.

A republic, by which I mean a government in which the scheme of representation takes place, opens a different prospect, and promises the cure for which we are seeking. Let us examine the points in which it varies from pure democracy, and we shall comprehend both the nature of the cure and the efficacy which it must derive from the union.

The two great points of difference, between a democracy and a republic, are, first, the delegation of the government, in the latter, to a small number of citizens, elected by the rest; secondly, the greater number of citizens, and greater sphere of country, over which the latter may be extended.

The effect of the first difference is, on the one hand, to refine and enlarge the public views, by passing them through the medium of a chosen body of citizens, whose wisdom may best discern the true interest of their country, and whose patriotism and love of justice, will be least likely to sacrifice it to temporary or partial considerations. Under such a regulation, it may well happen, that the public voice, pronounced by the representatives of the people, will be more consonant to the public good, than if pronounced by the people themselves, convened for the purpose. On the other hand the effect may be inverted. Men of factious tempers, of local prejudices, or of sinister designs, may by intrigue, by corruption, or by other means, first obtain the suffrages, and then betray the interest of the people. The question resulting is, whether small or extensive republics are most favorable to the election of proper guardians of the public weal; and it is clearly decided in favor of the latter by two obvious considerations.

In the first place, it is to be remarked that, however small the republic may be, the representatives must be raised to a certain number, in order to guard against the cabals of a few; and that however large it may be, they must be limited to a certain number, in order to guard against the confusion of a multitude. Hence, the number of representatives in the two cases not being in proportion to that of the constituents, and being proportionally greatest in the small republic, it follows, that if the proportion of fit characters be not less in the large than in the small republic, the former will present a greater option, and consequently a greater probability of a fit choice.

In the next place, as each Representative will be chosen by a greater number of citizens in the large than in the small Republic, it will be more difficult for unworthy candidates to practise with success the vicious arts, by which elections are too often carried; and the suffrages of the people being more free, will be more likely to center on men who possess the most attractive merit, and the most diffusive and established characters.

It must be confessed, that in this, as in most other cases, there is a mean, on both sides of which inconveniences will be found to lie. By enlarging too much the number of electors, you render the representative too little acquainted with all their local circumstances and lesser interests; as by reducing it too much, you render him unduly attached to these, and too little fit to comprehend and pursue great and national objects. The Federal Constitution forms a happy combination in this respect; the great and aggregate interests being referred to the national, the local and particular, to the state legislatures.

The other point of difference is, the greater number of citizens and extent of territory which may be brought within the compass of Republican, than of Democratic Government; and it is this circumstance principally which renders factious combinations less to be dreaded in the former, than in the latter. The smaller the society, the fewer probably will be the distinct parties and interests composing it; the fewer the distinct parties and interests, the more frequently will a majority be found of the same party; and the smaller the number of individuals composing a majority, and the smaller the compass within which they are placed, the more easily will they concert and execute their plans of oppression. Extend the sphere, and you take in a greater variety of parties and interests; you make it less probable that a majority of the whole will have a common motive to invade the rights of other citizens; or if such a common motive exists, it will be more difficult for all who feel it to discover their own strength, and to act in unison with each other. Besides other impediments, it may be remarked, that where there is a consciousness of unjust or dishonorable purposes, communication is always checked by distrust, in proportion to the number whose concurrence is necessary.

Hence it clearly appears, that the same advantage, which a Republic has over a Democracy, in controlling the effects of faction, is enjoyed by a large over a small Republic—is enjoyed by the Union over the States composing it. Does this advantage consist in the substitution of Representatives, whose enlightened views and virtuous sentiments render them superior to local prejudices, and to schemes of injustice? It will not be denied, that the Representation of the Union will be most likely to possess these requisite endowments. Does it consist in the greater security afforded by a greater variety of parties, against the event of any one party being able to outnumber and oppress the rest? In an equal degree does the increased variety of parties, comprised within the Union, increase this security. Does it, in fine, consist in the greater obstacles opposed to the concert and accomplishment of the secret wishes of an unjust and interested majority? Here, again, the extent of the Union gives it the most palpable advantage.

The influence of factious leaders may kindle a flame within their particular States, but will be unable to spread a general conflagration through the other States: a religious sect, may degenerate into a political faction in a part of the Confederacy but the variety of sects dispersed over the entire face of it, must secure the national Councils against any danger from that source: a rage for paper money, for an abolition of debts, for an equal division of property, or for any other improper or wicked project, will be less apt to pervade the whole body of the Union, than a particular member of it; in the same proportion as such a malady is more likely to taint a particular county or district, than an entire State.

In the extent and proper structure of the Union, therefore, we behold a Republican remedy for the diseases most incident to Republican Government. And according to the degree of pleasure and pride, we feel in being Republicans, ought to be our zeal in cherishing the spirit, and supporting the character of Federalists.

PUBLIUS

Federalist Paper No. 51

James Madison

FEBRUARY 6, 1788

To the People of the State of New York

To what expedient then shall we finally resort for maintaining in practice the necessary partition of power among the several departments, as laid down in the constitution? The only answer that can be given is, that as all these exterior provisions are found to be inadequate, the defect must be supplied, by so contriving the interior structure of the government, as that its several constituent parts may, by their mutual relations, be the means of keeping each other in their proper places. Without presuming to undertake a full development of this important idea, I will hazard a few general observations, which may perhaps place it in a clearer light, and enable us to form a more correct judgment of the principles and structure of the government planned by the convention.

In order to lay a due foundation for that separate and distinct exercise of the different powers of government, which to a certain extent, is admitted on all hands to be essential to the preservation of liberty, it is evident that each department should have a will of its own; and consequently should be so constituted, that the members of each should have as little agency as possible in the appointment of the members of the others. Were this principle rigorously adhered to, it would require that all the appointments for the supreme executive, legislative, and judiciary magistracies, should be drawn from the same fountain of authority, the people, through channels, having no communication whatever with one another. Perhaps such a plan of constructing the several departments would be less difficult in practice than it may in contemplation appear. Some difficulties however, and some additional expense, would attend the execution of it. Some deviations therefore from the principle must be admitted. In the constitution of the judiciary department in particular, it might be inexpedient to insist rigorously on the principle; first, because peculiar qualifications being essential in the members, the primary consideration ought to be to select that mode of choice, which best secures these qualifications; secondly, because the permanent tenure by which the appointments are held in that department, must soon destroy all sense of dependence on the authority conferring them.

It is equally evident that the members of each department should be as little dependent as possible on those of the others, for the emoluments annexed to their offices. Were the executive magistrate, or the judges, not independent of the legislature in this particular, their independence in every other would be merely nominal.

But the great security against a gradual concentration of the several powers in the same department, consists in giving to those who administer each department, the necessary constitutional means, and personal motives, to resist encroachments of the others. The provision for defense must in this, as in all other cases, be made commensurate to the danger of attack. Ambition must be made to counteract ambition. The interest of the man must be connected with the constitutional rights of the place. It may be a reflection on human nature, that such devices should be necessary to control the abuses of government. But what is government itself but the greatest of all reflections on human nature? If men were angels, no government would be necessary. If angels were to govern men, neither external nor internal controls on government would be necessary. In framing a government which is to be administered by men over men, the great difficulty lies in this: You must first enable the government to control the governed; and in the next place, oblige it to control itself. A dependence on the people is no doubt the primary control on the government; but experience has taught mankind the necessity of auxiliary precautions.

This policy of supplying by opposite and rival interests, the defect of better motives, might be traced through the whole system of human affairs, private as well as public. We see it particularly displayed in all the subordinate distributions of power; where the constant aim is to divide and arrange the several offices in such a manner as that each may be a check on the other; that the private interest of every individual, may be a sentinel over the public rights. These inventions of prudence cannot be less requisite in the distribution of the supreme powers of the state.

But it is not possible to give to each department an equal power of self defense. In republican government the legislative authority, necessarily, predominates. The remedy for this inconveniency is, to divide the legislature into different branches; and to render them by different modes of election, and different principles of action, as little connected with each other, as the nature of their common functions, and their common dependence on the society, will admit. It may even be necessary to guard against dangerous encroachments by still further precautions. As the weight of the legislative authority requires that it should be thus divided, the weakness of the executive may require, on the other hand, that it should be fortified. An absolute negative, on the legislature, appears at first view to be the natural defense with which the executive magistrate should be armed. But perhaps it would be neither altogether safe, nor alone sufficient. On ordinary occasions, it might not be exerted with the requisite firmness; and on extraordinary occasions, it might be perfidiously abused. May not this defect of an absolute negative be supplied, by some qualified connection between this weaker department, and the weaker branch of the stronger department, by which the latter may be led to support the constitutional rights of the former, without being too much detached from the rights of its own department?

If the principles on which these observations are founded be just, as I persuade myself they are, and they be applied as a criterion, to the several state constitutions, and to the federal constitution, it will be found, that if the latter does not perfectly correspond with them, the former are infinitely less able to bear such a test.

There are moreover two considerations particularly applicable to the federal system of America, which place that system in a very interesting point of view.

First. In a single republic, all the power surrendered by the people, is submitted to the administration of a single government; and usurpations are guarded against by a division of the government into distinct and separate departments. In the compound republic of America, the power surrendered by the people, is first divided between two distinct governments, and then the portion allotted to each, subdivided among distinct and separate departments. Hence a double security arises to the rights of the people. The different governments will control each other; at the same time that each will be controlled by itself.

Second. It is of great importance in a republic, not only to guard the society against the oppression of its rulers; but to guard one part of the society against the injustice of the other part. Different interests necessarily exist in different classes of citizens. If a majority be united by a common interest, the rights of the minority will be insecure. There are but two methods of providing against this evil: The one by creating a will in the community independent of the majority, that is, of the society itself; the other by comprehending in the society so many separate descriptions of citizens, as will render an unjust combination of a majority of the whole, very improbable, if not impracticable. The first method prevails in all governments possessing an hereditary or self appointed authority. This at best is but a precarious security; because a power independent of the society may as well espouse the unjust views of the major, as the rightful interests, of the minor party, and may possibly be turned against both parties. The second method will be exemplified in the federal republic of the United States. While all authority in it will be derived from and dependent on the society, the society itself will be broken into so many parts, interests and classes of citizens, that the rights of individuals or of the minority, will be in little danger from interested combinations of the majority. In a free government, the security for civil rights must be the same as for religious rights. It consists in the one case in the multiplicity of interests, and in the other, in the multiplicity of sects. The degree of security in both cases will depend on the number of interests and sects; and this may be presumed to depend on the extent of country and number of people comprehended under the same government. This view of the subject must particularly recommend a proper federal system to all the sincere and considerate friends of republican government: Since it shows that in exact proportion as the territory of the union may be formed into more circumscribed confederacies or states, oppressive combinations of a majority will be facilitated, the best security under the republican form, for the rights of every class of citizens, will be diminished; and consequently, the stability and independence of some member of the government, the only other security, must be proportionally increased. Justice is the end of government. It is the end of civil society. It ever has been, and ever will be pursued, until it be obtained, or until liberty be lost in the pursuit. In a society under the forms of which the stronger faction can readily unite and oppress the weaker, anarchy may as truly be said to reign, as in a state of nature where the weaker individual is not secured against the violence of the stronger: And as in the latter state even the stronger individuals are prompted by the uncertainty of their condition, to submit to a government which may protect the weak as well as themselves: So in the former state, will the more powerful factions or parties be gradually induced by a like motive, to wish for a government which will protect all parties, the weaker as well as the more powerful. It can be little doubted, that if the state of Rhode Island was separated from the confederacy, and left to itself, the insecurity of rights under the popular form of government within such narrow limits, would be displayed by such reiterated oppressions of factious majorities, that some power altogether independent of the people would soon be called for by the voice of the very factions whose misrule had proved the necessity of it. In the extended republic of the United States, and among the great variety of interests, parties and sects which it embraces, a coalition of a majority of the whole society could seldom take place on any other principles than those of justice and the general good; and there being thus less danger to a minor from the will of the major party, there must be less pretext also, to provide for the security of the former, by introducing into the government a will not dependent on the latter; or in other words, a will independent of the society itself. It is no less certain than it is important, notwithstanding the contrary opinions which have been entertained, that the larger the society, provided it lie within a practicable sphere, the more duly capable it will be of self government. And happily for the *republican cause,* the practicable sphere may be carried to a very great extent, by a judicious modification and mixture of the *federal principle.*

PUBLIUS

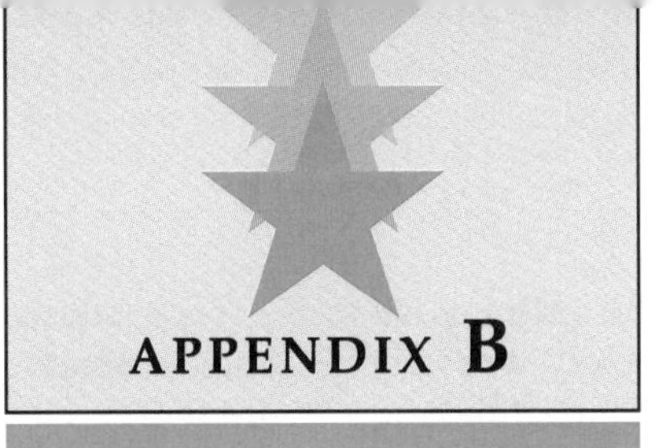

APPENDIX B

THE DECLARATION OF INDEPENDENCE

In Congress, July 4, 1776.

A Declaration by the Representatives of the United States of America, in General Congress assembled. When in the Course of human Events, it becomes necessary for one People to dissolve the Political Bonds which have connected them with another, and to assume among the Powers of the Earth, the separate and equal Station to which the Laws of Nature and of Nature's God entitle them, a decent Respect to the Opinions of Mankind requires that they should declare the causes which impel them to the Separation.

We hold these Truths to be self-evident, that all Men are created equal, that they are endowed by their Creator with certain unalienable Rights, that among these are Life, Liberty, and the Pursuit of Happiness—That to secure these Rights, Governments are instituted among Men, deriving their just Powers from the Consent of the Governed, that whenever any Form of Government becomes destructive of these Ends, it is the Right of the People to alter or abolish it, and to institute new Government, laying its Foundation on such Principles, and organizing its Powers in such Forms, as to them shall seem most likely to effect their Safety and Happiness. Prudence, indeed, will dictate that Governments long established should not be changed for light and transient Causes; and accordingly all Experience hath shewn, that Mankind are more disposed to suffer, while Evils are sufferable, than to right themselves by abolishing the Forms to which they are accustomed. But when a long Train of Abuses and Usurpations, pursuing invariably the same Object, evinces a Design to reduce them under absolute Despotism, it is their Right, it is their Duty, to throw off such Government, and to provide new Guards for their future Security. Such has been the patient Sufferance of these Colonies; and such is now the Necessity which constrains them to alter their former Systems of Government. The History of the present King of Great-Britain is a History of repeated injuries and Usurpations, all having in direct Object the Establishment of an absolute Tyranny over these States. To prove this, let Facts be submitted to a candid World.

He has refused his Assent to Laws, the most wholesome and necessary for the public Good.

He has forbidden his Governors to pass Laws of immediate and pressing Importance, unless suspended in their Operation till his Assent should be obtained; and when so suspended, he has utterly neglected to attend to them.

He has refused to pass other Laws for the Accommodation of large Districts of People, unless those People would relinquish the Right of Representation in the Legislature, a Right inestimable to them, and formidable to Tyrants only.

He has called together Legislative Bodies at Places unusual, uncomfortable, and distant from the Depository of their Public Records, for the sole Purpose of fatiguing them into Compliance with his Measures.

He has dissolved Representative Houses repeatedly, for opposing with manly Firmness his Invasions on the Rights of the People.

He has refused for a long Time, after such Dissolutions, to cause others to be elected; whereby the Legislative Powers, incapable of Annihilation, have returned to the People at large for their exercise; the State remaining in the mean time exposed to all the Dangers of Invasion from without, and Convulsions within.

He has endeavored to prevent the Population of these States; for that Purpose obstructing the Laws for Naturalization of Foreigners; refusing to pass others to encourage their Migrations hither, and raising the Conditions of new Appropriations of Lands.

He has obstructed the Administration of Justice, by refusing his Assent to Laws for establishing Judiciary Powers.

He has made Judges dependent on his Will alone, for the Tenure of their offices, and the Amount and payment of their Salaries.

He has erected a Multiple of new Offices, and sent higher Swarms of Officers to harrass our People, and eat out their Substance.

He has kept among us, in Times of Peace, Standing Armies, without the consent of our Legislatures.

He has affected to render the Military independent of, and superior to the Civil Power.

He has combined with others to subject us to a Jurisdiction foreign to our Constitution, and unacknowledged by our Laws; giving his Assent to their Acts of pretended Legislation:

For quartering large Bodies of Armed Troops among us:

For protecting them, by a mock Trial, from Punishment for any Murders which they should commit on the Inhabitants of these States:

For cutting off our Trade with all Parts of the World:

For imposing Taxes on us without our Consent:

For depriving us, in many cases, of the Benefits of Trial by Jury:

For transporting us beyond Seas to be tried for pretended Offences:

For abolishing the free System of English Laws in a neighboring Province, establishing therein an arbitrary Government, and enlarging its Boundaries, so as to render it at once an Example and fit Instrument for introducing the same absolute Rule into these Colonies:

For taking away our Charters, abolishing our most valuable Laws, and altering fundamentally the Forms of our Governments:

For suspending our own Legislatures, and declaring themselves invested with Power to legislate for us in all Cases whatsoever.

He has abdicated Government here, by declaring us out of his Protection and waging War against us.

He has plundered our Seas, ravaged our Coasts, burnt our towns, and destroyed the Lives of our People.

He is, at this Time, transporting large Armies of foreign Mercenaries to compleat the works of Death, Desolation, and Tyranny, already begun with circumstances of Cruelty and Perfidy, scarcely paralleled in the most barbarous Ages, and totally unworthy the Head of a civilized Nation.

He has constrained our fellow Citizens taken Captive on the high Seas to bear Arms against their Country, to become the Executioners of their Friends and Brethren, or to fall themselves by their Hands.

He has excited domestic Insurrections amongst us, and has endeavoured to bring on the Inhabitants of our Frontiers, the merciless Indian Savages, whose known Rule of Warfare, is an undistinguished Destruction, of all Ages, Sexes and Conditions.

In every stage of these Oppressions we have Petitioned for Redress in the most humble Terms: Our repeated Petitions have been answered only by repeated Injury. A Prince, whose Character is thus marked by every act which may define a Tyrant, is unfit to be the Ruler of a free People.

Nor have we been wanting in Attentions to our British Brethren. We have warned them from Time to Time of Attempts by their Legislature to extend an unwarrantable Jurisdiction over us. We have reminded them of the Circumstances of our Emigration and Settlement here. We have appealed to their native Justice and Magnanimity, and we have conjured them by the Ties of our common Kindred to disavow these Usurpations, which, would inevitably interrupt our Connections and Correspondence. They too have been deaf to the Voice of Justice and of Consanguinity. We must, therefore, acquiesce in the Necessity, which denounces our Separation, and hold them, as we hold the rest of Mankind, Enemies in War, in Peace, Friends.

We, therefore, the Representatives of the UNITED STATES OF AMERICA, in General Congress Assembled, appealing to the Supreme Judge of the World for the Rectitude of our Intentions, do, in the Name, and by Authority of the good People of these Colonies, solemnly Publish and Declare, That these United Colonies are, and of Right ought to be, Free and Independent States; that they are absolved from all Allegiance to the British Crown, and that all political Connection between them and the State of Great-Britain, is and ought to be totally dissolved; and that as Free and Independent States, they have full Power to levy War, conclude Peace, contract Alliances, establish Commerce, and to do all other Acts and Things which Independent States may of right do. And for the support of this declaration, with a firm Reliance on the Protection of divine Providence, we mutually pledge to each other our lives, our Fortunes, and our sacred Honor.

APPENDIX C

The Constitution of the United States of America*

We the people of the United States, in Order to form a more perfect Union, establish Justice, insure domestic Tranquility, provide for the common defence, promote the general Welfare, and secure the Blessings of Liberty to ourselves and our posterity, do ordain and establish this Constitution for the United States of America.

Article I

Section 1.

All legislative Powers herein granted shall be vested in a Congress of the United States, which shall consist of a Senate and House of Representatives.

Section 2.

The House of Representatives shall be composed of Members chosen every second Year by the People of the several States, and the Electors in each State shall have the Qualifications requisite for Electors of the most numerous Branch of the State Legislature.

No person shall be a Representative who shall not have attained to the Age of twenty five Years, and been seven Years a Citizen of the United States, and who shall not, when elected, be an Inhabitant of that State in which he shall be chosen.

Representatives and direct [Taxes][1] shall be apportioned among the several States which may be included within this Union, according to their respective Numbers [which shall be determined by adding to the whole Number of free Persons, including those bound to Service for a Term of Years, and excluding Indians not taxed, three fifths of all other Persons].[2] The actual Enumeration shall be made within three Years after the first Meeting of the Congress of the United States, and within every subsequent Term of ten Years, in such Manner as they shall by Law direct. The Number of Representatives shall not exceed one for every thirty Thousand, but each State shall have at Least one Representative; and until such enumeration shall be made, the State of New Hampshire shall be entitled to chuse three, Massachusetts eight, Rhode Island and Providence Plantations one, Connecticut five, New-York six, New Jersey four, Pennsylvania eight, Delaware one, Maryland six, Virginia ten, North Carolina five, South Carolina five, and Georgia three.

When vacancies happen in the Representation from any State, the Executive Authority thereof shall issue Writs of Election to fill such Vacancies.

The House of Representatives shall chuse their Speaker and other Officers; and shall have the sole Power of Impeachment.

*The spelling, capitalization, and punctuation of the original have been retained here. Brackets indicate passages that have been altered by amendments to the Constitution.

[1] Modified by the Sixteenth Amendment.
[2] Modified by the Fourteenth Amendment.

SECTION 3.

The Senate of the United States shall be composed of two Senators from each State [chosen by the Legislature thereof],[3] for six Years; and each Senator shall have one Vote.

Immediately after they shall be assembled in Consequence of the first Election, they shall be divided as equally as may be into three Classes. The Seats of the Senators of the first Class shall be vacated at the Expiration of the second Year, of the second Class at the Expiration of the fourth Year, and of the third Class at the Expiration of the sixth Year, so that one third may be chosen every second Year [and if Vacancies happen by Resignation, or otherwise, during the Recess of the Legislature of any State, the Executive thereof may make temporary Appointments until the next Meeting of the Legislature, which shall then fill such Vacancies.][4]

No Person shall be a Senator who shall not have attained to the Age of thirty Years, and been nine Years a Citizen of the United States, and who shall not, when elected, be an Inhabitant of that State for which he shall be chosen.

The Vice President of the United States shall be President of the Senate, but shall have no Vote, unless they be equally divided.

The Senate shall chuse their other Officers, and also a President pro tempore, in the Absence of the Vice President, or when he shall exercise the Office of President of the United States.

The Senate shall have the sole Power to try all Impeachments. When sitting for that Purpose, they shall be on Oath or Affirmation. When the President of the United States is tried, the Chief Justice shall preside: And no Person shall be convicted without the Concurrence of two thirds of the members present.

Judgment in Cases of Impeachment shall not extend further than to removal from Office, and disqualification to hold and enjoy any Office of honor, Trust or Profit under the United States; but the Party convicted shall nevertheless be liable and subject to Indictment, Trial, Judgment, and Punishment, according to Law.

[3]Repealed by the Seventeenth Amendment.
[4]Modified by the Seventeenth Amendment.

SECTION 4.

The Times, Places and Manner of holding Elections for Senators and Representatives, shall be prescribed in each State by the Legislature thereof; but the Congress may at any time by Law make or alter such Regulations, except as to the Places of chusing Senators.

[The Congress shall assemble at least once in every Year, and such Meeting shall be on the first Monday in December, unless they shall by Law appoint a different Day.][5]

SECTION 5.

Each House shall be the Judge of the Elections, Returns and Qualifications of its own Members, and a Majority of each shall constitute a Quorum to do Business; but a smaller Number may adjourn from day to day, and may be authorized to compel the Attendance of absent Members, in such Manner, and under such Penalties as each House may provide.

Each House may determine the Rules of its Proceedings, punish its Members for disorderly Behaviour, and, with the Concurrence of two thirds, expel a Member.

Each House shall keep a Journal of its Proceedings, and from time to time publish the same, excepting such Parts as may in their Judgment require Secrecy; and the Yeas and Nays of the Members of either House on any question shall, at the Desire of one fifth of those present, be entered on the Journal.

Neither House, during the Session of Congress, shall, without the Consent of the other, adjourn for more than three days, nor to any other Place than that in which the two Houses shall be sitting.

SECTION 6.

The Senators and Representatives shall receive a Compensation for their Services, to be ascertained by Law, and paid out of the Treasury of the United States. They shall in all Cases, except Treason, Felony and Breach of the Peace, be privileged from

[5]Changed by the Twentieth Amendment.

Arrest during their Attendance at the Session of their respective Houses, and in going to and returning from the same; and for any Speech or Debate in either House, they shall not be questioned in any other Place.

No Senator or Representative shall, during the Time for which he was elected, be appointed to any civil Office under the Authority of the United States, which shall have been created, or the Emoluments whereof shall have been encreased during such time; and no Person holding any Office under the United States, shall be a Member of either House during his Continuance in Office.

SECTION 7.

All Bills for raising Revenue shall originate in the House of Representatives; but the Senate may propose or concur with Amendments as on other Bills.

Every Bill which shall have passed the House of Representatives and the Senate, shall, before it become a Law, be presented to the President of the United States; If he approves he shall sign it, but if not he shall return it, with his Objections to that House in which it shall have originated, who shall enter the Objections at large on their Journal, and proceed to reconsider it. If after such Reconsideration two thirds of that House shall agree to pass the Bill, it shall be sent, together with the Objections, to the other House, by which it shall likewise be reconsidered, and if approved by two thirds of that House, it shall become a Law. But in all such Cases the Votes of both Houses shall be determined by yeas and Nays, and the Names of the Persons voting for and against the Bill shall be entered on the Journal of each House respectively. If any Bill shall not be returned by the President within ten Days (Sundays excepted) after it shall have been presented to him, the Same shall be a Law, in like Manner as if he had signed it, unless the Congress by their Adjournment prevent its Return, in which Case it shall not be a Law.

Every Order, Resolution, or Vote to which the Concurrence of the Senate and House of Representatives may be necessary (except on a question of Adjournment) shall be presented to the President of the United States; and before the Same shall take Effect, shall be approved by him, or being disapproved by him, shall be repassed by two thirds of the Senate and House of Representatives, according to the Rules and Limitations prescribed in the Case of a Bill.

SECTION 8.

The Congress shall have Power To lay and collect Taxes, Duties, Imposts and Excises, to pay the Debts and provide for the common Defence and general Welfare of the United States; but all Duties, Imposts and Excises shall be uniform throughout the United States;

To borrow Money on the credit of the United States;

To regulate Commerce with foreign Nations, and among the several States, and with the Indian Tribes;

To establish a uniform Rule of Naturalization, and uniform Laws on the subject of Bankruptcies throughout the United States;

To coin Money, regulate the Value thereof, and of foreign Coin, and fix the Standard of Weights and Measures.

To provide for the Punishment of counterfeiting the Securities and current Coin of the United States;

To establish Post Offices and post Roads;

To promote the Progress of Science and useful Arts, by securing for limited Times to Authors and Inventors the exclusive Right to their respective Writings and Discoveries;

To constitute Tribunals inferior to the supreme Court;

To define and punish Piracies and Felonies committed on the high Seas, and Offences against the Law of Nations;

To declare War, grant Letters of Marque and Reprisal, and make Rules concerning Captures on Land and Water;

To raise and support Armies, but no Appropriation of Money to that Use shall be for a longer Term than two Years;

To provide and maintain a Navy;

To make Rules for the Government and Regulation of the land and naval Forces;

To provide for calling forth the Militia to execute the Laws of the Union, suppress Insurrections and repel Invasions;

To provide for organizing, arming, and disciplining the Militia, and for governing such Part of them as may be employed in the Service of the United States, reserving to the States respectively, the Appointment of the Officers, and the Authority of training the Militia according to the discipline prescribed by Congress;

To exercise exclusive Legislation in all Cases whatsoever, over such District (not exceeding ten Miles square) as may, by Cession of particular States, and the Acceptance of Congress, become the Seat of the Government of the United States, and to exercise like Authority over all Places purchased by the Consent of the Legislature of the State in which the Same shall be, for the Erection of Forts, Magazines, Arsenals, dock-Yards, and other needful Buildings;—And

To make all Laws which shall be necessary and proper for carrying into Execution the foregoing Powers, and all other Powers vested by this Constitution in the Government of the United States, or in any Department or Officer thereof.

Section 9.

The Migration or Importation of such Persons as any of the States now existing shall think proper to admit, shall not be prohibited by the Congress prior to the Year one thousand eight hundred and eight, but a Tax or duty may be imposed on such Importation, not exceeding ten dollars for each Person.

The Privilege of the Writ of Habeas Corpus shall not be suspended, unless when in Cases of Rebellion or Invasion the public Safety may require it.

No Bill of Attainder or ex post facto Law shall be passed.

[No Capitation, or other direct, Tax shall be laid, unless in Proportion to the Census or Enumeration herein before directed to be taken.][6]

No Tax or Duty shall be laid on Articles exported from any State.

No Preference shall be given by any Regulation of Commerce or Revenue to the Ports of one State over those of another; nor shall Vessels bound to, or from, one State, be obliged to enter, clear, or pay Duties in another.

[6]Modified by the Sixteenth Amendment.

No Money shall be drawn from the Treasury, but in Consequence of Appropriations made by Law; and a regular Statement and Account of the Receipts and Expenditures of all public Money shall be published from time to time.

No Title of Nobility shall be granted by the United States; And no Person holding any Office of Profit or Trust under them, shall, without the Consent of the Congress, accept of any present, Emolument, Office, or Title, of any kind whatever, from any King, Prince, or foreign State.

Section 10.

No State shall enter into any Treaty, Alliance, or Confederation; grant Letters of Marque and Reprisal; coin Money; emit Bills of Credit; make any Thing but gold and silver Coin a Tender in Payment of Debts; pass any Bill of Attainder, ex post facto Law, or Law impairing the Obligation of Contracts, or grant any Title of Nobility.

No State shall, without the Consent of the Congress, lay any Imposts or Duties on Imports or Exports, except what may be absolutely necessary for executing its inspection Laws; and the net Produce of all Duties and Imposts, laid by any State on Imports or Exports, shall be for the Use of the Treasury of the United States; and all such Laws shall be subject to the Revision and Control of the Congress.

No State shall, without the Consent of Congress, lay any Duty of Tonnage, keep Troops, or Ships of War in time of Peace, enter into any Agreement or Compact with another State, or with a foreign Power or engage in War, unless actually invaded, or in such imminent Danger as will not admit of delay.

Article II

Section 1.

The executive Power shall be vested in a President of the United States of America. He shall hold his Office during the Term of four Years, and, together with the Vice President, chosen for the Same Term, be elected, as follows.

Each State shall appoint, in such Manner as the Legislature thereof may direct, a Number of Electors, equal to the whole Number of Senators and Representatives to which the State may be entitled in the Congress; but no Senator or Representative, or Person holding an Office of Trust or Profit under the United States, shall be appointed an Elector.

[The Electors shall meet in their respective States, and vote by Ballot for two Persons of whom one at least shall not be an Inhabitant of the same State with themselves. And they shall make a List of all the Persons voted for, and of the Number of Votes for each; which List they shall sign and certify, and transmit sealed to the Seat of the Government of the United States, directed to the President of the Senate. The President of the Senate shall, in the Presence of the Senate and House of Representatives, open all the Certificates, and the Votes shall then be counted. The Person having the greatest Number of Votes shall be the President, if such Number be a Majority of the whole Number of Electors appointed; and if there be more than one who have such Majority, and have an equal Number of Votes, then the House of Representatives shall immediately chuse by Ballot one of them for President; and if no Person have a Majority, then from the five highest on the List the said House shall in like Manner chuse the President. But in chusing the President, the Votes shall be taken by States, the Representation from each State having one Vote; A quorum for this Purpose shall consist of a Member or Members from two thirds of the States, and a Majority of all the States shall be necessary to a Choice. In every Case, after the Choice of the President, the Person having the greatest Number of Votes of the Electors shall be the Vice President. But if there should remain two or more who have equal Votes, the Senate shall chuse from them by Ballot the Vice President.][7]

The Congress may determine the Time of chusing the Electors, and the Day on which they shall give their Votes; which Day shall be the same throughout the United States.

No Person except a natural born Citizen, or a Citizen of the United States, at the time of the Adoption of this Constitution, shall be eligible to the Office of President; neither shall any Person be eligible to that Office who shall not have attained to the Age of thirty five Years, and been fourteen Years a Resident within the United States.

[In Case of the Removal of the President from Office, or of his Death, Resignation, or Inability to discharge the Powers and Duties of the said Office, the same shall devolve on the Vice President, and the Congress may by Law provide for the Case of Removal, Death, Resignation or Inability, both of the President and Vice President, declaring what Officer shall then act as President, and such Officer shall act accordingly, until the Disability be removed, or a President shall be elected.][8]

The President shall, at stated Times, receive for his Services, a Compensation, which shall neither be encreased nor diminished during the Period for which he shall have been elected, and he shall not receive within that Period any other Emolument from the United States, or any of them.

Before he enter on the Execution of his Office, he shall take the following Oath or Affirmation: —"I do solemnly swear (or affirm) that I will faithfully execute the Office of President of the United States, and will to the best of my Ability, preserve, protect and defend the Constitution of the United States."

SECTION 2.

The President shall be Commander in Chief of the Army and Navy of the United States, and of the Militia of the several States, when called into the actual Service of the United States; he may require the Opinion, in writing, of the Principal Officer in each of the executive Departments, upon any Subject relating to the Duties of their respective Offices, and he shall have Power to grant Reprieves and Pardons for Offences against the United States, except in Cases of Impeachment.

He shall have Power, by and with the Advice and Consent of the Senate, to make Treaties, provided two thirds of the Senators present concur; and he shall nominate, and by and with the Advice and Consent of the Senate, shall appoint Ambassadors, other public Ministers and Consuls, Judges of the supreme Court, and all other Officers of the

[7] Changed by the Twelfth Amendment.

[8] Modified by the Twenty-fifth Amendment.

United States, whose Appointments are not herein otherwise provided for, and which shall be established by Law; but the Congress may by Law vest the Appointment of such inferior Officers, as they think proper, in the President alone, in the Courts of Law, or in the Heads of Departments.

The President shall have Power to fill up all Vacancies that may happen during the Recess of the Senate, by granting Commissions which shall expire at the end of their next Session.

SECTION 3.

He shall from time to time give to the Congress Information of the State of the Union, and recommend to their Consideration such Measures as he shall judge necessary and expedient; he may, on extraordinary Occasions, convene both Houses, or either of them, and in Case of Disagreement between them, with Respect to the Time of Adjournment, he may adjourn them to such Times as he shall think proper; he shall receive Ambassadors and other public Ministers; he shall take Care that the Laws be faithfully executed, and shall Commission all the Officers of the United States.

SECTION 4.

The President, Vice President and all civil Officers of the United States, shall be removed from Office on Impeachment for, and Conviction of, Treason, Bribery, or other high Crimes and Misdemeanors.

Article III

SECTION 1.

The judicial Power of the United States, shall be vested in one supreme Court, and in such inferior Courts as the Congress may from time to time ordain and establish. The Judges, both of the supreme and inferior Courts, shall hold their Offices during good Behavior, and shall, at stated Times, receive for their Services, a Compensation, which shall not be diminished during their Continuance in Office.

SECTION 2.

The judicial Power shall extend to all Cases, in Law and Equity, arising under this Constitution, the Laws of the United States, and Treaties made, or which shall be made, under their Authority;—to all Cases affecting Ambassadors, other public Ministers and Consuls;—to all Cases of admiralty and maritime Jurisdiction;—to Controversies to which the United States shall be a Party;—to Controversies between two or more States; [—between a State and Citizens of another State;—][9] between Citizens of different States,—between Citizens of the same State claiming Lands under Grants of different States, [and between a state, or the Citizens thereof, and foreign States, Citizens or Subjects.][10]

In all Cases affecting Ambassadors, other public Ministers and Consuls, and those in which a State shall be Party, the supreme Court shall have original Jurisdiction. In all the other Cases before mentioned, the supreme Court shall have appellate Jurisdiction, both as to Law and Fact, with such Exceptions, and under such Regulations as the Congress shall make.

The Trial of all Crimes, except in Cases of Impeachment, shall be by Jury; and such Trial shall be held in the State where the said Crimes shall have been committed; but when not committed within any State, the Trial shall be at such Place or Places as the Congress may by Law have directed.

SECTION 3.

Treason against the United States, shall consist only in levying War against them, or in adhering to their Enemies, giving them Aid and Comfort. No Person shall be convicted of Treason unless on the Testimony of two Witnesses to the same overt Act, or on Confession in open Court.

The Congress shall have Power to declare the Punishment of Treason, but no Attainder of Treason shall work Corruption of Blood, or Forfeiture except during the Life of the Person attainted.

[9]Modified by the Eleventh Amendment.
[10]Modified by the Eleventh Amendment.

Article IV

SECTION 1.

Full Faith and Credit shall be given in each State to the public Acts, Records, and judicial Proceedings of every other State. And the Congress may by general Laws prescribe the Manner in which such Acts, Records and Proceedings shall be proved, and the Effect thereof.

SECTION 2.

The Citizens of each State shall be entitled to all Privileges and Immunities of Citizens in the several States.

A Person charged in any State with Treason, Felony, or other Crime, who shall flee from Justice, and be found in another State, shall on Demand of the executive Authority of the State from which he fled, be delivered up, to be removed to the State having Jurisdiction of the Crime.

[No Person held to Service or Labour in one State under the Laws thereof, escaping into another, shall, in Consequence of any Law or Regulation therein, be discharged from such Service or Labour, but shall be delivered up on Claim of the Party to whom such Service or Labour may be due.][11]

SECTION 3.

New States may be admitted by the Congress into this Union; but no new State shall be formed or erected within the Jurisdiction of any other State; nor any State be formed by the Junction of two or more States, or Parts of States, without the Consent of the Legislatures of the States concerned as well as of the Congress.

The Congress shall have Power to dispose of and make all needful Rules and Regulations respecting the Territory or other Property belonging to the United States; and nothing in this Constitution shall be so construed as to Prejudice any Claims of the United States, or of any particular State.

SECTION 4.

The United States shall guarantee to every State in this Union a Republican Form of Government, and shall protect each of them against Invasion, and on Application of the Legislature, or of the Executive (when the Legislature cannot be convened) against domestic Violence.

Article V

The Congress, whenever two thirds of both Houses shall deem it necessary, shall propose Amendments to this Constitution, or on the Application of the Legislatures of two thirds of the several States, shall call a Convention for proposing Amendments, which, in either Case, shall be valid to all Intents and Purposes, as Part of this Constitution, when ratified by the Legislatures of three fourths of the several States, or by Conventions in three fourths thereof, as the one or the other Mode of Ratification may be proposed by the Congress; Provided that no Amendment which may be made prior to the Year One thousand eight hundred and eight shall in any Manner affect the first and fourth Clauses in the Ninth Section of the first Article; and that no State, without its Consent, shall be deprived of its equal Suffrage in the Senate.

Article VI

All Debts contracted and Engagements entered into, before the Adoption of this Constitution, shall be as valid against the United States under this Constitution, as under the Confederation.

This Constitution, and the laws of the United States which shall be made in Pursuance thereof;

[11] Repealed by the Thirteenth Amendment.

and all Treaties made, or which shall be made, under the Authority of the United States, shall be the supreme Law of the Land; and the Judges in every State shall be bound thereby, any Thing in the Constitution or Laws of any State to the Contrary notwithstanding.

The Senators and Representatives before mentioned, and the Members of the several State Legislatures, and all executive and judicial Officers, both of the United States and of the several States, shall be bound by Oath or Affirmation, to support this Constitution: but no religious Test shall ever be required as a Qualification to any Office or public Trust under the United States.

Article VII

The Ratification of the Conventions of nine States, shall be sufficient for the Establishment of this Constitution between the States so ratifying the Same.

Done in Convention by the Unanimous Consent of the States present the Seventeenth Day of September in the Year of our Lord one thousand seven hundred and Eighty seven and of the Independence of the United States of America the Twelfth. IN WITNESS whereof we have hereunto subscribed our Names,

Attest

WILLIAM JACKSON
Secretary

GO. WASHINGTON
Presid[t]. and deputy from Virginia

DELAWARE

Geo. Read
Gunning Bedford jun
John Dickinson
Richard Basset
Jaco. Broom

MASSACHUSETTS

Nathaniel Gorham
Rufus King

CONNECTICUT

Wm. Saml. Johnson
Roger Sherman

NEW YORK

Alexander Hamilton

NEW JERSEY

Wh. Livingston
David Brearley.
Wm. Paterson.
John. Dayton

PENNSYLVANIA

B. Franklin
Thomas Mifflin
Robt. Morris
Geo. Clymer
Thos. FitzSimons
Jared Ingersoll
James Wilson.
Gouv. Morris

NEW HAMPSHIRE

John Langdon
Nicholas Gilman

MARYLAND

James McHenry
Dan of St. Thos. Jenifer
Danl. Carroll.

VIRGINIA

John Blair
James Madison Jr.

NORTH CAROLINA

Wm. Blount
Richd. Dobbs Spaight.
Hu. Williamson

SOUTH CAROLINA

J. Rutledge
Charles Cotesworth Pinckney
Charles Pinckney
Pierce Butler.

GEORGIA

William Few
Abr. Baldwin

Articles in addition to, and amendment of the Constitution of the United States of America, proposed by Congress and ratified by the Legislatures of the several states, pursuant to the Fifth Article of the original Constitution.

Amendment I[12]

Congress shall make no law respecting an establishment of religion, or prohibiting the free exercise thereof; or abridging the freedom of speech, or of the press; or the right of the people peaceably to assemble, and to petition the Government for a redress of grievances.

Amendment II

A well regulated militia, being necessary to the security of a free State, the right of the people to keep and bear arms, shall not be infringed.

Amendment III

No Soldier shall, in time of peace be quartered in any house, without the consent of the owner, nor in time of war, but in a manner to be prescribed by law.

Amendment IV

The right of the people to be secure in their persons, houses, papers, and effects, against unreasonable searches and seizures, shall not be violated, and no warrants shall issue, but upon probable cause, supported by oath or affirmation, and particularly describing the place to be searched, and the persons or things to be seized.

[12]The first ten amendments were passed by Congress on September 25, 1789, and were ratified on December 15, 1791.

Amendment V

No person shall be held to answer for a capital, or otherwise infamous crime, unless on a presentment or indictment or a Grand Jury, except in cases arising in the land or naval forces, or in the militia, when in actual service in time of war or public danger; nor shall any person be subject for the same offence to be twice put in jeopardy of life or limb; nor shall be compelled in any criminal case to be a witness against himself, nor be deprived of life, liberty, or property, without due process of law; nor shall private property be taken for public use, without just compensation.

Amendment VI

In all criminal prosecutions, the accused shall enjoy the right to a speedy and public trial, by an impartial jury of the State and district wherein the crime shall have been committed, which district shall have been previously ascertained by law, and to be informed of the nature and cause of the accusation; to be confronted with the witnesses against him; to have compulsory process for obtaining witnesses in his favor, and to have the assistance of counsel for his defence.

Amendment VII

In Suits at common law, where the value in controversy shall exceed twenty dollars, the right of trial by jury shall be preserved, and no fact tried by a jury, shall be otherwise reexamined in any Court of the United States, than according to the rules of the common law.

Amendment VIII

Excessive bail shall not be required, nor excessive fines imposed, nor cruel and unusual punishments inflicted.

Amendment IX

The enumeration in the Constitution, of certain rights, shall not be construed to deny or disparage others retained by the people.

Amendment X

The powers not delegated to the United States by the Constitution, nor prohibited by it to the States, are reserved to the States respectively, or to the people.

Amendment XI—(Ratified February 7, 1795)

The Judicial power of the United States shall not be construed to extend to any suit in law or equity, commenced or prosecuted against one of the United States by Citizens of another State, or by Citizens or Subjects of any Foreign State.

Amendment XII—(Ratified June 15, 1804)

The Electors shall meet in their respective states, and vote by ballot for President and Vice-President, one of whom, at least, shall not be an inhabitant of the same state with themselves; they shall name in their ballots the person voted for as President, and in distinct ballots the person voted for as Vice-President, and they shall make distinct lists of all persons voted for as President, and of all persons voted for as Vice-President, and of the number of votes for each, which lists they shall sign and certify, and transmit sealed to the seat of the government of the United States, directed to the President of the Senate;—The President of the Senate shall, in the presence of the Senate and House of Representatives, open all the certificates and the votes shall then be counted;—The person having the greatest number of votes for President, shall be the President, if such number be a majority of the whole number of Electors appointed; and if no person have such majority, then from the persons having the highest numbers not exceeding three on the list of those voted for as President, the House of Representatives shall choose immediately, by ballot, the President. But in choosing the President, the votes shall be taken by states, the representation from each state having one vote; a quorum for this purpose shall consist of a member or members from two-thirds of the states, and a majority of all the states shall be necessary to a choice. [And if the House of Representatives shall not choose a President whenever the right of choice shall devolve upon them, before the fourth day of March next following, then the Vice-President shall act as President, as in the case of the death or other constitutional disability of the President.][13]—The person having the greatest number of votes as Vice-President, shall be the Vice-President, if such number be a majority of the whole number of Electors appointed, and if no person have a majority, then from the two highest numbers on the list, the Senate shall choose the Vice-President; a quorum for the purpose shall consist of two-thirds of the whole number of Senators, and a majority of the whole number shall be necessary to a choice. But no person constitutionally ineligible to the office of President shall be eligible to that of Vice-President of the United States.

[13]Changed by the Twentieth Amendment.

Amendment XIII—(Ratified on December 6, 1865)

SECTION 1.

Neither slavery nor involuntary servitude, except as a punishment for crime whereof the party shall have been duly convicted, shall exist within the United States, or any place subject to their jurisdiction.

SECTION 2.

Congress shall have power to enforce this article by appropriate legislation.

Amendment XIV—(Ratified on July 9, 1868)

SECTION 1.

All persons born or naturalized in the United States, and subject to the jurisdiction thereof, are citizens of the United States and of the State wherein they reside. No State shall make or enforce any law which shall abridge the privileges or immunities of citizens of the United States; nor shall any State deprive any person of life, liberty, or property, without due process of law; nor deny to any person within its jurisdiction the equal protection of the laws.

SECTION 2.

Representatives shall be apportioned among the several States according to their respective numbers, counting the whole number of persons in each State, excluding Indians not taxed. But when the right to vote at any election for the choice of electors for President and Vice President of the United States, Representatives in Congress, the Executive and Judicial officers of a State, or the members of the Legislature thereof, is denied to any of the male inhabitants of such State, being [twenty-one][14] years of age, and citizens of the United States, or in any way abridged, except for participation in rebellion, or other crime, the basis of representation therein shall be reduced in the proportion which the number of such male citizens shall bear to the whole number of male citizens twenty-one years of age in such State.

SECTION 3.

No person shall be a Senator or Representative in Congress, or elector of President and Vice President, or hold any office, civil or military, under the United States, or under any State, who having previously taken an oath, as a member of Congress, or as an officer of the United States, or as a member of any State legislature, or as an executive or judicial officer of any State, to support the Constitution of the United States, shall have engaged in insurrection or rebellion against the same, or given aid or comfort to the enemies thereof. But Congress may by a vote of two-thirds of each House, remove such disability.

SECTION 4.

The validity of the public debt of the United States, authorized by law, including debts incurred for payment of pensions and bounties for services in suppressing insurrection or rebellion, shall not be questioned. But neither the United States nor any State shall assume or pay any debt or obligation incurred in aid of insurrection or rebellion against the United States, or any claim for the loss or emancipation of any slave, but all such debts, obligations and claims shall be held illegal and void.

SECTION 5.

The Congress shall have power to enforce, by appropriate legislation, the provisions of this article.

[14]Changed by the Twenty-sixth Amendment.

Amendment XV—(Ratified on February 3, 1870)

SECTION 1.

The right of citizens of the United States to vote shall not be denied or abridged by the United States or by any State on account of race, color, or previous condition of servitude.

SECTION 2.

The Congress shall have power to enforce this article by appropriate legislation.

Amendment XVI—(Ratified on February 3, 1913)

The Congress shall have power to lay and collect taxes on incomes, from whatever source derived, without apportionment among the several States, and without regard to any census or enumeration.

Amendment XVII—(Ratified on April 8, 1913)

The Senate of the United States shall be composed of two Senators from each State, elected by the people thereof, for six years; and each Senator shall have one vote. The electors in each State shall have the qualifications requisite for electors of the most numerous branch of the State legislatures.

When vacancies happen in the representation of any State in the Senate, the executive authority of such State shall issue writs of election to fill such vacancies: *Provided,* That the legislature of any State may empower the executive thereof to make temporary appointments until the people fill the vacancies by election as the legislature may direct.

This amendment shall not be so construed as to affect the election or term of any Senator chosen before it becomes valid as part of the Constitution.

Amendment XVIII—(Ratified on January 16, 1919)

SECTION 1.

After one year from the ratification of this article the manufacture, sale, or transportation of intoxicating liquors within, the importation thereof into, or the exportation thereof from the United States and all territory subject to the jurisdiction thereof for beverage purposes is hereby prohibited.

SECTION 2.

The Congress and the several States shall have concurrent power to enforce this article by appropriate legislation.

SECTION 3.

This article shall be inoperative unless it shall have been ratified as an amendment to the Constitution by the legislatures of the several States, as provided in the Constitution, within seven years from the date of the submission hereof to the States by the Congress.[15]

Amendment XIX—(Ratified on August 18, 1920)

The right of citizens of the United States to vote shall not be denied or abridged by the United States or by any State on account of sex.

Congress shall have power to enforce this article by appropriate legislation.

[15]The Eighteenth Amendment was repealed by the Twenty-first Amendment.

Amendment XX—(Ratified on January 23, 1933)

SECTION 1.

The terms of the President and Vice President shall end at noon on the 20th day of January, and the terms of Senators and Representatives at noon on the 3d day of January, of the years in which such terms would have ended if this article had not been ratified, and the terms of their successors shall then begin.

SECTION 2.

The Congress shall assemble at least once in every year, and such meeting shall begin at noon on the 3d day of January, unless they shall by law appoint a different day.

SECTION 3.

If, at the time fixed for the beginning of the term of the President, the President elect shall have died, the Vice President elect shall become President. If a President shall not have been chosen before the time fixed for the beginning of his term, or if the President elect shall have failed to qualify, then the Vice President elect shall act as President until a President shall have qualified; and the Congress may by law provide for the case wherein neither a President elect nor a Vice President elect shall have qualified, declaring who shall then act as President, or the manner in which one who is to act shall be selected, and such person shall act accordingly until a President or Vice President shall have qualified.

SECTION 4.

The Congress may by law provide for the case of the death of any of the persons from whom the House of Representatives may choose a President whenever the rights of choice shall have devolved upon them, and for the case of the death of any of the persons from whom the Senate may choose a Vice President whenever the right of choice shall have devolved upon them.

SECTION 5.

Sections 1 and 2 shall take effect on the 15th day of October following the ratification of this article.

SECTION 6.

This article shall be inoperative unless it shall have been ratified as an amendment to the Constitution by the legislatures of three-fourths of the several States within seven years from the date of its submission

Amendment XXI—(Ratified on December 5, 1933)

SECTION 1.

The eighteenth article of amendment to the Constitution of the United States is hereby repealed.

SECTION 2.

The transportation or importation into any State, Territory, or possession of the United States for delivery or use therein of intoxicating liquors, in violation of the laws thereof, is hereby prohibited.

SECTION 3.

This article shall be inoperative unless it shall have been ratified as an amendment to the Constitution by conventions in the several States, as provided in the Constitution, within seven years from the date of the submission hereof to the States by the Congress.

Amendment XXII—(Ratified on February 27, 1951)

No person shall be elected to the office of the President more than twice, and no person who has held the office of President, or acted as President, for more than two years of a term to which some other person was elected President shall be elected to the office of President more than once. But this Article shall not apply to any person holding the office of President when this Article was proposed by the Congress, and shall not prevent any person who may be holding the office of President, or acting as President, during the term within which this Article becomes operative from holding the office of President or acting as President during the remainder of such term.

Amendment XXIII – (Ratified on March 29, 1961)

SECTION 1.

The District constituting the seat of Government of the United States shall appoint in such manner as the Congress may direct:

A number of electors of President and Vice President equal to the whole number of Senators and Representatives in Congress to which the District would be entitled if it were a State, but in no event more than the least populous State; they shall be in addition to those appointed by the States, but they shall be considered, for the purposes of the election of President and Vice President, to be electors appointed by a State; and they shall meet in the District and perform such duties as provided by the twelfth article of amendment.

SECTION 2.

The Congress shall have power to enforce this article by appropriate legislation.

Amendment XXIV – (Ratified on January 23, 1964)

SECTION 1.

The right of citizens of the United States to vote in any primary or other election for President or Vice President, for electors for President or Vice President, or for Senator or Representative in Congress, shall not be denied or abridged by the United States or any State by reason of failure to pay any poll tax or other tax.

SECTION 2.

The Congress shall have power to enforce this article by appropriate legislation.

Amendment XXV – (Ratified on February 10, 1967)

SECTION 1.

In case of the removal of the President from office or of his death or resignation, the Vice President shall become President.

SECTION 2.

Whenever there is a vacancy in the office of the Vice President, the President shall nominate a Vice President who shall take office upon confirmation by a majority vote of both Houses of Congress.

SECTION 3.

Whenever the President transmits to the President pro tempore of the Senate and the Speaker of the House of Representatives his written declaration that he is unable to discharge the powers and duties of his office, and until he transmits to them a written declaration to the contrary, such powers and duties shall be discharged by the Vice President as Acting President.

SECTION 4.

Whenever the Vice President and a majority of either the principal officers of the executive departments or of such other body as Congress may by law provide, transmit to the President pro tempore of the Senate and the Speaker of the House of Representatives their written declaration that the President is unable to discharge the powers and duties of his office, the Vice President shall immediately assume the powers and duties of the office as Acting President.

Thereafter, when the President transmits to the President pro tempore of the Senate and the Speaker of the House of Representatives his written declaration that no inability exists, he shall resume the powers and duties of his office unless the Vice President and a majority of either the principal officers of the executive department or of such other body as Congress may by law provide, transmit within four days to the President pro tempore of the Senate and the Speaker of the House of Representatives their written declaration that the President is unable to discharge the powers and duties of his office. Thereupon Congress shall decide the issue, assembling within forty-eight hours for that purpose if not in session. If the Congress, within twenty-one days after receipt of the latter written declaration, or, if Congress is not in session, within twenty-one days after Congress is required to assemble, determines by two-thirds vote of both Houses that the President is unable to discharge the powers and duties of his office, the Vice President shall continue to discharge the same as Acting President; otherwise, the President shall resume the powers and duties of his office.

Amendment XXVI—(Ratified on July 1, 1971)

Section 1.

The right of citizens of the United States, who are eighteen years of age or older, to vote shall not be denied or abridged by the United States or by any State on account of age.

Section 2.

The Congress shall have power to enforce this article by appropriate legislation.

APPENDIX D

THE PRESIDENTS OF THE UNITED STATES

	Born	College or University	Religion	Occupation or Profession
1. George Washington	Feb. 22, 1732		Episcopalian	Planter
2. John Adams	Oct. 30, 1735	Harvard	Unitarian	Lawyer
3. Thomas Jefferson	Apr. 13, 1743	William and Mary	Unitarian*	Planter, lawyer
4. James Madison	Mar. 16, 1751	Princeton	Episcopalian	Lawyer
5. James Monroe	Apr. 28, 1758	William and Mary	Episcopalian	Lawyer
6. John Quincy Adams	July 11, 1767	Harvard	Unitarian	Lawyer
7. Andrew Jackson	Mar. 15, 1767		Presbyterian	Lawyer
8. Martin Van Buren	Dec. 5, 1782		Dutch Reformed	Lawyer
9. William H. Harrison	Feb. 9, 1773	Hampden-Sydney	Episcopalian	Soldier
10. John Tyler	Mar. 29, 1790	William and Mary	Episcopalian	Lawyer
11. James K. Polk	Nov. 2, 1795	U. of N. Carolina	Methodist	Lawyer
12. Zachary Taylor	Nov. 24, 1784		Episcopalian	Soldier
13. Millard Fillmore	Jan. 7, 1800		Unitarian	Lawyer
14. Franklin Pierce	Nov. 23, 1804	Bowdoin	Episcopalian	Lawyer
15. James Buchanan	Apr. 23, 1791	Dickinson	Presbyterian	Lawyer
16. Abraham Lincoln	Feb. 12, 1809		Presbyterian*	Lawyer
17. Andrew Johnson	Dec. 29, 1808		Methodist*	Tailor
18. Ulysses S. Grant	Apr. 27, 1822	U.S. Mil. Academy	Methodist	Soldier
19. Rutherford B. Hayes	Oct. 4, 1822	Kenyon	Methodist*	Lawyer
20. James A. Garfield	Nov. 19, 1831	Williams	Disciples of Christ	Lawyer
21. Chester A. Arthur	Oct. 5, 1829	Union	Episcopalian	Lawyer
22. Grover Cleveland	Mar. 18, 1837		Presbyterian	Lawyer
23. Benjamin Harrison	Aug. 20, 1833	Miami	Presbyterian	Lawyer
24. Grover Cleveland	Mar, 18, 1837		Presbyterian	Lawyer
25. William McKinley	Jan, 29, 1843	Allegheny College	Methodist	Lawyer
26. Theodore Roosevelt	Oct. 27, 1858	Harvard	Dutch Reformed	Author
27. William H. Taft	Sept. 15, 1857	Yale	Unitarian	Lawyer
28. Woodrow Wilson	Dec. 29, 1856	Princeton	Presbyterian	Educator
29. Warren G. Harding	Nov. 2, 1865		Baptist	Editor
30. Calvin Coolidge	July 4, 1872	Amherst	Congregationalist	Lawyer
31. Herbert C. Hoover	Aug. 10, 1874	Stanford	Friend (Quaker)	Engineer
32. Franklin D. Roosevelt	Jan. 30, 1882	Harvard	Episcopalian	Lawyer
33. Harry S Truman	May 8, 1884		Baptist	Businessman
34. Dwight D. Eisenhower	Oct. 14, 1890	U.S. Mil. Academy	Presbyterian	Soldier
35. John F. Kennedy	May 29, 1917	Harvard	Roman Catholic	Author
36. Lyndon B. Johnson	Aug. 27, 1908	Southwest Texas State	Disciples of Christ	Teacher
37. Richard M. Nixon	Jan. 9, 1913	Whittier	Friend (Quaker)	Lawyer
38. Gerald R. Ford‡	July 14, 1913	Michigan	Episcopalian	Lawyer
39. James E. Carter, Jr.	Oct. 1, 1924	U.S. Naval Academy	Baptist	Businessman
40. Ronald W. Reagan	Feb. 6, 1911	Eureka College	Disciples of Christ	Actor
41. George H.W. Bush	June 12, 1924	Yale	Episcopalian	Businessman

*Church preference; never joined any church

‡Inaugurated Aug. 9, 1974, to replace Nixon, who resigned the same day.

THE PRESIDENTS OF THE UNITED STATES

Political Party	Age at Inauguration	Served	Died	Age at Death	Vice-President	
1. None	57	1789–1797	Dec. 14, 1799	67	John Adams	(1789–1797)
2. Federalist	61	1797–1801	July 4, 1826	90	Thomas Jefferson	(1797–1801)
3. Democratic-Republican	57	1801–1809	July 4, 1826	83	Aaron Burr	(1801-1805)
					George Clinton	(1805–1809)
4. Democratic-Republican	57	1809–1817	June 28, 1836	85	George Clinton	(1809–1812)
					Elbridge Gerry	(1813–1814)
5. Democratic-Republican	58	1817–1825	July 4, 1831	73	Daniel D. Tompkins	(1817–1825)
6. Democratic-Republican	57	1825–1829	Feb. 23, 1848	80	John C. Calhoun	(1825–1829)
7. Democrat	61	1829-1837	June 8, 1845	78	John C. Calhoun	(1829-1832)
					Martin Van Buren	(1833–1837)
8. Democrat	54	1837–1841	July 24, 1862	79	Richard M. Johnson	(1837–1841)
9. Whig	68	1841	Apr. 4, 1841	68	John Tyler	(1841)
10. Whig	51	1841–1845	Jan. 18, 1862	71		
11. Democrat	49	1845–1849	June 15, 1849	53	George M. Dallas	(1845–1849)
12. Whig	64	1849–1850	July 9, 1850	65	Millard Fillmore	(1849–1850)
13. Whig	50	1850–1853	Mar. 8, 1874	74		
14. Democrat	48	1853–1857	Oct. 8, 1869	64	William R. King	(1853)
15. Democrat	65	1857–1861	June 1, 1868	77	John C. Breckenridge	(1857–1861)
16. Republican	52	1861–1865	Apr. 15, 1865	56	Hannibal Hamlin	(1861–1865)
					Andrew Johnson	(1865)
17. Nat'l Union†	56	1865–1869	July 31, 1875	66		
18. Republican	46	1869–1877	July 23, 1885	63	Schuyler Colfax	(1869–1873)
					Henry Wilson	(1873–1875)
19. Republican	54	1877–1881	Jan. 17, 1893	70	William A. Wheeler	(1887–1881)
20. Republican	49	1881	Sept. 19, 1881	49	Chester A. Arthur	(1881)
21. Republican	51	1881–1885	Nov. 18, 1886	57		
22. Democrat	47	1885–1889	June 24, 1908	71	Thomas A. Hendricks	(1885)
23. Republican	55	1889-1893	Mar. 13, 1901	67	Levi P. Morton	(1889-1893)
24. Democrat	55	1893-1897	June 24, 1908	71	Adlai E. Stevenson	(1893–1897)
25. Republican	54	1897–1901	Sept. 14, 1901	58	Garret A. Hobart	(1897–1899)
					Theodore Roosevelt	(1901)
26. Republican	42	1901–1909	Jan. 6, 1919	60	Charles W. Fairbanks	(1905–1909)
27. Republican	51	1901–1913	Mar. 8, 1930	72	James S. Sherman	(1901–1912)
28. Democrat	56	1913–1921	Feb. 3, 1924	67	Thomas R. Marshall	(1913–1921)
29. Republican	55	1921–1923	Aug. 2, 1923	57	Calvin Coolidge	(1921–1923)
30. Republican	51	1923–1929	Jan. 5, 1933	60	Charles G. Dawes	(1925–1929)
31. Republican	54	1929–1933	Oct. 20, 1964	90	Charles Curtis	(1929–1933)
32. Democrat	51	1933–1945	Apr. 12, 1945	63	John N. Garner	(1933–1941)
					Henry A. Wallace	(1941–1945)
					Harry S. Truman	(1945)
33. Democrat	60	1945–1953	Dec. 26, 1972	88	Alben W. Barkley	(1949–1953)
34. Republican	62	1953–1961	Mar. 28, 1969	78	Richard M. Nixon	(1953–1961)
35. Democrat	43	1961–1963	Nov. 22, 1963	46	Lyndon B. Johnson	(1961–19630
36. Democrat	55	1963–1969	Jan. 22, 1973	64	Hubert H. Humphrey	(1965–1969)
37. Republican	56	1969–1974			Spiro T. Agnew	(1969–1973)
					Gerald R. Ford**	(1973–1974)
38. Republican	61	1974–1977			Nelson A. Rockefeller§	(1974–1977)
39. Democrat	52	1977–1981			Walter F. Mondale	(1977–1981)
40. Republican	69	1981–1989			George H.W. Bush	(1981–1989)
41. Republican	64	1989–			James Danforth Quayle	(1989–)

†The National Union Party consisted of Republicans and War Democrats. Johnson was a Democrat.

**Inaugurated Dec. 6, 1973, to replace Agnew, who resigned Oct. 10, 1973.

§Inaugurated Dec. 19, 1974, to replace Ford, who became President Aug. 9, 1974.

GLOSSARY INDEX

Office of Personnel Management (OPM), 388
Old Age Survivors Disability Insurance (OASDI), 502
Operation Desert Shield, 538
Original jurisdiction, 416

Pack journalism, 253
Party discipline, 188
Party government, 380
Party in government, 186
Party in the electorate, 186
Party organizations, 186
Party platforms, 202
Peace dividend, 541
Pendleton Act, 387
Pentagon Papers case, 117
Perestroika, 534
Permissive pattern of opinion, 163
Platform committee, 226
Pluralism, 272
Police-patrol oversight, 407
Political action committees (PACs), 283
Political capital, 374
Political culture, 92
Political economy, 14
Political executives, 394
Political ideology, 173
Political participation, 175
Political protest, 176
Political socialization, 171
Politics, 13
Populist party, 192
Postmodern presidency, 329
Poverty line, 508
Presidency, 337
Presidential government, 380
Prior restraint, 116
Private goods, 273
Private property, 54
Proportional representation, 192
Proposition 13, 88
Public interest groups, 275
Public opinion, 160
Public policy, 13
Pyramid presidents, 344

Random sample, 168
Rational parties, 203
Reagan's New Federalism, 88
Realignment, 194
Reapportioned, 218
Reciprocity, 309
Recession, 475
Reconciliation, 454
Redistricting, 219
Regulatory Agencies, 391
Reinforcement, 249
Representation, 305
Representational role, 307
Resolutions, 310
Relative poverty, 508
Responsible parties, 201
Retrospective voting, 233
Revenue sharing, 88
Reynolds v. Sims (1964), 92
Right to privacy, 151
Rose garden strategy, 230
Rules Committee, 226

Schenck v. U.S., 113
School prayer amendment, 120
Sedition Act (1798), 112
Selective incorporation, 110
Selective perception, 249
Senior Executive Service (SES), 388
Seniority systems, 298
Separate but equal, 133
Separation of powers, 21, 39
Sequesters, 459
Sherman Antitrust Act (1890), 61
Single-issue groups, 274
Single-member districts, 192
Sit-in, 135
Smith, Adam, 55
Smith Act (1940), 114
Snowbelt, 96
Socialization and persuasion, 249
Social Security Act, 502
Speaker of the House of Representatives, 317
Special and Select Committees, 313
Specialization, 309
Souter, David, 429
Spoils system, 386
Standing committees, 313
Spring preview, 452
States' rights, 84
Stare decisis, 431
Strategic Arms Limitation Talks (SALT), 540
Strategic Arms Reductions Talks (START), 540
Subgovernments, 401
Subnational governments, 80
Suburbanization, 99
Succession laws, 365
Sunbelt, 96
Supplemental Security Income (SSI), 502
Supply-side economics, 66
Surveillance, 249

Tariffs, 481
Tax Indexing, 464
Tax Reform Act, 464
Technocrat, 400
Tenth Amendment, 82
Thirteenth Amendment, 132
Thirty-second spot, 22
Three-fifths compromise, 37
Total incorporation, 110
Totalitarian regime, 5
Trade deficit, 73
Traditional presidency, 329
Troika, 349
Truman Doctrine, 527
Twenty-fifth Amendment, 365
Two-thirds rule, 226

Unanimous consent agreements, 311
Underclass, 510
Unitary systems, 81

Vice-presidency, 342
Virginia Plan, 36
Voting Rights Act (1965), 138

War Powers Act, 367
Warsaw Pact, 528
Watergate, 363
White House staff, 337
White primary, 134
Wilson, Woodrow, 19
Window period, 223
Women's Christian Temperance Union (WCTU), 145
Women's Suffrage Movement, 145
Work ethic, 55
Workfare, 513

INDEX

Photo Credits

Section 1 **xxiv** Robert Kristofik/The Image Bank

Chapter 1 **2** Michael Sargent/The White House; **6** Michael McDermott/Black Star; **7** David Burnett/CPI; **8** The Bettmann Archive; **12** Gerry Verchetich/University of Minnesota; **17** Bill Fitz-Patrick/The White House; **18** Susan Biddle/The White House; **20** The Bettmann Archive

Chapter 2 **28** Dennis Brack/Black Star; **30** The Bettmann Archive; **34** The Granger Collection; **36** The Granger Collection; **44** The Bettmann Archive; **47** Philadelphia Convention and Visitors Bureau

Chapter 3 **50** The Bettmann Archive; **58** Library of Congress; **64** The Granger Collection; **67** Peter Turnley/Black Star; **70** The Bettmann Archive; **72** The Bettmann Archive; **74** Margaret Bourke-White/LIFE Magazine ©Time Warner, Inc.

Chapter 4 **79** George Hall/Woodfin Camp & Associates; **84** Spencer Grant/Photo Researchers; **87** The Bettmann Archive; **98** Chicago Historical Society; **100** AP/Wide World Photos; **102** AP/Wide World Photos

Chapter 5 **105** Bob Kusel/SIPA Press; **107** National Archives; **112** Chris Neidenthal/TIME Magazine; **113** James Steinberg/Photo Researchers; **119** Susan McCartney/Photo Researchers; **122** The Bettmann Archive; **125** Flip Schulke/Black Star

Chapter 6 **129** Library of Congress; **131** Jacques Chenet/Woodfin Camp & Associates; **136** UPI/Bettmann; **142** Tracy Woodward/*The Washington Times*; **145** The Bettmann Archive; **148** Margot Granitsas/Photo Researchers; **151** J.L. Atlan/Sygma

Section 2 **156** Chris Cross/UNIPHOTO

Chapter 7 **158** The Bettmann Archive; **163** Billy Barnes/UNIPHOTO; **165** Bill Pierce/Sygma; **169** The Bettmann Archive; **172** Art Attack/Photo Researchers; **177** Paul Conklin/UNIPHOTO

Chapter 8 **183** The Bettmann Archive; **186** Democratic National Convention; **191** Library of Congress; **194** The Bettmann Archive; **199** Democratic National Convention; **202** The Bettmann Archive

Chapter 9 **210** Sam Pierson, Jr./Photo Researchers; **212** Betsy Temple, Fresno/Telpaneca Sister City Project; **219** NYT Pictures; **222** Bob Daemmrich; **229** The Bettmann Archive; **233** The Bettmann Archive

Chapter 10 **242** The Bettmann Archive; **246** AP/Wide World Photos; **250** Paul Conklin/UNIPHOTO; **252** Susan Meiselas/Magnum; **257** The Bettmann Archive; **261** Steve Rubin/JB Pictures

Chapter 11 **269** Ira Wyman; **273** Tony Bacewicz/*The Hartford Courant*; **279** Mug Shots/The Stock Market; **282** NRA; **288** James Colburn/Photoreporters; **289** Terry Ashe/TIME Magazine

Section 3 **294** Susan Biddle/The White House

Chapter 12 **296** The Bettmann Archive; **299** Historical Pictures Service; **307** Charles Borniger; **313** Paul Conklin/UNIPHOTO; **318** Dirck Halstead/TIME Magazine

Chapter 13 **327** Washington Convention and Visitors Association; **332** AP/Wide World Photos; **338** Dave Valdez/The White House; **346** The White House; **347** Wally McNamee/Woodfin Camp & Associates; **353** Peter Turnley/Black Star

Chapter 14 **357** Carol T. Powers/The White House; **362** Larry Burrows/LIFE Magazine ©Time Warner, Inc.; **369** Mark Reinstein/UNIPHOTO; **374** Frost; **377** AP/Wide World Photos

Chapter 15 **384** Walter Bibikow/The Image Bank; **393** John Ficara/Woodfin Camp & Associates; **394** The Bettmann Archive; **400** AP/Wide World Photos; **410** Sam Pierson, Jr./Photo Researchers

Chapter 16 **414** The Bettmann Archive; **424** The Bettmann Archive; **428** Ken Heinen; **429** Dennis Brack/Black Star; **434** Ken Heinen; **436** Nina Berman/SIPA Press

Section 4 **442** Scott Andrews/SIPA Press

Chapter 17 **444** The Bettmann Archive; **447** Wally McNamee/Woodfin Camp & Associates; **453** Larry Downing/Woodfin Camp & Associates; **458** The Bettmann Archive; **466** The Bettmann Archive

Chapter 18 **470** The Bettmann Archive; **474** The Bettmann Archive; **478** Najlah Feanny/SABA; **483** Anthony Suau/Black Star; **488** Metropolitan Edison Company; **490** The Bettmann Archive

Chapter 19 **497** Edward Lettau/Photo Researchers; **501** The Bettmann Archive; **509** The Bettmann Archive; **514** Spencer Grant/Photo Researchers; **517** Larry Downing/Woodfin Camp & Associates

Chapter 20 **523** Chris Niedenthal/TIME Magazine; **525** Mark Peterson/JB Pictures; **529** R. Bossu/Sygma; **537** AP/Wide World Photos; **544** AP/Wide World Photos; **545** Jim Richardson/*Denver Post*